Taiwan

the Bradt Travel Guide

Steven Crook

edition
3

www.bradtguides.com

Bradt Travel Guides Ltd, UK
The Globe Pequot Press Inc, USA

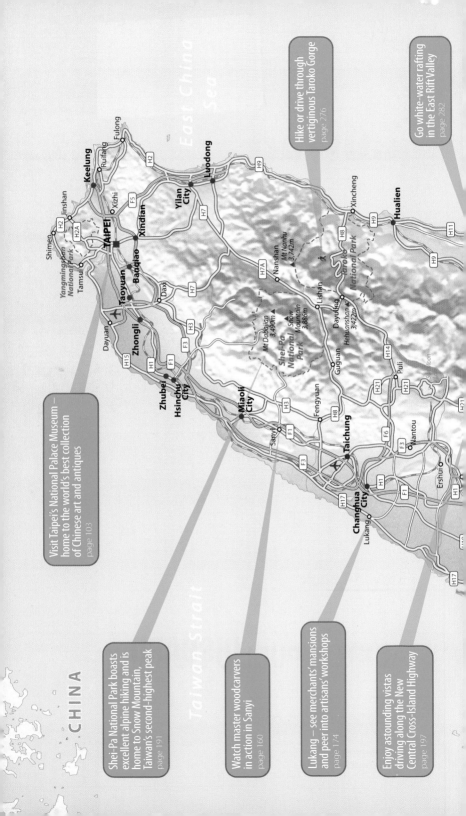

CHINA

East China Sea

Taiwan Strait

**Visit Taipei's National Palace Museum –
home to the world's best collection
of Chinese art and antiques**
page 103

**Hike or drive through
vertiginous Taroko Gorge**
page 276

**Go white-water rafting
in the East Rift Valley**
page 282

**Shei-Pa National Park boasts
excellent alpine hiking and is
home to Snow Mountain,
Taiwan's second-highest peak**
page 191

**Watch master woodcarvers
in action in Sanyi**
page 160

**Lukang – see merchants' mansions
and peer into artisans' workshops**
page 174

**Enjoy astounding vistas
driving along the New
Central Cross-Island Highway**
page 197

Shimen
Jinshan
Tamsui
Yangmingshan
National Park
Keelung
Ruifang
Fulong
Xizhi
H2
H2A
H2
F5
TAIPEI
Xindian
Banqiao
Taoyuan
Dayuan
Zhongli
Dax
H2A
Xizhi
Yilan
City
Luodong
H2
H9
H7
Nanshan
Mt Nanhu
3,742m
H7A
H7
F3
H3
Zhongli
Zhubei
Hsinchu
City
H1
F1
Dayuan
H15
H1
F1
Mt Dabajian
3,490m
Shei-Pa
National
Park
Snow
Mountain
3,886m
Lishan
Dayuling
Hehuanshan
3,422m
Taroko
National Park
H8
Xincheng
Hualien
H9
H9
H11
H9
Miaoli
City
F1
Sanyi
Fengyuan
Guguan
H3
H8
Taichung
H21
Puli
H21
H21
H14
H4
F3
F6
F1
Wantou
H1
Changhua
City
Lukang
H17
F1
Ershui
H1
H17

Tropic of Cancer

PACIFIC OCEAN

South China Sea

Bashi Channel

Penghu Islands

Orchid Island

Green Island

Little Liuqiu Island

Kenting National Park

Yushan National Park

Alishan National Scenic Area

Taijiang National Park

Mount Jade ▲ 3,952m
▲ 3,825m
▲ Xueyangshan 3,603m
Guanshan 3,666m ▲

Chenggong
Yuli
Fuli
Taitung City
Taimali
Daren
Chiayi City
Meishan
Jiaxian
Yujing
Qishan
Guanshan
Wutai
Pingtung City
Fangshan
Checheng
Hengchun
Kenting
Xinying
Neimen
Gangshan
Qigu
Beimen
Tainan
Kaohsiung

H11
H9
H23
H11
H20
H9
H9
H18
H29
H3
H3
H3
H1
H1
F3
F1
F3
H1
H17
H19
H26
H17
H17
H1
H1

N

50km
30 miles
0
0

Climb to the summit of Mount Jade – Taiwan's highest peak
page 196

Cycle along the Highway 11 coastal road admiring steep green hillsides and aboriginal villages
page 289

Look out for 1kg coconut crabs crossing the road on idyllic Green Island
page 327

Kenting National Park boasts superb beaches
page 264

Look for nesting green turtles on the windswept beaches of the Penghu Islands
page 302

Tainan, the former capital – famous for its delicacies and ornate temples
page 199

Foguangshan – one of Taiwan's leading Buddhist monasteries
page 247

Little Liuqiu Island – this coral chunk makes an excellent day trip
page 324

Taiwan
Don't
miss...

Raucous festivals
The annual Han Dan festival
in Taitung sees volunteers
take turns to have firecrackers
hurled at their bodies
(RM) page 298

Staggering mountains
At 3,952m, Mount Jade (or Yushan)
is the tallest peak in northeast Asia
(CL/D) page 196

Temple culture and architecture

Spectacularly made-up and attired *zhentou* troupes enliven temple events throughout Taiwan, but especially in the south

(RM) page 32

Biodiversity

The often-seen black-browed barbet lives up to its Chinese name, 'five-colour bird'

(RM) page 287

Taiwanese food

Taiwan's night markets appeal to the young and old, and are ideal places for budget travellers to fill up on local delicacies

(RM) page 62

Taiwan in colour

above   The National Palace Museum houses one of the world's finest collections of art, much of which once belonged to the Chinese emperors (TTB) page 103

left   Kaohsiung's Formosa Boulevard KMRT Station contains *The Dome of Light*, claimed to be the world's largest piece of glass art (CF) page 246

below   Taipei 101, once the world's tallest building at 509m, dominates the city skyline (CF) page 102

above Contrasting with the modernity of Taipei, Sanjiaoyong Old Street in Sanxia is lined with traditional shops and businesses (SJ/S) page 118

right The Holy Trinity Catholic Church in Yanshui has a roof and colourful murals akin to those in many Taiwanese temples (RM) page 223

below Dubbed 'Little Shanghai' in the 1930s, the quaint town of Jiufen retains much of its pre-World War II character (EP/S) page 129

AUTHOR

Educated in the UK, **Steven Crook** was backpacking through Asia in 1991 when he decided to go to Taiwan. He was running out of money and needed a job, but that wasn't the only reason. His geography teachers had never talked about the place and nobody he knew had ever been there. The prospect of visiting such an unfamiliar island was tantalising. He wasn't disappointed; he extended his stay and took up hiking. In 1996 he started writing about the country's mountains, temples and museums for newspapers and magazines. By 2009, when he accepted Bradt's offer to write a travel guide to Taiwan, he'd seen most of the country – but because he keeps discovering little museums, hiking trails and culinary delights, his 'to do, see and eat' list doesn't seem to be getting any shorter.

AUTHOR'S STORY

Writing the first edition of this guidebook and updating it twice has been a tremendous pleasure. The moments of confusion I've experienced are – possibly I'm rationalising here – key aspects of the Taiwan experience. The island's remarkable mountains and natural attractions are well known. But in the West, the incredible breadth and depth of Taiwan's cultures (I purposely use the plural) aren't so widely appreciated. There's nothing straightforward about the noisy parades that are central to popular religion, no glib explanations why during such events men may cut themselves with swords or scantily clad young women dance around poles. Trying to get to the bottom of things is an unending and sometimes frustrating journey, but underscores something I've felt every day for the better part of three decades: Taiwan may not always be beautiful and travelling here isn't without its niggles – but it's never dull.

When writing about Taiwan, it's hard not to fall back on clichés about 'east meeting west' and 'modernity blending with tradition'. After all, this is a country where businesspeople consult feng shui masters before laying out their offices and where high-school pupils pray to the god of education ahead of major exams. But the speed with which Taiwanese people adapt to change and the ease they show around imports of all kinds is striking. Most families have cars and new roads have shrunk the island. I appreciate the bullet train's speed and impressive bilingual service. Slower forms of transport are bargains considering just how safe, reliable and comfortable they are.

Like many guidebook writers, I care deeply about the destination. Hopefully, some of my missionary zeal shows through. But really my job is an excuse, the best one yet invented, to go everywhere. I've always wanted to see what's over the next hill and around every corner. I'm fortunate to have Taiwan, where the hills are numerous and where each corner – both literal and figurative – leads to many others.

PUBLISHER'S FOREWORD
Adrian Phillips, Managing Director

My eyes were opened to the attractions of Taiwan a few years ago during a presentation at World Travel Market; we saw slides of wildlife and mountains, and folk traditions untouched by the 21st-century slickness often associated with the country. Taiwan certainly got its hooks into Steven Crook. After visiting during a backpacking trip through Asia, he decided to make the country his home, and over 20 years later he remains filled with what he calls a 'missionary zeal'. It's fantastic to bring this third edition of his book to the shelves so he can continue to spread the word, introducing travellers to the pleasures of Taiwan's festivals and landscapes.

Third edition published June 2019
First published 2010
Bradt Travel Guides Ltd
31a High Street, Chesham, Bucks HP5 1BW, England
www.bradtguides.com
Print edition published in the USA by The Globe Pequot Press Inc, PO Box 480, Guilford, Connecticut 06437-0480

Photographs Alamy Stock Photos: robertharding (rh/A); Craig Ferguson (CF); Dreamstime.com: Chun-tso Lin (CL/D); Rich J Matheson (RM); Shutterstock.com: ThePonAek (TPA/S), CHC3537 (C/S), Richie Chan (RC/S), FenlioQ (F/S), Jakub Cejpek (JC/S), higrace (h/S), Sean Hsu (SH/S), Surachet Jo (SJ/S), Keitma (K/S), outcast85 (o/S), old apple (oa/S), phdwhite (p/S), Pinkcandy (PC/S), ESB Professional (EP/S), Sean Pavone (SP/S), The Perfect (TP/S), Rickshu (R/S), Wulong Tommy (WT/S), Nguyen Xuan Vu (NXV/S), wenliou (w/S), Shi Yali (SY/S), liou zojan (lz/S); SuperStock (SS); Taiwan Tourist Bureau (TTB)
Front cover Covered market, Jiufen (rh/A)
Back cover Foguangshan (PC/S); Taroko Gorge (h/S)
Title page Sun Moon Lake (h/S); Maroon oriole (oa/S); Taiwanese opera (CF)

Maps David McCutcheon FBCart.S. The following maps were based on materials kindly supplied by Compass Media Group: Hsinchu City, Kaohsiung Main Station, Kaohsiung Love River, Taichung City Centre, Tainan City Centre, Taipei Eastern, Taipei Northwest and Taipei Southwest.

Typeset by D & N Publishing, Baydon, Wiltshire and Ian Spick, Bradt Travel Guides
Production managed by Jellyfish Print Solutions; printed in India
Digital conversion by www.dataworks.co.in

Acknowledgements

The list has become so long and my fear of forgetting to include someone who's helped me so great that I've decided the best and fairest thing to do is this: let me hereby express my sincere gratitude to all the people who've shared their time and wisdom with me while travelling around Taiwan, whether it was for a minute or for a day, whether your information was spot-on or not quite what I needed. The country has changed tremendously in the quarter century I've lived here but one constant has been the hospitality Taiwanese people show to visitors (and long-term residents) from afar. It's folks like these who make exploring and writing about Taiwan such a pleasure.

I will name some names, however. Richard Foster and Rich J Matheson have been great friends and accomplices since years before they launched their current careers as, respectively, a birdwatching guide and a photographer. I also salute Stephen Flanigan and Cheryl Robbins for sharing their expertise. Among those who contacted me with suggestions or corrections, two names stand out: Tim Burford (author of Bradt's *Georgia* and *Uruguay* guides) and Sherman Cheng.

At Bradt, I'd like to thank Adrian Phillips, Laura Pidgley, Sue Cooper and Rachel Fielding for their patience and assistance throughout the commissioning and production of this guidebook.

This third edition is dedicated to my wife Irene and our son Conrad.

Contents

FEEDBACK REQUEST AND UPDATES WEBSITE

At Bradt Travel Guides we're aware that guidebooks start to go out of date on the day they're published – and that you, our readers, are out there in the field doing research of your own. You'll find out before us when a fine new family-run hotel opens or a favourite restaurant changes hands and goes downhill. So why not write and tell us about your experiences? Contact us on ✆ 01753 893444 or e info@bradtguides.com. We will forward emails to the author who may post updates on the Bradt website at w bradtupdates.com/taiwan. Alternatively, you can add a review of the book to w bradtguides.com or Amazon.

HOW TO USE THIS GUIDE

MAPS Taiwan's cities are dense mazes of side streets, lanes and back alleys. For reasons of space and clarity, urban maps in this book do not show every single thoroughfare. For the same reason, regional maps leave out many minor roads. Roads labelled 'F' are freeways; those with an 'E' are expressways; those labelled 'H' are highways. Roads with a number but no letter are slower and often narrower.

KEYS AND SYMBOLS Maps include alphabetical keys covering the locations of those places to stay, eat or drink that are featured in the book. Note that regional maps may not show all hotels and restaurants in the area: other establishments may be located in towns shown on the map.

GRIDS AND GRID REFERENCES Several maps use grid lines to allow easy location of sites. Map grid references are listed in square brackets after listings in the text, with page number followed by grid number, eg: [91 A1].

TRANSLATIONS Street and place names throughout this book are spelled according to *hanyu pinyin* except for certain places already known outside Taiwan by another spelling, such as Kaohsiung, Tamsui and Taroko Gorge. The pronunciation guide in parentheses after the name of each place or attraction is always *hanyu pinyin*. Chinese script has also been included for sights and places where relevant.

Introduction

As far as globetrotting tourists are concerned, Taiwan no longer flies under the radar. After decades of being known mainly for its economic success and its difficult relationship with China, the island has finally taken on its rightful role as a destination people choose to visit.

In a way, it's a shame Westerners no longer refer to this land as Formosa or Free China. The former name derives from a 16th-century description; Portuguese sailors bound for Japan are said to have called out '*ilha formosa*' – 'beautiful island' – when they glimpsed the towering cliffs and verdant hills of Taiwan's east. The main island, the size of Wales and Northern Ireland combined, retains a great deal of this natural beauty. There are so many mountains that the hundred peaks climbers try to bag – Taiwan's equivalent of Scotland's Munros – are all over 3,000m (9,842ft) high. And they're just the more accessible ones. In total, 258 summits top 3,000m. At 3,952m, Mount Jade is the highest peak in northeast Asia. Forests full of butterflies cover more than half the country. Coastal wetlands attract migratory waterbirds. Thanks to Taiwan's excellent transport system, it's possible to get from the latter to the former in just a few hours.

Many Taiwanese reject the 'China' label, even though the country's official name is the Republic of China. However, exploring Taiwan does give visitors an idea of what the giant on the other side of the Taiwan Strait could have been. Because certain traditions, in particular popular religion, have survived much better here than on the communist-ruled Chinese mainland, Taiwan is sometimes described as 'more Chinese than China'. There are Buddhist temples and Taoist clerics in every town and shrines in every village. Taipei's National Palace Museum remains the world's finest collection of Chinese artefacts. But I prefer to put it this way: Taiwan's society is much more than Chinese. The Han people who settled here from the 17th century onward found an island populated by Austronesian tribes. There was constant tension and frequent fighting but also trade and intermarriage. Between 1895 and 1945, Taiwan was ruled by Japan; Japanese food and architecture are still very evident. Taiwan was never colonised by a Western power yet there are smatterings of Americana, such as a love of baseball. If you're familiar with China, it's the differences between Taiwan and the mainland that'll strike you, not the similarities.

Some of the people browsing this book have been to Taiwan on business trips, possibly several times. Their memories may be of bleak industrial estates and heavy traffic, and they may be sceptical when people talk of Taiwan's beautiful landscapes, biodiversity and cultural treasures. The country is a bit like an ex-boxer struggling to convince the world he's now a poet. But the poetry exists, I promise you, in its natural environment and extraordinary festivals. Come and see it for yourself.

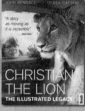

Part One

GENERAL INFORMATION

Location Taiwan is an island in northeast Asia, separated from China by the Taiwan Strait and located on the western edge of the Pacific Ocean.

Neighbouring countries Taiwan has maritime borders with China, Japan and the Philippines.

Size/Area 36,191km^2

Climate Semi-tropical in the north, tropical in the south with wet summers and mild winters

Status Republic

Population 23.57 million (2018). More than 96% of the population is of Han Chinese descent; around 2% is Austronesian.

Life expectancy 77.01 years (males), 83.62 (females)

Capital Taipei (population: 2.67 million)

Other main cities Taichung (population: 2.80 million), Kaohsiung (population: 2.77 million) and Tainan (population: 1.88 million)

Economy Free market with strong manufacturing and high-technology sectors

GDP US$579 billion (2017)

Languages/official language Mandarin (official), Taiwanese, Hakka, aboriginal languages

Religion Taoism and Buddhism with Christian and Muslim minorities

Currency New Taiwan dollar. Banknotes with a value of 100, 200, 500, 1,000 and NTD2,000; coins with a value of 1, 5, 10, 20 and NTD50.

Exchange rate £1 = NTD40.2, US$1 = NTD30.9, €1 = NTD34.9 (March 2019)

National airline/airport China Airlines/Taiwan Taoyuan International Airport (IATA: TPE)

International telephone code +886

Time Taiwan is 8 hours ahead of GMT (Greenwich Mean Time), 11 hours behind New York (Eastern Standard Time) and 15 hours ahead of Los Angeles (Pacific Standard Time). It's in the same time zone as the PRC and 1 hour ahead of Singapore. Sunrise and sunset times are listed on English-language pages of the Central Weather Bureau's website (w cwb.gov.tw).

Electrical voltage 110v/60Hz; two-pin plugs

Weights and measures Metric

Flag Red; the top left quarter is blue with a white star

National anthem *San Min Chu I* (*Three Principles of the People*)

National flower Plum blossom (*Prunus mei*)

National bird Taiwan blue magpie (*Urocissa caerulea*)

National sports Baseball and basketball

Public holidays On the Gregorian calendar: 1 January (Founding Day of the Republic), 28 February (Peace Memorial Day), 4 April (Children's Day), 5 April (Tomb-Sweeping Day), 1 May (Labour Day), 10 October (National Day). On the lunar calendar: January/February (Lunar New Year), June (Dragon Boat Festival), September (Mid-Autumn Festival).

1

Background Information

GEOGRAPHY

The country most outsiders and many of its own citizens call Taiwan, but which is officially the Republic of China (ROC), is in east Asia, southeast of the Chinese mainland and between Japan to the northeast and the Philippines to the south.

The ROC covers 36,191km², making it nearly twice as big as Wales but barely half the size of Tasmania. Compared with US states, it's a little larger than Maryland. What geographers define as Taiwan accounts for 95% of the ROC's land area. This main island is 394km long and 144km wide and shaped, Taiwanese often say, like a tobacco leaf. Taiwan includes the Penghu archipelago, Green Island, Orchid Island and a few other islets. In addition to these, the ROC controls three island clusters close to the Chinese coast (Kinmen, Matsu and Wuqiu) and the distant Pratas Islands. The Matsu Islands include the most northerly point of the ROC: Xiyin and Dongyin (two islands conjoined by a causeway) at 26°23'N. Pratas, three uninhabited atolls at 20°43'N and 116°42'E, is both the southernmost and westernmost outpost of the ROC. The Tropic of Cancer crosses Taiwan just south of the city of Chiayi.

It's Taiwan's mountains that stun visitors and create the most lasting impressions. Nearly one-third of the island is a kilometre or more above sea level. Some 10.3% reaches an elevation of 2,500m and 258 named peaks top 3,000m. Almost no humans live at these altitudes and only those willing to hike for days can properly experience this realm of alpine forests, wild animals and unique bird species.

There are five mountain ranges. The Central Mountain Range stretches four-fifths of the island's length. The Yushan Range, considered a separate entity because a river separates it from the Central Range, includes and is named after Taiwan's highest peak, Yushan or Mount Jade (3,952m). The Xueshan Range runs from the northeast coast to central Taiwan, a distance of 180km; its highest point is Taiwan's second-highest peak, Snow Mountain (3,886m). None of the peaks in the Alishan Range in Taiwan's southwest come close to 3,000m, but the area does include the famous resort from which it takes its name. The Coastal Mountain Range, which appeared when the Philippine Sea Plate collided with Taiwan, is just two million years old. The region between it and the interior mountains, the 180km-long East Rift Valley, is one of Taiwan's prettiest and most natural lowlands. There are extinct volcanoes near Taipei in Yangmingshan National Park. Several of Taiwan's outlying islands came into being because of undersea volcanic activity.

Because of the ongoing collision between the Philippine Sea Plate and the Asian Continental Plate, the entire island is rising at approximately four centimetres per year. Taiwan's location on the boundary of these two tectonic plates means it's vulnerable to earthquakes; 20th-century seismic events killed 8,000 people. There are benefits to being on the 'Pacific Ring of Fire', however – a string of beguiling mud volcanoes and an abundance of geothermal springs in which visitors can soak away stress.

According to some predictions, Taiwan's population will peak at 23.8 million in 2021 before starting to shrink, because the birth rate has for many years been among the lowest in the world. Even so, it's one of the most densely populated places on Earth. Nine out of ten Taiwanese live on the western plains and more reside in the north than the south.

The flattest and most fertile lands are the alluvial fans of rivers such as the 186km-long Zhuoshui (the island's longest waterway). Because of the island's topography and weather patterns – three-quarters of each year's total rain falls between May and October – Taiwan's rivers are short and often violent; only five waterways are more than 100km long. Natural lakes are few and tiny. Of Taiwan's six largest bodies of fresh water, five didn't exist at all until dams were built. Because of sedimentation and erosion, Taiwan is slowly gaining land along the west coast while losing it in the east. Climate change may lead to the inundation of parts of the western plains.

Considering almost every corner of the lowlands is used for agriculture, housing or industry, and that the camphor trade of the 18th and 19th centuries led to a massive felling of trees in the foothills, Taiwan has a remarkable amount of forest. Around 58% of the main island's land area is covered by trees or bamboo with hardwoods accounting for more than half of this area. While most of Taiwan's trees are in the highlands, in recent years there has been some reforestation on the western plains. Government efforts to preserve and expand tree cover have suffered setbacks. Landslides in the wake of 2009's Typhoon Morakot, for instance, swept an estimated 980,000 tonnes of branches, trunks and stumps into rivers.

CLIMATE

As you'd expect of a country that straddles the Tropic of Cancer, Taiwan is wet and warm. Seasons are distinct in terms both of temperature and the likelihood of rain. Daytime highs of 38°C have been recorded in urban areas during the summer. In December and January, northerners shiver as the mercury hovers around 10°C. The south doesn't get so cold, but jackets and gloves are essential if you're out early in the morning.

WHEN THE WIND BLOWS

The English word 'typhoon' is probably derived from one or another Chinese dialect; in Mandarin, these fearsome storms are called tái fēng. Typhoons form over the Pacific Ocean, hundreds of kilometres from land. Most then move due west, bringing heavy rain and dangerously strong winds to the islands (Taiwan, Okinawa, the Philippines) in their path. Typhoons tend to slow down when they hit land, but that doesn't make them any less deadly. In fact, because it's the rains they bring (and the consequent floods and landslides) that kill people and destroy property, some of the most destructive typhoons in Taiwan's recent history have been slow-moving storms that dumped immense quantities of water on fragile hillsides.

During a typical year there are 30 to 35 typhoons, of which three or four may hit Taiwan. Late July to mid-September is peak typhoon season, and even though Taiwan receives at least 72 hours' warning each time a typhoon approaches, the disruption to transport can still be severe. This is one reason why visitors do well to avoid Taiwan's summer.

VICTORIAN RAVES ABOUT TAIWAN'S SCENERY

Very seldom are precipices more startling than California's exquisite poetically beautiful land... or the majestic coastal cliffs of Scotland's Orkney's Hoy... or Portugal's Penha d'Águia 2,400-foot coastal cliffs... or Norway's encircling imposing coastal cliffs. But all are infinitesimal and not worth mentioning next to the enormous broken ridges of Formosa.

F H H Guillemard, British naturalist visiting Taiwan in 1882

I sat in the stern beside the helmsman – a good position for surveying the scene. It is grand at any time, but that night it was sublime. Long and high ranges of forest-clad mountains stood like dark perpendicular walls on the right. On the left lay a broad and boundless expanse of water.

George L Mackay, Canadian missionary travelling down Taiwan's east coast by rowboat in 1890

[The] guides hesitated about taking us any further, but... they at last unwillingly struck along a pathway leading due south through the jungle. This wood was even more beautiful than the one we had traversed on the east side of the peninsula. Very beautiful palms of two or three kinds, yellow Nepaul pepper, caladiums, the large-leaved Indian banyan, rattans, and guava bushes were in abundance. A beautiful orchid (*Phaloenopsis sanderiana*) grew on the trees, and we disturbed numbers of monkeys as we passed along.

Michael Beazeley, British traveller touring the south in 1875

Taiwan's annual average rainfall is 2,471mm. The north gets more than the south; the north's wet season is longer but less pronounced. A few places near Keelung receive close to 6,000mm of rain in a typical year. Taipei (an average of 170 rainy days per year) is noticeably wetter than central Kaohsiung (92 wet days each year). The ROC's outlying islands are relatively dry: Kinmen gets just 1,049mm of rain a year. Snowfall is uncommon below 2,000m in the northern half of Taiwan and below 3,000m in the south.

Taipei gets 1,408 hours of sunshine per year. Kaohsiung gets 2,082 hours, while in Tainan – where they used to produce salt by using sunshine to evaporate seawater – the annual average total is 2,264 hours. The days are relatively short, even in summer. In Taipei in early July, the sun rises about 05.10 and sets before 19.00. At the end of December, the times are around 06.40 and 17.20.

Taiwan's Central Weather Bureau publishes detailed English-language forecasts on their website (w cwb.gov.tw).

NATURAL HISTORY AND CONSERVATION

Taiwan has fantastic natural diversity in terms of topography, climate and soils. Of the world's 12 major soil types, 11 can be found in Taiwan. Consequently there's a wide range of habitats and these in turn nurture an astonishing variety of animals, birds, insects and plants. Rates of endemism are exceptionally high throughout the biosphere. A quarter of the country's 4,300 vascular plants are found nowhere else on Earth, and 55 of the 85 terrestrial mammals are endemic. A third of its reptile species and subspecies are unique, as are 42 of its 265 freshwater fishes, 11 of its 35 bats, 34 of the island's 56 stag-beetles, and 70% of its snails.

FAUNA

Mammals One of the easiest animals to spot is Taiwan's only primate, the **Formosan macaque** (*Macaca cyclopis*). Also known as the Formosan rock monkey, this endemic is distributed island-wide from sea level to at least 3,000m above sea level, but is most often spotted in foothills in the south and east. Macaques, who live in family groups usually numbering 20 to 40, have light brown fur often speckled with grey. Deep in the mountains there are larger animals such as **Formosan sambars** (*Rusa unicolor swinhoei*), a kind of deer, and **Formosan black bears** (*Ursus thibetanus formosanus*). The latter have distinctive V-shaped white marks on their chests and don't hibernate. Even though they've been known to steal food from hikers' packs while the humans are sleeping, they tend to keep a very low profile. Researchers fear this endemic subspecies will suffer the same fate as the **Formosan clouded leopard** (*Neofelis nebulosa brachyura*), a metre-long cat which hasn't been sighted since the late 1980s. Once hunted for its skin, it's now believed to be extinct.

Birds Thanks to its position on the East Asian–Australasian Flyway, Taiwan has fabulously varied birdlife. Fifty-three internationally recognised Important Bird Areas (IBAs) cover more than one-sixth of its land area. According to the most recent checklist issued by Taiwan's Chinese Wild Bird Federation (w www.bird. org.tw), 657 avian species, including vagrants and migrants, have been recorded in Taiwan and its minor islands. Among them, 28 are endemic species, while a further 55 are endemic subspecies. Many visiting birders have been able to add a dozen or more endemics, including the **Taiwan partridge** (*Arborophila crudigularis*) and the **mikado pheasant** (*Syrmaticus mikado*), to their 'life lists' during fortnight-long tours.

BIRDING IN TAIWAN   *Richard Foster*

As well as having a thriving local birdwatching scene, Taiwan has emerged as a key stop on the global birdwatcher's journey. Birders come with lists of species they hope to see, but leave impressed by much more than the island's avifauna. Taiwan's advantages include a hospitable population, good infrastructure, well-protected forests, no malaria or leeches, diverse habitats, great flora and butterflies – and all in a fairly compact area. It's possible to see most of Taiwan's 80-plus endemics and endemic subspecies, plus other outstanding birds, in just a few days.

The best places to see birds found only in Taiwan are the national forest recreation areas. For birding, the best known of these is Dasyueshan where **Swinhoe's pheasants** (*Lophura swinhoii*) are often spotted right next to the road. For wintering wetland birds I suggest Yilan County, Jincheng Lake (part of Hsinchu City's 17km Coastline Scenic Area) and Aogu Wetlands (see map, page 200) in Chiayi County.

There's good birding to be had even for visitors unable to get out of the lowland cities and into the high mountains. My favourite sites in central Taipei include the Botanical Garden – probably the easiest place in the world to spot the Malayan **night heron** (*Gorsachius melanolophus*) – and Daan Forest Park, where you should follow the bird photographers who are always there. At Chiang Kai-shek Memorial Hall, check the ponds and trees on the north, west, and south edges of the grounds. Huajiang Wild Duck Nature Park (see map, page 83) is less than 1km from the bustle of Longshan Temple in Wanhua. Further out, Guandu Nature Park (see map, page 80), further out but within walking distance of Guandu Station on

Throughout the western lowlands, visitors will notice white-headed birds in parks and larger white birds near rice fields and rivers. The latter are egrets. There has been some hybridisation between the former, light-vented **bulbuls** (*Pycnonotus sinensis formosae*), and an endemic variant, the black-capped **Styan's** bulbul (*Pycnonotus taivanus*). The **Eurasian tree sparrow** (*Passer montanus*) is ubiquitous, and in foothills the **crested serpent eagle** (*Spilornis cheela hoya*) is an important predator.

FLORA Many of Taiwan's most common wild flowers are invasive species. Among them are lantana of various colours, especially white, yellow and orange, the daisy-like **cobbler's pegs** (*Bidens pilosa*) and the flossflower (*Ageratum houstonianum*). The former, an aggressive weed, is used by some Taiwanese as a folk treatment for diabetes. The last has delicate pink blooms. *Mimosa pudica* is also widespread; this species isn't very interesting to look at but it does have touch-sensitive leaves that curl up when brushed.

CONSERVATION AND ENVIRONMENTAL ISSUES Taiwan is certainly a paradise for nature lovers – but a deeply troubled one. In recent years, air pollution has been the most talked-about environmental issue. The air quality in Taipei generally isn't bad, with the air quality index (AQI) value staying below 100 on the 500-point scale and qualifying as green (good) or yellow (not unhealthy). Across much of the western lowlands, however, it can be a very different story during the cooler, dryer months. Between Taoyuan and Pingtung, AQI values sometimes fall into the red zone (above 150) or even worse.

There's no doubt that a large proportion of the atmospheric pollution detected in Taiwan originates from the Chinese mainland. Taiwan's Environmental Protection

the metro's Red Line, has excellent facilities managed by the Wild Bird Society of Taipei (w wbst.org.tw).

My favourite site near Taipei is Wulai. Lots of good birds can be spotted amid the mid-elevation mountains here, among them the **Taiwan blue magpie** (*Urocissa caerulea*), and the **maroon oriole** (*Oriolus traillii*). From the main village follow either of the two rivers east or south. Further afield, the main lower part of Taroko Gorge can be good in winter, especially the side road to Buluowan and the hiking trail to Lianhua Pond. If possible drive the road westwards and upwards from Taroko towards Hehuanshan as both the scenery and the birding are incredible.

Good birding can be done throughout the year. That said, spring is best with autumn and winter being almost as good. Summer is a bit tougher – not only is the weather hotter, but most migrant species are absent. Don't miss Kenting around 10 October for the raptor migration – birders should go to Sheding Nature Park in the morning, then Manzhou around dusk.

Taiwan's minor islands offer numerous opportunities. Matsu National Scenic Area, especially Dongyin Island, is excellent for spotting migrants between mid-April and mid-May and again from mid-September to mid-October. For a change of scene and good winter birding (which even non-birders will enjoy), check out Kinmen County.

Richard Foster, who has seen more than 400 of the 657 bird species recorded in Taiwan, is founder and chief guide of Taiwan EcoTours (page 42).

Administration (EPA) attributes 34–42% of the dirty air to 'external sources'. To improve air quality, the EPA has been tackling everything from vehicle emissions to roadside restaurants (stir-frying produces a lot of dangerous particulates). Electric scooters are now common but few cars are hybrid or all-electric.

Reducing Taiwan's dependence on imported fossil fuels is proving very difficult. In 2017, nearly 47% of the country's electricity was generated by burning coal; almost 35% came from natural gas, while nuclear power accounted for a little over 8%. A mere 4.5% came from renewable sources, a pitiful total considering Taiwan is a leading manufacturer of solar cells and has superb conditions for photovoltaic power. The current government's determination to turn Taiwan into a 'nuclear-free' island by 2025 – a policy that became more popular after the Fukushima catastrophe in Japan in 2011 – makes curbing carbon emissions much harder.

As a non-member of the United Nations, Taiwan was excluded from the 2015 Paris Conference of Parties to the UN Framework Convention on Climate Change. However, that year Taiwan's parliament passed the Greenhouse Gas Reduction and Management Act, which sets out targets including a 50% cut in greenhouse-gas emissions by 2050 compared with 2005 levels. Per-capita CO^2 emissions were 11.73 tonnes in 2016, down from 12.34 tonnes in 2007 – but double the level in 1988 when fewer Taiwanese owned cars.

Environmental awareness has grown considerably over the past few decades, one reason being the air-quality issue. Yet Taiwan still has a lot of ground to make up. The Kuomintang (KMT) regime that ruled Taiwan through to 2000 had, for decades after 1949, a 'temporary home mentality': Chiang Kai-shek and his supporters regarded themselves as China's rightful government, and Taiwan was merely a base from which they would retake the mainland. They delivered rapid

KENTING NATIONAL PARK (w www.ktnp.gov.tw) As popular as Yangmingshan but for different reasons, Kenting has beaches, tropical forests and marine ecology. Land and sea area: 333km². See page 264.

KINMEN NATIONAL PARK (w www.kmnp.gov.tw) Comprising three parcels of coastline and one inland section, Kinmen's national park preserves the archipelago's architectural and military history as well as its natural allure. Land and sea area: 35km². See page 310.

TAIJIANG NATIONAL PARK (w www.tjnp.gov.tw) This littoral national park embraces tidal areas and wetlands rich in birdlife plus historic sites connected to Koxinga's arrival in Taiwan. Land and sea area: 393km². See page 219.

SOUTH PENGHU MARINE NATIONAL PARK (w www.marine.gov.tw) Established in 2014, Taiwan's newest national park covers several thinly populated islands in Penghu County and an area of ocean that attracts migratory birds, dolphins and sometimes whales. Land and sea area: 358km².

DONGSHA ATOLL MARINE NATIONAL PARK (w www.marine.gov.tw) This remote national park protects Pratas, the ROC's southernmost territory, and isn't currently open to tourists. The current emphasis is on conservation because the atolls have been damaged by fishing practices and global warming. Land and sea area: 3,537km².

economic development, but paid scant attention to preserving the island's land, air, water and biodiversity. The harvesting of old-growth forests continued until 1990.

Many local politicians like to be able to point to physical achievements while enriching their construction-industry backers. As a result, overdevelopment often takes the form of unnecessary roads and public facilities that become 'mosquito mansions' (the local term for white elephants). The private sector isn't much better; thanks to speculative building and investments, about 14% of Taiwan's 8.5 million residential properties are unoccupied.

The current administration has sent mixed signals as to its commitment to the environment. On the one hand, Tsai Ing-wen's cabinet has announced plans for a network of large-scale solar-power plants; on the other, her economics minister approved the renewal of a cement company's mining permit. The latter action was controversial because the site both abuts Taroko National Park and appears to have been stolen from indigenous people. Nevertheless, in certain respects progress is visible. Now almost everyone separates rubbish for recycling and understands the importance of conserving water and power. In cheap eateries, disposable cutlery is becoming less common; shark's fin has been taken off the menu at several notable restaurants; and more people are seeking out locally grown organic produce.

HISTORY

PREHISTORY In the early 1970s, archaeologists digging in southwest Taiwan unearthed seven skull fragments and two molars. Three of the skull pieces were dated to 30,000 years ago and thought to be the oldest human remains discovered in Taiwan. 'Zuozhen Man', so called because the discovery was made in what's now

BUDDHIST MERCY RELEASE

At ponds and lakes, visitors who read Chinese may notice signs prohibiting *fàng shēng* 放生. This term, usually translated as 'mercy release', describes a Buddhist custom of releasing captured animals or fish into the wild. The pious believe that by doing this, they can not only bring themselves longevity and good luck in this life, but can also make amends for sins committed in their previous lives. The tradition began long ago with spontaneous acts of compassion. If a monk came across a creature about to be sold for food, he would buy it and set it free. However, the modern version of mercy release is completely different, the majority of creatures involved being raised or caught solely so they can be sold to religious individuals who plan to release them. The practice is commonplace in Asian countries with substantial Buddhist populations.

In Taiwan, both native and non-native species are used for mercy release ceremonies. Fish, turtles, birds and even insects have been released in events organised by temples. Non-native creatures often die soon after being freed because they're unsuited to the local environment; there have been instances where freshwater turtles have been released into the ocean. Animals that don't perish may thrive and become competitors for food or mate with native species, threatening their gene pools. The **American bullfrog** (*Lithobates catesbeianus*), a foreign species often used in mercy releases, preys on the native **Taipei tree frog** (*Rhacophorus taipeianus*). Almost all of Taiwan's major rivers are infested with exotic species, while Sun Moon Lake has been invaded by foreign species to the point where native species are close to extinction. When Lotus Pond in Kaohsiung was emptied for cleaning in 2009, 95% of the fish removed were exotics. They were turned into fertiliser while local species were saved and released into nearby creeks.

It seems the practice of 'mercy release' is now declining. Much of the credit should go to animal-rights groups which have worked hard to educate Buddhists about the likely consequences of actions.

Tainan City's Zuozhen District, may have lived at a time when Taiwan was physically joined to the Eurasian landmass. However, the scientists who re-examined the fossils using different dating technology in 2015 concluded the remnants are 'merely' 3,000 years old.

Around 18,000 years ago sea levels began to rise and within 6,000 years Taiwan had become an island. Local palaeolithic and neolithic cultures developed. In parts of western Taiwan the Iron Age began about 2,000 years ago, while tribes in the east and deep in the interior continued to depend on stone implements.

FORMOSA The captain – some say it was the navigator – of a Portuguese vessel sailing past Taiwan to Japan in 1544 gave the island the name by which it was known until well into the 20th century: 'Ilha Formosa', Portuguese for 'beautiful island'. In recent years a version of this name, rendered in Chinese characters and pronounced slightly differently, has become popular within the country.

Taiwanese were trading internationally long before the arrival of Westerners. Indigenous people of Austronesian origin (page 23) bartered deer skins with Japanese merchants (who used them for harnesses and saddles) and sold deer meat to Chinese traders. Deer were hunted with snares, pitfalls and spears as well as bows and arrows.

DUTCH AND SPANISH RULE Having been refused permission to establish a commercial base on the Chinese coast or in the Penghu Islands, the Dutch East India Company (Vereenigde Oost-Indische Compagnie, VOC) was in 1624 allowed by the Ming Empire to found a small colony on Taiwan's southwest coast, at what is now Tainan. The Dutch called the location Tayouan, almost certainly a corruption of the aboriginal place name. This word eventually evolved into 'Taiwan' and came to be applied to the entire island. The VOC purchased locally grown sugar and rice for shipping to Japan. According to the company's records, in 1639 alone they collected almost 100,000 deer hides for export to Japan; not surprisingly, the vast herds seen by Dutch missionaries working in the interior soon disappeared. Wood, nutmeg, clove and pepper came in from southeast Asia; vessels arriving from Europe carried satin and linen and returned laden with silk and porcelain. To increase agricultural production, the Dutch encouraged peasants from the nearby Chinese province of Fujian to move to the Tainan area. Missionaries converted thousands of lowland aborigines to Christianity. Dutch-language schools were set up and several colonists married indigenous women.

The Spanish, rulers of the Philippines since 1565, had long hoped to expand northwards. In 1626, they established a base near Keelung. Their motives were economic, strategic and religious; the Dominicans who were part of the Spanish expedition are thought to have been the first Christian missionaries to set foot on Taiwan. The Spanish occupied a site in Tamsui in 1629 but abandoned it after less than a decade. Twelve years later the Dutch received intelligence that the Spanish garrison at Keelung had been weakened by redeployments and plague. They attacked and within days Taiwan's Spanish episode was over.

KOXINGA Were it not for one man, it's conceivable the Dutch would have retained Taiwan until World War II. That man was Zheng Chenggong, better known to Western historians as Koxinga. One of very few Chinese to figure in European histories written in the 17th century, he's been variously described as a ruthless pirate and an inept admiral. Born in Japan in 1624, his father was Chinese, his mother Japanese. He was fervent in his support for China's Ming Dynasty just as it was being overthrown by Manchu invaders from the north. The Manchus founded the Qing Dynasty in 1644 but Ming loyalists kept up the fight in China's south. Koxinga's father switched sides in 1646. China's new rulers ennobled him but because he failed to persuade his son to submit to the emperor, they executed him in 1661. Despite being awarded a prestigious title by the Qing in 1653 and occasionally negotiating with China's new rulers, Koxinga kept up a military campaign against the Manchus. The VOC knew of Koxinga because he traded with them to fund his struggle. When he fell sick, the Dutch colony sent its only physician to treat him. Koxinga refused to take the medicine the Dutchman prescribed.

In 1660, the VOC intercepted letters in which Koxinga made clear his desire to conquer Taiwan, which he'd never visited. On 2 April 1661, Koxinga's forces surrounded the Dutch strongholds, Fort Zeelandia and Fort Provintia in present-day Tainan. The garrison of the latter, caught unprepared and short of water, unconditionally surrendered on 4 April. Koxinga wasn't so lucky at Fort Zeelandia. Demands that the Dutch lay down arms were rebuffed; a series of cannon exchanges, Chinese efforts to storm the fortress and Dutch counter-raids followed. Although there was no prospect of a relief force arriving anytime soon, VOC Governor Frederik Coyett was determined to hold out. News of Koxinga's attack reached Batavia (now Jakarta in Indonesia) two months later, just after the VOC had sent Hermanus Clenk to replace Coyett. When Clenk arrived off the coast of Taiwan on 30 July, he realised the direness of the situation and made the less than admirable decision not to take up his new job. As Clenk fled back to Batavia, VOC reinforcements approached. The commander of this relief squadron was as cowardly as Clenk; promising to sail to Fujian and ask Qing generals there to come to the aid of the Dutch – something the former were showing a keen interest in doing – he instead headed directly for the safety of Batavia. By the end of the year there was little food left inside Fort Zeelandia and almost half of the 2,300 Europeans had died of wounds or disease. Several German mercenaries deserted; after one gave Koxinga information about the fort's layout, the Chinese made rapid military progress. Coyett signed the instrument of surrender on 1 February 1662. Under its terms the Dutch were allowed to leave with their personal possessions, VOC archives and sufficient provisions to reach Batavia. They left behind a substantial amount of money, merchandise and weaponry. But Koxinga's victory had been costly: more than one-third of the 25,000 men he'd led to Taiwan died in the battle for Fort Zeelandia.

Koxinga died suddenly on 23 June 1662, possibly of malaria. However, the anti-Manchu enclave was secure and the Kingdom of Dongning, as the mini-state styled itself, lasted another two decades. Koxinga's eldest son, Zheng Jing, ruled for most of this period. He continued his father's policies: skirmishing with imperial forces along the Chinese coast; smuggling so as to evade the Qing economic blockade; ordering his soldiers to fan out across the countryside and support themselves by farming; and trading with Japan. Like his father, he was committed to extirpating Christianity. Zheng Jing died in 1681 and was succeeded by his 12-year-old son, Zheng Keshuang.

CHINESE RULE Eager to finish off pro-Ming elements, the Qing Empire dispatched Shi Lang (1621–96) to retake the island. Shi, who had been planning the seizure of Taiwan since 1664, held a deep grudge against Koxinga's family. Initially a Ming loyalist, Shi went over to the Qing in 1646 after arguing with Koxinga; the latter responded to the defection by having Shi's father, brother and son put to death. A naval engagement near the Penghu Islands on 16–17 July 1683 was the only major battle in Shi's campaign. Within two months Zheng Keshuang had surrendered. He spent the rest of his life in comfortable captivity in Beijing.

The imperial court was divided over what to do with Taiwan. Some argued that the island's Chinese population should be evacuated back to the mainland. Others, including Shi, thought Taiwan should be retained. (He had a backup plan if the court rejected his advice: sell the island to the Dutch.) In 1684, Taiwan was made part of Fujian province. Officials were posted to the main settlements but they did little to develop the island's economy or improve the lives of its residents. For most of the following century, the authorities forbade family migration from the Chinese mainland to the island. Nonetheless, the Han population grew, as single Fujianese men arrived to seek their fortune.

For 150 years Taiwan's camphor forests were one of its main natural resources. The island was the world's foremost source of camphor, used for making balms and mothballs. This lucrative industry was an imperial monopoly; anyone caught felling a tree without permission was put to death. By 1811, at least two million people were living on the lowlands. Food was plentiful but malaria and other diseases killed so many people that, according to an idiom from the era, of every ten settlers 'just three remain; six are dead, and one has returned home'.

Banditry, clan warfare and ethnic strife plagued Taiwan until well into the 19th century. Different immigrant groups fought with each other and the island's indigenous inhabitants. Uprisings were common. In 1786, rebels led by Lin Shuang-wen (1756–88) took control of much of western Taiwan. Lin led a semi-religious secret society and proclaimed himself emperor. In 1788 he was captured, taken to Beijing and executed. Even though his movement caused thousands of deaths, the anti-Qing aspect of his campaign was regarded favourably by the Nationalists after World War II. A village in central Taiwan and two schools bear his name.

Most migrants were single men and gender imbalance was one cause of lawlessness. Because there were so few Han women, many settlers married aborigines. (DNA analysis suggests at least four out of five Hoklo and Hakka Taiwanese have some Austronesian ancestry.) Also, Taiwan was different from other parts of the Chinese Empire in that divorced or widowed women easily found new husbands. But that didn't alter the traditional preference for sons over daughters; European residents noted that female infanticide was still common in the 1860s.

If conditions were right junks could cross the Taiwan Strait in a day and a half, but gales sometimes blew ships off course and piracy was common until the second half of the 19th century. Boats were the only means of getting people or goods from one part of Taiwan to another; overland transport was unsafe and difficult on account of the lack of roads and the fast-flowing rivers that had to be crossed. Geographical obstacles meant few Han settlers made it to Taiwan's east. The indigenous tribes there were able to preserve their autonomy and culture until the Japanese occupation.

After yet another uprising was crushed in 1865, Taiwan gradually became more peaceful. A local gentry and scholar-literati class emerged in Tainan, Hsinchu and other settlements. Confucian academies were established. But corruption continued to be a massive problem. W A Pickering, a Briton who worked in Taiwan from 1863 to 1870, devoted an entire chapter of his book *Pioneering in Formosa: Recollections of Adventures among Mandarins, Wreckers and Head-hunting Savages* to the rapacity of the mandarins:

> The result of the misgovernment and oppression by the officials was that the resources of one of the most fertile islands in the world were being undeveloped or wasted, and instead of being a source of profit to the imperial government, Formosa was a drain upon its resources.

In December 1871 a ship from the Ryukyu Islands – then a semi-independent kingdom but soon annexed to Japan – was shipwrecked in south Taiwan. Three of those on board drowned. Of the 66 survivors, 54 were massacred by aborigines; the others escaped to a Han Chinese settlement and were repatriated. On behalf of the king of the Ryukyus, Japan demanded compensation. Beijing's response was curt: the Qing court bore no responsibility because the aborigines were beyond its jurisdiction. Tokyo then dispatched a 3,600-strong expeditionary force. Near Mudan, they fought and defeated the tribesmen on 22 May 1874. Japanese battle casualties were minimal, but one in six of the Japanese soldiers died of disease during the seven months they spent in Taiwan. The invaders didn't leave until the Qing court had paid an indemnity. Afterwards, the Qing tried to strengthen Taiwan's defences, but later events proved that these efforts were in vain.

In spring 1884 the Qing court clashed with France over Annam, now part of Vietnam. The French claimed it as a protectorate while China regarded it as a vassal state. To pressure the Qing court, in early October French forces occupied Keelung and attacked Tamsui. But the French found it difficult to quarantine the island as junks would cross the Taiwan Strait during the night and then dodge between islets and sandbars where the waters were too shallow for French warships to pursue them. The war ended with China recognising France's claims.

Following the French blockade, the Qing court began to pay much more attention to Taiwan. The island became a province in its own right in 1885; Liu Ming-chuan, who had led Qing forces in Taiwan during the Sino-French War, was the first governor. He ordered the building of a railroad between Taipei and Keelung, and in 1889 Taipei became the first city in the Chinese Empire to have electric lights along its streets and inside major buildings. Liu also introduced a postal system, had a telegraph cable laid between Tamsui and Xiamen and tried to reform taxation. He set up one government bureau to regulate the camphor and sulphur industries, and another to co-ordinate the search for oil. The creation of schools that taught foreign languages and science was encouraged; coastal fortifications were strengthened and soldiers given better training and equipment. After Liu was recalled to the mainland progress slowed. But Taiwanese hoping for another ruler who would shake things up didn't have to wait long.

CESSION TO JAPAN In August 1894 China and Japan went to war over Korea. For centuries Korea's kings had been paying tribute to China, but Japan – then in the throes of radical reforms which would lead to its emergence as a powerful industrial nation – forced the country to open itself to external trade. In June 1894 a Japanese expeditionary force installed a puppet Korean government which immediately asked Japan to remove Chinese soldiers from Korean soil. The Chinese, who were already leaving, were no match for well-trained, well-equipped Japanese units. By February 1895 the Japanese were pressing on into Manchuria; the following month they seized the Penghu Islands. The war came to a formal end on 17 April with the signing of the Treaty of Shimonoseki. Even though the Qing Dynasty controlled no more than half of Taiwan, they ceded the entire island, plus Penghu, to Japan in perpetuity.

With the tacit encouragement of the imperial court – or at least a faction in it – Qing officials in Taiwan declared the island's independence. Between 24 May, when the Republic of Taiwan was proclaimed, and 23 October, when the Japanese Army occupied Tainan, the state designed its own flag, had two presidents and issued postage stamps (they're considered quite collectable). It was not, as often claimed, Asia's first republic, but it was certainly another step in creating Taiwanese identity. The takeover was expensive in human lives with over 10,000 soldiers and civilians on the Taiwanese side dying; 164 Japanese soldiers were killed in combat, and another 4,642 died in accidents or from disease. Prince Yoshihisa Kitashirakawa, nominal commander of the expeditionary force, succumbed to malaria in Tainan on 5 November.

JAPANESE RULE The deaths of Prince Yoshihisa and a third of the men under his leadership made it clear that, if the Japanese were ever to benefit from their conquest, public health would have to improve. Yoshitaka Mori, a professor at Tokyo National University of Fine Arts and Music, has argued that the Japanese gained political legitimacy through infrastructure and public health improvements, and that Goto Shinpei (1857–1929), chief of civilian affairs in the colonial government from 1898 to 1906, was one of the era's most important personalities. Mori comments:

> Goto was the first person who understood the importance of controlling the population not only by coercive force but also through a kind of consensus. By introducing a way of Western urban planning, in particular the idea of public sanitation, he established magnificent governmental buildings, hospitals and schools to display Japanese authority. New buildings… functioned to stabilise upheaval… while he ordered the destruction of old traditional buildings which might evoke memories of Taiwanese past.

Goto thought major public buildings should be 'soldiers in civilian clothes' that would impress upon the local population the wisdom and might of the Japanese. He also established a system whereby opium could be sold only by licensed retailers and purchased only in limited quantities by registered smokers. There were 200,000 of the latter in 1904; by the end of 1922 that number had dwindled to fewer than 43,000. Goto's approach was both effective at curbing addiction and a way of aiding pro-Japan merchants, as the authorities made sure lucrative retail licences went only to supporters of the colonial regime. Camphor, salt, alcohol and tobacco monopolies ensured the colonial government's finances stayed in the black. Many Taiwanese recognise that, when it came to modernising their island, Japan did much of the heavy lifting.

When Japanese forces arrived in 1895 they found an island almost totally bereft of roads. The new rulers got to work right away; between early 1896 and the end of 1897 the total length of Taiwan's roads more than tripled. Kaohsiung and Keelung harbours were dredged and connected to the north–south railroad; bridges were built and schools were established; the lowlands were surveyed for tax purposes. But despite the power of the Japanese government machine, the colonial regime had no control over the mountainous interior and parts of the east coast.

To keep the indigenous population under control, the Japanese decided in 1914 to confiscate the rifles used by indigenous people to hunt deer and other animals. Between hunting expeditions, all guns were to be kept under lock and key in police stations. This policy and the deceitful methods the Japanese used in executing it outraged a Bunun chief called Raho Ari. In 1915 he and his clansmen massacred a police platoon at Dafen and then went into hiding near the upper reaches of the Laonong River, in what's now Yushan National Park. Tamaho, the village they founded there, grew into a community of 266 people as disaffected Bunun from elsewhere joined the rebels. Raho Ari remained a thorn in the side of the colonial authorities for two decades; he was able at will to breach the 'guardline' (a network of police stations and electric fences separating those areas under Japanese control from the wild interior) and launch guerrilla attacks on police stations, to kill Japanese and seize weapons and ammunition.

In the early years, Han insurgencies were also frequent. This prompted some Japanese parliamentarians to urge the sale of the island to whomever would take it off Tokyo's hands. In 1915 anti-Japanese factions in the southwest launched a rebellion that led to the deaths of over 1,000 Taiwanese plus hundreds of Japanese policemen and civilians. Many of those who participated in what came to be known as the Tapani Incident wore talismans which they believed made them invulnerable to modern weapons.

Inspired by the emergence of newly independent countries in eastern Europe and a Korean movement that pushed for self-determination and national identity, Taiwanese intellectuals and gentry founded the Taiwanese Cultural Association on 17 October 1921. The establishment of the TCA is seen as a landmark in the island's intellectual development and the emergence of a distinct Taiwanese (as opposed to Chinese or Japanese) identity. The association was suppressed in the late 1930s.

By autumn 1930 Mona Rudao, the educated son of a Sediq chief, was seething with rage. One of his sons had been insulted by a Japanese official and his youngest sister had been abandoned by her Japanese husband. Many other aborigines felt aggrieved: the colonial regime had taken away their guns and some of their ancestral lands, felled sacred trees and compelled tribesmen to labour for low wages on government projects. Japanese officers were notorious for expecting sexual favours from indigenous women. On 27 October 1930, Mona Rudao led a 300-strong band of warriors into the mountain town of Wushe where they attacked Japanese attending a school athletics event. The tribesmen were murderous but focused: 134 Japanese were killed but only two Han died. In response the Japanese assembled a massive force: 800 soldiers, 1,163 police officers and more than 1,300 paramilitaries recruited from other indigenous tribes. After two months of fighting, during which Japanese aircraft dropped poison gas on indigenous holdouts, the rebellion petered out. Mona Rudao ordered his people to commit suicide rather than surrender. Some 290 killed themselves. Of those who didn't at least a hundred were put to death after laying down their arms. They were beheaded by other aborigines in the pay of the Japanese as the latter awarded a bounty for each head. To ensure his enemies wouldn't have his head as a trophy, Mona Rudao took his own life in a remote cave on 1 December. His remains were found four years later and put on public display in Taipei. He wasn't given a proper burial until 1981.

After the outbreak of the Second Sino-Japanese War in 1937, the Japanese government launched the 'Kominka Movement', an attempt to erase Han identity in Taiwan and promote loyalty to the emperor in Tokyo. Over a thousand shrines were demolished or confiscated as part of an ineffective effort to replace local religion with Japanese beliefs. (Several had been destroyed earlier in the colonial period to make way for roads or public buildings.) Local periodicals were ordered to stop publishing Chinese-language supplements. The movement's promotion of the Japanese language and Japanese names was fairly successful: by 1945, two out of three Taiwanese could speak Japanese, and one in 14 had taken Japanese names. Among the latter was Lee Teng-hui, ROC president from 1988 to 2000, who until 1945 was known as Iwasato Masao.

WORLD WAR II Throughout the war, Japan treated Taiwan as a secure rear area where soldiers could be trained and POWs held (see box, page 130). Farmers were obliged to sell their rice to the colonial government; as in previous times of scarcity, sweet potatoes became the main carbohydrate. Production of rubber and timber were increased. In the final months, thousands of Taiwanese civilians died as the US Air Force bombed harbours and factories. Just as war made British society more egalitarian, so the conscription of Japanese nationals and the rapid expansion of industry opened up skilled positions previously closed to Taiwanese.

More than 200,000 Taiwanese joined the Japanese armed forces, some less willingly than others. Lee Teng-hui spent a short time in the Imperial Japanese Army; his elder brother was killed in the Philippines in 1945 while serving as a petty officer in the Imperial Japanese Navy. Several thousand indigenous men served in combat units. One of them, an Amis tribesman called Attun Palalin, got separated from his unit during a battle in what's now Indonesia. He survived for decades by hunting and gathering. It wasn't until November 1974 that he learned the war was over and he could return to his home village. During the war, around 2,000 Taiwanese females were kidnapped or tricked into becoming 'comfort women' forced to provide sexual services to Japanese soldiers.

NATIONALIST TAKEOVER At the end of the war, Taiwan became part of the Republic of China (ROC), the state created on the Chinese mainland when the last emperor was overthrown in 1911. On 25 October 1945, the last Japanese governor-general of Taiwan formally handed control of the island to Chen Yi, a Nationalist general whom Chiang Kai-shek had chosen to administer the island. Many Taiwanese were cautiously hopeful, but for some this optimism evaporated the moment they set eyes on the Nationalist army. Compared with the Japanese, KMT soldiers were slovenly and ill-disciplined. Taiwan's economy was already in a sorry state and Chen's mismanagement made the situation worse. He and his staff, whom many Taiwanese regarded as carpetbaggers, brought with them rampant corruption and hyperinflation.

Native Taiwanese were outraged by the favouritism Chen showed to his fellow mainlanders and by the looting of assets left behind by the Japanese. Public anger finally exploded on 27 February 1947 when Taipei citizens witnessed tobacco monopoly bureau agents beating an elderly widow whom they'd caught selling contraband cigarettes. The police responded to an impromptu demonstration with gunfire. Civilians were killed but the protests snowballed. As news of the violence spread there were uprisings across the island. It's said the majority of victims in the following week were mainlanders killed by native mobs.

Taiwanese leaders formed a committee and drew up a list of grievances. They met with Chen who requested ten days to consider their proposals. Secretly, the governor sent for extra troops to crush the rebellion. Taipei returned to semi-normality – but when Nationalist reinforcements arrived on 8 March, shooting began immediately. College students who'd formed peacekeeping teams surrendered their weapons as ordered and were then executed without trial. Hundreds of bodies were dumped in Keelung Harbour. Up to 28,000 people died in what's known as the 2-28 Incident (after the date protesters began attacking government offices, assaulting and in some cases killing those inside).

Aware that Communists, Taiwan independence supporters and others were trying to undermine the regime, the Nationalist authorities cracked down on all forms of political dissent. In the wake of the 2-28 Incident, up to 80% of city- and county-level elites 'disappeared from the political field' (to use the words of a report produced for the government-backed 2-28 Memorial Foundation). According to another study, around 140,000 people were detained and at least 3,000 executed. Many were sent to Green Island. Among them were mainlanders who'd fled to Taiwan with the Nationalists, Japanese-educated Taiwanese intellectuals, aborigines and even high school students. Some had been trying to subvert the government. Some had campaigned peacefully for political reforms. Many, it's now known, were completely innocent and victims either of the regime's paranoia or ambitious officials.

RETREAT TO TAIWAN By late 1948 it was clear that Chiang Kai-shek was losing the civil war against Mao Zedong's Chinese Communist Party. On 10 December 1949, Chiang and his son, Chiang Ching-kuo, arrived in Taiwan. They brought with them the ROC's gold reserves and some of the regime's political prisoners. The following March the elder Chiang resumed the ROC presidency, which he'd stepped down from a year earlier in order to lead the Nationalist armed forces. Between 1946 and the early 1950s, an estimated 2.2 million mainland Chinese fled to Taiwan, almost half of them being soldiers. Thousands more arrived later via Hong Kong and Burma. These refugees weren't the only people cut off from their families and hometowns; some Taiwanese studying or doing business on the mainland in 1949 were stranded there until restrictions on travel were relaxed in the late 1980s. While Chiang consolidated his control of Taiwan, many observers predicted a communist invasion of the island. However, a few days after the Korean War broke out on 25 June 1950, President Harry S Truman ordered the US Navy to patrol the Taiwan Strait and prevent a resumption of the Communist–KMT conflict.

One of the reasons the Nationalists lost the Chinese Civil War was their failure to address the needs of China's vast and impoverished rural population. Land reform efforts achieved little, and it was left to the Communists to seize and redistribute farmland. Apparently having learned a lesson – and no doubt keen to diminish the power of Taiwan's Japanese-influenced landed gentry – the KMT quickly implemented a 'land to the tiller' policy that revolutionised Taiwan's economy. The first step was to reduce rent, abolish the practice of paying rent in advance, and force landowners to grant six-year leases rather than the usual one or two years. Tenant farmers gained both income and security. Secondly, land that had previously belonged to the Japanese colonial government was sold off cheaply. Thirdly, major landowners were compelled to hand fields over to their tenants. The former were compensated: a little cash, some shares in state-owned companies and 'industrial revenue bonds' – government-backed vouchers that were worthless unless they were invested in some kind of business. A great many ex-landlords used these vouchers to set up factories that made goods for export.

On 23 August 1958, communist forces began an intense bombardment of Kinmen, the KMT-held front-line island better known in the West as Quemoy. Planning to seize the island, the Communists fired 474,900 shells during the 44-day battle. There were four naval clashes and numerous dogfights between ROC and PRC jets. The exhausted Communists suspended their campaign on 5 October, but until 1979 the two sides made a habit of shelling each other on alternate days. Often the shells contained propaganda leaflets rather than high explosives.

INDUSTRIALISATION By 1940 manufacturing was contributing more to the economy than agriculture, yet it wasn't until the late 1950s that Taiwan ceased depending on exports of sugar and bananas. Manufactured goods weren't just for foreign markets: refrigerators, rice cookers and electric fans were popular with domestic consumers. Clothes and shoes underpinned the economy in the 1960s; in the following decade Taiwan was the world's leading producer of tennis racquets and sunglasses. The population grew from under eight million in 1950 to 14.6 million in 1970 and women entered the labour market in record numbers. However, economic progress wasn't matched by democratic reforms. Peng Ming-min (b1923), a dissident who stood for the presidency in 1996, described political conditions in his 1972 book *A Taste of Freedom*:

> [The claim that Chiang's regime] represented a 'government of China' was an absurd fiction which amounted to a gigantic hoax. This fiction enabled the Nationalist government to maintain two levels of organisation, the so-called 'national government' in which all positions of effective power were reserved for [mainlanders]… and a subordinate provincial administration partially open to Formosan participation. Over 80% of the national budget was spent on military affairs, including elaborate secret police organisations… The Formosans who constitute 85% of the population [had] less than 3% representation in the national legislature… Advocates of birth control are considered defeatists, and a high birth rate is encouraged only to produce conscript soldiers for Chiang's armies twenty years hence.

THE END OF THE 20TH CENTURY Chiang Kai-shek died on 5 April 1975 and was succeeded by Vice President Yen Chia-kan (1905–93). Like Chiang, Yen was a mainlander who'd retreated to Taiwan in 1949. When Yen's term ended in 1978, Chiang's only biological son, the Russian-educated Chiang Ching-kuo, became president. Throughout his premiership and presidency, the younger Chiang promoted several Taiwan-born officials to high office. His first vice president, Hsieh Tung-min (1908–2001), was a Taiwanese who'd moved to the Chinese mainland in 1925. Another of his protégés, agricultural economist Lee Teng-hui (b1923), had a very different background. Lee, who has never visited the Chinese mainland let alone lived there, received a Japanese education and often speaks of the affinity he felt for Japan.

According to Jack F Williams, an American geographer who wrote an academic paper titled *Sugar: The Sweetener in Taiwan's Development*, sugarcane was already growing in Taiwan when the Dutch set up their trading base in Tainan in 1624. The VOC recognised sugar's potential as a cash crop and encouraged Han migrants to plant more. Koxinga continued where the Dutch had left off and exported sugar to Japan. During Qing rule the industry grew but slowly; after 1895, however, production surged as Japanese entrepreneurs, backed by the colonial government, built modern refineries and expanded the area under cultivation. By 1920 sugar accounted for 65% of Taiwan's exports; by 1950 this figure was 80%. Since the late 1950s the industry has shrunk to a fraction of its former size because other countries are able to produce sugar more cheaply. Yet sugar has left a noticeable physical imprint on the landscape, and not only in the shape of imposing refinery buildings. Most of the large fields in the south used to be sugar plantations and Taiwan Sugar Corp remains one of the country's largest landowners.

On 15 December 1978, Washington and Beijing announced they were establishing formal diplomatic relations and that US military bases in Taiwan would close. The American move, intended to encircle the Soviet Union, left many Taiwanese feeling betrayed. The following year the US Congress passed the Taiwan Relations Act, a law stipulating that Washington–Taipei contact and co-operation – including arms sales – would continue, albeit on a semi-official basis.

Democracy activists launched a magazine called *Meilidao* (literally 'beautiful island', but in English sometimes called *Formosa*). The government, jittery after the rupturing of diplomatic ties with the US, had already decided to ban this publication when its Kaohsiung office applied for permission to hold a seminar marking Human Rights Day on 10 December 1979. The application was rejected but the organisers went ahead regardless. Demonstrators clashed with police and soldiers, and the authorities used the riot as a pretext to round up most of Taiwan's dissidents. More than 50 individuals were tried for their role in what was soon dubbed the 'Kaohsiung Incident' or the 'Meilidao Incident', or for harbouring fugitives. The trials were a watershed for Taiwan's democracy movement; not only were the accused able to make long speeches during proceedings attended by foreign reporters, but a second generation of activists – the lawyers defending them – caught the public eye. One of the latter, Chen Shui-bian (b1950), became Taiwan's first non-KMT president in 2000. The Meilidao Incident is commemorated in the Chinese name of Kaohsiung's Formosa Boulevard metro station.

For a long time 'Made in Taiwan' meant cheap and shoddy, but since the 1970s Taiwanese companies have been successfully 'moving up the chain', producing more sophisticated items and innovating rather than imitating. From the mid 1980s until the Asian Financial Crisis of 1997, exports of high-tech products such as computer peripherals and memory chips powered an economic boom. In 1950, living standards in Taiwan were on a par with those in India. Within two decades the island had overtaken Argentina in terms of real household incomes. In recent years international rankings of GDP per capita, adjusted for purchasing power parity, place Taiwan on a par with Australia, ahead of the UK and Japan. However, because Taiwanese families need to spend much more on their children's education and save greater amounts for their old age compared with British families, in reality they aren't more affluent.

During the final two years of Chiang Ching-kuo's presidency, Taiwan moved towards democracy. Martial law was lifted in 1987, as was a ban on the formation of new political parties (there are now over 300). Opponents of the KMT established the Democratic Progressive Party. Taiwan's parliament ceased to be a rubber-stamp body, but proceedings were often marred by demonstrations and fights as lawmakers threw shoes and chairs at each other, smashed microphones or draped banners across the furniture.

Lee Teng-hui became the appointed mayor of Taipei in 1978 and vice president in 1984. When he took the top job after Chiang Ching-kuo's death on 13 January 1988 he wasn't expected to wield real power. But within a few years he'd skilfully sidelined his opponents within the KMT and the military, and brought like-minded people into his cabinet. Constitutional measures called 'Temporary Provisions Effective During the Period of Communist Rebellion' were cancelled. For the first time in its history, those making Taiwan's laws had actually been elected by the island's people. While paying lip service to the ideal of unification, Lee embarked on a 'Taiwan First' path that riled Beijing but won him a landslide when the first direct presidential elections were held in 1996.

At 01.47 on 21 September 1999, people throughout Taiwan were roused from their sleep by a tremor measuring 7.3 on the Richter scale. Near the epicentre of what's often referred to as the 9-21 earthquake, in the central Taiwan township of Jiji, there was great devastation. Some 2,416 people died and 11,443 were seriously injured. Almost 100,000 buildings collapsed or were damaged beyond repair.

POST-MILLENNIUM EVENTS Barred by the constitution from seeking another term, Lee selected Vice President Lien Chan to be the KMT candidate in the 2000 presidential election, prompting KMT heavyweight James Soong to run as an independent. Lien's campaign failed to take off and Soong was harmed by corruption allegations. Chen Shui-bian, a former Taipei mayor running for the opposition Democratic Progressive Party, won with 39% of the vote. His running mate, ex-dissident Annette Lu, became Taiwan's first female vice president. Chen's election dismayed Beijing, which continued to block Taipei's efforts to take part in international organisations such as the United Nations. Many pan-greens (see box, opposite) thought a new era was about to unfold, but governing the country in the face of KMT obstruction wasn't easy. The KMT and its allies used their majority in parliament to thwart many of Chen's initiatives.

Chen's first term in office was marred by a weak economy, yet symbolic changes that underscored Taiwan's separate identity – such as adding the word 'Taiwan' to ROC passports – seemed genuinely popular. In the weeks before the 2004 presidential election, opinion polls showed Chen neck-and-neck with Lien Chan (who'd recruited James Soong as his running mate). The day before voting, Chen was campaigning in Tainan when a lone gunman fired from the crowd. Both Chen and Vice President Lu were slightly wounded; the gunman escaped and committed suicide ten days later. Chen won the election by fewer than 30,000 votes out of almost 13 million cast. Some blue politicians insisted the shooting was staged to generate sympathy votes, but failed to provide any evidence to back up their claim.

During his term as Taipei mayor, Chen changed the name of Jieshou Road (which honoured Chiang Kai-shek) to Ketagalan Boulevard (after one of Taiwan's lowland aboriginal tribes). After reaching the presidency, he continued pushing for 'localisation' and 'name rectification'. The word 'China' was dropped from the names of government-owned companies and the post office. But during his second

Politically, Taiwan is divided into two camps: the blues and the greens. The former faction is dominated by the Kuomintang (KMT), the Chinese Nationalist Party founded by Dr Sun Yat-sen (see box, page 103) and led for decades by Chiang Kai-shek. The greens (not to be confused with the environmentalist Green Party of Taiwan) are the Democratic Progressive Party (DPP) and other supporters of independence and localisation. The DPP's Tsai Ing-wen, who led the party between 2008 and 2012 and again from 2014, was elected Taiwan's first female president in 2016.

term, Chen's approval ratings sank as first his wife, and then his son-in-law, were embroiled in corruption scandals.

Few people were surprised when the KMT's Ma Ying-jeou (b1950) beat the DPP's Frank Hsieh in the presidential election on 22 March 2008. Ma, whose campaign had focused on economic issues and his own squeaky-clean image, got 58% of the vote. Prosecutors barred the outgoing president from leaving the country and on 11 September 2009 Chen was sentenced to life in prison for money laundering, embezzlement and accepting bribes. Following appeals and trials on related charges, Chen's sentence was reduced to 19 years; in early 2015 he was released on medical parole.

On the evening of 6 August 2009, local governments around Taiwan announced that schools and offices would not open the following day because of the approach of Typhoon Morakot. The rain began falling and didn't stop until some parts of the south had received an unbelievable 2,900mm (almost ten feet) of precipitation in 72 hours. Dozens of mountain communities were cut off by landslides and thousands of people had to be rescued by helicopter. By the end of the week 700 people were dead or missing.

Despite Beijing's insistence that Taiwan is part of China, and its refusal to renounce the use of force against the island, the Ma administration quickly signed several non-political agreements with the PRC. Scheduled direct flights between Taiwan and cities on the mainland got underway and PRC tourists began visiting Taiwan in large numbers. A trade pact inked by Taipei and Beijing stirred controversy. Supporters said it would give Taiwanese companies greater access to the vast mainland market, while critics argued it would make Taiwan even more dependent on China and erode the island's sovereignty.

Ma won a second term in office in early 2012. However, anger over soaring house prices, stagnating wages, government land grabs and a wiretapping scandal soon pushed his popularity ratings below 10%. In 2014, both major political parties were blindsided by the intervention of a group of young activists who became known as the 'Sunflower Movement'. Angered that KMT lawmakers were trying to rush through another China–Taiwan trade deal, protestors invaded the parliament building on the evening of 18 March and brought proceedings to a halt. Led by college students, the 'sunflowers' stood firm for 23 days, enjoying huge public support, before winning concessions and making a negotiated withdrawal. The activists' anti-KMT resolve was one reason (a food safety scandal was another) for the DPP landslide win in local elections later in 2014.

The DPP's Tsai Ing-wen (b1957) cruised to a comfortable victory in the 2016 presidential election. Tsai, who has never married, holds a PhD from the London School of Economics. Being a quarter Paiwan, she is the first president with indigenous ancestry and also made history by becoming the first female national leader in Asia who isn't the widow, daughter or sister of a previous leader. Inevitably, some people are disappointed with her performance since taking office and re-election in 2020 isn't guaranteed. Nevertheless, civil society in Taiwan remains stronger than almost anywhere else in Asia. Every day, newspapers embarrass the authorities and citizens protest without fear.

GOVERNMENT AND POLITICS

Taiwan is a republic. The head of state is the president, directly elected by citizens aged 20 and above every four years. Presidents are limited to two consecutive terms. Taiwan's president since 2016 has been Tsai Ing-wen of the DPP.

The president appoints a premier (prime minister) who heads the cabinet. Unlike in the UK, cabinet members aren't members of parliament. The Legislative Yuan, as the parliament is called, has 113 members – 73 elected from single-member, first-past-the-post constituencies, 34 allocated proportionally to parties that obtain more than 5% of the national vote, and six reserved for indigenous people. Each citizen has two votes: one in his or her local constituency and one for a national party list. At the time of writing, the DPP held 69 seats, giving them a comfortable majority in the Legislative Yuan.

ECONOMY

Taiwanese often say they work so hard and focus so much on business because the island has no natural resources. That's true in the modern industrial sense: Taiwan has no oil and only tiny amounts of natural gas; the north's coal, gold and copper mines closed decades ago; and the island's forests are no longer logged on any significant scale. Yet the influx of Han Chinese immigrants in the 18th and 19th centuries was due largely to the presence of camphor, plus enough water to make intensive agriculture possible.

Taiwan has moved on from its days as an island of manufacturers who export low-cost goods, although you'll still see plenty of factories. It has a well-developed capitalist economy; thousands of new companies emerge each year while thousands of old ones hit the wall. Barriers to entry are low so many Taiwanese try their hand at running a small enterprise. It isn't unusual for restaurants and shops to open without any kind of business licence. Rules and regulations are often ignored until the business grows to a size where officialdom starts to take an interest.

Economic growth is now slower than in the halcyon 1980s. In 2017, Taiwan's GDP was US$579 billion, making it the 22nd-largest economy in the world. In recent years, many of Taiwan's largest corporations have shifted manufacturing operations overseas (to China or other low-wage countries) while keeping their head offices and research and development divisions in Taiwan. Service industries, including tourism, now employ more than half the working population. Agriculture accounts for less than 2% of GDP; most farmers are over 60 years old. The transition from a factory-based economy to a more diverse and advanced economy hasn't been easy for older, less-educated individuals. In 2018, unemployment was around 3.5%.

Taiwan's reliance on the USA as an export market (it used to take almost half of its exports) has been replaced by economic dependence on the only country that threatens it militarily. China and Hong Kong now take more than 40% of Taiwan's exports. The mainland has also absorbed over US$100 billion in Taiwanese investment (official figures, which don't include investments routed through third countries, are much lower).

PEOPLE

Travellers passing through Taiwan can be forgiven for assuming it's a homogeneous society. Compared with Japan or Hong Kong, Taiwan's Western and Asian expatriate populations are small and there are very few people of African origin. Taiwanese society has often and recently fractured along ethnic lines. The aborigines tried to defend their land against Han Chinese settlers. Within the Han majority, Hoklo from one county in Fujian fought Hoklo from another county. For decades after World War II, there was considerable friction between the Hoklo majority and the ruling class dominated by recent immigrants from the Chinese mainland.

Ethnic relations are now fairly harmonious and intermarriage, along with internal migration, is blurring the lines between population groups. However, children of 'mixed marriages' often fail to learn languages other than Mandarin and Taiwanese.

THE INDIGENOUS PEOPLE Taiwan's original inhabitants number just over 560,000 and make up nearly 2.4% of the population. The ROC government recognises 16 tribes, the largest being the Amis with around 210,000 members, the Paiwan (101,000) and the Atayal (90,000). Other groups are lobbying for similar status, as it opens the door to subsidies and other benefits. At the time of writing, the Siraya in Tainan (see box, page 216) were nearing the end of a court battle that may well result in central government recognition of the tribe.

Taiwan's indigenous people are of Austronesian origin. In fact, some scholars claim Taiwan is where the Austronesian branch of humanity started out (see box, page 26). Formerly classified as 'mountain compatriots' – and still often stereotyped as hard-drinking, poorly educated but kind-hearted mountain-dwelling folk – the aborigines farmed and hunted on the lowlands until Han settlers forced them to relocate to the interior. There was a great deal of intermarriage between early settlers and indigenous people. Also, many of the latter abandoned their original names and languages to better fit into Han-dominated mainstream society.

The Japanese were intolerant of cultural practices they regarded as barbaric, such as the tattooing of faces and hands. A few very elderly Atayal, Sediq and Truku women still bear the traditional cheek tattoos of their tribes. Indigenous cultures survive in villages in mountain areas and in east Taiwan. However, few indigenous people under the age of 40 speak their ancestral tongue fluently, even among those who participate enthusiastically in the many and varied tribal festivals. Traditional clothing is worn only on special occasions and most aboriginal homes resemble the concrete boxes found in lowland towns.

Taiwanese who have indigenous ancestry are now less likely to hide the fact. Despite affirmative action and other government help, indigenous people continue to be considerably poorer and less well educated than other Taiwanese, although they're prominent in pop music and professional sport.

THE HOKLO PEOPLE A unified Hoklo ('Taiwanese') identity is a relatively recent thing. Well into the 19th century, many Hoklo people identified themselves as being Quanzhou folk or Zhangzhou folk rather than Hoklo or Taiwanese. (Quanzhou and Zhangzhou were prefectures in Qing-era Fujian.) During the Japanese occupation and the subsequent Nationalist dictatorship, these sub-ethnic groups coalesced. Taiwanese of Hoklo descent account for around 70% of the population. Some

Taiwan is a highly educated society yet some ancient superstitions are showing incredible staying power. More than a few Taiwanese will tell you the future is sometimes foretold in dreams and that evil spirits threaten the well-being of the living.

The fear of ghosts is widespread among those of Fujianese descent. Because those who died suddenly – especially suicides, murder victims and those who drowned – are thought to haunt the spot where they died, estate agents are required by law to disclose details of any 'violent events' that took place in the properties they're trying to sell. If a murder victim is buried before his or her killer is brought to justice, the family of the deceased may inter that person with a knife in one hand and an axe in the other, so the dead person's spirit may better hunt down the killer.

Just as the number 13 is unlucky in the West, quite a few Taiwanese avoid renting or buying fourth-floor apartments because the Mandarin word for 'four' (sì) sounds similar to the word for 'death' (sǐ). Such homophones are central to several beliefs. Taoist priests who officiate at funerals sometimes present surviving relatives with nails. These are believed to help the younger generation beget sons and continue the family line because in Taiwanese the word for 'nail' sounds like the word for 'son' – both are pronounced *ding*. These nails aren't to be used, however, especially if there's a pregnant woman in the house. Hammering nails into the wall of a house where there's a mother-to-be may harm the unborn baby, it's said.

call themselves 'true Taiwanese' or even 'native Taiwanese' to the annoyance of Austronesian indigenous people.

THE HAKKA PEOPLE Like Hoklo Taiwanese, the Hakka are Han Chinese. Their origins are unclear but it's believed they emerged as a distinct sub-ethnic group, speaking their own language and following a unique set of customs, as they moved *en masse* from central China to the south in a series of migrations between the 4th and 17th centuries. Unlike most Han Chinese, the Hakka never practised foot-binding. Because they've had to relocate so often and they've sometimes faced persecution, the Hakka are often compared to the Jews. Like the Jews, they've a reputation for working hard, living frugally and encouraging their children to study hard. Hakka started arriving in Taiwan in the early 18th century.

Taiwan's Hakka are concentrated in the hilly region between Zhongli and the Dajia River, and in a few towns in the south, notably Meinong. Since the late 19th century many Hakka have migrated to the big cities or to east Taiwan. English-language information about Hakka culture can be found at w www.hakka.gov.tw.

THE MAINLANDERS In the 1950s, officials, soldiers, civilians and their families who fled from the mainland – together with their Taiwan-born children – accounted for a quarter of the island's population (9.4 million in 1957). This diverse group included Shanghai tycoons, Buddhist monks and Muslims from China's far west. In traditional Han thinking, one's ancestry and identity comes from one's father; for this reason, many ROC citizens who have a Taiwanese mother and have never visited the PRC are considered mainlanders. Most mainlanders settled in the larger cities but some ended up in remote mountain areas where they worked on road-building projects or did farmwork. All but a few of the old soldiers have passed away and the military dependants' villages where they lived have been demolished. Owing to high rates of intermarriage, coupled with a reluctance to highlight mainlander ancestry now that the political wind blows from a different direction, the distinctive 'mainlander demographic' that dominated the government and military has more or less disappeared, even though over 300,000 PRC citizens have married Taiwanese in recent years.

ASIAN IMMIGRANTS For decades, ethnic Chinese from Malaysia, Myanmar and other countries have been coming to Taiwan to study. Many have stayed on, found jobs, married and had children. Since the 1990s, many Taiwanese men have sought wives abroad, especially from Vietnam. There are also contingents of Filipinos, Thais and Indonesians. Mainland Chinese who've relocated to Taiwan in recent years, usually because they've married an ROC citizen, are another minority. In recent years, one in 11 of the island's newborns has had at least one non-Taiwanese parent.

LANGUAGE

MANDARIN In theory, Taiwan and China share a common official language: Mandarin Chinese. In the PRC it's known as Pǔtōnghuà ('common language') while in Taiwan it's called Guóyǔ ('national language'). In reality, Taiwan Mandarin and mainland Mandarin are somewhat like American English and British English: people from one side usually have no problems communicating with folk from the other but there are differences in pronunciation and word use. The 'curled-tongue' accent so common in northern China is almost unknown in Taiwan except among people originally from certain parts of the mainland. Also, Taiwanese learn traditional ('long form') characters at school whereas mainlanders are taught simplified ('short form') characters. The latter are quicker to write but, say critics, much of the original beauty and nuance is lost.

In terms of grammar, Mandarin is beautifully simple. There are no cases or genders and verbs do not conjugate. Nouns stay the same whether they're singular or plural.

Pronunciation is difficult to master because the correct tone (pitch) must be used for each syllable. There are four tones plus a fifth, seldom-used neutral tone. Using an incorrect tone can convey a very different meaning from the one intended. For instance, *bēi* means 'cup' while *běi* means 'north'. Several words have both the same pronunciation and the same tone. Lǐ is a very common surname, for example, but one online dictionary lists 17 other words that sound exactly the same. Taken out of context, individual words are easily misunderstood, even by native Mandarin speakers.

With the exception of a few old people, everyone in Taiwan understands Mandarin, though not all are capable of or willing to speak it.

TAIWANESE The language many people call Taiwanese is a form of Hokkien, the language spoken in much of Fujian, the Chinese province from whence most of Taiwan's early Han settlers came. The language has various names in Taiwan including Taigi, Holo, Táiwānhuà and Mǐnnányǔ. It has eight tones. In rural areas, especially in the south, it's the most commonly used language.

Taiwanese and Mandarin are mutually unintelligible. However, there are several similarities, just as many English words are close to their German equivalents. Words borrowed from Japanese are frequently used; one you might hear is *o-to-bai*, meaning 'motorbike'.

Between the 1950s and 1980s the KMT discouraged the use of Taiwanese. Students who spoke it in the classroom were punished and few Taiwanese-language TV shows

1

were aired. Nowadays many soap operas, news reports and talk shows are entirely or mostly in Taiwanese. Some citizens still feel that speaking Taiwanese is low class. However, they're outnumbered by those who speak it proudly as an expression of their self or national identity. However, fluency in Taiwanese is no longer a clear marker of a person's ethnic or political affiliation. Some people with mixed mainlander/local parentage habitually speak Taiwanese. Also, quite a few young people who are 100% Taiwanese on both sides don't speak the language well. Nonetheless, those running for elected office must have some fluency in Taiwanese, whatever their politics.

HAKKA The language of Taiwan's Hakka minority isn't mutually intelligible with either Mandarin or Taiwanese. An archaic language that retains features of Chinese as it was spoken more than a thousand years ago, it's more closely related to Cantonese (Hong Kong's main language) than Mandarin. Taiwan's government subsidises a Hakka-language TV station and Hakka-language courses in schools, yet the tongue is gradually losing ground to Mandarin and Taiwanese. Of the five Hakka accents most widely spoken in Taiwan, four can be traced back to particular counties in Guangdong.

INDIGENOUS LANGUAGES Unlike the three Han languages commonly spoken in Taiwan (Mandarin, Taiwanese and Hakka), what are known as the Formosan Austronesian languages don't have tones. Nor, until the arrival of the Dutch in the 17th century, did they have any written form.

TAIWAN: CRADLE OF AUSTRONESIA?

If some academics are right, millions of people in southeast Asia, the Pacific and New Zealand have some Taiwanese ancestry. The theory that Austronesian populations can trace their origins to Taiwan, first proposed a quarter of a century ago, gained credence in 2009 with the publication of two intriguing studies. One focused on words and languages, the other on germs.

It's not known when proto-Austronesians reached Taiwan, but most scholars are convinced they came from the Chinese mainland. According to a team at the University of Auckland, computer analyses of the core vocabularies of 400 Austronesian languages 'clearly show that the origin of the entire Austronesian language family can be dated back to Taiwan around 5,200 years ago'. A millennium on, the team concluded, Austronesians from Taiwan settled in the Philippines. From there, they spread rapidly across Polynesia. Several waves of migrants reached Hawaii and New Zealand between AD500 and 1300. Easter Island may have been reached as early as AD300, or as late as 1200.

A multi-national investigation of stomach bacteria reached very similar conclusions. Germs evolve like plants and animals, and by comparing gut bacteria taken from Taiwanese aborigines with samples from Polynesians and New Guineans, scientists were able to chart the way in which a certain microbe linked to various stomach ailments has mutated and diversified. This medical evidence correlates well with archaeological discoveries throughout the Pacific. However, studies of human DNA suggest the islands of southeast Asia were inhabited before Taiwan, and that climate change prompted proto-Austronesians to disperse in several directions, including north to Taiwan, within the past 10,000 years.

CALENDARS AND ZODIACS

Taiwanese companies, schools and government offices follow the Gregorian calendar. Most people work or go to school from Monday to Friday and have Saturday and Sunday off. However, official dates are counted from the establishment of the Republic of China in 1912. The year 2018 was therefore ROC year 107; 2019 is year 108.

What's often called the lunar calendar and sometimes referred to as the farmers' calendar is still very important, however. If you look closely at any diary or calendar made in Taiwan, you'll see the lunar date printed below the Gregorian date. The timing of many holidays and festivals depends on this calendar, which is actually lunisolar (in that it indicates both the moon phase and the time of the solar year). Certain religious practices, such as burning joss paper (see box, page 98) and not eating meat (see box, page 62), are observed on the first and 15th day of every lunar month. The lunar calendar is 354 days long. So it doesn't fall out of sync with the 365-day astronomical year, an intercalary (additional or 'leap') month is added to the lunar calendar about once every three years. The formula used to calculate when an extra month is required is very complex, so it's not as predictable as the quadrennial addition of February 29 to the Gregorian calendar.

The most important days on the lunar calendar are those at the very end of one lunar year and at the beginning of the next. This period, usually called Chinese New Year or Lunar New Year, is celebrated by ethnic Chinese communities throughout the world. The Chinese animal zodiac follows the lunar calendar, not the Gregorian calendar. Babies who came into the world on 3 February 2019 were born in the Year of the Dog; those born a week later are Year of the Pig kids. The other creatures in the 12-year cycle are: rat, ox, tiger, rabbit, dragon, snake, horse, goat, monkey and rooster.

The amazing diversity of Taiwan's indigenous languages fascinates linguists and endows them with a significance far beyond the small number of speakers (perhaps 300,000 aboriginals and a handful of foreign Christian missionaries). Just as many researchers think Taiwan was the wellspring from which Austronesian peoples and cultures originated, many linguists believe Taiwan was the root of the entire Austronesian language family, a grouping that includes the national languages of Indonesia, Malaysia and the Philippines, plus hundreds more languages spoken in places as far apart as Madagascar, Hawaii and New Zealand. According to Robert A Blust, a professor at the University of Hawaii, Austronesian languages can be divided into ten branches, nine of which exist only in Taiwan, and that all Austronesian languages spoken outside Taiwan (including the language of Orchid Island's indigenous Tao people) belong to the Malayo-Polynesian branch, which embraces more than 1,200 languages spoken by over 350 million people.

Of the 26 Austronesian languages known to have been spoken in Taiwan, ten have died out. At least four more are on the verge of extinction.

RELIGION

Religion in Taiwan is a bit like the island's politics: noisy, turbulent and inescapable. However, unlike the hate-filled relationship between the blue and green camps (see box, page 21), the various faiths, sects and cults seem to get along well. Many people are extremely pious, to be sure, but just as many seem to treat religion like they do life insurance – something that's so important they wouldn't do without it, but which needs to be attended to just once or twice a year.

No more than one in ten Taiwanese practises a religion that excludes other faiths, be it a 'pure' form of Buddhism, Christianity or Islam. The majority of pious Taiwanese follow a blend of Taoism, Buddhism and popular beliefs. The proportions vary from person to person and are impossible to estimate, even for

TEMPLE ARCHITECTURE

As with churches and mosques, Chinese temples are laid out in accordance with certain architectural conventions. From the visitor's perspective, the first of these concerns the three doorways at the front. The doors are always painted red – Taiwan's temples are dominated by shades of red and gold – and usually they're decorated with colourful full-body portraits of General Qin and General Yuchi. This duo, who lived in the Tang Dynasty, became 'door gods' because of their ability to repel demons. The lion statues in temple forecourts have a similar protective function; the lion pawing a ball is male, while the one with a cub is female. The door on the right, the 'dragon door', is the correct entrance to use. The one on the left, the 'tiger door', is the doorway by which you should leave. You shouldn't enter by the central portal as it's reserved for supernatural entities. The red wooden planks that lie across the bottom of each doorway are there to stop evil spirits from getting inside.

Larger temples have internal courtyards and small towers on either side. The tower on the right contains a bell; the one on the left has a large drum. These days, temple bells and drums are usually struck mechanically rather than by hand. In smaller shrines the bell and drum are within the main chamber, attached to the wall or the ceiling.

Most temples have at least three altars; some have a dozen. They're obvious and, as you'd expect, the central altar is dedicated to the temple's main deity. In front of each altar there's an offertory table on which you're likely to see joss paper, fruit, incense and candles. It may be difficult to get a really good look at the icons themselves as they're often behind steel bars or a Perspex screen. The bars prevent theft – precious idols have been stolen or kidnapped – while the screens keep them from getting sooty. Ancient temples typically also contain other important relics, among them carved stone censers (modern censers are usually made of steel) and inscribed boards. The latter, rectangular boards hung from rafters, bear auspicious four-character slogans plus the name of the person (often an emperor or president) who donated it to the temple and the date the donation was made.

Many Buddhist houses of worship are beautiful in their simplicity. By contrast, temples where popular religion is practised (see box, page 30) are made as opulent as possible. In the eyes of those who build and decorate such shrines, less is never more. In many temples, the stone columns and wooden beams have been carved to resemble dragons and other creatures. The exteriors and roofs are often bedecked with ceramic figurines; many of the latter are mass-produced but some are superb examples of *koji* glazed earthenware (page 227). Identifying the legendary characters and understanding the meaning of each animal greatly enhances a temple visit; a tour guide who can explain these things is worth his or her fee.

a given individual, because, 'All three of these strains… have contributed heavily to [Taiwan's] religious life, and their interpenetration is so extensive as to prevent a thorough sorting of the elements one might associate with each in its "primal" state' (David K Jordan, *Gods, Ghosts & Ancestors*).

Taiwan has an estimated 30,000 non-Christian houses of worship. In these shrines you'll see spirit images representing the Jade Emperor, Mazu and other deities of Chinese origin, plus icons that represent supernatural or divine entities propitiated only in Taiwan, such as the Yimin worshipped by Hakka people (see box, page 152). Guanyin, the Buddhist goddess of compassion, can be found in a great many non-Buddhist shrines. However, Buddhist temples don't generally accommodate images of popular gods. Taoist rituals are conducted in mainstream shrines, before private altars and, as part of funerals or exorcisms, inside ordinary homes.

Popular religion in Taiwan includes thousands of divine or supernatural personalities; one tally puts the number of deities at approximately 36,000. Some have always been gods but many are like Christian saints in that they were ordinary humans who led exemplary lives. After death their reputations grew as miracles were attributed to them. There are several instances of Chinese emperors issuing edicts stating that a certain deceased individual had become a god, a process more akin to ratification than promotion. In temples you'll also see depictions of supernatural individuals who aren't venerated – such as Mazu's two cohorts – and a few animals who are, such as Lord Tiger, whose effigy is usually on the floor beside an altar.

There are several explanations for the fantastic richness of the island's religious life. Firstly, most Taiwanese trace their ancestry to Fujian, a province regarded as the most superstitious part of China. The dangers faced by early migrants, such as the perilous sea crossing, epidemics and headhunting aborigines, made them cling even more tightly to their incense and icons. The Japanese colonial regime's Kominka Movement (page 16) was a direct attack on popular religious beliefs, and the postwar Chinese Nationalist dictatorship discouraged what it branded 'excessive and wasteful' temple practices, but neither of these episodes can be compared to the decades-long vehement suppression of religion throughout the communist-ruled mainland. Rising income and better education since World War II hasn't led to growing secularism. If anything, temples have been a major beneficiary of Taiwan's prosperity. Not only do people have more money to donate, but it's said the pace and uncertainty of modern life induces them to seek answers from gods or gurus. Whatever the reasons, traditional religion in Taiwan shows no signs of decline.

TAIWAN'S MAJOR RELIGIONS Because of the overlap between Buddhism, Taoism and what might be called the Common Religion or the Popular Religion (see box, page 30), estimating the size of each religion's following is very difficult.

Confucianism isn't a religion but rather a system of ethics that stresses propriety and respect for one's elders and betters. Confucian temples are best viewed as memorials to the philosopher and his most notable disciples. In them, Confucius is always represented by a tablet. In some mainstream shrines, however, statuettes of the sage are worshipped alongside popular deities.

Taoism This religion grew out of a philosophy, founded by Chinese philosopher Laozi, who lived in the 4th or 6th century BC and is now one of the religion's deities. Tao (*dào* in Mandarin) means 'the path' or 'the direction', but in a religious context it's sometimes translated as 'the flow of the universe'; Taoism stresses going with that flow, not fighting the current. The three core principles can be summarised as kindness, frugality and modesty. The central Taoist text is the *Tao Te Ching*,

The religions of Greater China (Taoism, Buddhism and Confucianism) are often collectively called the 'Three Teachings', and these major textual traditions dominate the written record, having influenced the governments and literate elites of Chinese societies, as well as, to varying but limited degrees, communities as a whole. However, these religions have never been the main religion of society. Confucianism in particular – as a comprehensive ideological and ritual system – never extended beyond the gentry, and it was far less influential on the cultural life of the great majority of Chinese than either Buddhism or Taoism.

The most universal and socially unifying form of religious culture never had a name of its own, just like the religion of the ancient Romans, which is today simply referred to as 'Roman religion'. But given the plurality of religious traditions in China, we cannot simply call it 'Chinese (or *huá* 華) religion', meaning that most scholars have come to call it the Chinese Popular Religion – though I and others prefer to call it the Common Religion, as it was shared by all classes of society, and amid stylistic and regional varieties, the religion formed the common basis of a shared culture from village, town and city to the imperial court.

The closest name in Chinese historical texts for this foundational strata of the religious culture is *shè huì* 社會, literally 'the gathering to worship the Community Earth God'. The ritual cycles of the local *shè huì* formed the primary institution that joined different family and professional groups of society to become a shared community.

With good reason, most Taiwanese people call this nameless and universal 'popular religion' of society as a whole 'Taoism', though this requires some unpacking. 'Religious' Taoism (the only Taoism that ever existed as a historical entity

attributed to Laozi. The Jade Emperor is a notable member of the Taoist pantheon often worshipped in local temples.

Buddhism

Buddhism spread from India to China more than 2,000 years ago and was brought to Taiwan by Han migrants in the 17th century. As in China, Buddhism in Taiwan is part of the Mahāyāna ('Great Vehicle') tradition. Until the 1960s Buddhism was less popular than Taoism and mainstream religion but recently it has enjoyed rapid resurgence. Dharma Drum Mountain, one of the island's major Buddhist associations, claims its membership increased tenfold between 1993 and 2008. The most prominent forms of Buddhism in Taiwan are Pure Land Buddhism (which scholars say appeals to those who grew up surrounded by Taoism) and Zen (*Chán* in Mandarin). In the 1930s and 1940s, the colonial authorities tried unsuccessfully to promote Shintoism in Taiwan; during that era Japanese Buddhism made some inroads. The Tibetan Tantric form of Buddhism has attracted followers in recent years, but it's the tendency of Taiwanese Buddhists to engage in charitable acts around the world and social activism at home that gives them their high profile.

I-Kuan Tao

This faith claims to have over 800,000 adherents on the island but is little known in the West. Founded in China in the 1930s, I-Kuan Tao draws on Buddhism, Taoism and Confucianism and requires followers to be non-smoking, teetotal and vegetarian. It is notable for its stance on other religions: Christianity and Islam are regarded as valid equals; depictions of Jesus and Muhammad can be seen in some I-Kuan Tao shrines (such as Holy Glory Temple; page 218) alongside in Chinese society) began in the late Han Dynasty as a religious reform movement that sought to replace the popular worship of deified human beings with their own Taoist system of celestial, stellar and cosmic deities, organised into a bureaucratic imperial administration. The newly revealed divinities of Taoism were heavenly beings untouched by death, who rejected the offerings of meat that the deified human gods and environmental spirits of local society traditionally demanded. But as Taoism gradually evolved from a closed theocratic community to become part of society at large, Taoists increasingly sought to secure their position in the cultural world they inhabited by adopting the local gods of society into the lower ranks of the Taoist hierarchy as military protector spirits and local administrators in a Taoist 'sacred empire'. In this way, from the Song Dynasty (CE960-1279) onward, the Taoist Church and its ordained priesthood came to provide a kind of spiritual central government. According to that system, the local gods of the Popular Religion were given legitimate status as faithful servants of Heaven under the Jade Emperor and the still higher gods of the Taoist cosmos, the Three Pure Ones. Hence the entire system of local temples has, for the most part, become integrated into a Taoist cosmos in which the high Taoist divinities are always elevated above the deified human beings and terrestrial spirits of the Popular Religion.

Stephen M Flanigan is a historian of religions (MA and PhD from the University of Hawaii) who specialises in Taoism and the way of the Ritual Master, the Tantric-Taoist priest of the temple gods and their mediums. He has lived in Tainan for many years, and is well known in the community as the only Westerner to ever learn the ritual repertoire of the Ritual Master.

the Maitreya Buddha and Guan Gong. Because of its secretive nature, the sect was illegal in Taiwan from the 1950s until 1987, although there was little active repression for most of this period.

Christianity Christianity arrived in Taiwan in the 17th century with the Dutch and the Spanish but it didn't put down deep roots. The British and North American missionaries who arrived after 1860, like George L Mackay (see box, page 138), had to start afresh. Thanks to their medical and educational work, within two decades they were accepted by society at large. However, the number of converts remains very small, something that many observers attribute to the emphasis in Han Chinese culture on filial respect and ancestor worship. Taiwanese who convert are sometimes accused of not respecting their elders and abandoning their ancestors. No more than 5% of Taiwan's Han population is Christian. Among indigenous people, conversion efforts have been much more successful – over half are Protestant and a significant minority are Roman Catholic.

GODS AND GODDESSES In addition to praying to their gods, many Taiwanese still offer sacrifices to their ancestors. In the traditional scheme of things, neglecting deceased relatives isn't just disrespectful to one's forebears but also dangerous to oneself. Dissatisfied ancestors, it's said, have the ability to inflict misfortune.

Mazu 媽祖 Taiwan's most prominent deity, Mazu (formerly spelled 'Matsu') is said to have been born Lim Vo'g Niu (in Mandarin, Lin Mo-niang) in Meizhou, a

Adding fantastic colour and vigour to Taiwan's religious life are the island's several hundred *zhentou* troupes who march or perform in temple precincts and during processions throughout the country. The majority of these groups participate in religious festivals because they represent specific supernatural personalities or reenact particular legends, but a number are there simply to entertain.

Some zhentou members are highly trained professionals who tour for a living but most are amateurs with kinship ties to a particular temple. For many sightseers and all shutterbugs, these gaudily made-up, ornately dressed squads of young men (a few recently formed troupes are female) are the highlight of temple parades. During religious celebrations, zhentou members strut, swagger and wave mock weapons. They're menacing yet fascinating; in the minds of many Taiwanese, they're synonymous with juvenile delinquency and gang culture – a perception that some cultural organisations, notably Ten Drum Art Percussion Group, are working hard to recast.

Of the many types of zhentou, perhaps the easiest to recognise are the *Bajiajiang* ('Eight Generals'). Four members of each octet play the role of 'infernal generals' while the others represent the gods of the seasons. In addition to fabulous headgear and face paint, they carry ritual items such as fans on which protective spells have been written. They're forbidden to smile, and some troupes traditionally require their members to avoid funerals, disease and menstruating women in the three days before they appear in public.

fishing community in Fujian, on the 23rd day of the third lunar month in AD960. Her birthday is celebrated throughout the ROC and there's an especially large event in and around Dajia (see box, page 171).

By the time she was in her early teens, Mazu had an excellent grasp of Buddhist and Confucian texts. She used her powers to heal the sick and exorcise evil spirits but refused to marry. Her most famous achievement came at the age of 16 when her father and brothers, then far away on a fishing expedition, were caught in a tremendous storm. She slipped into a trance just as the storm was at its fiercest and after she regained consciousness her father and brothers returned home safely, swearing Mazu had projected herself out into the ocean to save them. An alternative legend has it that she saved her brothers, but because she was disturbed during her trance she let go of her father who then drowned. According to another version, she swam out to sea and searched for her father, but drowned and was washed ashore in the Matsu Islands. Many believe that when she was about 27, she told her family she was going to leave this world, climbed a nearby mountain and ascended to the heavens.

Mazu also persuaded two mischief-making demons to 'go straight' and become her servants. Altars dedicated to the goddess are very often flanked by human-sized statues of these two: Shunfeng Er ('ears that hear the wind') and Qianli Yan ('eyes that see a thousand leagues'). Mazu herself is often depicted with a rather plump face partially hidden by a veil of beads.

Fujianese migrants sailing to Taiwan often carried effigies of Mazu with them to ensure a safe crossing. Koxinga certainly brought with him a number of icons, as did Shi Lang, the Qing general who brought Taiwan into the imperial fold. Over time, Mazu has become much more than the patron saint of seafarers, and many Taiwanese who venture nowhere near the ocean seek her blessings in times of plenty and her aid in times of distress. More than 800 shrines around the ROC are dedicated to Mazu; many are named Tiānhòu Gōng 天后宫, meaning 'Queen of Heaven Temple'.

Guan Gong 關公 Also known as Guan Di or Guan Yu, this deity is traditionally depicted with a red face and wielding a weapon somewhat like a halberd. He's one of the most prominent deities in Chinese religion and one of the highest-ranking former mortals in the pantheon. A general who lived more than 1,800 years ago, he's worshipped by police officers, gangsters, businesspeople and others who revere his steadfast loyalty and righteousness.

Land gods 土地公 Also known as 'earth gods', these lowly figures in the celestial hierarchy are the equivalent of village or borough chiefs. Like their human counterparts, their powers are limited to a particular place. There are tens of thousands of land-god shrines throughout Taiwan's countryside; some are sizeable but many are no bigger than dog kennels. Most are quite basic and contain little more than a censer and a table or shelf where an idol has been placed. The land god is often depicted as wearing a mandarin's hat and robe, and sometimes he carries a staff (because he's believed to patrol his area of responsibility on foot) or a gold ingot (a symbol of prosperity).

Traditional graves incorporate small land-god shrines, found at the front left as you face the gravestone. Land gods are also worshipped in major temples, almost always under the name Fude Zhengshen 福德正神, which means 'Blessed and Benevolent Righteous God'. Land gods have birthdays, the most common dates being the second day of the second lunar month and the 15th day of the eighth lunar month.

City gods Just as there are thousands of land gods, there are numerous city and town gods too. Each one is called Chéng Huáng Yé 城隍爺; *chéng* means 'city wall', *huáng* means 'moat' and *yé* means 'lord'. Every settlement in Taiwan that used to be walled – and a few such as Lukang that were not – has a city-god temple. In some places the city god is explicitly identified with a human official who once served in that locale and who was posthumously deified. Like land gods, city gods have no powers beyond their territory. They're worshipped by members of the public as well as local bureaucrats. Notable city-god temples can be found in Hsinchu, Chiayi and Tainan.

Wang Ye 王爺 The words *wáng yé* mean 'royal lord' but this name is more honorific than accurate – the only royal connection is that the original 360 of the many hundreds of spirits in this category were musicians and scholars employed by Emperor Taizong (reigned AD626–649). They've been joined by, among others, Koxinga and a Japanese police officer who served in colonial-era Taiwan, who committed suicide as he was unwilling to follow orders to extort money from locals. Because he later appeared in a village chief's dream and warned of an impending epidemic, peasants in the area began worshipping him. He's a typical Wang Ye in the sense he's believed to possess plague-defeating powers.

The Wang Ye cult is stronger in Taiwan than elsewhere in Greater China because of plague-expelling customs in Fujian. Whenever coastal communities in that province were afflicted by disease, they'd place Wang Ye icons on boats and set them adrift. Prevailing currents carried many of these vessels to southwest Taiwan, which has more than two-thirds of the ROC's 1,200-plus Wang Ye shrines, including its best known, Nankunshen Daitian Temple. Knowing exactly what these boats were, Han people living along Taiwan's coastline received them with a mixture of fear and awe; they knew that ignoring the Wang Ye was to tempt fate, so they built shrines

Divination has been an aspect of Chinese religious life since the beginning of the country's long history, when tortoise shells were heated and the resulting cracks 'read' in a process called pyromancy. In modern Taiwan, the most popular method of divination is the casting of pairs of blocks made of wood or bamboo. Because these blocks – known in Taiwanese as *poe* – are crescent shaped, they're sometimes called 'moon boards' in English. You'll see *poe* cast in temples (a process known as *pua-poe*) and before ancestor shrines in private homes. Typical blocks are 10–15cm long, painted red and placed on the altar when not in use. One side of each block is flat and the other is rounded: a critical difference as casting these boards is somewhat like tossing a coin. The procedure is straightforward: a worshipper kneels, formulates his request (which he may whisper but is unlikely to utter aloud, and which is more often a statement than a question), cups the blocks in his hands, stands up and then lets the blocks drop from waist height. If only one lands rounded side up, this signals divine confirmation of the statement. If both land on their flat sides (rounded sides up), the deity is refuting the statement. If they both come to rest rounded side down, this shows the god is amused by the question. For a worshipper to be sure, he needs three consecutive confirmations. If he doesn't get them he may reformulate his request or give up.

Another common way of seeking supernatural advice is to draw lots. The lots are numbered bamboo slats – often 60 of them – placed in a cylinder on or beside an altar. Supplicants pick up the cylinder, give it a good shake and then pull out the slat sticking out the furthest. They read the number and, after casting *poe* to confirm it's correct, take a sheet of paper out of a drawer or off a numbered hook. Each sheet bears a message 30 to 60 characters in length. Because the language is frequently obscure or archaic, the volunteers who look after temples are often asked to assist with interpretation.

to house them and made offerings of incense. Rather than set icons on a vessel and push it out to sea, Taiwan's coastal communities have tended to construct elaborate votive boats and then set them ablaze. The most spectacular of these boat burnings is the triennial event in Donggang (see box, page 262).

The Old Man Under the Moon 月下老人 Shrines dedicated to this Cupid-like deity are especially busy ahead of Qixi, the traditional midsummer lovers' day. Each altar to this god has a bowl of short red threads that symbolise the traditional belief that each person is tied to and destined to eventually find his or her life partner; every lonely heart who seeks his help takes a thread home. In recent years, many of those who find love thanks to his intervention return to express their gratitude and leave behind a photo from their wedding.

The Jade Emperor 玉皇 Taoism's chief deity is like the chairman of the board – acknowledged to be the boss but seldom seen on the shop floor. Although he's said to reign over heaven, hell and humanity in the way the emperors of old used to rule China, the Jade Emperor is less prominent in local temples than Mazu or Guan Gong. Icons of the Jade Emperor usually have him seated on a throne and wearing imperial robes and a flat-topped crown. The jade tablet he clasps before his chest is a symbol of his authority. His birthday is the ninth day after Lunar New Year.

The Yellow Emperor 黃帝 Not to be confused with the Jade Emperor, the Yellow Emperor was a legendary sovereign who ruled China 4,700 years ago. He's said to have refined the crop cultivation methods used ever since by Chinese people; the invention of chopsticks is attributed to one of his concubines. At the age of 100 he attained immortality. He's worshipped not only for his contributions to Chinese civilisation but also because he's considered the forefather of all Han people.

EDUCATION

Formal education is valued highly by Taiwanese and those who hold postgraduate degrees from famous universities are revered. The adult literacy rate is more than 98%; most of those who can't read or write are rural women over 60 years old.

Children are expected to study hard; many parents have an unhealthy obsession with their offspring's test results and class rankings. A generation or two ago, only sons were pushed hard, but today young females are under as much pressure to do well at school as males. Schooling is compulsory between the ages of six and 18, and most kids attend kindergarten for two or three years before entering primary school and the majority continue in full-time education until their early 20s. City kids aged ten and over spend several evenings per week in cram schools where they review, preview and supplement school lessons.

University courses last four years. Because the birth rate has plunged, less well-known colleges are struggling to attract students and as a result, foreigners interested in studying in Taiwan can find some attractive scholarship opportunities. Information can be obtained from the Foundation for International Co-operation in Higher Education of Taiwan (w fichet.org.tw) and the government's Study In Taiwan website (w studyintaiwan.org).

STUDYING MANDARIN IN TAIWAN

Since China's emergence as an economic superpower, ambitious young Westerners have been travelling to the PRC to learn spoken Mandarin and written Chinese. This is a relatively recent phenomenon; before the late 1970s few outsiders, mostly elite students from China's allies in the developing world, were admitted by PRC colleges. Teaching Chinese is now big business, but China isn't necessarily the best place to go. Some of Taiwan's language schools, notably National Taiwan Normal University's Mandarin Training Centre (w mtc.ntnu.edu.tw) and the privately run Taipei Language Institute (w tli.com.tw), have more than half a century of experience.

While it's true that many Taiwanese people habitually speak languages other than Mandarin, the same is true in many parts of the mainland. In the PRC, Chinese is taught using *hanyu pinyin* (a way of rendering Mandarin sounds in the Latin alphabet, now widely used in Taiwan for road and place names). In Taiwan, *zhuyin fuhao* (a set of 37 phonic symbols) is used to teach both foreign adults and local primary school pupils. Some strongly prefer one system over another; you probably won't know which works best for you until you've tried both.

Students on a limited budget shouldn't rule out Taiwan, as the south of the island can be cheaper than Beijing or Shanghai. There's another reason why you may prefer living in Taiwan: you can say what you like about government policy and the country's politicians without having to worry about the consequences for yourself or those you associate with.

Economic growth coupled with the lifting of martial law and the return of thousands of Taiwanese who've lived or studied abroad has led to an explosion in artistic endeavour and a proliferation of high-profile cultural events. During the Chiang dictatorship (page 16), the government's cultural policies were heavy-handed. Classical Chinese culture and ethics were promoted, with local Taiwanese customs ignored or derided as backward. Some allowance was made for indigenous Austronesian traditions but the overriding goal was to inculcate Chinese identity throughout the population and prepare the ROC's citizenry for the eventual defeat of Communism and the retaking of the mainland.

A massive transformation began in the early 1990s. Political pluralism was matched by growing interest in local and minority customs. Museums, school books and television programmes began to focus on the truly local rather than the glories of old China. School curricula were rewritten to include a lot more of Taiwan's history, geography and literature and less of China's. Every city and county now has a cultural centre that hosts concerts, plays and other performances. Indigenous artists and performers are among those who have benefited from this paradigm shift.

Years ago, one writer described Taiwan as a 'cultural Titicaca', a lake into which many rivers flow but none leave. Nowadays, only the first part of this characterisation is true. Fujianese religious beliefs are still a massive influence. Japanese fashions, cartoons and comic books continue to be popular. Aspects of US popular culture – especially rap and hip-hop and the clothes and dance moves that go with them – are conspicuous. South Korean pop music and soap operas have made inroads. And just as the KMT toned down its efforts to promote a certain version of Chinese culture, exchanges with the mainland began exposing Taiwanese to trends on the other side of the Taiwan Strait. Also, the worldview of Taiwanese people is no longer dominated by the US and Japan. In recent years, tens of thousands of Taiwanese have studied in the UK. A great many Taiwanese have been abroad for business or pleasure.

Several Taiwanese pop singers have achieved stardom in the PRC and southeast Asia. Cloud Gate Dance Theatre (w cloudgate.org.tw) has toured the world, as has the Ten Drum Art Percussion Group (w ten-hsieh.com.tw; page 217). Until the surprise success of Wu Ming-yi's environmentalist fantasy *The Man with the Compound Eyes* (page 343), Taiwanese literature hadn't made much of an impact in the West.

It's in cinema that artists from Taiwan have had the greatest international successes, double Oscar-winner Ang Lee (b1954) being perhaps the most famous Taiwanese person in the world. According to Michael Berry, professor of Contemporary Chinese Cultural Studies at the University of California and the author of several books on Chinese-language cinema: 'An incredible array of unique and powerful cinematic voices have emerged from Taiwan over the past several decades [offering] a rich series of perspectives on Taiwan's history and society, while, at the same time, using their films to provide broad and profound statements about the human condition.' Taiwan-based filmmakers who've won acclaim overseas include Hou Hsiao-hsien (b1947), Edward Yang (1947–2007), Malaysian-born Tsai Ming-liang (b1957) and Chang Tso-chi (b1961). Others have achieved great successes at home. Doze Niu's 2010 gangster melodrama *Monga* was set in Taipei's Wanhua District, while the box-office success of the 2008 romance *Cape No. 7* made it possible for director Wei Te-sheng (b1969) to secure funding for his 2011 epic *Warriors of the Rainbow: Seediq Bale*. The latter, released in two parts totalling more than 4½ hours, depicts the Wushe uprising of 1930 (page 15).

2

Practical Information

WHEN TO VISIT

Even if you're sure you can endure the heat and humidity of a Taiwanese summer, avoid July, August and early September because of the typhoons that blow in from the Pacific. From late June to the end of August, thousands of local college students crowd Kenting National Park and Green Island. Yet for those who can handle the temperatures Taiwan's summers are wonderfully vivid: the skies are blue, the rivers are full and mountain peaks are clearly visible from the lowlands, and butterflies and flowers are abundant. Overall, October to March is the best period to visit because temperatures are comfortable and there's little chance of getting caught in a downpour. That said, it can get downright frigid in the mountains. Because of landslides, mountain areas are occasionally inaccessible during the summer wet season. The best times of year for high-altitude hiking – or any kind of mountain exploration – are October to November and the early spring. During the colder months, excursions to Penghu County and Orchid Island are less pleasant and more prone to delays. People with very sensitive respiratory systems should avoid Taiwan's southern lowlands during the winter because air quality declines during the season's long dry spells. Don't come around Lunar New Year, when accommodation rates go through the roof, trains get booked out and the roads are jammed with sightseers and people visiting relatives. For the same reason, it's worth checking if any public holidays fall on a Monday or Friday, creating a long weekend.

HIGHLIGHTS

Your first impressions of Taiwan may be of overcrowded urban areas and a bewildering lack of English once you leave the airport but with a little nudging (and this book) the door to the treasure house opens. Taiwan not only has a tremendous range of attractions – cultural, scenic and ecological – but also great depth in every category. Two weeks isn't nearly enough to do justice to its mountains, museums, minorities, temples or birds.

A PERSONAL TOP SIX: NATURE AND THE OUTDOORS

East Taiwan Hualien to Taitung by Highway 11 is many cyclists' favourite, but the inland route brings you closer to the region's indigenous population. See page 289.

Little Liuqiu Island This coral chunk is near enough to Kaohsiung to make an excellent day trip, yet far enough from 'mainland' Taiwan to have a completely different vibe. See page 324.

New Central Cross-Island Highway The high-altitude road that connects Sun Moon Lake with Yushan National Park and Alishan more than justifies renting a car or hiring a driver. See page 197.

Penghu County Straight, empty roads link sandy beaches, crumbling coral houses and superb windsurfing spots. See page 302.

Snow Mountain Taiwan's number two peak in terms of height is a world-class three-day hike offering stunning vistas. See page 192.

Taroko Gorge You'll understand why this place is called a 'must-see' as soon as you reach Swallow Grotto or the Tunnel of Nine Turns. See page 276.

A PERSONAL TOP SIX: CULTURE AND MANMADE ATTRACTIONS

Temple culture The fervour and colour of Taiwan's *tang-ki* (page 221) and *zhentou* (see box, page 32) are unforgettable.

Kinmen County Staggeringly quaint villages scarred by Cold War battles. See page 310.

EXPLORING TAIWAN'S INDIGENOUS COMMUNITIES   *Cheryl Robbins*

There are several hundred indigenous communities all over Taiwan. They are often close-knit, friendly places, with an average population of just a few hundred. Some are located high in the mountains, reached by narrow, winding roads, while others are situated along the coast or near popular tourist areas. If joining a tour group, renting a car or hiring a driver, reaching these communities is not difficult, but finding them using public transport can be somewhat inconvenient; there may be only one or two scheduled bus departures per day or sometimes no bus service at all. If staying in a guesthouse run by a local family, ask the owner to pick you up from the nearest train station, bus station or bus stop.

One point is worth noting: Taiwan is a small, well-developed island and there are few places that can be considered truly remote. This means that indigenous people and communities have long had interactions with mainstream society, and thus you shouldn't expect to see 'primitive' lifestyles. Taiwan's indigenous people wear contemporary clothing, except during special ceremonies, and most live in homes made of brick and cement, similar to those seen in other parts of Taiwan.

Although the very traditional way of life has all but disappeared, there are still a number of reasons to visit indigenous communities. Firstly, these communities are located in areas of natural beauty and offer ecotourism and sports opportunities such as hiking, white-water rafting, paragliding, swimming, surfing and river tracing. Such places are often home to certified ecotourism guides who can lead challenging hikes or less taxing local ecological tours. In many indigenous communities, native Austronesian languages (page 26) are still spoken. Chinese is spoken by almost everyone but few people speak English. This should not deter non-Chinese speakers, however, as indigenous people are generally very hospitable and a smile goes a long way.

Secondly, in indigenous areas there are often opportunities to interact with local people. Some have opened guesthouses, usually just a few spare rooms in or

Lukang Get lost in the backstreets of Taiwan's living museum. See page 174.

National Museum of Taiwan History Whether you know nothing about Taiwan's past or have immersed yourself in the subject, you'll find this museum very satisfying. See page 216.

National Palace Museum The cream of the artistic output of one of the world's oldest and most accomplished civilisations. See page 103.

Tainan's Martial Rites Temple The most exquisite shrine in a city famous for temples, a place of supreme tranquillity and refinement. See page 212.

SUGGESTED ITINERARIES

Spend weekdays exploring the countryside, the mountains and little towns like Lukang and Tamsui; spend weekends and national holidays in the major cities. Many scenic spots are all but deserted in the middle of the week; room rates are lower and there are some discounts on admission charges. Note that many museums close on Mondays.

adjacent to their own homes. Guesthouse owners often serve as guides and can help tourists gain insights into the community's attractions and people. Walking through a community, you'll often see residents chatting or barbecuing. Don't be surprised if you're invited to join in.

Thirdly, many indigenous community-development associations are working to revive various aspects of their culture, such as the growing of millet, a traditional staple crop, or the production of handicrafts such as glass beads and wood carving. In addition, there are opportunities to see ceremonies that have been performed for centuries, during which villages take on a festive atmosphere as those working and studying in urban areas return to join in. They wear traditional clothing and make use of traditional items, such as the Paiwan tribe's double drinking cup and the Saisiyat tribe's hip bells. Native-language traditional songs and traditional dances are performed. Outsiders are sometimes allowed to join the dance circle.

Finally, indigenous cuisine differs greatly from other cuisines in Taiwan. Traditionally, indigenous people hunted and fished and grew millet and taro root. They also gathered wild greens and flavoured their food with locally obtained herbs such as Aralia and mountain peppercorn (also known as *maqaw*). Restaurants in indigenous communities serve cuisine that includes local ingredients prepared using traditional and modern methods. All in all, indigenous communities offer unique experiences different from the rest of Taiwan and are well worth adding to your itinerary.

Cheryl Robbins (e specialtytourstaiwan@gmail.com) is a veteran translator, journalist and Taiwan-licensed tour guide originally from the US. She is the author of three guidebooks to Taiwan's indigenous areas and operates w tribe-asia.com. Since 2013, she has been offering tour packages to Taiwan's indigenous areas in co-operation with various travel agencies.

2

A LONG WEEKEND As many Asia-based Western expatriates are discovering, a long weekend in Taiwan is very feasible. Fly to Taipei for culture or Kaohsiung for outdoors adventure. The capital has more than enough shops, restaurants and museums to keep you out of mischief, and for glimpses of tradition you needn't go beyond the city limits. Baoan and Longshan temples are among Taiwan's most interesting shrines. Dihua Street, where business is still done the way it was a hundred years ago, nicely counterpoints the city's department stores and boutiques. Central Kaohsiung has its attractions but if time's limited, speed away from the city, either towards the hills, or down to the beaches and beautiful hinterland of Kenting National Park.

ONE WEEK Try to hit at least two but not more than three of the following: Taipei, Tainan, Taroko Gorge and somewhere in the high mountains. If you restrict yourself to the northwest, you'll probably be able to take in the woodcarving centre of Sanyi and possibly an indigenous village. Those staying in the south should get their own transport, and drive or ride towards Taitung. The return leg to Kaohsiung can be via Kenting National Park.

TWO WEEKS Ease yourself in with a full three days in and near your city of arrival, then rent a car or a motorcycle for a week so you can traverse the Central Mountain Range by whichever road takes your fancy. When you reach the east coast stop at a hot springs if the weather's cool, or a mountain creek if it isn't. Spend up to three days in Taroko Gorge. To find solitude or something close to it, arrive on Green Island or Orchid Island on a weekday. Consider hiking into the eastern part of Yushan National Park before heading back to western Taiwan by any mountain road you haven't already seen. If you've no intention of braving the roads, get to grips with the bus schedule or find a tour operator who can transport you to and around the hills. Do this because if you leave having seen only the places served by trains, you won't have seen the best of Taiwan.

TOUR OPERATORS AND TOURIST INFORMATION

Taiwan isn't always an easy country to explore. Language is often a problem and if you're going far from the major cities – which you should if you want to find the island's true flavours – comprehending bus schedules and finding food you like can be frustrating. Using a local travel agent or tour guide can smooth the way and will often save you money as well as time. Not only will they overcome the language barrier and steer you towards the best (but not necessarily the most famous) attractions, they'll also know where in the back country you can find vegetarian food and even where there are toilets you can sit on as opposed to the kind you squat over.

UK

Bamboo Travel 020 7720 9285; e info@ bambootravel.co.uk; w bambootravel.co.uk. Organises longish tours inc a self-drive excursion, 'Treasures of Taiwan' (14 days from £3,395) & 'Taiwan in Style' (15 days from £4,895).
Birdfinders 01258 839066; e info@ birdfinders.co.uk; w birdfinders.co.uk. Their 13-day birdwatching trip (£3,495) includes Taroko

National Park, Orchid Island, Kenting & high-altitude forests.
Black Tomato 020 7426 9888; e info@ blacktomato.co.uk; w blacktomato.com. Among tour options is the 7-night 'From Lakeside to Mountains' (from £3,650) & a 9-night 'Best of' (from £2,250). Both prices exclude flights.
China Holidays 020 7487 2999; e sales@ chinaholidays.co.uk; w chinaholidays.co.uk. Offers

a 15-day comprehensive tour (from £2,895) & can tailor itineraries for small groups.

Cox and Kings 📞020 3813 9531; e info@ coxandkings.co.uk; w coxandkings.co.uk. The 11-day/9-night 'Beautiful Island' tour includes the National Palace Museum & other Taipei sights, Alishan, Foguangshan & Meinong. Prices start at £2,595.

Cultural Tours 📞020 7636 7906; e info@ culturaltours.co.uk; w culturaltours.co.uk. Offers a rather rushed 4-day itinerary that crams in Sun Moon Lake, Tainan, Kenting & Taroko Gorge.

Eastravel 📞01473 214305; e info@eastravel. co.uk; w eastravel.co.uk. Can tailor itineraries of various lengths inc self-drive trips & self-guided rail adventures.

Greentours 📞01298 83563; e enquiries@ greentours.co.uk; w greentours.co.uk. Organises tours that introduce Taiwan's fauna & flora.

Intrepid Travel 📞0808 274 5111; e enquiries@ intrepidtravel.com; w intrepidtravel.com. Both the 11-day 'Explore Taiwan' (from £1,945) and the 8-day 'Taiwan Food Expedition' (from £1,590) inc Sun Moon Lake.

Ours Travel 📞020 7388 8955; e sales@ ourstravel.com; w ourstravel.com. Has a strong Taiwan focus & offers discounted air fares as well as tours & services to Taiwanese living or studying in the UK. Various options for those wanting short (up to 5 days) tours of Taiwan.

Regent Holidays 📞020 7666 1258; e regent@ regentholidays.co.uk; w regent-holidays.co.uk. Offers a range of tours that inc rail travel, national parks & night markets.

US AND CANADA

All State Travel Inc 📞626 854 1636; e allstate_ travel@yahoo.com; w enjoyingtaiwan.com. Offers cheap flights with stopovers in Beijing or Shanghai as well as tour packages lasting 5–9 days with an emphasis on Taiwan's eastern half.

Royal Scenic 📞905 946 2228; e info@royalscenic. com; w royalscenic.com. Runs tours that combine Taiwan with Hong Kong, Shanghai or Tokyo.

AUSTRALIA

Taiwan Holidays 📞2 9267 1308; e sales@ taiwanholidays.com.au; w taiwanholidays.com. au. Taiwanese-staffed agency with a wide range of transfers, stopovers & tours; other useful services inc selling rail passes.

LOCAL TRAVEL AGENTS AND TOUR GUIDES

The businesses listed here cover several regions, & some can make arrangements for any part of the country. English-speaking tour guides specialising in one town or region are listed in the relevant chapters in the guide.

Blue Skies Adventures Mark Roche, 10th Flr 7, Lane 43, Jianan St, Kaohsiung; 📞07 389 0795; m 0982 858 316; e blueskiesadventures@ yahoo.com; w blueskiestaiwan.com. Has years of experience running high-mountain hikes & offers guided & self-guided bike tours; rents road & touring bikes in all sizes.

Cheryl Robbins m 0923 151 965; e specialtytourstaiwan@gmail.com. Originally from California, this ROC-licensed tour guide & travel writer specialises in Taiwan's indigenous areas & cultures.

Edison Travel Service 4th Flr 190 Songjiang Rd, Taipei; 📞02 2563 5313; e paul@edison.com. tw, edisontravelservice@gmail.com. Regular tours with English-speaking guides. Can provide rentals with drivers & assist with hotel reservations & domestic & international flight bookings.

Golden Foundation Tours 5th Flr 142 Zhongxiao E Rd Sec 4, Taipei; 📞02 2773 3266; e gftour@gftours.com.tw; w gftours.com.tw. This agency has partnered with some of Europe's major travel companies. Can help with hotel & public transport reservations, special-interest tours & conventions.

Hualien Outdoors Matt Hopkins, 2-16 Guolian 5th Rd, Hualien; 📞03 833 9037; m 0989 512 380; e hualienoutdoors@gmail.com; w hualienoutdoors.org. This expat-run company runs river tracing, hiking & tea-focused trips in & around Hualien & Taroko Gorge National Park.

Life of Taiwan 9, Lane 38, Qianfong Rd, Tainan; 📞06 208 8173; m 0939 626 382; e contact@ lifeoftaiwan.com; w lifeoftaiwan.com. Organises bespoke high-end tours for small groups interested in Taiwan's culture, food & natural attractions.

MyTaiwanTour 4th Flr 103 Nanchang Rd Sec 2, Taipei; 📞02 2523 3881; e service@mytaiwantour. com; w www.mytaiwantour.com. Professional English-speaking tour guides take you off the beaten path with 1- to 5-day packages that can be booked & paid for online.

RoundTaiwanRound ✆03 857 1005; m 0918 485
041; e service@roundtaiwanround.com; w rtaiwanr.
com. Provides customised single- & multi-day
trips with English-speaking guides throughout
the country plus adventure tours, accommodation
booking, car hire & travel photography.
Taiwan Adventures 9th Flr 628 Songshan
Road, Taipei; ✆02 2346 5867; m 0983 212 499;
e info@taiwan-adventures.com; w taiwan-

adventures.com. This Anglo-American company
specialises in hiking, canyoning & rafting
expeditions.
Taiwan EcoTours m 0938 337 710;
e taiwanecotours@gmail.com; w taiwanbirding.
com. Richard Foster has several years' experience
guiding birders around Taiwan & outlying islands.
Can arrange extensions to other parts of Asia.

TOURIST INFORMATION Taiwan's Tourism Bureau (w taiwan.net.tw) administers the country's 13 national scenic areas with an emphasis on promotion rather than conservation. The ROC's national parks are run by the Ministry of the Interior, while forest recreation areas come under the aegis of the Forestry Bureau, part of the Council of Agriculture. The Tourism Bureau or the semi-official Taiwan Visitors Association has representatives in the US, Japan, Germany and a few other places but not in the UK; contact information for these offices can be found on the bureau's website.

Because local visitor information centres and travel service centres are run by various organisations – among them national scenic areas and local governments – service quality, information accuracy, and English ability is uneven. At a minimum, you should be able to get bilingual maps and leaflets about the area; at best they'll answer all your transport queries and even telephone homestays on your behalf. See page 87 for centres based in the capital.

RED TAPE

Nationals of the UK, USA, Canada, Australia, Ireland, Japan, New Zealand and more than 20 other European countries can stay in the ROC for up to 90 days without a visa. Malaysians and Singaporeans can stay for up to 30 days. As well as tourists, visa-free entry can be used by those coming for business reasons or to receive medical treatment. However, if you're intending to work, teach or engage in missionary activities, you should contact an ROC embassy or representative office well in advance to find out what kind of visa you should apply for. See the Bureau of Consular Affairs website (w boca.gov.tw) for information about visa-free entry, visa fees and online application forms.

CUSTOMS REGULATIONS Taiwan's customs regulations are similar to those of other countries. Cold War-era rules barring visitors from bringing in newspapers or books printed in communist China were scrapped years ago. If you've more than a litre of alcoholic drinks, 200 cigarettes, 25 cigars or a pound of tobacco, declare it when you enter the ROC. You shouldn't bring in more than US$20,000 in gold (or US$10,000 in cash or other foreign currencies) or more than NTD100,000 in Taiwanese money. For Chinese currency, the limit is RMB20,000. Full details are available at w www.customs.gov.tw.

There's a tax-refund system for foreign visitors who shop at participating stores. If you spend more than NTD3,000 in a single day at any of these shops no more than 30 days before your departure, and you take the items with you when you leave Taiwan, you can reclaim the 5% VAT at the airport prior to boarding your flight. Complete details, along with a searchable list of participating shops and department stores, can be found at w www.taxrefund.net.tw.

EMBASSIES For a list of embassies and consulates in Taiwan (all in Taipei), see **w** embassypages.com/taiwan.

GETTING THERE AND AWAY

BY AIR Taiwan makes for a good stopover if you're flying between Australia and Japan or South Korea or from North America to Singapore or Malaysia.

The bulk of scheduled international flights land at Taiwan Taoyuan International Airport near Taipei or Kaohsiung International Airport, the former handling all long-haul flights. Both Taichung and Taipei Songshan airports handle several flights to east and southeast Asia per day. Flights between Taiwan and the Chinese mainland are classed as neither full international flights nor domestic flights.

Airlines

From the UK

✈ **Cathay Pacific w** cathaypacific.com. Flies Heathrow to Hong Kong up to 4 times daily & Manchester to Hong Kong 5 times weekly. From Hong Kong passengers have several options daily on to Taoyuan & Kaohsiung.

✈ **China Airlines w** www.china-airlines.com. Taiwan's flag carrier resumed direct, non-stop London–Taoyuan flights at the end of 2017, this time flying in & out of Gatwick 5 times each week.

✈ **China Eastern Airlines w** ceair.com. This PRC carrier offers inexpensive tickets but very long flights from Heathrow & Gatwick to Taiwan, connecting in Shanghai.

✈ **Emirates w** emirates.com. Daily flights between Dubai & Taoyuan, & from Dubai to 6 airports in the UK.

✈ **EVA Air w** www.evaair.com. The better of Taiwan's airlines flies from London Heathrow to Taoyuan via Bangkok daily.

✈ **Qatar Airways w** qatarairways.com. Offer flights from Heathrow, Gatwick, Birmingham, Edinburgh & Manchester to Taoyuan or Kaohsiung, but you'll need to change in Doha & Hong Kong.

✈ **Singapore Airlines w** singaporeair.com. A good option between Heathrow & Taoyuan but less convenient if you want to arrive at Kaohsiung.

From Ireland There aren't any direct flights to Taiwan from Ireland. An alternative to connecting at London Heathrow is Emirates:

✈ **Emirates w** emirates.com. Flies from Dublin with a connection in Dubai, then on to Taoyuan.

From the rest of Europe

✈ **China Airlines w** www.china-airlines.com. Has about 20 flights each week between Taoyuan & Amsterdam, Frankfurt, Rome & Vienna.

✈ **EVA Air w** evaair.com. Flies from Amsterdam, Paris & Vienna to Taoyuan.

From China Direct flights across the Taiwan Strait are with PRC airlines or Taiwan's China Airlines, EVA Air & other minor carriers. The PRC airlines & related agents include:

✈ **Air China w** www.airchina.com.cn

✈ **China Eastern Airlines w** ceair.com

✈ **China Southern Airlines w** csair.com

✈ **Shandong Airlines w** sda.cn

From the US and Canada

✈ **China Airlines w** china-airlines.com. Flies non-stop from New York JFK, Los Angeles, San Francisco, Honolulu & Vancouver to Taoyuan.

✈ **EVA Air w** evaair.com. Flies non-stop from New York, Los Angeles, San Francisco, Seattle, Chicago, Houston, Toronto & Vancouver to Taoyuan.

✈ **United Airlines w** united.com. Has direct San Francisco–Taoyuan flights. Flying with United to Taoyuan via Tokyo may save you time compared with other routes where you need to change in Hong Kong.

From Australia and New Zealand Cheaper options, which include a change of plane in southeast Asia or China, include:

✈ **China Southern Airlines w** csair.com

✈ **Garuda Indonesia w** garuda-indonesia.com

Practical Information GETTING THERE AND AWAY

2

Budget airlines If you're planning a multi-country trip through Asia, the following airlines may come in useful:

✈ **Air Asia** w airasia.com
✈ **HK Express** w hkexpress.com

✈ **Peach** w www.flypeach.com
✈ **Scoot** w flyscoot.com
✈ **Tigerair Taiwan** w www.tigerairtw.com
✈ **Vietjet** w vietjetair.com

Main airports Taiwan Taoyuan International Airport (TPE) (TPE; ✆ 398 3728; w www.taoyuan-airport.com) is Taiwan's busiest airport, 28km due west of Taipei, and is where long-haul flights land. Known between its inauguration in 1979 and 2006 as Chiang Kai-shek International Airport, the facility was renamed as part of the Chen Shui-bian administration's push to remove symbols of the KMT era (page 20). It's a reasonably smart and well-equipped airport and not intimidatingly huge, and you'll find bank kiosks, post offices, travel information counters and car-hire desks (page 57) in both terminals. Most Hong Kong and southeast Asian carriers use T1 (✆ 273 5081) while long-haul and mainland Chinese airlines use the newer and nicer T2 (✆ 273 5086). Don't worry if you arrive at the wrong terminal for your flight out – a free mini-train connects the two. Terminal 3 will open in stages after 2020.

The modestly sized **Kaohsiung International Airport (KHH)** is properly staffed so you can be sure of getting through customs and immigration quickly and then on to Tainan or Kenting. For more details see page 237.

Airport transfers

By Taoyuan Metro/Airport MRT Each terminal has its own station on the Taoyuan metro line, which currently runs between Taipei Main Station and the outskirts of Zhongli. Travel time from T1 or T2 to Taipei Main Station is 36–50 minutes (6 departures per hr; ⊕ 05.59–23.36 daily; NTD160). Taoyuan metro is a separate entity from Taipei Metro, so to save the hassle of buying another ticket when transferring from one to the other, consider buying a 48- or 72-hour pass at the airport that covers both systems (NTD520/600).

By HSR Taoyuan HSR Station is 11km from the airport and 18km from central Taoyuan. It takes 20 minutes to get from T1 or T2 to the HSR station via the Taoyuan metro (5 departures per hr; ⊕ 05.57–23.55 daily; NTD35). To/from Taipei by HSR takes around 20 minutes (NTD160); to/from Kaohsiung Zuoying takes around 1¾ hours (NTD1,330).

By bus Various services link the airport with central Taipei (takes about 1hr; NTD93–145) and if you're aiming for a specific part of the capital, ask before buying your ticket as there are several routes and one may stop right outside your hotel. There are also frequent departures to Taichung, including the #1623, #1860 and #5503 (⊕ 06.00–01.10 daily; takes 2¼hrs; NTD280). Until mid evening, local buses set off for Taoyuan (#5059, every 30mins; 40mins; NTD53) and Zhongli (#5089, every hr; 40mins; NTD62), departing from and terminating at stops very near the TRA stations.

By road Freeway 2, which links to both Freeway 1 and Freeway 3, leads directly to the airport. Freeway 1 is preferable if your initial destination is Taipei or Hsinchu, but Freeway 3 is usually less crowded.

Expect to pay at least NTD1,200 for a taxi from the airport to central Taipei, which takes around 45 minutes.

BY SEA The number of visitors arriving by sea has jumped and there are now several regular ferry services between Taiwan and the Chinese mainland, including from Kinmen (page 311), Taichung Harbour and Bali near Taipei. A number of cruise companies drop anchor in Keelung for a day while sailing around east Asia and the South Pacific:

⛴ **Costa Cruises** w costacruise.com		⛴ **Regent Seven Seas** w www.rssc.com
⛴ **Oceania Cruises** w oceaniacruises.com		⛴ **Star Cruises** w starcruises.com
⛴ **Princess Cruises** w princess.com		⛴ **Yachts of Seabourn** w seabourn.com

HEALTH   *with Dr Felicity Nicholson*

Taiwan is a healthy place but visitors should take some precautions, including taking out adequate insurance before leaving home.

INOCULATIONS No vaccinations are required except yellow fever, and then only if you're coming from a yellow-fever endemic area such as sub-Saharan Africa or South America, as there is no risk of disease in Taiwan. It is wise to be up to date with standard vaccinations including diphtheria, tetanus and polio given in the UK as one vaccine (Revaxis), and also measles, mumps and rubella. Vaccination against hepatitis A, and possibly hepatitis B, rabies and Japanese encephalitis are advisable depending on your length of stay. Taiwan has a high prevalence of hepatitis B so vaccination would be recommended for those working in medical settings and with children, as well as for those playing contact sports. The course comprises three vaccines given over a minimum of 21 days for those aged 16 and over; younger travellers require a minimum of eight weeks to be vaccinated effectively. The Japanese encephalitis vaccine (Ixiaro) is recommended for those staying in rural parts of the country, and consists of two doses ideally given one month apart, so ensure that you have enough time if you need it. Taiwan also has one of the highest incidences of hepatitis A in the world; one dose of the vaccine will provide cover for one year and can then be boosted to extend protection to around 25 years.

MEDICAL CONCERNS

Rabies After half a century with no cases, rabies re-emerged in Taiwan in 2013. Almost all recent cases have been in ferret-badgers (*Melogale moschata*), but there has been a case in a puppy that was bitten by a ferret-badger. So far there have been no human infections, but if you're bitten or scratched by any mammal do seek medical treatment as soon as possible. Rabies is also found in the bat population.

Tuberculosis The TB rate in Taiwan is low, but the BCG vaccination would be recommended in certain circumstances (ie: unvaccinated children who are under 16 and will be staying for three months).

Malaria Mosquitoes can be a threat. Taiwan long ago eradicated malaria but there are sometimes outbreaks of dengue fever, usually in the south. Dengue fever is transmitted by day-biting mosquitoes and there is no vaccine or tablet to prevent it. DEET-based insect repellents (50–55% DEET) should be used on all exposed skin day and night.

Tick-borne diseases There is the possibility of getting Lyme disease in Taiwan. Most cases of the disease have been imported, but research has shown

Ticks should ideally be removed complete, and as soon as possible, to reduce the chance of infection. You can use special tick tweezers, which can be bought in good travel shops, or failing this with your finger nails, grasping the tick as close to your body as possible, and pulling it away steadily and firmly at right angles to your skin without jerking or twisting. Irritants (eg: Olbas oil) or lit cigarettes are to be discouraged since they can cause the ticks to regurgitate and therefore increase the risk of disease. Once the tick is removed, if possible douse the wound with alcohol (any spirit will do), soap and water, or iodine. If you are travelling with small children, remember to check their heads, and particularly behind the ears, for ticks. Spreading redness around the bite and/or fever and/or aching joints after a tick bite imply that you have an infection that requires antibiotic treatment. In this case seek medical advice.

that the *Borrelia spirochaete* that causes the disease is found in mammals in Taiwan, so the chance of infection exists. If you are walking in forested areas of Taiwan in the spring and summer months, it is wise to take precautions (see box, above).

Japanese encephalitis This viral infection is transmitted by the night-biting *Culex* mosquitoes that pick up the virus from pigs and wading birds in and around rice-growing areas. The peak season for transmission is April to October, and it is unusual for travellers to get infected outside of these months. There is no treatment for Japanese encephalitis and the mortality rate is up to 30%. Vaccination is recommended for longer stays of a month or more, but may also be wise for shorter stays in rural areas during the peak months. Two doses of the vaccine (Ixiaro) are given about a month apart but shorter courses are available when time is limited. The initial course lasts for two years but a booster given before age 65 will last for another ten.

OTHER HEALTH ISSUES
Food preparation and drinking water Individuals with delicate stomachs should be OK if they exercise common sense. Night markets and roadside eateries aren't necessarily less sanitary than proper restaurants. If a place looks popular, that's usually a sign that the food is clean as well as tasty. Also, high turnover means food isn't left lying around.

Almost every hotel and homestay provides boiled tap water free of charge for guests. This is what most Taiwanese people drink, though it's debatable whether it's good for you long term. For short-term visitors, however, it's an acceptable alternative to buying mineral water.

Environmental factors Because of the high population density, coughs and colds sometimes spread quickly; this is why many Taiwanese wear masks on trains and in other crowded places. If you visit during the hot season, do always carry with you a long-sleeved shirt or cardigan. If you're sightseeing in a city you'll find yourself constantly entering and leaving air-conditioned areas and the temperature changes may give you a chill. In the countryside, be prepared for big differences between midday and late afternoon temperatures.

Any prolonged immobility, including travel by land or air, can result in deep-vein thrombosis (DVT) with the risk of embolus to the lungs. Certain factors can increase the risk and these include:

- History of DVT or pulmonary embolism
- Recent surgery to pelvic region or legs
- Cancer
- Stroke
- Heart disease
- Inherited tendency to clot (thrombophilia)
- Obesity
- Pregnancy
- Hormone therapy
- Older age
- Being over 1.83m (6ft) or under 1.52m (5ft)

A DVT causes painful swelling and redness of the calf or sometimes the thigh. It is only dangerous if a clot travels to the lungs (pulmonary embolus). Symptoms of a pulmonary embolus – which commonly start three to ten days after a long flight – include chest pain, shortness of breath, and sometimes coughing up small amounts of blood. Anyone who thinks that they might have a DVT needs to see a doctor immediately.

PREVENTION OF DVT
- Wear loose comfortable clothing
- Do anti-DVT exercises and move around when possible
- Drink plenty of fluids during the flight
- Avoid taking sleeping pills unless you are able to lie flat
- Avoid excessive tea, coffee and alcohol
- Consider wearing flight socks or support stockings, widely available from pharmacies

If you think you are at increased risk of a clot, ask your doctor if it is safe to travel.

In regions with heavy industry and lots of motor vehicles, such as parts of Kaohsiung, air quality is often an issue, especially in the dry winter months. Secondhand smoke is a very minor problem; smoking is now barred in restaurants, pubs and other enclosed places.

Public toilets The good news is that Taiwan has plenty of public toilets, they're almost always free and they're generally quite clean. You'll find them in parks, petrol stations, railway stations and temples. The bad news is that some toilets are marked in Chinese only and toilet paper and soap are seldom provided. Carry your own, like the Taiwanese do. Also, you should get used to using squat-style toilets, which are standard outside the major cities. Squatting is more hygienic and said to be better for your bowels. If you can't or won't use this kind of plumbing fixture, seek out a bathroom in a department store or fast-food restaurant. If there's a wastepaper basket next to the toilet, put used toilet paper and sanitary items in it, not in the toilet. In many older buildings the plumbing may get blocked if you toss paper down the toilet. Also, many guesthouses and hotels in the countryside have septic tanks instead of sewer connections, and these systems don't deal with paper well. Consider carrying alcohol swabs or some kind of sanitising gel. These are useful for cleaning your hands if you come across a tap that's run dry (this sometimes happens on trains) as well as wiping cutlery before eating or the tops of soda cans before drinking.

GETTING TREATED

Clinics and pharmacies In small towns and cities you'll find plenty of clinics (⏰ 09.00–noon & 15.00–20.00 daily). Many doctors but few other health professionals speak English. In major hospitals they'll probably assign an English speaker to see you to the right department. Prescription medicines are dispensed on site.

Major hospitals also have commercial pharmacies where you can buy over-the-counter medicines, aspirin, contraceptives and other items.

Paying for treatment At clinics and hospitals you'll be expected to pay a registration fee before seeing the doctor, and for any medicines immediately afterwards. Bring your passport and cash as few places accept credit cards. Treatment is inexpensive by European standards and an absolute bargain compared with the US. You'll be given a receipt but it might be entirely in Chinese. At major hospitals they'll be able to provide you with a document in English which you can submit when making an insurance claim.

TRAVEL CLINICS AND HEALTH INFORMATION A full list of current travel clinic websites worldwide is available on w istm.org. For other journey preparation information, consult w travelhealthpro.org.uk (UK) or w wwwnc.cdc.gov/travel (US). Information about various medications may be found on w netdoctor.co.uk/travel. All advice found online should be used in conjunction with expert advice received prior to or during travel.

SAFETY

Taiwan is one of the world's safest countries for tourists. Street crime isn't a big issue, even late at night, and there's little danger of being harassed by a drunk. That said, homeowners do take precautions against burglary – hence the metal bars over windows and balconies – and pickpockets work festival and night-market crowds.

Traffic is the major threat to your well-being. Be very careful when crossing roads. Don't just look both ways, look in every direction as two-wheelers often use the pavements or pedestrian crossings. There are two reasons why self-driving visitors should think twice before stopping at what appears to be the aftermath of a traffic accident: lawsuits and robberies. If you take an individual to hospital, you may later be held responsible for their death or injuries. Also, criminals have been known to stage fake-crash scenes on quiet country roads and beg passing drivers to stop. Good Samaritans have, for their trouble, been robbed and had their vehicles stolen. Up-to-date advice from the Foreign Office can be found at w gov.uk/foreign-travel-advice/taiwan.

NATURAL HAZARDS Taiwan suffers both earthquakes and typhoons but these shouldn't stop you visiting. If you cycle or hike in the lowlands or the foothills, keep an eye out for aggressive dogs. If you're confronted by one, pick up a stone or some gravel. In the countryside you should also be wary of but not paranoid about snakes (six poisonous species are fairly common) and hornets. The latter have been known to kill people.

POLICE Taiwan's police force (☏ 110) doesn't have a stellar reputation for efficiency or enforcement but as a foreign visitor you can expect courtesy and assistance. All police stations are marked in English as well as Chinese. Few officers speak good English but if you go into a larger station you've a much better chance of finding someone who can communicate.

DRUGS Taiwan has strict drugs laws and death sentences are possible for smugglers and dealers. The police are empowered to force those they suspect of using illegal drugs to take a urine test. If the test comes up positive for amphetamines, ecstasy or another controlled substance, the individual may be sent to a detention centre for up to 30 days of compulsory detoxification. This is an administrative action, not a judicial procedure, so there's no appeal.

IN AN EMERGENCY Call ☏ 110 for police or ☏ 119 if there's a fire or an ambulance is needed. Operators may not understand English, so you may prefer to call the 24-hour 'information for foreigners' hotline (☏ 0800 024 111).

WOMEN TRAVELLERS Apart from being careful when taking taxis by themselves late at night, female tourists needn't take any exceptional precautions. Western women rate Taiwan highly in terms of hassle-free travelling.

LGBT TRAVELLERS Attitudes to homosexuality have changed dramatically in the past two decades. There are now gay venues in the major cities and an annual gay-pride parade in Taipei. However, many gay men still face immense pressure from traditional parents to marry and continue the family line; the consequences of this form the basis of Ang Lee's 1993 film *The Wedding Banquet*. Some gay women come up against the traditional notion that an unmarried adult woman is somehow incomplete. However, the number of women (straight or gay) remaining unmarried well into their thirties has soared in recent years.

There's a chance Taiwan will become the first country in Asia to allow same-sex marriage. In May 2017, the highest court ruled that same-sex couples have a right to marry under the constitution and that the parliament has two years to amend the marriage laws to align with this. If this is not done, same-sex couples will be able to have their unions registered as marriages and be treated as such by law. Marriage equality remains an uphill battle, however. At the time of writing, a bill to legalise same-sex marriage has been drafted but not passed, and groups opposed to marriage equality won two non-binding referendums in November 2018.

One of the few prominent individuals to have come out is Lin Hwai-min, founder of Cloud Gate Dance Theatre (page 36). In 2016, the new administration appointed Audrey Tang (b1981), a transgender woman who describes herself as an anarchist, to a minister-without-portfolio position with responsibility for digital communications and the sharing economy.

Local gay organisations include the Taiwan Tongzhi Hotline Association (w hotline.org.tw). English speakers will find w travelgayasia.com useful.

TRAVELLING WITH CHILDREN Taiwan is a safe and welcoming destination for travellers with children. In restaurants, temples and shops, Taiwanese people show

2

great tolerance towards kids who are noisy or fidgety. Children with Western features attract plenty of positive attention. Parents must, of course, take steps to protect their children against Taiwan's traffic, strong sunshine and mosquitoes, but in terms of food, cleanliness and general public health, Taiwan isn't a dangerous place.

If you plan to use a pushchair for any distance, be prepared for an obstacle course. In many places in urban Taiwan the pavement isn't flat or doesn't exist at all. Also, it isn't unusual for shopkeepers to pile so much merchandise on the pavement that pedestrians are forced to detour into the road. Parents with babies will find there are few nappy-changing stations except those at department stores, large supermarkets, metro stations and some train stations.

Anyone with a young child knows it's essential to bring an extra set of clothes, including shoes, when going away from your base for more than a few hours. Taiwan's countryside has lot of places where kids can play safely – but they're likely to get dusty, muddy or sweaty. Making sure your children stay hydrated is also important, and this is another area in which Taiwan's 24/7 shopping culture is a boon for travellers. Even the smallest towns have convenience stores that stock milk and juices as well as mineral water, not to mention snacks that can help fill the stomachs of youngsters unimpressed by local cuisine.

Finding child-friendly accommodation is sometimes an issue. Five-star hotels and top-end resorts are invariably safe and comfortable, but may not match your budget and may not exist near your destination. Hotels in city centres are convenient but rooms are often small and sometimes noisy. Moreover, parents putting teenage children in a separate room may have cause for concern when they turn on the television: one or more channels may be devoted to hardcore pornography. The recent explosion in homestays is a boon for travellers with children. Unfortunately, many of these places are like ordinary Taiwanese homes in that they have tiled floors – hard surfaces for an infant to take a tumble on. Few homestays have lifts, which can be a problem if you're upstairs and your kids are still in pushchairs. Wherever you're staying, careful examination of your room as soon as you get inside is advisable. Childproofing your hotel room is much the same as childproofing your home, and some parents may want to take along safety devices such as cupboard latches.

On both high-speed and conventional trains, very young children can travel for free if they don't need a seat, and primary school-age youngsters can get half-price tickets. Few taxis are equipped with child-safety seats, but car-hire companies say they can provide them if given some notice. If you do drive yourself, make use of the service stations along the highways as they are normally very family-friendly places with playgrounds and other distractions.

TRAVELLERS WITH A DISABILITY Taiwan isn't the world's most wheelchair-friendly society, but it's come a long way in recent years. Public buildings and larger hotels almost always have ramp access. However, where pavements do exist, obstacles (parked cars, moving motorcycles, street vendors) often force wheelchair users out into the road.

Physically challenged travellers are advised to take trains rather than buses wherever possible, as railway workers have been trained to give assistance to the disabled and visually impaired as they get on and off trains. Tipping for this service is not necessary or expected. Note, though, that the substantial discounts train and bus operators extend to disabled citizens aren't always offered to foreign visitors.

The UK's **gov.uk** website (w gov.uk/guidance/foreign-travel-for-disabled-people) provides general advice and practical information for travellers with disabilities

The steps visitors to Taiwan should take to minimise the environmental impact of their trip aren't so different from what travellers everywhere should be doing. When you make a purchase, refuse excess packaging. Separate your rubbish so as much as possible can be recycled; if you're unsure what kind of trash goes into which bin – few litter bins have bilingual labels – just ask. Use public transport wherever possible and, to save on 'food miles', eat local produce rather than imported foods. If you want to practise 'sustainable eating', you should avoid fish and sea creatures which are critical to reef ecosystems.

Re-use plastic bags as often as possible, because food-and-drink vendors tend to wrap every purchase in a fresh bag. Some travellers carry their own chopsticks and spoon (or knife and fork) rather than use disposable utensils made of bamboo or plastic. In Taiwan's hot weather you'll be consuming a lot of liquids, so rather than buying several bottles of mineral water each day, bring a canteen and refill it at public water fountains in bus, train and metro stations (and many temples). Not using more water than you need when bathing and washing clothes is important as Taiwan often suffers water shortages. Rainfall per square kilometre is more than three times the global average, but because of Taiwan's dense population, per-capita precipitation is less than one-eighth of the world's average.

preparing for overseas travel. **Accessible Journeys** (w disabilitytravel.com) is a comprehensive US site written by wheelchair users who have been researching wheelchair-accessible travel full-time since 1985. There are many tips and useful contacts (including lists of travel agents on request) for slow walkers, wheelchair travellers and their families, plus informative articles, including pieces on disabled travelling worldwide. The company also organises group tours. **Global Access News** (w globalaccessnews.com/index.htm) provides general travel information, reviews and tips for travelling with a disability. The **Society for Accessible Travel and Hospitality** (w sath.org) also provides some general information.

WHAT TO TAKE

There's very little you can't buy in Taiwan, but when deciding what and how many clothes to bring, bear in mind that Taiwanese people are generally shorter and thinner than Westerners, so you may not find something in your size. Even if you're coming during the hot season, do bring a light jacket, cardigan or shawl – something that's easy to put on and take off – as you'll probably be entering and leaving air-conditioned buildings several times a day. Winter visitors should be prepared for surprisingly low temperatures indoors as well as outside. Even in the mountains, there are plenty of hotels without any sort of heating. Bring multiple layers rather than thick sweaters, as between breakfast and early afternoon the mercury may rise by as much as 15°C.

Good walking shoes are essential for urban and rural exploring. Very few Taiwanese temples expect visitors to remove their footwear, so don't worry if your favourite boots require a lot of lacing. If you're not bringing sandals, consider buying a cheap pair while in Taiwan for evening trips to the convenience store and times when your feet need fresh air.

ELECTRICITY

Taiwan's domestic electricity supply is 110v/60Hz. Plugs are American-style and have two parallel flat prongs. Adaptors can be bought from electrical-goods shops or borrowed from hotels.

MONEY

Taiwan's currency is the New Taiwan dollar, abbreviated throughout this guidebook as NTD. In Mandarin, NT dollars are called *táibì*. When quoting a price, however, most people use the word *kuài*, as in *yī bǎi kuài* (NTD100).

The NTD comes in banknotes of 100, 200, 500, 1,000 and 2,000, and coins of 1, 5, 10, 20 and 50. The NTD1 and NTD50 coins are copper; the NTD20 has a bronze ring and cupro-nickel centre; the NTD5 and NTD10 coins are cupro-nickel. The NTD200 and NTD2,000 notes and NTD20 coin are seldom used. Keeping a pocketful of coins is a good idea as bus journeys usually have to be paid for with exact change, and sometimes taxi drivers aren't able to break large-denomination notes.

EXCHANGING MONEY Outside of banks, major post offices and big hotels, your money-changing options are very limited. Unlike in some other Asian countries, money-changing kiosks are almost unknown in Taiwan. Some department stores are able to change US dollars, euros, Japanese yen and Chinese RMB. Annoyingly, some of the banks that have 'authorised foreign exchange' signs outside are unable to change foreign notes into local currency. If it's after 15.30 and you need to change money, try a major hotel or a department store. Differences in terms of exchange rates are minimal, so don't waste time walking from one bank to another comparing rates.

When buying NT dollars, you're likely to get a better rate of exchange in Taiwan than in your home country, so consider waiting until you've arrived and then changing money at the airport. The banks inside Taoyuan and Kaohsiung airports keep very long hours for the convenience of international travellers.

CASH MACHINES Most of Taiwan's ATMs give you the option of Chinese or English instructions. Many but not all accept debit cards or credit cards issued overseas, so carrying enough cash to see you through the day is always a good idea. If you're heading somewhere remote – such as an island or a mountain village – take enough for that segment of your holiday.

PEOPLE AND PEAKS IN YOUR WALLET

The head on the NTD1, 5 and 10 coins belongs to Chiang Kai-shek, although the latter is only for coins minted before 2011. Newer NTD10 coins have Sun Yat-sen (see box, page 103), who also appears on the NTD50 coin and NTD100 note. The NTD20 coin shows aboriginal chieftain Mona Rudao (page 15) and Tao canoes from Orchid Island. The NTD200 note bears a likeness of Chiang Kai-shek together with the Presidential Office; the NTD500 features youngsters playing baseball, sika deer and Mount Dabajian. One side of the NTD1,000 shows a group of schoolchildren examining a globe; the other has a mikado pheasant in the foreground and the main peak of Mount Jade. The NTD2,000 note shows a locally made space satellite, the Formosan landlocked salmon (see box, page 194) and Mount Nanhu.

CREDIT CARDS Do bring your credit cards as you'll find them very useful in major hotels, better restaurants and for buying train tickets. Credit cards tend not to be accepted in small eateries or homestays.

DISCOUNT CARDS If you have an International Student Identity Card, bring it. You'll get discounts at museums, forest recreation areas and other places.

BANKS Except for branches in the international airports, all banks keep the same opening hours, 09.00 to 15.30 Monday to Friday. Three of the largest local banks are: Mega International Commercial Bank (Mega) (**w** megabank.com.tw), Bank of Taiwan (**w** www.bot.com.tw) – not to be confused with Taiwan's central bank – and First Bank (**w** www.firstbank.com.tw).

BUDGETING

Taiwan isn't nearly as expensive for travellers as destinations such as western Europe or Japan, but nor is it as inexpensive as southeast Asia. Public transport and eating out are bargains; accommodation will probably account for over half of your daily expenditure.

SCRIMPING If you take advantage of discounted intercity bus tickets, stay in cheaper hotels and hostels and eat what local people eat, a couple could spend less than NTD2,500 per day and still have a most enjoyable trip.

MODEST A daily budget of NTD2,000 per person is enough for reasonable hotel or homestay accommodation, transport that's convenient (such as occasionally renting a motorcycle), tickets to all the museums and other attractions you'd like to see, plus some upmarket meals.

LUXURY Hiring a car or paying a local tour operator to show you exactly what you want to see will greatly enhance your Taiwan experience. Jumping in and out of taxis in places like Tainan can save lots of time and isn't likely to add more than NTD800 to your day's spending. If you're happy to fork out NTD5,000 or more per night on hotels, you'll be able to stay in establishments that aren't just comfortable places to sleep but which add an extra layer of enjoyment and relaxation to your trip. Eating out is seldom expensive, so even gourmands and those who require Western meals are unlikely to spend more than NTD1,000 per person per day on food.

Practical Information BUDGETING

2

DISCOUNTS FOR THE OLD AND YOUNG

At many attractions in Taiwan, including museums and forest recreation areas, senior citizens, full-time students (adults and children) and those with disabilities quality for half-price tickets. However, foreign seniors aren't always given discounts available to their local counterparts. Throughout *Part Two* of this book, if more than one admission price is listed, the first is for standard entry while the second is the discounted rate for the elderly, students and people with disabilities . Sometimes a third, even cheaper ticket price is listed. This is unlikely to apply to foreign visitors; often it's for servicemen and police officers only. University students should show their student ID when asking for discounted tickets; seniors who look youthful should have their passports ready.

TIPPING There's very little tipping in Taiwan. When using a porter at an airport or a high-end hotel, it's usual to tip NTD100 per piece of luggage moved. Many upmarket restaurants and hotels add a 10% service charge; there's no need to add anything more.

GETTING AROUND

Public transport in Taiwan is safe, inexpensive, reliable and comfortable. Smoking is not permitted on buses or trains or inside stations. Foreign visitors may encounter language problems, but the information in this guidebook combined with the kindness of many Taiwanese (both transport workers and passing strangers) should ensure you get from one place to another smoothly. When taking any kind of bus or train, don't lose your ticket, as you'll need to show it – or run it through a machine – at your destination. Senior citizens holding discounted tickets on account of their age may be asked to provide ID showing their date of birth.

BY AIR Tourists are likely to fly only if they're heading to the east or one of the outlying islands. If weather conditions are right, flying Taipei–Taitung or Kaohsiung–Hualien is worth every penny of the fare for the stirring views you'll get of Taiwan's mountains and coastline. Flight times and ticket prices are listed in *Part Two* of this book.

BY FERRY The boats that link Taiwan's mainland island with Penghu County, the Matsu Islands, Green Island and Orchid Island are a good option if you have plenty of time or dislike flying. There's no civilian boat service to Kinmen County. If you're heading to Little Liuqiu, the ferry from Donggang is your only option. Short-distance boat journeys include Tamsui–Bali and the ferry to Kaohsiung's Cijin Island.

BY TRAIN Taiwan has two railway systems: TRA and HSR.

Taiwan Railway Administration (TRA) The TRA is the government-owned conventional railway network. The Keelung–Kaohsiung line is divided into 'mountain' and 'ocean' routes. Just south of Hsinchu, the railroad splits: the

Vast amounts of energy have been devoted to the romanisation question: how should Taiwan render Chinese place names in the Latin alphabet? The issue boils down to this: should it use the system invented in the PRC and adopted by the UN, *hanyu pinyin*, or should it use a home-grown system called *tongyong pinyin*? Many of the 'greens' (see box, page 21) favour *tongyong pinyin* whereas the 'blues' support the adoption of *hanyu pinyin*. However, no administration has fully embraced one system over another, which is why Taipei remains Taipei (in *hanyu pinyin* it should be Taibei) and Kaohsiung continues to be spelled that way (*hanyu pinyin*: Gaoxiong).

Throughout this book I've used *hanyu pinyin* except for those places already known outside Taiwan by another spelling (Taroko Gorge and Hsinchu, for instance) and a few places consistently spelled in a special way (such as certain aboriginal villages). The pronunciation guide that appears in parentheses after the name of each place or attraction is always *hanyu pinyin*.

Spelling mistakes sometimes appear on road signs and on leaflets given out to foreign tourists. Inconsistencies are rife: what one website labels Nanhu Big Mountain may elsewhere be spelled Nanhudashan (*dà* is Mandarin for 'big', *shān* means 'mountain'). Common alternative spellings are noted in *Part Two*. Sometimes a little imagination helps: if you suspect that Banqiao, Banciao and Panchiao are the same place, you'd be right.

Mountain Line goes inland via Miaoli and Sanyi, while the Ocean Line hugs the coast and bypasses Taichung. Trains to east Taiwan take the North Link via Yilan or the South Link via Pingtung. Branch lines serve Pingxi in New Taipei City, Neiwan near Hsinchu and Jiji in Nantou County. There are also useful short rail lines between the TRA and HSR stations in Tainan and Hsinchu. Fares depend on distance and the type of train. A journey during rush hour is no more expensive than travelling off-peak but you may have to stand up. Over short distances TRA services are often quicker than buses. Over long distances, intercity buses are faster and cheaper.

Train types Non-local trains are classed as Puyuma, Taroko, Tze-Chiang (TC) or Chu-Kuang (CK). The first two are the fastest; on them seat reservations are essential and no standing passengers are allowed. TC services make fewer stops than CK trains. At the time of writing, the one-way fare between Taipei and Kaohsiung was NTD843 by Puyuma (takes 3½hrs), also NTD843 by TC (a little under 5hrs) and NTD650 by CK (nearly 7hrs).

Local trains stop at all or almost all stations along shorter routes but are considerably cheaper. Kaohsiung–Chiayi by TC (takes less than 1½hrs) is NTD245; by local train (over 2hrs) it's NTD158.

Getting tickets In many stations one ticket window (⊕ usually 06.00–23.00 daily) is marked 'For English'. Before approaching the clerk, it's a good idea to write down the romanised name of the station you want to go to and the departure time. When you buy tickets for an express train, seat reservations are made automatically at no extra charge. If no seats are available, the clerk will tell you and may suggest a later train. If you stick to your original plan, your ticket will be marked 'no seat' but you can search for a space once you're on board.

You can buy tickets for express services up to 12 days in advance from any station, not only the one you'll be departing from. Buying tickets ahead of time is no cheaper than getting them at the last minute, but it's a very good idea if you plan to travel at the weekend or on a national holiday, or on a Puyuma or Taroko express. Getting a round-trip ticket is slightly cheaper than buying two one-way tickets. Credit cards are accepted. Tickets bought from a clerk have all the pertinent information in both English and Chinese.

Tickets bought from vending machines are in Chinese only and do not come with seat reservations. If you're in a rush and there's a long queue for tickets, get a ticket from a vending machine. It doesn't matter if it's for a lower class of train or for only part of the journey; you can upgrade and/or extend it on board. To do this, find the ticket inspector and say *bǔ piào*. Confirm your destination and he'll issue a new ticket; you'll need to pay cash for the upgrade. If you get on a train without any kind of ticket, you'll be asked to pay a surcharge.

There's no need to get fresh tickets if you miss a train for which you've reservations as tickets are valid on any train going to the same destination, although your seat reservation can't be transferred, and you may be required to pay for an upgrade.

Students can get a TR Pass (NTD599 for five consecutive days) entitling them to unlimited travel on all trains except Puyuma, Taroko and TC expresses. Seven- and ten-day versions are also available; passes can be purchased at major stations for immediate use.

Baggage Most stations have lifts for disabled passengers and those with heavy bags. Major TRA stations have baggage services offices (🕐 08.00–20.00 daily) where you can ship your bicycle or motorcycle. For a small fee and a bit of paperwork, you can also leave bags for a few hours or a few days. In many stations there are lockers, costing NTD50 for 3 hours or part thereof.

While your stuff is pretty safe on Taiwanese trains, do of course carry your valuables with you if you leave your carriage to visit the bathroom.

Food and drink On long-distance TRA trains there's a trolley service but the pickings are slim, so you're advised to stock up before you get on board. Drinking water is sometimes available on expresses but you'd do well to bring liquids.

High-speed Railway (HSR)
Taiwan's bullet train covers the 349km between Nangang in Taipei and Zuoying in Kaohsiung in as little as 1 hour 45 minutes. Every train stops at Taipei Main Station, Banqiao and Taichung; many services skip Taoyuan, Hsinchu, Miaoli, Taichung, Changhua, Yunlin, Chiayi and Tainan.

There are around four southbound departures per hour from Taipei Main Station (🕐 06.30–22.16 daily). If you buy your ticket eight or more days in advance, you may be able to get as much as 35% off, bringing the price of a standard Taipei–Kaohsiung ticket down from NTD1,490 to NTD965. Business class (bigger seats, power outlet for your laptop, free coffee and newspapers) is 30% more expensive. HSR tickets can be bought online and at stations (from staff or from vending machines that accept credit cards and cash).

BY BUS There are several bus companies and they compete on price and comfort level. All coaches are air conditioned; many intercity services are equipped with personal entertainment systems that show TV programmes and movies but these may not include English-language options. Major operators such as Kuo-Kuang and Ubus serve small towns such as Puli and Lukang as well as the big cities. Unfortunately, few companies have much English-language information on their websites, so you may need to go to the bus station and get timetable details in person. If heading from one big city to another there's usually no need to book ahead. Services are frequent and discount fares are often available midweek.

By tourist shuttle and tour bus Two government-sponsored bus systems have made exploring some parts of Taiwan much easier for visitors who don't wish to drive. Taiwan Tourist Shuttle (w www.taiwantrip.com.tw) services are much like regular buses except the routes were designed with sightseers in mind. On some, it's possible to get a one-day jump-on/jump-off ticket. Taiwan Tour Bus (w taiwantourbus.com.tw) excursions last half or a whole day, with a guide on board who can introduce points of interest along the way. These tours can be a good way of seeing places like Taroko Gorge but you should review the information on the website carefully as reservations are necessary and English-speaking guides aren't available on all routes. Payment is usually made in advance by credit card or PayPal.

By city bus Useful local bus routes are mentioned throughout the guide. Buses are air conditioned and on most eating and drinking aren't allowed. Greater Taipei has a good bus network, as does Kaohsiung (in both cities most services operate ⊕ 06.30–20.30 daily; one-way fares NTD12–30). Compared with getting around by metro, urban bus travel is slow but you'll see much more.

BY CAR If you can deal with the way some Taiwanese people drive and can accept dense traffic in urban areas, consider getting your own vehicle for part of your stay.

Cars and motorcycles are supposed to drive on the right; outside the big cities, many two-wheelers use whichever side of the road is most convenient. Driving can be frustrating and stressful. At junctions, always observe what some call the 'lights plus one' rule – before moving forward, assume one more motorist or motorcyclist will try to rush across, despite the lights being against him. If an oncoming car flashes its headlights at you, it means you should give way, not (as in the UK) that the driver is letting you go first. Drivers and passengers are now required by law to wear seat belts at all times. Don't drink and drive; the alcohol limit for drivers in Taiwan is lower than in the UK.

Self-driving tourists should refer to the bus journey times listed in *Part Two* and not assume they can move significantly quicker. In many mountain areas you're required to keep your headlights on regardless of conditions.

Hiring a car Car-rental businesses and their locations are listed on page 58 and in *Part Two* of this guidebook; almost all insist on seeing an International Driving Permit as well as your passport. Expect to pay around NTD2,500 per day for a 1,600cc Nissan Tiida and NTD3,600 per day for a Toyota Sienta which can take up to seven people.

When hiring a car, a credit card is usually the only acceptable means of payment and you'll probably be required to sign a blank credit-card voucher to cover any fines that might be processed after your departure (they may not show up until three months later).

If your car or motorcycle disappears, go into any police station and give them the licence number. If it was towed rather than stolen, they can find out very quickly and call you a taxi to where it's been impounded.

There are three vehicle-rental offices inside Taoyuan Airport:

It's worth getting to grips with Taiwan's road-numbering system as there's potential for confusion. For instance, two separate north–south roads bear the number 3. On Freeway 3 you can cruise comfortably at over 100km/h; the other, Highway 3, is a winding country road on which you'd do well to average 50km/h.

Motorcycles and bicycles aren't allowed on freeways, which are like British motorways. The usual freeway speed limit is 110km/h; on other roads it's normally 50 or 60km/h. Speed traps are common and on freeways cameras also catch those driving too close to the vehicle in front. By law, cars travelling at 100km/h must be at least 50m behind the vehicle ahead. There are no traffic lights on freeways.

There are also several expressways which are almost as fast as freeways. Most of them run east–west and link the two north–south freeways. An exception is Expressway 61, which hugs the west coast between Bali in the north and Tainan in the south.

Avis Taiwan Arrivals, T2; 656 5990 ext 112, 113; e booking@avis-taiwan.com; w avis-taiwan.com; 06.00–midnight daily
Ching Bing Auto Leasing Arrivals, T1; 398 3979; e order@chingbing.com.tw; w chingbing.com.tw; 06.00–00.30 daily

Hotai Leasing Corp Arrivals, T2; 398 3636; e x034@mail.hotaimotor.com.tw; w www.easyrent.com.tw/English; 05.00–midnight daily

BY MOTORCYCLE Most Taiwanese ride step-through scooters. These Vespa-type machines are fully automatic and come in a few different sizes, the most common being 50cc and 125cc. If you're on your own, neither large nor heavy, don't have much luggage and don't intend to stray far from the city, a 50cc scooter will do you fine. If you expect to cover more than 100km in a day, carry a passenger or climb serious hills, rent a 125cc.

How to ride The fundamental rules are obvious but bear repeating: be careful, obey traffic laws regardless of what you see other people doing, don't ride when tired or intoxicated and always wear a helmet; rental businesses provide helmets for no additional cost. If dust and fumes bother you, do as the locals do and wear a mask. There are simple cloth masks which can be washed when they get grimy and hospital-style masks with carbon filters; the latter are said to be better at blocking nasty particulates. Even if bright sunshine isn't a problem for you, do wear some form of eye protection. Grit or insects – Taiwan has plenty of both – may get in your eyes.

Hiring a motorcycle Rental businesses are often found near train stations but tend not to have English signs. Many will turn you away even if you have an international licence. Often this isn't xenophobia; more often it's because the rental business doesn't want to get stuck with having to pay fines for traffic violations committed by customers they can't later track down. This problem wouldn't exist if more motorcycle-rental businesses accepted credit cards.

If you succeed in renting a scooter, before hitting the road confirm whether it takes '92' (two-star petrol) or '95' (four-star). You'll be lucky if there's more than a tiny amount of fuel in the tank, so make the nearest petrol station your first objective. Renting a scooter for 24 hours typically costs NTD400. Read the section on the opposite page for additional tips.

Hiring an e-scooter or e-bike Many motorcycle- and bicycle-rental outlets also offer electric scooters, which can be hired without a licence (you may have to leave your passport as a deposit) and are fine for touring the local area. While they are a bit cheaper than petrol-powered scooters, they are neither sufficiently powerful nor comfortable for long-distance travel.

BY TAXI Taiwan's taxi industry has become more professional in recent years, yet very few drivers understand English (so carry your destination's name or address in Chinese) and women are advised against taking taxis by themselves late at night.

All legal taxis are yellow. Unless you're travelling a long distance, or from an airport or in the mountains – in which case the driver may ask for a flat fee – the fare is calculated by a clearly visible meter. At the time of writing, taxis in Taipei charged NTD70 for the first 1.25km, plus NTD5 for each additional 200m or 1 minute 20 seconds spent waiting. A 4km daytime journey in normal traffic therefore costs at least NTD140. There are small extra charges late at night, around Lunar New Year and if you have lots of luggage. In other cities, slightly different formulas are used to tot up taxi fares – you may see the meter starting at NTD100. Some taxis accept payment by EasyCard (see box, page 54).

Uber (w uber.com) has run into legal problems in Taiwan but at the time of writing was operating in conjunction with licensed local partners. Tripool (w tripool.app) is a Taiwanese startup promising inexpensive point-to-point travel in vehicles that can take up to seven people and their luggage.

HITCHHIKING Hitchhiking isn't at all common in Taiwan, but solo foreign travellers will find it relatively easy to get a lift in more rural and mountainous areas. You may be expected to practise English with the driver's children, and you may have snacks and drinks forced on you, but you'll come away agreeing that Taiwanese people are some of the friendliest and most helpful in the world.

ON FOOT Walking can be quite pleasurable in Taipei and Kaohsiung but in many other places the pavements are narrow and often cluttered with vendors, piles of merchandise and parked motorcycles. Look both ways before crossing any roads.

BY BICYCLE Taiwan's cyclists have a lot to contend with: heat, unpredictable drivers and pollution (consider buying a disposable mask; supermarkets and convenience stores sell them). Despite these factors, Taiwan is an excellent place for a cycling holiday. Roads are well maintained and drivers are used to sharing the carriageway with two-wheelers. There's lots to see wherever you go and countless places where you can stop for a drink or a snack. At certain 7-Eleven convenience stores it's possible to borrow a bike pump (look for the bike-pump sign outside), but if you can't find one of these, try a police station.

Folding bikes that have been properly bagged can be taken on any TRA local train and certain expresses at no extra cost. Cyclists travelling with unbagged, non-folding bicycles are allowed on most but not all local trains at many but not all stations. The charge for the bike is half the adult fare. After buying your tickets be sure to be on the platform several minutes before departure as the guard will need to show you which carriage you should sit in.

Practical Information GETTING AROUND

2

Bagged non-folding bikes can be taken on HSR trains for free. Bagged and/or folding bicycles are allowed on metro trains in Taipei and Kaohsiung; this is free but unfeasible during rush hours. Folding bikes go for free on Kuo-Kuang intercity buses; non-folding bicycles are charged half price.

ACCOMMODATION

Compared with other travel expenses, accommodation in Taiwan isn't cheap. Hotel prices are almost always quoted in New Taiwan dollars (NTD). Credit cards are accepted by top- and mid-range hotels but often not by budget inns, homestays or campsites. Bargaining is occasionally possible at motels and mid-range places.

Rather than kettles in every room, in some establishments you'll find filtered-water machines in the lobby or corridor. These provide both room-temperature and piping-hot water. The buttons may be labelled in Chinese only, so be careful not to get scalded.

HOTELS Travellers willing to pay NTD3,000 or more per night will have plenty of options. In smaller towns and resorts you may struggle to find a hotel that has both personality and staff with a good grasp of English. In all major towns, inexpensive hotels (often costing less than NTD1,500 per night) can be found near TRA stations. These places vary hugely in quality and you should be prepared to visit a few before choosing one. Air conditioning and cable TV are standard; if there's a deficiency it's likely to be the hot-water system. In cheaper inns, hot water is only available in the evening, as Taiwanese tend to bathe after dinner.

HOMESTAYS AND B&BS Homestays (*mínsù* 民宿) can be found throughout rural Taiwan, and in many you can learn a lot from the host family about local customs, lifestyles and ecology. A huge variety of establishments call themselves homestays. Some, including several in Kinmen County and the Matsu Islands, occupy well-kept traditional buildings that would be tourist attractions even if they weren't bed-and-breakfasts. Some newer homestays were purpose-built and are very luxurious; a few places that call themselves B&Bs don't, oddly, offer breakfast. Many homestays in remote areas offer dinner to those who book it in advance but you may be expected to eat quite early. Even in low season, rooms should be booked before arrival as many owners have farms to tend to and errands to run.

Foreign travellers face two language-related obstacles when it comes to homestays. Few bosses speak English and some establishments are hard to find if you can't read Chinese signs. It's worthwhile looking through an establishment's website before making a reservation, even if the site has no English, as pictures of the guest rooms are useful when judging whether a place meets your standards.

MOTELS Locals will tell you motels prosper by providing places where people can conduct extramarital affairs. This perhaps explains why so many motels have large comfortable beds and are absolutely soundproof – just what you want for a good night's rest. For self-driving travellers, motels are a value-for-money alternative. They'd be an even better option if more were located in city centres or proper countryside rather than dull suburbs.

YOUTH HOSTELS Taiwan's hostelling scene includes 'youth activity centres' managed by the quasi-official China Youth Corps (an organisation which until 2000 bore the magnificent moniker, 'China Youth Anti-Communist National Salvation Corps'), establishments accredited by the Taiwan Youth Hostel Association (w yh. org.tw), the local Hostelling International affiliate, Church-run hostels and various private-sector operations. Both inexpensive private rooms and dorm beds can be booked through w hostels.com.

MOUNTAIN SHELTERS If you do any serious hiking you'll probably stay in mountain shelters. In some you can sleep for free but bunk space should be booked ahead of time. For a few, such as Paiyun Lodge on Mount Jade, you pay when you make the booking. Comfort levels vary greatly and depend on how new the structure is and how many people you're sharing with. In many, no bedding is provided. The toilets may be grim and you shouldn't expect shower facilities. Many shelters have a water supply but this isn't always reliable; you may have to walk a considerable distance to fill your bottles.

ACCOMMODATION PRICE CODES

Accommodation listings are laid out in decreasing price order, under the following categories: Luxury, Upmarket, Mid-range, Budget and Shoestring. The following key gives an indication of prices. Prices are based on a double room per night in high season, including any taxes and service charges.

Luxury	$$$$$	NTD7,000+
Upmarket	$$$$	NTD4,500–6,999
Mid-range	$$$	NTD2,500–4,499
Budget	$$	NTD1,000–2,499
Shoestring	$	<NTD1,000

CAMPSITES Well-organised campsites with shower facilities can be found throughout east Taiwan, in Kenting National Park and several other places. Expect to pay around NTD200 per person per night. It's not worth dragging a high-quality tent all the way from your home country when a standard Taiwanese two-person tent, which you can buy from a hypermarket for less than NTD2,000, will do perfectly well. Some campsites rent out tents. It goes without saying that the drier, cooler winter months are the best time to camp. A useful website is w www. taiwancamping.net.

EATING AND DRINKING

Taiwanese eat a lot and eat often, so it isn't surprising that around one in six is overweight. Many young women, however, are stick-thin. As in other east Asian countries, rice and noodles are staples. Sweet potatoes and yams are secondary sources of carbohydrates. As you'd expect on an island, seafood is common; much of the fish, however, is farmed rather than caught in the ocean. There's a good selection of vegetables, especially cabbage, carrots, turnips and cucumbers. Vegetables are often fried with crushed garlic rather than boiled or steamed. Sweetcorn and various beans are common.

Pork is the most frequently eaten meat and those following a kosher or halal diet should assume that meat sauces are pork-based unless stated otherwise. Chicken and mutton are also popular. Most of the beef eaten in Taiwan is imported, and part of the population – perhaps one in ten – never eats beef. This prohibition dates from pre-industrial times when cattle and water buffalo were protected because they were needed for ploughing and manure. Goose and duck are easy to find. You may also have chances to try turtle, pigeon, frog, snake or snails – but not dog meat, the sale of which has been illegal since 2003.

TAIWANESE CUISINE No longer regarded as a subset of or inferior to China's culinary traditions, Taiwanese cooking emphasises neither spiciness nor sourness. Dishes are usually steamed, stewed or stir-fried. Taiwanese make the most of local seafood, and of the fresh ingredients that are available year-round. Rice was once thought to be very important indeed, but consumption has fallen dramatically in

MOCK MEAT FOR VEGETARIANS

Vegetarian food (sù shí 素食) is easy to find throughout Taiwan, even in small towns. Visitors who don't read any Chinese can look for restaurants displaying the swastika, a Buddhist symbol that denotes vegetarianism. Nowadays, the number of Taiwanese who don't eat meat for the sake of their health probably exceeds the number who follow a vegetarian diet for purely religious reasons. The latter also avoid strong-smelling vegetables such as garlic, leeks, shallots and onions; these are considered undesirable because they excite the senses. Lay Buddhists tend to be vegetarian on the first and 15th days of each lunar month. Relatively few Taiwanese vegetarians are motivated purely by a concern for animal welfare.

In many vegetarian restaurants, you'll see 'fake meat' – slabs of vegetable protein (soy, wheat gluten or mushrooms) that have been shaped, coloured and cooked to resemble beef patties, sausages, juicy steaks, ribs or mince. They don't taste much like real meat, but they're often delicious all the same.

Restaurant listings are laid out in decreasing price order, under the following categories: Expensive, Above average, Mid-range, Cheap and cheerful and Rock bottom. The following key (also on the inside front cover) gives an indication of prices. Prices are based on the cost of a main course (including tax) per person.

Expensive	$$$$$	NTD1,000+
Above average	$$$$	NTD500–999
Mid-range	$$$	NTD250–499
Cheap and cheerful	$$	NTD100–249
Rock bottom	$	<NTD100

the past few decades as wheat-based alternatives became widely available. Even so, few Taiwanese go 48 hours without eating a bowl or two of steamed polished white rice (*bái fàn* 白飯). Noodles (*miàn* 麵) are common; they're usually served 'dry' with gravy (*gān miàn* 乾麵) or with chunks of meat in a soup. Taiwanese cuisine also has a vast range of broths and consommés that differ from European soups in that the liquid is often clear and somewhat oily, and the ingredients (which may include large pieces of bone) aren't finely chopped.

Breakfast (*zǎo cān* 早餐) Few Western visitors find the traditional Taiwanese breakfast of rice gruel, pickles, peanuts and dried shredded pork appetising. If you're staying in an upmarket establishment you can expect a full breakfast buffet, but if you're not you may want to buy something the evening before. In towns and cities there are plenty of breakfast eateries (🕐 05.30–11.00 daily) that sell hot, inexpensive items like egg pancakes (*dàn bǐng*, you can ask to have bacon and/or cheese added) and hamburgers (*hàn bǎo*, usually pork). Hot coffee is usually available, though it may come in a can. At least once during your stay try cruller sticks, a type of unsweetened doughnut, and hot soya milk. Some find this type of food a little too greasy, but on cold mornings it's just the ticket.

Lunch (*wǔ cān* 午餐) and dinner (*wǎn cān* 晚餐) The foods eaten at lunchtime are very similar to those eaten at dinnertime. Lunchtime is usually noon–13.30, though many restaurants open earlier and close later, if at all. In small towns and mountain areas, you might struggle to get a hot meal after 19.30.

In many eating establishments the menu is either pasted on the wall or resembles a form with boxes that you tick. Because English-language menus (abbreviated EM throughout this guide) are rare, you'll be making good use of the *Eating and drinking* section of the *Language* appendix in this book (page 337). Pointing at what someone else is eating and holding up a finger or two to indicate quantity won't offend anyone.

Local-style buffets are especially convenient for those who don't speak Mandarin. They can be found throughout urban areas and vary considerably in terms of freshness and cleanliness. At one you'll see anywhere between a dozen and 50 different trays of food, with everything from meat to fish to vegetables. Because the food gets cold quickly and the choicest items go quickly, it pays to arrive early – 11.30 for lunch, 17.30 for dinner. Grab a paper plate (or box if you want to take the food away) and use tongs to pick up whatever takes your fancy. At the end of the line you'll be offered white rice; the cashier will then either weigh your plate or just take a look and come up with a figure. Unless you've really piled the food on, the meal shouldn't cost more than NTD150.

MAINLAND CUISINE In Taiwan's bigger cities you'll find restaurants that specialise in Shanghainese, Cantonese, Hunanese and other mainland Chinese styles of cooking. The oldest were founded by refugees who fled to Taiwan in the late 1940s.

HAKKA COOKING Hakka food isn't to everyone's liking because it's saltier, greasier and more vinegary than mainstream Taiwanese cuisine. Hakka meals are usually based around steamed white rice. However, one of the most popular dishes in Hakka regions is a kind of broad noodle made from rice flour and called *ban-tiao*. Fried with slivers of pork and carrot, or boiled and then served in soup or dry with a few slices of meat on top, a bowl of ban-tiao makes for a tasty lunch.

INDIGENOUS CUISINES Visitors should seize any chance they have to try indigenous foods. They're available nowhere else in the world and, in the opinion of many people, indigenous cooking tastes very good indeed.

Indigenous feasts often include roasted or barbecued meat (some of it obtained by hunting), small fish and shrimp taken from mountain streams, and vegetables quite different from those seen in the lowlands (see box, page 39).

Until a few decades ago, millet was a staple food in many indigenous communities. To some extent it's been replaced by rice, but at festival time millet-based dishes are prominent. It's during such events that you'll see the most authentic indigenous foods, including items not offered in restaurants. Among the Bunun tribe, raw pickled flying-squirrel intestines are considered a special delicacy, as is what's called 'stinky meat' – game that's begun to rot after being left in the trap a little too long. It's barbecued, fried with garlic and ginger, then served with a spicy sauce. For indigenous families in remote mountain communities, hunting and gathering remain important ways of obtaining food.

COOKING Taiwanese are passionate about local and international food. If you're interested in learning how to cook yourself, the following teachers all speak excellent English:

Ivy Chen w kitchenivy.com   **Calvin Tu** w gotucook.wixsite.com/cookingclass
Jodie Tsao w kitchen.j321.com

EATING OUT Taiwan has an astonishing range of roadside stalls, cheap eateries, mid-range restaurants and pretentious dining establishments. In the listings in *Part*

WHAT'S IN THE BOTTLES?

In many local eateries condiments are available on every table, although salt and pepper aren't always among them. Vinegar, soy sauce and chillies are easy to recognise, but Western visitors shouldn't expect red plastic bottles to contain ketchup (often it's spicy sauce) or yellow ones to be filled with mustard (usually it's *jiàng yóu gāo*, a thick brown sauce made from soy sauce). Green bottles are likely to contain a liquid version of wasabi, a mustard-like condiment often used in Japanese cooking.

TEA IN FREE CHINA

Tea is Taiwan's traditional beverage. Unlike their Japanese counterparts, Taiwanese tea aficionados don't follow any rigid ceremonies when brewing and sipping the beverage. They do, however, discard the very first brew each time as a matter of course.

Despite the growing popularity of coffee and herbal infusions, per-capita tea consumption has climbed steadily since the 1980s. Thanks to its climatic and topographical variations, the island can grow a wide range of teas, but it's the various oolongs that excite tea drinkers from afar. Despite this, domestic production is now much lower than in the 1970s and more than half of the tea drunk in Taiwan is imported from low-wage countries. Cheap tea is turned into packaged drinks for supermarkets and convenience stores; local teas tend to be much more expensive. Demand from China has driven up prices and growers of prize-winning teas are often able to sell their harvests for more than NTD100,000 per kg. However, a number of vendors have been caught passing off imported tea as premium Taiwanese oolong.

There's nothing new about foreign interest in Taiwanese tea. From the 1860s, north Taiwan saw an export-driven tea boom. North America and southeast Asia were the major markets; beneficiaries included Western businessmen living in Tamsui, Han merchants in Dadaocheng (that part of Taipei near Baoan Temple) and plantation owners in Maokong and elsewhere. There were losers, too. In an early example of globalisation having dire effects on indigenous peoples, the demand for tea led to aborigines being pushed off their ancestral lands.

Two, rather than identify and describe Taiwan's best restaurants – a task that would take more than one lifetime – I've tried to present a cross-section of the dining scene, including the excellent, the typical-yet-tasty and what (to Western if not local sensibilities) is downright bizarre.

SNACKS In night markets (pages 91 and 133) and alongside busy roads you'll find vendors who offer a vast range of tasty snacks, many of which are deep-fried and slathered with sauce. If you'd rather eat something healthier, buy fruit. Prices and availability vary according to the season, but local bananas seem to be sold year-round, as are imported apples, plus peaches and pears grown in the mountains. Taiwanese guavas, mangoes and pineapples are exceptionally good and quite unlike those sold in supermarkets in the West.

DRINKS Nobody in Taiwan drinks tap water without first boiling or filtering it, but if you do drink some unboiled or unfiltered water by mistake – when brushing your teeth, say – don't worry too much about it. You won't be stricken with diarrhoea or something worse. The problem isn't so much nasty bacteria as industrial pollutants and the state of water tanks and pipes. Almost all hotels and homestays will provide drinking water that's been boiled and/or filtered. There's no need to avoid the ice that comes with freshly squeezed juices and other drinks. If you do suffer from stomach problems while in Taiwan, it's likely to be a result of the kind of food you've been eating, not the cleanliness of the place where the food was prepared.

In addition to the usual fizzy soft drinks and supermarket fruit juices, Taiwan has an excellent selection of fresh fruit and vegetable juices, plus milkshakes made with local fruit like papaya, pineapple and mango. Cold tea is drunk in huge quantities; a Taiwanese invention variously known as 'bubble milk tea' or 'pearl milk tea' (cold black tea mixed with milk and tapioca balls) has caught on overseas.

Taiwan Beer, a lager best drunk cold, is the most popular alcoholic tipple with more than 60% of the beer market. Popular imported brands include Heineken and Kirin (a Japanese brew). In many restaurants you'll see refrigerators full of beer and other cold drinks. Just help yourself; the staff will add the cost to your bill. Red wine is far more popular than white wine and there are several local wineries. The best-known spirit is *kaoliang* – the Chinese name means 'sorghum', which is its main ingredient – and it's made in Kinmen County and the Matsu Islands. Kavalan whiskey, made in Yilan County, has won awards in both the UK and US.

PUBLIC HOLIDAYS AND FESTIVALS

Banks and government offices close on national holidays. If a national holiday falls on a Saturday or Sunday, many private companies will take the following Monday off. If it falls on a Monday, museums and other attractions that normally close on Mondays will stay open and take Tuesday off instead.

Taiwan has hundreds of festivals. Many are strictly local affairs and more than a few were concocted by mayors looking to generate income and publicity for their townships. Many annual religious events are tied to the lunar calendar (see box, page 27). For indigenous festivals, the precise date may vary from one year to the next and from one village to another.

NATIONAL HOLIDAYS

Founding Day (1 January) Rather than marking the beginning of a new year on the Gregorian calendar, this holiday celebrates the establishment of the Republic of China on 1 January 1912.

Lunar New Year (6 or more days including w/ends in late January or early February) Chinese Lunar New Year is somewhat like the Christmas/New Year period in the UK. Most employers close for a week but for the retail & hospitality sectors it's a very busy time. Ahead of the Lunar New Year, people clean their homes & try to settle all their debts. Families dine together on New Year's Eve, then relax the following day. On the second day, married women visit their parents.

2-28 Peace Memorial Day (28 February) This day commemorates the massacres of 1947 (page 17).

Tomb Sweeping Day (5 April) On this day many Taiwanese return to their hometowns to clean their ancestors' graves, make offerings & burn joss paper. The day before it is also a national holiday called Children's Day.

Dragon Boat Festival (fifth day of the fifth lunar month) This festival usually falls in early Jun & celebrates Qu Yuan, a poet-politician who

2,300 years ago committed suicide as a protest against corruption. Highly competitive dragon-boat races are held in several cities & people eat sticky rice triangles called *zòng zǐ*.

Mid-Autumn Festival (15th day of the eighth lunar month) This isn't so much a public celebration as a chance for families to get together, let off fireworks, admire the full moon & share stodgy pastries called 'mooncakes'.

Double Ten Day (10 October) This holiday marks the beginning of the 1911 uprising in central China that toppled the Qing Dynasty & led to the founding of the ROC.

IMPORTANT NON-HOLIDAYS

Valentine's Day (14 February) Without any official encouragement whatsoever, Valentine's Day has become one of the most important days of the year for young Taiwanese, who celebrate the day with fancy meals & trips to the cinema.

Lantern Festival (15th day of the first lunar month) Traditionally the climax of the Lunar New Year festivities, Lantern Festival is now a major event in its own right featuring fireworks displays, the carrying of decorated lanterns through the streets & the release of lanterns into the night sky at various places including Pingxi near Taipei. Many of the lanterns are shaped or painted to resemble that year's zodiac animal (see box, page 27). Far more exciting are 2 events held on the same day as Lantern Festival but historically unrelated to it: Yanshui's Beehive Fireworks Festival (see box, page 222) & the Bombing of Han Dan in Taitung City (see box, page 298).

Guanyin's Birthday (19th day of the second lunar month) The birthday of the Buddhist goddess of mercy is celebrated in temples with solemn prayers, in homes with vegetarian feasts &, incongruously, with displays of fighting skills in the town of Neimen (see box, page 249).

Bunun Ear-shooting Festival (late April or early May) This is one of Taiwan's most popular indigenous festivals. The precise date varies from year to year & events are held in a number of locations including Lidao (page 288) & Namasia. In addition to feasting & music, there are contests of skill & strength. Young males try to prove they deserve the respect accorded full adults by hitting animal ears hung on trees; bows & arrows are used, not guns.

Mazu's Birthday (23rd day of the third lunar month) The birthday of the sea goddess is celebrated with gusto at Dajia (see box, page 171) & other Mazu temples around the country.

Guan Gong's Birthday (13th day of the fifth lunar month) This god's birthday is marked by his devotees at major shrines including Tainan's Martial Rites Temple & Taipei's Longshan Temple.

Amis Harvest Festivals (July or August) Indigenous villages in east Taiwan celebrate the abundance of harvest time with singing, dancing & feasting (see box, page 284).

Ghost Month (seventh lunar month) On the first day of the month the gates of Hell are believed to open & the spirits of the dead return to the human world. Huge offerings are made to the wandering ghosts lest they cause mayhem. The living are concerned not only with their ancestors but with all inhabitants of the afterworld. Because accidents & deaths that occur in Ghost Month are sometimes blamed on troublesome ghosts, during this period the traditionally minded avoid getting married, opening new businesses or moving house. Ghost Month is important in Chinese communities throughout Asia. In Taiwan, Keelung is the best place to see the action.

Pasta'ai Ceremony (15th day of the tenth lunar month) This biennial event, one of Taiwan's better-known indigenous traditions, is in effect an apology by the Saisiyat tribe to the spirits of those they massacred hundreds of years ago (see box, page 160).

SHOPPING

Taiwan has countless shops of all sizes and descriptions. Morning markets open before dawn and stay active until lunchtime, and many towns also have afternoon markets where you can find a similar range of fruit, vegetables, meat and fish (but not bread or dairy products). Department stores typically run 10.00–22.00 while supermarkets often open earlier. Bookshops keep similar hours to department stores; all the bookshops listed in *Part Two* stock English-language titles. Family-run corner shops keep long hours in cities but may close soon after dinner in rural areas. Taiwan's bakeries are best visited late in the afternoon. All of these places tend to open seven days a week throughout the year, closing for no more than three days around the Lunar New Year. Convenience stores which stay open 24/7 are ubiquitous (see box, page 68).

Taiwan's economic miracle was founded on manufacturing. The island's prosperity stems from making and exporting practical consumer goods, items that have found their way to every corner of the world. Taiwanese people are rightfully proud of this, but it does mean visitors are sometimes hard-pressed to find charming and distinctive mementos they can take home and share. Everything sold in Taiwan, it often seems, is available everywhere else. Even though a lot of electronic products are made in Taiwan or made in factories owned by Taiwanese companies, don't expect huge savings on such goods. Also, English-language manuals and software may not be available.

It's said Taiwan has the highest density of 24-hour convenience stores in the world and it's hard to imagine how the country would function without 7-Eleven and Family Mart, the two main chains. In addition to buying breakfast in the morning and beer at night (Taiwan has an admirably *laissez-faire* approach to booze sales), locals stop by to pay their household bills, send parcels and buy concert tickets.

Many foreign visitors gain a profound appreciation of convenience stores. Can't face tepid rice gruel for breakfast? Get a bagel and a hot coffee from your nearest convenience store. Flat tyre on your bicycle? Look for a 7-Eleven displaying the bike-pump symbol and ask for help. Parking fees to pay? Something needs to be xeroxed or faxed? 7-Eleven or Family Mart. Looking for an English-language newspaper or imported beer? Convenience stores are often the best bet. Need hot water to make up a bottle for your infant or some tea for yourself? Any 7-Eleven will allow you to fill your Thermos or tin mug with piping-hot water for free.

Indigenous art isn't widely available in the big cities but you'll come across it in places like Sandimen and throughout the east. Good options include glass-bead jewellery and textiles. Tribe Asia (w tribe-asia.com) sells high-quality and authentic indigenous crafts via the internet.

If you want to buy presents but are bereft of ideas, Taipei's National Cultural and Creative Gift Centre (page 94) is an excellent place to start. The gift shops in major museums are also worth browsing. As befits a great repository, the National Palace Museum has an excellent on-site store with reproductions of paintings and other treasures exhibited in the museum.

ARTS AND ENTERTAINMENT

Like many other nationalities, Taiwanese spend much of their free time watching television, going to the cinema, playing computer games, shopping and listening to popular music. That said, substantial numbers of people pay to attend classes in traditional ink painting, oil painting (which took off during the Japanese occupation) or calligraphy. The last has no real parallel in the West; in Taiwan and China it's considered an art form in its own right and remains extremely popular.

The grassroots live music scene isn't as developed as it is in the West, but dramatic performances (including Taiwanese opera; see box, page 127) and concerts are frequent in the major cities. Puppetry, modernised versions of which can be seen on local television, is often performed as part of religious celebrations.

Religious art continues to be a massive influence on stone carving, woodcarving and painting around the island. Many of Taiwan's most innovative artists cut their teeth decorating temples. Exceptions include indigenous artists who work with ceramics, driftwood or glass beads (page 259).

To find out about gallery openings, museum exhibitions and live performances, scan the *Taipei Times* newspaper or ask at any visitor information centre.

MUSEUMS The majority of exhibition venues are open 09.00–17.00 Tuesday–Sunday. Notable museums include:

Lukang Folk Arts Museum Many of the items come from one of Taiwan's richest families but they still count as folk artefacts. See page 179.

National Museum of Taiwan History Covers every episode in the island's past. See page 216.

National Palace Museum Rightfully regarded as one of the world's greatest collections. See page 103.

National Taiwan Museum of Fine Arts A strong permanent collection & worthwhile rotating exhibitions. See page 170.

Shung Ye Museum of Formosan Aborigines By far the best of the island's several indigenous-theme museums. See page 106.

Taipei Fine Arts Museum Stresses modern artists & their works. See page 101.

Taiwan Theatre Museum Has displays on opera & puppetry. See page 126.

ARCHITECTURE

Sometimes it seems as if all of Taiwan's architectural energies and talent have gone into the design and construction of houses of worship. Urban areas are often bleak and untidy; many houses are drab concrete boxes. That said, architecture buffs will find a great deal to enjoy.

Until well into the 19th century, most Taiwanese lived in bamboo huts or wood-framed wattle-and-daub homes. Only in a handful of places, including some indigenous villages (pages 255 and 260), were stone houses common. Following the Japanese takeover, reinforced-concrete European–Japanese buildings began appearing. After World War II, Chiang Kai-shek's regime emphasised 'Northern Palace' architecture (like Beijing's Forbidden City) featuring glazed roof tiles and elaborate dougong brackets. Many historic structures were demolished during the postwar rush for development. Since the 1980s, however, preservation laws and civic organisations have saved a good number of Taiwan's heritage buildings.

TOP-RANK TEMPLES

Baoan Temple This feast for the eyes is Taipei's most interesting shrine. See page 100.

Buddha Memorial Centre An imposing combination of Chinese, Indian & modern styles. See page 248.

DOS AND DON'TS WHEN VISITING TEMPLES

Many temples are extremely wealthy thanks to their Taiwanese supporters. Very few charge admission; visitors are only expected to drop something in the donation box if they pray or throw divining blocks (see box, page 34).

Don't hesitate to go into any temple if it looks interesting, even if you're dressed very casually and there are people praying inside. The caretaker may well have his feet up, his back to the altar and be watching baseball on television. There's no need to cover your head or your shoulders. Behave as you would in any other place of worship. Don't smoke, eat or drink; keep your voice down; don't point at people or effigies; and don't touch the offerings, which typically include fruit and glasses of rice wine. Be sensitive when taking photos. Removing your hat is a good idea but it isn't necessary to remove symbols of your own religion. In most temples you needn't take off your shoes.

Don't take meat or fish into a place of worship that might be Buddhist; vegetarianism is a tenet of the religion. In other temples you'll often see meat among the offerings. Women shouldn't enter a temple when they're menstruating.

Chung Tai Chan Monastery Striking from afar & engrossing close up. See page 190.

Longshan Temple Not the busiest place of worship in Lukang but certainly the greatest in artistic terms. See page 98.

Martial Rites Temple Perhaps the very finest shrine in Tainan, a city overflowing with classic temples. See page 212.

Tzu Yun Temple With its Japanese-influenced shape & high-altitude location, Alishan's loveliest place of worship is a rarity among Taiwanese temples. See page 234.

TRADITIONAL HOMES AND MANSIONS

Erkan ancient residences A mostly abandoned village located in windswept Penghu County. See page 308.

Jinshi Mansion Dilapidated but still impressive, this is one of Hsinchu's most important relics. See page 149.

Kinmen's South Fujianese houses The county has preserved hundreds of alluring single-storey abodes. See page 310.

Matsu's villages Qinbi & Jinsha are notable for their stone dwellings. See page 322.

Xinhua Old Street A well-preserved & still-lively 1930s commercial thoroughfare in Tainan. See page 217.

JAPANESE-ERA LANDMARKS

Angered by Tokyo's decision in 1972 to establish diplomatic ties with the PRC, Chiang Kai-shek's regime decreed that all colonial-era relics glorifying Japanese rule should be removed & that other remnants of the period should never be repaired. The policy was reversed in the late 1980s & colonial-era structures are now cherished.

The Japanese legacy in Tainan The colonists left a deep imprint on Taiwan's oldest city (page 215).

Put to new uses National Taiwan Museum, Futai Street Mansion, the Museum of Contemporary Art & the National Museum of Taiwanese Literature all date from the colonial period.

Shintoism Japan's state religion didn't make much headway in Taiwan but there's an intact former Shinto shrine in Taoyuan City & the ruins of another outside Jinguashi.

Railway stations The TRA station in Hsinchu & the former station in Taichung date from before World War II.

NATIONALIST EDIFICES

Chiang Kai-shek Memorial Hall Whatever your feelings about the generalissimo, his memorial is unique. See page 97.

Grand Hotel This Taipei landmark is a good example of 'Northern Palace' architecture rendered in rebar & concrete. See page 89.

National Revolutionary Martyrs Shrine This place was intended to be sober, even severe, & the architects succeeded. See page 106.

21ST-CENTURY CONSTRUCTION

Beitou Branch of Taipei City Library This wooden structure is a model of style as well as sustainability. See page 108.

Lanyang Museum Inspired by the slant of rock strata, this museum looks as if it's sinking into a wetland. See page 126.

Paper Dome A recycled building set in a place of great natural beauty. See page 190.

Taipei 101 What used to be the world's tallest building still pulls in shoppers & tourists. See page 102.

SPORTS AND ACTIVITIES

Taiwan is a sports underachiever. Despite the achievements of Chi Cheng (a female sprinter who set three world records in one week in 1970) and baseball professionals playing in the USA, Taiwan's impact in the international sporting arena has been minimal. This isn't because Taiwanese teams and individuals are forced for political reasons to compete under the absurd moniker 'Chinese-Taipei'. Rather, it's the result of an education system that stresses test scores at the expense of overall development and an environment that until recently lacked sports facilities.

It wasn't until 2004 that the island's sports stars struck Olympic gold, winning two in the martial art taekwondo. At the Rio Summer Games in 2016, one gold (women's weightlifting) and two bronze medals (women's weightlifting and the women's archery team event) were won. At the time of writing, Taiwan's most prominent sports star was Tai Tzu-ying (b1994), the world's top-ranked female badminton player.

Long term, things are looking up, thanks to government investment in training and infrastructure and a population that's becoming more outdoorsy. In 2009, Kaohsiung did an excellent job of hosting the eighth World Games, an Olympics-style event that features sports not on the Olympic roster such as karate and orienteering. Later the same year, Taipei was the venue for the 21st Deaflympics. In 2017, Taipei hosted the 29th Summer Universiade.

BASEBALL Taiwan's national sport is baseball. Taiwanese players who've become stars in the US Baseball Major League are a source of immense national pride. However, Taiwan's own baseball league has been rocked by match-fixing scandals, and the national team's performance in recent international competitions has been patchy, but includes an Olympic silver medal (1992) and an Asian Games gold (2006).

BASKETBALL Taiwan's foremost participation sport is played in schools and parks everywhere. There's a national league but some of its stars have joined better-paying teams in China. Jeremy Lin, an American of Taiwanese descent now playing for the Houston Rockets, became a Taiwanese hero after his stunning debut in the US National Basketball Association league in early 2012.

CAMPING Sleeping under canvas is popular in Kenting National Park as well as the mountains. See page 62 for details.

CLIMBING With the exception of some highly rated spots along the northeast coast, rock climbing isn't nearly as popular as you might expect given Taiwan's mountainous landscape.

CYCLING AND MOUNTAIN BIKING In terms of rental and repair businesses, bicycle-only trails and ordinary roads suitable for bikers, Taiwan has excellent infrastructure for cyclists. See also page 59.

ECOTOURISM Taiwan has a tremendous variety of butterflies, fireflies and other insects. Other curiosities you might see include freshwater scorpions, flying squirrels and landlocked salmon (see box, page 194). Whale watching is popular off the east coast (see box, page 292). Probably the most popular form of ecotourism is birdwatching (see box, page 6).

GOLF Golf has been played on the island since the Japanese occupation and several Taiwanese golfers have made a splash in international competitions, most recently Yani Tseng (b1989). For 109 consecutive weeks until early 2013, Tseng was the world's top-ranked female golfer. Taiwan has dozens of golf courses; see w golfworldmap.com for details. The better ones charge non-members around NTD3,500 for green and caddie fees.

HIKING Taiwan is a hiker's dream. The island's mountains are numerous, steep and extremely scenic yet the vast majority of trails demand no technical climbing skills. You'll have no problems finding a route that meets your requirements. Yangmingshan National Park has plenty of family-friendly paths while Yushan and Shei-Pa national parks offer multi-day treks through expedition country.

Before beginning any hike longer than a kilometre or two, take note of weather conditions and make sure you've snacks, water and sun protection. Don't leave the path; more than one Western tourist has disappeared without trace in recent years and others have got themselves into sticky situations. Rely on your eyes as well as your map; the fact that a route is clearly marked on a map doesn't mean it's survived recent typhoons and tremors. If it looks too dangerous to proceed, turn back.

If you're venturing deep into the interior or to peaks more than 3,000m high, check what permits are legally required and get them. Hikers who don't and later have to be rescued may well be billed for the rescue effort – and helicopters don't come cheap.

HOT SPRINGS Geothermal activity has given Taiwan more than 120 natural spas. Each spring has a slightly different mineral content, odour and colour. There are scalding sulphurous springs, cold bubbling springs, mud spas and clear-water springs. Some, like those at Xinbeitou and Zhiben, have become highly developed resorts. Others are more or less natural, and consist of nothing more than a riverside pool without changing rooms or other facilities.

The springs in Xinbeitou and on Yangmingshan are acidic and sulphuric. Natural spas in other parts of Taiwan tend to be carbonatic and rich in dissolved sodium, magnesium, potassium and calcium. The medicinal claims made for many hot springs should be taken with a pinch of sulphur but there's no doubt a soak can relieve stress and ease chronic body aches. At the end of a long hike, of course, a few hours in a hot spring is nothing short of blissful.

PARAGLIDING Taiwan has wind and hills and therefore paragliding. The best places are near Puli in the very centre of the island and Luye in the southeast.

RAFTING Letting the current sweep you through the white-water rapids of the Xiuguluan River is a fun way to cool off at the height of summer (see box, page 286).

WATERSPORTS Warm water and consistent winds make Penghu County a world-class **windsurfing** venue, while much of Taiwan's west coast is good for **kitesurfing**. The **snorkelling** around Green Island, Orchid Island and Kenting National Park is first-rate.

Taiwan's coastline offers **scuba diving** enthusiasts a range of different environments. In the south, year-round diving in water temperatures of 21–30°C is enjoyable. In the north, winter diving is only possible with a thicker wetsuit. There are several good soft-coral sites and some healthy hard-coral sites. Of Kenting's 50-odd dive locations, one is a soft-coral site at a depth of 6–10m depth near Houbihu called 'the flower garden'. Little Liuqiu has fantastic undersea corals and is well known among Taiwanese divers for turtles. Green Island and Orchid Island offer some of Taiwan's best diving. Between January and March, Green Island also offers a hammerhead shark dive at depths of 30–35m as the hammerheads migrate in large schools and come up from deeper water after hunting.

PHOTOGRAPHY

Taiwan is visually fascinating and there are very few laws or taboos limiting what a photographer is allowed to capture on film or a memory card. In addition to superb mountain and coastal landscapes, the cities are beehives of activity filled with memorable structures, signs and posters. Shutterbugs also adore Taiwan's many colourful festivals. Even if the weather isn't ideal, you'll find the warmth of

Taiwan's people encouraging. Very few people will refuse permission if you ask to take snaps of their shops, their products or even themselves at work.

If people are kneeling under a roadside tarpaulin, they're attending a funeral. At other religious and semi-religious events, however, it's fine to shoot away. Almost certainly, you won't be the only one taking photos. You should always have your camera ready for immediate use. You never know what you'll find around the next corner. It could be a roadside vendor selling vegetables you've never seen before, a dramatic display of religious fervour, a traditional wedding banquet, or a family letting off firecrackers to celebrate their son winning a place at a top university.

MEDIA AND COMMUNICATIONS

PRINT The most popular Chinese-language newspapers in Taiwan include *Apple Daily* (w tw.appledaily.com), which often features gory photos of road accidents and computer-generated graphics showing how crimes were committed, and *Liberty Times* (w ltn.com.tw), which is altogether more serious and a staunch backer of the green camp (see box, page 21).

English-language press Taiwan's only English-language print daily is the pro-green *Taipei Times* (w taipeitimes.com), which can be found in convenience stores and bookshops. The online-only *Taiwan News* (w taiwannews.com.tw) is often sensationalist yet sometimes runs pieces of interest to visitors, while the more thoughtful Chinese-language *Commonwealth Magazine* posts translations of much of its content online (w english.cw.com.tw).

The Ministry of Foreign Affairs publishes a substantial English-language bimonthly called *Taiwan Review*, which is well worth seeking out if you've a serious interest in Taiwanese art or social issues (articles and other news items can be read online at w taiwantoday.tw. The American Chamber of Commerce in Taipei publishes a monthly, *Taiwan Business Topics* (w amcham.com.tw), which can be found in some bookshops and ventures beyond dry business subjects; each year, one issue is devoted to travel and culture and another to fine dining.

ONLINE The News Lens (w thenewslens.com) publishes a blend of original and shared content in Chinese and English.

TELEVISION Taiwan has dozens of television stations covering every demographic, and most broadcast a mix of Mandarin- and Taiwanese-language programming. The government's PTS (Public Television System) often shows documentaries and popular TV series from other countries. Many hotels have cable TV with CNN, HBO, Sky News and other international channels.

RADIO Turn the dial and you'll come across plenty of Mandarin- and Taiwanese-language radio stations offering a blend of talk, music and news. The government-funded Radio Taiwan International (w rti.org.tw) broadcasts in 13 languages including English on shortwave and the internet. Taiwan's only English-language FM station, ICRT (100.7FM; w www.icrt.com.tw), plays mostly middle-of-the-road pop and rock. The hourly newscasts include weather and Taipei-centric traffic reports.

TELEPHONE Public phones are easy to find in train and bus stations and outside convenience stores. Some take coins (NTD1 gets you a 1-minute local call) but for most you'll need a stored-value card (at least NTD100) which you can buy from any convenience store. To call abroad, dial 002 then the country code:

Australia +61	**Ireland** +353
Canada +1	**New Zealand** +64
China +86	**UK** +44
Hong Kong +852	**USA** +1

City and county codes When calling Taiwan from overseas, drop the zero from the area code. When calling Taipei, you should thus dial 886 (Taiwan's country code) followed by 2 (area code, minus the zero), then the phone number.

Useful and emergency telephone numbers The government-run 24-hour Information For Foreigners hotline (✆ 0800 024 111) is free of charge, as is the 24-hour tourist information line (✆ 0800 011 765). Both are very useful; if they can't find the information you want immediately they'll call you back, usually within 30 minutes. The emergency services are at ✆ 110 (police) and ✆ 119 (fire and ambulance) but little English is spoken. Taipei's English-speaking police can be contacted at ✆ 02 2556 6007.

Mobile phones Mobile-telephone coverage throughout Taiwan is excellent, although you may encounter blind spots in the mountains. If you have an international 'roaming' account, bring your phone with you and it should work normally. If you don't, consider getting a temporary account (in the form of a prepaid SIM card to put in your phone) from one of the phone-company counters at Taiwan Taoyuan or Kaohsiung airports. Ten days' unlimited data typically costs NTD500.

POST OFFICES All post offices have green shopfronts, and most bear the single English word 'Post'. You'll find them on major roads in every city and small town and most open 08.30–17.00 Monday–Friday; some also open 09.00–noon on Saturday. At many branches it's possible to change US dollars, euros and Japanese yen. When sending mail within Taiwan, or from overseas to Taiwan, do ask a friend to write the destination and return addresses in Chinese. In theory, a letter bearing an address written entirely in romanised script should reach the intended recipient, but because of spelling inconsistencies this doesn't always happen. When sending something out of Taiwan, write the destination country in Chinese or English, not another language.

INTERNET Wi-Fi and 4G broadband are now commonplace and the few surviving internet cafés (*wǎng kā* 網咖) are used by gamers. If you're carrying a laptop, you're better off looking for a restaurant or coffee shop that offers wireless internet access. Many do but may not have an English sign; ask the staff if they have Wi-Fi (*wúxiàn wǎnglù* 無線網路).

Foreign visitors can get free Wi-Fi access by registering online or showing their passport at certain travel-service and visitor-information centres. They'll receive a password enabling them to go online at iTaiwan (w itaiwan.gov.tw) hotspots at government offices and transport hubs.

MAPS

Road maps of Taiwan go out of date quickly for two reasons. Typhoons sometimes close or destroy mountain routes, and the government is obsessed with road-building. If you plan to drive or ride any significant distance, go to a visitor centre and grab the free regional maps covering the north, south, centre and east. If you have special interests, it's worth contacting the Tourism Bureau or one of its overseas offices before you arrive and seeing what they can come up with.

BUSINESS

Office workers are usually at their desks 09.00–17.00 Monday to Friday, sometimes earlier, often later. Lunch lasts at least an hour, from midday, and is regarded by many as sacrosanct. If you wander into a company or a government office at that time you might find most people sleeping or absent. English and Japanese are widely spoken in Taiwanese business circles, and lots of Chinese tea is drunk. If you'd rather not drink tea, ask for water instead. Many companies operate as normal on public holidays, but don't try to get any business done in the three or four days before the Lunar New Year or the week afterwards.

USEFUL CONTACTS/WEBSITES

American Chamber of Commerce in Taipei Suite 706, 7th Flr, 129 Minsheng E Rd Sec 3, Taipei 10596; ☎+886 2 2718 8226; e amcham@ amcham.com.tw; w www.amcham.com.tw **British Chamber of Commerce in Taipei** 26th Flr, 9–11 Songgao Rd, Taipei 11073; ☎+886 2 2720 1919; e info@bcctaipei.com; w bcctaipei. com

Bureau of Foreign Trade w www.trade.gov.tw **European Chamber of Commerce Taipei** 11th Flr 285 Zhongxiao E Rd Sec 4, Taipei 10692; ☎+886 2 2740 0236; w ecct.com.tw **The Ministry of Economic Affairs** w www. moea.gov.tw **The Ministry of Foreign Affairs** w mofa.gov. tw

CULTURAL ETIQUETTE

Taiwanese people are open-minded and aware that people from the West do many things differently. You may get stared at during your trip but this doesn't mean offence has been taken.

GREETINGS Mandarin is quite straightforward when it comes to greeting people. Usually people say nǐ hǎo (literally 'you good?' but meaning 'hello'). Sometimes they'll use the more polite and formal nín hǎo. When entering a shop or restaurant, it's not necessary to do anything more than smile at whoever's behind the counter. Shaking hands is common in business circles. If you're from a culture where greeting a lady by kissing her cheek is normal, restrain yourself while in Taiwan.

ALCOHOL Taiwan is quite free and easy when it comes to where and when you can buy and consume alcoholic drinks. Labourers can sometimes be seen drinking beer during the day; drinking in public places like parks and train stations is legal yet considered low class.

If drinking with Taiwanese friends, it's polite to top up their glasses before refilling your own. At formal events like wedding banquets, expect frequent toasts. You'll be expected to join in, but sipping tea or juice rather than an alcoholic beverage is perfectly acceptable.

Sometimes complete strangers will invite you to sit and drink with them; refuse politely if you don't wish to join them. The importance of not drinking and driving is now widely understood.

HOSPITALITY Taiwanese are extremely friendly to visitors from the West and Japan. If you're invited to a Taiwanese person's home, do bring a gift of some kind. Fruit is a good option but avoid cheaper varieties like bananas and guavas; go for a box of imported peaches or cherries. If you plan to bring alcohol, buy a decent whisky or red wine. Whatever you do, don't bring a clock as it implies you want the recipient to die! Don't be surprised if your host initially refuses your gift; he or she is being polite. Offer it again and eventually it'll be accepted. Say hello (in English or Mandarin) to everyone you see in the house but don't be surprised or offended if the very oldest or very youngest present doesn't seem to acknowledge your greeting. They may well be shy and unsure how to deal with a foreigner. However, it's just as likely that your hosts will ask you lots of questions about your work, your spouse or partner and what you think of Taiwan.

Take your shoes off when you arrive; you'll be offered a pair of plastic beach sandals (which English-speaking Taiwanese often call 'slippers') to wear inside the house. You'll probably be shown to the living room, which is where many families take their meals. Don't be shocked if old newspaper is used instead of a tablecloth and the TV stays on throughout the meal.

In most respects Taiwanese people aren't so different from Westerners, so it's hard to go wrong. Compliment your host's cooking (or choice of restaurant if you eat out), make sure everyone knows you've had a good time and make sure you don't stay too late if people need to work or attend school the next day.

TRAVELLING POSITIVELY

Taiwan isn't a conspicuously poor society, though you will see a few homeless people sleeping rough in the cities and families living in dilapidated houses. The worst social problems – which include poverty, unemployment, alcoholism and youngsters failing to complete high school – tend to be in the most remote parts of the country. For many visiting Westerners, the sorry state of Taiwan's animals is the most obvious and distressing issue.

CHARITIES
Noordhoff Craniofacial Foundation w www. nncf.org. Founded by a now-retired American missionary-doctor who specialised in repairing cleft lips & palates, this foundation subsidises surgery & postoperative care for young children with facial deformities. Donations welcome.
Taiwan SPCA ✆ 02 2738 2130; e spca@spca. org.tw; w spca.org.tw. Taipei-based Taiwan SPCA is an expat-inspired animal welfare group that welcomes volunteers for rescues, CNR & educational events.
World Vision Taiwan 6th Flr 133 Minsheng E Rd Sec 4, Taipei 105; ✆ 02 2175 1995; e pr@ worldvision.org.tw; w www.worldvision.org.tw. This international Christian organisation matches sponsors with children in Taiwan (especially in indigenous areas) & elsewhere, & does relief work in the wake of typhoons & other disasters. Donations welcome.

WWOOF Taiwan e info@wwooftaiwan.com; w wwooftaiwan.com. Part of the WWOOF (World Wide Opportunities on Organic Farms) network, this group can arrange for you to stay & work on an organic farm. If you're not already a member you can join in Taiwan (NTD800 for a year), after which board & lodging is free.

ENVIRONMENTAL CONTACTS IN TAIWAN
Citizen of the Earth 9th Flr, 198 Boai 2nd Rd, Zuoying, Kaohsiung; ✆ 07 556 1585; e cet@cet-taiwan.org; w cet-taiwan.org. One of the most active environmental groups in south Taiwan with a focus on issues of industrial structure, deforestation, habitat protection, climate change & ecology education.
Environment & Animal Society of Taiwan (EAST) 18 Lane 84, Hexing Rd, Taipei; ✆ 02 2236 9735; e eastfree@east.org.tw; w east.org.tw. This

animal welfare group has campaigned against the consumption of shark fin soup & Buddhist 'mercy release' (see box, page 10).

Green Party 6th Flr, 28 Beiping E Rd, Taipei; ☎02 2392 0508; e greenpartytaiwan@gmail.com; w greenparty.org.tw. This small pro-environment group should not be confused with the 'greens' who favour Taiwan's independence from China (see box, page 21).

Greenpeace 109 Chongqing S Rd Sec 1, Taipei; ☎02 2361 2351; e inquiry.tw@greenpeace. org; w greenpeace.org/taiwan/zh. Greenpeace engages in volunteer training, fundraising, publicity & work on their own & with local environmental groups on oceans/fishing & nuclear issues.

Society of Wilderness (SOW) 204 Zhaoan St, Taipei; ☎02 2307 1568; e sow@sow.org.

tw; w www.sow.org.tw. This conservation & nature education group also takes on plots of undeveloped land where nature can revive & manage itself.

Taiwan Environmental Protection Union 2nd Flr, 107 Tingzhou Rd Sec 3, Taipei; ☎02 2363 6419; e tepu.org@msa.hinet.net; w www.tepu. org.tw. One of the oldest registered associations dedicated to environmental issues; has a strong focus on anti-nuclear activities.

Wild at Heart Legal Defense Association 6th Flr, 106 Huaining St, Taipei; ☎02 2382 5789; e comment@wildatheart.org.tw; w wildatheart. org.tw. The 1st environmental advocacy organisation in Taiwan with full-time lawyers & specialising in policy & legal action on behalf of indigenous groups dispossessed of their land & on behalf of wildlife whose habitats are threatened.

SEND US YOUR SNAPS!

We'd love to follow your adventures using our *Taiwan* guide – why not tag us in your photos and stories via Twitter (🐦 @BradtGuides) and Instagram (📷 @bradtguides)? Alternatively, you can upload your photos directly to the gallery on the Taiwan destination page via our website (w bradtguides.com/taiwan).

Part Two

THE GUIDE

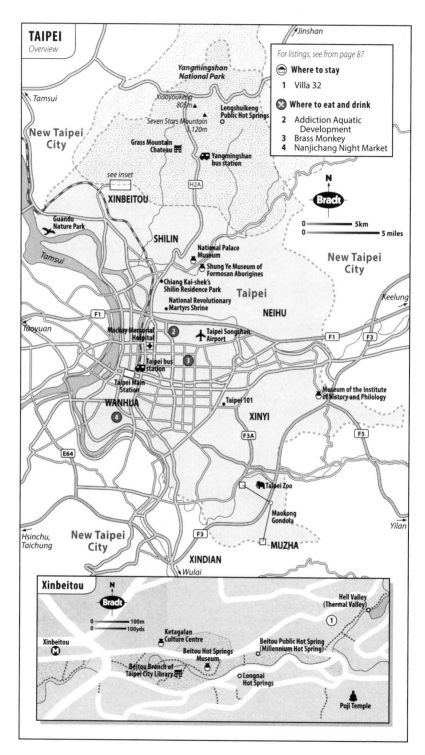

TAIPEI
Overview

Jinshan

Tamsui

Yangmingshan National Park

New Taipei City

Xiaoyoukeng 805m ▲

Lengshuikeng Public Hot Springs

Seven Stars Mountain 1120m

Grass Mountain Chateau 🏯

Yangmingshan bus station 🚌

see inset

H2A

XINBEITOU

Guandu Nature Park

SHILIN

Tamsui

F1

Taoyuan

National Palace Museum

Shung Ye Museum of Formosan Aborigines

● **Chiang Kai-shek's Shilin Residence Park**

National Revolutionary ● **Martyrs Shrine**

Taipei

New Taipei City

Keelung

NEIHU

F1   F3

Mackay Memorial Hospital ✚

❷

✈ **Taipei Songshan Airport**

Taipei bus station 🚌

❸

Taipei Main Station 🚆

WANHUA

❹

● **Taipei 101**

XINYI

F3A

Museum of the Institute of History and Philology

F5

E64

Taipei Zoo 🐼

Maokong Gondola

Yilan

Hsinchu, Taichung

New Taipei City

F3

MUZHA

XINDIAN

◀ *Wulai*

For listings, see from page 87

⬭ **Where to stay**
1 Villa 32

✖ **Where to eat and drink**
2 Addiction Aquatic Development
3 Brass Monkey
4 Nanjichang Night Market

N

Bradt

0 ───────── 5km
0 ───────── 5 miles

Xinbeitou

N

Bradt

0 ──────── 100m
0 ──────── 100yds

Xinbeitou Ⓜ

Ketagalan Culture Centre ♨

Beitou Hot Springs Museum ♨

Beitou Branch of Taipei City Library 🏛

◯ **Longnai Hot Springs**

Beitou Public Hot Spring (Millennium Hot Spring)

Hell Valley (Thermal Valley) ◯

① 1

🛕 **Puji Temple**

3

Taipei 台北

Telephone code 02

Twenty-first-century Taipei is a delightful metropolis in which to spend time. It's safe and easy to get around and there's plenty to see and do in multiple categories including museums, temples, gastronomy, nature rambles and shopping.

Taiwan's capital, often compared with Hong Kong or Singapore and found lacking, is the nearest Greater China has to a renaissance city. The money-making here is avid, to be sure, but feels less visceral than in Hong Kong. Compared with Singapore, far less English is spoken but more genuine friendliness is expressed. There's greater freedom and civility here than in any other Han-majority metropolis. With 2.67 million people, Taipei will never rival London, Paris or Tokyo in artistic output or economic significance, but, it certainly holds its own when compared with Asian cities twice the size – and thanks to the mountains that limit Taipei's sprawl, getting lungfuls of fresh air and eyefuls of green forest isn't difficult.

Relatively few of Taipei's buildings are older than the Chiang Kai-shek Memorial Hall (completed in 1980) yet the city is streaked with veins of antiquity. The richest of these are in Wanhua, a down-at-heel, Taiwan-as-Formosa-used-to-be neighbourhood, and the riverside district called Dadaocheng.

For many, the mere fact that Taipei has the world-class National Palace Museum justifies time in the capital. Visitors shouldn't, however, obsess about that stupendous repository to the exclusion of other attractions, such as the exquisite Baoan Temple. Nor should they pack their schedule with too much sightseeing, as one of Taipei's most pleasurable pastimes is simply lingering on a busy street and watching passers-by: office workers in the latest fashions, Buddhist nuns, Tibetan monks, southeast Asian labourers and swarms of college and high-school students.

HISTORY

Han migrants settled near the coast in the 17th century and gradually made their way upriver. In 1709, the imperial authorities – aware that population pressure in Fujian could lead to unrest – approved a scheme to develop the Taipei Basin. Migrants poured in and within half a century the area's native inhabitants, the Ketagalan tribe, were being forced to cede ground to Han Chinese settlers. As the latter increased in number, the former intermarried with the newcomers, assimilated or migrated. Within a century they'd disappeared as a distinct ethnic group.

Like London, modern Taipei is to some extent an agglomeration of villages and small towns. In the mid-19th century, one of these towns, Wanhua (now part of the capital's southwest), was a large, dynamic settlement. The merchants of Wanhua saw their counterparts in Dadaocheng (the area around Dihua Street) as upstarts and there was an ethnic component to this rivalry. Immigrants from different parts of Fujian had clashed violently in Wanhua in 1853. The losers, among them merchants, fled to the newer riverside community at Dadaocheng, which they called Twatutia. Tea was the commodity that powered Dadaocheng's growth and enabled it to overtake Wanhua.

The place name Taipei (Táiběi in Mandarin, meaning 'north Taiwan') first appeared on maps in 1875 when the imperial court reorganised Taiwan's system of prefectures and subprefectures. The seat of the new Taipei prefecture was located between Wanhua and Dadaocheng for the same reasons Ottawa was chosen to be Canada's capital: it was a compromise between two powerful blocs and there was space to build.

In June 1895, the Japanese Army entered Taipei without firing a shot. The colonial regime set about tearing down the city's walls, widening and straightening roads and commissioning public buildings, among them the Japanese governor-general's office, which is now the Presidential Office. The National Taiwan Museum also dates from the colonial era. Taihoku (the city's Japanese name) quickly overtook Tainan and Taichung in terms of size and wealth, but it suffered substantial damage from American air raids in 1945.

In 1949, the influx of retreating Nationalists changed the face of Taipei society. Certain neighbourhoods came to be dominated by mainlanders and their children, but because of intermarriage and the demolition of the purpose-built cantonments where KMT soldiers lived with their dependants, ethnic boundaries are no longer so apparent. The mainlanders brought with them their customs and cuisines and turned the city into a microcosm of China.

For years, the Nationalist government regarded Taipei as a mere 'temporary capital' from which they would plot the retaking of the mainland. As a result little was spent on public works; well into the 1980s, the state of Taipei was an embarrassment. However, in the past two decades there's been great improvement. The sprawl (less than 40 years ago, the district where Taipei 101 now stands was mostly vegetable plots and graveyards) is criss-crossed by metro lines. It's a testament to Taiwan's maturity and stability that in recent years, landmark events in the capital have not been protests or riots, but inaugurations of infrastructure projects and museum openings.

GETTING THERE AND AWAY

BY AIR What's officially known as Taipei Airport, but which most locals and expatriates refer to as Songshan Airport (✆ 8770 3430; w www.tsa.gov.tw), handles domestic flights to Hualien, Taitung, Penghu, Kinmen and Matsu (for one-way fares, see the entries on those destinations) as well as international flights to mainland China, Japan and Hong Kong. More than a dozen city bus lines stop right outside the airport, and it is on the Taipei Metro's Brown Line.

BY HSR The high-speed rail system shares Taipei Main Station [83 F1] with TRA. Journey times are about an hour to Taichung (NTD700) and between 1 hour 34 minutes and 2 hours 14 minutes to Kaohsiung Zuoying (NTD1,490). There are three or more southbound bullet-train services per hour (⊕ 06.26–22.16 daily). The majority skip Miaoli, Changhua and Yunlin, and several don't stop at Hsinchu, Chiayi or Tainan.

BY TRA From Taipei Main Station, two or three expresses leave for Kaohsiung every hour between dawn and early evening every day of the week (takes up to 7hrs; NTD650–843). Fastest of all are the Puyuma trains, of which there are currently two in either direction daily (takes 3½hrs; NTD843). All southbound expresses on the Mountain Line (page 54) stop at Taichung (takes up to 3¼hrs; NTD289–375). There are no overnight expresses.

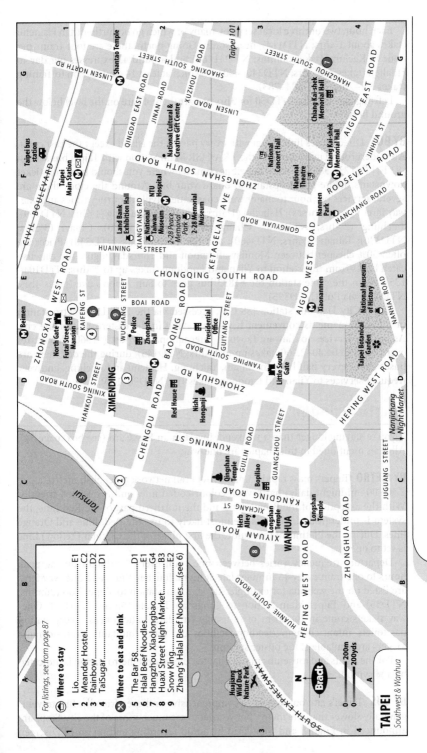

Taipei GETTING THERE AND AWAY

TAIPEI
Southwest & Wanhua

For listings, see from page 87

🛈 **Where to stay**
1 Lio E1
2 Meander Hostel C2
3 Rainbow D2
4 TaiSugar D1

✕ **Where to eat and drink**
5 The Bar 58 .... D1
6 Halal Beef Noodles E1
7 Hangzhou Xiaolongbao .. G4
8 Huaxi Street Night Market .. B3
9 Snow King E2
Zhang's Halal Beef Noodles ....(see 6)

Taipei 101

Shantao Temple

National Cultural & Creative Gift Centre

Chiang Kai-shek Memorial Hall

National Concert Hall

National Theatre

Chiang Kai-shek Memorial Hall

Taipei bus station

Taipei Main Station

Land Bank Exhibition Hall

National Taiwan Museum

NTU Hospital

2-28 Peace Memorial Park

2-28 Memorial Museum

Nanmen Park

Beimen

North Gate
Futai Street Mansion

Police
Zhongshan Hall

Presidential Office

Ximen

Red House
Nishi Honganji

Little South Gate

National Museum of History

Xiaonanmen

Taipei Botanical Garden

XIMENDING

Qingshan Temple
Bopiliao

Herb Alley

Longshan Temple

Longshan Temple

WANHUA

Huajiang Wild Duck Nature Park

Nanjichang Night Market

200m
200yds

N

Bradt

Each hour, two or three local services, many of which go no further than Hsinchu (takes about 1¾hrs; NTD114), head south. Going north, there are four trains per hour to Keelung (takes 50mins; NTD41–64) and around 43 expresses per day to Hualien (takes 2–3½hrs; NTD340–440), of which at least 14 continue on to Taitung (takes 3½–7hrs; NTD604–783).

Left-luggage lockers (NTD50 for 3hrs or part thereof) are on the level below the ground floor.

BY BUS Direct buses link Taipei with every part of the island except the east coast. An underground mall connects the TRA/HSR Main Station with Taipei bus station [83 F1] (✆ 7733 5888; w www.taipeibus.com.tw) where you should buy your ticket downstairs before going upstairs to board your bus. Around the clock there are several services per hour to major west-coast cities (typical journey times and one-way fares in parentheses): Hsinchu (1½hrs; NTD130); Zhudong (1½hrs; NTD159); Taichung (2¾hrs; NTD260); Changhua (3¼hrs; NTD300); Chiayi (3½hrs; NTD330); Tainan (4¼hrs; NTD460); and Kaohsiung (5hrs; NTD530). Prices are often 30% cheaper between Monday afternoon and Thursday night. You can also catch buses from this station to Yilan and Luodong (takes up to 1¼hrs; NTD104–135). From the same station the #1833 bus goes to Sun Moon Lake (takes 4hrs; NTD470) via Puli (NTD395).

Taipei City Hall bus station [88 G1], accessed via the Blue Line metro station of the same name, is convenient if you're staying in the eastern half of the city. As well as services to Taiwan Taoyuan International Airport (#1960; departures every ½hr; ⊕ 04.40–23.00; takes up to 1¼hrs; NTD145), during the day there are buses about every half hour to Tainan, Taichung, Hsinchu and Keelung, and very frequent services to Yilan and Luodong (takes 1hr; NTD90–120).

GETTING AROUND

If you're staying longer than a weekend, invest in an EasyCard (see box, page 54). All fares mentioned in this chapter are one-way.

BY METRO Taipei's mass rapid-transit (MRT) rail network (w english.metro.taipei; ⊕ 06.00–midnight daily) has several colour-coded lines and is disabled-friendly. With the exception of the Brown Line and the northern part of the Red Line, the system is underground. Tourists are most likely to use the Red, Blue and Orange lines. During the lifetime of this guide, the first phase of the Circular (Yellow) Line is set to open.

Departure frequency varies between one train every 2 minutes during peak hours to one train every 15 minutes late at night. Journey times and one-way fares are listed on the website; for example: Taipei Main Station to Taipei Zoo (26mins; NTD35) and Taipei Main Station to Longshan Temple (5mins; NTD20). One-way tickets come in the form of re-usable circular plastic tokens. Every station has toilets, infant changing/feeding facilities and water fountains. Coin-operated lockers are available at the busier stations.

For the sights and museums in this chapter, the nearest metro station is indicated by a 🚇 symbol.

BY BUS Taipei's city bus system is comprehensive and user-friendly. Bus travel is generally slower than the metro, but you get to see much more of the city. Stops are announced in English and Mandarin by audio recording and on an LED screen

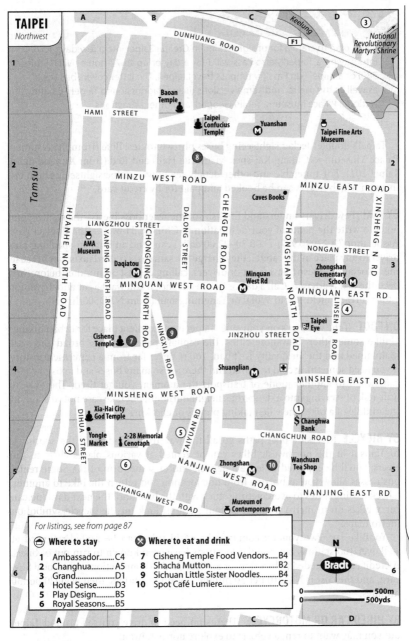

For listings, see from page 87

TAIPEI
Northwest

Where to stay
1 Ambassador........C4
2 Changhua...........A5
3 Grand.................D1
4 Hotel Sense.........D3
5 Play Design........B5
6 Royal Seasons.....B5

Where to eat and drink
7 Cisheng Temple Food Vendors.....B4
8 Shacha Mutton....................................B2
9 Sichuan Little Sister Noodles..........B4
10 Spot Café Lumiere..............................C5

Taipei GETTING AROUND

3

above the driver. During peak hours you may have to stand, although older or more unsteady travellers may find that someone will give up their seat for them. Bus journeys cost NTD15 per section with most journeys being a single section. On some buses you pay when you board; on others, you pay when getting off. Useful services starting out near Taipei Main Station include the #260 to Yangmingshan and #295 to Taipei Zoo.

If you plan to cram a lot of sightseeing in Greater Taipei into a few days, look into buying a Taipei Metro Pass valid for a day or up to 72 hours (NTD150–380) or a Taipei Fun Pass (w funpass.travel.taipei). The latter covers bus travel as well as the metro, and some versions include admission to Taipei 101, the National Palace Museum, Yehliu Geopark and other attractions.

Taipei's double-decker sightseeing buses ply two routes: Blue (from the National Palace Museum to Chiang Kai-shek Memorial Hall) and Red (from Ximending to Taipei 101). For timetable and other details see w www.taipeisightseeing.com.tw, through which tickets can be booked and paid for by credit card.

BY TAXI Few drivers understand English so whenever possible ask the staff at your hotel to write the name of your destination in Chinese. However, the English Taxi Association (☏ 2799 7997; ⊕ 08.30–22.00 daily) can send an English-speaking taxi driver to any place in the capital; they charge the same as standard taxis, but because the association doesn't have a lot of drivers, calling at least 30 minutes before you need the taxi is advised. Call a day or two in advance if you want a car and driver for a tour further afield, say to Wulai or Yangmingshan (from NTD500/hr).

ON FOOT If the weather's on your side, Taipei is an excellent place for urban hiking. Unlike some other Taiwanese cities, the capital's pavements are broad and well maintained and the air quality isn't bad. You're never far from a convenience store if you need something cold to drink, and there are so many buses and taxis that you can switch to another mode of transport the moment you get tired. There's very little risk of straying into a dangerous neighbourhood, but take care not to stand in the middle of a bike lane when taking photos or checking your map.

BY BICYCLE Riverside bike paths go all the way from Xindian in the southeast to Tamsui in the northwest. Bikes can be rented at various places close to the rivers; you'll be expected to leave a deposit and/or some form of ID. Some rental businesses allow you to borrow from one location and return the bike to another. Check closing times to avoid getting stuck with the bike until the next day. You can carry bikes on to metro trains at certain stations; look for the bicycle symbol on metro maps.

YouBike (w www.youbike.com.tw) shared bicycles can be rented/returned at well over 100 stations but popular locations have been known to run out of bikes. A credit card is needed to hire one, or an EasyCard in conjunction with a local SIM card, and the cost is NTD10 per 30 minutes for up to 4 hours, then NTD20 per 30 minutes.

BY HIRED CAR OR MOTORCYCLE There's no need to drive yourself around Taipei but you may want to rent a vehicle to explore north Taiwan.

🚗 **Avis Budget** Taoyuan Airport MRT ticket barrier at Taipei Main Station; ☏ 6620 6620 ext 124; w avis-taiwan.com; ⊕ 10.00–19.00 daily. Standard rentals & leasing; can arrange chauffeur services to/from airport or further afield.

🚗 **Car Plus Auto Leasing** 71–1 Jianguo N Rd Sec 1; ☏ 2502 1389; w www.car-plus.com. tw; ⊕ 08.30–20.30 daily. General-use car hire & long-term leasing; near Songjiang Nanjing metro station.

🚗 **Hotai Leasing** [83 F1] Ground Flr, Taipei Main Station; 📞 2375 6000; w www.easyrent.com.tw; ⊕ 07.00–23.00 daily. Can provide limousines with chauffeurs as well as conventional rentals.

🚲 **Bike Farm** m 0926 283 300; e bikefarmbikes@gmail.com; w bikefarm.net.

Tourist-friendly rental business needing 24hrs' notice for motorcycle/scooter rentals. Renting a 125cc bike & helmet for the minimum 4 days costs NTD2,000 plus NTD7,000 deposit. Pickup from Taipower Building metro station; delivery to your hotel for a fee.

TOURIST INFORMATION

There are several visitor information centres, the most useful being those in Taipei Main Station [83 F1] (⊕ 08.00–20.00 daily), Songshan Airport (⊕ 08.00–20.00 daily), Maokong gondola station (⊕ 09.00–18.00 Tue–Fri, 08.30–20.00 Sat–Sun) and in the following metro stations: Beitou (⊕ 09.00–18.00 daily), Jiantan and Ximen [83 D2] (both ⊕ 11.00–20.00 Mon–Fri, 11.00–21.00 Sat–Sun). It's also worth checking out Taipei City Government's tourism website: w taipeitravel.net/en.

🏠 WHERE TO STAY

Accommodation in Taipei isn't cheap but there's a good range of options and English is spoken at almost every establishment. Because the metro is so convenient, any of the neighbourhoods shown on the street maps in this chapter could serve as your base.

SOUTHWEST TAIPEI

🏠 **TaiSugar Hotel** [83 D1] (68 rooms) 39 Zhonghua Rd Sec 1; 📞 2388 5522; e taipeihotel@taisugar.com.tw; w www.taipeihotel-tsc.com.tw; 🚇 Ximen. This hotel is the antithesis of so many in Ximending that offer modish but rabbit-hutch rooms. By contrast, TaiSugar's guestrooms are all decent sizes & (as you might expect of an establishment owned by the state-run sugar company) fixtures & fittings are solid if conservative. Overall one of the best accommodation bargains in central Taipei. B/fast inc. **$$$**

🏠 **Lio Hotel** [83 E1] (37 rooms) 9 Yanping S Rd; 📞 2314 5296; e lio.hotel@gmail.com; w www.liohotel.com.tw; 🚇 Ximen. The sgl rooms here (NTD1,300) are probably the best deal in central Taipei for solo travellers who can do without windows & bathtubs, but want something better than a hostel. The rooms are clean, quiet & decorated in pastel shades & soft golds. Decent b/fast inc. **$$**

🏠 **Meander Hostel** [83 C2] (7 rooms & 5 dorms) 163 Chengdu Rd; 📞 2383 1334; e info@meander.com.tw; w meander.com.tw; 🚇 Ximen. Not the most central accommodation option in this part of the city (you'll need to walk 700m to Ximen Station) but the dorm beds (from NTD600

inc a highly rated b/fast) are no more expensive than in many far less attractive places. Rooms for 2, 3 or 4 ppl start at a little over NTD2,000. There's no lift but everything else is just about perfect. The staff organise activities through which guests can learn more about Taiwan, such as making pineapple cakes, plus excursions to nearby sights. **$$**

🏠 **Rainbow Hotel** [83 D2] (70 rooms) 36 Hanzhong St; 📞 2311 9193; e rainbow2009@kimo.com; w www.rainbowhoteltaipei.com.tw; 🚇 Ximen. The décor is unimaginative but the Rainbow's location in the heart of Ximending, the size of its rooms & some competitive prices make it an attractive option. Suites for 3, 4 & 5 ppl available. B/fast inc. **$$**

NORTHWEST TAIPEI

🏠 **Ambassador Hotel** [85 C4] (416 rooms) 63 Zhongshan N Rd Sec 2; 📞 2551 111; w taipei.ambassadorhotel.com.tw; 🚇 Shuanglian. Thanks to frequent renovations & an unswerving focus on friendly service, Taiwan's oldest 5-star hotel (established 1963) continues to be at the top of its game. Room décor is elegant rather than flashy & the beds are rated as among the city's most comfortable. In summer, request a room beside the small outdoor swimming pool. Long-running

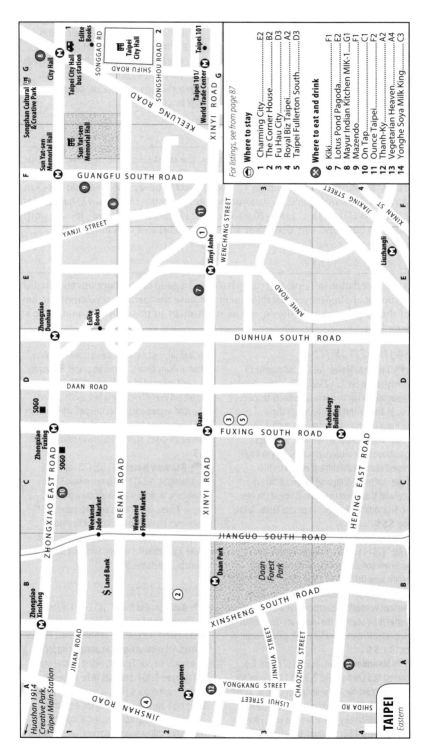

TAIPEI
Eastern

For listings, see from page 87

🛏 **Where to stay**
1 Charming City.................E2
2 The Corner House............B2
3 Fu Hau City.....................D3
4 Royal Biz Taipei...............A2
5 Taipei Fullerton South.....D3

🍴 **Where to eat and drink**
6 Kiki..................................F1
7 Lotus Pond Pagoda..........E2
8 Mayur Indian Kitchen MIK-1...G1
9 Mazendo..........................F1
10 On Tap............................C1
11 Ounce Taipei...................F2
12 Thanh-Ky........................A4
13 Vegetarian Heaven..........A4
14 Yonghe Soya Milk King.....C3

in-house restaurants offer Cantonese, Sichuan & other cuisines. For a blowout, try **Cut Steakhouse** (🕾 2571 0389; 🕐 11.30–15.00 & 18.00–22.30 daily; EM; $$$$) which serves dry-aged US & Australian beef & has been consistently praised by *Wine Spectator* magazine. Most deals inc buffet b/fast. $$$$$

🏠 **Grand Hotel** [85 D1] (490 rooms) 1 Zhongshan N Rd Sec 4; 🕾 2886 8888; e reservations@grand-hotel.org; w www. grand-hotel.org; 🚇 Jiantan. Built at the behest of Madame Chiang Kai-shek, who wanted a hotel befitting ambassadors & world leaders, the Grand Hotel has had numerous ups & downs since its opening in 1952. Service standards are still a tad old-fashioned but the hotel has modernised extensively in recent years while retaining the conservative décor & massive lobby that give this landmark considerable retro appeal. The better rooms have balconies with fine views. The free shuttle minibus to Yuanshan metro station saves a 15min walk to Jiantan metro station. B/fast optional. $$$$$

🏠 **Hotel Sense** [85 D3] (79 rooms) 477 Linsen N Rd; 🕾 7743 1000; e info@hotelsense.com. tw; w www.hotelsense.com.tw; 🚇 Zhongshan Elementary School. Although the black-&-grey lobby is a shrine to the Art Deco movement, the styling in the guestrooms isn't quite so strong. Nevertheless, there are huge doors, distinctive bathtubs & high-tech toilets, & TVs can be swivelled & watched from the bed or the sofa. The superior rooms lack windows; all but 1 of the deluxe rooms (ideal for 3 ppl) has a large balcony. B/fast usually inc but you can save a little money by opting out. $$$$

🏠 **Play Design Hotel** [85 B5] (5 rooms) Floor 5, 156–2 Taiyuan Rd; 🕾 2555 5930; e info@ playdesignhotel.com; w www.playdesignhotel. com; 🚇 Zhongshan. Within walking distance of Dihua St but not super-convenient if you expect to use the metro a lot, this hotel appeals to those looking for something different. Its highly original design has won awards, with each room reflecting a different theme (1 being crowd-funding). No b/fast available but the neighbourhood isn't short of eateries. $$$$

🏠 **Royal Seasons Hotel** [85 B5] (113 rooms) 326 & 330 Nanjing W Rd; 🕾 2555 6488; e rsvn. tp.nw@royalseasons.com; w royalseasons.com; 🚇 Zhongshan. Occupying 2 properties separated

by a narrow lane, this hotel has rooms that vary greatly in terms of décor; visit the website if you're particular about hand-painted furniture, cabinets inlaid with mother-of-pearl & patterned carpeting. Not every room has a window but each comes with a smartphone guests can carry with them while exploring Taipei. Free shuttle bus to company's sister hotel in Xinbeitou [map, page 80]. Not all deals inc b/fast. $$$$

🏠 **Changhua Hotel** [85 A5] (24 rooms) 49 Xining N Rd; 🕾 2555 2268; e changhuahotel49@ gmail.com; w www.changhuahotel49.com.tw; 🚇 Beimen. Named after the city in central Taiwan where the owner grew up, this budget inn has an excellent location if you're planning to explore the older parts of the capital. The hallways are a little tatty but the rooms themselves are adequate & clean if small, sleeping 2 ppl only. Walk-in rates start at NTD1,580; it's often possible to get prices 30% lower by booking through a 3rd-party website. $$

EASTERN TAIPEI

🏠 **Taipei Fullerton South** [88 D3] (100 rooms) 41 Fuxing S Rd Sec 2; 🕾 2703 1234; e service2@taipeifullerton.com.tw; w taipeifullerton.com.tw; 🚇 Daan. This boutique hotel, which turns down tour groups so it can focus on its core market of international business travellers, is distinguished by the elegance that oozes from every corner & a narrow yet soaring atrium. Rooms at the back of the building have views of Taipei 101. Coffee & tea available to guests around the clock in the lobby lounge. Sauna & gym. B/fast inc. $$$$

🏠 **Charming City Hotel** [88 E2] (90 rooms) 295 Xinyi Rd Sec 4; 🕾 2704 9546; e service@ city-hotel.com.tw; w www.city-hotel.com. tw; 🚇 Xinyi Anhe. Often fully booked because of its proximity to Taipei World Trade Centre, this friendly establishment – part of a chain of 10 hotels around Taipei – sometimes discounts room rates to below NTD3,000 inc b/fast. If you need a bathtub say so when booking, otherwise you might be given a very slightly cheaper room without one. $$$

🏠 **The Corner House** [88 B2] (48 rooms) 10 Lane 157, Xinsheng S Rd Sec 1; 🕾 2704 5888; e sales@thecornerhouse.com.tw; w thecornerhouse.com.tw; 🚇 Daan Park. Rooms here can often be had for a little over NTD3,000 per night & inc a healthy b/fast – splendid value for a hotel of this quality & location. Larger business dbls come with kitchenettes. Self-service laundry & fitness centre. Within 1km of Yongkang St's restaurants & 300m from Daan Park metro station on the Red Line. **$$$**

🏠 **Fu Hau City Hotel** [88 D3] (40 rooms) 9 Fuxing S Rd; 📞2325 0722; w fuhauhotel.com. tw; 🚇 Daan. This quiet, tasteful establishment has smallish rooms without many frills but couldn't be closer to the metro's Red & Brown lines. NTD600 to add a 3rd bed. B/fast inc. **$$$**

🏠 **Royal Biz Taipei** [88 A2] (48 rooms) 71 Jinshan S Rd; 📞2397 9399; e service@royalbiz. com.tw; w royalbiz.com.tw; 🚇 Dongmen. Popular due to its proximity to the Yongkang St dining district & an excellent choice if you want accommodation that's a cut above but won't break the bank. Rooms are spacious & quite plush. Free tea & coffee in the lobby around the clock, free fruit & snacks in guestrooms. Buffet b/fast inc. **$$$**

XINBEITOU

🏠 **Villa 32** 三二行館 [map, page 80] (5 suites) 32 Zhongshan Rd; 📞6611 8888; e info@ villa32.com; w www.villa32.com; 🚇 Xinbeitou. Separated from the outside world by walls & tall trees, this 5,000m² property is a place to pamper yourself. The interior features great amounts of teak & stone & the Japanese-style quarters have *tatami* mats & sliding paper doors. Suites start at around NTD19,000 inc b/fast, 3 of which are Western-style, inc the very spacious 2-floor Azure Room. If you don't have money to burn, consider treating yourself to a daytime package that includes 4hrs in the public hot-spring pool & a meal; the Italian fusion cuisine served in The Restaurant is among the best in Taipei (reservations required; EM & extensive wine list; **$$$$$**). Admission to Villa 32's public pools (no swimsuits allowed; ⏰ 10.00–23.00 daily) is by reservation only. Private hot-spring rooms (max 2 ppl for 1½hrs) cost from NTD2,600. Spa services available. No under-16s. **$$$$$**

✖ WHERE TO EAT AND DRINK

Taipei has Taiwan's most diverse dining scene, and not only because of its sizeable population and prosperity. Many of the Chinese mainlanders who fled to Taiwan after 1949 sold hometown delicacies in order to survive; the more successful ones converted their roadside stalls into proper restaurants. From the 1960s onwards, Taipei was also where businesspeople would wine and dine customers and suppliers from Japan, North America and other parts of the world. For a couple of generations, sashimi, steak and other non-Taiwanese foods have been filtering down into the mainstream diet.

For scores of additional recommendations, take a look at A Hungry Girl's Guide To Taipei (w hungryintaipei.blogspot.tw) and Taipei Vegetarians (🖪 @taipeivegetarians).

SOUTHWEST TAIPEI

✖ **Halal Beef Noodles** 清真黃牛肉麵 館 [83 E1] 23 Yanping S Rd; 📞2331 8203; ⏰ 10.30–20.00 daily; 🚇 Ximen. Popular with Taipei's southeast Asian expatriates, this clean & bright restaurant offers over 100 beef-noodle & beef-soup permutations (NTD100–190). Carbohydrate options are standard noodles, braised noodles, soya vermicelli & dense crouton-like 'bread' cubes. The EM also lists beef knuckle (NTD200), fried noodles with beef sauce (NTD80), fried or boiled beef dumplings, vegetables & other items. Next door is another halal eatery, which is older & almost as good: **Zhang's Halal Beef**

Noodles 張家清真黃牛肉麵館 [83 E1] (21 Yanping S Rd; 📞2331 2791; ⏰ 10.00–19.15 daily; 🚇 Ximen; **$$**), which was founded by a Muslim who fled to Taiwan with the KMT army. The sesame-paste noodles are served with beef gravy instead of pork, but sadly it lacks an EM. **$$**

✖ **Hangzhou Xiaolongbao** 杭州小籠湯 包 [83 G4] 19 Hangzhou S Rd Sec 2; 📞2393 1757; w thebestxiaolongbao.com; ⏰ 11.00–22.00 daily; 🚇 Chiang Kai-shek Memorial Hall. This perpetually busy restaurant's claim that it's 'as cheap as street food' isn't quite accurate, but the dumplings & dim sum are still good value for money. EM. 2nd branch with a very similar menu not far from Songshan

Airport [map, page 80] (118 Minsheng E Rd Sec 3; ✆6613 0666; ⏰ 11.00–21.00 daily). $$

✕ **Snow King** 雪王 [83 E2] 65 Wuchang St Sec 1; ✆2331 8415; **w** www.snowking.com. tw; ⏰ noon–20.00 daily; 🚇 Ximen. A place for lovers of bizarre foods, Snow King has been selling strangely flavoured homemade ice creams for more than 60 years. They don't just serve flavours that Westerners find odd, like fried peanut or green bean – we're talking curry, sesame-oil chicken & others. Prices are NTD85–150 for a medium-sized bowl. There's no English sign at street level, so look for the doorway bearing the phone number & go up the stairs. EM. $$

✕ **Huaxi Street Night Market** 華西街 觀光夜市 [83 B3] Huaxi & Guangzhou sts; ⏰ approx 17.00–midnight daily; 🚇 Longshan Temple. Formerly known to Westerners as 'snake alley' on account of the half-dozen restaurants where limbless reptiles were slaughtered, skinned & cooked, this neighbourhood is not nearly as lively or seedy as it once was. The last of the snake eateries closed down in spring 2018, so there's now nowhere men keen to boost their virility can drink snake-bile mixed with wine (a concoction said to be an aphrodisiac), or where gonzo gourmands can try snake blood, snake urine or even snake semen. Still, if you're satisfied with *guabao* 刈包 (a so-called 'Taiwanese hamburger' that is actually pork belly in a steamed bun) & other mainstream delicacies, you won't leave hungry. $

✕ **Nanjichang Night Market** 南機場夜市 [map, page 80] Lane 307, Zhonghua Rd Sec 2; ⏰ 18.00–midnight daily; 🚇 Longshan Temple. Less convenient to reach compared with Huaxi St but a better choice if you want to try a good range of street foods, with some healthy options in addition to the usual deep-fried snacks. The freshly made fruit juices (when guavas are in season, order a big cup of *bàlè zhī* 芭樂汁, typically NTD50) are good for washing down sesame chicken (*mayóu jī* 麻油雞, from NTD100 per portion). Rather than YouBike or a 1km walk from Longshan Temple or Xiaonanmen stations, consider taking a #212 bus (departs every 30mins; ⏰ 06.00–22.00 daily; stops at several central locations inc Taipei Main Station, from where it takes 15mins; NTD15) or the more frequent #223 (⏰ 05.00–22.00 daily; NTD15–30). The latter can be boarded in Shilin & at Daqiaotou metro station. $

🍷 **The Bar 58** [83 D1] 58 Kaifeng St Sec 2; ✆2388 8580; ⏰ 18.30–01.00 daily; 🚇 Ximen. Far from spacious but offers a very wide selection of Taiwanese & overseas craft beers & some draught options (most priced NTD200–270). Dinner options inc pizzas, chicken dishes & other Western favourites (NTD240–420). EM. $$$

NORTHWEST TAIPEI

✕ **Spot Café Lumiere** [85 C5] 18 Zhongshan N Rd Sec 2; ✆2562 5612; **w** www.spot.org.tw; ⏰ 10.00–midnight daily; 🚇 Zhongshan. This landmark building dates from 1925 & resembles an antebellum mansion in the south of the US, which is appropriate as the US ambassador lived here 1953–79. It's not just a good place to stop for a coffee – it doubles as a cinema showing art-house films (schedule on the website). There aren't many brunch/meal options but the choice of desserts & hot drinks is impressive. Imported & craft beers from NTD200. Indoor & outdoor seating. EM. $$$

✕ **Shacha Mutton** 沙茶羊肉 [85 B2] 241 Dalong St; **m** 0935 611 175; ⏰ 17.00–22.00 daily; 🚇 Yuanshan. Smack in the middle of a street packed with eateries & evening vendors, this no-frills restaurant near Baoan Temple serves tasty mutton with rice (NTD70), noodles or in soups. The EM pasted on the wall doesn't tell the whole story – there's also fried sheep tripe (NTD200) & a few non-mutton dishes such as fried shrimps (NTD200). $$

✕ **Cisheng Temple Food Vendors** [85 B4] Lane 49, Baoan St; ⏰ varies; 🚇 Daqiaotou. The shacks in front of Cisheng Temple don't look very inviting & the groups of oldish men drinking beer well before midday might put you off. However, the hot foods here are authentic & inexpensive, & it's worth seeking out the vendor that makes & serves nothing but *jī juǎn* 雞捲. Don't be led astray by the 1st character, which means 'chicken'; the main ingredient is pork paste, deep-fried in a tofu-skin wrapping, then served with a sweet-spicy dip. A single serving (NTD50) is enough for 3 ppl to enjoy a proper tasting. The neighbouring stand sells a few different soups but their most interesting dish is a type of shrimp/pork dim sum often called *siu mai* (*shāo mài* 燒賣, NTD50 for 4 open-topped dumplings). Other vendors offer fish stew, smoked shark meat & braised pork on rice. No EMs. $–$$

✕ Sichuan Little Sister Noodles 川妹仔麵館 [85 B4] 139 Ningxia Rd; m 0903 396 971; ⊕ 09.00–21.00 Mon–Sat, 09.00–14.00 Sun; 🚇 Daqiaotou. This low-key eatery hasn't been in business very long but has gained a reputation for decent Szechuan-style beef noodles 川牛肉麵 (NTD120), Szechuan wontons in spicy red oil (*hóng yóu chāoshǒu* 红油抄手, NTD70) or clear oil (*bái yóu chāoshǒu* 白油抄手, NTD70) & other dishes popular in China's southwest. No EM. **$–$$**

EASTERN TAIPEI

✕ Lotus Pond Pagoda 蓮池閣素菜餐廳 [88 E2] Basement, 153 Xinyi Rd Sec 4; 2703 5612; w lck888.com; ⊕ 11.30–14.00 & 17.30–21.00 Thu–Tue, 17.30–21.00 Wed; 🚇 Xinye Anhe. Accessed via the side road between Changhwa & Union banks, this upmarket 100%-vegetarian buffet offers close to 100 different & delicious items inc a salad bar; dim sum; spicy tofu hotpot; 'sashimi' made of konnyaku; 'eel' sushi; & teriyaki 'chicken'. Vegans should note that the ice creams, cakes & pastries are made with eggs & milk. Items are labelled in Chinese only so it helps to be adventurous. NTD550/275 adult/child under 140cm; 10% service charge added to every bill. **$$$$**

✕ Kiki Restaurant KIKI 餐廳 [88 F1] 47 Lane 280, Guangfu S Rd; 2781 4250; ⊕ 11.50–15.00 & 17.15–22.00 daily; 🚇 Sun Yat-sen Memorial Hall. The Szechuan cuisine served here isn't absolutely authentic – nor does it claim to be – but it's so good that reservations are a necessity. Most items are priced NTD200–400; mitigate the spiciness of meat & tofu dishes by ordering vegetables such as plain stir-fried water-spinach (NTD180) or stir-fried bitter melon with salted egg (NTD220). EM. **$$$**

✕ Mayur Indian Kitchen MIK-1 馬友友印度廚房 [88 G1] 350–5 Keelung Rd Sec 1; 2720 0011; w indianfoodtaiwan.com; ⊕ 11.30–15.00 & 17.00– 21.30 daily; 🚇 City Hall. What's perhaps the city's best Indian food is served here & at other MIK branches (see website for locations & different menus), founded by a chef from the subcontinent whose experience in 5-star hotels shows through in both food & service. You'll find both north & south Indian dishes on the à la carte menu (mains around NTD250), which includes an especially good lamb curry. Among drink options are Indian milk tea (NTD55) & several beers (from NTD95) inc Kingfisher. EM. **$$$**

✕ Mazendo 麻膳堂 [88 F1] 24 Lane 280, Guangfu S Rd; 2773 5559; w www.mazendo.com.tw; ⊕ 11.00–22.00 daily; 🚇 Sun Yat-sen Memorial Hall. Located in a neighborhood full of decent but mostly pricey places to eat, this branch of Mazendo (there are 8 others in Greater Taipei) offers solid rice & noodle dishes featuring beef, pork & mutton; nothing costs more than NTD200. Especially good is the mala mutton soup (NTD180), the goaty odour that some find off-putting being balanced by duck-blood curd, tofu skin & bean sprouts. You'll be asked how spicy you want it; 'a little' is enough for most. Try also the pork-sesame dumplings (NTD80). EM. **$$$**

✕ Thanh-Ky 誠記 [88 A2] 1 Lane 6, Yongkang St; 2321 1579; ⊕ 11.00–23.00 daily; 🚇 Dongmen. Run by ethnic Chinese originally from Vietnam, Thanh-Ky is one of Yongkang St's most popular eateries & for good reason. The *pho* (Vietnamese beef noodles) is excellent, as are the deep-fried starters. Vietnamese desserts such as jackfruit in coconut milk also available. Further down the same lane there's another branch (⊕ 11.30–14.00 & 17.30–21.30 daily). EM with pictures. **$$**

✕ Vegetarian Heaven 素食天地 [88 A4] 182 Heping E Rd Sec 1; 2363 8662; ⊕ 11.00–14.00 & 17.00–20.00 daily; 🚇 Guting. A buffet-style restaurant where you help yourself from 30-odd dishes of vegetables & tofu-based items, then take your plate to the counter for weighing & payment, Vegetarian Heaven is a true paradise for non-meat eaters on a budget & others who prefer potato salad to rice. Bottomless bowls of free soup. A good feed costs about NTD140 pp. **$$**

✕ Yonghe Soya Milk King 永和豆漿大王 [88 C3] 102 Fuxing S Rd Sec 2; 2703 5051; ⊕ 24hrs Mon–Sat, noon–midnight Sun; 🚇 Daan/Technology Building. Among the upsides of going to a place that does such great business are reliably fresh & crispy crullers, but a downside is a floor very often littered with discarded chopsticks & other debris. The food preparation area is kept clean & there's an EM. If you need carbohydrates, you can't do better than a cruller folded into a sesame flatbread (*shāobǐng yóutiáo* 燒餅油條, NTD30). Yonghe is an island-wide chain, but not every branch is as good as this outpost. **$**

🍷 On Tap [88 C1] 21 Alley 11, Lane 216, Zhongxiao E Rd Sec 4; 2741 5365;

w ontaptaipei.com; ⏲ 17.00–02.00 Mon–Fri, 11.00–02.00 Sat–Sun; 🚇 Zhongxiao Fuxing. Serving ales & ciders as well as lagers, On Tap is as close to a British pub as you'll find in Taipei. Happy-hour specials until 20.00 every day. Indoor & outdoor seating; live sports on a big screen. Salads (from NTD220), burgers (NTD300–420) & other Western staples plus finger foods. $$$

🍸 **Ounce Taipei** [88 F2] 309 Xinyi Rd Sec 4; ✆ 2703 7761; 🅵 @OunceTaipei; ⏲ 17.30–01.00 Sun–Thu, 17.30–03.00 Fri–Sat; 🚇 Xinyi Anhe. A place for classic & cutting-edge cocktails, access to this speakeasy-style bar is through a coffee shop. For specials like barrel-aged cocktails & new acquisitions see their Facebook page; dozens of the liquors here are available nowhere else in Taiwan. Expect to pay around NTD400 per drink. $$$

ELSEWHERE IN THE CITY

🍴 **Addiction Aquatic Development** 上引水產 [map, page 80] 18 Alley 2, Lane 410, Minzu E Rd; ✆ 2508 1268; w www.addiction. com.tw; ⏲ varies; 🚇 Zhongshan Junior High School. A former fish market transformed into an exceptionally elegant place where high-end seafood is both sold raw & served in 6 distinctive restaurants, AAD draws so many gourmets that a fair number have complained about waiting times, having to stand to eat & no credit cards being accepted. An enjoyable walk-through experience thanks to its lobster-filled tanks & shelves full of premium sakés, it is a prime example of the Japanese-influenced design ethos widely adored in Taiwan. $$$

🍸 **Brass Monkey** [map, page 80] 166 Fuxing N Rd; ✆ 2547 5050; w www.brassmonkeytaipei. com; ⏲ 11.00–01.00 Sun–Wed, 11.00–02.00 Thu–Sat; 🚇 Nanjing Fuxing. One of the city's longest-running expat bars (open since 2003), this serves typical pub mains inc burgers, pasta & schnitzel from NTD330, plus curries from NTD390. If you're planning to come here to watch a major sporting event, book ahead by phone or website. $$$

ENTERTAINMENT

Taipei has no shortage of concert venues, exhibition halls and cinemas. The English-language *Taipei Times* is a good source of information about upcoming events, as are the leaflets you can pick up at metro stations and visitor information centres. The following venues are of particular interest.

Huashan 1914 Creative Park 華山 1914 文化創意產業園區 [88 A1] 1 Bade Rd Sec 1; ✆ 2358 1914; w www.huashan1914. com; most shops ⏲ noon–21.00 Tue–Sun; 🚇 Zhongxiao Xinsheng. A century-old former winery (hence the '1914') originally slated for demolition, Huashan's empty warehouses were illegally taken over by a theatre troupe in the late 1990s. Now run by a foundation on behalf of the government, the park hosts concerts, workshops & art exhibitions, & has a number of shops & bars.

Songshan Cultural and Creative Park 松山文創園區營運中心 [88 G1] Lane 553, Zhongxiao E Rd; ✆ 2765 1388; w www. songshanculturalpark.org; ⏲ exhibition halls 09.00–18.00, grounds 08.00–22.00 daily; 🚇 Sun Yat-sen Memorial Hall. The surviving part of a 1930s tobacco-processing complex (much was cleared to make space for Taipei Dome,

a controversial infrastructure project bogged down in lawsuits), this park hosts a range of cultural events & is the permanent home of the Taiwan Design Museum (✆ 2745 8199 ext 382; ⏲ 09.30–17.30 Tue–Sun; admission NTD50/30) where you can learn about some notable made-in-Taiwan products.

Taipei Eye 台北戲棚 [85 D4] 113 Zhongshan N Rd Sec 2; ✆ 2568 2677; w www.taipeieye. com; ⏲ shows begin 20.00 Mon, Wed, Fri & Sat; 🚇 Zhongshan Elementary School. Of special interest to visitors from overseas, Taipei Eye offers performances featuring easy-to-digest portions of Beijing & Taiwanese opera, puppetry, local folk music & aboriginal dance. The Mon/Wed/Fri shows (NTD550/275) last an hour; those on Sat (NTD880/440) are 90mins. English & Japanese subtitles; after the show, the performers mingle with the audience. Enter Taiwan Cement Hall from Jinzhou St.

SHOPPING

For fashion, tech toys and other mainstream items, shopaholics should head to Nanjing West Road or Zhongxiao East Road Section 4. For more traditional items, Wanhua and Dihua Street are good hunting grounds.

DEPARTMENT STORES

Taipei's department stores follow the Japanese model, right down to lift operators who greet you with put-on smiles.

SOGO [88 C/D1] 300 Zhongxiao E Rd Sec 3 & 45 Zhongxiao E Rd Sec 4; ☎2776 5555; w www. sogo.com.tw; ⊕ 11.00–21.30 daily; ☒ Zhongxiao Fuxing. These 2 department stores, one on either side of Zhongxiao Fuxing metro station, have the usual brands & clean, well-lit food courts (but not much English on the menus).

Taipei 101 Mall [88 G2] Xinyi & Shifu rds; ☎8101 7777; w www.taipei-101.com.tw; ⊕ 11.00– 21.30 daily; ☒ Taipei 101/World Trade Centre. 5 floors of shops to max out your credit card & a basement with some good-value eating options.

SOUVENIRS

National Cultural and Creative Gift Centre [83 F2] 1 Xuzhou Rd; ☎2393 3655; w giftcenter. tw; ⊕ 09.30–18.00 daily; ☒ NTU Hospital. This government-sponsored non-profit organisation aids local handicraft industries by marketing their products. The mart has a massive inventory inc jade items, leather art, porcelain & hand puppets. At the time of writing the website was Chinese only but the centre's multi-lingual staff can accept orders & arrange shipping by telephone.

Weekend Jade Market 建國假日玉花市 [88 B1] Jianguo S & Renai rds; ⊕ approx 09.00– 17.00 Sat–Sun; ☒ Zhongxiao Xinsheng. Said to be one of the largest jade markets in the world, several hundred vendors gather here & sell not only jade items but also semi-precious stones, coral jewellery & Buddha statues. If you continue walking southwards you'll come to Taipei's main flower market, where you'll see orchids, bonsai & all kinds of cut flowers.

GIVE YOUR FEET A TREAT

In recent years, going for a foot massage in Taipei has become a must-do for tourists. At the end of a long day of sightseeing and/or shopping, sitting down for a reflexology session is indeed a pleasure, and seldom an expensive one. A full hour, which normally includes some shoulder and back pummelling, is unlikely to cost more than NTD800.

Contrary to what some people assume, a foot massage isn't holistic, each area of each foot being associated with a specific part of the human body. In many establishments, charts of the right and left soles are displayed, showing the differences between the two sides, just as the human body is asymmetrical. The pressure points for the heart and spleen are on the right foot, while the actual organs are slightly to the left of each person's midline. Pressure zones for the appendix and liver (located on the right side of the body) are on the left foot. The nose is linked to the outer side of both big toes, while massaging the toes helps the ears, eyes and sinuses – and, some claim, the brain.

There are several foot-massage parlours in Ximending but you'll find them in every part of the city. In each place the procedure is much the same: you'll be asked to take off your shoes and socks, then shown to a barcalounger-type armchair. Before any massaging begins, you soak your feet in a small tub filled with herb-infused hot water. If things get painful, say *xiǎo lì yī diǎn* ('a little less vigour, please!').

TEA

Many tourists take boxes of Taiwan's excellent teas home with them. The capital's most famous tea dealers – among them shops which claim to have been in business since the 1840s – are concentrated in the city's northwest.

Wanchuan Tea Shop 萬全茶行 [85 D5] 4 Lane 13, Nanjing E Rd Sec 1; ☎2521 4247; ⏰ 09.00–noon & 13.30–midnight daily; 🚇 Zhongshan. Some English is spoken at this long-established shop, which has won awards for its oolongs & oriental beauty teas.

BOOKSHOPS

The following have English-language books & magazines:

Caves Books [85 C2] 58 Zhongshan N Rd Sec 3; ☎2599 1169; ⏰ 11.00–20.00 daily; 🚇 Yuanshan
Eslite Books Several branches around the city, including:
[88 G1] 11 Songgao Rd; ☎8789 3388; ⏰ 11.00–22.00 daily; 🚇 City Hall
[88 E1] 245 Dunhua S Rd Sec 1; ☎2775 5977; ⏰ 24hrs daily; 🚇 Zhongxiao Dunhua
[83 F1] Underground shopping mall at Taipei Main Station; ☎6632 8168; ⏰ 10.00–22.30 daily

OTHER PRACTICALITIES

BANKS AND CHANGING MONEY

Taipei has scores of banks. Money can also be changed in major hotels & some department stores & in all 3 of the post office branches mentioned here.

$ Changhwa Bank [85 C5] 57 Zhongshan N Rd Sec 2
$ Land Bank [88 B1] 29 Renai Rd Sec 3; 🚇 Zhongxiao Xinsheng

MEDICAL

✚ **Mackay Memorial Hospital** [map, page 80] 92 Zhongshan Rd Sec 2; ☎2543 3535; w post.mmh.org.tw/english; ⏰ 24hrs daily; 🚇 Shuanglian

POLICE

Main police station [83 D2] 96 Yanping S Rd; ☎2381 8251, 2556 6007; in emergencies call ☎110; 🚇 Ximen

POST

✉ **General post office** [83 E1] 114 Zhongxiao W Rd Sec 1; ⏰ 08.00–21.00 Mon–Fri, 08.30–16.30 Sat; 🚇 Taipei Main Station
✉ **Taipei Main Station** [83 F1] ⏰ 08.00–18.30 Mon–Fri, 09.00–noon Sat
✉ **National Palace Museum** [map, page 80] ⏰ 08.30–17.00 Sun–Fri, 08.30–20.30 Sat

WHAT TO SEE AND DO

Taiwan's capital isn't the oldest city on the island and postwar growth has dramatically changed its appearance. Despite this, a great deal of history remains here, not far from modern landmarks like Taipei 101 and the Chinese Nationalist memorial halls.

SOUTHWEST TAIPEI Sights are listed in the order you're likely to reach them if starting out on foot from Taipei Main Station.

Taipei's city gates Taipei's walls, completed in 1884 after the settlement was made capital of Taiwan province, once enclosed an area south of the railway station, but they were demolished in the first decade of the Japanese colonial era. The **North Gate** 北門 [83 E1] (Zhongxiao W & Yanping S rds) is the only element to retain its original appearance, and the **Little South Gate** 小南門 [83 D3] (Aiguo & Yanping S rds) was heavily modified in 1966 on the orders of KMT leaders who thought the original wasn't 'Chinese' enough.

Futai Street Mansion 撫臺街洋樓 [83 E1] (26 Yanping S Rd; ⊕ 10.00–18.00 Mon–Sat; free admission; 🚊 Taipei Main Station) Originally the headquarters of a Japanese-owned construction company, then the offices of a newspaper, this two-floor century-old stone building is now a small but engrossing museum devoted to aspects of Taipei's history.

Ximending 西門町 **(Xīméndīng)** The best place on the island to see Taiwan's Japanese-influenced youth culture, Ximending is a pedestrian shopping zone full of fashion shops, cinemas, tattoo parlours and places to eat. At the beginning of the Japanese colonial era, Ximending ('west gate district') was an undeveloped area just outside the city's west gate, but by World War I it had become Taipei's main entertainment district. The most elegant landmark is the **Red House** 西門紅樓 [83 D2] (w www.redhouse.org.tw; ⊕ 11.00–21.30 Tue–Sun; free admission; 🚊 Ximen), built as a theatre in 1908 and now billed as a 'market for artists and designers'. It's been pointed out that the octagonal front part resembles a Buddhist lotus in shape, while the rear part, viewed from above, is shaped like a crucifix.

Nishi Honganji 西本願寺 [83 D2] (174 Zhonghua Rd Sec 1) The remnants of this colonial-era Buddhist temple aren't much to look at, but this makes a good spot to sit down and chill for a while if you're hoofing it between Wanhua and Ximending.

Zhongshan Hall 中山堂 [83 D2] (98 Yanping S Rd; ✆ 2381 3137; w www. csh.taipei.gov.tw; ⊕ 09.30–21.00 daily; free admission except during concerts; 🚊 Ximen) Completed in 1936 to honour Japan's Emperor Hirohito (reigned 1926–89) but now named after Sun Yat-sen (see box, page 103), this Spanish Islamic building is where the final Japanese governor-general of Taiwan surrendered to one of Chiang Kai-shek's generals on 25 October 1945. It houses a quintessentially Taiwanese work of art: *Water Buffaloes*, a plaster relief executed by Huang Tu-shui (1895–1930) that depicts a rural scene of water buffaloes, banana trees and naked infants, and the main hall is now a venue for concerts and conferences. If you decide to eat at the plush **Fortress Café** (2nd Flr; ✆ 2331 1186; ⊕ 10.00–21.00 daily; EM, lists Western & Taiwanese dishes & afternoon tea sets; $$$) you can sup indoors or on the balcony from which Chiang addressed his subjects on several occasions.

National Taiwan Museum 國立台灣博物館 [83 E2] (2 Xiangyang Rd; ✆ 2382 2566; w en.ntm.gov.tw; ⊕ 09.30–17.00 Tue–Sun; admission to main bldg & Land Bank Exhibition Hall NTD30/15; 🚊 NTU Hospital) Made partly of stone imported from Japan, this impressive edifice was built 1913–15 to commemorate the achievements of colonial governor Kodama Gentaro and his right-hand man, Goto Shinpei (page 14). It now contains a mix of permanent and temporary exhibitions, with especially strong natural history and indigenous-artefact sections; look out for the Bunun calendar etched on a piece of wood. In recent years the museum has expanded across the road into the **Land Bank Exhibition Hall** [83 E2] and to **Nanmen Park** [83 F4] (1 Nanchang Rd Sec 1), both of which keep the same opening hours as the main building although there's a separate charge for the latter (NTD20/10). The former is filled with information about dinosaurs, fossils and land reform after World War II; the latter has a permanent exhibition about the camphor industry. Sometime after 2020, the museum is set to gain additional space beside Beimen metro station [83 D1].

2–28 Peace Memorial Park 二二八和平紀念公園 [83 E/F2] (🕐 24hrs daily; 🚇 NTU Hospital)

Except for the Japanese-era National Taiwan Museum and the starkly modern 2-28 Memorial Monument, this is a very Chinese park, full of ponds and pavilions. It's actually Taiwan's oldest city park, dating from 1908, and its historical and social significance goes beyond urban planning. The former radio station in the southeastern corner was seized by protesters just after 28 February 1947 and now houses the **2-28 Memorial Museum** [83 F2] (📞 2389 7228; 🕐 10.00–17.00 Tue–Sun; admission NTD20), which doesn't contain much English and is strictly for history mavens curious about the Japanese era and the following years. In the 1960s and 1970s the park was one of the few places in the capital where gay men could gather in safety.

Chiang Kai-shek Memorial Hall 中正紀念堂 (Zhōngzhèng Jìniàntáng)

[83 G4] (📞 2343 1100; w www.cksmh.gov.tw; 🕐 09.00–18.00 daily; 🚇 Chiang Kai-shek Memorial Hall) There's much more to this complex – inaugurated on 5 April 1980, the fifth anniversary of the dictator's death – than quasi-classical Chinese architecture and spit-and-polish military policemen. Taipei citizens come here to attend cultural events (the two brown-roofed buildings are the National Theatre and National Concert Hall), to practise martial arts or hip-hop dance moves, or to find a secluded park bench they can share with a lover or a good book.

The blue-roofed, white-sided tower at the eastern end of the site is the memorial proper. At the time of writing, the exhibition rooms directly beneath the immense bronze image of the generalissimo outlined the high points of Chiang's career while skating over personal topics such as his Methodism and his first two wives. If the DPP (see box, page 21) wins the 2020 elections, it's very possible the hall will be renamed and other traces of Chiang excised from public places.

Taipei Botanical Garden 台北植物園 (Táiběi Zhíwùyuán)

[83 D4] (Cnr of Nanhai & Heping W rds; w tpbg.tfri.gov.tw; 🕐 05.30–22.00 daily; free admission; 🚇 Xiaonanmen, leave by Exit 3) Established at the very beginning of the colonial era, these gardens cover just 8ha but have almost 2,000 different tree and plant species, not to mention birds like the Japanese white eye (*Zosterops japonicus*); the resident avians are remarkably tolerant of human admirers and photographers. The garden's very detailed bilingual website will engross the green-fingered.

By the southeastern corner of the garden, the **National Museum of History** 國立歷史博物館 [83 E4] (w www.nmh.gov.tw) is closed until mid 2021 for comprehensive renovations. When it reopens, its exhibitions are likely to again focus on ancient China.

WANHUA 萬華

Many Taiwanese toponyms have been dragged through multiple languages. Wanhua is the Mandarin pronunciation of two characters chosen by the Japanese colonial authorities because, when pronounced in standard Japanese, they came close to imitating the name actually used by the area's inhabitants, Mangka (sometimes spelled Manka, Monga or Bangkah). That 19th-century place name, which has been revived in recent years, was itself derived from an indigenous term meaning 'canoe'. In the early days of Han settlement, Ketagalan tribesmen would bring their boats downstream and barter vegetables and charcoal for Chinese products.

These days, Taipei citizens consider Wanhua a less-than-ideal district in which to live. Coming here from east Taipei, you'll notice the people are less fashionably dressed, the cars are older and the buildings scruffier. For tourists, however, Wanhua

Many Taiwanese honour their gods and ancestors by burning incense and joss paper, especially the small sheets of yellow paper many Westerners call 'ghost money'. Taoists do it more often and in greater quantities than Buddhists and for slightly different reasons. According to both religions, the living have an obligation to take care of the deceased by making offerings of fruit and other foods, and by sending them spirit currency (the dead have living expenses, it's believed). Adherents of mainstream religion have an additional motive: because it's widely believed that burning joss paper brings a person good luck, businesspeople often place tables of offerings in front of their shops or offices and order their employees to *bài bài* (pray) and burn bundles of spirit currency in portable braziers.

During Ghost Month (page 67), huge quantities of ghost money are sacrificed to keep troublesome spirits at bay. Just as there are several types of incense, there are different kinds of joss paper for different rituals. Paper which is to be burned for a funeral is folded in a special way, sometimes to resemble a lotus, other times into the shape of a ship. Once made by hand from rice straw, joss paper is now mass-produced in factories and lots of chemicals are used – so many, in fact, that the government has warned that those who burn joss paper risk inhaling dangerous quantities of nitrogen oxide, benzene and toluene.

Environmentalists have promoted online 'virtual ghost-money burning' services and the burning of 'spirit credit cards', which the dead can use in the after-world instead of banknotes. Some shrines, including Longshan Temple (see below), no longer permit the on-site burning of joss paper, while a handful of others have installed wet scrubbers, devices that force smoke through a dense particle-capturing mist. Unfortunately, at least one study has found these scrubbers make no significant difference to the quantity of carcinogenic emissions. Master Cheng Yen, founder of the Buddhist Compassion Relief Tzu Chi Foundation (page 275), has said that sincerity and virtue are far more important than burning joss paper. Reforms, however, have yet to make much of a dent in the tradition.

is fascinating – rich in history, architecture and traditional culture. Longshan Temple, best accessed from the metro station of the same name, is a logical place to start.

Longshan Temple 龍山寺 (Lóngshān Sì) [83 C3] (🕐 06.00–22.00 daily; 🚇 Longshan Temple) Named after a shrine in Jinjiang County, Fujian – the ancestral district of many of those who settled in Wanhua in the 18th century – Longshan Temple is the only place of worship in Taipei City that comes close to Baoan Temple in terms of art, history and ongoing religious action. Religious practices here lean towards Buddhism, Guanyin being the centre of attention since the temple was established in 1738. Guan Gong, who as usual has a red face, is on the left at the back and Mazu is the main deity in the rear chamber. She was installed here in 1793 at the behest of a merchants' guild whose members often made the dangerous voyage between Taiwan and the Chinese mainland. If you visit in the evening you'll see a queue of young people at the back on the left, waiting to pray to the Old Man Under the Moon (page 34).

There used to be a pond in front of the temple's main entrance because a feng shui expert determined the temple was the abode of a beautiful female spirit and that she should have a 'mirror' in which she could gaze at her own countenance. However, in 1923 the Japanese colonial authorities decided the pond was a health hazard and ordered it filled in and turned into a park. The current main structure, completed in 1959, replaced a building wrecked by American bombs during World War II.

The section of Xiyuan Road nearest Longshan Temple has 20-odd shops selling Buddha statuettes and religious accoutrements.

Herb Alley 青草巷 [83 C3] (Lane 224, Xichang St; ⏱ approx 08.00–20.00 daily; 🚇 Longshan Temple) At least seven of the businesses here have been dealing in medicinal and culinary herbs for over 100 years, and wandering down this lane is an olfactory and visual pleasure. When people became sick in the 18th and 19th centuries, they were as likely to consult a spirit medium as a physician, who would ask a deity for a 'prescription' that would then be filled here. Nowadays the herbs are purchased for culinary use.

Bopiliao 剝皮寮 [83 C3] (Lane 173, Kangding Rd; 🚇 Longshan Temple) The name of this renovated neighbourhood, one of Taipei's oldest, gives a clue as to what used to be the main industry. Bopiliao means 'the hut where bark is peeled

MACKAY IN WANHUA

Nowhere did the missionary work of George L Mackay (see box, page 138) face greater opposition than in Wanhua. Referring to the settlement by its Holo name, he described his forays into the city in his book *From Far Formosa*:

Bangkah was the Gibraltar of heathenism in north Formosa… thoroughly Chinese and intensely anti-foreign in all its interests and sympathies. The citizens… are materialistic, superstitious dollar-seekers. At every visit, when passing through their streets, we are maligned, jeered at and abused. Hundreds of children run ahead, yelling with derisive shouts; others follow, pelting us with orange peel, mud and rotten eggs… the authorities of Bangkah issued proclamations calling on all citizens, on pain of imprisonment or death, not to rent, lease or sell either houses or other property to the barbarian missionary.

In December 1877, Mackay did find a place he could rent – but xenophobic local merchants paid lepers and beggars to harass the missionary and his associates. After a mob invaded the premises, tore tiles from the roof and bricks out of the walls, the British consul rushed to the scene and demanded the local mandarin meet the Chinese Empire's treaty obligations and ensure Mackay's safety. Protected by Chinese soldiers, Mackay built a mission station on the same site. Nevertheless, active opposition continued: Taiwanese who dared attend meetings were boycotted, and in 1879 Mackay's wife was almost blinded when a man taking part in an 'idolatrous procession' shoved a burning torch into her face. It was another decade before Christians were to feel safe in Wanhua, but by 1893 Mackay was being carried through the streets in a sedan chair and presented with honorary parasols by civil and military officials.

off', and two centuries ago this was where tree trunks imported from China were stripped of their bark so they could be used for building. Taiwan didn't lack for trees in that era, but Han settlers considered logging in the headhunter-dominated foothills far too dangerous. The restored 19th-century buildings are appealing but mostly empty. In 1966, just after Taiwan's baby boom peaked, the elementary school that lies on the north side of the neighbourhood had more than 11,000 students.

Qingshan Temple 青山宮 [83 B3] (218 Guiyang St Sec 2; ⏰ 05.30–21.20 daily; 🚇 Longshan Temple) Named after and dedicated to the King of Qingshan, a general in Fujian almost 1,800 years ago who was promoted to godhood in the 12th century, this house of worship was founded in 1854. In that year, an icon of the king was being carried through this neighbourhood by fishermen when the statue suddenly became too heavy to move. By divination the king's followers determined he wished to stay in this place, so a shrine was built. The king's birthday, the 22nd day of the tenth lunar month, is one of Wanhua's most important annual events. Of the associated rituals, the most impressive is a nighttime parade that the pious believe can draw out and eradicate evil spirits and bad luck. The ground floor of this temple has a tremendous collection of effigies notable for their fearsome countenances and collar-length eyebrows. Seek out one on the right as you enter: one half of his face has a normal Chinese complexion but the other half is black with a red eyebrow; his title is given as Sī Yáng Yīn 司陽陰, literally 'controller of yin and yang'. The Jade Emperor commands centre stage on the top floor where, on the right, there's an idol of the Lord of the South Pole Star, and on the left you'll find the Lord of the North Pole Star.

NORTHWEST TAIPEI
Baoan Temple 保安宮 (Bǎoān Gōng) [85 B1] (61 Hami St; ⏰ 06.00–22.00 daily; 🚇 Yuanshan) In artistic terms, this 200-year-old temple is without doubt one of Taiwan's finest places of worship. The quality of its 1995–2002 restoration received international recognition in the form of an honourable mention in the 2003 UNESCO Asia-Pacific Heritage Awards for Culture Conservation. Come at dusk if you can, and spend time appreciating the door gods, the fabulously ornate carved screens and the large murals on the outside of the central shrine painted by Pan Li-shui (see box, opposite). The main shrine in the centre of the courtyard is dedicated to Baosheng Dadi ('the life-guarding emperor'), a god of justice, sustenance and medicine who was born as Wu Dao in Fujian in AD979; a Taoist physician, it's said he once brought a skeleton back to life. Deified by a local cult soon after his death, he was fast-tracked for full godhood during the Ming Dynasty (1368–1644) after his intercession cured an emperor's concubine of cancer. His prominence in Taiwan dates from 1699 when he was credited with bringing an epidemic under control.

The god's birthday falls on the 15th day of the third lunar month and is celebrated with the Baosheng Cultural Festival. The temple's name isn't derived from the deity's title. Instead it means 'keeping Tongan folk safe', the founders having come from Fujian's Tongan County. Other deities worshipped include Shennong, the god of farming and putative inventor of the hoe, plough and irrigation; you'll recognise this chubby fellow because he holds rice stalks. Near the temple, bilingual information panels explain how this neighbourhood came to be called Dalongdong and why Hami Street used to be known as Sishisikan Street (literally 'street of 44 thresholds').

Baoan Temple showcases several works by Pan Li-shui (1914–95), one of Taiwan's most famous temple artists. His father, Pan Chun-yuan (d1972) was also a noted painter, but during the Kominka Movement (page 16) a lack of work forced the pair to design advertisements for a living. Pan Li-shui's son Pan Yue-xiong (b1943) assisted his father in the 1960s and 1970s and continues to work on restoration projects. None of his descendants, however, have carried on the tradition.

Taipei Confucius Temple 台北孔廟 **(Kǒngzǐ Miào)** [85 B2] (275 Dalong St; w www.ct.taipei.gov.tw; ◷ 08.30–21.00 Tue–Sun & national holidays; exhibition rooms close 17.00; 🚇 Yuanshan) After the warmth and embellishment of Baoan Temple, the capital's Confucian shrine comes across as grand but a little desolate. Within, the sage is represented by a simple tablet; in Baoan Temple he gets a small statue. Built in 1925–39 on the site of an earlier Confucian shrine, the complex contains various multimedia displays and static exhibitions. An especially good one explains the traditional instruments and ceremonial music heard each 28 September during the grand rites that mark Confucius's birthday.

Taipei Fine Arts Museum 台北市立美術館 **(Táiběi Shìlì Měishùguǎn)** [85 D2] (181 Zhongshan N Rd Sec 3; ☏ 2595 7656; w www.tfam.museum; ◷ 09.30–17.30 Tue–Fri & Sun, 09.30–20.30 Sat; admission NTD30/15; 🚇 Yuanshan) Exhibitions at TFAM lean towards the modern and usually highlight Taiwanese artists, including some who live abroad.

Cisheng Temple 慈聖宮 **(Císhèng Gōng)** [85 B4] During the late 19th century, it's said, day labourers used to gather here before dawn in the hope of getting some work; there's been a conglomeration of vendors selling hot foods ever since (page 91). While you're here, do go to the very back of the shrine via the right-hand corridor to see the sealed well in which a 'dragon spirit' is believed to dwell.

Dihua Street 迪化街 **(Díhuà Jiē)** [85 A5] A hub of traditional commerce, Dihua Street is where local families go in the run-up to Lunar New Year to buy ritual items and special treats. In recent years the street has seen quite a bit of gentrification – a good thing, as several of the oldest, grandest merchant homes were on the verge of collapse a couple of decades ago, but today the architecture is very photogenic. You'll soon find and smell the dried fruits, medicinal herbs and other goods associated with the street. **Yongle Market** 永樂市場 (21 Dihua St Sec 1; most shops ◷ approx 09.30–18.00 daily; 🚇 Beimen), housed in an ugly building near the southern end of the street, is dominated by fabrics and tailoring services. Aside from the metro, the frequent #302 bus stops at Daqiaotou on the Orange Line, which is a 1.1km walk from Yongle Market; it's also a convenient way to get to Baoan Temple. Walking north, you'll come across Baroque features such as shields, laurels, crenellations and even minarets; the façade of the herbal medicine clinic at number 71 on Section 1 bears ginseng embossments.

On Dihua Street and in other old Taipei neighbourhoods you'll come across 'urban regeneration stations' (URS) – pre-1945 dwellings that the city government has rehabilitated and turned into art spaces and cultural-creative industry outposts. Tourists are welcome to wander in, enjoy the architecture and peruse displays.

Taipei WHAT TO SEE AND DO

3

Vintage buildings and colourful shops make it worthwhile continuing as far as Liangzhou Street. Near the junction, **AMA Museum** 阿嬤家和平與女性人權館 [85 A3] (256 Dihua St Sec 1; ⏱ 10.00–17.00 Tue–Sun; admission NTD100/80; 🚇 Daqiaotou) is only worth entering if you've a special interest in the issue of 'comfort women' (page 16).

XiaHai City God Temple 霞海城隍廟 [85 A4] (61 Dihua St Sec 1; ⏱ 06.16–19.47 daily; 🚇 Beimen) The excellent bilingual labelling within Taipei's best-known city-god temple makes it a highly digestible stop. The city god himself is a generalist who can bestow peace, prosperity, happiness and good weather, and he's kept company by effigies representing his wife (note the offerings of cosmetics), Mazu, the Old Man Under the Moon and others. This representation of the Old Man is thought to be particularly efficacious: the temple claims that more than 20 couples tie the knot each day thanks to his efforts. The city-god icon arrived in Mangka from China in 1821. During ethnic clashes in 1853, the effigy was evacuated to its current location. It was a bloody retreat and the 38 men who died while protecting the god are enshrined here as Yiyonggong ('brave guards').

Museum of Contemporary Art 台北當代藝術館 [85 C5] (39 Changan W Rd; ☎2552 3720; w www.mocataipei.org.tw; ⏱ 10.00–18.00 Tue–Sun; admission NTD50/free, also free for families 10.00–noon Sat–Sun & national holidays; 🚇 Zhongshan) As with TFAM (page 101), visits to MOCA can be hit-or-miss affairs depending on your tastes and what's showing. The website lists current and upcoming exhibitions.

2–28 Memorial Cenotaph [85 B5] (Lane 185, Nanjing W Rd) This simple bilingual plaque is a dignified reminder that the 2-28 Incident of 1947 (page 17) erupted at this very spot.

EASTERN TAIPEI
Taipei 101 台北101 (**Yī Líng Yī**) [88 G4] (7 Xinyi Rd Sec 5; w taipei-101.com. tw; 🚇 Taipei 101/World Trade Centre) Formerly the world's tallest structure at 509m including antenna, Taipei 101 is surely memorable if not especially beautiful. Divided into segments each of eight floors, the building was designed by architect C Y Lee to mimic the shape of bamboo, which not only grows well throughout Taiwan but is also a symbol throughout the Chinese world of longevity and resilience. Much has been written about the meaning of the motifs that can be seen on the side of the tower, how feng shui considerations influenced the design and how the structure was made typhoon- and earthquake-proof.

To visit the **Observatory** on the 91st floor (⏱ 09.00–22.00 daily; admission NTD600/540) go to the fifth floor of the mall; to avoid wasting time queuing for tickets, book at least one day ahead through the website. However, if conditions aren't good, the view simply isn't worth the steep admission charge. The exit route is unnecessarily long, having been designed to maximise visitors' exposure to various shops. Security has been tight since 2007, when Austrian BASE jumper Felix Baumgartner (who now holds the world skydiving record after jumping from the very edge of the Earth's stratosphere) leapt from the viewing deck, landed safely in a nearby car park and fled the country before he could be arrested. The adjacent **mall** (⏱ 11.00–21.30 daily) has five floors of fancy shops and an impressive range of eating options.

Sun Yat-sen Memorial Hall 國父紀念館 (**Guófù Jìniànguǎn**) [88 F1] (☎2758 8008; w www.yatsen.gov.tw/en; ⏱ 09.00–18.00 daily; free admission; 🚇 Sun Yat-sen

Memorial Hall) This memorial to the Republic of China's founding father (see box, above), completed in 1972, is less ostentatious than the Chiang Kai-shek Memorial Hall, the roof being less than half the height of the Chiang edifice. Architect Wang Da-hong purposely avoided both Western conventions and Chinese palatial architecture to invoke Sun's belief that neither a return to China's past nor slavish imitation of the West could solve the nation's problems. The historical displays inside barely touch on Taiwan – which isn't surprising as Sun made just three brief visits to the island – but among the heirlooms and photographs you're sure to find some things of interest. Exit 4 of Sun Yat-sen Memorial Hall metro station leads to the northwestern corner of the 11.5ha grounds; work your way around to the front entrance facing Renai Road where, each hour on the hour, the changing of the military police detachment draws a small crowd. The guards are there to protect a larger-than-life bronze statue of Sun.

Daan Forest Park 大安森林公園 (Dà'ān Sēnlín Gōngyuán) [88 B3] (Jianguo
S & Xinyi rds; ⊙ 24hrs daily; free admission; 🚇 Daan Park) Over half a century passed between this 26ha site being officially designated parkland and it beginning to resemble a park. Like many empty spaces, it was occupied by refugees in the wake of KMT's chaotic withdrawal from the Chinese mainland in 1949. The squatters and their descendants weren't removed until the mid 1990s, since when the trees have matured and multiple bird species have taken up residence.

TAIPEI SUBURBS

Museum fans (and visitors encountering awful weather) may want to spend an entire day in Shilin and a half day venturing out to Nangang. If it's dry yet cold, consider a walking tour of Xinbeitou followed by a hot-springs soak.

SHILIN 士林
National Palace Museum 國立故宮博物院 (Gù Gōng) (📞6610 3600; w npm.
gov.tw/en; ⊙ 08.30–18.30 Sun–Thu, 08.30–21.00 Fri–Sat; admission NTD350, free for under-18s & disabled, free for everyone on 1 Jan, 18 May, 27 Sep, 10 Oct, 17 Oct & Lantern Festival) Rightly considered to have one of the world's finest collections, the NPM is colossally rewarding for anyone interested in east Asian art. It derives

its name from the fact that much of this magnificent accumulation used to be the personal collection of the Chinese emperors; collecting was an imperial habit from the Song Dynasty (AD960–1279) onward. When the Qing Dynasty gave way to the Republic of China in 1911, the last emperor was permitted to remain in the Forbidden City for more than a decade. During this period numerous items were pilfered and sold by eunuchs and other retainers. After the ex-emperor was expelled from his palace in 1924, the original NPM was established in the Forbidden City. However, because Japan was expanding its sphere of influence in north China, in 1933 the most valuable treasures were packed up and moved away, which were then moved several more times during World War II and the subsequent civil war. By the beginning of 1949 most had been transported to Keelung. Only in 1965, with the opening of the current building, were the treasures put on display once again.

The NPM collection is constantly growing as a result of purchases and donations. By mid 2018 the museum held 697,740 items, among which were 212,329 rare books, 386,865 Qing-era archival documents and 11,501 documents in the Manchu, Mongolian and Tibetan languages. The vaults contain also 6,227 bronzes, 6,656 paintings, 3,707 calligraphic works, 25,560 ceramics and 13,478 jade items (see box, below). Some of these artefacts have never been displayed because they're too fragile or they've not yet been sufficiently researched.

Many of the prettiest pieces in the collection were gifts from Chinese officials hoping to curry favour with the emperor, others were tributes from vassal states such as Tibet. A few, such as the timepieces cherished by Qing rulers, were gifts from Western diplomats. Not all of the works executed in China were undertaken by Chinese artists – a number of paintings, the most famous being *A Hundred Steeds*, are the accomplishments of Giuseppe Castiglione (1688–1766), an Italian Jesuit missionary who became a court painter in Beijing.

Getting a general idea of what's here and lingering over displays that catch your eye requires at least 3 hours inside; don't be surprised if the museum ends up taking

JADE IN OLD CHINA AND PREHISTORIC TAIWAN

Some of the oldest pieces in the NPM's collection are made of jade, a material which in ancient times was believed to have semi-magical properties and was often turned into ritual or ceremonial items. Jade may be white, green, brown or even reddish. Carved into blades, discs, dragons or figurines of humans or gods, several of the pieces in the museum have endured for 7,000 years. Jade artefacts were also highly valued by the indigenous Beinan culture that thrived in southeast Taiwan over 2,000 years ago (page 297).

Jade was treasured for its toughness and beauty and valued more highly than gold. Jade thumb rings were popular during the Ming and Qing dynasties as wearing them showed one didn't engage in physical labour. It remains a popular material in 21st-century Taiwan, particularly for making bracelets and pendants. However, some of what was considered to be 'jade' in the China of old doesn't fall into the modern definition. According to geologists, 'true' jade is either nephrite or jadeite, both of which are semi-precious stones. The former used to be mined in considerable quantities in China itself, as well as in prehistoric and postwar Taiwan, while the latter was imported from what's now Burma. Ancient Chinese regarded any beautiful stone as jade, and faux-jades included serpentine, soapstone, topaz and quartz.

On some of the paintings and calligraphy scrolls in the NPM, you may notice as many as 60 red imprints. These are the names of personages who have, at one time or another, owned the item and used their personal seals to mark their property. In the China of yore, such additions were thought of as enhancements rather than defacements, and in the margins you may even see short comments written by previous owners.

Personal seals have been used by Han people for more than 2,500 years. Even in 21st-century Taiwan, documents and cheques are more often sealed than signed. Most of the name stamps you'll see being used in banks and offices are machine-carved and made of wood, bamboo or even plastic, but the NPM has a number of exquisite seals (or 'chops' as they're sometimes called) carved from jade or cast from bronze. Bat motifs, a symbol of luck, are a common feature. Some fist-sized seals bear dragon sculptures or excerpts from poems.

over the day. Those with special interests would do well to look at the NPM's very thorough website before they arrive.

There's no additional charge for the twice-daily (⊕ 10.00 & 15.00) English-language tours but online reservation at least two days before visiting is required. Tours last 1–2 hours and most guides are amenable to requests and very willing to answer questions. They're especially good at explaining the symbolism of shapes and motifs; for example, presenting someone with an object that incorporates the 12 animals of the Chinese zodiac signified that you wished him or her a long life, while paintings that depicted travel implied scholarship, because one had to go far afield to acquire knowledge. When the tour has finished you're free to backtrack and revisit galleries at your own pace. If you'd rather rent an English-language audio guide (NTD150 for adults' version, NTD50 for children's version; deposit ID or NTD1,000), these can be booked online; alternatively the audio files can be downloaded for free from the museum's website so there's no need to rent a player if you have a suitable device. If you've time to kill before the start of a tour, spend it in the coffee shop on the east side of the main building's first floor (⊕ 09.00–18.00 Sun–Thu, 09.00–21.00 Fri–Sat; $) or in the gift shop at level B1. The latter has an excellent range of souvenirs for every budget.

Once you enter the museum proper, the Orientation Gallery, on the same level as the entrance, is a logical place to begin. Timelines put China's various dynasties and kingdoms in chronological order and relate those eras to what was happening in other parts of the world. On the same floor, you'll notice that the icons and statues in 'Compassion and Wisdom: Religious Sculptural Arts' are exclusively Buddhist; you won't find any popular or Taoist gods. Some of the most striking pieces in this gallery are of Tibetan origin. Elsewhere on the first floor there's a permanent exhibition of Qing-era curio boxes and other items under the title 'A Garland of Treasures: Masterpieces of Precious Crafts in the Museum Collection'.

One of the principal displays on the second floor focuses on kneaded-clay ceramics, another on porcelains. On the third floor, 'Rituals Cast in Brilliance: Masterpieces of Bronzes' features some truly ancient bronzeware. Another permanent exhibition focuses on jade masterpieces (see box, opposite).

If you get hungry but aren't ready to leave the museum, head to **Silks Palace** (◣ 2882 9393; ⊕ 11.00–21.30 daily). The second basement level of the restaurant offers Taiwanese favourites ($), while on the first floor, most of the options are

Taipei TAIPEI SUBURBS

3

Cantonese (\$\$\$). Banquet menus on the second and third floors start at NTD1,380 per diner.

Note: you can gain free entry to the NPM Southern Branch (page 229) with a ticket stub from the Taipei NPM that's no more than three months old.

Getting there and away Most visitors ride the metro's Red Line to Shilin (from Taipei Main Station takes 11mins; NTD25) then one of the frequent #304, #255 or R30 buses to the museum (takes about 15mins; NTD15). Bus #304 goes all the way to the museum from Zhonghua Road near Ximending (takes 40mins; NTD30). A taxi from Shilin metro station shouldn't cost more than NTD200.

Shung Ye Museum of Formosan Aborigines 順益台灣原住民博物館 (282 Zhishan Rd Sec 2; ✆ 2841 2611; w www.museum.org.tw; ☺ 09.00–17.00 Tue–Sun; admission NTD150/100) Taiwan's foremost collection of indigenous artefacts is less than 200m from the NPM; if you plan to visit both museums, buy a joint ticket at either place for NTD400. English-language tours for groups and specialists can be arranged if the museum is given at least a week's notice. The core of the collection was donated by C F Lin, a Han Taiwanese businessman who over many years acquired 800-plus aboriginal artefacts, most of them from the Atayal, Paiwan and Tao tribes. The museum, which opened in 1994, now has a collection of almost 2,000 ethnological items, among them canoes from Orchid Island and finely woven clothes. One absorbing section about tattooing features tools and describes the process in detail. Men earned arm, chest and back tattoos by hunting; women were tattooed on the face or hands if they could weave well. There are also smoking pipes (several tribes grew their own tobacco), a Paiwan bronze dagger, pots in which Paiwan people believed their ancestors dwelt, and carved wooden twin-cups used by southern tribes to toast deals or seal alliances. By drinking from the same utensil, chiefs could show they trusted each other.

Chiang Kai-shek's Shilin Residence Park 士林官邸 (Shìlín Guāndǐ) (60 Fulin Rd; ☺ 09.30–noon & 13.30–17.00 Tue–Sun but often closed on national holidays; free admission to grounds, admission NTD100/50) After the Chinese Nationalists were forced to retreat to Taiwan after losing the Chinese Civil War in 1949 (page 17), Chiang appropriated or had built for himself at least 20 grand houses and villas in various parts of the island. The 9.3ha of gardens that surround this abode – the dictator's main residence in the 1960s and early 1970s – were opened to the public in 1996; the house remained off-limits until after Madame Chiang Kai-shek (1898–2003), who regarded it as her personal property, passed away. The interior is hardly palatial but you'll see the living room where the Chiangs relaxed and some of the antiques that decorated their home as well as the upstairs bedroom where the generalissimo died in 1975.

Visitor numbers are restricted so be sure to reserve a ticket in advance if you plan to come at the weekend. During the week it's usually possible to roll up and join a tour within an hour; while waiting, take a look at the Methodist chapel where the ROC's first couple often prayed.

Getting there and away It's a 10-minute walk from Shilin metro station, or you can hop on a bus from there heading to the National Palace Museum.

National Revolutionary Martyrs Shrine 忠烈祠 (Zhōngliè Cí) (139 Beian Rd; ☺ 09.00–17.00 daily except 28–29 Mar & 2–3 Sep; free admission) This

shrine, consecrated in 1969, is sacred ground for hardcore Chinese Nationalists. In architectural terms, it's cut from the same cloth as the Chiang and Sun memorial halls; it has the same kind of entrance gate as the former and a sanctuary topped with the same glazed tiles as the latter. The approach to the sanctuary is lined with ROC flags. Once there, you'll notice an ornate entranceway, the main hall (off-limits to visitors), one shrine for civilians on the right and another for soldiers on the left. More than 99% of the 400,000-plus martyrs commemorated here were military personnel, and more than three-quarters of them died fighting the Japanese during World War II. The KMT launched sporadic military operations against the communist mainland for years following their retreat to Taiwan and among those enshrined here are spies, saboteurs and reconnaissance pilots. Martyrs are listed on wooden tablets, each one carrying up to 75 names. Some died before the establishment of the ROC in anti-Qing uprisings, others perished fighting the Communists. Some of the photos are prison mugshots; at least one was taken after the firing squad had done its work. The profiles, many of which are bilingual, make for interesting reading. Memorial tablets are grouped according to era and region, but unfortunately these categories aren't labelled in English. One such section is devoted to 251 Taiwanese who died resisting Japan's 1895–1945 colonial rule of the island. If the history doesn't interest you, the hourly changing of the guard might. The slow-motion goose-stepping and rapid twirling of rifles is done with absolute and engrossing precision. These young men, who must keep their weight between 64 and 66kg, deserve the round of applause they get at the end of each ceremony.

Getting there and away Buses from Yuanshan metro station on the Red Line (from Taipei Main Station takes 6mins; NTD20) include #247 and #287 (both depart every 20mins; NTD15), which stop outside the shrine.

XINBEITOU 新北投 **(XĪN BĚITÓU)** Named Xinbeitou ('New Beitou') to distinguish it from an older neighbourhood called 'Beitou' closer to the Tamsui River, Xinbeitou is pressed up against the southwestern edge of Yangmingshan National Park. It's a geothermal hotspot: super-hot sulphur-tainted acidic water spews out of the rocks and into public pools and the bathtubs of dozens of hotels. The Ketagalan people, the lowland tribe that dominated the Taipei Basin until the 1700s, knew about and made good use of the scalding waters. They called the Beitou-Xinbeitou area Paktaaw (meaning 'witch'), which eventually morphed into today's place name. It was outsiders who understood the tourist potential of the springs: a German businessman who enjoyed a soak during an 1893 visit returned the following year to open a clubhouse. A Japanese entrepreneur followed suit in 1896.

Exploring Xinbeitou on foot is enjoyable as there's plenty of shade, not much traffic, fine mountain views and good walkways on both sides of the stream that gurgles down the hill. The sights described here can be seen in a leisurely few hours if you do a loop, proceeding up Zhongshan Road as far as Hell Valley, then returning to the metro station via Wenquan Road and Guangming Road. It's hard to get lost.

Getting there and away Take the Red Line to Beitou then change trains for Xinbeitou (about 30mins from Taipei Main Station; NTD35). Bus #230, which runs between the Yangmingshan stop and Beitou metro station, goes through Xinbeitou.

What to see and do
Ketagalan Culture Centre 凱達格蘭文化館 (3–1 Zhongshan Rd; w www. ketagalan.taipei.gov.tw; ⏰ 09.00–17.00 Tue–Sun, closed national holidays; free

admission) Cross the road in front of Xinbeitou metro station and walk towards the park, and if you follow Zhongshan Road for just over 100m, you'll see this centre on your left. Supported by the city government, it's named after the long-gone lowland tribe and hosts brief but worthwhile displays about Taiwan's aboriginal groups and temporary exhibitions of indigenous art.

Beitou Branch of Taipei City Library 台北市立圖書館北投分館 (251 Guangming Rd; ⏰ 08.30–21.00 Tue–Sat, 09.00–17.00 Sun–Mon, closed 1st Thu each month) If you were hoping to pop into this attractive wooden building across the park from the Ketagalan Cultural Centre and browse magazines in frigid comfort, you might be disappointed. There's very little air conditioning because the library is one of Taiwan's most energy-efficient buildings and has won prizes for sustainable design. Large windows let natural light and breezes in; the roof collects rainwater for flushing toilets and watering plants. Nevertheless, it isn't as green as it could be; the timber was shipped all the way from North America. Note, too, that there are no bike racks due to the library's park location, where these are banned. As in all Taiwanese libraries, you'll find quite a few English-language books mixed in with Chinese titles.

Beitou Hot Springs Museum 北投溫泉博物館 (2 Zhongshan Rd; ✆ 2893 9981; ⏰ 09.00–17.00 Tue–Sun, closed national holidays; free admission) Continue walking along Zhongshan Road to find this small museum, a 1913 replica of one of Japan's most famous bathhouses. The displays inside include lots of geological information about Taiwan's natural spas, and the original bathing pool can be seen downstairs, though no-one has soaked here for decades. The columns and arches are akin to those in a Turkish bath, but the stained-glass windows come as a surprise. Just up the road there's an open-air bath that's still in use: **Beitou Public Hot Spring aka Millennium Hot Spring** (6 Zhongshan Rd; ⏰ 05.30–22.00 daily; closes briefly for cleaning every 2hrs; admission NTD40), where bathers are required to wear swimsuits and shower caps.

Hell Valley aka Thermal Valley 地熱谷 *(Dìrè Gǔ)* (⏰ 09.00–17.00 Tue–Sun; free admission) About 300m beyond Millennium Hot Spring is one of Taipei's most impressive natural sights, a cloudy blue-green pond that emits dense miasmas of steam. The fence is there to stop people getting too close, as falling in would probably be fatal – the water temperature is seldom lower than 90°C. There's no mention of hell in the Chinese place name, which means simply 'geothermal gully'.

Puji Temple 普濟寺 (112 Wenquan Rd; ⏰ 08.00–17.00 daily) This exquisite Japanese-style temple is obscured by trees and accessed via stone steps. The gate near the road is to keep out stray dogs; human visitors are welcome to tour the grounds but shouldn't enter the shrine itself, which is dedicated to Guanyin. The temple was founded in 1905 by the Shingon sect, a form of Japanese Buddhism. The current structure, a picture of grace, dates from the early 1930s. The frame and walls are juniper; the roof is hip-and-gable style. Among those memorialised here are colonial-era railway workers who died in the line of duty.

Longnai Hot Springs 瀧乃湯 (244 Guangming Rd; ⏰ 06.30–21.00 Thu–Tue; admission NTD150) Almost lost amid much taller and newer buildings, Longnai (sometimes styled 'Longnice') offers a thoroughly traditional bathing experience.

There are two pools inside this slightly decrepit pre-World War II bungalow, one for each gender, plus a private room where two people can soak in privacy for an hour for NTD400. No swimsuits are needed but you should have your own towel. The water temperature is usually 41–46°C. From Longnai, it's less than 500m back to Xinbeitou metro station.

NANGANG 南港
Museum of the Institute of History and Philology 歷史文物陳列館 (130 Academia Rd Sec 2; ✆ 2652 3180; w museum.sinica.edu.tw; ⏰ 09.30–16.30 Wed & Sat–Sun; free admission) The small but excellent MIHP is on the campus of Academia Sinica, Taiwan's national academy and the country's leading research establishment in several fields. The collection here includes Koxinga-era maps and memorials relating to Taiwan, as well as early paintings of indigenous people. Even if you've no great interest in China, you'll find intriguing the truly ancient oracle bones, the 2,000-year-old letters, reports and weather records written on bamboo slips by soldiers and officials posted to the empire's northwest, and the various skulls and weapons.

If you've made the trek out to this corner of Taipei, you may want to also visit the **Museum of the Institute of Ethnology** (✆ 2652 3303; w www.ioe.sinica.edu.tw; ⏰ 09.30–16.30 Wed & Sat–Sun; free admission). It's next door to the MIHP and engrossing for aficionados of indigenous culture.

Getting there and away Take the Blue Line to Nangang metro station (18mins from Taipei Main Station; NTD30) then bus #212, #270 or Blue 25 (frequent departures; takes 15mins; NTD15). Get off when you see on your left the Latin words 'Academia Sinica'. Bilingual signs will guide you around the campus.

MUZHA 木柵
Taipei Zoo 臺北市立動物園 (w english.zoo.gov.taipei; ⏰ 09.00–17.00 daily except Lunar New Year's Eve, indoor areas close some Mon; admission NTD60/30) This zoo has some of Taiwan's best-known animals, including Formosan black bears, and a superb insectarium. Children adore the place and for nature-focused adults it's very worthwhile. To get there, take the Brown Line to Taipei Zoo metro station (from Taipei Main Station takes 26mins; NTD35).

Maokong Gondola 動物園站水舞區 (w english.gondola.taipei; ⏰ 09.00–21.00 Tue–Sun; NTD120/50 one-way) This highly recommended 4.03km-long cable-car journey takes 25 minutes one-way and, in good weather, the views are excellent; in bad weather (such as when typhoons are in the vicinity) service is suspended. Passengers board near Taipei Zoo's ticket office and the second of the four stations is inside the zoo. The final stop, Maokong, is 299m above sea level and in the heart of one of Taiwan's oldest tea-growing areas. As well as dozens of places where you can enjoy tea and snacks, there are short hiking trails. You can get maps of the vicinity from the visitor information centres at both terminus stations. Gondola riders can save money by using an EasyCard (see box, page 54) or a Taipei Fun Pass (see box, page 86).

YANGMINGSHAN NATIONAL PARK 陽明山國家公園 (YÁNGMÍNGSHĀN GUÓJIĀ GŌNGYUÁN)

If you've seen Taiwan's Central Mountain Range, the hills and dormant volcanoes of this 11,455ha national park – almost equally divided between the cities of Taipei and New Taipei – are unlikely to leave you gasping in awe. However, if you're here for birds, butterflies and half-day hikes you'll certainly enjoy the park. Twitchers have a good chance of ticking off one of Taiwan's endemic species, the Taiwan blue magpie (*Urocissa caerulea*). Lepidopterologists, if they come in late spring, will have a field day with the park's 150-plus butterfly species.

Because of its proximity to Taipei, convenient public transport and user-friendly bilingual signage, parts of the park get overrun at weekends. Midweek you'll still meet plenty of hikers, but there's an upside to this – you needn't worry about getting lost or stranded. During the colder months, many Taiwanese drive up so they can enjoy the park's hot springs. Each year, usually from late February, there's a month-long flower festival.

Yangmingshan's original name was Grass Mountain, a reference to the tall grasses that cover many of the slopes and summits. After World War II it was renamed in honour of Wang Yang-ming (1472–1529), a Confucianist philosopher.

GETTING THERE, AWAY AND AROUND
By bus The two main services to Yangmingshan Bus Terminal are #230 from Beitou metro station (departs every 30mins before 17.00, every 45mins after 17.00; ⊕ 05.30–22.35 daily; takes 30mins; NTD15) and #260 (departs every 15–20mins, less often after 19.00; ⊕ 05.40–22.30 daily; takes at least 35mins; NTD30) from Taipei Main Station via Jiantan metro station. There's also the Red 5 from Jiantan metro station (departs every 5–15mins; ⊕ 05.30–00.40 daily; takes 25mins; NTD15). On all routes, the first bus of the day is often packed with retirees going hiking, and at weekends you'll probably have to queue for a spot on a bus heading back to the city. To get to Xiaoyoukeng and Lengshuikeng and other points of interest use Leisure Bus #108 (departs every 30mins; ⊕ 07.00–17.30 daily; NTD15), while to see a good amount of the park without having to do any walking, take bus #1717 all the way to Jinshan (departs hourly; ⊕ 06.00–18.45 daily; takes 1¼hrs; NTD145) from where you can explore the north coast (page 135). Convenient boarding spots are near NTU Hospital metro station and Taipei Fine Arts Museum.

By car, motorcycle or bicycle From Taipei, there's no practical alternative to Highway 2A. Before driving into the park, call the tourist hotline (✆ 0800 011 765) to find out if traffic controls are in place because of festivals or other special events. On weekdays, parking near the main attractions isn't difficult but at the weekend it can get crowded.

TOURIST INFORMATION The main visitor centre (✆ 2861 5741; ⊕ 08.30–16.30 daily, closed last Mon each month), 10 minutes' walk from Yangmingshan Bus Terminal, dispenses bilingual maps, leaflets and advice. For more information, visit the national park website (w english.ymsnp.gov.tw).

WHAT TO SEE AND DO Hikers should be properly prepared in terms of footwear, clothing, snacks and water.

Grass Mountain Chateau 草山行館 (Cǎoshān Xíng Guǎn) (89 Hudi Rd; ✆ 2862 2404; w www.grassmountainchateau.com.tw; ⊕ 10.00–17.00 Tue–Sun; admission NTD30) Yet another of Chiang Kai-shek's hideaways, this single-storey chateau was built in 1920 by a Japanese sugar corporation. Three years later, Crown Prince Hirohito (later Japan's emperor) spent a few hours here during a tour of Taiwan. The original chateau was destroyed by arson in 2007 but the replica is faithful in

every detail and incorporates stones and timbers retrieved from the ruins. The four adjacent buildings, which used to house Chiang's bodyguards and assistants, are occasionally open for exhibitions. The restaurant (⏰ 11.00–17.00 Tue–Sun; EM; $$$$) commands magnificent views and offers Taiwanese set meals for around NTD400, as well as waffles, teas and other treats.

Getting there and away Walking here from Yangmingshan bus station takes about 20 minutes and it's level most of the way. Take Hushan Road rather than the highway towards Jinshan. The Small 8 and Small 9 minibuses (both depart about every 40mins; NTD15) shuttle between Zhuzihu 竹子湖 and the Red Line's Shipai and Beitou metro stations.

Seven Stars Mountain 七星山 (Qīxīngshān)
The tallest point within the park, the 1,120m-high peak of Seven Stars Mountain is a fine spot from which to gaze over Taipei City and the mouth of the Tamsui River. The ascent begins at the park's main visitor centre. No map is required – all you need are reasonably strong legs. Allow 4 hours to reach the top, take in the spectacular view and make your way down. Energetic hikers can continue northwest to Xiaoyoukeng or eastward to Lengshuikeng. Both descents take no more than an hour.

Xiaoyoukeng 小油坑
The fumaroles of Xiaoyoukeng have been spewing steam and sulphur for millennia, staining the land yellow-green and creating the park's single most striking sight. As long ago as the early 16th century, Ketagalan indigenous people were mining the sulphur and bartering it with Han Chinese merchants. If you take a #1717 bus (see opposite), you'll see the main vent on your right. Hikers coming from Seven Stars Mountain often use this bus service to get back to Taipei.

Lengshuikeng Public Hot Springs 冷水坑溫泉
(⏰ 09.00–17.00 daily; free admission) Lengshuikeng means 'cool water hole' and it's true that the water here doesn't scald like some other natural spas and, at approximately 40°C, it's a pleasant temperature for bathing after a hike. The sulphur content is very high, hence the water's milky appearance. There is a pool for each gender; swimsuits aren't required. If you're travelling on bus #1717 you'll need to walk 1.7km from Highway 2A; the side road is clearly signposted. There's paid parking very close to the hot springs.

UPDATES WEBSITE

You can post your comments and recommendations, and read feedback and updates from other readers online at **w** bradtupdates.com/taiwan.

4

North Taiwan

Most international visitors fly into Taoyuan and head directly to Taipei or other parts of the country, bypassing a region that deserves at least three days in any two-week itinerary. For our purposes, north Taiwan consists of the two vast and rapidly growing municipalities of New Taipei (land area: 2,053km²; population a shade below four million) and Taoyuan (1,221km²; population approaching 2.2 million), the harbour city of Keelung City (133km²; 371,000 people) and Yilan County (2,143km²; 457,000 people).

New Taipei encircles the capital and is a microcosm of Taiwan, with densely populated urban areas, the historic districts of Tamsui and Sanxi, steep uplands dotted with tiny aboriginal villages and everything in between. The lowland portion of Taoyuan is heavily industrialised while the inland half boasts the attractive old town of Daxi, indigenous villages and scenery that's more than pleasing. Yilan, by contrast, was largely spared in the small-factory revolution that powered Taiwan's economic miracle but damaged its environment, and remains home to the indigenous enclave of Wulai. The rugged north and northeast coasts abound in memorable landscapes, although gritty yet historic Keelung is the kind of city you'll either love or hate.

The region is also home to the beautiful but little-used North Cross-Island Highway that links Yilan with Taoyuan; this mountain route, certainly one of north Taiwan's highlights, deserves to be taken slowly.

TAOYUAN 桃園 (TÁOYUÁN) *Telephone code 03*

It's hard to picture Taoyuan as an orchard full of blossoming peach trees, but that's how this manufacturing centre looked two centuries ago, hence its bucolic name: *táo* (peach) *yuán* (garden). The pioneers who settled hereabouts in the late 1700s dubbed it Humaozhuang, meaning 'the terrace covered by plants with leaves as sharp as tigers' teeth'. They cleared the land to grow rice, vegetables and – of course – peaches. Since World War II, however, agriculture has taken a back seat to car-making and electronics, and there's no compelling reason for travellers heading to or emerging from the airport to get embroiled in central Taoyuan or neighbouring Zhongli 中壢 unless they're using TRA services to get to their next destination. Those planning to drive across the North Cross-Island Highway may well prefer to stay on the freeway and follow the signs to Daxi.

GETTING THERE AND AWAY For details on how to get to Taoyuan from the airport, see page 44.

By car Central Taoyuan is 25km southwest of Taipei and 141km northeast of Taichung, best accessed by Freeway 1.

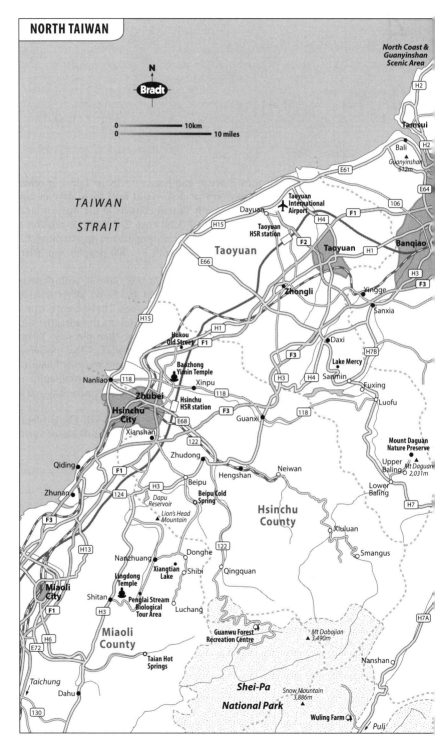

NORTH TAIWAN

N
Bradt

0 ————— 10km
0 ————— 10 miles

North Coast &
Guanyinshan
Scenic Area

*TAIWAN
STRAIT*

Tamsui

Bali
*Guanyinshan
612m*

Taoyuan
International
Airport

Dayuan

Taoyuan
HSR station

Taoyuan

Banqiao

Zhongli

Yingge

Sanxia

Hukou
Old Street

Daxi

Baozhong
Yimin Temple

Lake Mercy

Nanliao

Xinpu

Sanmin

Fuxing

Zhubei

Luofu

Hsinchu
City

Hsinchu
HSR station

Xianshan

Guanxi

Mount Daguan
Nature Preserve

Upper
Baling   *Mt Daguan
2,031m*

Qiding

Zhudong

Neiwan

Lower
Baling

Zhunan

Beipu

Hengshan

Xiuluan

*Dapu
Reservoir*

Beipu Cold
Spring

Hsinchu
County

Smangus

*Lion's Head
Mountain*

Nanzhuang

Donghe

Qingquan

Lingdong
Temple

Xiangtian
Lake   Shibi

Miaoli
City

Shitan

Penglai Stream
Biological
Tour Area

Luchang

Taichung

Miaoli
County

Guanwu Forest
Recreation Centre

*Mt Dabajian
3,490m*

Nanshan

Taian Hot
Springs

Dahu

Shei-Pa
National Park

*Snow Mountain
3,886m*

Wuling Farm

Puli

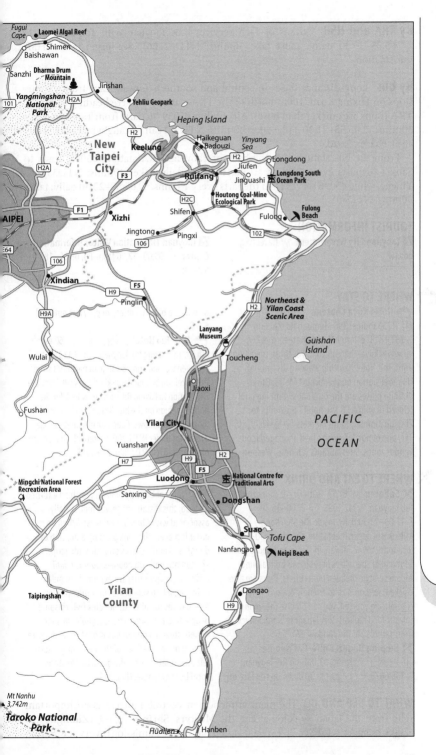

115

By TRA and HSR Dozens of TRA services link Taoyuan with Taipei (departs ⊕ 05.35–23.30 daily; most take 36mins; NTD42–66). See page 44 for HSR information.

By bus Long-distance buses to central and southern Taiwan leave from various stops on Fuxing Road, 100m north of the TRA station. If you're heading to Taipei, TRA trains are quicker than buses. Airport bus #5059 (departs from Taoyuan every 30mins; ⊕ 05.55–21.30 daily; takes 40mins; NTD53) can be caught by Hotel Today at 81 Fuxing Road.

From the bus station near the back of Taoyuan TRA station, #5005 heads to Sanxia (departs every 20mins; ⊕ 06.10–22.30 daily; takes 40mins; NTD35) via Yingge, while #5096 serves Daxi (departs every 15mins; ⊕ 05.50–22.30 daily; takes 30mins; NTD40).

TOURIST INFORMATION

🛈 Taoyuan City Government w travel.tycg. gov.tw

🛈 Taoyuan TRA Station Visitor Information Center ⊕ 09.00–17.00 Mon–Fri, 08.00–18.00 Sat–Sun

🏠 WHERE TO STAY

🏠 Hotel Kuva Chateau 古華花園飯店 (255 rooms) 398 Minquan Rd, Zhongli; ✆ 281 1818; e hotel@kuva-chateau.com.tw; w www.kuva-chateau.com. For those travelling light, this hotel is within walking distance of Huanbei station on the Airport Metro. Other definite pluses are the outdoor swimming pool (closed in winter) & the hotel's proximity to Zhongli Xinming Night Markets 中壢新明夜市, one of north Taiwan's best-managed food-vendor zones. 3 restaurants (Chinese, Western & Thai) & a bakery/coffee shop. B/fast optional. **$$$**

🏠 Hsin Tao Hotel 欣桃大旅社 (60 rooms) 8th Flr, 180 Fuxing Rd, Taoyuan; ✆ 333 1131. Smack between the Shinkong & Tonlin department stores, this hotel can be found quickly if you walk from the TRA station to Fuxing Rd; turn left & look for the hotel sign high on the bldg's side. It's clean but few rooms have windows. Couples can sometimes get a room for under NTD1,200 & rooms sleeping 4 can often be had for NTD1,800. Wi-Fi. **$$**

✕ WHERE TO EAT AND DRINK

✕ Saboten 勝博殿 10th Flr, 19 Zhongzheng Rd, Taoyuan; ✆ 332 1088; ⊕ 11.00–15.30 & 17.00–21.30 daily. Inside the Shin Kong Mitsukoshi department store, this chain (30+ locations around Taiwan, inc Taoyuan Airport Terminal 2) specialises in set meals built around Japanese-style breaded pork cutlets. There are also chicken, salmon & child-friendly options. Before committing yourself, you can browse the *sampuru* (plastic food replicas; this Japanese word derives from 'sample') in the window. EM. **$$$**

✕ Beiping Dagezi Knife-Cut Noodles 北平大個子刀削麵 7 Datong Rd, Taoyuan; ✆ 335 6678; ⊕ 11.00–20.30 daily. On the face of it just another brightly lit eatery with a TV turned up loud, this restaurant serves food usually associated with China's northwest. When an order is placed, the cook picks up a big slab of dough & skilfully carves off inch-wide strips. The tomato pork-rib noodles (*fānqié páigǔ miàn* 番茄排骨麵) are extremely popular. Help yourself to side dishes of tofu or pickles. Alternatives to knife-cut noodles (which some people find too hard to be enjoyable) include ramen, steamed dumplings & beef soup. If you're coming out of the front of the TRA station, turn left immediately after the department store. Local beer available. No EM. **$$**

WHAT TO SEE AND DO The main attraction in central Taoyuan is an important relic from the Japanese colonial era: the **Martyrs' Shrine** 忠烈祠 (**Zhōngliè Cí**) (200 Chenggong Rd Sec 2; ⊕ 09.00–17.00 daily; free admission). Very few Shinto places of worship survived Nationalist rule and this is certainly the largest and most accessible. Information boards explain the functions of the buildings and the meanings of the statues. Completed by the Japanese in 1938 as a temple worshipping Amaterasu, the mythical ancestress of Japan's royal family, it also honoured Prince Yoshihisa Kitashirakawa, the imperial relative who died of malaria while leading Japan's 1895 takeover. Made largely of cypress, the structure is classically Japanese in that it reflects the strong cultural influence on Japan of China's Tang Dynasty. During the 1970s it was the subject of a long dispute between preservationists and those who wanted it demolished because they saw it as a hated reminder of Japanese rule. The compromise eventually reached saw the buildings saved but converted into a shrine for heroes from Taiwan's past. Koxinga is here, as are Liu Yong-fu (the second and final president of the Republic of Taiwan in 1895; page 14) and Qiu Feng-jia, who led local soldiers against the Japanese. Every 29 March there's a memorial ceremony, and for the other 364 days it's a place where people go to stroll among cherry trees and enjoy views over the city. To get here, take bus L101 (departs from 99 Fuxing Rd every 20mins/60mins on weekdays/weekends; NTD18) and get off about 10 minutes later at the hospital. Follow the road as it curves uphill and very soon you'll see a broad stairway on the right.

SANXIA 三峽 AND YINGGE 鶯歌 *Telephone code 02*

Twin towns separated by the Dahan River, Sanxia (population: 116,000) and Yingge (population: 86,000) are associated, respectively, with traditional architecture and ceramics. Sanxia means 'three gorges', but if you arrive on a clear day it's the nearby mountains rather than the narrow streams that will impress you. An abundance of natural resources – camphor, coal, tea and timber – powered the town's growth; indigo dyeing was a major industry, thanks to abundances of clean water and *Goldfussia formosanus*, a wild plant from which the dye was extracted. By 1930, however, trains and lorries had replaced riverboats as the main means of shifting goods around north Taiwan and Sanxia was soon eclipsed by upstart towns like Taoyuan.

Yingge is to Taiwan what Stoke-on-Trent used to be to England: the home of the pottery industry. Today, however, most of the pottery produced here is decorative rather than practical, so tourists come here in search of elegant teapots and other souvenirs.

GETTING THERE AND AWAY
By TRA Yingge is well served by trains, which from Taipei takes under half an hour (NTD31–37) and from Taoyuan less than 10 minutes (NTD15–18).

By bus Options to Sanxia include the #908 (departs every 8–20mins; ⏰ 06.00–22.00 daily; takes 40mins; NTD30) to/from Jingan metro station on Taipei's Orange and Circular lines, and the #916 (departs every 6–20mins; ⏰ 06.00–23.30 daily; takes 45mins; NTD30) to/from Yongning metro station on the Blue Line.

From Taoyuan, bus #5005 (departs every 20mins; ⏰ 06.10–21.30 daily) follows a winding route to Sanxia (takes 40mins; NTD35) with stops en route very near Yingge Ceramics Old Street, Yingge TRA station and the ceramics museum.

By car or motorcycle Self-drivers should take Freeway 3 to the Sanxia–Yingge exit at km5, from where it's just over 1km to the centre of Sanxia's Zushi Temple and slightly further to Yingge Ceramics Museum. If you're bound for the east coast, follow the signs from Sanxia to Dapu and then Sanmin. This road, Highway 7B, joins up with the North Cross-Island Highway near Sanmin.

✗ **WHERE TO EAT AND DRINK** Sanxia's signature *niújiǎo bāo* 牛角包 – chewy croissants that come in various flavours including adzuki bean, chocolate, coffee, and pineapple – are sold by bakeries near Zushi Temple.

WHAT TO SEE AND DO Finding your way around Sanxia is a cinch thanks to bilingual map boards and signposts. If you've come by car, look for somewhere to park before you reach the town centre, then tackle the sights in the following order.

Sanxia Historical Relics Hall 三峽歷史文物館 (18 Zhongshan Rd; ⏰ 09.00–17.00 Tue–Sun; free admission) This small museum (which at the time of writing lacked English-language labelling) displays a model of the low-tech, labour-intensive process by which camphor trunks were cut up and heated to produce an oil prized for its medicinal and insect-repelling properties. Upstairs, there are intriguing photos of the town as it used to look.

Zushi Temple 祖師廟 (Zǔshī Miào) (⏰ 04.00–23.00 daily) The shrine that many regard as the very pinnacle of religious art in Taiwan is, you may think at first, grossly overrated. Patches of crudely painted concrete are visible, as is messy wiring. But if you go over the wood and stone carvings column by column and inch by inch, you'll be won over. In addition to the usual dragons and sages, there are crabs and other crustaceans, fish, owls, pangolins, elephants and a whole orchestra of musicians. The gold-leaf-bedecked ceiling of the central chamber, where incense is offered to Zushi, is breathtakingly ornate. Meaning 'divine progenitor', Zushi is the godly name of Chen Zhaoying, a 13th-century government official honoured for his bravery at a time when the Mongols were invading China. The temple was established in 1769, flattened during fighting between Japanese forces and Taiwanese militia in 1895, then rebuilt in 1899. A major renovation effort was begun in 1947 under the supervision of Li Mei-shu (1902–83), a local politician and acclaimed painter, but since his death progress has stalled and cheaper contractors employed.

Sanjiaoyong Street 三角湧老街 (Sānjiǎoyǒng Lǎo Jiē) Sanxia's oldest thoroughfare and former business hub has been reborn as a touristy 'old street' and reverted to its pre-1945 name. By far the largest building on the 260m-long street is a hangar-like temple, but it's the redbrick Baroque-style shop-houses that catch the eye. Several of them are more than a century old, although the street's distinctive look didn't appear until around 1915, when the colonial authorities ordered gutters to be added for reasons of public health. The declared doctrine of the 2004–06 renovation was 'original architecture, original materials', which meant firing hundreds of mud bricks for internal partitions and straightening sagging roofs. However, residents were permitted to build additional floors so long as façades were preserved and the classical appearance of the street maintained. Embellishments of vases (a symbol of peace – in both Mandarin and Taiwanese the word for vase sounds similar to the word for peace), lotuses, dragons and lions were redone. The street and the alleyways that lead off it have been paved with chiselled (rather than machined) granite slabs, and even unavoidable modern features such as manhole covers and house numbers have been made to look as traditional as possible.

Yingge Ceramics production in Yingge is said to have started in 1804 thanks to a favourable combination of local clay, plentiful wood and the arrival of a master potter from south China. Unable to compete with low-wage countries, Taiwan's potters now focus on upmarket decorative items. Those wanting to purchase some to take home will want to head to **Yingge Ceramics Old Street** 陶瓷老街 (shops ⏰ approx 10.00–20.00 daily) on the northern side of the Dahan River near Yingge TRA station. Although the street isn't especially old, it is a good place to pick up teapots and other fragile souvenirs. Elsewhere, the bleak but highly rated **Yingge Ceramics Museum** 鶯歌陶瓷博物館 (**Yīnggē Táocí Bówùguǎn**) (200 Wenhua Rd; ✆ 8677 2727; w ceramics.ntpc.gov.tw; ⏰ 09.30–17.00 Mon–Fri, 09.30–18.00 Sat–Sun, closed 1st Mon each month; admission NTD80) covers everything from the production of roof tiles in 17th-century Taiwan and ceramic art to the use of ceramics in electronics and medicine. The English wording outside the museum is tiny, so keep your eyes peeled if you're driving or approaching by bus.

WULAI 烏來 (WULÁI) *Telephone code 02*

Wulai covers more land than Taipei City, but because over 90% of the district is mountainous it has just 6,300 residents. A third are Atayal (alternative spellings of Wulai, such as Urai and Ulay, are closer to the indigenous pronunciation than the current place name) and their culture is evident in the restaurants that line Wulai's main street, as well as in the small tribal museum.

Wulai's hillsides are covered by mixed forest and drained by boulder-filled azure creeks. For reasons of safety and hygiene, the free hot-spring pools beside the river were demolished a few years ago. Since then, enterprising soakers have gone upriver and moved rocks and gravel to create new pools – the waters are colourless and don't have a strong smell – although these disappear after heavy rains and those who use them could, in theory, face hefty fines if the authorities decided to crack down. In addition to the springs, there are excellent opportunities for ecotourism as Wulai is one of the best year-round butterflying areas in north Taiwan and birdwatchers will find plenty of reasons to twitch.

GETTING THERE AND AWAY
By car or motorcycle Self drivers should take Highway 9A from Xindian, but note that headlights must be kept on beyond Xindian.

By public transport Take the Taipei Metro Green Line to Xindian (takes 22mins from Taipei Main Station; NTD30) then board bus #849 (4–6 departures per hr; ⏰ 05.30–21.40 daily; takes 30mins; NTD30) to the busiest part of Wulai. If you'd rather not travel below the streets, you can also board #849 at Taipei Main Station or the Chiang Kai-shek Memorial Hall.

TOURIST INFORMATION
There are visitor information centres at Xindian metro station, in Wulai Village and at Wulai Waterfall (all ⏰ 09.00–17.30 daily).

WHERE TO STAY AND EAT
In addition to the following, mid-range hotels and typical Taiwanese eateries can be found in and around the main village.

🏠 **Volando Urai Spring Spa & Resort** 馥蘭 朵烏來渡假酒店 (23 rooms) 176 Xinwu Rd Sec 5; ✆ 2661 6555; e fo@volandourai.com. tw; w volandospringpark.com. Slate, granite & some delicate examples of Atayal weaving lend this place an air of quiet refinement. Staying here isn't cheap by any standards – during the peak winter season the smallest suite will set you back NTD16,000 & you may want to spend a little more for 'Grand View' rooms that are both grand & perfectly positioned for views over the river. Inc b/fast, a gourmet dinner & afternoon tea. No under-12s. Coming from Taipei, the Spring Park is on the right 1km before Wutai's main village, just past the 13km marker on Highway 9A. Free shuttle buses pick up guests from Xindian metro station if booked beforehand. $$$$$

✖ **Atayal Grandma** 泰雅婆婆美食店 14 Wulai St; 📞 2661 6371; ⊕ 10.00–21.00 daily. Located beside Wulai Atayal Museum – look for this restaurant's bamboo-bedecked walls – this is the best known of Wulai's indigenous eateries thanks to local & international media coverage; Andrew Zimmern is among those who has eaten here. Like many of the restaurants around here, seasoned rice in a bamboo tube (*zhú tǒng fàn* 竹筒飯) is a popular offering. Mountain boar (*shān zhū ròu* 山豬) can be quite delicious, while vegetable options include bamboo shoots & yams. If you're brave enough, order a portion of *damamian* 的麼面 – a mixture of raw pork, rice & salt that's been fermented in a jar for 2 weeks at room temperature. If you don't want a meal, at least try the millet- &/or maqaw-flavoured ice creams. No EM, but some English understood. $$

WHAT TO SEE AND DO If nature takes priority over hot springs, ask at the visitor centre about hiking and birding trails.

Wulai Atayal Museum 烏來泰雅民族博物館 (12 Wulai St; 📞 2661 8162; w atayal.ntpc.gov.tw; ⊕ 09.30–17.00 daily, closed 1st Mon every month; free admission)

In addition to clothes, tools and model houses, this museum offers bilingual displays that touch on local indigenous history, religion, festivals and ecological practices – all of which are endangered in Wulai, in large part because outsiders dominate the local tourist trade. If you've arrived by bus, the museum is on the main street on the right-hand side of the road. Look for the huge carved face above the entrance.

Wulai Waterfall 烏來瀑布

Some 80m from top to bottom, this is the highest waterfall in north Taiwan and pretty if not breathtaking. Getting here is a 25-minute walk from Wulai's main street, or a 1.6km, 6-minute ride on the mini-train, or 'log cart' as bilingual signs refer to it; departures are according to demand (⊕ 09.00–17.00 daily; NTD50 one-way).

Neidong Forest Recreation Area 內洞森林遊樂區 (w recreation.forest.gov.tw/RA_E/RA_03.html; ⊕ 08.00–17.00 daily; admission NTD65/40 Mon–Fri, NTD80/40 Sat–Sun)

If you walk upstream beyond Wulai Waterfall, after around 45 minutes you'll come to this 1,191ha forest recreation area. The falls here are lower but prettier than Wulai's main cascade. On the easy-to-follow hiking trails, the longest of which is 2.2km, you may spot creatures such as the endemic Meintein tree frog (*Kurixalus idiootocus*) as well as lots of interesting insects and birds. Flora includes wild ginger and begonias.

Fushan 福山

This tiny village marks the end of the paved road and the starting point of three hiking trails. The 2.4km **Kalamoji Trail** 卡拉莫基步道 will bring you to the entrance of the much longer **Hapen Ancient Trail** 哈盆古道, which is part of a centuries-old path that once connected Atayal communities in Greater Taipei with tribe members in Yilan. A footbridge just below the village leads to the 17.5km **Fuba Cross-Ridge National Trail** 福巴越嶺國家步道, so named because it connects Fushan with Upper Baling in Taoyuan (page 123). At the time of writing, both Hapen and Fuba trails were closed due to typhoon damage, so check their status and permit requirements (call the tourist information hotline ❧0800 011 765) well before venturing deep into the mountains.

There's no public transport to Fushan; a taxi one-way from the bus stop at Wulai costs a fixed NTD600. Don't depend on being able to get supplies or a meal in Fushan.

NORTH CROSS-ISLAND HIGHWAY 北橫公路 *Telephone code 03*

Inland of Daxi, Highway 7 – known as the North Cross-Island Highway – heads eastwards through the indigenous settlements of Fuxing District towards Yilan County. While not as breathtaking as its equivalents in central Taiwan and the south, it's at least reliably open and a very pleasant way to approach the northeast.

GETTING THERE AND AROUND

By bus There are several options, but none travel the length of the North Cross-Island Highway. From Yongning metro station on Taipei's Blue Line, the #710 (departs every 40mins; ⊕ 06.50–22.00 daily; takes 25mins; NTD77) will take you very close to Daxi's old streets. Service #5096 connects Daxi with the bus station behind Taoyuan TRA station (departs every 15mins; ⊕ 05.50–21.50 daily; takes 30mins; NTD40).

Buses going inland of Daxi will stop at Lake Mercy if you tell the driver when boarding; #5104 connects Daxi with Fuxing (7 departures daily; ⊕ 06.40–21.15; takes 45mins; NTD49). The less frequent #5093, #5105 and #5106 also serve Lake Mercy and Fuxing.

The only buses that get close to Lalashan/Mount Daguan are the #5090 (departs from Taoyuan at 06.50 only; takes at least 2hrs; NTD194) and the #5091 (departs from Zhongli at 10.35 only; takes 2hrs; NTD192). From the final stop you'll still need to walk for more than 20 minutes to the nature reserve. Both buses go via Daxi, Lake Mercy and Fuxing.

By car or motorcycle Take Freeway 3 to the Daxi exit at km62. Motorcyclists should take Highway 4 from Sanxia or Highway 3 if you're approaching from the south.

TOURIST INFORMATION

🛈 **Taoyuan City Government** w travel.tycg. gov.tw

🛈 **Cihu Visitor Centre** Cihu car park; ⊕ 09.00–17.00 daily. Offers information & answers questions about the entire region.

WHERE TO STAY AND EAT Because the local water is thought to be ideal for tofu production, Daxi has become synonymous with *dòu gān*, firm dried tofu that's been braised in a blend of soy sauce, star anise, cumin and other ingredients. If you need supplies for the mountains, buy a packet or two of *dòu gān* to nibble on while hiking; there are spicy and other variants. If you have time, try some freshly braised, piping-hot artisanal *dòu gān* at one of the shops in Daxi's old quarter. Carrying supplies is a very good idea as beyond Fuxing you'll struggle to find a hot meal.

🏠 **Ming Chi Shan Zhuang** 明池山莊 (111 rooms) km68 Hwy 7; ❧989 4104; w makauy.lealeahotel.com. Across the road from Mingchi National Forest Recreation Area (to which guests get free entry), the accommodation here is in wood cabins & rooms in the main bldg. The former are nicer than the latter but getting to some of them involves more than a few steps. Rooms & suites for 2, 4 or 8 ppl; midweek a couple will pay around NTD4,200 for a room,

4

b/fast & dinner. Meals can also be ordered à la carte. **$$$$**

🏠 **Fuhsing Youth Activity Centre** (57 rooms) Fuxing Vlg; ☏ 382 2276; e service-fsyac@cyc.tw; w fuhsing.cyh.org.tw. There's no missing this place, the largest building in Fuxing situated at the end of a road chock-a-block with eateries. The centre has relatively few rooms for couples & tends to fill up with school groups at w/ends & throughout summer. The VIP rooms on the corner (NTD6,000) have spectacular views over the valley but some might feel the wall-to-ceiling windows don't provide enough privacy. Room rates are 20% lower on w/days. English spoken & b/fast inc. There are superb views over the river from the restaurant-coffee shop (🕑 07.00–22.00 daily; EM; **$$**). **$$$**

WHAT TO SEE AND DO This section assumes visitors are starting from Daxi, with sights covered from west to east.

Daxi 大溪 A major inland port shipping tea and camphor throughout the Qing era, Daxi (literally 'big stream') hasn't been the same since the construction of a nearby dam in the 1960s left the Dahan River barely deep enough for a kayak. Goods now arrive and leave in lorries rather than boats, but the town's old quarter still reflects the good old days. Before World War II, **Heping Road** 和平路 was known as Lower Street and **Zhongyang Road** 中央路 was Upper Street. Together they formed the business hub of the town and its hinterland, and the century-old Baroque-style merchant houses along these roads incorporate Greek, Roman and Taiwanese elements. You're unlikely to find much that's truly traditional beneath the redbrick archways; the dried-tofu shops perhaps come closest. If you continue to where Heping Road makes a 90-degree turn, you'll get good views of the river and the stone steps up which stevedores used to lug cargo.

A few hundred metres to the south, in **Zhongzheng Park**, there's a 1950s building in which Chiang Kai-shek occasionally stayed; it should be open to the public as a restaurant/display space by the time you read this. Elsewhere in the park there's a statue of Chiang riding a horse.

Lake Mercy 慈湖 **(Cíhú)** Chiang Kai-shek adored the scenery just inland of Daxi because it reminded him of his hometown on the Chinese mainland. However, it was more than just a holiday retreat – the generalissimo had it fitted out as an emergency command centre from which he could direct operations against Mao's Communists. Just inland of km6 on Highway 7, park your vehicle (NTD50 for cars, NTD20 for motorcycles) or get off the bus at what's variously called **Cihu Park**, **Cihu Sculpture Memorial Park** or **Chiang Kai-shek Statue Park** 慈湖蔣公銅像公園 (🕑 08.00–17.00 daily; free admission). This repository displays more than 200 Chiang Kai-shek statues 'donated' ('discarded' would be a more accurate word) by various cities and towns. Just two decades ago almost every campus and park in Taiwan had a bronze, stone or cement representation of Chiang; districts run by the Democratic Progressive Party were the first to remove these relics of the dictator. Chiang is joined by two-dozen statues of Sun Yat-sen (see box, page 103) and two of Chiang Ching-kuo (page 18). Many of the statues have been painted shades of blue or brown – purely for aesthetic reasons, it seems.

From the statue collection, it's a delightful 800m walk to **Cihu Mausoleum** 慈湖陵寢 (🕑 09.00–17.00 Wed–Mon; free admission to the grounds) where Chiang Kai-shek's remains still lie in state. At the time of writing, there seemed little impetus to give him a permanent burial – something he said shouldn't happen until China is unified under a non-communist government. Following a 2018 incident in which activists splashed red paint on Chiang's sarcophagus, visitors are no longer allowed inside the mausoleum itself.

Fuxing 復興 If you're heading all the way across the North Cross-Island Highway, this sizeable village (elevation: 410m) is the last place you can enjoy any semblance of urban 'bustle', and then only at the weekend. The main drag has a post office and plenty of restaurants, some of which serve Atayal food and sell bottles of sweet, cloudy millet liquor (*xiǎo mǐ jiǔ* 小米酒), as well as a youth activity centre with rooms (see opposite). Filling up at the petrol station (⊕ 07.00–19.00 daily) here is a good idea if you're continuing all the way to Yilan. You'll notice that many of the signposts around Fuxing are bilingual – Chinese and romanised Atayal.

Luofu 羅浮 More a series of scattered hamlets than a proper village, Luofu has a prominent church and, near km22.5, a 36km-long back road that goes on to Guanxi near Beipu. For about 13km beyond Fuxing, the highway hardly climbs at all. Between Luofu and Lower Baling the landscape is defined by high cliffs and a river that never runs straight.

Lower Baling 下巴陵 Coming from the western side of the island, the traffic thins out a lot as soon as you pass Lower Baling because the bulk of tourists head north for Mount Daguan or the peach-growing area of **Upper Baling** 上巴陵. Lower Baling is a tiny place but it has a couple of places to eat; from there it's 72km to Yilan City. The eastern half of the North Cross-Island Highway is a journey through sublime temperate forest; when you stop, you're likely to hear only birdsong. There are no villages and, apart from the road, few signs of humanity. The road's highest point, 1,140m above sea level, is where it crosses the boundary between Taoyuan and Yilan.

Mount Daguan Nature Preserve 達觀山自然保護區 **(Dáguānshān Zìrán Bǎohùqū)** (⊕ 06.00–17.00 daily; admission NTD100/50) Still widely known and signposted by an alternative name, Lalashan 拉拉山, this reserve encompasses a grove of monster trees, and an easy-to-follow 3.7km trail passes 22 of these ancient cypresses. The oldest has been here for 2,800 years; the tallest is 55m. The climate is often wet, misty and cold, so bring an umbrella and a jacket as well as food and drink as not much is available inside.

Mingchi National Forest Recreation Area 明池森林遊樂區 **(Míngchí Sēnlín Yóulèqū)** (☎ 989 4106; ⊕ 08.00–17.00 daily; admission NTD120/60/10) Located in the most beautiful section of the North Cross-Island Highway, this forest reserve takes its name, literally 'shining pool', from a small lake. The surrounding woodlands deserve much more of your time than that body of water; they're full of strange ferns, curious herbs and wild orchids. The highest part of the recreation area is 1,700m above sea level. See page 121 for details of a hotel in the forest.

YILAN COUNTY 宜蘭縣 (YÍLÁN XIÀN) *Telephone code 03*

Almost all of Yilan County's residents live on the Lanyang Plain, a waterway that broadens into an impressive torrent as it makes its way from Mount Nanhu (3,742m, Taiwan's eighth-highest peak) to the Pacific Ocean. Named after the Lanyang River, the plain is a fertile flatland where rice, watermelons and spring onions grow well. Thanks to Freeway 5, most of the county is now less than an hour from Taipei, a fact that draws second-homers and day trippers.

The region is thick with rural homestays, but if you prefer an urban base then Luodong 羅東, south of the river, has an edge over Yilan City 宜蘭市 on the north bank. The latter is somewhat larger (population 96,000 compared with 72,000) and home to the enjoyable Taiwan Theatre Museum, but the former is nearer the National Centre for Traditional Arts and those driving through en route to Hualien may like to stretch their legs at Luodong Forestry Culture Garden.

HISTORY The area that's now called Yilan County has seen a succession of human inhabitants. The Atayal were driven from the lowlands into the mountains by another indigenous tribe, the Kavalan, who were themselves displaced by Han settlers from the 1790s onward and now cling to their culture in a handful of settlements further south. A British adventurer named James Horn appeared on the coast in 1868. Bankrolled by Western merchants who hoped he could recover the bodies of Europeans lost in a shipwreck, he married the daughter of an aboriginal chief and attempted to establish a colony. China protested this incursion and pressured the British consul to order Horn to leave; he agreed to do so, but drowned while trying to board the boat sent to take him to Tamsui.

Until well into the 20th century, the county was quite isolated from the rest of Taiwan. Some very local customs appeared, including the performing art now known as Taiwanese opera (see box, page 127). Even today, many Yilan natives speak Taiwanese with a distinctive accent.

GETTING THERE AND AROUND

By TRA Most Taipei–Yilan City trains take less than 1½ hours (over 40 departures; ⊕ 05.28–21.43 daily; NTD140–218). There's at least one train per hour to Hualien (⊕ 05.32–23.01 daily; NTD143–223), the fastest of which take an hour. Within the county, about 16 trains per day link Yilan City with Dongao via Luodong (⊕ 05.32–23.01 daily; takes 30mins; NTD44–52).

By bus Services #1570, #1571 and #1572 link Yilan and Luodong with Taipei City Hall bus station (up to 7 departures per hr; ⊕ 05.20–23.00 daily; takes 1hr; NTD128), the last of which also stops in Jiaoxi. Buses #1915, #1916 and #1917 (very frequent departures; ⊕ 05.15–00.55 daily; takes up to 1¼hrs; NTD141–165) go to/from Taipei bus station.

From Yuanshan metro station on Taipei's Red Line (and via Nangang TRA/metro station), buses leave for Toucheng (#1877; departs hrly; ⊕ 06.25–21.05 daily; NTD125) and Yilan (#1878; departs every 20mins; ⊕ 06.00–22.30 daily; NTD125); the journey time for both is around 90 minutes. The #1879 (at least hrly; ⊕ 06.00–22.30 daily) also sets out from Yuanshan for Luodong (NTD135) and Suao (NTD185) before terminating at Nanfangao (takes 2¼hrs; NTD185). If you'd rather travel along the coast road, take the daily #1812 service (departs at 14.20 from Daqiaotou metro station on Taipei's Orange MRT line) via Badouzi (page 134) and the National Centre for Traditional Arts (NCFTA) – but not central Yilan or Luodong – to Nanfangao (takes 3¼hrs; NTD198). The bus leaves Nanfangao for Taipei at 06.35.

The #1751 Yilan–Lishan service runs twice a day (departs from Yilan at 07.30 & 12.40, from Lishan at 08.30 & 13.30; takes 4hrs; NTD352), stopping at Wuling Farm on the way.

Within the county, the #1766 (around 23 departures daily) can be boarded at Wushi Harbour, Yilan City or Suaoxin railway station, but you're more likely to use it to get from Luodong to Nanfangao (takes 45mins; NTD56). Your best bet for getting to/from the NCFTA is the #21 Taiwan Tourist Shuttle Dongshan River

Route, which also serves Luodong Forestry Culture Garden and Luodong TRA station (departs from the station hrly; ⊕ 08.30–18.00 daily; NTD29).

By car Freeway 5 is by far the quickest way of driving from northwest Taiwan to Yilan County – from central Taipei it often takes just 1 hour – but the North Cross-Island Highway (page 121) offers better scenery. The road between Suao and Hualien (the Suhua Highway) is vulnerable to landslides and sometimes closed; this situation should improve as additional tunnels are opened over the next few years.

By motorcycle or bicycle Before the opening of Freeway 5, cars and lorries had to choose between a long coastal route and Highway 9, a slow-but-scenic road through the mountains via Pinglin, a pretty tea-growing region. The freeway now handles the great bulk of traffic, leaving Highway 9 for drivers with time on their hands, motorcyclists and determined cyclists. Via Highway 9, it takes around 2 hours to drive from central Taipei to central Yilan. Two-wheelers tackling the Suhua Highway to Hualien need strong nerves; the road is twisting and often busy.

TOURIST INFORMATION

i Northeast and Yilan Coast National Scenic Area w www.necoast-nsa.gov.tw
i Wushi Harbour Visitor Centre Between Lanyang Museum & Wushi Harbour; ⊕ 09.00–17.00 Tue–Sun & national holidays that are Mon

i Yilan TRA Station Visitor Information Centre ⊕ 09.00–20.00 daily

WHERE TO STAY AND EAT

The Dew B&B 晨露庄 (9 rooms) 363 Wuhan 5th Rd, Dongshan; m 0910 058 080; e thedew363@gmail.com; w thedew.com.tw. Yilan County has an unbelievable number of homestays, but The Dew stands out for being exceptionally clean & having English-speaking owners who can help book tickets for whale-watching trips (see box, page 292) & other activities. The family has 3 locations, all near Luodong; guests can borrow bikes for free. Inc b/fast & unlimited tea/coffee. **$$$**

Jidong Inn 集東旅社 (13 rooms) 150 Suhua Rd Sec 3, Dongao; ☎ 998 6164; ☐ @tungao.039986164. Basic rooms (all with AC & private bath) start at NTD1,000 for 2 ppl, NTD1,700 for 3 ppl & NTD2,000 for 4 ppl. No English sign & hardly any English spoken, but friendly staff nonetheless. Right on the main road but there's very little traffic after 23.00. **$$**

Loya Herb Art Hotel 樂亞香草藝術旅店 (68 rooms) 68 Linsen Rd, Luodong; ☎ 955 1910; e loya.herbart@gmail.com; w herbartloya.com.tw. Smallish rooms, some of which lack windows, but with new, well-maintained fittings throughout

& rates that seldom top NTD2,400. Good location for the bus & train stations, night market & forestry garden. Gym (⊕ 09.00–21.00 daily) & bikes you can borrow. Decent b/fast inc. **$$**

✗ CangJiu Winery Next to Toucheng Farm, near km129 Hwy 2; ☎ 977 8555; w cjwine.com; ⊕ 09.00–18.00 daily, reservations required after 18.00. Several of the wines produced here are non-grape, made instead with kumquat or grains. Many ingredients are grown in the valley & among problems faced by English-speaking founder Jack Cho are wild pigs who butt trees (to make ripe fruit fall to the ground) so violently the trees sometimes topple over. Alcohol can be enjoyed alongside lamb chops, steaks, chicken, grilled salmon & other dishes served with local vegetables (from NTD350). If you drink too much, stay at Toucheng Farm (82 rooms inc some for groups; ☎ 977 2222; w tcfarm.com.tw; **$$$** inc b/fast), owned by the same family & a shortish downhill walk from the winery. Bilingual signs point the way to both from Hwy 2. Admission to the winery is NTD100/50, redeemable if you buy wine or order food. **$$$**

WHAT TO SEE AND DO

Lanyang Museum 蘭陽博物館 (km134 Hwy 2; ☎ 977 9700; w www.lym.gov.tw; ⊕ 09.00–17.00 Thu–Tue; admission NTD100/50) Unless you wish to delve deep into the past of Yilan County, you're likely to find the award-winning design of this museum, situated next to Wushi Harbour, more exciting than the displays inside, which cover the region's nature, history and culture.

Guishan Island 龜山島 (⊕ 1 Mar–30 Nov) Meaning 'turtle mountain island', this 2.9km² islet can be seen from many points along the coast, and when viewed from around Luodong it does indeed resemble a south-facing turtle. Home to a tiny fishing community until 1977, when the population was evacuated so sensitive military equipment could be installed, Guishan Island is now open to limited numbers of ecotourists who come to see the lizards, birds and plants. Just offshore, there are active undersea volcanic vents. Overnight stays are not permitted and visitors must apply in advance for permits; this can be done with the help of a Chinese speaker through the **Yilan Guishan Island Whalewatching Shipping Center** (☎ 950 8199). Tours last around 4 hours, including time on the boat, and cost around NTD1,700 per adult.

Taiwan Theatre Museum 台灣戲劇博物館 (101 Fuxing Rd Sec 2, Yilan City; ☎ 932 2440; ⊕ 09.00–noon & 13.00–17.00 Tue–Sun; free admission) This little-known museum, 20 minutes' walk from Yilan railway station, provides an excellent introduction to Taiwanese opera (see box, opposite) and other performing arts. On Saturday afternoons, there's a chance you'll see a local troupe rehearsing in costume. The second floor has a collection of more than 100 traditional glove and string puppets that will beguile photographers; the ones dressed as ROC soldiers featured in anti-communist propaganda puppet shows in the 1950s and 1960s.

Luodong Forestry Culture Garden 羅東林業文化園區 (118 Zhongzheng N Rd, Luodong; ☎ 954 5114; w www.forest.gov.tw/EN/0000222; ⊕ 08.00–17.00 daily; free admission) Trees taken from the mountains of the northeast were processed here, 900m from Luodong railway station, between 1905 and the 1980s. The most impressive sight is the 5.6ha log pond, in which Formosan red false cypresses and certain other types of timber were stored to prevent the wood from cracking or warping during the summer; the massive semi-submerged trunks make it look like a devastated woodland. Some of the site's Japanese-style buildings date from the 1920s and now house displays of black-and-white photos and heirlooms such as stoves and tools. The narrow-gauge railroad that brought timber down from more than 2,000m above sea level terminated here and six old locomotives – a few of which burned wood rather than coal or diesel – have been preserved.

National Centre for Traditional Arts 國立傳統藝術中心 **(Guólì Chuántǒng Yìshù Zhōngxīn)** (km155 Hwy 2; ☎ 970 5815; w px-sunmake.org.tw; ⊕ 09.00–18.00 daily; admission NTD150/100/75, parking NTD50) This theme park endeavours to preserve and transmit local customs and art forms. Stages, exhibition halls and replica buildings are spread over 24ha and visitors will enjoy the short performances given at frequent intervals each day; typically you'll be able to take in shadow and glove puppetry, acrobatics, a 19th-century wedding procession, dance and Taiwanese opera. Most of the schedules and displays are in Chinese only, so reserve an English-speaking guide (send an email via the website or get a Chinese speaker to call) a week or more in advance. The Folk Art Boulevard is

Said to have originated in Yilan County, Taiwanese opera isn't an especially accessible art form. Visitors who stumble across productions usually find them baffling, garish and over the top. Shrine performances, which often celebrate the birthdays of local deities, are typically low-budget affairs. The stage is the back of a customised flatbed truck, and usually just two or three actors are on it at any one moment. There's no orchestra, nor even any live vocals; the somewhat jaded performers mime to a recorded (and ear-splittingly loud) soundtrack. The lyrics are entirely in Taiwanese and rich in slang and idioms. Like Beijing opera, the Taiwanese version is properly performed to the accompaniment of traditional instruments such as three-stringed banjos and bamboo flutes, plus the gongs and drums that punctuate dialogues and provide fierce backing for the sessions of acrobatics that represent combat. Much of the movement on a Chinese opera stage – be it Beijing, Taiwanese or another regional variant – is symbolic rather than realistic. The audience understands that purposeful striding in circles means the actor is undertaking a long journey, whereas hands clasped behind one's back is a show of bravery. Taiwan's best-known opera troupe is Ming Hwa Yuan; extracts from their performances can be found on YouTube.

lined with craft showrooms worth investigating even if you're not an ardent shopper. To escape the crowds, cross one of the small bridges and head to Scholar Huang's House, a traditional courtyard abode built in 1877 in what's now Yilan City that was dismantled and reassembled here some years back; the displays inside are very worthwhile. The food court (⏱ 09.00–18.00 daily) has a good selection of reasonably priced meals and snacks; there's also a convenience store and a coffee shop.

Nanfangao 南方澳 Taiwan is a fisheries superpower and Nanfangao is a key fishing port with a dramatic natural setting. As you'd expect, it has several seafood restaurants but communicating your wishes can be difficult; the main foreign language spoken hereabouts is Indonesian because many southeast Asians work on Taiwanese fishing vessels. The easiest way to get here is by bus #1766 (or the slightly more frequent Red 2) from Yilan or Luodong, passing the cargo port/naval base of **Suao** 蘇澳. If you're driving or riding you may want to stop at the VIC just past km168 on Highway 2. Bus passengers should stay on until the final stop then walk 800m around a dock often crammed with boats to **Neipi Beach** 內埤海 滩. Swimming is not permitted but in good weather there are stirring views to the south. Continuing to the headland nearest the Pacific then following the road north past a couple of boatyards for a total of 700m will bring you to **Tofu Cape** 豆腐岬, where some of the rocks really do resemble slabs of tofu. From there, take the road bridge (safe for pedestrians lingering to take photos) over the harbour. This way it's another 1km from the cape to the information centre but from the bridge you'll get a bird's-eye look at this unkempt yet interesting town and its fleet. For transport back to Luodong, turn left to the bus stop opposite the temple.

Dongao 東澳 This oceanside Atayal community makes for a decent half-day excursion by train from Luodong or Hualien. It's also a fine place to break the long Taipei–Hualien drive, but railway tourists thinking of stopping here for a few hours should travel light; the train station lacks lockers and there's no certainty the

4

police will let you leave luggage at their station while you explore. Overnighting is a possibility (page 125) as the 'high street' (turn left when you exit the station) has a few eateries and shops. On the inland side of the main road you'll find (in this order) the police station, post office, convenience store and a Catholic church. Take the side road between the church and the school into the village and follow it until a Chinese-only sign points right to **Dongyue Cold Spring** 東岳湧泉. Cross the river and you'll spot the cold-spring park on your left; total distance from the station is 1km. At the time of writing the spring was officially closed, meaning no facilities, but there's nothing to stop you from enjoying a dip; the water looked very clean.

You may want to leave the spring until after you've worked up a sweat walking 20-odd minutes to the coast for captivating views of the bay, or taking the shorter but steeper option of hiking up **Snake Mountain** 蛇山. The steps at the beginning of the trail are marked by a large inscribed boulder at the back of the village; take these to a concrete track, then follow the gravel path. The observation deck at the top affords good views of the cold spring, the railway line and an elevated stretch of the Suhua Highway that should be in commission by the time you read this.

THE NORTHEAST *Telephone code 02*

Taiwan's richest coal, gold and copper deposits lay beneath the hills east and southeast of Keelung. Old mining settlements like Jiufen, Jinguashi and the tiny towns served by the Pingxi Branch Railway are now well and truly on the tourist map and make for good day trips if you're staying in Greater Taipei. Note, though, that it can get busy during the summer and at weekends, when you may have to stand up on buses and trains.

GETTING THERE AND AROUND

By TRA From Taipei, many local trains and occasional expresses stop at Ruifang (🕐 05.28–22.45 daily; takes around 45mins; NTD49–76) from where you can take a bus to Jiufen or Jinguashi or change trains for Houtong, Pingxi or Shenao. There are 16 services each way daily on the Pingxi Branch Railway; Ruifang to Jingtong taking up to an hour (NTD30). Jump-on/jump-off day passes (NTD80/40) can be purchased at Ruifang and Taipei Main Railway Station. Each day, nearly 30 Yilan-bound trains stop at Fulong (takes around 1¼hrs from Taipei; NTD83–128).

By bus From Zhongxiao Fuxing metro station in Taipei, the #1062 heads to Jinguashi via Jiufen (departs every 20mins; 🕐 07.00–21.10 daily; takes 1½hrs; NTD90). The #788 leaves from near Keelung TRA station (departs every 15mins; 🕐 05.25–21.55 daily) and serves Ruifang and Jiufen with most services terminating at Jinguashi (takes 40mins; NTD30). If you want to explore the north coast in depth, consider using the Golden Fulong Tourist Shuttle (w www.gold-fulong.com. tw) to reach Jiufen, Longdong and other attractions.

By car, motorcycle or bicycle If you're approaching on either freeway, Expressway 62 allows you to bypass Keelung and head straight for Ruifang. Road 102 leaves central Keelung for Ruifang and then Jiufen and Jinguashi. An extremely steep, twisting short cut connects Jinguashi and Highway 2, which stays very close to the ocean all the way to Yilan County.

By taxi The local government has fixed a rate of NTD205 between Ruifang TRA station and Jiufen and NTD270 between the station and Jinguashi.

TOURIST INFORMATION There are visitor information centres at Ruifang TRA station (⌚ 09.00–18.00 daily), Fulong (⌚ 09.00–17.00 daily), Jiufen (⌚ 09.00–18.00 daily) and Jinguashi (⌚ 09.30–17.00 daily). Also try the website of the Northeast and Yilan Coast National Scenic Area (w necoast-nsa.gov.tw).

🏠 **WHERE TO STAY AND EAT** Unless you've a strong desire to wake up to views over the coast (there are dozens of homestays in Jiufen and nearby, although the pleasure doesn't come cheap), you may prefer to stay in central Taipei and take day trips in this region.

There's no shortage of snack vendors in Pingxi and Jiufen, and in the latter you'll find restaurants and teahouses with excellent views if unremarkable food. During the week, the pickings may be slim in Jinguashi and Houtong, so bring a picnic.

✗ **Ruifang Food Court** 2 Lane 35, Minsheng St, Ruifang District; ☎ 2496 5670; ⌚ individual vendors vary; w www.ruifangfoodcourt.com.tw. The local government deserves a pat on the back for gathering nearly 20 food businesses under 1 roof & helping them devise EMs. There's a lot of decent inexpensive local food here, plus a place that specialises in burgers & others that do beancurd pudding, sushi & vegetarian fare. AC. **$–$$**

WHAT TO SEE AND DO
The northeast coast Allow an hour to drive from Yilan County to Keelung on Highway 2, not including sightseeing and bathroom breaks.

Fulong Beach 福隆海水浴場 (⌚ May–Sep 08.00–18.00 daily; admission NTD100/80) is a long, broad stretch of sand where people swim, canoe, surf and windsurf; equipment can be rented. Expect crowds during summer weekends, the annual Hohaiyan Rock Festival (usually held in late June) and sand-sculpture competitions. The town of Fulong doesn't lack for eating and accommodation options.

Beside the unmissable white buildings near km88, child-friendly **Longdong South Ocean Park** 龍洞南口海洋公園 (⌚ 08.00–18.00 daily; admission NTD120/100, parking NTD50/20) has saltwater pools of varying sizes and depths good for swimming, paddling and searching for starfish and crabs. Visitors can rent snorkelling gear and there's an on-site restaurant (EM; meals from NTD70). The 70m-high sandstone cliffs around Longdong offer excellent rock climbing and bouldering with 500-plus routes; if you're seriously interested in the sport in Taiwan, look for the guidebook and articles written by Matt Robertson. At km78.5, look inland and you'll see immense black cement pipes snaking up the mountainside; these once discharged noxious gases from a 13-storey copper refinery, the remains of which are now known as the Thirteen Levels (not open to the public). Minerals washed out from the area's abandoned mines have stained the nearby creek orange-gold and colour part of the ocean; the latter has been dubbed **Yinyang Sea** 陰陽海.

At km75, the **'Bats Crossing'** sign asks drivers to take care because each summer over half a million female common bent-wing bats (*Miniopterus schreibersii*) gather in two nearby disused mines to give birth. During the season, mighty swarms of bats emerge at dusk to feed on insects.

Jiufen 九份 **(Jiǔfèn)** So bustling in the 1930s that outsiders nicknamed it 'Little Shanghai', this former mining town went through hard times before it was rescued from obscurity by the 1989 film *A City of Sadness* and from economic oblivion by the tourists who've been pouring in ever since. The quaint streets retain a fair bit of its pre-World War II character but if anything wins you over, it'll be the superb views down towards the sea. If you prefer exercise to crowds, hike up Mount Keelung. Reaching the top of this 587m-high mountain takes healthy folks less than half an hour. The trailhead, just beyond the centre of Jiufen on Road 102, is clearly marked; the path itself is mainly stone steps. Unless the weather's poor, from the top you'll enjoy tremendous views of Heping Island and other points on the coast. Heavy traffic and expensive parking fees (typically NTD200 for 2hrs) means driving here is often a bad idea; see page 128 for public transport options.

Gold Museum 黃金博物館 (↘ 2496 2800; w gep-en.ntpc.gov.tw; ⊕ 09.00–17.00 Mon–Fri, 09.00–18.00 Sat–Sun, closed 1st Mon every month; admission NTD80) Like Jiufen, **Jinguashi** 金瓜石 lost much of its population when mineral extraction ceased in the early 1980s. Embracing most of the town, the museum now preserves a great deal of industrial infrastructure; those fascinated by economic history will want to spend half a day touring the two exhibition buildings (in one you can touch a 220.3kg gold ingot), Japanese-era dormitories and other sites. The section of mine shaft open to the public (additional admission charge NTD50) is too clean and well lit to be convincing, but that's the only criticism that can be made of the park. Particularly appealing are the windswept ruins of a Shinto shrine, perched on a mountain ledge 15 minutes' walk above the town. During World War II, Jinguashi was the site of a prisoner-of-war camp (see box, below), where a memorial was unveiled in 1997 and Remembrance Day events are held each year.

Houtong Coal-Mine Ecological Park 猴硐煤礦博物園區 (↘ 2497 4143; ⊕ 08.00–18.00 daily; free admission) If you liked Jinguashi, drive or take a local train to **Houtong** 猴硐 (1hr travel time & NTD56–67 from Taipei; 6mins & NTD15 from Ruifang) for an extra dose of industrial archaeology. Get a leaflet

---

ALLIED POWS IN WARTIME TAIWAN

During World War II, more than 4,300 Allied prisoners-of-war were detained in Taiwan, then part of the Japanese Empire. The majority were British soldiers who surrendered when Singapore fell on 15 February 1942. As in other parts of Asia, many POWs suffered neglect and cruelty at the hands of the Japanese.

Kinkaseki – as Jinguashi was known before 1945 – was the most notorious of the 16 sites in Taiwan where POWs were held. Prisoners were forced to descend 800 steps into a sweltering mine shaft each morning, work hard through the day and then return to a camp where they were often beaten or tortured. Of the first 523 POWs sent to the mine, more than 400 succumbed to tropical diseases, rockfalls and exhaustion. One survivor, Cardiff-born Jack Edwards (1918–2006), wrote a moving book about his experiences called *Banzai You Bastards!*

The Taiwan POW Camps Memorial Society (w powtaiwan.org) has organised visits to Kinkaseki by former prisoners and maintains an online directory with the names, ranks and other details of those held in Taiwan. In recent years, the society has unveiled memorials at the sites of several other POW camps around the island.

from the information centre near the station and start walking. The Geology House and Commemorative House of Miners are the most distant sights but especially absorbing; some buildings close on Mondays.

Pingxi Branch Railway 平溪支線 Like Taiwan's other branch railways, this 12.9km-long spur was built so the resources of the interior could be more easily exploited. Coal deposits were discovered in 1907 near Jingtong, the terminus of the branch line, but large-scale mining didn't begin until 1918. At one point, 14 collieries employed 80% of the area's adult males. The track, completed in 1921, goes through six tunnels and over 15 bridges, with plenty of good scenery along the way (see page 128 for fares and other details). It's best to avoid summer weekends when trains are so packed you'll be lucky see anything let alone get a seat; aim instead for midweek, and for good views of dense forest and pretty streams sit on the right when setting out from Ruifang, after which there are eight stops. The fourth stop is the tiny town of **Shifen** 十分, where the railroad doubles as the main street, and the waterfall 20 minutes' walk away is one of Taiwan's widest.

The penultimate stop of **Pingxi** 平溪 is synonymous with sky lanterns – bamboo or wire frames covered with paper that are propelled upwards by the heat of the wick burning inside. Originally used in the bandit-ridden 19th century by remote households wanting to tell their neighbours all was well, the custom is now popular with young couples who paint their wishes on the sides of a lantern (from NTD100 each) then watch it float into the distance. Romantic, to be sure, but lantern remnants end up in trees and streams. The custom has spread to many parts of Taiwan, including nearby Shifen. If you'd rather not backtrack through Ruifang, take bus #795 (departs every 40mins; ⊕ 04.50–22.40 daily; takes 1¼hrs; NTD45) from Shifen, Pingxi or Jingtong to Muzha metro station in southwestern Taipei.

Shenao Branch Railway 深澳支線 Another treat for train enthusiasts, this 4.7km-long railroad heads north from Ruifang to Haikeguan (named after, but not especially near, the National Museum of Marine Science and Technology; page 134) before terminating at Badouzi, 1.7km from the fishing harbour of the same name. The seaside views at the latter are very agreeable. Between 1967 and 2007 trains on this branch line carried coal to power stations; there were also passenger services until 1989. Each weekday, eight trains set out from Ruifang (⊕ 09.32–17.15; takes 13mins; NTD15), with a few additional trains at the weekend.

KEELUNG 基隆 (JĪLÓNG) *Telephone code 02*

Before setting aside time for north Taiwan's most important port, know this: Keelung is much like any other Taiwanese city, only more so. Noisier, messier, more crowded and more confusing. Squashed between the ocean and craggy mountains, the city gets notorious amounts of rain and as a result the concrete is stained, there's mould in dark corners and moss on the rooftops. Keelung is neither quaint nor pretty, but it does have a wealth of abandoned fortifications and rich local culture.

HISTORY Keelung has had as much history as precipitation. The first outsiders to show an interest were the Spanish, who, in 1626, established an outpost on a nearby islet and began trading with the indigenous population. After losing their Tainan base to Koxinga, the Dutch attempted a comeback here in 1663; they gave up after

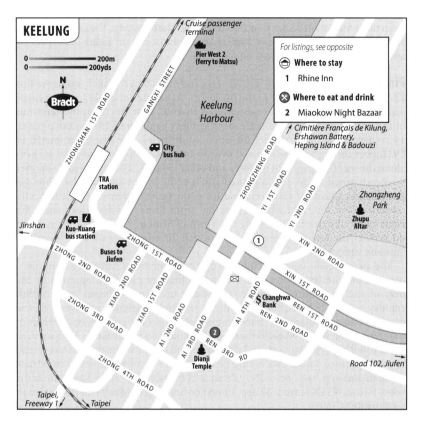

0 ——————— 200m
0 ——————— 200yds

N

Bradt

Cruise passenger terminal

Pier West 2 (ferry to Matsu)

Keelung Harbour

For listings, see opposite

🏠 **Where to stay**
1   Rhine Inn

❌ **Where to eat and drink**
2   Miaokow Night Bazaar

Cimitière Français de Kilung, Ershawan Battery, Heping Island & Badouzi

City bus hub

TRA station

Zhongzheng Park

Zhupu Altar

Jinshan ←

Kuo-Kuang bus station

Buses to Jiufen

Changhwa Bank

Dianji Temple

Road 102, Jiufen →

Taipei, Freeway 1 ↓   ↘ Taipei

GANGXI STREET
ZHONGSHAN 1ST ROAD
ZHONGZHENG ROAD
YI 1ST ROAD
YI 2ND ROAD
XIN 2ND ROAD
XIN 1ST ROAD
ZHONG 1ST ROAD
ZHONG 2ND ROAD
ZHONG 3RD ROAD
XIAO 2ND ROAD
XIAO 1ST ROAD
AI 2ND ROAD
AI 3RD ROAD
AI 4TH ROAD
REN 1ST ROAD
REN 2ND ROAD
REN 3RD RD
ZHONG 4TH ROAD

a profitless half-decade. Relatively few Han Chinese came this way until the late 18th century, as established sea routes led them instead to the southwest or what's now Wanhua. During the First Opium War (1839–42), Royal Navy and British East India Company vessels shelled the port but all three British attempts to land troops were fought off.

Two Fujianese communities dominated the Keelung area: those who traced their origins to Zhangzhou and others whose ancestors came from Quanzhou. In addition to minor cultural and linguistic differences, these two groups sacrificed to different Taoist deities. In 1851, disputes between the two sides over stray cattle and access to fresh water escalated into full-scale ethnic warfare. Local worthies finally brokered a peace deal that included burying the hundreds of dead and joint rites each Ghost Month to propitiate the deceased. In recent decades the event has grown into a joyous, raucous festival that encompasses parades and folk-art performances as well as food, drink and entertainment for the ghosts. If you happen to be in the north at the right time, it's worth diverting to Keelung to take in what's now called the Mid-Summer Ghost Festival.

Keelung was opened to foreign trade in 1860 and the arrival of coal-burning steamships jump-started the hinterland's mining industry (page 130). French marines and foreign legionnaires occupied the town for nine months during the Sino-French War. Chinese forces successfully contained the French, who during the stalemate lost far more men to cholera and typhoid than enemy action. The French cemetery is perhaps the city's most anomalous sight.

During and after the Japanese occupation, Keelung developed rapidly. It's still very much a working harbour, but in the past few years the authorities have begun transforming it into a cruise-ship destination.

GETTING THERE AND AROUND

By TRA Few northbound expresses reach Keelung but local services from Taipei (🕐 05.50–23.45 daily; takes 45mins; NTD41–64) are frequent. If you're coming from the east coast, change trains at Badu or Qidu between Keelung and Taipei.

By bus Kuo-Kuang's #1813 service sets out from Taipei every 20 minutes (🕐 05.30–22.30 daily; takes around 45mins; NTD55), and outside of rush hours these are more frequent and quicker than trains. There are also services from Taipei City Hall bus station (page 84). Coastal services include #862 to/from Tamsui (departs every 30mins; 🕐 06.00–20.00 daily; takes 2hrs; NTD120) and #790 to/from Jinshan (departs every 20mins; 🕐 05.50–22.50 daily; takes 40mins; NTD45) via Yehliu. The #788 service leaves from near the TRA station for Jiufen via Ruifang (🕐 05.35–21.35 daily; 40mins; NTD30) every 20 minutes.

Keelung's most useful intercity bus services are #101 to Heping Island (takes 20mins) and #103 to Badouzi (takes 30mins), both of which depart about every 20 minutes (🕐 06.00–23.00 daily; NTD15 one-way) from near the TRA station.

By boat For details of the overnight ferry to the Matsu Islands, see page 319.

By car Both Freeway 1 and Freeway 3 will take you into the heart of the city, but because of parking issues and traffic density you're strongly advised to use public transport.

By motorcycle or bicycle From Keelung, Road 102 provides access to Jiufen and Jinguashi and on to attractive but less-touristy parts of New Taipei City.

TOURIST INFORMATION

ℹ️ **Keelung City Government** w www.klcg. gov.tw

ℹ️ **Keelung Visitor Information Centre** At Keelung TRA station; 🕐 09.00–17.00 daily

🏠 **WHERE TO STAY AND EAT** *Map, opposite*

🏠 **Rhine Inn** (67 rooms) 17th Flr, 177 Xin 1st Rd; 📞 2425 7766; w rhineinn.com.tw. Occupying several floors of Keelung's tallest building (there's a cinema downstairs), the Rhine's rooms aren't huge but they are comfortably appointed & several have excellent harbour views. B/fast inc. **$$$**

✖️ **Miaokow Night Bazaar** 廟口夜市 Ren 3rd Rd, between Ai 3rd & Ai 4th rds; 🕐 24hrs daily. 'Miaokow' means 'temple's entrance' & this night market is now much more famous than the shrine around which vendors began gathering

in the late Qing Dynasty (page 134). Its success means the 60-odd stalls in the 'official' section are joined each evening by at least 100 others around the end of Ai 4th Rd that's nearest the river. Almost every one of the former has a bilingual sign, but some of these leave you none the wiser. For instance, 'salted porridge' is more usually called *congee*. Few have EMs or English-speaking workers. Following your nose would be a good idea but for all the competing smells; if you look around you're bound to find a soup or snack that you'll enjoy. **$**

OTHER PRACTICALITIES

💲 **Changhwa Bank** 60 Ai 4th Rd

✉️ **General post office** 130 Ai 3rd Rd; 🕐 08.30–19.00 Mon–Fri, 09.00–noon Sat

WHAT TO SEE AND DO If you're using public transport, it makes sense to begin at Badouzi or Heping Island and then move towards the city centre.

Badouzi 八斗子 Recent tourism-related developments near this fishing town include the **National Museum of Marine Science and Technology** 國立海洋科技 博物館 (☎2469 6000; w www.nmmst.gov.tw; ⊕ 09.00–17.00 Mon–Fri, 09.00–18.00 Sat–Sun; admission NTD200/140), which aims to educate schoolkids and others about marine biology and oceanography. Several colour-coded walking routes have been marked out for visitors to follow; taking the blue route from Highway 2 near the museum and then the green route over the headlands is recommended. City bus #103 terminates outside the museum and from here you can catch buses on to Longdong and Fulong.

Heping Island 和平島 Formerly called Sheliao Island, this is where the Spanish established their first base in Taiwan (page 11). Nowadays much of this 4km² island, reached by city bus #101 and linked to the city by a causeway, is crowded with drab houses. However, if you keep walking and enter **Ho-Ping Island Hi Park** 和平島 公園 (⊕ 08.00–17.00 daily, Apr–Oct until 19.00; admission NTD60/40) you'll find peculiar rock formations, saltwater swimming pools (⊕ Jun–Oct) and a somewhat underwhelming cave where graffiti left by 17th-century Dutch sailors has been discovered. It's easy to spend a few hours in the park and kids will enjoy themselves immensely. The castle-like structure inside the park is an unconvincing replica of a Spanish fort; inside you can get meals and soft drinks.

Ershawan Battery (Haimen Tianxian) 海門天險 (⊕ 24hrs daily; free admission) At km64 on Highway 2 you'll see steps going up the forested hillside. Take these and within 10 minutes you'll find yourself at Ershawan Battery, a ridgetop defence post established by the Qing authorities during the First Opium War (1839–42). Little remains of the original encampment but the views over the harbour are good and bilingual information boards provide some history. From here, you can continue on to **Zhongzheng Park** 中正公園, 20 minutes' gentle strolling away, where there's a seven-storey-high **Guanyin statue and Zhupu Altar** 主普壇 (⊕ 07.00–19.00 daily), an important venue for ceremonies during the Mid-Summer Ghost Festival (page 132). Both the altar and the small on-site museum devoted to the festival stay closed during Ghost Month.

Cimetière Français de Kilung 法國公墓 (101 Zhongzheng Rd; ⊕ 24hrs daily; free admission) The graves of French servicemen who died in the Keelung area during the Sino-French War (page 14) were moved to this spot, about 100m north of the stairs leading to Ershawan Battery, in 1909. A handful of tombs originally in the Penghu Islands were relocated here in 1953. Many of the 600-plus French soldiers interred here were North Africans and presumably Muslims, yet none of the ten gravestones or memorials acknowledge religions other than Christianity.

Dianji Temple 奠濟宮 (⊕ 06.00–22.00 daily) Visiting the shrine that gives Miaokow Night Bazaar (page 133) its name is especially worthwhile around the 15th day of the second lunar month, the birthday of Kaizhang Shengwang, a revered ancestor and patron deity of those who trace their origins to Zhangzhou. The temple was founded in 1873 on land donated by Lin Ben-yuan, one of the Qing era's most successful merchants.

The coastline between Keelung and Tamsui is as green and rugged as that of Ireland. None of the towns here are particularly large (or special) and in winter the weather is often like Ireland's – cold, wet and blustery. However, fans of strange landforms will enjoy themselves at Laomei and Yehliu, while those into culture and art can look forward to a major monastery and a museum. Brace yourself for heavy traffic at weekends and on national holidays.

GETTING THERE AND AROUND

By bus The #1717 Taipei–Jinshan service (page 110) is a beautifully scenic way of reaching the north coast. The buses that ply Highway 2 (pages 133 and 139) are frequent and can drop you within walking distance of most attractions. Kuo-Kuang's #1815 service from Taipei (departs every 20mins; ⊕ 05.00–21.00 daily) makes stops at Yehliu (1¼hrs; NTD99), Jinshan (1½hrs; NTD128) and Dharma Drum Mountain (1¾hrs; NTD142).

By car or motorcycle From central Taipei, Highway 2A will take you through Yangmingshan National Park, but call the tourist information hotline (📞 0800 011 765) in advance as sometimes there are traffic controls when approaching from central Taipei. Away from the coast, there are some pretty back roads on which it's easy to get lost.

TOURIST INFORMATION

🄻 Baishawan Beach Visitor Information Centre ⊕ 09.00–17.00 daily
🄻 North Coast and Guanyinshan National Scenic Area w www.northguan-nsa.gov.tw

🄻 Yehliu Visitor Information Centre ⊕ 08.00–17.00 daily

WHAT TO SEE AND DO Attractions are listed in the order you'll encounter them if starting out from Keelung.

Yehliu Geopark 野柳地質公園 **(Yěliǔ Dìzhì Gōngyuán)** 📞 2492 2016; w www.ylgeopark.org.tw; ⊕ 08.00–17.00 daily; admission NTD80/40) The single-most popular tourist destination on the north coast, this natural wonderland is a place geologists and kids adore. There are sometimes queues to see the park's most famous sight, the Queen's Head, so named because it resembles the famous bust of Nefertiti. Just as engrossing are the caves, hoodoos, pot-holes, overhangs, honeycombed outcrops, and rocks marked with swirls or concentric ripples, all of which are the result of wind and wave erosion. The peninsula is 1.7km long, so be prepared for some walking.

Jinshan 金山 This pleasant little town is just off the coast. After getting off the bus, you'll need to walk for the better part of an hour if you want to see the ocean from the end of the cape, but the hike is recommended. Follow the signs to the Twin Candlesticks, a pair of unwieldy-looking 60m-high rock columns just offshore. The Yehliu promontory is clearly visible 5km to the southeast. When returning to the town centre, a convenient and enjoyable place to try Jinshan's iron-rich hot springs is **The Governor-General's Hot Spring** (196 Minsheng Rd; 📞 2408 2628; w www.warmspring.com.tw; ⊕ 09.00–midnight daily, meals available 11.30–14.15 & 17.00–20.00 Mon–Fri, 11.30–20.00 Sat–Sun; NTD300/180 Mon–Fri, NTD350/250 Sat–Sun, swimsuits required). Built in 1939 on the orders of the Japanese viceroy as a place

North Taiwan   **THE NORTH COAST**

4

for entertaining dignitaries, it was used for much of the postwar period as an army outpost. As well as an outdoor hot spring and cold pool, there are private rooms and gender-segregated ocean-view pools on the fourth floor (swimsuits not required).

Dharma Drum Mountain 法鼓山 **(Fǎgǔshān)** ✎ 2498 7171; w ddm.org.tw; ⊕ 09.00–16.00 daily) One of Taiwan's religious landmarks, DDM was established in 1989 and grew out of a Buddhist monastery led by the Venerable Chan Master Sheng-Yen (1930–2009). The complex now includes two universities, a college, a memorial hall, exhibition rooms and a network of walking paths. Free half-day and one-day English-language tours, recommended for those interested in religion and/or meditation, can be arranged if notification is made at least ten days ahead (e vedus@ddmf.org.tw). Casual visitors are welcome and will find plenty of English-language signs and leaflets, but note that smoking or consuming meat or alcohol isn't allowed in the complex and photography isn't permitted indoors. If you don't want to drive, take bus #1815 (page 135) from Taipei.

Laomei Algal Reef 老梅海岸 Laomei is a rather forlorn seaside village but if it's low tide, head down to the beach and turn left – you'll be able to see something rather odd and, depending on the season, potentially very photogenic. Wave erosion has cut deep grooves into a large patch of bedrock and the humps that run down to the water are covered with multiple layers of dark green algae. When the algae die, their limestone skeletons remain in place and new algae grows on top of them. Imagine rows of boulders covered with moss, emerging from the ocean. Tide times can be checked online (w cwb.gov.tw) – click on 'forecast', then 'fishery' then 'tidal forecast'. Find 'New Taipei City, Shimen' on the list to see tide details for 30 days ahead. Walking from Laomei's bus stop to the reef, then around Fugui Cape and back to Highway 2 takes around an hour.

Fugui Cape 富貴角 **(Fùguì Jiǎo)** Taiwan's most northerly point – the ROC controls territory significantly further north in the Matsu Islands – is about 30 minutes from Tamsui by bus. The place name is a Mandarin derivation of a Taiwanese transliteration of a 17th-century Dutch term meaning 'small peninsula'. This gorse-covered promontory was created millions of years ago when volcanism in what's now Yangmingshan National Park hurled lava and rocks as far as the coast. Among them are windkanter boulders recognisable by their sharp edges, the result of erosion by sand-bearing northeasterlies. Neither the peninsula's radar base nor its lighthouse are open to the public. On the western side of the cape, take a look at the small harbour where just-caught lobsters and crabs try to escape from plastic tubs outside seafood restaurants (no EMs; confirm prices before taking a seat).

Baishawan 白沙灣 Come here in the summer and you'll find hundreds of people enjoying this beach, one of the nicest in north Taiwan. Baishawan means 'white sandy bay' and the name is spot on – the sand is fine, clean and pale. There are places to eat, drink coffee and rent surfboards.

TAMSUI 淡水 (DÀNSHUǏ) *Telephone code 02*

Nowadays a suburb of the capital with 170,000 inhabitants, but for much of its history a town bigger and more important than Taipei, Tamsui has been able to retain a good amount of its historic character. In recent years the old spelling 'Tamsui' has made a government-sponsored comeback, but you may see 'Danshui'

TAMSUI

Golf course

UNIVERSITY

Yangmingshan National Park

XUEFU ROAD

Yinshan Temple

Buses to Keelung

Leqi Bicycles

Central Taipei (21km)

Buses to Jinshan

Tamsui MRT Station

M

Tamsui Cultural Park

YINGZHUAN ROAD

Sanzhi (23km)

ZHONGSHAN NORTH ROAD

CHONGJIAN STREET

XINSHENG STREET

XINMIN STREET

Mackay's Grave

Foreigners' Cemetery

ZHENLI STREET

Oxford College

Fort San Domingo

Little White House

Former Residence of Tada Eikichi

3

Tamsui Church

Mackay Hospital

SANMIN ST

MACKAY ST

1

Fuyou Temple

Cooperative Bank

2

TAMSUI OLD ST

ZHONGZHENG ROAD

ZHONGZHENG ROAD

Ferries to Bali

Tamsui

For listings, see from page 139

Where to stay

1 Taipei Travellers Hostel

Where to eat and drink

2 Kekou Fish Balls
3 Tamsui Traditional Agei

N

Bradt

0   200m
0   200yds

George Leslie Mackay, the first Canadian to serve overseas as a Christian missionary, entered Taiwan's history when he disembarked at Takao (now Kaohsiung) on 29 December 1871. The eldest son of Scottish Highlanders, Mackay had studied at seminaries in Canada, the United States and Scotland. He was only 27 when he was dispatched to Taiwan by the Canadian Presbyterian Church.

Within days of his arrival, Mackay was picking up Taiwanese words from a British Presbyterian. From Takao, he sailed north to Tamsui, reaching the town on 9 March 1872, where he worked day and night to master the Taiwanese language. As soon as he became semi-proficient, he began to preach to whoever was willing to listen, and to debate ethics and religion with the educated elite. 'The proud, conceited literati would enter my room, open my Bibles and other books, throw them on the floor and then strut out with a grunt of contempt', he recalled in *From Far Formosa*, the 1896 book he wrote about his missionary experiences. But it was from among this group that he made his first convert, a young man who went on to play an important role in the spreading of Christianity in north Taiwan.

Among non-Christian Taiwanese, Mackay is revered for his educational and medical work. While touring the countryside he offered his services as a dentist, pulling more than 21,000 teeth, which he always returned to their owners, lest he be accused of sorcery. Two of Tamsui's landmark schools were founded by Mackay: Aletheia University (until 1999 known as Tamsui Oxford College after Oxford County in Ontario, Mackay's birthplace) and Tamkang High School. Mackay Memorial Hospital, which he established in 1880, now has more than 1,000 beds.

Mackay's name will always be linked with Tamsui (which in *From Far Formosa* he described as 'a smoky, dirty town'), but during his first seven years in Taiwan he stayed there a total of just 175 days. The rest of the time was spent travelling, usually on foot. He became something of a polymath; as well as a preacher, doctor and dentist, he became an architect who designed 60 churches and a civil engineer who supervised the building of them.

There can be no doubt that Mackay was incredibly courageous and physically very tough. He survived bouts of malaria and meningitis. *From Far Formosa* suggests a man absolutely convinced he was doing God's work, and who believed non-Christian Taiwanese were 'hopelessly blinded' by Taoism's 'spirit-superstition and wretched incantations'. Yet in some ways Mackay was ahead of his time; he married a Taiwanese woman in an era when miscegenation was frowned upon in the West, and he publicly denounced as 'unjust and un-Christian' the head-tax levied on Chinese (and only Chinese) entering Canada. Mackay's evident love for Taiwan continues to endear him to Taiwanese and his story is told in primary school textbooks.

on some signs. The attractions – among them schools, graves and a fortress-turned-consulate – are clustered more or less within walking distance of each other.

HISTORY By the late 18th century, Tamsui (meaning 'fresh water', also the name of the river that drains the Taipei Basin and flows past the town) was growing fast thanks to strong trade links with the Chinese mainland. Between 1859 and 1895, when Japan took control of Taiwan, the Treaty of Tientsin gave traders from the British Empire, Russia, the United States and France special rights and protections in Tamsui. Among them was John Dodd, an English merchant who arrived in 1864 and who played a key role in the development of Taiwan's tea industry (see box, page 65). He was living in the town when it was blockaded and shelled by the French during the Sino-French War of 1884–85. He wrote extensively about that period and also about Taiwan's indigenous people and flora. However, his life and achievements are overshadowed by those of another Tamsui-based expatriate, Canadian-born missionary George L Mackay (see box, opposite). Like many harbours on the west coast, Tamsui's port suffered from silting. By the 1920s, almost all ships bound for north Taiwan anchored instead in Keelung's deep-water harbour.

GETTING THERE AND AROUND

By metro or light rail Taipei metro's Red Line links Taipei Main Station with Tamsui (departs every 5mins; ⏱ 06.00–23.48 daily; takes 37mins; NTD50). The Danhai Light Railway should be up and running by the time this book appears but the first phase, connecting with the Red Line at Hongshulin metro station, won't be of much use to tourists as it'll serve residential areas away from the old town centre.

By bus Tamsui's bus stops are on both sides of the main road just outside the metro station. The #862 to Keelung (departs every 30mins; ⏱ 05.50–20.30 daily; takes 2hrs; NTD120) and the equally frequent #863 to Jinshan (⏱ 05.40–21.30 daily; takes 1¼hrs; NTD75) are convenient for touring the north coast. Within Tamsui, the Red 26 bus (departs every 10mins; ⏱ 05.40–00.40 daily; NTD15) goes westward from the metro station, down Zhongshan and Wenhua roads, stopping very near Fort San Domingo.

By boat Small ferries (passenger and bike only) cross the Tamsui River to Bali at least every 15 minutes (⏱ 07.00–21.00 daily; takes 10mins; NTD20 one-way, return NTD39).

By car or motorcycle You're unlikely to drive to Tamsui, but if you do, start your search for a parking spot on Wenhua Road. If that fails, try west of Fort San Domingo.

By bicycle Very near Tamsui metro station, decent bikes are available at **Leqi Bicycles** (☏ 2626 3233; ⏱ 10.00–19.00 Mon–Fri, 09.00–19.00 Sat–Sun & national holidays). Daily rates are NTD100–350.

TOURIST INFORMATION

🛈 **Tamsui Historical Museum** (online only) **w** en.tshs.ntpc.gov.tw

🛈 **Tamsui Visitor Information Centre** Tamsui metro station; ⏱ 08.30–18.30 daily

WHERE TO STAY AND EAT *Map, page 137*

🏠 **Taipei Travellers Hostel** (3 dorms) 22 Sanmin St; ☏ 2625 8222; **e** booking@ taipeitravelers.com; **w** taipeitravelers.com. Modern, conveniently located & legal unlike many other Taiwan hostels (so likely to be around for a while), this offers the usual pros & cons of city-centre hostel living. A bed in a 6- or 8-ppl

dorm can often be had for NTD600, inc basic b/ fast. **$**

✕ **Kekou Fish Balls** 可口魚丸 232 Zhongzheng Rd; ☏ 2623 3579; ⏱ 08.00–19.00 daily. The riverside zone is packed with vendors selling deep-fried delights, but for the most delectable wontons this writer has ever tried do stop here if walking to Fort San Domingo. A small portion of wontons in soup is NTD35; the same price gets you fish balls in soup or a sampler of 3 wontons & 2 fish balls. No EM but everything is prepared in the open so just point. $

✗ **Tamsui Traditional Agei** 淡水老牌阿給 6–1 Zhenli St; ☎ 2621 1785; ⏰ 05.00–14.00 Tue–Sun. This plain-jane eatery specialises in *agei*,

bun-sized chunks of tofu that are stuffed with glass noodles & fish paste then deep fried (NTD40). Said to have been invented on this very street in the mid 1960s, *agei* is now sold at several locations in Tamsui. The Chinese-only menu also lists fish-ball soup, soya milk & surprisingly thick slices of toasted bread. $

OTHER PRACTICALITIES

$ **Co-operative Bank** 119 Zhongzheng Rd

✉ **Post office** 203 Zhongzheng Rd; ⏰ 08.30–17.30 Mon–Fri, 09.00–noon Sat

WHAT TO SEE AND DO Tamsui abounds in physical reminders of the past. Some, like the temples, were established by Han settlers and their descendants, but there's a whole slew of locations associated with Mackay and the other Westerners who made Tamsui their home. What's called **Tamsui Old Street** 淡水老街 is a stretch of Zhongzheng Road that isn't especially old or interesting. It does, however, lead to several of the town's major sights and many of its eateries. Temples aside, most of Tamsui's attractions are closed on the first Monday of each month, Lunar New Year's Eve and Lunar New Year's Day.

Tamsui Cultural Park 淡水文化園區 (⏰ 09.00–18.00 Tue–Sun; free admission)
The restored warehouses southeast of Tamsui metro station date from the 1860s and were owned by Shell Petroleum (now Royal Dutch Shell) between 1897 and 2001. Most now serve as exhibition spaces or community classrooms but some oil-trade relics are on display in the Shell Story House.

Yinshan Temple 鄞山寺 (15 Denggong Rd; ⏰ 05.00–19.00 daily) Tamsui's most
beautiful shrine was founded in 1822 and is especially worth visiting after dark when the exterior is illuminated. It's one of two shrines in Taiwan dedicated to Dingguang Buddha (the other being in Changhua City), a 10th-century deified Chinese monk, and the effigy of a meditating monk presents quite a contrast to the fearsome-looking bearded gods seen in most temples.

Fuyou Temple 福佑宮 (200 Zhongzheng Rd; ⏰ 05.00–20.45 daily) This
atmospheric Mazu shrine has a notable relic – a battered-looking inscribed board that hangs from a ceiling beam in the middle of the main chamber. Conferred by order of Emperor Guangxu just after the Sino-French War (page 14), it makes public his recognition of and appreciation for Mazu's apparent intercession on behalf of the Chinese side during the conflict. It reads (from right to left, which is often but not always the case with written Chinese) *yì tiān chāo yòu*, meaning 'bright heaven's blessing'.

Mackay Street 馬偕街 One of very few roads in Taiwan named after someone
not of Han Chinese descent, this short thoroughfare has a pair of buildings related to the missionary: Mackay's original **clinic** (6 Mackay St; ⏰ not open to the public) and **Tamsui Church** (8 Mackay St; ⏰ for services only). The latter was designed by his son who followed in his father's footsteps and served as a missionary here before and after World War II. If you take the footbridge over Wenhua Road you'll come to the **Former Residence of Tada Eikichi** 多田榮吉故居 (⏰ 09.30–17.30 daily;

free admission). Tada, a Japanese civil servant, was the appointed chief of Tamsui township when this house was built in 1934; its dimensions are modest but the view across the estuary is priceless. Visitors hoping for additional glimpses of the Tamsui of old should explore both **Chongjian Street** 重建街 and **Sanmin Street** 三民街.

Foreigners' Cemetery 外僑墓園 (Cnr of Xinmin St & Lane 3, Zhenli St; ⊕ during school hrs; free admission)

At least 75 and perhaps as many as 81 Westerners were interred in this graveyard, about the size of two tennis courts, between 1867 and 1974. Among the 19 Americans and 15 Britons buried here are missionaries, infants, soldiers, sailors and a diplomat. There are also Germans, Spaniards, Portuguese and French. The tombs are now well cared for but for much of the 1980s, after the US Embassy in Taipei closed down, the plot was ownerless and neglected. If you enter via the school gates on Xinmin Street, you'll pass the memorial to George L Mackay and the tombs of the missionary and some of his family members.

Oxford College 牛津學堂 (32 Zhenli St; ⊕ 09.00–17.00 daily, campus ⊕ 07.00–22.00 daily; free admission)

The original 1882 redbrick building, now surrounded by the modern buildings of Aletheia University, is an attractive blend of Taiwanese residential and Western ecclesiastical architecture. Presbyterian Church-related photos and documents are displayed inside. A side gate allows access between the university and Fort San Domingo.

Fort San Domingo 紅毛城 (Hóngmáo Chéng) (⊕ 09.30–17.00 Mon–Fri, 09.30–18.00 Sat–Sun; admission NTD80)

With its miniature turrets and red walls, Tamsui's most popular attraction resembles a Victorian folly, but this square fortress has been around since 1646. It was built by the Dutch East India Company and some sources refer to it by its Dutch name, Fort Antonio. In that era Taiwanese referred to Europeans as 'red-haired barbarians', so locals dubbed the building *hóngmáo chéng*, meaning 'castle of the red-haired folk'. The current Western moniker is actually the name given by the Spanish to the stockade that stood here in the 1630s. For much of the 18th century, imperial troops were stationed in the building. In 1867, the British government turned the site into their main Taiwan consulate, having agreed to pay an annual rent of 10 taels of silver (equivalent to 12 Troy ounces). They renovated the fort and built a lovely two-floor consular residence next door; the latter has several bricks marked 'VR 1891', VR being Queen Victoria.

There's quite a bit to see inside these buildings, including wall safes, a stove for burning documents and cells for detaining British nationals (who were immune to local laws but could be punished by UK courts). The consulate was closed 1941–46 because of World War II. The British government recognised the communist regime in Beijing in 1950 but kept this consulate open, putting the British diplomats based here in an awkward situation; they had to avoid contact with officials of the ROC's central government, and communicated only with Taiwan's provincial authorities. The consulate was closed in 1972 as part of a deal whereby the UK upgraded its Beijing mission to embassy status. Hold on to your ticket as it'll get you into a few other attractions for free, such as the nearly **Little White House** 小白宮 (15 Zhenli St; ⊕ 09.30–17.00 Tue–Fri, 09.30–18.00 Sat–Sun), built as a residence/office for a customs official sometime after 1869.

Bali 八里 (Bālǐ)

Even if you've no time to explore the district opposite Tamsui, consider taking the boat (page 139) across the estuary for the views you'll get of

Yangmingshan National Park to the east and the 612m-high **Guanyinshan** 觀音山 to the south. The latter mountain, part of the North Coast and Guanyinshan National Scenic Area (w northguan-nsa.gov.tw), is the loftiest of the eight peaks in Taiwan named after the Buddhist goddess. If it's low tide, take a close look at the mudflats near Bali's ferry dock – you'll notice hundreds of fiddler crabs and dozens of finger-length mudskippers.

Bike-rental businesses (from NTD80/hr) can be found near the dock; a pleasant 3.5km-long bike trail path passes mangrove swamps on its way to **Shisanhang Museum of Archaeology** 十三行博物館 (2619 1313; w en.sshm.ntpc.gov. tw; ⊕ 09.30–17.00 daily; admission NTD80), which preserves artefacts of the prehistoric Shisanhang culture, who smelted iron and buried their dead hereabouts 500 to 1,800 years ago. One alternative to cycling is the Red 13 bus (departs every 30mins; ⊕ 08.00–21.00 daily; takes 25mins; NTD15) that departs from the Red Line's Guandu metro station to the museum via Bali's ferry dock.

5

Hakka Country

The northwestern counties of Hsinchu and Miaoli (combined population 1.54 million, land area 3,351km²) form Taiwan's Hakka heartland. Because much of the terrain is unsuitable for growing rice, Fujianese migrants historically preferred to go elsewhere and, as a consequence, the interior remained undeveloped until Hakka settlers began to arrive in the late 18th century. These days you won't hear the Hakka language spoken very much in Hsinchu City, a prosperous place whose historic side isn't well known. Never a purely Hakka settlement, its booming hi-tech industries have drawn migrants from every corner of the ROC, as well as thousands of foreigners. However, if you venture into the hilly townships that characterise this part of Taiwan, you'll have plenty of chances to meet Hakka people who still use their mother tongue on a daily basis and whose lives, like those of their grandparents, revolve around extended families, farming, the local temple and traditional festivals like the annual celebration of the Yimin militiamen's bravery.

Just as they struggled against an unfavourable natural environment, Hakka settlers also faced indigenous opposition. They traded with, competed against and often fought Atayal and Saisiyat aborigines, eventually pushing them deeper into the highlands. Beipu, once a fortified frontier town, is popular now for its quaintness. Sanyi has become a renowned woodcarving centre, while Nanzhuang offers an appealing blend of Hakka and indigenous cultures and natural attractions. Aboriginal clans cling to their way of life in the eastern third of the region; their villages are rewarding but somewhat difficult places to visit. English-language information about Hakka culture can be found at **w** www.hakka.gov.tw.

HSINCHU CITY 新竹市 (XĪNZHÚ SHÌ) *Telephone code 03*

Just as Taiwan is still better known for its exports than its rich culture and natural beauty, Hsinchu's recent economic achievements – evidenced by the semi-conductor foundries, optoelectronics companies and computer-peripheral makers hosted by Hsinchu Science-based Industrial Park – have been so impressive that few outsiders are aware of its long history and alluring colonial-era buildings, or know that the local government has succeeded in translating its prosperity into tangible quality-of-life improvements. This is a shame: in my opinion, Hsinchu (population 441,000) is the most interesting west-coast city between Taipei and Tainan, and it is easy to spend an entire day exploring the city centre on foot.

HISTORY Fujianese, who've been settling hereabouts since at least 1711, called the town Tekkham (in Mandarin, Zhuqian), meaning 'bamboo barricade'. There was no barricade and the presence of bamboo was nothing more than a coincidence because – like many 17th- and 18th-century place names – Tekkham was a simply loose Chinese rendering of the name used by the area's indigenous inhabitants; in

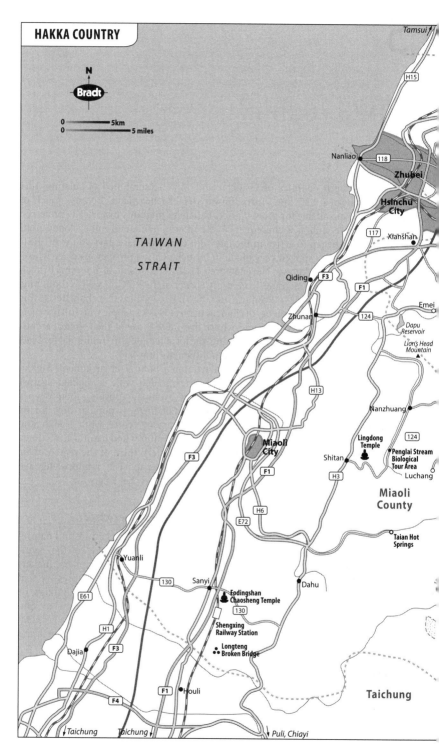

HAKKA COUNTRY

N

Bradt

0 ——— 5km
0 ——— 5 miles

TAIWAN

STRAIT

Tamsui

H15

Nanliao 118
Zhubei

Hsinchu
City

117 Xianshan

Qiding F3
F1

Emei

Zhunan 124
Dapu
Reservoir

Lion's Head
Mountain

H13

Nanzhuang

Lingdong
Temple 124

Miaoli
City Shitan Penglai Stream
Biological
Tour Area

F1 H3 Luchang

H6 Miaoli
County

E72

Taian Hot
Springs

Yuanli

130 Sanyi Dahu

E61

Fodingshan
Chaosheng Temple

130

Shengxing
Railway Station

H1

Longteng
Broken Bridge

Dajia F3

Taichung

F1 Houli

F4

Taichung Taichung Puli, Chiayi

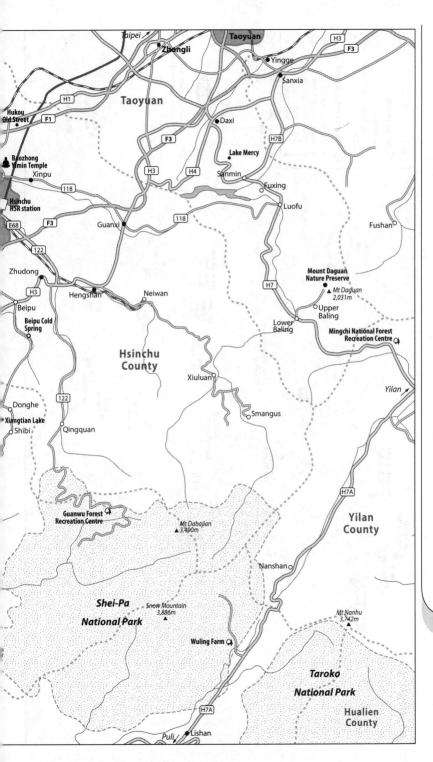

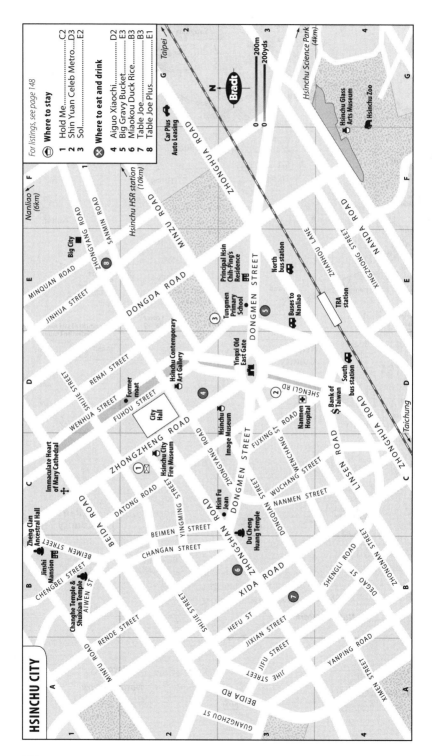

HSINCHU CITY

For listings, see page 148

Where to stay

1	Hold Me.................	C2
2	Shin Yuan Celeb Metro...D3	
3	Sol.........................	E2

Where to eat and drink

4	Aiguo Xiaochi...........	D2
5	Big Gravy Bucket........	E3
6	Miaokou Duck Rice......	B3
7	Table Joe.................	B3
8	Table Joe Plus...........	E1

Car Plus
Auto Leasing

Taipei

200m
200yds

Hsinchu Science Park
(4km)

Hsinchu Glass
Arts Museum

Hsinchu Zoo

Nanliao
(6km)

Big City

Hsinchu HSR station
(10km)

MINQUAN ROAD

ZHONGYANG ROAD

SANMIN ROAD

JINHUA STREET

DONGDA ROAD

MINZU ROAD

ZHONGHUA ROAD

Principal Hsin
Chih-Ping's
Residence

North
bus station

DONGMEN STREET

Tungmen
Primary
School

Buses to
Nanliao

TRA
station

ZHANHOU LANE

XINGZHONG STREET

NANDA ROAD

Hsinchu Contemporary
Art Gallery

Former
moat

WENHUA STREET

RENAI STREET

FUHOU STREET

Yingxi Old
East Gate

DONGMEN STREET

SHENGLI RD

South
bus station

Bank of
Taiwan

City
Hall

ZHONGZHENG ROAD

Hsinchu
Image Museum

Hsin Fu
Jean

ZHONGYANG ROAD

FUXING ST

Nanmen
Hospital

NANMEN STREET

WUCHANG STREET

LINSEN ROAD

SHENGLI ROAD

ZHONGHUA ROAD

Taichung

Immaculate Heart
of Mary Cathedral

Zheng Clan
Ancestral Hall

Jinshi
Mansion

Changhe Temple &
Shuixian Temple

CHENGBEI STREET

AIWEN ST

BEIDA ROAD

DATONG ROAD

BEIMEN STREET

YINGMING STREET

BEIMEN
STREET

CHANGAN STREET

Hsinchu City
Fire Museum

ZHONGSHAN ROAD

Du Cheng
Huang Temple

XIDA ROAD

SHILI STREET

HEFU ST

JIXIAN STREET

JIFU STREET

JIHE STREET

SHENGLI ROAD

DEGAO ST

ZHONGNAN STREET

YANPING ROAD

XIMIN STREET

MINFU ROAD

RENDE STREET

BEIDA RD

GUANGZHOU ST

Bradt

N

the language of the local Taokas tribe it meant 'seashore'. The Taokas moved away or assimilated as the Han town developed. Then, as now, the population was a mix of Fujianese and Hakka. In the first quarter of the 19th century, when Taipei was still a brusque frontier community, Tekkham had several schools and an active group of literati. One of the latter, Zheng Yong-xi (1788–1858), became in 1823 the first Taiwan-born candidate to pass the highest-level imperial examination for scholar-bureaucrats, thus gaining the title *jinshi*. Zheng and his clan left their mark on Hsinchu, as the city was renamed in 1880. In 1826, Zheng successfully lobbied the Qing court for permission to construct a 2.7km-long brick-and-stone wall around the town, promising it would be financed entirely by citizens' donations. Visitors can still see a small part of that wall (most was torn down during the Japanese colonial era), the house where Zheng lived and the shrine where his descendants worship their ancestors.

GETTING THERE AND AROUND All fares mentioned in this chapter are one-way.

By HSR Frequent trains to/from Taipei take just over half an hour (NTD290), but early morning and evening services are often packed with commuters. To/from Kaohsiung Zuoying (NTD1,200) takes 1½ hours. The quickest way to get into the city centre from the HSR station, located 11km to the east, is by the TRA Liujia Branch Line (departs every 30mins; ⊕ 06.19–23.02 daily; 19mins; NTD16), but City Bus #182 (approx every 40mins; ⊕ 06.10–21.10 daily; 25mins; NTD15) also runs between the two.

By TRA Expresses from both Taipei (NTD137–177) and Taichung (NTD152–197) take just over an hour. Most of the sights marked on the map are within 20 minutes' walk of the TRA station [146 E4].

By bus The Taipei-bound #9003 leaves from Hsinchu's South bus station [146 D4] (departs every 6–10mins; ⊕ 05.20–23.08 daily; 1½hrs; NTD130), which is where you can also board the frequent #5608 bus to Zhudong if you're headed for Beipu. From the North bus station [146 E3] there are services to Zhongli via Hukou, Fangliao and other small towns in Hsinchu's hinterland.

To get to Nanliao on the coast, take city bus #15 (departs every 20mins; ⊕ 06.20–22.00 daily; 20mins; NTD15) from the stop on Minzu Road near the TRA station [146 E3].

By car and motorcycle By Freeway 1, Hsinchu is 70km south of Taipei and 83km north of Taichung. Parking in the city centre shouldn't be a problem.

For those on two wheels, consider taking Highway 15 near the coast if coming from the north.

🚗 **Car Plus Auto Leasing** [146 G2] 315 Zhonghua Rd Sec 1; ☏515 3528; w car-plus.com. tw; ⊕ 08.30–20.30 daily. General-use car rentals & long-term leasing. There's also a counter inside Hsinchu HSR station (⊕ 07.00–22.00 daily).

TOURIST INFORMATION
ℹ **Hsinchu City Government Travel**
w tourism.hccg.org.tw

ℹ **Hsinchu Visitor Centre** Hsinchu TRA station; ⊕ 09.00–20.00 daily
ℹ **Liujia Visitor Information Centre** Liujia TRA station; ⊕ 09.00–17.00 daily

🏠 WHERE TO STAY

🏠 **Shin Yuan Celeb Metro Hotel** [146 D3] (35 rooms) 20 Datong Rd; ☎ 521 1888; e service@shinyuan-hotel.com.tw; w shinyuan-hotel.com.tw. The glitzier yet quieter sibling of the 75-room Shin Yuan Hotel (11 Datong Rd), the Celeb Metro branch has rooms awash with shiny golds & yellows. Chic bathrooms (white pebble floors, traditional wooden buckets) are standard. B/fast inc. **$$$**

🏠 **Sol Hotel** [146 E2] (152 rooms) 10 Wenhua St; ☎ 534 7266; e room@solhotel.com.tw; w solhotel.com.tw. Aimed very much at business travellers but good for tourists on account of its central yet quiet location & reasonable prices, Sol's rooms were decorated by someone who understands that less is more & restraint shows good taste. Gym & self-service laundry. B/fast inc. **$$$**

🏠 **Hold Me Hotel** [146 C2] (21 rooms) 11th Flr, 107 Zhongzheng Rd; ☎ 521 3333; e holdmehotel@yahoo.com.tw; w www.hmhotel.com.tw. Very quiet, very central & by Hsinchu's relatively expensive standards very good value, although the rooms aren't overlarge. B/fast inc. **$$**

✘ WHERE TO EAT AND DRINK

The 40-plus food vendors clustered around Cheng Huang Temple serve a good range of Taiwanese snacks and hot, filling dishes; specialities include the city's excellent pork meatballs (*xīnzhú gòng wán* 新竹摃丸) in a clear soup and rice noodles. Don't expect EMs but some places have picture menus; most items are under NTD70.

✘ **Aiguo Xiaochi** 愛國小吃 [146 D2] 1001 Dongmen Market; ☎ 524 9612; ⏰ 11.00–19.00 Mon–Fri. Eat here & market-goers will assume you're a long-term resident who knows where some of the city's best Hakka/Taiwanese home cooking is served. Now run by the founder's grandson; no EM so enlist a Chinese speaker or this book's language appendix. Only 2 tables, so you may have to wait for a seat. **$$**

✘ **Miaokou Duck Rice** 廟口鴨香飯 [146 B3] 142 Zhongshan Rd; ☎ 523 1190; ⏰ 10.30–15.00 & 15.30–21.30 Thu–Tue. If your love of superbly prepared duck outweighs any dislike of crowds or noise, do try this eatery. A portion of the signature 'fragrant duck meat on rice' (*yā xiāng fàn* 鴨香飯, NTD60) may not contain enough meat for duck addicts who should consider also ordering a plate of boneless duck (*qùgǔ yāròu* 去骨鴨肉, NTD150). Noodle & vermicelli options; stir-fried vegetables start at NTD35 & soups at NTD40. **$$**

✘ **Table Joe** [146 B3] 102 Hefu St; ☎ 527 8150; ⏰ 10.00–21.00 daily. Probably the best place in the city for burgers, onion rings & other Western staples, Table Joe attracts a youngish crowd & offers tourists home-from-home hospitality. **Table Joe Plus** [146 E1] (25 Sanmin Rd; ☎ 535 6070) keeps the same hours but has a slightly different menu. EM. **$$**

✘ **Big Gravy Bucket** 大滷桶 [146 E3] 322 Minzu Rd; ☎ 523 0609; ⏰ 15.30–21.00 Mon–Sat, noon–21.00 Sun. If you've a mind to try *lǔ wèi* 魯味 – the category of food items that includes chickens' feet, ducks' hearts, tempura, various soy products & unidentifiable animal organs – this is a good place to do it. No language skills are needed; simply grab a pair of tongs & put the sausages, meatballs, etc, you want in a plastic basin, then wait while they're cut up, heated & sprinkled with spring onion. This kind of food goes very well with beer. None is sold but the staff say it's OK to bring in drinks from outside & there's no corkage. **$**

SHOPPING

Big City [146 E1] 229 Zhongyang Rd; ☎ 623 8000; w fecityonline.com; ⏰ 11.00–21.30 daily. Reasons to visit Hsinchu's biggest mall include a hypermarket & gourmet deli (both in the basement), a cinema (4th Flr), English-language books & magazines (5th Flr) as well as 20-odd places to get a meal (4th & 7th flrs).

Hsin Fu Jean 新復珍 [146 C3] 6 Beimen St; ⏰ 08.00–22.30 daily. The flagship store of a traditional cake-maker that has been in business since 1898 welcomes international visitors with English-language leaflets & samples to taste (no obligation to buy). Their signature product is a flaky pastry called chuchan cake; the filling is mostly ground pork but it's the zesty green onions that make this baked delight memorable. The company also sells walnut cake, *mochi* (a snack made from pounded glutinous rice) & rice puffs.

OTHER PRACTICALITIES
$ Bank of Taiwan [146 D4] 29 Linsen Rd
✚ Nanmen Hospital [146 D3] 20 Linsen Rd;
📞 528 6456; ⏰ 24hrs daily

✉ Post office [146 C2] 2 Yingming St;
⏰ 08.00–17.30 Mon–Fri

WHAT TO SEE AND DO
Yingxi Old East Gate 迎曦東門城 [146 D3] Most of the city wall was torn down in 1902, so this gate, the only remnant, is now treasured as an emblem of Hsinchu. A double-eave structure that looks best at night when floodlit, it's sometimes used as a concert venue. After being pressed into service as a sewer, a long section of what used to be Hsinchu's moat has been cleaned up and beautified with banyans, flowerbeds and stepping stones. As an urban creek it's now every bit as attractive as Seoul's famous Cheonggyecheon – and it cost the taxpayer far less.

Du Cheng Huang Temple 都城隍廟 **(Dū Chéng Huáng Miào)** [146 C3] (75 Zhongshan Rd; w www.weiling.org.tw; ⏰ 04.30–22.30 daily) Since 1889 the deity venerated here has been seen as the divine equivalent of a provincial governor, thus outranking every other city god in Taiwan. He's also unique in having two sons; effigies of them are at the very back of the temple, on the left of the city god's wife, while fertility goddess Zhusheng Niang Niang is on her right. Established in 1748, the temple also features a huge iron abacus (to remind people that the gods tally their righteous deeds and sins), but the real stars are the statues – the *Six Generals*, the *Two Judges* and others. Pick up a bilingual leaflet from the supervisor's desk to find out who's who. If you can, come in the early evening when the temple is full of families who pray and burn joss paper before eating at the food stalls that surround the temple.

Beimen Street 北門街 [146 C2] Not long ago this thoroughfare was an authentic 'old street' lined with two-floor colonial-era merchant houses behind which stood even older structures. Sadly, the neighbourhood has suffered from neglect and piecemeal development, but it's still worth walking north from Du Cheng Huang Temple to get whiffs of old Taiwan. Numbers 59 and 96 are in excellent shape, and at number 109, you'll find a shop selling *bùdàixì* puppets. Where Beimen Street meets Aiwen Street 愛文街 there's a pair of small yet photogenic shrines, **Changhe Temple** 長和宮 and **Shuixian Temple** 水仙宮 [146 B1]; information boards out front have all the facts. If you can't get enough of characterful backstreets, explore Aiwen Street and nearby Chengbei Street 城北街.

Zheng Yong-xi (page 147) commissioned the construction of **Jinshi Mansion** 進士第 [146 B1] in 1838. This magnificent yet decrepit residence at number 163 was, at the time of writing, covered by a steel frame to prevent further deterioration. Other segments bear numbers 167 to 179 and one reason why proposals to renovate this five-courtyard complex have come to nothing is that ownership is divided among scores of Zheng's descendants. Damaged by fire during World War II, the mansion – classed as a national relic – has never been formally open to the public. Nonetheless, the intricate stone-lattice windows and exquisitely carved dragons and flowers can be appreciated from the street. At number 185, the **Zheng Clan Ancestral Hall** 鄭氏家廟 [146 B1], which dates from 1853, is where descendants of the scholar-official worship their illustrious ancestor and other forefathers. It's in far better condition than the mansion yet invariably locked up. The two stone banner-holders outside show the clan produced not one but two *jinshi*.

Hakka Country   HSINCHU CITY

5

149

Hsinchu City Hall 新竹州廳 [146 D2] (120 Zhongzheng Rd) Built between 1925 and 1932, what's also known as Hsinchu Old Prefectural Hall is a tasteful two-storey stucco-redbrick edifice. The mayor and other senior officials still work here so it's best you stay outside.

Hsinchu City Fire Museum 消防博物館 [146 C2] (4 Zhongshan Rd; ⏰ 09.00–17.00 Sun & Tue–Fri, 09.00–21.00 Sat; free admission) The most interesting thing about this museum, directly across the road from the prefectural hall and part of a functioning fire station, isn't what's displayed in the small bilingual exhibition room but the well outside from which the firemen of yesteryear drew water before setting off to fight fires in neighbourhoods that lacked hydrants.

Hsinchu Contemporary Art Gallery 新竹市美術館 [146 D2] (116 Zhongyang Rd; ☎ 524 7218; ⏰ 09.00–17.00 Tue–Sun; free admission) A building of similar vintage and style to the fire museum – and boasting a gorgeous if tiny *porte-cochère* – lies just around the corner from the government hall. Exhibitions change every two or three months.

Immaculate Heart of Mary Cathedral 北大天主堂 [146 C1] (156 Zhongzheng Rd; ☎ 525 6057; ⏰ for services only) Many of Taiwan's Catholic churches incorporate elements of Chinese 'Northern Palace' architecture, but the design of this 1957 landmark is emphatically Western.

Hsinchu Image Museum 影像博物館 [146 D3] (65 Zhongzheng Rd; ☎ 528 5840; ⏰ 09.00–noon & 14.00–21.00 Tue–Sun; admission to museum or film NTD20/10) Built in 1933 as the city's first modern cinema (and the first building in Taiwan with air conditioning), the displays about Taiwan's film industry aren't half as appealing as the opportunity to watch a movie (often Chinese language but with English subtitles) in stylish Art Deco surroundings. Screenings begin at 19.00 every day except Monday; there are also matinees at the weekend.

Principal Hsin Chih-Ping's Residence 辛志平校長故居 [146 E3] (32 Dongmen St; ⏰ 09.00–17.00 Tue–Sun; free admission) Almost a century old and formerly the home of a noted educator whose name is often rendered Xin Zhi-ping, this carefully restored bungalow is a good example of colonial-era Japanese architecture and comes complete with sliding rice-paper panels and a Japanese-style garden.

Hsinchu Glass Arts Museum 新竹市玻璃工藝博物館 [146 F4] Located in the same park as the city's zoo and Confucian shrine, this museum – undergoing renovation at the time of writing – celebrates Hsinchu's tradition of glass-making. At one point, 80% of the lights decorating North American Christmas trees were made in the Hsinchu area.

AROUND HSINCHU
Nanliao 南寮 Even though it abuts the coast, Hsinchu is seldom thought of as a maritime city, and the old fishing settlement of Nanliao to the north feels like a separate town. Bike trails run from here into Miaoli County, and the entire scenic area is designated as an Important Bird Area on account of the Kentish plovers (*Charadrius alexandrinus*) and Saunders's gulls (*Chroicocephalus saundersi*) that winter here. City bus #15 is an alternative to driving or riding out to Nanliao.

Qiding 崎頂 Just outside the city in the northwestern corner of Miaoli County, Qiding is easily reached by local train (departs at least every 30mins from Hsinchu; 05.00–23.29 daily; NTD21 one-way), car or motorcycle. The station is 100m inland of Expressway 61; when you get off the train follow the signs to the Landscape Platform 5 minutes' walk away for views up and down the coast. More engaging sights lie down in the village behind (where there are some magnificent but dilapidated traditional courtyard houses) and at the bottom of the stairs. Go down to the path beside the railway line and turn right; walking north brings you to a pair of tunnels. When the railway was double-tracked and moved closer to the sea in the early 1970s, the tunnels were preserved as solid examples of Japanese colonial infrastructure. The first tunnel is 67m long, and just before you enter the 131m-long second tunnel, look closely at the arched brickwork: US warplanes strafed the railway in the closing months of World War II and bullet holes can still be seen.

Baozhong Yimin Temple 褒忠亭義民廟 (Bāozhōng Tíng Yìmín Miào)

(Yimin & Baozhong rds, Xinpu; ⏱ 07.00–21.00 daily) The most important place of worship for many of Taiwan's Hakka citizens, this temple differs from the majority of shrines in that it isn't dedicated to an individual who lived and was deified in China centuries ago, or to a legendary figure like the Jade Emperor, but rather to men who died fighting to protect Hakka settlements here in Taiwan during the 18th and 19th centuries. When Lin Shuang-wen's rebels (page 12) moved to seize granaries in the region, 1,300 Hakka volunteers took up arms, calling themselves the 'Yimin Army' (*yìmín* meaning 'upholding faithfulness and honesty'). After repelling Lin's men they fought alongside Hoklo Taiwanese and aborigines to liberate nearby towns.

There's a reason why Taiwan's most important Yimin shrine is in a backwater. The bodies of 200-plus Yimin killed fighting Lin's forces were loaded on to ox carts so they could be interred in their home villages, but after stopping to rest where the temple now stands, the oxen refused to go any further. Through prayer and divination, the convoy's leaders determined the dead Yimin wished to be buried at this very spot, and so set about building a tomb and a makeshift shrine. A second tomb was added in the 1860s after more than 100 Yimin soldiers died battling another major uprising; these two mass graves are in the overbuilt, decrepit yet beguiling garden behind the temple. The shrine's original memorial tablets were destroyed in 1895 when Japanese troops clashed with Taiwanese irregulars. The temple is unusual in that it lacks effigies of deities; even Guan Gong is represented by a simple tablet.

Thousands of people come here between the 18th and 20th of the seventh lunar month each year for the Hakka Yimin Festival, during which it's traditional to sacrifice minced chicken or duck (not whole fowl as is usual in Taiwanese rites) or sliced pork. If you attend, you're likely to witness a highly controversial religious practice: the display of 'divine pigs'. These enormous swine are fed (often forcibly and sometimes with sand and iron-filings, critics allege) until they're so big they're unable to walk. The root cause of this cruelty is vanity – the heavier the pig, the greater the prestige of the family who raised it.

Getting there and away Without your own wheels it's difficult. If you're driving from Hsinchu City, get on Road 117 just inland of the TRA station and follow it southeast then northeast for 20–25 minutes. The Fast #5 minibus (departs every 30mins; ⏱ 07.10–20.45 daily; 15mins; NTD15) is a direct service from Hsinchu HSR station. Between the temple and central Hsinchu you're limited to the nine #5621 buses each day to Zhubei TRA station (20mins; NTD25) – good if you're heading north – and another 20-odd minutes to the centre of Hsinchu (NTD45).

Hukou Old Street 湖口老街 **(Húkǒu Lǎojiē)** Popular with domestic sightseers, Hukou Old Street is of limited appeal unless you've a special interest in urban conservation. Almost all the 200-plus houses here are two-floor shop-house combinations dating from around 1915, most of which are now family homes, although a few businesses sell souvenirs or meals. The street owes its existence to the north–south railroad; a station used to stand where there's now a Catholic church. When the tracks were shifted seaward after World War II, businesses moved out or withered away, and there was neither the incentive nor the money to rebuild. A comprehensive government-funded renovation has restored aspects of the street's original appearance. Power, telephone and TV cables are underground and neither air-conditioning units nor rooftop water tanks are visible from the street. Many houses have traditional wooden sliding doors rather than vertical metal shutters.

Getting there and away Self-drivers should take Freeway 1 to the Hukou exit then drive north on Highway 1 for 3km. Buses include the #5676 Hsinchu–Zhongli service (18 departures per day; ⊕ 05.50–20.40; takes around 40mins from Hsinchu or Zhongli; NTD54/75 from Hsinchu/Zhongli), which stops on Highway 1, a few minutes' walk from the old street. Several but not all of the less frequent #5612 and #5613 services go into central Hsinchu; be sure to confirm the destination before paying.

EAST OF HSINCHU

Winning scenery and appealing villages make this region a delight to explore if you've your own transport, and more than justify getting to grips with bus and train schedules and routes. If you've time for just one of these places, head for delightfully historic Beipu; if minimising public-transport hassle is a priority, opt for Neiwan.

GETTING THERE AND AROUND Self-drivers will arrive via Highway 3, and minor roads linking Beipu with Lion's Head Mountain and Nanzhuang are clearly signposted in English. For details of public transport, see the individual sections.

TOURIST INFORMATION
🛈 **Lion's Head Mountain Visitor Information Centre** ⊕ 08.30–17.30 daily

🛈 **Tri-Mountain National Scenic Area** w www.trimt-nsa.gov.tw

---

RIGHTEOUS HAKKA MARTYRS

Yimin worship is central to the spiritual life of Taiwan's Hakka population and the spirits of the Yimin have evolved into all-purpose deities. During 19th-century droughts and epidemics people prayed to them for relief. When Hakka pioneers moved deeper into the mountains they besought the Yimin to protect them from aboriginal headhunters. A newer custom appeared when compulsory military service was introduced in the early 1950s – young men receiving their call-up papers would, before reporting for duty, visit a Yimin shrine and ask the spirits to look out for them.

Nowadays the Yimin festival is celebrated over several days during the summer in dozens of towns and villages throughout the Hsinchu region.

NEIWAN 內灣 This little riverside town, 258m above sea level, is the end point of the 27.9km-long **Neiwan Branch Railway**, originally built to serve the timber and coal industries but now used by commuters from Hsinchu. Travel on a weekday after rush hour to avoid packed carriages. Inland of Zhudong the landscape is appealingly rural yet there's little point in getting off the train before the terminus. The scenery is pleasant and, if you stay after dusk in late spring, you're likely to see fireflies.

Once in Neiwan, cross the tracks and make your way up to the police station. Built in 1938, it looks its age, unlike many remnants of that era. If you want to take photos of trains as they leave or arrive, the steps leading up to the police station is the best (and safest) place to stand. Then walk down into the town proper, stopping perhaps for a steamed-rice dumpling flavoured with local ginger (NTD20 each; vegetarian versions available). Two vendors specialise in these dense but tasty leaf-wrapped snacks: Mother Luo's Wild Ginger Zongzi is right across the road from the station entrance (89 Zhongzheng Rd; ⏰ varies) while Auntie Zhan's (105 Zhongzheng Rd; ⏰ 10.00–19.00 daily) is several doors down on the right. If you continue a little further you'll find **Neiwan Forest Industry Exhibition Hall** 林務局內灣林業展示館 (11 Datong Rd; ⏰ 09.00–17.00 Wed–Sun; free admission) in a stand-alone building on the corner. There's no English inside, but the black-and-white photos taken more than 60 years ago are engrossing.

The quaint **former cinema** in the heart of the town is now a restaurant (227 Zhongzheng Rd; ⏰ 11.00–19.00 daily; **$$$**), remarkable only because diners can watch Chinese-language movies while enjoying Hakka-style dishes. A better place to laze is **New Hakka Cultural Park** 好客好品希望工場 (⏰ 10.00–17.00 Wed–Mon; admission NTD50, redeemable if you spend money inside), where there's a café selling hot and cold drinks and snacks (**$$**), as well as on-site handicrafts production. The park is best reached by turning left when you exit the railway station, walking 80m and going through the tunnel on the left. This takes you under the tracks; turn left when you emerge.

Getting there and away
Four of the six daily trains that go all the way from Hsinchu to Neiwan (1hr; NTD42) depart before 08.00 so you'll likely change at Zhuzhong (hrly departures to Neiwan; ⏰ 08.46–21.52; 42mins; NTD30). A day pass, good for both the Neiwan Branch Railway and the Liujia Branch Railway (page 147), costs NTD95.

Where to stay and eat
Migration Café & B&B 遷徙∣咖啡&民宿 (3 rooms) 18 Heping St; m 0983 332 511; e migrationbb2015@gmail.com; w migrationbb2015.wixsite.com/migrationbb2015. English is spoken at this small but characterful house in the heart of Neiwan.

All the rooms are delightful but the cheapest is tiny. Midweek, the 4-person room upstairs is often priced around NTD4,000. B/fast inc; the café (⏰ 11.00–18.00 daily) serves a wide range of hot & cold drinks (from NTD120) & a few meal options; EM. **$$$**

BEIPU 北埔 (**BĚIPŬ**) Like Tainan and Lukang, Beipu (population 9,400, 98% Hakka) is a place where the past can still be seen and touched, though it's actually much younger than those two bastions of tradition. Given the circumstances in which the town was founded in 1835 – armed Hakka settlers forced out the original Atayal inhabitants – it's not surprising that for decades afterwards the townsfolk didn't feel safe at night. In addition to the usual walls and gates, Beipu's pioneers deployed a guileful way of protecting the settlement. The town's streets were covered with stone slabs, most of which were fixed in place. A few weren't, however, and made a loud 'clunk' when stepped on. Locals knew where to step, of course, but intruders trying to infiltrate couldn't help but set off these 'alarm stones'.

During the colonial era, coal turned Beipu into a boom town where miners blew their wages in wine shops and brothels. These days the businesses that thrive are altogether more salubrious and, as often as not, aimed squarely at incoming tourists. **Citian Temple** 慈天宮 (1 Beipu St; ⊕ 05.30–19.00 daily) is at the heart of Beipu's historic quarter. Local folk come to this shrine to worship Guanyin and the Three Mountain Kings. The latter, represented by a tablet on the left, are deities revered by Hakka people throughout east and southeast Asia. Nearby, at 14 Miaoqian Street, you'll find a shop (⊕ 08.00–18.00 daily) that sells various oils, including black sesame, tea seed and camphor, the last of which was a key commodity in Taiwan in the 18th and 19th centuries. Making 3,600cc of camphor oil requires 100kg of wood; these days many of the shop's customers are dog-owners who rub it into their pets' fur to repel insects.

Three landmark buildings stand with 100m of the temple. Parts of the exquisitely photogenic mansion called **Tianshuitang** 天水堂 (1 Zhongzheng Rd; ⊕ not open to the public) date from the 1830s. **Jinguangfu** 金廣福公館 (6 Zhongzheng Rd; ⊕ 09.00–17.00 daily; admission NTD30) – sometimes spelled 'Ching Kwang Fu' – was once the head office (and is named after) the joint venture that opened Beipu to Han settlement, a group so-named because it brought together Fujianese businessmen with Hakka originally from Guangdong. There's very little English inside so pick up a bilingual leaflet. Near the entrance, look for the knee-high snipers' loopholes through which residents could shoot at intruders without killing them, thereby avoiding the legal consequences of causing a death. The two-storey **Jiang A-Xin House** 姜阿新洋樓 (10 Beipu St) was built just after World War II by a scion of the town's most famous family, and by the time you read this renovation work should be finished and the building open to the public.

If you're getting about by car or motorcycle, do explore the hills southeast of the town as the scenery along County Road 37 to Donghe (page 159) is lovely. The 'official' **Beipu Cold Spring** 北埔冷泉 is at km13.5 but because it gets very crowded on summer weekends, many locals head a little further south to cool off in the river.

Getting there and away For Beipu, go first to Zhudong by #5608 from Hsinchu's South bus station (departs every 15mins; ⊕ 06.00–22.30; NTD51) or by #1820 from Taipei (departs every 20–30mins; 2hrs; ⊕ 06.10–22.30; NTD159). In Zhudong board #5610 (departs every 30mins; ⊕ 06.00–20.00; NTD25) for the final stage of the journey. At the weekend, the last bus back to Zhudong leaves at 18.55.

⌂ Where to stay and eat

⌂ **HaveFun** 海福坊 (2 rooms) 9 Lane 16, Gongyuan St; m 0955 313 130; w penrita6.wixsite. com/havefun. Hidden in the backstreets of old Beipu, this old & characterful homestay is usually booked as a whole so a family or group of friends can enjoy the kitchen & living room (NTD3,000–3,600 for 2 adults & 2 children). English spoken. **$$$**

✗ **Old Street Bantiao** 老街板條 31 Miaoqian St; ☎ 580 3871; ⊕ 09.00–17.00 Thu–Tue, a bit later Sat–Sun. Some Beipu restaurants fake old but this one doesn't have to as its photogenic home has been around for a century.

Within, sections of wall have been stripped of plaster to show the original daub, bricks & stones. The menu features Hakka staples inc ban-tiao (NTD60), Hakka stir fry (NTD150), 'countryside chicken' (tǔjī 土雞, NTD150–250), & vegetable fern (guòmāo 過貓 – a vegetable listed in the Slow Food Foundation's Ark of Taste – NTD110). No EM but some English spoken. **$$**

✗ **Dinghao Dishes** 頂好小吃店 27 Beipu St; ☎ 580 2719; ⊕ 09.00–18.30 daily. Nearly a century old, this restaurant's food wins plaudits for authentic flavours but not generous portions. The

Just as Hakka people have a distinctive way of cooking, they also have a special way of preparing tea. In several of Beipu's restaurants, tourists can try their hand at making *léi chá* 擂茶 (literally 'pounded tea'), which involves a lot of elbow work but is also good fun. If you order a set you'll be brought the ingredients on a tray plus a mortar and pestle with which to grind them.

The recipe varies from one establishment to the next but often includes sesame seeds, pine nuts, peanuts, sunflower seeds, crispy rice and peppermint as well as dried tea leaves. Once you've reduced everything but the rice to a fine paste, added piping hot water and a spoonful of soybean powder, and stirred the resulting concoction, you'll have something that looks like pea soup. Throw in the rice and it's ready to drink. The taste is very different from tea you're used to, of course, and it isn't to everyone's liking – but it'll be a cuppa you'll remember for quite some time.

names of several noodle, rice vermicelli & ban-tiao dishes (NTD55 & up) inc the characters *zhàcài ròu sī* 榨菜肉絲 meaning they incorporate pickled mustard greens & shredded pork. The menu also lists beef noodles, wontons & Hakka-style *tāng yuán* (NTD75). No EM. **$**

LION'S HEAD MOUNTAIN 獅頭山 **(SHĪTÓUSHĀN)** Excursions to Beipu can easily be combined with a visit to this segment of the Tri-Mountain National Scenic Area. None of the mountain's hiking trails are especially challenging, but they do offer a chance to get close to nature and see picturesque Buddhist shrines and monasteries established more than a century ago. The best known, **Cyuanhua Temple** 勸化堂 **(Quànhuà Táng)** (⊕ 05.00–19.00 daily), offers food and accommodation (see below). The visitor information centre on the northern side of the mountain can provide a detailed English-language map-leaflet with distances and altitudes (the highest point is 492m above sea level) and can help with arranging accommodation. Those who approach from the south may have to depend on the bilingual signposts, of which there are more than enough.

So long as you reach the information centre before noon you'll be able to explore the area thoroughly, dally a little at each of the sights, and still make it to the bus stop on Road 124 in plenty of time to either return to Hsinchu or continue on to Nanzhuang. If you're up early, try to at least get to **Yuanguang Temple** 元光寺; although it's one of the plainer shrines on the mountain, from the forecourt it's often possible to see the Hsinchu–Zhubei sprawl.

Getting there and away The Tourist Shuttle #5700 Lion's Head Mountain Route (departs hrly on the hour ⊕ 08.00–15.00 Mon–Fri, every 30mins ⊕ 08.00–16.00 Sat–Sun), departs from Zhubei TRA station, stopping at Hsinchu HSR station 19 minutes later, Beipu Old Street an hour after initial departure (NTD82), and reaching Lion's Head Mountain Visitor Centre after 1½ hours on the road (NTD112). The first bus leaving Lion's Head Mountain is at 10.00; final departure is at 17.00 on weekdays, 18.00 at the weekend. Some Tourist Shuttle buses in the Nanzhuang area will also get you to Lion's Head Mountain.

 Where to stay and eat

Cyuanhua Temple Pilgrims Lodge 獅山香客大樓 (72 rooms) ☏ 037 822 563. The main accommodation option on Lion's Head Mountain is next to & operated by Cyuanhua Temple. Across the border in Miaoli County, so you'll need to add the area code 037 if calling from Hsinchu or further afield. Some English is spoken, but maybe ask the VIC to help you book a room & meals. The rooms (NTD1,000 for 2 ppl; some take 3, 4 or 6 ppl) aren't 5-star but not nearly so austere as you expect at a religious institution. Simple but filling vegetarian meals are available & free of charge (🕘 b/fast 06.30–07.30, lunch noon–14.00 & dinner 17.30–18.30), but do make a small donation if you're satisfied. The bldg is a bit of a walk from the nearest car park/bus stop so don't carry too much luggage. **$$**

EMEI 峨眉 This thinly populated township is a short drive from Beipu but tricky to explore by public transport. Motorists can park near the elementary school in Fuxing 富興 and take a look at the old tea-processing factory that's now the photogenic **Fuxing Tea Demonstration Centre** 富興茶葉文化館 (🕘 09.00–17.00 Tue–Sun; free admission). There's no English sign outside; look for the old tree bent at 45 degrees right in front of a traditional double doorway. From here, walk south down Lane 8, Taiping Street to a footbridge that crosses part of **Dapu Reservoir** 大埔水庫. The immense building on the other side is **Nature Loving Wonderland** 大自然文化世界 (w naturelovingwonderland.org; free admission), a Buddhist landmark completed in 2011 and best known for the world's tallest bronze statue of the Maitreya Buddha (72m including base). Visiting rules are complex so go online well ahead of time if you've a serious interest. If you get inside, expect proselytising from the guides. Advance bookings aren't required for the adjacent **Hall of Buddha Maitreya** 彌勒殿 (🕘 09.00–11.30 & 13.30–16.30 Tue–Fri, 09.00–17.00 Sat–Sun; free admission) in which visitors can see statues of the Maitreya Buddha, Guanyin and Guan Gong.

THE ABORIGINAL INTERIOR

Adventurous self-drivers may want to visit indigenous communities located deep in the mountainous interior of Hsinchu and Miaoli counties.

GETTING THERE AND AROUND You'll need your own car and strong nerves because road conditions are often poor; only highly experienced riders should attempt to reach these places by motorcycle. Having lots of time is essential as distances on maps and signposts are deceptive; the final 16km to Smangus, for instance, often takes an hour. None of these destinations can realistically be done as day trips from the lowlands; accommodation options are mentioned below.

For Qingquan, take Highway 3 to Hengshan then Road 122 south. To reach Xiuluan and Smangus, follow Highway 3 northeast away from Hsinchu City until you see signs to Neiwan; beyond Neiwan the route is clearly signposted. The turn-off to Taian is north of Dahu.

QINGQUAN 清泉 This mostly Atayal village is best known among Taiwanese for being the place where Manchurian warlord Zhang Xueliang (1901–2001) was kept in detention between 1946 and 1959. Arrested in 1936 on the orders of Chiang Kai-shek, whom he had kidnapped and coerced into an alliance with China's Communists, Zhang was variously a soldier, politician, opium addict and womaniser (Mussolini's eldest daughter was one of his lovers). He endured more than half a century under house arrest in various locations before spending his final years in Hawaii. Zhang Xueliang's Former Residence (🕘 09.00–17.00 Tue–Sun; free admission) is a beautiful reconstruction of the house where Zhang and his wife stayed. In addition to hot springs and homestays, Qingquan has an inexpensive hostel operated by the local Catholic church. The priest is an American who's lived here since the 1970s and speaks Atayal.

XIULUAN 秀巒 The toponym means 'elegant mountain ranges' but the nearby peaks are often lost in fog. The village's free, 100% natural hot-spring pools are beside the river. To go beyond this tiny settlement you'll need to obtain a mountain permit at the police checkpoint; the procedure is straightforward but you'll need to show your passport.

SMANGUS 司馬庫斯 This village, which lies at an elevation of around 1,600m, has been an Atayal settlement on and off for well over a century. Like many other indigenous groups, the clan that regards this as their ancestral land were forced by the Japanese colonial regime to move to a lower elevation so they could be more easily controlled. After 1945 they returned, but for decades living conditions were extremely tough. Electricity didn't come to the village until 1979 and there wasn't a proper road before 1995. Villagers have responded to the recent tourism boom by establishing a Church-affiliated co-operative that shares homestay and restaurant revenues in a way that's designed to encourage young people to remain part of the community. Get a Chinese speaker to contact the visitor centre (✆ 03 584 7688; w smangus.org) in advance if you want to arrange accommodation and/or meals. Smangus's main attraction is a grove of giant trees, one of which is an estimated 2,500 years old. Because the villagers are Christians they don't, unlike their forebears, consider the trees to be sacred. Reaching the grove and then returning to the village is a proper hike that takes the better part of a day.

TAIAN HOT SPRINGS 泰安溫泉 Between Dahu and Nanzhuang, Road 62 leads inland from Highway 3 to a resort where you can enjoy some challenging day hikes before soaking. The springs themselves are clear, odourless, carbonic and weakly acidic; to enjoy them you'll need to stay in one of Taian's mid-range hotels.

NANZHUANG 南庄 (NÁNZHUĀNG) *Telephone code 037*

Well and truly discovered by domestic tourists, the Nanzhuang area has a slew of scenic, cultural and ecological attractions. The town itself is a good spot to explore on foot and get a meal, but Penglai and the tiny aboriginal villages beyond Donghe are more attractive places to spend the night. The valleys inland of Nanzhuang are home to a branch of one of Taiwan's smallest aboriginal tribes, the 6,600-strong Saisiyat.

GETTING THERE AND AROUND
By car, motorcycle or bicycle Self-drivers should take Highway 3 then Road 124. Cyclists should know that coming from the south involves steeper gradients than approaching from the north, and that in either direction it's a challenging route.

By bus The #5804 leaves central Hsinchu for Nanzhuang every hour (⊕ 08.10–20.50 daily; 1¼hrs; NTD148). To get beyond Nanzhuang, you'll need to make use of Taiwan Tourist Shuttles; a one-day pass (NTD150) covers Nanzhuang (#5805; 9 services daily), Xiangtian Lake (#5824; 8 daily), and Xianshan (#5822; 8 daily) routes. The first of these takes nearly an hour to get from the back (east) exit of Zhunan TRA station to Nanzhuang via Lion's Head Mountain Historic Trail Entrance 獅頭山古道口站 on Road 124, where you should get off if you're heading to Cyuanhua Temple. From Nanzhuang to Xiangtian Lake can take half an hour in heavy traffic, and to Xianshan the journey time is often 40 minutes.

TOURIST INFORMATION

🛈 Miaoli County Culture and Tourism Bureau w miaolitravel.net

🛈 Nanzhuang Visitor Centre Near Nanzhuang Market; ⏰ 08.30–17.30 daily

🏠 WHERE TO STAY

🏠 Good-Mountain Good-Water Cabins & Homestay 好山好水景觀木屋民宿 (17 rooms) 536 Penglai Vlg; ✆ 825 789; w gmgw.com. tw. The rooms & cabins for 2, 4 or 6 ppl are pretty comfortable & every evening the manager leads a Chinese-language ecotour of the grounds, still highly enjoyable even if you don't speak a word. You can expect to see various moths, frogs (Penglai has 17 of Taiwan's 32 amphibian species), freshwater crabs & shrimp & possibly flying squirrels. The creek that runs through the grounds is clean enough for children to play in & there are camping spots with electricity. Good Mountain is on the left if you're coming from Nanzhuang, less than 100m down a side road near km33.5 on Road 124. B/fast inc. **$$$**

🏠 Lily Village 百合山莊 (12 rooms) km31 Rd 124; ✆ 825 822; w lilyvillage.com.tw. Popular with well-off Taiwanese & surrounded by farmland, Lily has largish modern rooms & is equidistant between Penglai & Nanzhuang; look for the fake windmill on the right if you're coming from the latter. B/fast inc; the in-house restaurant offers a good range of meals but these must be booked at least a day in advance. **$$$**

🏠 Olive Tree 橄欖樹 (10 rooms) 76 Div 42, Penglai Vlg; m 0919 822 379; e ot822379@ yahoo.com; w olive-tree.idv.tw. More English is understood here than at many Miaoli homestays, but that's not the only reason to stay in this country retreat; it's extremely comfortable & strolling in any direction is a pleasure. Rooms for 2 ppl or 4 ppl. B/fast inc; other meals can be ordered. Take the side road that goes downhill at km37.5 on Road 124; the junction is cluttered by colourful signs for nearby B&Bs. You'll pass Olive Tree on the way to the 42 Fen Ping Trail (see opposite). **$$$**

🍴 WHERE TO EAT AND DRINK

🍴 Songhe Market Delicacies 松鶴市場小吃 Inside Nanzhuang market bldg; ✆ 822 435; ⏰ 06.00–17.00 daily. The best of the eateries inside the busy traditional market, this friendly establishment is located at the back & serves up Hakka stir fry (NTD200), various soups (from NTD35), plus ban-tiao & other noodles (from NTD45). Their signature dish is pig-skin & rice (*zhū pí fàn* 豬皮飯, NTD50 for a small portion). No EM. **$$**

🍴 Xianshan Xiancao 仙山仙草 62 Shitan Old St, Shitan; ✆ 932 318; ⏰ 08.00–17.30 daily. Almost everything on the menu here features *xiāncǎo*, a jelly made from Chinese mesona (*Platostoma palustre*, a distant relative of mint sometimes translated as 'grass jelly'). In the days of yore a folk remedy for heat stroke, *xiāncǎo* is now usually enjoyed as a dessert. A bowl of iced jelly with milk, mung beans, adzuki beans, sweet potato, taro, &/or powdered peanuts (NTD45–80) is just the ticket in warm weather. If you need something more substantial, order one of the meat sets, such as *xiāncǎo*-flavoured hot pot, ramen or dumplings (NTD180–330). No EM. **$$**

🍴 Mother Tian Douhua 田媽媽豆花 Next to Presbyterian church, Nanzhuang; ⏰ 10.00–17.00 daily. A good bet if you want something to eat while avoiding the crowds around the old street & the market, this eatery sells only hot & cold bean-curd pudding (*dòuhuā* 豆花, NTD35–40) & flavour options inc peanut, tapioca balls & mung bean. Mother Tian isn't the owner but rather the name of a government scheme that encourages rural women to monetise their cooking skills & knowledge of local produce by selling homemade delicacies. Go up the stairs across the road from the visitor centre; you'll find it at the top on your right. **$**

WHAT TO SEE AND DO Road 124 leads right through Nanzhuang. You'll have no problems finding the pedestrians-only 'Old Street' across the road from the visitor centre and market building. Cyclists should know that beyond Nanzhuang the road climbs gradually all the way to Xianshan then drops steeply to Shitan.

Nanzhuang Old Street 南庄老街 (Nánzhuāng Lǎo jiē) Before joining the

herd as it shops, photographs and eats its way through what's also known as Sweet

Osmanthus Alley 桂花巷, do notice the spring where, in the olden days, townsfolk would come to do their laundry, using the rutted stone slabs as washboards. A few residents still use it for its original purpose but you're more likely to see tourists washing their kids' sticky fingers. Few of the local specialities sold near here are labelled in English, but this matters not one jot. If something looks good and you're offered a morsel-sized sample, accept it – there's no obligation to buy. The most picturesque building along the street is a wooden former post office over a hundred years old.

Donghe 東河 Reached by Road 21, a 14.5km-long dead end, Donghe is a multi-cultural mix of Hakka, Hoklo, Atayal and Saisiyat households. Just past the elementary school, a former logging-company office has been renovated and turned into the **Walo Industrial Culture Gallery** 瓦祿產業文化館 (✆ 823 050; ⊕ 09.00–17.00 Wed–Sun; free admission), which sells local souvenirs and hot drinks (from NTD80).

Xiangtian Lake 向天湖 **(Xiàngtiān Hú)** Although the drive up is scenic, there's little reason for you to go out of your way to this indigenous settlement 738m above sea level unless you've a great interest in the Pasta'ai Ceremony (page 67). The ceremony and related traditions are a key part of the poorly executed yet to-a-degree informative **Saisiyat Folklore Museum** 賽夏族民俗文物館 (✆ 825 024; ⊕ 09.00–17.00 Tue–Sun; admission NTD30). Displays are bilingual, after a fashion.

Shibi 石壁 A few minutes beyond Donghe on Road 21, Shibi is notable for the rough cliffs that line both sides of the valley; the Chinese and indigenous ('Raisinay') toponyms both mean 'rocky wall'. **Raisinay Dyeing and Weaving Workshop** 石壁染織工坊 (w raisinay.com; ⊕ 09.00–17.00 Mon & Wed–Sat) sells waistcoats, pencil cases and other high-quality pieces, and the owners also run a six-room B&B (✆ 821 255; **$$**).

Shensian Valley 神仙谷 **(Shénxiān Gǔ)** The main attraction between Shibi and Luchang is the confluence of three streams where rushing torrents have cut and smoothed a series of gullies far too dangerous to swim in. Nature makes quite a racket here; in addition to the non-stop crash of water on rock, birds babble and cicadas buzz. The footbridge across the river leads to a trail that goes 2.2km downstream; this path has been closed in the past due to typhoon damage, so you may have to retrace your steps rather than complete a loop.

Luchang 鹿場 Formerly a thriving mining-and-logging settlement, this tiny village has few residents nowadays, and there's little to do but enjoy superb views down the valley and buy locally grown high-mountain produce. The old police station, a remnant of the colonial government's efforts to control the indigenous population, has been renovated.

Penglai Stream Biological Tour Area 蓬萊溪自然生態園區 (⊕ 24hrs daily; free admission) Fishing has been banned in this nature reserve, also known as Penglai Creek Ecology Park, since 2001. It's easy to spend an hour on the riverside wooden walkway, spotting grey herons and clusters of butterflies. Peer into the water and you've an excellent chance of seeing schools of fish, among them two endemic species: *Acrossocheilus paradoxus*, sometimes known as the Taiwan stone minnow, and *Candidia barbata*. The former is a silvery dark-grey colour and grows up to 10cm in length, while the latter is of a similar size but greenish. If the car park is full, continue a further 3km south to the **42 Fen Ping Trail** 四十二分坪步道

DANCING FOR DEAD DWARFS

One element of Saisiyat culture has become well known within Taiwan: the biennial Pasta'ai Ceremony. Held in the middle of the 10th lunar month of each even-numbered year, the four-day/three-night festival is intended to appease the spirits of an extinct tribe called the 'short people'. According to Saisiyat tradition, these dwarfs taught the Saisiyat how to farm. Relations between the two groups were harmonious until, it's said, a Saisiyat woman was raped by one of the dwarfs. A brief war followed; the victorious Saisiyat exterminated their enemies but soon suffered a series of grave misfortunes.

Tribal leaders, believing the spirits of the short people were wreaking revenge, decided to hold the Pasta'ai. The importance of the festival to the tribe can be seen from what happened when local clergy urged Christian tribespeople not to participate. The majority, it's reported, have stopped attending church services. An especially impressive version of the event, which features rites to welcome the spirits, offerings, prayers and dancing, is held every ten years. The next super Pasta'ai will be in the autumn of 2026.

(🕘 24hrs daily; free admission). The turn off at km37.5 on Road 124 is easy to find – look for the cluster of bilingual B&B signs – and from there you'll soon come to a small car park within sight of the Penglai Creek. Half an hour is usually enough for a slow stroll enjoying the surroundings but if it's summertime and you're into dragonflies you may stay over an hour.

Xianshan 仙山 The only reason to stop here, roughly equidistant between 42 Fen Ping Trail and Shitan, is to appreciate the often-superb view from **Lingdong Temple** 靈洞宮. The shrine itself (dedicated to Guan Gong) is neither particularly old nor interesting but thanks to the number of visitors it attracts, the sheltered mini-market (🕘 10.00–18.00 daily) is your best hope for hot food (many options; no EM; **$**) between Shitan and Nanzhuang. The trail up the hill (the summit is 967m above sea level) to the right of the temple is divided into two parts; the first is a mere 490m in length but has 1,052 steps, while the second features an additional 1,200 steps over a distance of 630m.

Shitan 獅潭 There's little reason to stop in this tiny town unless you want to enjoy a refreshing bowl of *xiāncǎo* (page 158) or refuel. The petrol station (🕘 07.00–18.00 daily) is on Highway 3, 1km north of the junction with Road 124. The Presbyterian church here was founded by George L Mackay (see box, page 138), who pulled rotten teeth from the mouths of converts and potential converts during an 1873 church-planting expedition.

SANYI 三義 (SĀNYÌ) *Telephone code 037*

Taiwan's foremost woodcarving centre and its surroundings make for an excellent day trip from Taichung or Hsinchu, but if possible, stay overnight so you can give the area the time it deserves. The woodcarving industry began here during the early part of the Japanese colonial period when the local camphor forests were heavily logged. Roots and stumps were plentiful and carvings made by local artisans were popular with Taiwanese and Japanese Buddhists. Americans were important customers after World War II: Catholics commissioned sculptures of the Virgin

Mary while soldiers based in Taiwan picked up souvenirs. Each summer there are exhibitions and competitions.

In addition, gorgeous valleys and forest-covered hills lie to the east of Sanyi, but to explore them you'll need your own car or motorcycle or to be a determined cyclist.

GETTING THERE AND AROUND

By car, motorcycle or bicycle By Freeway 1, Sanyi is 125km south of Taipei, 28km north of Taichung. Those on two wheels should, if possible, arrive or leave by the splendidly scenic Road 130 (page 162).

By TRA At least one local train in either direction per hour stops at Sanyi, with typical journey times being 53 minutes from Hsinchu (NTD77) and 33 minutes from Taichung (NTD50). The station is 2.5km north of the Wood Sculpture Museum, a taxi to which shouldn't cost more than NTD150.

By bus Compared with the train, bus #5664 from Miaoli (departs about hrly; ⊕ 07.05–21.40 daily; 40mins; NTD64) stops on Shuimei Street but it's still a good uphill walk from Highway 13 to the museum.

TOURIST INFORMATION

☑ Miaoli County Culture and Tourism Bureau w miaolitravel.net

WHERE TO STAY AND EAT

⌂ Teafate 茗緣居 (5 rooms) Junction of Rd 130 & Rd 119; ☏ 787 8985; w www.teafate.com. tw. No English sign but this stand-alone 2-storey bldg is easy to find if you're coming from Sanyi, although it's a good 1.2km from the busiest part of town. The owners are quite old & don't speak much English but they're very helpful, & evening meals can be provided. A room for 2 costs NTD1,880– 2,400 inc b/fast. **$$**

✕ Jinbang Noodle Restaurant 金榜麵 館 170–7 Zhongzheng Rd, Sanyi; ☏ 873 567; ⊕ 07.00–20.00 daily. Come early because this place is so popular with locals you might have trouble finding a table. Serves Hakka dishes inc ban-tiao with pork or beef. Many dishes priced under NTD90; portions are quite large. The menu also features pig's head meat (zhū tóu ròu 豬頭肉) & ducks' heads (yā tóu 鴨頭), plus safer bets like wonton soup. **$$**

WHAT TO SEE AND DO Over 100 shops sell woodcarvings in the town, and they range from stores packed with mass-produced souvenirs to exclusive galleries. Two neighbourhoods in particular are dominated by workshops and showrooms and you'll have no problems finding either. One, **Shuimei Street** 水美街, is just north of the freeway exit around km49 and 50 on Highway 13. The other, **Guangsheng Village** 廣聲新城, is a newer part of town where you'll also find Sanyi's popular museum.

Sanyi Wood Sculpture Museum 三義木雕博物館 (Sānyì Mùdiāo Bówùguǎn)

(☏ 876 009; w wood.mlc.gov.tw; ⊕ 09.00–17.00 Tue–Sun; admission NTD80) Not a place to be rushed, this museum has galleries on four floors and is permeated by woody aromas. Among the hundreds of religious, practical, decorative and abstract carvings are exquisite prize-winning works by local artists. The most interesting sections are those devoted to the history of the art in China, aboriginal woodcarving and temple carving. Finding the museum isn't that easy as some of the signs are Chinese only, use a different English name or are hidden behind foliage. On weekdays it's often possible to park for free right outside the museum.

April Snow Path 四月雪小徑 If you face the museum, you'll see the start of this short hiking trail to your right – so named because each spring white Tung-tree blossoms make it look as though snow has fallen on the hillside. Ten minutes of brisk uphill walking brings you to a tea plantation. For additional exercise, turn left when you reach the concrete track.

Shengxing Railway Station 勝興火車站 At 402m above sea level, this station used to be the highest point on the north–south railroad. Trains now take a straighter route nearer the sea, but the colonial-era wooden station building remains in place. Special trains pulled by steam locomotives can be ridden between May and August; ask at Sanyi's visitor centre or call the tourist hotline (☎ 0800 011 765). The village here is very quaint and makes the most of its rustic appeal. It does get packed with people at times, in particular during the **Hakka Tung Blossom Festival** (w tung. hakka.gov.tw). Vehicles can be parked in one of the village's car parks or on the main road (NTD50; no time limit).

Longteng Broken Bridge 龍騰斷橋 Completed in 1909, Longteng Bridge was damaged beyond repair in the terrible earthquake of 1935 (see box, above). The only arch to survive that disaster collapsed during 1999's big quake, after which the site was declared a national monument. It's hard to explain the attraction of this ruin, which from a distance resembles a row of giant mushrooms, yet it and the surrounding hills are certainly appealing. To reach this bridge drive through Shengxing Village and follow the road for 5km. Hikers have the option of a slightly shorter and much flatter route: tramp along the railway tracks through the 725m-long tunnel by the station and you'll reach the bridge in about an hour.

Road 130 This route links the coastal lowlands with Highway 3, meeting the latter south of Dahu 大湖, a town famous for its strawberries. The inland section of Road 130 is exceptionally pretty and at least a dozen homestays (most signposted in Chinese only) can be found between km17 and km22. Near km17.5, a turn-off on the right goes uphill for approximately 1km to **Fodingshan Chaosheng Temple** 佛頂山朝聖寺 (⏲ 06.00–18.00 daily), a newish Buddhist place of worship that shows strong Japanese influences; the gardens are delightful and offer nice views of the nearby hills. A little further along Road 130 there are spots where, if you come in the middle of spring, impressive clusters of fireflies can be seen.

6

Central Taiwan

Central Taiwan, which covers 8,685km², consists of the municipality of Taichung and the counties of Nantou, Changhua and Yunlin. A quarter of the region's 5.25 million people live in central Taichung, a modern metropolis that dominates the interior's economy. Cleaved by powerful rivers and rippled with hills, central Taiwan didn't see much development before the arrival of the Japanese as the first few waves of Han migrants stayed close to the coast. Today, Lukang, where the Japanese traded and prayed, remains one of Taiwan's most fascinating towns, while Changhua, a Qing prefectural capital for 150 years, has preserved a good part of its history.

Most of the region's other attractions are deep in the interior. Sun Moon Lake has long been one of Taiwan's most popular tourist destinations. Around Hehuanshan, mountain scenery can be enjoyed without having to get out of your car or off your motorcycle. If you feel the need to lace up your boots and do some serious hiking, there are few better places in east Asia than Yushan and Shei-Pa national parks. The former embraces Taiwan's highest peak, Mount Jade, and an expanse of expedition country that will have experienced trekkers salivating, while Shei-Pa includes Snow Mountain, the island's second-highest peak. Visit either reserve and you'll agree made-in-Taiwan alpine views are world class.

TAICHUNG 台中 (TÁIZHŌNG) *Telephone code 04*

Ever so briefly Taiwan's capital, Taichung is often overlooked by travellers, despite having worthwhile museums and a very wide range of eating options. It's thus a good place to be when the weather's bad, but that seldom happens as the city is blessed with an equitable climate. Some visitors base themselves here while exploring Sanyi, Lukang and other small towns.

HISTORY For more than a century from the 1720s, the plot of land that's now Taichung Park was an army training ground called Datun ('big mound'). In 1885, Liu Ming-chuan's proposal that the site be developed into the administrative centre of the new provincial government was approved by the Qing court. However, little progress was made before Liu left Taiwan six years later, and Taipei's role as interim capital was eventually formalised.

Under Japanese rule, Taichung – then known as Taichu – grew rapidly. Buildings from that era dot the city, but apart from the railway station there are few grand structures. From the 1960s onwards, Taichung prospered as thousands of local entrepreneurs set up small factories making clothes, electric fans and other common consumer goods. These days, in terms of being aspirational, fashion-conscious and outward-looking, Taichung's people aren't far behind the citizens of Taipei.

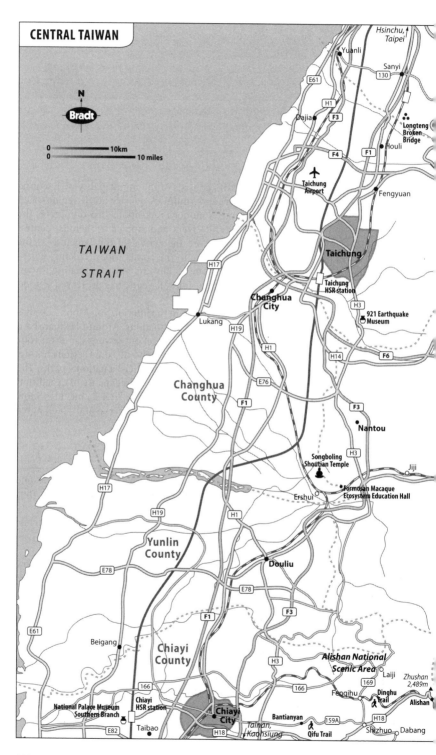

CENTRAL TAIWAN

Hsinchu,
Taipei

Yuanli

Sanyi

E61 · 130

H1

Dajia · F3

Longteng
Broken
Bridge

F4 · F1 · Houli

Taichung
Airport

Fengyuan

TAIWAN

STRAIT

H17

Taichung

Taichung
HSR station

Changhua
City

H3

Lukang

921 Earthquake
Museum

H19

H1

H14 · F6

Changhua
County

E76

F1

F3

Nantou

H3

Songboling
Shoutian Temple

Jiji

Formosan Macaque
Ecosystem Education Hall

H17

Ershui

H19

H1

Yunlin
County

Douliu

E78

E78

F3

E61

Beigang

F1

Chiayi
County

H3

Alishan National
Scenic Area

Laiji

Zhushan
2,489m

166

169

Fengihu

Dinghu
Trail

Alishan

Chiayi
HSR station

National Palace Museum
Southern Branch

166

Chiayi
City

Bantianyan

159A

H18

Taibao

Tainan,
Kaohsiung

Qifu Trail

Shizhuo

Dabang

E82

H18

N
Bradt

0 ——— 10km
0 ——— 10 miles

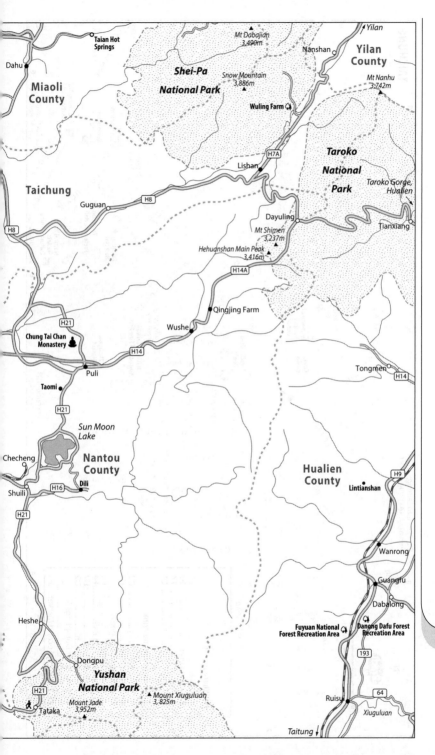

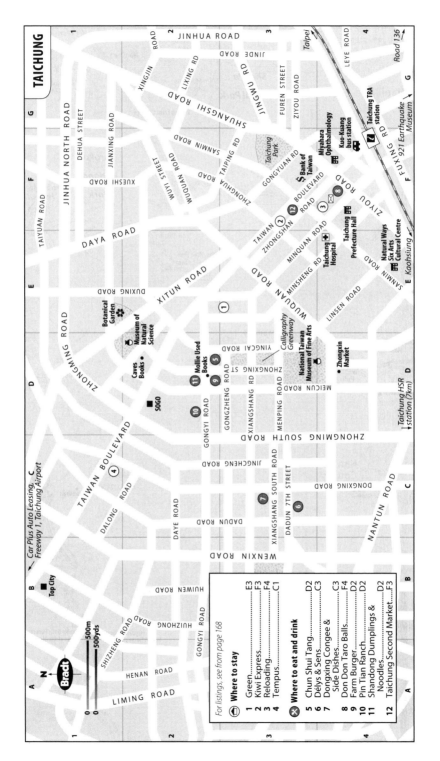

TAICHUNG

N

0   500m
0   500yds

Where to stay
1   Green.................................E3
2   Kiwi Express.....................F3
3   Reloading.........................F4
4   Tempus..............................C1

Where to eat and drink
5   Chun Shui Tang..............D2
6   Délys & Sens....................C3
7   Dongxing Congee &
     Side Dishes...................C3
8   Don Don Taro Balls........F4
9   Farm Burger....................D2
10   Pin Tian Ranch...............D2
11   Shandong Dumplings &
     Noodles.......................D2
12   Taichung Second Market.....F3

For listings, see from page 168

Top City

Car Plus Auto Leasing,
Freeway 1, Taichung Airport

Botanical Garden

Museum of Natural Science

Caves Books

SOGO

Mollie Used Books

Calligraphy Greenway

National Taiwan Museum of Fine Arts

Zhongxin Market

Bank of Taiwan

Taichung Park

Miyahara Ophthalmology

Kuo-Kuang bus station

Taichung TRA station

921 Earthquake Museum

Taichung Hospital

Taichung Prefecture Hall

Natural Ways Six Arts Cultural Centre

Taichung HSR station (7km)

Taipei

Road 136

GETTING THERE AND AWAY

By air Taichung Airport (IATA: RMQ; ☏2615 5000; w www.tca.gov.tw) has flights to/from Vietnam, Japan, Hong Kong and several mainland Chinese cities, as well as domestic services to the outlying islands. The airport, 20km northwest of the city centre, can be reached by bus #9 from the TRA station (departs every 20mins; ⊕ 05.50–22.10 daily; takes at least 1hr; NTD49). A taxi from the TRA or HSR stations will cost around NTD500. There's a visitor information centre (⊕ 09.00–18.00 daily) and a place to change money (⊕ 06.00–23.00 daily).

By HSR Taichung HSR station is 11km south of the city centre. Trains to/from Taipei take an hour (NTD700), and a little less to/from Kaohsiung Zuoying (NTD790). As well as bus services to various parts of the metropolis and Taichung's airport, fairly frequent direct buses link the HSR station with Lukang, Puli and Sun Moon Lake. The bus stops are downstairs and labelled in English. To get from the HSR station to central Taichung, take a local train from Xinwuri TRA station (11mins; NTD15).

By TRA Puyuma services to Taipei (currently 5 daily; 1¾hrs; NTD375) are quicker than other expresses (hrly departures; ⊕ 05.56–21.46 daily; 2½hrs; NTD289–375). Expresses to Kaohsiung take the better part of 3 hours (hrly departures; ⊕ 05.42–21.43 daily; NTD361–469).

By bus Kuo-Kuang services include four to/from Taipei per hour (⊕ 05.00–23.00 daily; takes 3hrs; NTD290), a bus every half hour to Tainan (⊕ 06.10–21.45; 2½hrs; NTD250) and about as frequently to Chiayi (⊕ 06.00–22.00; 1¾hrs; NTD190). During the same period, Kuo-Kuang also has at least one bus per hour to/from Kaohsiung (NTD330), Pingtung (NTD350) and Hsinchu (NTD160). Also useful is the direct bus to Taoyuan Airport (departs at least hrly; ⊕ 01.00–21.50; 2½hrs; NTD280). Other bus companies offer similar services near the TRA station, so shop around as cheap promotional fares are often available.

Buses arriving from Taipei and other cities usually stop at Chaoma bus station very near Freeway 1 and then at various points along Taiwan Boulevard before terminating near the TRA station [166 F4]. Direct buses to/from Lukang, Sun Moon Lake and Puli leave from other stops near the TRA station; for details ask at the visitor information centre.

By car, motorcycle or bicycle Taichung is 153km south of Taipei and 189km north of Kaohsiung, and Freeway 1's Taichung Interchange at km178 is the most convenient way for cars to approach the centre. If you're heading for the mountains from Taichung, consider taking Road 136. Beyond the suburbs, it's scenic and rather steep.

GETTING AROUND

By bus Taichung's bus system is extensive but confusing, so many visitors rely on taxis. From the HSR station, there's a good chance #159 (departs every 20mins; ⊕ 06.35–00.10 daily) will get you near your hotel as it passes SOGO and the Museum of Natural Science. One-way fares start at NTD20/11.

By car If you need to hire a vehicle, Car Plus Auto Leasing [166 B1] (w www.car-plus.com.tw) has an office just outside the centre (826 Taiwan Bd Sec 3; ☏2703 2912; ⊕ 08.30–20.30 daily), as well as counters at the HSR Station and Taichung Airport (☏2615 5233; ⊕ 08.30–20.30 daily).

By metro By the time you read this, the Green Line of the Taichung Metro should be up and running. It'll make getting to Taichung HSR station much quicker.

TOURIST INFORMATION

🛈 **Taichung City Government** w eng. taichung.gov.tw

🛈 **Taichung TRA Station Visitor Information Centre** [166 F4] 📞2221 2126; ⏰ 09.00–17.00 daily

🏠 WHERE TO STAY

🏠 **Tempus Hotel** [166 C1] (334 rooms) 689 Taiwan Bd Sec 2 (lobby accessed from Dongxing Rd); 📞2326 8008; e tempus@tempus.com.tw; w tempus.com.tw. Many of the rooms in Taichung's plushest hotel have huge windows & good city views. Guests have free use of the fitness centre, swimming pool & sauna & needn't pay to join aerobics & yoga classes. The club also has a children's play area. The hotel has a bar & a bakery; the better of the 2 restaurants is perhaps **Ali Seafood** (⏰ 11.30–14.00 & 17.30–21.00 daily; EM; **$$$$$**). Both dining venues offers a good choice of European & New World wines. Buffet b/fast inc. **$$$$**

🏠 **Green Hotel** [166 E3] (36 rooms) 126 Minsheng N Rd; 📞2301 0011; e service@greenhotel.com.tw; w greenhotel.com.tw. This new hotel (opened in 2017) is in a quiet neighbourhood within 20mins' walking distance of many restaurants & both major museums. Rooms are mid-sized & have adequate natural light. Inc b/

fast, use of bikes & access to laundry facilities (soap provided). Midweek prices often below NTD2,500. **$$$**

🏠 **Kiwi Express Hotel** [166 F3] (43 rooms) 441 Taiwan Bd Sec 1; 📞2229 4466; w rs-kiwihotel.com. This decent budget inn (part of a chain with 4 other Taichung branches) has a good location for those getting around by bus & helpful English-speaking staff. The rooms lack character – hardly an issue with rates sometimes below NTD1,000 – & not all have a window or bathtub. Guests can borrow bikes from the hotel & use the PC in the lobby. B/fast inc. **$$**

🏠 **Reloading Hotel** [166 F4] (47 rooms) 55 Zhongshan Rd; 📞222 17668; e reloading.hotel@gmail.com; w reloading-hotel.com. If you're happy with walls & furnishings that are overwhelmingly white, you'll probably love this place on account of its location & cleanliness. The prices aren't at all bad, too – a room for 4 ppl can sometimes be had for just over NTD2,000. Simple b/fast inc. **$$**

✘ WHERE TO EAT AND DRINK

For additional dining and drinking ideas, pick up a copy of *Compass*, a free pocket-sized bilingual 'what's on' magazine available in hotel lobbies, restaurants and bars throughout the city. The magazine can be read online at w taiwanfun.com.

✘ **Chun Shui Tang** 春水堂 [166 D2] 17 Lane, 155 Gongyi Rd; 📞2302 8530; w chunshuitang.com.tw; ⏰ 08.30–22.30 daily. One of 2 establishments with a credible claim to have invented bubble tea, Chun Shui Tang has grown into a chain with 45 branches around Taiwan & several in Japan. Drinks take up half the menu; the famous Pearl Milk Tea (NTD70–160) is a good bit pricier than versions sold by competitors, but tea aficionados say the leaves used are palpably better. The food selection inc many Taiwanese favourites (NTD80–200), set meals that come with rice & a drink (from NTD260) & inexpensive side dishes, all of which are tasty. There's another convenient branch in the grounds of the **National**

Taiwan Museum of Fine Arts [166 D4] (⏰ 11.00–22.00 daily). **$$$**

✘ **Farm Burger** 田樂 [166 D2] 128 Gongzheng Rd; 📞2305 0507; ⏰ 11.00–21.30 daily. Hidden between 2 bldgs, Farm Burger's part-retro part-Nordic décor & fusion dishes attract a young crowd; at the w/end you may be turned away unless you reserve. The menu (no EM but some English spoken) has around 30 beef, chicken, fish, pork sausage & tofu options (NTD160–330) made from quality ingredients. Add NTD70 for salad & a drink; what you might assume to be cubes of cheese in the former are, in fact, tofu. **$$$**

✘ **Pin Tian Ranch** 品田牧場 [166 D2] 152–1 Gongyi Rd; 📞2326 3800; ⏰ 11.30–14.00 &

17.30–21.00 daily. Very reliable Japanese-style pork chops, curries & salt-grilled mackerel meal sets. Quiet ambience & sensitive service make this a good escape from the heat & noise on the streets. EM. **$$$**

✕ Dongxing Congee & Side Dishes 東興清粥小菜 [166 C3] 19 Dongxing Rd Sec 2; ☎2473 5817; ⏰ 08.00–midnight daily. A good bet if you're vegetarian or you've missed the lunch rush but want a good choice of greens, this help-yourself-then-pay eatery also has plenty of tofu, fish, pork & chicken. Get rice or congee at the point of payment & enjoy the unlimited barley tea. Only the hungriest will spend more than NTD120 pp. AC. **$$**

✕ Shandong Dumplings & Noodles 山東餃子牛肉麵 [166 D2] 96 Gongyi Rd; ☎2321 5955; ⏰ 11.00–21.00 daily. Consistently good north Chinese dishes inc fried dumplings (*běifāng guōtiē* 北方鍋貼, NTD120 for 6) & various kinds of beef noodle soup, among them the Signature Half-Rib Beef Noodles (*zhāopái bànjīn bànròu miàn* 招牌半筋半肉麵, NTD190). More Taiwanese in flavour are the curried noodles/rice with beef (NTD130) or chicken (NTD90) & the seasonal greens (NTD40). Additional seating upstairs. **$$**

✕ Don Don Taro Balls 東東芋圓 [166 F4] 63 Shifu Rd; ☎2227 5678; ⏰ 10.00–22.00 daily. Selling variations of a traditional dessert that features chewy chunks of taro & sweet potato with a warm yam paste, Don Don lacks an EM but has a colour-coding system: choose orange if you like pineapple, green for mung beans & Chinese mesona jelly, & black for jelly with tapioca balls. Each bowl (NTD50) is big enough to be shared by 2 ppl. To better enjoy the taste of each ingredient (no sweetener is added) resist the temptation to stir everything in with the bed of shaved ice before you've sampled a few morsels. **$**

✕ Taichung Second Market 台中第二市場 [166 F3] Corner of Taiwan Bd Sec 1 & Sanmin Rd. This general market is gradually becoming more tourist orientated but the cheap eats are well worth a look. One of the more interesting is vendor #175, which specialises in shallow-fried 'turnip cake' (*càitóu guǒ* 菜頭粿, NTD40 inc fried egg) & various traditional soups like pig-blood soup (*zhūxiě tāng* 豬血湯, NTD25). For non-oily food, try Foolish Master Soup Dumplings (portion of 7 dumplings NTD55). Both face Sanmin Rd, & tend to shut shop around 18.00 daily. **$**

♀ Délys & Sens 得梨思法式料理 [166 C3] 151 Dadun 7th St; ☎2471 0033; ⏰ 11.30–22.00 Wed–Mon. This French–Taiwanese-owned restaurant/patisserie serves budget-busting but top-notch meals. A good number of people come after dining elsewhere to make the most of the quality desserts, imported beers & highly rated cocktails. **$$$$$**

SHOPPING

Caves Books [166 D2] 12 Guanqian Rd; ☎2326 5559; ⏰ 10.30–22.00 daily

Mollie Used Books [166 D2] Basement, 161 Gongyi Rd; ☎2305 0288; ⏰ noon–22.00 daily

Top City [166 B1] 251 Taiwan Bd Sec 3; ☎3702 2168; w www.feds.com.tw/tw/53; ⏰ 11.00–22.00 daily. Eating options inside this department store cover much of Asia & there's also a cinema.

SOGO [166 D2] 459 Taiwan Bd Sec 2; ⏰ 11.00–22.00 daily. A useful landmark with the usual brands.

OTHER PRACTICALITIES

$ Bank of Taiwan [166 F3] 276 Taiwan Bd Sec 1

✚ Taichung Hospital [166 E4] 199 Minquan Rd; ☎2229 4411; ⏰ 24hrs daily

✉ Post office [166 F4] 86 Minquan Rd; ⏰ 07.30–21.00 Mon–Fri, 08.30–16.30 Sat, 08.30–noon Sun

WHAT TO SEE AND DO Taichung looks and feels relatively modern. Rather than temples, the key attractions are colonial landmarks and museums.

Japanese-era heritage buildings Architecture aficionados will find four colonial-era landmarks in the old city centre worth a look. A 1917 renaissance-style beauty, the former **Taichung Railway Station** 舊台中車站 [166 F4] at the eastern end of Taiwan Boulevard is the most impressive of the five surviving 'classical' railway stations in Taiwan. In late 2016 it was superseded by the vast and unpopular building behind as part of a project to elevate the tracks, eliminate level crossings and add five commuter stations. A few minutes' walk away stands **Miyahara Ophthalmology** 宮原眼科 [166 F4] (20 Zhongshan Rd), built for a Japanese ophthalmologist Takekuma Miyahara in 1927, a redbrick structure that served for decades as an eye hospital. A decade ago, when it was in a terrible state due to neglect, typhoons and earthquakes, a confectionary company bought it. The renovation-reimagining they bankrolled was inspired, it seems, by the Harry Potter films and steampunk science fiction. Lots of people come here for the gourmet ice cream (⊕ 10.00–22.00 daily; from NTD90) but if you want to sit down you'll need to go to the restaurant upstairs (⊕ 11.00–22.00 daily; min charge NTD380 pp; **$$$**), which serves Taiwanese-style steamed and stir-fried dishes. Downstairs you can buy gift boxes of pineapple cakes and oolong tea.

To reach the other two sights, you'll need to walk westwards. Designed by Moriyama Matsunosuke and resembling in form and original function Moriyama's National Museum of Taiwan Literature, **Taichung Prefecture Hall** 台中州廳 [166 F4] (99 Minquan Rd; ⊕ 09.00–17.30 daily; free admission) was built in stages between 1913 and 1934. Bureaucrats still work here so if you want to look around inside you'll need to sign in with the security guard. The whitewashed frontage is the main attraction, however, and it's often used as a backdrop by local couples taking pre-wedding photos. The **Natural Ways Six Arts Cultural Centre** 道禾六藝文化館 [166 E4] (33 Linsen Rd; ☏ 2375 9366; ⊕ 09.00–17.00 Tue–Sun; free admission) is a reconstruction of the dojo and an office that formed part of Taichung's prison between 1937 and 1992. The name alludes to the six disciplines Confucius regarded as key to a good education.

Museum of Natural Science 國立自然科學博物館 [166 D2] (1 Guanqian Rd; ☏ 2322 6940; w www.nmns.edu.tw; ⊕ 09.00–17.00 Tue–Sun; admission NTD100/70) Themes explored in this high-quality and child-friendly museum go beyond straightforward geo-science and biology to embrace local spiritual life and herbal medicine. Separate tickets are sold for the 3D (NTD70) and IMAX (NTD100) cinemas; the website has details of film showings as well as current and upcoming exhibitions (all are bilingual). The museum manages the adjacent **Botanical Garden** 台中植物園 (⊕ 06.00–22.00 daily; free admission), which covers 4.5ha and hosts 800 plant species. Allot some time for the garden's 31m-high hothouse (⊕ 09.00–17.00 Tue–Sun; admission NTD20) where there's an indoor rainforest ecosystem complete with waterfall.

National Taiwan Museum of Fine Arts 國立台灣美術館 (Guólì Táiwān Měishùguǎn) [166 D4] (2 Wuquan W Rd Sec 1; ☏ 2372 3552; w www.ntmofa. gov.tw; ⊕ 09.00–17.00 Tue–Fri, 09.00–18.00 Sat–Sun; free admission except for special exhibitions) The range of styles and materials is broad here; amid the oil paintings, gouache, ink on paper and acrylic works are landscapes and abstract images. Important works by Chen Cheng-po (page 224), Li Mei-shu (page 118), Pan Chun-yuan (see box, page 101), and Yuyu Yang (1926–97) are included, as well as by Richard Lin (1933–2011), a minimalist who spent his most productive years in the UK. Be sure to scrutinise the works displayed on the third floor; all were executed in Taiwan or by Taiwanese artists overseas. Visitors are welcome to borrow an English-language audio guide (free; show ID). Check the website ahead of time to see if there are any special exhibitions that match your interests.

Zhongxin Market 忠信市場 (Zhōngxìn Shìchǎng) [166 D4] (⊕ varies) An odd mix of arty cafés and blue-collar hovels across the road from the Fine Arts Museum, this dank building hosts a small traditional market that winds up well

What's claimed to be the largest regular religious event in the world outside India begins and ends each spring in Dajia, a town of 78,000 people in the northwestern part of Taichung. To celebrate Mazu's birthday, an immense procession (now marketed as the Taichung City Mazu International Festival) sets out on foot from Jenn Lann Temple and makes its way southwards. Over the course of eight days, a palanquin bearing the shrine's revered Mazu icon is carried 300km through towns and villages, stopping to accept offerings at dozens of shrines and roadside altars on the way. When the parade reaches Fengtian Temple, 14km northwest of Chiayi City, the palanquin turns around and begins the return leg.

Up to 200,000 people attend the start of the procession and a million or more watch or join in over the following days. Many are fervent believers; others are hoping to gain good luck, or simply want to enjoy the spectacle, which includes puppet and opera performances, dragon and lion dances, children's games and martial-arts demonstrations. Each year a handful of devotees walks the entire distance. Some people push their way through the crowd and try to touch the palanquin; every day hundreds prostrate themselves on the road ahead of the procession so the icon is carried over them. Both are ways of winning the sea goddess's blessing.

before lunchtime. Later in the day, especially at the weekend, it's possible to sniff out some good coffee.

921 Earthquake Museum 九二一地震教育園區 (Jiǔèryī Dìzhèn Jiàoyù Yuánqū) [166 G4] (46 Zhongzheng Rd, Wufeng; ☎ 04 2339 0906; w 921emt.nmns. edu.tw; ⊕ 09.00–17.00 Tue–Sun; admission NTD50/30, free before 10.00 Wed) This museum, a good stop on the road between Taichung and Sun Moon Lake, was built on the site of a high school campus wrecked by the strongest tremor to strike Taiwan in the 20th century (page 20). The quake left the school's running track corrugated with ridges, which made for one of the disaster's most enduring images. These, together with several devastated classrooms, have been preserved as part of an engrossing yet sobering exhibition. There's a great deal of information about why and how earthquakes occur, as well as specific details of the 1999 disaster. If you've never felt a temblor, head for the Quake Experience Theatre. Kids will enjoy the 3D film presentations.

The museum is just a half-hour drive south of the city. The nearest freeway interchange is Wufeng at km211 on Freeway 3. Turn right on to Highway 3 and proceed to km197 where you'll see signs to the museum. Several buses from central Taichung stop nearby, the most convenient from Taichung TRA station being #50 (departs every 10–15mins; ⊕ 05.40–22.10 daily; 40mins; NTD38), which terminates right outside the museum.

CHANGHUA CITY 彰化市 (ZHĀNGHUÀ SHÌ) Telephone code 04

Best known for the Buddha statue atop Mount Bagua, Changhua comes as a pleasant surprise to many people. This city of 250,000 people boasts more Qing-era relics than nearby Taichung, as well as one of Taiwan's three most important Confucian temples, but it's the hilltop Buddha, a relatively recent addition to the landscape, which really pulls in the tourists.

HISTORY Changhua rose to prominence in 1723 when it was made capital of one of Taiwan's three prefectures. Half a century later, Lin Shuang-wen (page 12) launched his rebellion just north of here and proclaimed himself emperor after seizing the town.

The decisive engagement of Japan's takeover of Taiwan was fought around Mount Bagua on 27 August 1895. The Taiwanese, who had modern artillery dug in on the slopes of the hill, were unable to hold back the invaders. Two senior commanders and more than 1,000 local soldiers died in the fighting, but rather than press the advantage the Japanese paused for more than a month to regroup and await reinforcements – a delay that proved costly. September is always hot and wet, and diseases, notably malaria, killed more than 2,000 Japanese. Seventy years later a mass grave containing 679 bodies – presumably Taiwanese casualties – was unearthed and turned into a memorial park.

GETTING THERE AND AROUND

By HSR Each hour, one northbound and one southbound bullet train stops at Changhua HSR station. Although travel time from Taipei (⊕ 07.11–21.56; 1¼hrs; NTD820) is shorter by HSR than by TRA, the station's location makes arriving by TRA a much better idea.

By TRA Almost all north–south expresses stop in Changhua. Expresses to/from Taipei take less than 3 hours (NTD320–415), while all trains to/from Taichung take less than half an hour (NTD26–40) with many stopping en route at Xinwuri (NTD15) for Taichung HSR station. Changhua TRA station has a baggage services office (⊕ 08.00–20.00 daily) where you can store luggage while exploring Changhua or Lukang.

By bus Kuo-Kuang buses #1828 and #1829 connect Taipei with Changhua (5 or 6 departures per hr; ⊕ 06.00–22.00 daily; 3¼hrs; NTD300), while services linking with Lukang include #6909, #6933 and #6934 (departures every 15mins; ⊕ 06.20–22.50 daily; 40mins; NTD49).

By car By Freeway 1 Changhua is 20km south of Taichung, 173km south of Taipei and 169km north of Kaohsiung. Parking in central Changhua isn't easy so consider finding a spot on Mount Bagua and walking the 15 or so minutes from there to the Confucius Temple.

By bicycle or motorcycle For ambitious cyclists willing to tackle some hills, Road 139 is an excellent way to approach the city from the south via Mount Bagua. To hire a motorcycle in Changhua City, try **Zheng Jie** (576 Zhongzheng Rd Sec 1; ☏ 725 5052; ⊕ 06.00–01.00 daily) on the left as you exit the TRA station. If you'd rather pedal than walk around the city, there's a **YouBike** (w chcg.youbike.com.tw) station right outside the TRA station.

TOURIST INFORMATION

i **Changhua City Government** w www.changhua.gov.tw
i **Changhua Visitor Information Centre** Inside the TRA station; ⊕ 08.30–17.30 daily

i **Mount Bagua Visitor Information Centre** Guashan Rd; ⊕ 08.30–17.30 daily

WHERE TO STAY AND EAT

🏠 **Taiwan Hotel** (45 rooms) 48 Zhongzheng Rd Sec 2; ☏ 722 4681; e hoteltaiwan047@ gmail.com; w hoteltaiwan.com.tw. Thoroughly renovated since the last edition of this book,

Taiwan Hotel is clean, friendly & very central. 3-person rooms can often be had for less than NTD3,000, & although all have cable TV not every room has a window. Good location if you find Changhua's nightlife dull – you can either jump on a train to Taichung or go to the cinema next door. B/fast inc. **$$**

✗ **Ah-Chang's Meat Circles** 阿璋肉圓 144 Changan St; ☎722 9517; ⏰ 06.00–21.00 daily. Changhua's most famous eatery is on the corner of Changan St & Chenleng Rd & serves the city's best-known local delicacy, something that's often translated as 'meatballs' but which bear little resemblance to the equivalent in Italian cooking. For a start, they're not spheres so much as thick discs, so glutinous you'll need a fork to break them apart. 1 meat circle (*ròu yuán* 肉圓, NTD35) is usually enough unless you're exceptionally hungry. Add a dash of spicy sauce & order a bowl of dragon-marrow soup (*lónggǔ suǐ tāng* 龍骨髓湯, NTD35), which, despite its name, is actually a consommé poured over steamed egg, slivers of mushrooms & a few medicinal herbs. AC, no EM. **$**

✗ **Changhua Vegetarian Food** 彰化素食 117 Changan St; ☎723 6427; ⏰ 07.30–20.30 daily. Good noodle dishes, tofu & mock meat, & unlike many restaurants in this price range, the interior has AC. No EM. There are lots of good, inexpensive eateries in this neighbourhood, 300m southeast of the TRA station. Changan St runs south from Guangfu Rd. **$**

OTHER PRACTICALITIES

$ Hua Nan 152 Guangfu Rd

✉ **Post office** 130 Guangfu Rd; ⏰ 08.30–21.00 Mon–Fri, 09.00–noon Sat

WHAT TO SEE AND DO To begin a walking tour, walk east from the TRA station down Guangfu Road to Minsheng Road, then turn south, from where it's 650m to the first of the attractions listed below.

Yuanqing Hall 元清觀 (207 Minsheng Rd; ⏰ 06.30–21.00 daily) The main chamber of this 1763 temple, dedicated to the Jade Emperor, was, in April 2006, gutted by a fire so ruinous many Changhua folk feared the shrine would lose its status as a national relic. Thankfully the principal icons survived the blaze and were placed on makeshift altars so the faithful wouldn't be inconvenienced during reconstruction. Inaugurated at the beginning of 2012, the temple has several new beams and panels easily distinguishable by clean, bright colours and expert brushwork. Across the junction from the temple on the corner of Minsheng Road, there's a traditional *tatami*-maker (202 Minsheng Rd; ⏰ 08.00–20.00 daily). *Tatamis* are hard straw mattresses 7–8cm thick; the word is Japanese but has been part of the local vocabulary since the colonial era.

Confucius Temple 孔子廟 (**Kǒngzǐ Miào**) (30 Kongmen Rd; ⏰ 08.00–17.30 daily, closed nat hols) The entrance to Changhua's most stately edifice is a few doors down from the *tatami* store. Peeling paint and faded decorations give this place an aura of genuine antiquity that's appealing yet melancholy. Founded in 1726, it was expanded in 1830, partly dismantled during the Japanese occupation and then restored to its 1830 dimensions in 1978. There's almost nothing in the way of labels or information panels, but hunt around and you should find an informative bilingual booklet that explains the history and meaning of every memorial tablet and architectural feature. To continue the walking tour, on leaving the Confucius Temple, turn left and left again, past the main doorway that is opened only on 28 September, the sage's birthday.

Red-haired Well 紅毛井 Follow Kongmen Road east to Zhongshan Road then turn left, and within a minute or two you'll spot an off-white Japanese-era Art

Deco building, **Changhua Arts Hall** 彰化藝術館 (⊕ 09.00–17.00 Tue–Sun; free admission). Set back from the road, squeezed between the arts hall and a sprawling hillside grave, you'll see what's now a land-god shrine. The sealed well in front of it gets its name because it's said to have been dug in the 17th century by employees of the Dutch East India Company – in that era, Europeans were referred to as 'red-haired barbarians'. To get to Mount Bagua from here, take the stairway behind the library to the top; it's a short but invigorating walk with plenty of shade.

Mount Bagua 八卦山 (Bāguàshān)

This isn't much of a mountain, the peak being just 97m above sea level, but the ridge extends south for more than 30km and often you can see as far as the wind turbines that dot the coast. Named after the 'Eight Trigrams' that feature prominently in Taoist cosmology, the mountain's best-known landmark is **The Great Buddha** (exhibition ⊕ 08.00–20.00 daily, surrounding park ⊕ 24hrs daily; free admission). Up close it's more attractive than a simple written description – 23m high, made of concrete and painted a very dark brown – might suggest. The **Mount Bagua Skywalk** (free admission) is a recent addition to the landscape; from either end you can walk southward and down the hill towards Gongyuan Road, where you'll find three very different buildings almost side by side.

Jiexiao Shrine 節孝祠

(51 Gongyuan Rd; ⊕ 09.00–noon Tue & Sun only) It's a pity this temple, founded in the 1880s to celebrate central Taiwan's 'chaste and filial women', keeps such limited opening hours; it's an unusually restful and alluring place of worship. In addition to the usual incense and fruit, cosmetics often feature among offerings made here. The adjacent Changhua **Wude Hall** 彰化市武德殿 (usually open for exhibitions) is an elegant former *butokuden* built by the colonial authorities around 1920 to encourage residents to practice kendo and other martial arts. Working your way back towards the city centre you'll next come to the very modern-looking **Changhua County Art Museum** 彰化縣立美術館 (⊕ 09.00–17.00 Tue–Sun; free admission) in which you may find something of interest.

LUKANG 鹿港 (LÙGĂNG) *Telephone code 04*

Touristy yet crammed to the gills with genuine culture and antiquity, Lukang (often spelled 'Lugang') is rightfully one of Taiwan's most popular lowland destinations. It's hard to believe now, but from the mid-18th century to the last quarter of the 19th century, this out-of-the-way town (population now 87,000) was Taiwan's second-largest city. In that era, Tainan and Lukang were like Taipei and Kaohsiung now – the former focused on politics and government, the latter obsessed with commerce. While not quite frozen in time, Lukang has preserved enough of its physical past to make it a worth an entire day. The town is easy to reach by bus and almost every sight is within walking distance of the core.

HISTORY The characters *lù* and *găng* together mean 'deer harbour' and the most often given explanation of this town's name is that it was a place where the indigenous Babuza people hunted for deer. However, some think Lukang is a corruption of the aboriginal place name, Rokau-an. Lukang already had a well-established Han population in 1685, the year Qing authorities began posting coastguards at the mouth of the Lukang River to combat piracy and smuggling.

The settlement enjoyed rapid growth after the completion in 1719 of a huge privately financed irrigation system in the town's hinterland. Rice production rose dramatically and Lukang's merchants began shipping the surplus to Fujian. Soon

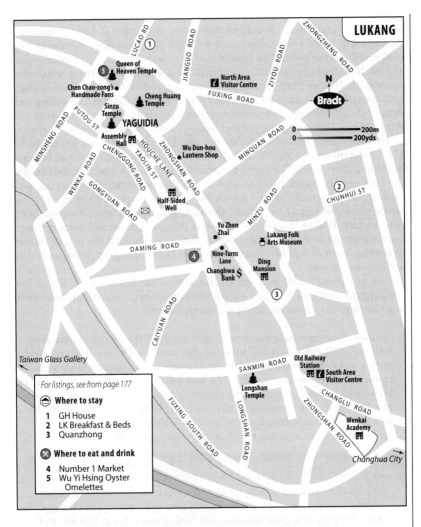

For listings, see from page 177

Where to stay

1 GH House
2 LK Breakfast & Beds
3 Quanzhong

Where to eat and drink

4 Number 1 Market
5 Wu Yi Hsing Oyster
   Omelettes

more than 3,500 ships were using the port each year. The harbour here was never very good – larger sailing ships could enter only at high tide and it was inaccessible to the steamers which replaced them – but it was the best in central Taiwan. Donald R DeGlopper, an American anthropologist who did fieldwork in Lukang, describes a bustling commercial centre in *Lukang: A City and Its Trading System*:

Lukang's prosperity and indeed its very existence depended on a trading system that exchanged the rice, sugar and fibre (hemp, ramie) of central Taiwan for the cloth, crockery and other manufactured goods of southern Fujian… During the 19th century Lukang was a city of wholesalers and middlemen, with many large firms devoted to trade in rice, sugar, cloth, timber, pottery, fish and other commodities. Oxcarts and gangs of porters moved through its narrow streets and hundreds of workers loaded and unloaded the bamboo rafts and small boats that were rowed or poled into its shallow inner harbour. The merchants lived in solid, multi-storey houses, the very bricks and tiles of which had been imported from Fujian.

So many Fujianese lived in Lukang that locals nicknamed it Little Quanzhou. Business and politics were dominated by eight *jiāo*, groupings somewhat like medieval European guilds. One consisted of merchants who imported stone, wood and silk from Quanzhou; another comprised those who exported rice and sugar to, and imported timber from, the Kinmen archipelago and the Fujian towns of Xiamen and Zhangzhou. A third guild imported salted fish products from Guangdong and Penghu; the others focused on peanut and sesame oil, cloth, dye, sugar, and groceries. Produce from Taiwan's interior reached Lukang by ox cart or on the backs of porters.

The shape-shifting nature of Taiwan's coastline caused serious problems. In 1717, the harbour was narrow and choked with silt, but by 1740 it had become broad and deep again. The town's fortunes began to decline precipitously before the 19th century ended, partly as a result of sediment blocking the port but also because the growth of Taiwan's population left little surplus rice to export. The Japanese colonial regime reorganised the island's economy to meet the needs of its new masters. Trading links with Fujian were disrupted; roads and trains replaced coastal shipping as the principal means of moving goods from one part of Taiwan to another. Many of the town's entrepreneurs packed their bags for Taipei and other arriviste settlements.

One of Lukang's most interesting customs died out before World War II but DeGlopper was able to interview some who'd participated (taken from *Blood, Luck and Clanship: The Annual Rockfight at Lukang, Taiwan*):

> The men of Lukang would gather every year on one day in the early spring, line up by surname, and throw rocks at their fellows of other surnames. They were thus throwing rocks at and dodging rocks thrown by men who were in other contexts their in-laws, mother's brothers, business partners, old school friends [etc]… The rock fight was a festive public occasion; women and children watched and cheered; vendors sold snacks. Blood was shed and teeth lost, but… no one was ever killed. [Some people said] folks back then had different thoughts and believed that if blood was not shed in the spring, then the community might suffer bad luck during the coming year.

LUKANG FOLK AND THEIR MUSLIM ANCESTORS

The Muslim cemetery is long gone and it's extremely unlikely you'll see anyone wearing a burqa, but a number of Lukang's most eminent families, among them the original owners of the Ding Mansion (page 180), were of Muslim origin. Their ancestors arrived in the 17th and 18th centuries from Quanzhou in Fujian, where Arab and Persian merchants had been living for centuries before the opening of Taiwan.

Many were already partly assimilated into Han society before reaching Taiwan where, isolated from the large Muslim communities on the Chinese coast, they gradually lost their traditions. However, a few households still possess Korans that they can't read, but which they recognise as sacred. It's said they wash those who've just died in an Islamic manner and wrap the deceased in simple white shrouds, rather than the multiple layers of clothing decreed by Han custom. Moreover, when making offerings to their ancestors, they purposely exclude pork. Aware that their house of worship stands where there was once a mosque, this taboo is also observed by some of those who make offerings at Beitou Guocuo Baoan Temple, less than 300m north of the Queen of Heaven Temple.

GETTING THERE AND AROUND All the sights listed can be reached on foot; it's 1.5km from the Queen of Heaven Temple to Wenkai Academy. You can **rent a YouBike** (page 86) at Lukang Folk Arts Museum and other locations.

By bus Ubus service #1652 leaves Taipei bus station at least seven times **per day** for Lukang (⊕ 08.20–20.20; 3½hrs; NTD380). Plenty of services link Changhua City with Lukang including #6909, #6933 and #6934 (departures every 15mins; ⊕ 06.20–22.50 daily; 40mins; NTD49).

The Taiwan Tourist Shuttle Bus Lukang Route (departs from Taichung HSR station 5 times per day; ⊕ 10.00–18.00 Mon–Fri, 09.00–18.00 Sat–Sun) covers some of Changhua City's sights and terminates at Taiwan Glass Gallery. A timetable, list of stops and fare details are at w taiwantrip.com.tw.

By car, motorcycle or bicycle Just 14km from Changhua, Lukang is linked with both north–south freeways by Expressway 76 and Expressway 61. Driving around the town itself isn't advisable as the streets are narrow and often packed with pilgrims and vendors, but parking near the Queen of Heaven Temple or Wenkai Academy usually isn't difficult. For those on two wheels, Highway 17, which approaches Lukang from both north and south, is flat and takes you through typical lowland scenery.

TOURIST INFORMATION

i **Lukang Township Government** w www.lukang.gov.tw

i **North Area Visitor Centre** 488 Fuxing Rd; ⊕ 10.00–17.00 daily

i **South Area Visitor Centre** 110 Changlu Rd Sec 8; ⊕ 09.00–17.00 daily

WHERE TO STAY *Map, page 175*

GH House (8 rooms) 63 Gonghou Ln; ☏777 8080; e ghhouse63@gmail.com; w www.ghhouse.com.tw. Opened at the end of 2017, this purpose-built homestay offers rooms for 2 or 3 ppl, a nice back garden & a café open to outsiders (drinks from NTD80). **$$$**

LK Breakfast & Beds (14 rooms) 46 Chunhui St; ☏777 4446; e meilkbnb@gmail.com; w lkbnb.com.tw. This 6-storey bldg was Lukang's tallest when it was built in 1976 as an industrialist's wedding gift to his son. The latter's English-speaking sister has turned the house into a tasteful homestay with wooden floors, sparkling bathrooms & a wonderful roof space where guests can enjoy late afternoon breezes. Rooms for 2, 3, 4 or 6 ppl. Free car parking & adorable resident canines. Bike loan & b/fast inc. **$$$**

Quanzhong Hotel (10 rooms) 104 Zhongshan Rd; ☏777 2640. An old budget establishment but the owners keep it clean & the location is excellent. All rooms have en-suite bathrooms & AC, priced NTD900–1,600; note that weekdays are cheaper than weekends. No b/fast. **$$**

WHERE TO EAT AND DRINK *Map, page 175*

Near the Queen of Heaven Temple, you'll find several vendors hawking one of Lukang's best-known specialities, called 'cow's tongue' (*niú shé bǐng* 牛舌餅). It's actually a flat sweetbread stuffed with a sugary paste and sprinkled with sesame seeds. If you'd like to try one before committing yourself to a whole packet, several shops sell individual biscuits (NTD10).

Number 1 Market 第一市場 Daming & Minzu rds; ⊕ varies. The hungry & intrepid should head here, ideally noon midday, for hot traditional foods. No EMs; if it looks good, point to order. **$**

Wu Yi Hsing Oyster Omelettes 吳益興蚵仔煎 432 Zhongshan Rd; ☏777 2627;

🕐 08.00–21.00 daily. In addition to oyster omelettes (NTD60), this large & very busy eatery serves up oysters pan-fried with rice vermicelli (*chǎo hé mǐfěn* 炒蚵米粉, NTD70), plus various fried-rice & fried-noodle dishes (NTD40–70). If you want nothing more than a snack, go for the savoury daikon cake (*luóbo gāo* 蘿蔔糕, NTD25). $

SHOPPING

Chen Chao-zong's Handmade Fans 陳朝宗手工扇 Cnr of Zhongshan & Lucao rds; 🕻777 5629; 🕐 08.00–17.00 daily. Mr Chen has been making & hand-painting fans like those favoured by the ladies of yesteryear for decades; prices start at NTD500.

Wu Dun-hou Lantern Shop 吳敦厚燈鋪 310 Zhongshan Rd; 🕻763 1877; 🕐 09.00–noon & 14.00–22.00 daily. This shop showcases the kind of hand-painted bamboo-framed paper lanterns that earned the eponymous Mr Wu (1924–2017) an international reputation. Aleksandr Solzhenitsyn & Lady Gaga are among those who've left Taiwan with one of his lanterns in their luggage.

Yu Zhen Zhai 玉珍齋鳳眼糕 168 Minzu Rd; 🕻777 3672; 🕐 08.00–22.00 daily. Lukang's best-known bakery sells traditional pastries in colourful presentation boxes. Flavours include pineapple, mung bean, vanilla, chocolate & sesame. Prices start at NTD80.

OTHER PRACTICALITIES

$ **Changhwa Bank** 137 Zhongshan Rd

✉ **Post office** 1 Chenggong Rd; 🕐 08.00–17.30 Mon–Fri, 08.30–noon Sat–Sun

WHAT TO SEE AND DO Lukang has plenty of bilingual signs, so finding your way around isn't difficult.

Queen of Heaven Temple 天后宮 (Tiānhòu Gōng) (🕐 06.00–22.00 daily)

Like other super-popular shrines – which some English signs refer to as 'Tien-hou Temple' – this isn't a place for the nervous of disposition. It's riotously lively at weekends; the temple's mechanised drums are extremely loud and pilgrims set off strings of firecrackers in the forecourt. A second or two after each outburst, you'll see a mini-mushroom cloud rising skyward. Don't let the people or noise distract you, and remember to look up as you enter – there are some splendid woodcarvings above the doors. The entire interior has a delightfully timeworn quality, not to mention ceilings absolutely encrusted with soot from the incense that's been burned here. The shop near the back of the complex sells a range of practical Mazu-themed souvenirs including T-shirts, mugs and baseball caps. The claim often made that this temple was established in 1590 isn't quite accurate; Lukang residents were certainly worshipping Mazu at that time, but it was another half-century before any kind of permanent structure appeared. The temple's small, black-faced Mazu icon is especially valued as it's said to have been brought to Taiwan by Shi Lang (page 12).

Cheng Huang Temple 城隍廟 (366 Zhongshan Rd; 🕐 06.00–21.00 daily) Locals

come to this ornate shrine for various reasons, one being that the resident deities are said to be exceptionally good at resolving cases of theft. One of their greatest successes was the recovery of valuable proprietary items lost by a major Taiwanese computer company. The stone lions just outside the temple, you'll notice, are secured to the pavement by welded iron bars. According to temple staff, this is because they're 'valuable relics, many hundreds of years old', and liable to be stolen. The town god may be a superb detective, it seems, but he isn't much of a security guard.

Across the street from the temple there used to be a small plaza called Yaguidia, which in Taiwanese means 'courtyard of the hungry ghosts'. The name didn't come about because of any supernatural activity; rather, it's where at the end of long voyages sailors and fishermen would come to enjoy their first proper meal in days. The seafarers ate with such gusto that locals nicknamed them 'hungry ghosts'. There's nothing to be seen nowadays but a Chinese-language information board.

Lukang's old streets

Putou and Yaolin streets, along with several nearby lanes, have never been widened for cars. During Lukang's heyday, many of the town's shipping agents and merchants lived hereabouts, and several of the homes are now souvenir shops but a few are uninhabited and crumbling. Hoping their sons would be as academically successful as the man who built Ding Mansion (page 180), the first few generations living at 8 Yaolin Street would order the youngsters to take their books and brushes to the attic, then remove the ladder that provided the only access. One of Lukang's most popular photo opportunities is **Half-Sided Well** 半邊井 (12 Yaolin St). In the 18th and 19th centuries, it wasn't unusual for rich households to dig private wells; the family here wanted the convenience of a water source near their front door but were public-spirited enough to have it straddle the boundary of their land so their neighbours could also draw water.

The main attraction on Putou Street is the **Sinzu Temple** 新祖宮 (96 Putou St; ⏰ 07.00–20.00 daily). Also known as the Official Queen of Heaven Temple, this shrine's name doesn't imply that the main Queen of Heaven Temple is illegitimate or that the Mazu worshipped there is an imposter. Instead, it reflects the official shrine's unique background – it's the only Mazu temple in Taiwan founded by order of the authorities, the edict being issued by the imperial court in 1788 because the general who crushed Lin Shuang-wen's revolt (page 12) believed Mazu had aided his campaign. For several decades only government officials could worship here but later it was opened to the public. Nearby, the 1928 **Assembly Hall** (aka Lukang Literary Arts Hall) 鹿港藝文館 (72 Putou St; ⏰ 10.00–18.00 Tue–Sun) is a whitewashed anomaly amid the neighbourhood's red and brown bricks. Inside, local artists' works are displayed and sold.

Zhongshan Road's traditional shops

Once called 'See-No-Sky Street' because it was so narrow and shops' awnings blocked the sunlight, Zhongshan Road 中山路 was widened during the colonial era. There are several well-preserved Japanese-era shops with Art Deco features, the most impressive of which is Yu Zhen Zhai's three-story flagship store (see opposite) on the corner of Minzu Road. Traditional apothecaries continue to trade at numbers 196 and 389. In the early 18th century seawater was less than 100m from this thoroughfare; the ocean is now about 3km away.

Lukang Folk Arts Museum

鹿港民俗文物館 (Access via Lane 74, Zhongshan Rd; ☎ 777 2019; w lukangarts.org.tw; ⏰ 09.00–17.00 daily; admission NTD130/70) This museum is housed in a beautiful Baroque mansion built in 1913–19 for the Koo family. Major landowners during the Japanese era, the Koos branched out into cement and other industries after World War II and remain one of Taiwan's most important business clans. In 1973 the family donated the house and many of the 6,000 items inside to establish the museum, where there are now books, documents, portraits, musical instruments, antique pieces of furniture and traditional garments. There's plenty of English inside and while the museum is certainly worthwhile, it's been criticised for presenting a version of Taiwan's history that stresses migration from China while neglecting indigenous, Japanese and other influences.

Nine-Turns Lane 九曲巷 **(Jiǔqū Xiàng)** This backstreet, which doesn't merit more than a quick look, can be accessed from near the Number 1 Market; the entrance is on the right of the florist's at 163 Minzu Road. It's said the curves and sharp corners were intended to block harsh, sand-bearing winter winds, but there's an unintended and unpleasant consequence: in summertime it's often stifling.

Ding Mansion 丁家古厝 **(Dīng Jiā Gǔcuò)** (132 Zhongshan Rd; ⏰ 09.00–17.00 Tue–Sun; free admission) The façade is 1920s but behind it stands a sensitively restored residence built in 1893 by Ding Shou-quan, who'd just passed the highest level of China's imperial civil-service examinations to become a *jinshi* ('presented scholar'). The red and gold tablet high above the doorway to the central chamber bears those two characters, symbolising the status he'd achieved. The mansion is just 4.5m wide but 77m deep; there are three courtyards and a back door that leads to the entrance of Lukang Folk Arts Museum.

Old Railway Station 火車站前 (110 Changlu Rd Sec 8; ⏰ 09.00–17.00 daily) It's often said that Lukang's great and good lobbied against a rail connection early in the colonial period and so condemned the town to backwater status. However, no-one seems to have objected in 1911 when a Japanese-owned sugar company laid narrow-gauge tracks and built a station within 150m of Longshan Temple. After World War II, Taiwan Sugar Corp (see box, page 19) operated passenger services from this point. The building stood empty between the 1970s and 2011, when it was revamped as a tourist attraction; children will enjoy clambering over the preserved diesel locomotive.

Longshan Temple 龍山寺 **(Lóngshān Sì)** (⏰ 05.30–21.30 daily) Undoubtedly one of Taiwan's most inspiring places of worship and likely the oldest Buddhist shrine on the island, Longshan Temple (founded 600m north of its current location in 1653) is a splendid example of traditional religious architecture. Like the finest European cathedrals, construction took generations. Despite serious earthquake damage in 1795, 1848 and 1999, the temple retains a tremendous sense of antiquity as well as considerable beauty.

The original seated Guanyin icon was over 1,200 years old when it was destroyed in a fire in 1921. Its replacement, now in the main hall, was for years relegated to a side chamber at the behest of Japanese Buddhists backed by the colonial authorities. The complex boasts 99 doorways of all shapes yet its most famous feature is neither a portal nor an effigy, but rather a sublime octagonal ceiling in the front pavilion. Designed to fool malign spirits into thinking the temple is in fact underwater (and thus impervious to arson attempts), a mass of carved and painted wood converges on the whiskery face of a dragon. Do also pay attention to the temple's windows – several, especially those at the front, are wooden screens of exceptional delicacy and embellishment.

Wenkai Academy 文開書院 **(Wénkāi Shūyuàn)** (⏰ 09.00–17.30 daily; free admission) Whether they're the starting point of your tour or the final sight, the academy and its adjacent Wu and Wen temples deserve to be taken in slowly. There's little in the way of labelling so you won't learn much but this is a delightful place to linger and much loved by photographers. The academy was established in 1827 to prepare students for imperial civil-service examinations, success in which brought tremendous prestige for candidates' families, such as the Dings (see above).

Between the crowded lowlands and the high mountains, some of central Taiwan's nicest countryside can be found between the outskirts of Taichung and the small town of Jiji.

GETTING THERE AND AWAY

By car, motorcycle or bicycle Drivers in a hurry should take Freeway 3 to the Mingjian exit at km236, then Highway 16. Motorcyclists are spoiled for choice as the region has several attractive roads including 131 and 139. There's one bike-hire office (✆ 08.00–18.00 daily; NTD50/hr or NTD100/day) right outside Ershui TRA station and at least four very near Jiji TRA station (bicycles NTD100/day, electric scooters NTD350/day).

By TRA Ershui, the terminus for the Jiji Branch Railway (page 182), is well served by mainline services, with expresses to/from Taipei (3–4hrs; NTD376–487); Kaohsiung (under 3hrs; NTD275) and Taichung (under 1hr; NTD72–87). Ershui has a baggage office (✆ 08.00–20.00 daily).

By bus The #6333 links central Taichung with Shuili (departs about every 30mins; ✆ 05.35–22.35 daily; 1¼hrs; NTD194), stopping right outside the Endemic Species Research Institute in Jiji (NTD169) en route; not every service goes via Taichung HSR station. From Shuili, Highway 21 leads north to Sun Moon Lake and south to the New Central Cross-Island Highway, and from the bus stops on Minquan Road – turn left if you're coming from the TRA stop – there are infrequent local buses to Sun Moon Lake, Puli and Dongpu.

TOURIST INFORMATION The website of Tri-Mountain National Scenic Area (w trimt-nsa.gov.tw) has information about Ershui and around; click on 'Baguashan'. There are also information centres in Ershui (TRA station; ✆ 09.00–17.00 Mon–Fri, 08.00–17.00 Sat–Sun & nat hols) and Checheng (next to the log pond; ✆ 09.00–17.00 daily).

WHERE TO STAY

Kurumba Jiji B&B (5 rooms) 46 Bazhang St, Jiji; m 0933 135 497; e kurumbajiji@ gmail.com; w kurumba.com.tw. Brand new & impeccably clean, this easy-to-find B&B is 100m south of the railroad. Some guestrooms (inc 1 of the 4-ppl rooms) have large balconies. Rated very highly by families with young children; extra bed for a child under 12 costs NTD600. Inc b/fast & use of bicycles. **$$$**

Mountain Fish Water Boutique Hotel (29 rooms) 205 Chenggong Rd, Jiji; ✆ 049

276 1000; w www.mfwhotel.com.tw. This modern hotel is a good deal, having chic rooms with pleasant views over the valley & midweek rates sometimes below NTD2,700. Those on the 6th Flr (1 is for 8 ppl, the other for 6) also boast high ceilings, 180° panorama windows & massive square bathtubs. To find this hotel, go north from the TRA station until you reach Chenggong Rd. On your right you'll see a swimming pool with jacuzzi & waterslide that guests can use for free; the hotel is beside it. B/fast inc. **$$$**

WHERE TO EAT AND DRINK
Plenty of snack vendors and small eateries can be found close to Ershui and Jiji TRA stations.

Bazhang Beef Noodles 八張牛肉麵 11 Lane 291, Wenxin St, Jiji; ✆ 049 276 4539; ✆ 10.30–14.30 & 16.30–20.00 Mon–Sat. A

logical stop if you're moving between Wuchang Temple & Mingsin Academy, this revered eatery is located on a quiet residential street. The customer base is locals rather than tourists but city types will feel comfortable in the spacious eating area (AC). The signature beef noodles (*niúròu miàn* 牛肉麵, NTD120) is a decent-sized bowl with a generous amount of tender meat. Alternatives inc braised *lŭ wèi* & boiled dumplings (NTD5 each). $$

🖵 **Blue Cloud Ice Shop** 雲製冰城 130 Bazhang Rd, Jiji; ☎049 276 2957; ⏰ 08.00–18.00

daily. This prize-winning ice-lolly maker near Wuchang Temple serves up some interesting flavours inc pineapple, taro milk (*yùtóu niúnăi bīng* 芋頭牛奶冰) & milk with sweetcorn (*yùmĭ niúnăi bīng* 玉米牛奶冰). You won't complain about the prices – the most expensive lollies are less than NTD20. $

WHAT TO SEE AND DO

Jiji Branch Railway 集集線火車
This 29.7km-long branch line was built in 1920 to transport materials and machinery for hydro-electric plants into the interior, and to carry sugar and timber out to the lowlands. A long-established tourist attraction, the branch railway veers inland from the main north–south line at **Ershui** 二水 and follows the course of Taiwan's longest river, the **Zhuoshui** 濁水 (literally, 'turbid water'). Few visitors get off at the three stops between Ershui and Jiji: **Yuanquan** 源泉火車站 is attractively bucolic; Zhuoshui is less interesting than quaint, compact **Longquan** 龍泉. On reaching **Jiji** 集集, the town served by the fourth of the line's six stops, the done thing is to take photos of the 1933 station building. It fell down in the big earthquake but was carefully reassembled using the original beams and planks, plus roof tiles salvaged from Japanese-era ruins elsewhere. The rest of the town has been rebuilt since 1999's earthquake, but not entirely – one of its most memorable attractions is the semi-collapsed Wuchang Temple (see opposite). If you want to rent a bicycle, look left and right as you exit the railway station. On the edge of Jiji, the Endemic Species Research Institute (see opposite) is a must for ecotourists.

There are a dozen services in each direction daily between Ershui and Checheng (departures from Ershui ⏰ 06.00–20.15), some of which set out from Taichung and also serve Xinwuri TRA station/Taichung HSR station. A one-way ticket costs NTD44; a one-day jump-on/jump-off pass for the branch line is NTD80. Even if you're too lazy to get off the train and explore, you'll find the hour-long journey an agreeable way to spend a few hours. In addition to mountain and river views, you'll catch sight of farms and forests before arriving at the ex-logging village of **Checheng** 車埕, which has preserved some of its timber-handling facilities. The railway can be done as a day trip from Taichung or Chiayi. Note: there's nowhere to change money along the line.

Songboling Shoutian Temple 松柏嶺受天宮
(⏰ 06.00–21.00 daily) A fine view over the plains rewards those who walk or drive up to this ridgetop shrine. The 2.2km-long **Kengneikeng Forest Trail** 坑內坑森林步 ends at the temple, and finding the trailhead, 2.3km north of Ershui TRA station, isn't difficult. Along the path, hikers are likely to encounter macaques that are neither aggressive nor scared of humans.

Formosan Macaque Ecosystem Education Hall 台灣獼猴生態教育館
(km43.2 Rd 152; ☎04 879 7640; ⏰ 09.00–17.00 Tue–Sun; free admission) To reach this hall, which has good English-language displays about Taiwan's only monkey species, you'll need to drive or cycle east from Ershui, shadowing the branch railway beyond Yuanquan TRA station, for 7.5km. The butterfly conservation area behind the hall has pretty insects, but for real macaques you're better off heading for the hills near Shoutian Temple.

Wuchang Temple 武昌宮 (🕐 06.00–20.00 daily) The Lord of the North Pole, also known as Xuanwu or Xuantian Shangdi, is the key deity in the town's largest hall of worship, inaugurated in late 2013 to replace a shrine wrecked by the 21 September earthquake. The previous edition of this temple remains where it partly collapsed, and a memorable sight it is too. Most of the ground-floor walls gave way, pulling many of the roof decorations down to head-height. Visitors are free to walk up to this odd and much-photographed attraction at any time of day or night, but going inside isn't permitted for safety reasons.

Endemic Species Research Institute 特有生物研究保育中心 **(Téyǒu Shēngwù Yánjiū Bǎoyù Zhōngxīn)** (📞 049 276 1331; w tesri.tesri.gov.tw) This government-run research body is on the right if you're driving out of Jiji on the main road to Shuili. Much of it (including the wildlife first-aid station) is off-limits to the public, but the **Conservation Education Centre** (🕐 09.00–16.30 Tue–Sun, closed 1–10 Jun & 1–10 Dec; admission NTD60/30, free for students every Tue) provides an excellent introduction to Taiwan's astonishing biodiversity. The island's unique birds receive a lot of attention but rates of endemism are much higher in other parts of the biosphere. The displays describe the threats these special creatures face and what ordinary people can do to help preserve the environment. Almost everything inside is bilingual. The adjacent **Ecological Education Park** (🕐 08.30–16.30 daily; free admission) is divided in various sections including aquatic plants, grassland, broad-leaf forest and ferns. In the summer, expect to see some stunning dragonflies – but be ready for mosquitoes.

Mingsin Academy of Classical Learning 明新書院 (🕐 08.00–20.00 daily; free admission) Founded in 1878 and moved to its present location next to the ESRI in 1908, this academy was endowed by businessmen who made fortunes from camphor. Literacy and Confucianism were among the subjects taught here, and even now, students come here to pray to the deity Wenchang Dijun. Like several other buildings in the area, the academy had to be rebuilt after the 21 September earthquake. It's a pretty little complex of single-storey buildings deserving of a quick look.

SUN MOON LAKE 日月潭 (RÌYUÈ TÁN) *Telephone code 049*

What's often but incorrectly described as Taiwan's largest natural lake (its current dimensions are a result of human engineering) falls into the 'touristy-but-pretty' category. It's a lovely place to visit but if you don't make it here, you needn't feel you've missed something unique.

Covering 8km², the lake assumed its modern shape and size in the early 1930s when the Japanese colonial regime dammed the basin as part of a hydro-electricity project. Supposedly, the eastern part is round like the sun while the southern section resembles a sickle moon. The surface is 748m above sea level and the waters up to 30m deep. Rising waters forced members of the Thao, a tiny indigenous ethnic group, to leave Lalu Island in the southwestern quarter of the lake they call Zintun. This islet, which shrank further as a result of the 21 September earthquake, is where the Thao believe their ancestral spirits dwell. Nowadays the tribe's main home is Ita Thao, a settlement on the southeastern shores of the lake.

Sun Moon Lake is good to visit any time of year, but unless you're planning to take part it's best to avoid the area on the day of the annual mass cross-lake swim, usually held in September. Swimming is prohibited at all other times.

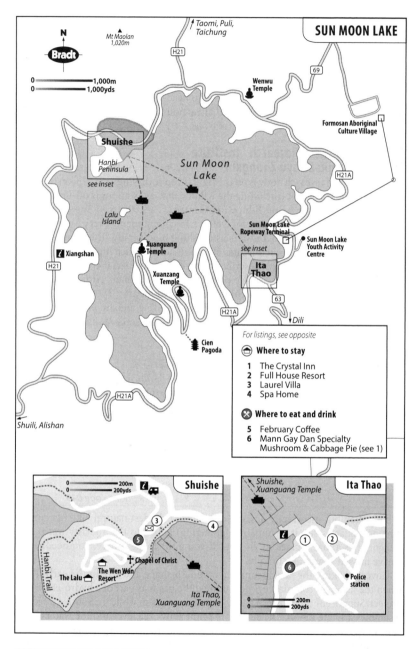

Sun Moon Lake

N

Bradt

Mt Maolan 1,020m

→ Taomi, Puli, Taichung

H21

0 ———— 1,000m
0 ———— 1,000yds

Wenwu Temple

H21

69

Formosan Aboriginal Culture Village

Shuishe

Hanbi Peninsula
see inset

Sun Moon Lake

H21A

Lalu Island

i Xiangshan

H21

Xuanguang Temple

Sun Moon Lake Ropeway Terminal

Sun Moon Lake Youth Activity Centre

see inset

Ita Thao

Xuanzang Temple

63

H21A

↓ Dili

Cien Pagoda

H21A

Shuili, Alishan

For listings, see opposite

⬤ **Where to stay**

1 The Crystal Inn
2 Full House Resort
3 Laurel Villa
4 Spa Home

✖ **Where to eat and drink**

5 February Coffee
6 Mann Gay Dan Specialty Mushroom & Cabbage Pie (see 1)

Shuishe

0 ——— 200m
0 ——— 200yds

i

③
④
⑤
✉
† Chapel of Christ

Hanbi Trail

The Lalu
The Wen Wan Resort

Ita Thao, Xuanguang Temple

Ita Thao

↑ Shuishe, Xuanguang Temple

i
① ②
⑥
● Police station

0 ——— 200m
0 ——— 200yds

GETTING THERE AND AWAY

By car, motorcycle or bicycle Drivers in a hurry can use Freeway 6 to Puli then Highway 21, although two-wheelers may want to avoid this route because the traffic can be heavy. A scenic but steep alternative is Road 131 from Puli then Local Road 69, which joins Highway 21A near Wenwu Temple. If you can, leave the area by Local Road 63 (page 187).

above   At the Bunun Ear-shooting Festival, tribesmen try to hit animal ears hung from trees using bows and arrows (RM) page 67

right   A Rukai bride during her wedding procession; the majority of this indigenous group live in Pingtung County (RM) page 259

below   Indigenous festivals often include demonstrations of hunting skills (RM)

above Yingge has long been the country's foremost producer of ceramics; these days the town's output is decorative rather than practical (SS) page 119

left Taiwanese opera performances typically feature bright make-up and costumes, traditional instruments and symbolic gestures (CF) page 127

below Meinong is renowned for its painted oil-paper parasols (SY/S) page 251

bottom Tea-pickers gather oolong tea leaves more than 1,000m above sea level in Greater Alishan (W/S) page 65

above Artisanal food producers are found in every community, among them noodle-makers who dry their pasta under the sun (Iz/S)

right A woodcarver at work in Lukang, a historic town filled with traditional buildings and lifestyles (RM) page 174

below The annual Beehive Fireworks Festival in Yanshui takes the Taiwanese love of explosions to new extremes (RM) page 222

above left With its breathtaking scenery, Taroko Gorge is understandably one of the country's biggest tourist attractions (TPA/S) 276

above right Cyclists looking for a challenge will be in their element in Taiwan, with routes ranging from sea level to mountain passes that climb to over 3,000m (SS) page 71

left Kenting National Park is much more than just a beach resort, encompassing windswept coastlines and conservation zones (o/S) page 264

below Set amid mountains and with shores punctuated by temples, Sun Moon Lake is popular for bike rides and boat trips (h/S) page 183

right   Caoshan Moonscape World is a uniquely desolate area of badlands; in certain lights the eroded hillocks and steep ravines look truly lunar (RM) page 218

below left   Over a century old, Alishan Forest Railway is one of the highest in the world (SH/S) page 227

below right   A highlight of Taiwan's rugged uplands, Snow Mountain is one of the country's most enticing peaks when it comes to hiking (SS) page 192

bottom   Yehliu Geopark is a natural wonderland with an array of curious rock formations caused by wind and wave erosion (NXV/S) page 135

above left   One of Taiwan's leading monastic organisations, Foguangshan runs a TV station, several publishing houses, homes for children and the elderly, and overseas branches (SS) page 247

top right   The fabulously ornate ceiling in Lukang's Longshan Temple (RM) page 180

above right   Guan Gong is one of the most important deities in Chinese religion (RM) page 33

bottom   One of the most beautiful places of worship in Taiwan, Taipei's Baoan Temple is a UNESCO-recognised architectural treasure (RC/S) page 100

above   Inaugurated on the fifth anniversary of the dictator's death, Chiang Kai-shek Memorial Hall is one of Taipei's most striking landmarks (JC/S) page 97

right   Built by the Dutch and besieged by Ming Dynasty loyalists fleeing China, Fort Zeelandia in Tainan is a key location in Taiwan's history (K/S) page 206

below   The shrines and pagodas that surround Kaohsiung's Lotus Pond are riotously colourful (SP/S) page 246

Taiwan is a haven for birdwatchers, with over 25 endemic avian species (page 6).

above left   Greater painted snipe (*Rostratula benghalensis*) (R/S)

above right Swinhoe's pheasant (*Lophura swinhoii*) (WT/S)

left   Steere's babbler (*Liocichla steerii*) (p/S)

below left   Maroon oriole (*Oriolus trailli*) (oa/S)

below right Taiwan blue magpie (*Urocissa caerulea*) (F/S)

By bus All buses arrive and depart from beside the visitor information centre in Shuishe. Each day Kuo-Kuang has at least six #1833 services (⊕ 07.00–17.00; 4hrs; NTD470) from Taipei. From Taichung TRA station via Taichung HSR station, around 20 #6670 services per day go to Sun Moon Lake via Puli (⊕ 07.48–19.48; about 1½hrs; NTD202), from where there's at least one #6668 service each hour (⊕ 06.05–21.00 daily; 40mins; NTD54). Leaving Sun Moon Lake, the last bus back to Taichung departs at 19.25 and to Puli at 21.30.

The #6739 Sun Moon Lake–Alishan bus leaves Shuishe at 08.00 and 09.00 (3½hrs; NTD350). Seats can be booked in advance (an English-language form can be found online at w www.ylbus.com.tw/news/file/1/1569.pdf).

GETTING AROUND

By bus You can download the timetable of the #6669 'Round-the-Lake Bus' from the scenic area website (w www.sunmoonlake.gov.tw) or get a copy from the visitor centre. Jump-on/jump-off tickets are NTD80 and valid for one day (19 buses daily Mon–Fri; 22 buses daily at w/ends & nat hols; ⊕ 06.40–17.20). Only eight go beyond Ita Thao to Xuanguang Temple. Before each stop a multi-lingual announcement is made, but remember to press the bell or the driver may not stop.

By boat Tourist boats cruise between Shuishe, Ita Thao and Xuanguang Temple (departures every 15–30mins; ⊕ approx 09.00–17.30 daily). The official price is NTD100 per journey but discounts are often available. Depending on how people there are in your group and your bargaining skills, chartering a boat for an hour or so can be as cheap as NTD1,500 midweek.

By motorcycle or bicycle The scenic area website (w www.sunmoonlake.gov.tw) has details of bike paths. Going all the way around the lake (total distance: 33km) can be done very comfortably in a day but heavy traffic means weekends are best avoided. To hire a bike, head for Giant (in the visitor centre basement; ⊕ May–Oct 06.00–19.00, Nov–Apr 07.00–18.00, closed Thu); weekday rentals begin at NTD150 per day; on weekends, you'll pay NTD200 for 2 hours. All bikes hired here must be returned here. Cheaper bikes can be hired from shops nearby including Meilidaai Bike Hire (25 Lane 12, Zhongxing Rd; ☏ 285 5295; ⊕ 06.30–18.00 daily).

You can also hire 125cc and e-scooters in Shuishe and Ita Thao; typical rates for the former are NTD500 per day or NTD600 per 24 hours, while the latter are slightly cheaper.

By cable car The **Sun Moon Lake Ropeway** (⊕ 10.30–16.00 Mon–Fri, 10.00–16.30 Sat–Sun & nat hols; journey time 7mins; round-trip NTD300/250), a 1.88km-long cable-car system, is a spectacular way of arriving on the lake's eastern shore a short walk from Ita Thao (page 187). Parking at the ropeway's lakeside station costs NTD100 for cars, NTD20 for motorcycles.

TOURIST INFORMATION Sun Moon Lake National Scenic Area (☏ 285 5668; w www.sunmoonlake.gov.tw) runs visitor information centres in Shuishe, Ita Thao and Xiangshan (all ⊕ 09.00–17.00 daily).

WHERE TO STAY *Map, opposite*

Shuishe

🏠 **Spa Home** (9 rooms) ☏ 285 5166; w spahome.com.tw. If you really want lake views but dislike larger hotels, this could be your best option. The staff go well out of their way to assist. Excellent b/fast inc. **$$$$**

Laurel Villa (9 rooms) 28 Mingsheng St; 285 5765; e laurel.villa@gmail.com; w laurelvilla.com.tw. The property was given a top-to-bottom renovation & restyling in 2017 (inc installation of a lift) but the bilingual host family are as helpful as ever, even organising early-morning bike rides for guests. B/fast inc. **$$$**

Ita Thao

The Crystal Inn (20 rooms) 700 8188; e service@thecrystal.com.tw; w www.thecrystal.com.tw. This boutique hotel has a waterside location & rooms that are strikingly designed, spacious & extremely comfortable; all beds are king-size plus. Request a lake-view room. B/fast inc; dinner is optional (restaurant open to non-guests; EM; **$$$$**). There's a smallish gym (09.00–22.30 daily) & an observation deck

that's especially pleasant just after dawn. Prices sometimes drop below NTD4,000. **$$$$**

Full House Resort 日月潭富豪群渡假民宿 (10 rooms) 285 0307; e a2850307@yahoo.com.tw; w fhsml.idv.tw. Ita Thao has 2 large, chalet-type hotels; Full House is the one that's smaller & set back from the water's edge. The English sign is small & little English spoken within, but if you're sick of concrete & tiles, you'll adore the wooden walls, floors & ceilings here. Comfortable, distinctive rooms & a lobby that's filled with artworks collected by the owner. The lobby doubles as an eating area but many of those dining here (11.00–22.00 daily; EM; **$$$**) prefer the lush garden. The menu is geared to groups; teas, coffees & beers from NTD150. B/fast inc. **$$$**

✗ WHERE TO EAT AND DRINK *Map, page 184*

✗ February Coffee 二月咖啡 Between Mingsheng St & the Hanbi Trail, Shuishe; 285 5471; 11.00–21.00 Wed–Mon. A good bet if you want Western food but don't want to pay 5-star-hotel prices for it. Choice of pastas plus snacks like French fries, as well as coffees, teas & beers. Indoor & outdoor seating. EM. **$$**

✗ Mann Gay Dan Specialty Restaurant 瑪蓋旦風味餐廳 42 Fengnian St, Ita Thao; 285 0523; 09.00–19.30 Thu–Tue. This long-standing indigenous restaurant is a big hit with local tourists who wolf down platefuls of freshwater shrimp, barbecued meat & high-mountain vegetables. Ordering is by sets designed

for 2–8 ppl that work out at NTD350–500 pp. No EM but the menu has pictures. Local beers & liquors available; indoor & outdoor seating. The newer bldg has AC but no view & may be closed on weekdays. **$$**

✗ Mushroom & Cabbage Pie 香菇高麗菜包 111 Wenhua St, Ita Thao; 285 0082; approx 10.00–19.00 daily. A few tables under a tarpaulin & just 2 or 3 deep-fried items – none of them remotely Austronesian in flavour – but this vendor is perhaps Ita Thao's best. Point to order a round cabbage & mushroom pie &/or a cylindrical boar-meat & cheese pie. Both are NTD45 each & delicious. No EM. **$**

OTHER PRACTICALITIES There are no banks at Sun Moon Lake, but you'll find ATMs in Shuishe and Ita Thao. There's a post office in Shuishe (36 Mingsheng St; 08.30–12.30 & 13.00–16.30 Mon–Fri).

WHAT TO SEE AND DO At Sun Moon Lake, the whole is very much more than the sum of its parts, and spending a sunny day circumnavigating the lake is highly recommended. Because there's relatively little to be seen south of Shuishe, visitors starting from there tend to look at the Hanbi Peninsula first before moving clockwise.

Hanbi Trail 涵碧步道 This 1.5km-long waterside path goes around a small finger of land on which Chiang Kai-shek spent a fair bit of time. The dictator's retreat is long gone and the peninsula is now the location of two very swanky hotels, **The Lalu** (96 rooms; 285 5311; w www.thelalu.com.tw; **$$$$$** inc b/fast, meals available) and **The Wen Wan Resort** (92 rooms; 285 5555; w thewenwan.com; **$$$$$** b/fast & dinner optional). The latter is more ostentatious (the curving 'mast' on the exterior is coated with 15kg of gold leaf) but the former has far better food. The **Chapel of Christ** 耶穌堂 near the Wen Wan is a Romanesque-style place of worship completed in 1971 for the convenience of Chiang, his wife and their entourage. The surrounding trees presumably made assassination from a distance less likely.

Wenwu Temple 文武廟 (⊕ 24hrs daily) Dedicated to both Confucius (the *wén*, or literary, part of its name) and Guan Gong (the *wǔ*, or martial, element), this sizeable house of worship replaced two temples that were inundated when the water level rose. The interior has several superbly decorated beams but you'll find the view over the lake from the roof more alluring. Do explore some of the hiking trails near here as you can get away from the road and down to the water's edge. None are longer than 600m.

Sun Moon Lake Ropeway 日月潭纜車 This very scenic cable-car ride (page 185) links the lake with the **Formosan Aboriginal Culture Village** 九族文化村 (\ 289 5361; w nine.com.tw; ⊕ 08.00–17.00 daily; admission NTD850/650/420), where indigenous heritage is presented in an amusement park setting. The terminal, within walking distance of Ita Thao, has a coffee shop (EM; $) and a restaurant (EM; $$); there are lots of tables where you can sit and take in the view. Across the road from the terminal is **Sun Moon Lake Youth Activity Centre** 日月潭青年活動中心 (75 rooms; \ 285 0070; w sun.cyh.org.tw; $$ inc b/fast, meals available for groups $$), which has very pleasant grounds open to non-guests.

Ita Thao 伊達邵 Were it not for the souvenir sellers who don pseudo-aboriginal clothing during peak season, you'd never guess this village is the 'capital' of the Thao indigenous people. About 60 of the households here are registered as members of the tribe; as in other parts of Taiwan, many of the businesses are run by lowlanders of Han descent.

Just south of Ita Thao's police station, Local Road 63 heads into the mountains to and beyond Tannan, a Bunun settlement. Minor landslides are frequent – watch out for rocks on the tarmac – but this very scenic and little-used route is almost always open all the way to **Dili** 地利 on Highway 16. The total distance is 11.5km; being mostly downhill it's ideal for cyclists. East of Dili, Highway 16 is often in terrible disrepair, but west to Shuili the going is usually fine.

Xuanzang Temple 玄奘寺 **and Xuanguang Temple** 玄光寺 (both ⊕ 05.30–19.30 daily) Linked by an 850m-long hiking trail, these two shrines hold relics associated with Xuan Zang (AD602–664), a Buddhist monk revered for travelling to India and translating religious texts. Between the 4th and 7th centuries AD at least 3,000 Chinese Buddhists set out for the subcontinent; perhaps 80 reached their destination and Xuan Zang was one of just 15 known to have survived the return journey. Nine hundred years after his death, his adventures were retold in a classic Chinese novel, *Journey to the West*, which inspired a 1970s Japanese television series shown in English-speaking countries under the title *Monkey*.

Cien Pagoda 慈恩塔 (⊕ 09.00–16.30 daily; free admission) Commissioned by Chiang Kai-shek as a memorial to his mother, Cien Pagoda never gets as crowded as the attractions on the lake's north side, and the panoramic views from the upper floors more than justify climbing the stairs. The top of the pagoda is exactly 1,000m above sea level.

From whichever direction you approach Sun Moon Lake, you'll see hillside plantations of thin palm trees up to 20m tall. These are betel-nut trees (*Areca catechu*), though the 'nuts' are in fact dark-green, walnut-sized fruit. If chewed, betel nut is a stimulant, which is why it's popular with lorry and taxi drivers and others who work long hours. It warms the body and sometimes causes the chewer to break out in a sweat. Masticating on a nut causes the mouth to salivate. This fluid should not be swallowed; the red splotches sometimes seen on roads are betel-nut expectorations. In aboriginal cultures, betel nut has long had a ritual as well as recreational role.

Preparing the nuts for sale (each one has to be slit open, filled with lime paste and wrapped in a leaf that comes from a different kind of plant) is a major industry that employs tens of thousands of people, women mostly. Thousands of roadside stands around the island sell betel nut, alongside cigarettes, beer, soft drinks and mineral water.

Compared with the general population, heavy users of betel nut suffer very high rates of oral cancer. Non-users also have good reasons to worry about the nut's popularity. Compared with woodlands, betel-nut plantations retain very little moisture, partly because their leaves are too small to shade the topsoil. Consequently, whenever there's a heavy downpour, the run-off is sudden and massive. Moreover, the palms have shallow roots and are thus easy to dislodge. During typhoons and tropical storms, groves on steep slopes quickly turn into landslide zones. Successive governments have vowed to crack down on illegal betel-nut plantations in mountain areas, and according to official data some progress has been made. In 2015, the island grew an estimated 113,000 tonnes of the nut, 14% less than in 2010. In terms of total betel-nut production, Taiwan is second only to India, and betel nut remains Taiwan's number-two cash crop – rice is number one.

PULI TO LISHAN *Telephone code 049*

The important transport hub of **Puli** 埔里 lacks major attractions, but within striking distance there's a monumental Buddhist shrine as well as some of the island's most captivating mountain scenery. Now that Highway 8 is again fully open, travellers heading to **Lishan** 梨山 need not take the spectacular detour over Highway 14A. However, the latter remains one of Taiwan's most thrilling drives, the highest stretch of tarmac in the country climbing above the treeline to an elevation of 3,275m. The landscapes are always excellent and sometimes snow causes traffic jams as lowland Taiwanese rush to the hills for a once-in-a-lifetime snowman-making experience. At Dayuling, you can proceed to Lishan and then Wuling Farm or turn east towards Taroko Gorge.

GETTING THERE AND AROUND

By car or motorcycle It's a shade under 100km from Puli to Lishan; expect the going to be slow and keep your headlights on at all times. There are petrol stations in Wushe, at km11 on Highway 14A and in Lishan (all ☉ approx 08.00–18.00 daily).

By bus Around 25 services per day link Puli with Wushe (#6658, 6659 & 6664; departures 05.40–18.45 daily; takes 50mins; NTD83), and a dozen continue on to

Qingjing Farm (⊕ 06.00–16.35 daily; journey time from Puli 1¼hrs; NTD118), meaning you can savour the mountains for a couple of hours before boarding #6506, a daily service to Lishan. This bus sets out from Fengyuan bus station, less than 100m from Fengyuan TRA station, at 09.10 and follows Highway 8 then Highway 21, where the good scenery begins. The bus, which can be boarded at Puli at 10.45, reaches Dayuling at 12.50 (NTD449) and Lishan at 14.00 (NTD546). It's also possible to board this bus at Qingjing Farm or Hehuanshan but only if you get a Chinese speaker to call the bus company (✆ 04 2523 4175) during office hours the day before. In the opposite direction, the bus leaves Lishan at 08.00, stops in Dayuling an hour later and gets back to Fengyuan at 13.20.

For an alternative route between Lishan and Taichung TRA station, take bus #850 to Guguan (departs about hrly; ⊕ 06.00–20.00 daily; 1hr 50mins; NTD177), and from there catch bus #865 to Lishan (departs 06.45, 11.45 & 16.15 daily; 1hr 30mins; NTD119). Buses leave Lishan for Guguan at 06.10, 11.10 and 15.40.

For details of buses between Dayuling and Taroko Gorge, see page 278. For Lishan–Wuling Farm services, see page 124.

TOURIST INFORMATION There's a visitor information centre in Lishan (near the bus stop; ⊕ 08.30–17.30 daily). Hehuanshan is part of Taroko National Park (w www.taroko.gov.tw) but Lishan falls under the Tri-Mountain National Scenic Area (w trimt-nsa.gov.tw).

WHERE TO STAY AND EAT Entrepreneurs have opened dozens of homestays between Wushe and Qingjing Farm, several of which offer lavish mountain views, sumptuous comfort and reasonable midweek prices, but little English is spoken. Be sure to carry provisions as between Qingjing Farm and Lishan there's nothing but a few vendors on Hehuanshan. For budget lodgings, try the small hotels on the main road in Lishan.

Lishan Guest House (97 rooms) ✆2598 0887; w lishanguesthouse.com.tw. One of Chiang Kai-shek's country retreats (he had at least 20), this impossible-to-miss complex near Lishan's petrol station is a low-rise version of Taipei's Grand Hotel. Outside, gaudy red columns hold up a glazed-tile roof, but the guestrooms are modern & spacious, although not all have bathtubs. Located at the western end of the town, a stone's throw from the visitor information centre & bus stop, this hotel isn't a bad deal given that English is spoken & room rates are often discounted. Dinner & lunch available (NTD900 for 2 ppl). **$$$$**

Herblife Homestay 草本生活家地址 (7 rooms) Taomi Vlg; ✆291 3551; m 0913 809 823; w herblife.okgo.tw. If you're driving or walking into Taomi, go past the elementary school & you'll immediately see this homestay's butterfly-motif sign on the right, directly opposite the km9 marker on Local Road 68. The gorgeous garden & pristine interior more than make up for a lack of English. Inc b/fast & dinner, featuring many home-grown ingredients. Non-guests can enjoy the highly rated country fare; expect to pay around NTD500 pp; no EM. **$$$**

Minglan Garden Homestay 名蘭楓香花園民宿 (9 rooms) ✆280 2251; w minlan. emmm.tw. Popular with birders, Minglan is situated 1,100m above sea level, about 1km before Wushe if you're approaching from Puli (look for a side road on the right just where the main road swings left), Minglan's common balcony & most of its rooms look over the valley where the owners grow medicinal herbs, vegetables & bamboo. Bookings seldom needed midweek when rooms can often be had for NTD2,240. For weekends (from NTD3,200) get a Chinese speaker to make a reservation. Groups may like the 8-person & 12-person rooms. B/fast inc. The same family operates a good-value Taiwanese-style restaurant, also called Minglan, in the centre of Wushe (⊕ 11.00–20.30 daily; no EM; **$$**). **$$$**

OTHER PRACTICALITIES There are banks in Puli and a post office in Wushe (⊕ 08.00–16.30 Mon–Fri) where you can change money.

WHAT TO SEE AND DO
Paper Dome 紙教堂 (Taomi Vlg; w paperdome.blogspot.com; ⊕ 09.30–17.30 Sun–Tue & Fri, 09.30–20.00 Sat & nat hols; admission NTD120/60) Almost two-thirds of the buildings in Taomi, 6km southwest of Puli, were destroyed in the 21 September earthquake, but the village has successfully reinvented itself as an ecotourism destination and now has over a dozen B&Bs. Contrary to its Chinese name, which means 'Puli's paper church', the Paper Dome isn't now a place of worship. What makes it special are the materials used in its construction and the fact it's a recycled building in the truest sense of the word. Its original owners, a Catholic church in Japan, decided it was no longer big enough for their purposes. Some years after dismantling it, they donated the pieces – principally 58 columns, each 32.5cm in diameter and 5m high, made from laminated and fireproofed layers of recycled paper – to this village. A Taiwanese charity reassembled it and added an exterior membrane of steel and waterproof polycarbonate. It's quite special and best seen around dusk. The site includes artificial wetlands, a coffee shop, a restaurant and a craft shop.

Taomi Village is between Puli and Sun Moon Lake at km51.5 on Highway 21. Coming from Puli, turn right off the highway, then left, and you'll very soon see the dome and places where you can park. Buses between Puli and Sun Moon Lake will stop here if you forewarn the driver.

Chung Tai Chan Monastery 中台禪寺 **(Zhōng Tái Chán Sì)** (Turn west at km39 Hwy 21; ☏ 2930 215; e ctworld@mail.ctcm.org.tw; w ctworld.org.tw; ⊕ 08.00–17.30 daily) Designed by C Y Lee, the architect behind Taipei 101, this edifice is especially impressive if you come in the middle of the afternoon and stay until it gets dark, when the exterior is lit up. Casual visitors usually see only the Hall of the Four Heavenly Kings (dominated by 12m-high black granite statues of a quartet of guardian deities) and the adjacent Great Majestic Hall. Call or email several days in advance for a guided tour (free, donations welcome) of the entire complex and an explanation of the sect's brand of Chan (better known in the West as Zen) Buddhism. Within the complex, **Chung Tai Museum** (w ctmuseum.org; ⊕ 09.30–17.30, closed 2nd & 4th Mon each month but open all nat hols; admission NTD100/70) displays Buddhist art and artefacts. Driving here from Puli is a cinch, but if you're coming from the north the turn off is less obvious.

Wushe 霧社 **(Wùshè)** This small town, 1,180m above sea level and known to Sediq tribespeople as Paran, is where Mona Rudao launched his uprising against the Japanese in 1930 (page 15). If you're coming from Puli, you'll see the white archway of the Wushe Incident Memorial Park on the left just before reaching the town centre. Do stock up on provisions here as between Qingjing Farm and Lishan there's nothing but a few vendors on Hehuanshan.

Qingjing Farm 清境農場 (km10 Hwy 14A; w cingjing.gov.tw; ⊕ 08.00–17.00 daily; admission NTD200/120) Established by the KMT regime in the early 1960s as a place where veterans of the Chinese Civil War could settle down, Qingjing Farm's current inhabitants include descendants of anti-communist guerrillas who waged war in the mainland's southwest long after Chiang Kai-shek retreated to Taiwan. The farm's sheep and pasturelands are a big hit with Taiwanese and southeast Asian tourists; Western visitors tend to go for the scenery and birdlife.

Sanjiaofong Trail 三角崙步道 (km17.3 Hwy 14A) It's easy to miss the entrance to this 780m-long trail but if you're in the mood for a jaunt, look for a brown-and-white sign on the right as you're heading towards Dayuling. You'll want a hat for the first bit as there's no shade but soon you'll be ascending through forest. Allow an hour to do this spot justice.

Hehuanshan 合歡山 Anyone with good legs can knock off the main peak of Taiwan's 34th-highest mountain (oddly, at 3,416m it's very slightly lower than the north and east peaks) and return to the trailhead near km30.8 on Highway 14A in around 2 hours. Getting to the north peak, which many regard as more worthwhile, takes up to 4 hours; the scenery is good in every direction and in April and May the mountain's rhododendrons are in bloom. An easy hike hereabouts is the 750m-long path to top of **Mount Shimen** 石門山 (3,237m). If you're heading north on Highway 14A, the trailhead is on your right near km33.4. There's a small car park on the left-hand (western) side of the road.

Lishan 梨山 (Líshān) (km86 Hwy 8) The smartest structure in this spread-out little town is the Presbyterian church, as many other buildings look as though they were hastily assembled using sheets of corrugated metal. Also, the frames that support thousands of apple and pear trees on the hillsides hereabouts do nothing to enhance the area's appearance. However, if you decide to stay you'll find some pleasant trails (one starts right behind Lishan Guest House) and some very pleasing vistas.

SHEI-PA NATIONAL PARK 雪霸國家公園 (XUĚBÀ GUÓJIĀ GŌNGYUÁN)

With 51 mountain peaks above 3,000m, Shei-Pa National Park features some of Taiwan's very best alpine scenery. Because this 76,850ha park is entirely in the subtropics and the lowest spot is 760m above sea level, temperatures often go very low. Typically, the mornings are gloriously clear but the weather in the afternoons is often cloudy or wet, while blizzards are a possibility in wintertime.

The park gets its English name from peculiar renderings of its two most notable peaks: Snow Mountain (variously known as Syueshan, Hsuehshan and Mount Xue) and Mount Dabajian (sometimes Dabajian Mountain). The former is Taiwan's second-highest mountain; at 3,886m (12,749ft) it's just 66m shorter than Jade Mountain. Mount Dabajian, which reaches 3,490m, has – from some directions at least – a distinctive cylindrical appearance. It's also considered a holy spot by Atayal and Saisiyat aborigines. The first recorded ascent was by a team of Japanese climbers in 1927; one of them, Numai Tetsutaro, later described the crest-line between Mount Dabajian and Snow Mountain as a 'holy ridge'. This name has stuck and serious hikers may want to consider spending up to ten days doing what's now called the Holy Ridge 'O' Route. Another popular trek is Snow Mountain West Ridge Trail, which takes six days.

Because the park sprawls across county boundaries, telephone codes are included in listings.

GETTING THERE AND AWAY The only part of the park accessible by public transport is Wuling Farm and its hinterland, although once there you'll need to walk or rent a bike. For self-drivers, it's 24km from Lishan to Wuling and 57km from Wuling to Qilan, from where you can continue on to Yilan City or turn right on to the North Cross-Island Highway. Thick mists are very common between Wuling and Nanshan so keep your headlights on. There are petrol stations at Lishan and Nanshan (both ⊕ 08.00–18.00 daily).

TOURIST INFORMATION AND LOCAL TOUR OPERATORS There is a visitor centre at Wuling Farm (near the bus station; ⊕ 09.00–16.30 Tue–Sun), and the headquarters of Shei-Pa National Park (w spnp.gov.tw) doubles as Wenshui Visitor Centre (Fuxing Vlg, Dahu, Miaoli County; ☎ 037 996 100; ⊕ 09.00–16.30 Tue–Sun, open on nat hols that are Mon). Taiwan Adventures (☎ 02 2346 5867; m 0983 212 499; e info@taiwan-adventures.com; w taiwan-adventures.com) organises regular group and private trips to Snow Mountain and other peaks in the national park.

WHERE TO STAY AND EAT Information about Wuling Farm's campsite is at w www2. wuling-farm.com.tw/en/camp/index.php. Meals are available in the hotel listed here and there are shops in Lishan but it would be wise to bring some supplies. Hikers heading into the uplands usually stay in basic huts managed by the national parks; for some, reservations can be made when applying for mountain permits.

⌂ Hoya Inn Wuling (24 rooms) ☎ 04 2590 1399; e inn@hoyaresort.com.tw; w www. hoyaresort.com.tw/inn. Alternatively known as Wuling Lodge, this inn is the cheapest & cosiest accommodation option inside Wuling Farm. It's also in a much better location – a stone's throw from the trail to Taoshan Waterfall – for those planning to explore on foot. However, if you arrive by public transport you'll need to figure out a way of covering the 5.3km from the bus stop. If you walk you can drop into the Taiwan Salmon Eco Centre en route. Outside of the summer & Lunar New Year peak seasons, solo travellers can get a bed in one of the 6-person dorms for NTD700 (NTD900 at w/ends). B/fast inc. **$$$**

WHAT TO SEE AND DO

Snow Mountain 雪山 **(Xuěshān)** Even if you're here only because you couldn't get permits for Mount Jade, there's absolutely no reason to feel you're settling for second-best. Hiking up Snow Mountain is far too good an experience to be considered a consolation prize; in terms of scenic and ecological variety – not to mention pleasurable exertion – it's every bit as good as its taller compatriot. By Taiwan's standards it does snow fairly often here but that's not how the mountain got its name. The Atayal named it Sekoan, meaning 'broken cliffs'; it's a toponym you'll understand if you get close to the summit. The first Han people to know about the mountain adapted the indigenous name, then shortened it.

Because the trailhead is located within Wuling Farm (see opposite), hikers need to pay admission even if they stay in their vehicle until the service station (elevation: 2,140m) where permits are inspected. The station's bathrooms are the last ones until Chika Cabin (2,463m), a good hour's walk away. It takes 5 or more hours to get from Chika Cabin to 369 Cabin (3,100m) and the trail passes very close to Snow Mountain's east peak (3,201m). Many hikers set out from 369 Cabin well before dawn and try to reach the top, 4 hours' walk away, before sunrise.

Along the trail bilingual information boards introduce the fauna and flora, and explain various phenomena, such as why the rocks on one side of the valley have shattered into smaller pieces than those on the other side (it's the result of freezing and thawing). Birds include Taiwan flamecrests (*Regulus goodfellowi*), tiny but colourful warblers, and vinaceous rosefinches (*Carpodacus vinaceus*). The last hang around the cabins, picking up crumbs left by humans.

Climbing to and returning from the peak can be done in two days if you get an early start, but spending three days on the mountain is usual and advisable. Proper equipment and provisions are essential as the cabins (both are free) lack bedding and cooking facilities. Both national park and police permits are required and enforcement is strict. Beds in the two cabins must be booked in advance, so don't change your itinerary on a whim.

Mount Dabajian 大霸尖山 **(Dàbàjiānshān)** This mountain is accessed via Qingquan (page 156) and Guanwu National Forest Recreation Area (⏰ 24hrs daily; free admission); there's no public transport anywhere near the trailhead. Some call the mountain 'Taiwan's Matterhorn', but in terms of shape it's more akin to an immense plinth than a pyramid. Like the Matterhorn, Mount Dabajian should not be underestimated; allow three full days and don't go if you're not in good shape. Permits are required and hikers aren't allowed through the checkpoint after 11.00 because the first day involves a 19km march to Jiujiu Hut (2,700m above sea level) where there are dormitories and kitchen facilities. To make the first day less brutal, many groups camp near the 15km point, saving a gruelling ascent for the following morning. From Jiujiu Hut, approaching Mount Dabajian involves skirting or going over four 3,000m-plus peaks. The actual summit is off-limits, as the rock layer is too unstable to support the ladders and chains hikers would need to reach the very top. That may put off peak baggers but, in clear weather the superb views to be had along the way more than make up for any lack of bragging rights.

Wuling Farm 武陵農場 **(Wǔlíng Nóngchǎng)** (3km from the turn off at km54 Hwy 7A; ✆ 04 2590 1259; w www2.wuling-farm.com.tw; ⏰ 08.00–17.00 daily; admission NTD130/80 Mon–Fri, NTD160/80 Sat–Sun & nat hols; parking NTD50/10) Also known as Wuling National Forest Recreation Area, this area's history is similar to that of Qingjing Farm (page 190) but it's seen far less development. Many of the peach and apple orchards established in the 1960s have been taken back by the national park and planted with native trees. The lower parts of the recreation area (1,740–2,100m above sea level) have lots of red and green maples, oaks and gum trees, and there are also vast clusters of pine trees. Cherry and plum blossoms appear around the end of winter and are a magnet for domestic tourists.

Wuling is the starting point of some truly excellent hikes, including the ascent of Snow Mountain (see opposite). Even if the mountain isn't on your itinerary, consider driving up to the trailhead for the views you'll get over the area. For those without their own vehicles, the 2-hour minibus tour (NTD150 pp) is a good way of seeing the recreation area. There's also a free guided walking tour; for details see the farm's website. Bicycles can be rented from a shop (⏰ 08.00–17.30 daily) next to the bus station; prices range from NTD100 for a bike for 2 hours to NTD400 per hour for a three-person electric tricycle.

Tourists are barred from approaching Qijiawan Creek, the main waterway, to protect its population of Formosan landlocked salmon (see box, page 194) from human disturbance. Artificially propagated salmon can be seen near the bus station in the **Taiwan Salmon Eco Centre** (⏰ 09.00–noon & 13.00–17.00 Tue–Sun; free admission), where displays cover their feeding and breeding habits but don't include much English. The only place where visitors are allowed close enough to the creek to glimpse wild fish is 2.4km beyond the visitors' centre, at what maps call the Salmon Observatory. Distinguishing salmon from the other three fish species that inhabit the creek is close to impossible, however.

No permits are required for the 4.3km hike to **Taoshan Waterfall** 桃山瀑布. The concrete footpath, shaded by pine trees, climbs gradually to 2,250m above sea level.

Allow at least 3 hours to get to the fall and back, and set out before breakfast to beat the crowds. Very near the start, you'll get lovely views of Qijiawan Creek and the forest from a footbridge.

YUSHAN NATIONAL PARK 玉山國家公園
(YÙSHĀN GUÓJIĀ GŌNGYUÁN) *Telephone code 049*

Taiwan's largest national park covers 1,055km², 3% of the country's land area, and is named after the island's highest peak. Both the park and the mountain are called *yù* (jade) *shān* (mountain) in Mandarin. The park's official English name is Yushan but many English-language publications refer to the mountain itself as Mount Jade (3,952m); for the sake of clarity this guidebook does the same.

Large tracts of the park are totally unspoiled. Roads don't penetrate beyond the northwest and southwest corners; and it's only in the past few years that ordinary hikers (as opposed to fully equipped expeditions) have been able to cross the park from west to east. Those who get into the core of the reserve, which takes three or four days of walking, have an excellent chance of seeing some of the park's 28 mammal species. Black bears aren't easy to spot, but Formosan serows (*Capricornis swinhoei*) and Formosan sambars gather near water sources, and Reeves's muntjacs can be heard yapping after dark.

The park's only permanent human settlements are the mainly Bunun communities of Dongpu and Meishan. The former, a well-developed hot-springs resort in the park's northwest, is 1,120m above sea level; the latter has been hard to access since Typhoon Morakot wrecked the South Cross-Island Highway. Much of the park is traditional Bunun stomping ground and it's from this tribe that the mountain porters who work on Mount Jade are recruited.

For all kinds of visitors – not just tourists who don't want to stray far from their vehicles – Tataka is a highlight. The New Central Cross-Island Highway crests here at 2,610m above sea level and there are truly stunning views of Taiwan's highest uplands. If you're climbing Mount Jade, you'll almost certainly start from here. For details of the eastern segment of Yushan National Park, see page 287.

GETTING THERE AND AWAY

By car, motorcycle or bicycle Tataka is 21km from Alishan via Highway 18 and 71km from Shuili via Highway 21. The nearest petrol stations are those in Alishan and in Heshe at km102 on Highway 21. Dongpu (approximately 1,200m above sea level) is reached by Highway 21 to Heshe, then Local Road 60.

By bus The #6739 Sun Moon Lake–Tataka–Alishan bus service sets out from Sun Moon Lake at 08.00 and 09.00. It reaches Tataka about 3 hours later and Alishan about half an hour after that. From Alishan, buses depart at 13.00 and 14.00. Sun Moon Lake's Shuishe bus stop to Tataka costs NTD276 one-way; Alishan to Tataka is NTD73. You're advised to book your seat a few days or more in advance; an English-language form can be found online at w www.ntbus.com.tw/6739order-en.doc.

Several of Alishan's hotels offer to take guests to Tataka (NTD300 return) to see the sunrise there instead of Zhushan.

TOURIST INFORMATION

Tataka Visitor Centre km145 Hwy 21;
⊕ 09.00–16.30 daily. Birders & butterfly enthusiasts should check out the exhibitions here.

Yushan National Park Headquarters 515 Zhongshan Rd Sec 1, Shuili; 277 3121; w ysnp. gov.tw; ⊕ 09.00–16.30 daily. As well as collecting maps & information, you can apply for mountain permits in person at this office.

TOUR OPERATORS If you hope to climb Mount Jade, engaging a specialist tour operator to organise permits, transport, meals and equipment is strongly recommended.

Blue Skies Adventures 07 389 0795; m 0982 858 316; e blueskiesadventures@yahoo.com; w blueskiestaiwan.com. Has organised multiple ascents of Mount Jade & treks to other parts of the park.

Taiwan Adventures 02 2346 5867; m 0983 212 499; e info@taiwan-adventures.com; w taiwan-adventures.com. Another experienced outfit.

WHERE TO STAY AND EAT There are plenty of eating options and hotels in Dongpu but they aren't convenient for the Tataka area. The restaurant inside Tataka Visitor Centre (⊕ 09.00–16.30 daily; $$) serves meals and hot drinks, but bringing instant noodles and cutlery as a backup is a good idea; the visitor centre can provide piping-hot water.

 Dongpu Hostel (3 dorms) km108 Hwy 18; 270 2213. With 106 tightly packed beds (NTD300 pp), those who opt to sleep here shouldn't expect a fabulous night's rest. However, the location is perfect for exploring Tataka & enjoying the sunset & sunrise views. You may be sharing with a hiking group that rises before dawn to tackle Mount Jade, but you could have the place all to yourself. Bedding provided. The shower facilities are rudimentary & seldom used. Call ahead if you want a meal cooked for you (dinner NTD200, b/fast NTD80). Guests who bring their own food are welcome to use the kitchen. **$**

WHAT TO SEE AND DO It's 15km from Alishan to the park's western boundary.

Lulin Sacred Tree 鹿林神木 (km102 Hwy 18) This tree, a 2,700-year-old, 43m-high Formosan cypress (*Chamaecyparis formosensis*), is very close to but almost invisible from the road. Look for the sign and stairs on the left as you're coming from Alishan.

Shishan Lookout 石山觀景點 (km104.2 Hwy 18) Just past the national park boundary marker there's a service centre that's only sporadically open. Near the km105 marker you'll see a net strung across the road, put there to help macaques cross safely. What park literature calls 'inappropriate interactions' between the animals and human visitors have caused changes in the former's behaviour, including incidents in which macaques have vandalised cars when the occupants didn't give them food.

Mount Lulin 鹿林山 (Trailhead at km106.5 Hwy 18) A good option if you lack the time or permits for Mount Jade but have plenty of energy, hiking to the top of Mount Lulin (elevation: 2,845m) requires nothing more than decent legs and proper footwear. It's possible to then hike northeast to **Mount Linjhih** 麟趾山 (2,854m) without returning to the highway. Permits aren't required for either peak.

Tataka 塔塔加 **(Tǎtǎjiā)** (km145 Hwy 21) Highways 18 and 21 meet at this point, 2,610m above sea level. Parking, dropping into the visitor centre and then exploring the various trails – or simply strolling along the main road – are highly recommended. The botanically minded will enjoy the bilingual information boards that introduce tree and plant species. One, the Formosan pieris (*Pieris taiwanensis hayata*), is an endemic evergreen shrub with leaves that aborigines used to mash and use as an organic pesticide.

Mount Dongpu 東埔山 (Trailhead at km144.2 Hwy 21) Allow 30 minutes to reach the summit of this 2,782m-high mountain and plenty of additional time for taking in the wondrous panoramas. Mount Jade is clearly visible to the southeast.

Mount Jade 玉山 **(Yùshān)** This is the peak everyone wants to bag. Permit applications should be made several weeks in advance; because they often exceed the fixed daily quota by a ratio of 10:1, a lottery is used to decide who gets to climb the mountain. Visitor numbers are kept down to protect the mountain's fragile ecology and also because there isn't much space in Paiyun Lodge (92 beds in 8 dorms; NTD480 pp). Apart from limited camping options, the lodge is the only accommodation between the trailhead and the peak. It's much easier to get permits for midweek dates than for weekends, but applications must be submitted well in advance. The process can be completed online (start at **w** npm.cpami.gov.tw/en) but it's best to get a hiking outfit (page 195) to do the 'paperwork' for you. Mount Jade and some other trails in the national park are closed to the public for a month each year, sometime between January and March. The precise dates vary from year to year and may be brought forward or extended because of weather conditions.

Most hikers spend two days and one night on Mount Jade and scale the main peak only. Before beginning the walk to Paiyun Lodge it's necessary to go to the police checkpoint (⌚ 06.00–18.00 daily) to have your permits inspected. You're advised to fill your water bottles there, especially if you're tramping the 2.8km to the actual trailhead at Tataka Anbu (*ānbù* is Mandarin for 'saddle'). Private vehicles are not allowed past the checkpoint; the only alternative to walking is to jump on one of the minibuses that shuttle between the highway, the checkpoint and the saddle (NTD100 pp one-way). From Tataka Anbu (2,600m) it's 8.5km to Paiyun Lodge. The track to Mount Jade is to the left. The surfaced road dropping down to the south is only open to scientific researchers. Soon after stepping on to the trail, you'll likely see Taiwan laughing thrushes (*Garrulax morrisonianus*) scampering ahead of you; they've become totally unafraid of humans.

The hike to Paiyun Lodge is straightforward and very enjoyable. Along the way there are two toilets and a few shelters where you can rest. At km2.7 you'll see the trailhead for Yushan Front Peak (3,236m). This side trail is steep so allow up to 3 hours to get to the top and come back down to the main path. In a few places along the main trail, wooden walkways have been built and there are precipitous drops on the right side. These sections are quite safe so long as you pay attention to where you're putting your feet.

When you reach Paiyun Lodge (3,415m), you'll be shown to your bunks. The lodge has a reliable water supply but the electricity may not be on 24 hours so keep your torch handy through the night. Hikers aren't permitted to cook for themselves, but hot water is available very early in the morning so can you make coffee before going up to the peak. Various meal options are available but must be booked in advance; one package includes dinner, pre-dawn breakfast, brunch after summitting, and use of a sleeping bag for NTD850. Carrying up or renting a sleeping bag (NTD300) is essential. If you've arrived at the lodge with time and energy to spare, Mount Jade West Peak (3,528m) awaits. The round trip takes 2–3 hours; carry a torch and extra clothing as you might not make it back before dusk. Once the sun has set there's nothing to do at Paiyun Lodge and it gets very cold very quickly. Even if you don't feel sleepy you should turn in early as a courtesy to the majority who hope to reach the summit before sunrise.

The 2.4km journey from the lodge to the summit takes even the fastest hikers well over an hour. Most people rise early enough to eat some breakfast before heading out into the darkness. Watch out for ice on the path. In the dark it isn't difficult to lose the trail as it zigzags between trees and juniper bushes. If the ground feels unusually rough you may have blundered off the track, and if that happens, retrace your steps carefully. Some 700m beyond Paiyun Lodge the trail forks. Keep left if you're aiming for the summit; going right will take you to Mount Jade South Peak (3,844m). It's another 1.7km to the main peak. Take it slowly; where chains have been fixed in place you should pay careful attention to your footing and stick to the established route. There's a caged section where a metal frame protects hikers from falling rocks. The trail splits just before the summit. Left goes to the weather station on Mount Jade North Peak (3,858m); right leads to the peak. It can be extremely windy at this point, as it often is on the peak itself. Whatever the conditions, the mood among hikers who make it to the top is invariably exuberant. Expect yelping, shouting and singing as the sun makes its appearance. Don't rush down the mountain afterwards. Search out a sheltered spot a little below the summit where you can enjoy views over scores of high mountains – and pat yourself on the back for reaching east Asia's highest point.

New Central Cross-Island Highway 新中橫 The road between Tataka and Shuili Highway 21 is known as the New Central Cross-Island Highway, despite the fact that it doesn't go across the island. This road, which you'll take if you visit the hot-springs resort of **Dongpu** 東埔, offers one of Taiwan's finest mountain driving experiences but make sure you have enough petrol, food and drinks before setting out. Also, ask about road conditions as the highway is sometimes damaged by landslides. For safety's sake the section between km110 and km145 is typically closed to civilian traffic between 17.30 and 07.00.

Batongguan Historic Trail 八通關古道 The 90km trek from Dongpu in the west to near Yuli in the east is neither the longest nor most difficult in Taiwan. It is, however, an incredible way to spend a week (or more, if you choose to tack

Is it Mount Jade, Jade Mountain, Mount Yu or Yushan? To the Tsou tribe, it's Pattonkan – but the official toponym Batongguan actually refers to a different place, a high-altitude meadow where hikers on multi-day treks often camp.

The mountain would surely have been seen by the Dutch from their base in 17th-century Tainan, yet there's no record of it acquiring a Dutch name. From the 1860s until after World War II, English speakers referred to the mountain as Mount Morrison, although it's unclear whether this name honoured Robert Morrison (1782–1834), a Scotsman and pioneering missionary in China, or a ship's captain who recorded sighting the mountain while anchored near Tainan.

Between 1900 and 1945, the mountain's official name was Niitakayama, Japanese for 'new high mountain' and an admission that Taiwan's highest peak was taller than Japan's beloved Mount Fuji. The phrase *Niitakayama nobore* ('Climb Niitakayama') has been notorious since 1941 – it was the code sent out by Imperial Japanese Navy headquarters on 7 December, instructing its fleet to attack Pearl Harbor the following day.

on an ascent of Mount Jade from the north) in true wilderness. The trail, blazed in 1920–21 by the Japanese authorities so they could better monitor and control the aborigines, wasn't the first formal route through the Central Mountain Range. A previous path, established in 1875 on the orders of the Qing imperial court, has long been unusable. Tents aren't needed as there are shelters along the route, which is clearly marked. Self-sufficiency in terms of provisions is essential, and you shouldn't contemplate tackling this route (part of which was officially closed at the time of writing) unless you've plenty of hiking experience.

For additional online content, articles, photos and more on Taiwan, why not visit w bradtguides.com/taiwan?

7

Southwest Taiwan

Southwest Taiwan comprises Tainan, Chiayi City and Chiayi County (combined land area: 4,153km²; population: 2.66 million). The municipality of Tainan embraces the ancient city and its hinterland of small towns and farming villages. Chiayi City is surrounded by a county of the same name; the latter stretches from fishing villages that face the Taiwan Strait to the western face of Mount Jade. The region enjoys mild winters, the weather being dry and almost always sunny between October and March.

Most of the Han migrants who sailed for Taiwan in the 17th and early 18th centuries landed on the island's southwest coastline for three reasons: prevailing winds, flat land suitable for rice cultivation and a modicum of established civilisation. Tainan, renowned for its shrines and other antiquities, has the lion's share of points of interest. If you've any curiosity about Taiwan's past, this old city is a must-visit deserving a minimum of two whole days.

There are yet more historic buildings and lively temples in Chiayi City. The former, however, is more often used as a launch pad for trips to Alishan and other places in the mountainous interior. A tourist destination since the Japanese colonial era, Alishan's cool weather and temperate woodlands are profoundly soothing. From the resort it's possible to make forays into Yushan National Park.

TAINAN 台南 (TÁINÁN) Telephone code 06

Visiting Tainan is essential if you hope to learn about Taiwanese history, religion or traditional life. Comparisons to Kyoto are often made and aren't far off the mark; Taiwan's former capital has more government-recognised first-grade relics than any other city, and on every street there are signs of the pre-industrial past. However, Tainan is easier to navigate than Japan's cultural treasure house. Even though the population of Tainan's urban core is around 750,000, most of the sights are within walking distance of one another. It's a place where temples don't charge admission and where sightseers often find themselves far outnumbered by those visiting for reasons of piety. Among Taiwanese, Tainan is as famous for its snack foods as it is for traditional culture, and although Westerners may find many of these delicacies rather odd, the brave and the gluttonous will have a field day.

HISTORY Small numbers of Han Chinese, among them traders, fugitives and pirates, were living alongside the indigenous inhabitants when the Dutch arrived here in 1624 (page 11). The trickle of Han settlers turned into a flood when the VOC began offering incentives – oxen, seeds and tools – to Fujianese willing to cross the Taiwan Strait and work the land. The Dutch used thoroughly modern methods to attract immigrants: they promised tax holidays and advertised through local entrepreneurs on the Chinese coast. While the 38 years of VOC control set

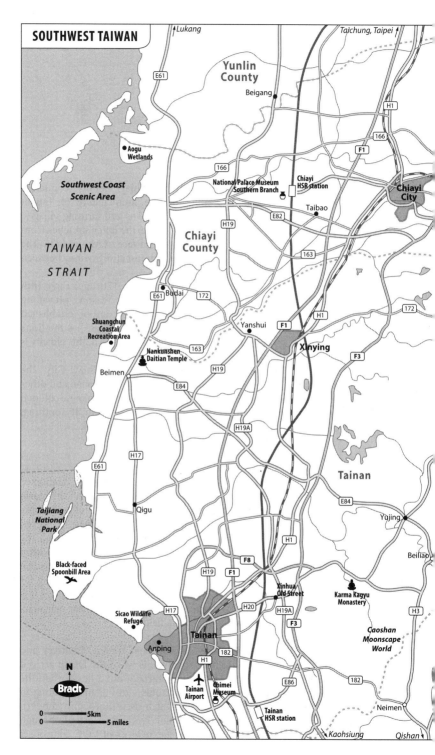

SOUTHWEST TAIWAN

↑Lukang

Taichung, Taipei ↗

Yunlin County

Beigang

E61

H1

166

F1

Aogu Wetlands

National Palace Museum Southern Branch

Chiayi HSR station

Chiayi City

166

Southwest Coast Scenic Area

Taibao

H19

E82

TAIWAN

Chiayi County

STRAIT

163

E61 Budai

172

Shuangchun Coastal Recreation Area

Yanshui

F1

H1

172

Nankunshen Daitian Temple

163

Xinying

F3

Beimen

H19

E84

H17

H19A

E61

Tainan

Qigu

E84

Yujing

Taijiang National Park

H1

Beiliao

Black-faced Spoonbill Area

F8

Xinhua Old Street

Karma Kagyu Monastery

H3

H19

F1

Sicao Wildlife Refuge

H17

H20

H19A

Caoshan Moonscape World

F3

Tainan

Anping

182

N

H1

Bradt

Tainan Airport

Chimei Museum

E86

182

Neimen

0 ——— 5km

Tainan HSR station

0 ——— 5 miles

↙Kaohsiung

Qishan ↘

200

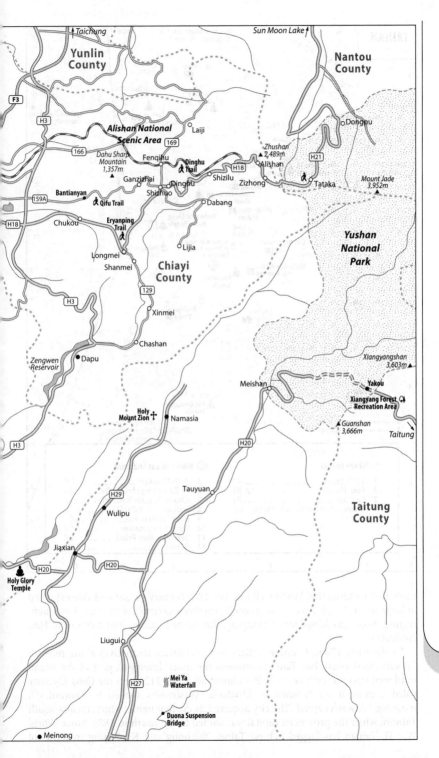

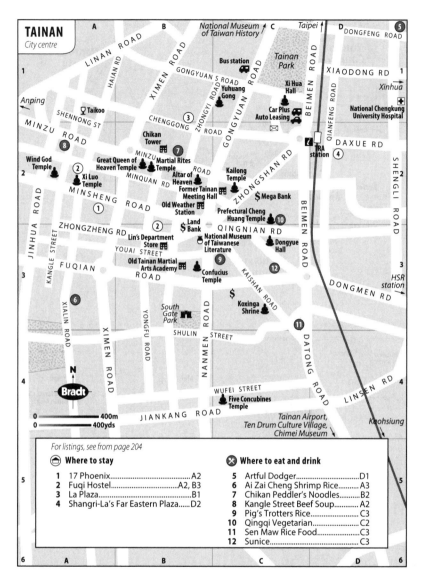

economic patterns that lasted well into the 18th century (sugar and rice exported in large quantities, tobacco and ginger in smaller amounts), it was the subsequent regime, Koxinga's Kingdom of Donging, that turned Tainan into a centre of Han civilisation.

By the early 1700s, Chinese settlers had established themselves along most of Taiwan's west coast, but Tainan remained the most developed part of the island until well into the 19th century. For almost all of the 212 years the Qing Dynasty ruled Tainan, it was known as Táiwānfǔ (Westerners spelled it 'Taiwanfoo'), meaning 'Taiwan's capital'. The city acquired its current name, which means 'south Taiwan', when the provincial capital was shifted to the north in 1885. Since World War II, Tainan has lagged behind Taipei, Taichung and Kaohsiung in terms of economic development yet succeeded in preserving a great deal of its character. On 6 February 2016, an earthquake – the most serious to strike Taiwan for almost 20 years – killed 117 people in Greater Tainan but left almost all of its landmarks undamaged.

GETTING THERE AND AWAY All fares mentioned in this chapter are one-way.

By air Up to three flights per day to Magong and a similar number to Kinmen leave from Tainan Airport (IATA code: TNN; ☎ 260 1016; w www.tna.gov.tw), 6km south of the city centre. In addition to daily flights to Hong Kong and Ho Chi Minh City, there are two flights per week to Osaka. A taxi from the airport to central Tainan costs around NTD250.

By HSR There are three trains to Taipei each hour (1½–2hrs; NTD1,350), and every northbound service stops at Taichung (38–53mins; NTD650). Tainan HSR station is an inconvenient 14km southeast of the city centre (which means it's not worth using the HSR if you're heading to Kaohsiung) but a TRA branch line (departs every 30mins; ⊕ 05.30–23.18 daily; 24mins; NTD25) connects the city centre with Shalun TRA station, which is right next door. Shuttle buses from the HSR station into the city centre are much slower.

By TRA Puyuma expresses to/from Taipei take little more than 3 hours but services are few (2 daily at the time of writing; NTD738) and they're often booked out. TC and CK trains need a minimum of 4¼ hours to reach Taipei (NTD569–738), to/from Taichung takes 2 hours (NTD363), and trains to/from Kaohsiung seldom take more than an hour (NTD68–106). If you're travelling light you can walk from the TRA station [202 D2] to many of Tainan's hotels and attractions.

By bus By the time you read this, Tainan's new bus station [202 C1] should be open and handling all intercity services. Kuo-Kuang's #1837 goes hourly to/from Taipei (⊕ 00.20–23.00 daily; 4¼hrs; NTD460) while the #1871 heads to Taichung (departs every 45mins; ⊕ 06.10–22.45 daily; 2½hrs; NTD250). Other bus companies offer similar routes, and discounts are common midweek.

By car or motorcycle By Freeway 1 Tainan is 302km south of Taipei and 40km north of Kaohsiung. Two-wheelers may want to approach via Highway 17, a road that runs near the coast south to Kaohsiung and north through Beimen into Chiayi County.

GETTING AROUND
By bus City bus #2 links the TRA station with Anping (departs every 20mins; ⊕ 06.00–22.00 daily; 25mins; NTD18) and stops very close to Confucius Temple and Five Concubines Temple. Two Tourist Shuttle services pick up passengers in front of Tainan TRA station (both NTD18 one-way): #88 to Anping (departs hrly Mon–Fri, every 30mins Sat–Sun; ⊕ 09.00–18.00) and the less frequent #99 to Qigu. Some of the latter go as far afield as the Black-faced Spoonbill Area in Taijiang National Park.

If you expect to do a lot of bus travel, look into getting a Tainan Fun Pass (w tainan.funcard.com.tw), which covers the double-decker Tainan Sightseeing Bus (w tainancitybus.com.tw), the #88 and #99, admission to certain attractions within the city and discounts at selected shops. The pass can be bought online and used via a smartphone.

By car, motorcycle or bicycle

There are several hire outlets in the city. Note that motorcycle-rental shops near the front and back of the TRA station usually insist on a local driving licence.

🚗 Car Plus Auto Leasing [202 C1] 111 Beimen Rd Sec 2; ⊕ 223 5566; w car-plus.com.tw; ⊕ 08.30–20.30 daily. General-use car rentals & long-term leasing. Also has a counter inside Tainan HSR station.

🚲 Dragon Bike [map, page 207] 120 Anbei Rd; 🔧228 5472; ⊕ 10.00–19.00 Thu–Tue. Standard bikes from NTD100/day.

🚲 T-Bike w tbike.tainan.gov.tw. The local government's bike-sharing scheme has expanded to more than 50 stations. EasyCards & credit cards accepted; NTD10/30mins, NTD100 for entire day.

TOURIST INFORMATION

The bilingual walking-guide maps and information boards found around the city centre are exceptionally useful.

ℹ️ Anping Visitor Information Centre [map, page 207] 790 Anping Rd; ⊕ 10.00–18.30 Tue–Sun
ℹ️ Office of English as the Second Official Language w oeasol.tainan.gov.tw. This city government unit has initiated various projects to make life easier for foreign visitors & residents, inc providing free Wi-Fi in major temples & detailed audio guides that can be downloaded or streamed.

ℹ️ Tainan City Government Tourism Bureau w www.twtainan.net
ℹ️ Tainan City Guide w tainancity.wordpress.com. Unofficial & not updated since 2012, but still informative regarding tourist attractions.
ℹ️ Tainan HSR Station Visitor Information Centre ⊕ 09.30–18.00 daily
ℹ️ Tainan TRA Station Visitor Information Centre [202 C2] ⊕ 07.30–19.00 daily

WHERE TO STAY

🏠 Shangri-La's Far Eastern Plaza Hotel 香格里拉台南遠東國際大飯店 [202 D2] (333 rooms) 89 Daxue Rd West Sec; 🔧702 8888; e sltn@shangri-la.com; w shangri-la.com/en/tainan/fareasternplazashangrila. Located in the steel-&-glass cylinder behind Tainan TRA station, guestrooms (11th to 37th flrs) in this 5-star hotel offer excellent city views & are a pleasing change from the boxiness of many other Taiwanese offerings thanks to the curve of the outer wall. Black-&-white photos of the city add a local touch to each room. The largest suites are 50m². Health club inc sauna & gym; the heart-shaped swimming pool is outdoors but heated in the winter (⊕ 06.00–23.00). B/fast inc. Café at **Far Eastern** (10th Flr; EM; **$$$$**) is likely the best buffet in the city. **$$$$**

🏠 17 Phoenix 捉鳳凰 [202 A2] (2 suites) 11 Lane 296, Haian Rd Sec 2; m 0980 716 478; w 17phoenix.com. Delightful split-level accommodation in 2 ultra-central locations (the other being Shennong St; both have living rooms & basic kitchens). Lots of wood & old character. For 2 ppl, midweek prices go as low as NTD2,300. **$$$**

🏠 La Plaza Hotel 天下大飯店 [202 B1] (103 rooms) 202 Chenggong Rd; 🔧229 0271;

w laplaza.com.tw. The popularity of this hotel (with Japanese business travellers in particular) is entirely understandable. The absolutely spotless & well-appointed rooms can often be had for less than NTD2,000. There's a fitness centre, a self-service laundry room & guests can borrow bikes for free. Some of the 3-person rooms have balconies & small living rooms. B/fast inc, served in the 8th-flr restaurant that also offers steaks, salads & other dishes (⊕ 11.30–14.00 & 17.30–20.30 daily; EM; **$$**). **$$$**

🏠 Fuqi Hostel 福憩背包客棧 [202 B3] (3 dorms, 1 room) 76 Zhongzheng Rd; 🔧703 4543; e fuqi.tainan@gmail.com; w fuqitainanhostelen.blogspot.com. While offering 28 beds for as little as NTD450 pp per night, the English-speaking owners of this hostel have succeeded in keeping some of this building's 1940s character, although that also means narrow, steep stairs (cyclists hoping to bring their bikes indoors might struggle). The only private room (NTD1,200) accommodates 2 ppl on *tatami* beds; shared bathroom. Coin-operated washing machine & dryer. Reception ⊕ 09.00–21.00 daily but 24hr security. The same team have expanded to 91 Heping St [202 A2] where there's a 3-ppl room (NTD1,950), a 4-ppl room for female guests only (NTD2,400) & a 6-bed dorm (NTD530 pp). **$**

✖ WHERE TO EAT AND DRINK
City centre

✖ Chikan Peddler's Noodles
赤崁擔仔麵 [202 B2] 180 Minzu Rd Sec 2; 📞 220 5336; **w** chikan.com.tw; 🕐 11.00–14.00 & 17.00–21.00 daily. The emphasis here is on traditional recipes cooked with high-quality ingredients. The eponymous danzai noodles (*dānzǐ miàn* 擔仔麵, served with minced pork & a single shrimp, NTD65) are extremely tasty but portions are small so order some extra items. Desserts inc bean curd & shaved ice. The wooden ceiling beams aren't original but not everything here is artifice: the tables & chairs downstairs are genuinely time-worn & look like they were retrieved from a primary school. Long-legged diners will feel more comfortable upstairs; both floors have AC. EM. **$$**

✖ Kangle Street Beef Soup
康樂街牛肉湯 [202 A2] 325 Kangle St; 📞 227 0579; 🕐 04.30–13.30 & 16.30–midnight Wed–Mon. The beef soups (NTD110/160 for small/large portion) consist of nothing but stock & thin slices of meat that are raw until a few moments before serving; neither onions nor greens are added. Cow's lung & cow's heart are also available, fried or in soup (all NTD130), & there's a beef version of the old favourite, braised meat on white rice (*niúrouzao fan* 牛肉燥飯, NTD30). The meat is sourced from a ranch on the northern outskirts of the city. **$$**

✖ Pig's Trotters Rice
豬腳飯 [202 C3] 41 Nanmen Rd; 📞 221 3455; 🕐 11.00–14.00 & 17.00–20.00 Tue–Sun. A real treat for those who adore pork, this little restaurant (eat inside or out front) serves large bowls filled with steamed rice, Hakka pickle, stewed bamboo & succulent pigs' trotters (NTD90/100). If that's not enough, get a portion of vegetables (NTD30) or a bowl of *dòubāo tāng* 豆包湯 (NTD35), a soup that contains fried tofu balls. **$$**

✖ Ai Zai Cheng Shrimp Rice
矮仔成蝦仁飯 [202 A3] 66 Haian Rd Sec 1; 📞 220 1897; 🕐 08.30–19.30 Wed–Mon. In business since 1922, this simple eatery serves up portions of rice topped with shrimps cooked on a charcoal grill (NTD50), egg-drop soup made with duck eggs (NTD30) & other side dishes such as sausages & *miso* soup (NTD10–65). AC. Pay when you order at the counter. Soft drinks available. **$**

✖ Qingqi Vegetarian
清祺素食 [202 C2] 135 Qingnian Rd; 📞 228 5781; 🕐 05.00–11.30 & 14.00–21.00 daily. This long-established eatery serves excellent & inexpensive meatless dim sum throughout the day. Help yourself from what's kept warm in the circular bamboo steamers out front, order noodles if you're especially hungry & take your selection to the counter inside where you pay. The bright lights & white-tile walls may remind you of an old hospital, but for many the cleanliness is a draw. **$**

✖ Sen Maw Rice Food
森茂碗粿 [202 C3] 317 Kaishan Rd; 📞 214 3389; 🕐 07.00–19.00 Thu–Tue. Going since the early 1980s, Sen Maw specialises in the savoury pudding-type dish known in Taiwanese as *waguei* 碗粿. Add spicy sauce or crushed garlic according to your preference & wash it down with a bowl of meatball soup. An ideal mid-afternoon snack if you expect to eat a late dinner. **$**

✖ Sunice
太陽牌冰店 [202 C3] 41 Minquan Rd Sec 1; 📞 225 9375; 🕐 10.00–21.30 daily. What's served here isn't quite high-calorie ice cream nor the crushed ice that's so popular during Taiwan's summers, but something in between. It's very refreshing & 19 flavours are available, among them conventional tastes like mango & strawberry as well as more radical options inc walnut & egg yolk, yam & rice cake. They've been doing this for half a century & have it down pat. If you want to keep moving, go for an ice lolly. **$**

♀ Artful Dodger
[202 D1] 181 Dongfeng Rd; 📞 237 0370; 🕐 11.30–10.00 Sun–Thu, 11.30–23.00 Fri–Sat. As much a restaurant as a watering hole, the English-/Welsh-owned Artful Dodger does good pies, fish & chips & more sophisticated dishes like mussels cooked in garlic butter & white wine. Often shows major sport events on TV. Outdoor tables. Reasonably priced draught & bottled beers. EM. **$$$**

Anping *Map, page 207*

✖ Chen's Oyster Rolls
陳家蚵捲 786 Anping Rd; 📞 222 9661; 🕐 10.00–21.00 daily. Where traditional foods are assembled using modern technology rather than legions of kitchen staff, Chen's gets packed with customers most

lunchtimes. In addition to the signature oyster rolls & omelettes, there are shrimp rolls (best with a squirt of wasabi) & soups. Portions are snack-sized, so order 2 or 3 items pp if you've a serious appetite. EM but you may have to hunt for it. $

✖ **Chou's Shrimp Rolls** 周氏蝦捲 408–1 Anping Rd; ☎ 280 1304; ⊕ 10.00–21.30 daily. Don't expect much olde-worlde atmosphere at Anping's best-known seafood eatery, where it seems every aspect of preparation & serving has been optimised by efficiency experts. The good thing is you won't have to wait long & the food is consistently excellent, especially the signature

rolls. A single portion of the famous shrimp rolls (*xiā juǎn* 蝦捲) doesn't make a meal so also order meatballs or soup. There's a small branch closer to Fort Zeelandia at 125 Anping Rd (☎ 229 2618; ⊕ 09.30–19.00 daily). $

🍴 **Ruhfu Bakery** 熱富安平伴手禮 133 Anping Rd; ☎ 224 3729; ⊕ 08.00–23.00 daily. Ruhfu isn't the only bakery around here making traditional pastries & confectionaries, nor is it the only one to sell shrimp crackers that, at the end of a day, pair well with cold beer. However, it's one of very few to have English labelling so you know which items contain mung beans or pork floss & which are filled with pineapple jam. $

OTHER PRACTICALITIES

$ **Mega Bank** [202 C2] 90 Zhongshan Rd
✚ **National Chengkung University Hospital** [202 D1] 138 Shengli Rd; ☎ 235 3535; w www. hosp.ncku.edu.tw; ⊕ 24hrs daily

✉ **General post office** [202 C2] 6 Chenggong Rd; ⊕ 08.30–20.00 Mon–Fri, 09.00–noon Sat. Money can be changed in the banking section next door (⊕ 08.00–18.00 Mon–Fri).

WHAT TO SEE AND DO Because there's so much to take in, major attractions have been thematically arranged as four separate walking tours.

Anping 安平 [map, opposite] The cradle of Han Chinese civilisation in Taiwan and the first European base on the island, Anping – the name means 'place of peace' and was chosen by Koxinga himself – has a wealth of physical remains from the 17th–19th centuries. After the Dutch were expelled, the English East India Company cut a deal with Koxinga's son and set up a trade base. The venture didn't prosper, however, and so between 1682 and 1864, when Anping was opened to foreign trade, the port handled coastal and cross-Strait shipping only. Because Anping has been a backwater since the late 19th century, much of its old character has survived.

Fort Zeelandia aka Anping Old Fort 安平古堡 (***Ānpíng Gǔbǎo***) (⊕ 08.30–17.30 daily; admission NTD50/25) What you see here is very different from what existed during the Dutch era. The original bastion – completed in 1634 and named after the ship on which the first VOC governor arrived – had a much larger footprint than the current site. Inside the fort you'll find models showing the original layout and features such as the Protestant chapel (Catholics had to worship in secret), the governor's residence and the execution ground just beyond the outer wall. However, typhoons, earthquakes and the appropriation of building materials meant that, by the beginning of the 20th century, little was left of the Dutch structure.

The museum in the building on the left gives a thorough overview of both the fort's history and technical aspects of its construction. Pottery shards – some Dutch, others Chinese – retrieved during archaeological excavations are displayed, and the ultimate fate of Frederik Coyett, the Swedish-born governor who surrendered to Koxinga in 1662 (page 11), is described. On his return to Batavia he was blamed for the loss of the Taiwan colony, and subsequently arrested and imprisoned. (In fact he had repeatedly warned his superiors that Koxinga was a threat; just prior to

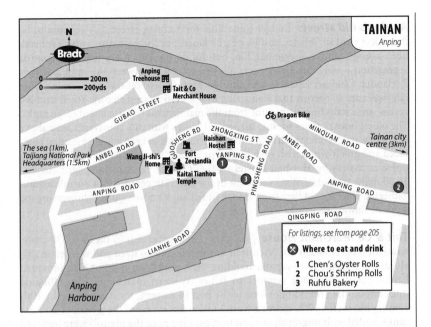

Koxinga's attack, the VOC had resolved to replace him with someone less 'alarmist'.) When Coyett finally made it back to Europe, he tried to clear his name by authoring a self-serving account of his governorship and the siege.

Right behind the museum stands the largest surviving section of the original fortress. A massive brick-and-coral wall, it looks weathered and truly battered yet ready to survive another few centuries. Climb the steps inside the watchtower (a 20th-century addition) for views towards the city and the coast. None of the cannons arrayed near the watchtower date from the Dutch era, although the least-corroded one is almost 300 years old and could, in its day, fire a small cannonball 2km.

Kaitai Tianhou Temple 開台天后宮 (33 Guosheng Rd; ⊕ 05.00–22.00 daily) The green glazed roof tiles of this shrine can be seen from Fort Zeelandia and the current structure, completed in 1976, is exceptionally intricate and colourful. It's claimed the main Mazu icon inside is more than a millennium old and was brought to Taiwan by Koxinga himself. If so, the statuette has been lucky to survive as since its founding in 1668, the temple has moved more than once, caught fire and been demolished on the orders of the Japanese colonial authorities.

Wang Ji-shi's Home 王雞屎洋樓 (2 Lane 35, Guosheng Rd; ⊕ not open to the public) It is possible that Wang wanted a house that would distract attention from his given name, which literally meant 'chicken droppings'. The fact his parents named him thus suggests he was a sickly baby; they may have believed – as many did in Taiwan at that time – that a more grandiose name would arouse the jealousy of disease-spreading spirits. As an adult Wang did well in the salt trade, and his 1937 two-storey abode continues to excite architecture buffs. Octagonal windows face the fort, but to see the façade you'll have to duck down the tiny alley on the building's left. Since his death in 1948, Wang has been venerated as a land god in the dingy shrine just around the corner.

Anping's old streets Budget some time for Yanping Street 延平街, said to be the oldest road in Taiwan, and its nearby lanes. For the past two centuries there's been a small temple at number 106, but during the Dutch era this site signified segregation – only Europeans were allowed to reside between this spot and Fort Zeelandia; Chinese, Japanese and aborigines were kept on the inland side. Some alleyways are so narrow that wandering tourists risk grazed elbows. You'll stumble across stone slabs that likely came from the mainland as ballast aboard cargo junks. The oldest houses are modest L-shaped structures with tiny courtyards, and above the doorways of some you'll spot sword-lion motifs that keep evil at bay; often blue-faced and green-whiskered, each lion grips a blade between its teeth while staring down at passers-by. **Haishan Hostel** 海山館 (7 Lane 52, Xiaozhong St; ⊕ 09.00–17.00 daily; free admission) was built in the late 17th century as a dormitory and gathering place for soldiers from Haitan in Fujian. It's now a gallery showcasing the work of Taiwanese artists.

Tait & Co Merchant House 德記洋行 (194 Anbei Rd; ⊕ 08.30–17.30 daily; admission NTD50/25) The Victorian businessmen who lived and worked in this elegant two-floor, 130-year-old building dealt mainly in tea, but also provided banking and insurance services to fellow Western merchants. The bilingual museum on the ground floor, one of the best in Anping, focuses not on the 19th century but on the 17th. Extracts from VOC archives record the arrival of Chinese junks loaded with migrants, salt and iron cooking pots; the utensils were bartered with aborigines for deer skins and meat. The Dutch were fond of making laws: neither indigenous people nor Chinese settlers were allowed to own a hunting dog without a licence; another licence was needed for snaring deer; and gambling was forbidden.

It's thought that some of the bricks used to build the ruined warehouse behind the Tait office were purloined from the ruins of Fort Zeelandia. As at many other ancient buildings in Anping, the warehouse's bricks were stuck in place with a cement made from glutinous rice, cane sugar and the ash of oyster shells. The building, where salt was stored between about 1911 and the 1970s, is now known as **Anping Treehouse** 安平樹屋 (⊕ same opening hrs; admission inc in the Tait ticket) on account of the huge banyans that have grown through the roof. The way in which roots have climbed walls and grown across openings is almost surreal, so make a point of exploring every corner of the building.

Koxinga's capital
After evicting the Dutch, Koxinga and his successors set about creating the institutions essential to a 'pretender' regime, such as shrines to Confucius and the various gods of Chinese Popular Religion.

Confucius Temple 孔子廟 ***(Kǒngzǐ Miào)*** [202 B3] (2 Nanmen Rd; w confucius.culture.tw; ⊕ inner courtyard 08.00–17.30 daily, closed during Tomb Sweeping, Dragon Boat & Mid-Autumn festivals, grounds 24hrs daily; admission free to the grounds, NTD25 to the inner courtyard) Possibly the most sublimely beautiful historical building in Taiwan, Tainan's Confucius Temple is a genuine must-see. Founded by Koxinga's son in 1665 and central to the Ming loyalists' efforts to preserve and transmit classical Chinese values, the temple functioned as both a school and a shrine where the sage was – and each 28 September continues to be – venerated. Calligraphy tablets donated by six of Taiwan's presidents hang in the inner sanctum, and every year on the seventh day of the seventh lunar month teenagers in traditional garb ride here on horseback and offer incense to Confucius as part of the Qixi rite (see box, page 214). At the time of writing, the temple was open as usual despite renovation work expected to continue into 2019.

By the main gate on Nanmen Road, note the inscription on your right as you face the temple grounds, which orders visitors on horseback to dismount before entering. It's in both Chinese and Manchurian; the latter, an official language of the Qing court, resembles written Tibetan. The stone archway across the road dates from 1777 and celebrates the role of the Confucius Temple in cultivating literati.

Koxinga Shrine 延平郡王祠 *(Yánpíng Jùnwángcí)* [202 C3] (152 Kaishan Rd; ⊕ 09.00–17.30 daily) Koxinga died before the mini-state he established was a year old. Like many other Chinese historical figures, his spirit was worshipped not only by his descendants but also by those convinced such a great man must have godly powers. The manicured grounds that surround the shrine are very attractive even for those with no interest in the man or the cult. History buffs should spend their time inside the shrine itself rather than the adjacent museum (⊕ 09.00–17.00 Tue–Sun; free admission) as the information panels contain some fascinating snippets: Koxinga's Japanese mother committed suicide in 1646 rather than suffer the indignity of being captured by the Manchus (his father, however, defected to the invaders); the Qing authorities moved Koxinga's grave to Fujian in 1699; and, for the first few decades of Qing rule, local people worshipped the Ming loyalist under the pseudonym 'Prince Zhu' to avoid angering the island's new rulers. His birthday is still celebrated on the 16th day of the first lunar month.

In time Koxinga as a historical figure was rehabilitated. In 1874, an imperial official on an inspection tour of Taiwan noted how this long-dead enemy of the Qing was still revered by Tainan residents, and consequently recommended to the court that permission be given to upgrade the existing shrine. The emperor gave his consent the following year and at the same time ratified Koxinga's status as a god. The Japanese, keen to stress Koxinga's connections to their country, converted the site into a Shinto jinja. This was unacceptable to the Chinese Nationalists and in the early 1960s they replaced it with the current building. A statue of Koxinga, seated as if on a throne, takes centre stage; offerings of incense and fruit are made each day. More than a hundred of his most loyal and trusted lieutenants are also commemorated here.

Dongyue Hall 東嶽殿 [202 C3] (110 Minquan Rd Sec 1; ⊕ 05.30–21.30 daily) When 19th-century missionary George L Mackay described religion in Taiwan as being 'of the same kind and quality as the heathenism of China… the same poisonous mixture, the same dark, damning nightmare', he was likely thinking of sites like this – a cramped and spooky place of worship named after Emperor Dongyue, a god whose job description includes making sure sinners get their just deserts. Other deities worshipped here include underworld generals and ministers, but the main object of veneration is King Dizang (Sanskrit name Ksitigarbha), the Buddhist bodhisattva of those in hell. Because King Dizang is believed to have power over monsters and mischief-making demons, disaster victims sometimes beg him for relief. However, the majority of those praying here are relatives of the recently deceased, petitioning the emperor in an effort to minimise their loved ones' suffering in the after-world.

Some of the posthumous torments wrongdoers can anticipate are depicted in the temple's graphic wall murals, which show terrified prisoners being chopped into pieces and fed to wolves or dropped on spikes. The first version of this temple shrine was a thatched hut built in 1673. Early followers included some of

Tainan is a city of gods, the living gods of the settlers who brought their protector deities and the way of the spirits with them from Fujian. While traditional religion thrives across Taiwan, in Tainan these traditions are particularly strong, fed by deep roots of a long and unbroken history. Tainan is unique among all of the formerly walled cities of the Ming and Qing empires in that the fortunes of history and cultural vitality have together enabled the people to preserve their rich religious ecosystem better than any other urban centre of the traditional Chinese Empire.

Tainan was damaged by American bombing during World War II, and impacted by urban development throughout the Japanese and postwar periods, yet the religious culture in the city and its rural hinterland was protected from the wars and other ravages of the 20th century. Following Taiwan's economic take-off, as in earlier historical periods of prosperity, new wealth was enthusiastically invested in temple construction and ritual celebrations. The revolutionaries in mainland China believed that the traditional religious culture had to be destroyed for the country to become modern, yet Taiwan has proven them wrong, and shown that traditional religious life in no way conflicts with modern economic life, but rather reinforces the ideals of honour, mutual trust and honesty on which trade and social order depend. Today, most factories in Taiwan have altars and shrines dedicated to the gods and goddesses their ancestors brought with them centuries ago from Fujian. As Taiwan has grown and transformed, the gods of the Taiwanese people have remained an essential part of Taiwanese society itself.

In Tainan's temples, and in the basic act of temple worship, one can readily observe the historical arrangement among Popular and Taoist gods. To pray to the gods means to burn incense, and when people have lit enough incense sticks for all of the censers in a temple, they always face outside, away from the gods of the temple, and worship the Lord of Heaven 天公, aka the Jade Emperor. They offer the first three sticks of incense to the Lord of Heaven, who has his own dedicated incense burner outside (or symbolically facing outward) at every temple, before proceeding inside to sacrifice incense to whichever deities they hope can help them. The Jade Emperor has two temples of his own in Tainan: the Altar of Heaven (page 214) and the Yuhuang Gong 玉皇宮 [202 C1], but in neither do we find any of the deified human beings of the Popular Religion. Instead, together with the Jade Emperor are the higher gods of Taoism, among them the Three Pure Ones, and several stellar deities.

Despite the tremendous influence of Buddhism, Taiwan's overall religious system is fundamentally organised around the symbols and rites of Taoism. To call the entire religious complex 'Taoism' acknowledges an important fact: that for 1,000 years, the gods of local society have been incorporated into a Taoist sacred empire, whose contours are visible not only in the major Taoist offering ceremonies that culminate religious life in the community, but each and every time worshippers burn incense.

Much more needs to be said about this Taoist Popular Religion. One important concept within the religion is what scholars have called the 'bureaucratic metaphor'. As a reflection of how power in traditional society was organised, the temples of the gods are much like government offices, with prayers and

Koxinga's soldiers who would offer incense to the emperor and then wear packets of incense ash as amulets for protection against the pestilence then rife in Taiwan. This temple's special atmosphere is heightened by a lack of direct natural light, communication conveyed to heaven by divine messengers in the same way as the terrestrial administration, while spirit-bailiffs and spirit-soldiers enforce order at the local level, just as the imperial state relied on the power of compulsion to quell bandits and enforce the law. Taoism in particular promoted this bureaucratic vision of the spirit world, in which Taoist priests submit written documents to the celestial administration by burning them. Naturally, the spirit world has an economy every bit as monetised as that of early modern China. Accordingly, the burning of spirit-money is an important practice, as the delivery of messages, the provisioning of armies, and the handling of requests in the spirit world all require money, just as in the material world. In many ways the religion closely mirrors the society from which it sprang, and it envisions a spiritual cosmos modelled on the ways power was constructed and wielded in traditional society.

Temple alliances are reflected in the sequences of ritual performance, from how people worship and pray in temples, to how temples celebrate their rites and festivals. Of these, the birthdays of the gods form the primary rhythm around which religious life is structured. The gods themselves are highly immanent, and communicate with their temple communities by directly manifesting through spirit-mediums, or by several forms of spirit-writing, as well as through divination blocks, which every worshipper can make use of to ask the gods for advice. The gods, together with their temple communities, have an engaging social life, and so many temple events involve gods calling on one another, hosting one another as guests, gathering to witness a Taoist offering ceremony, or making pilgrimage to the ancestral temple from where the soul inhabiting a temple's spirit-image was born. In these social events of the gods one can often see the many different forms of sacred performance art and ceremonial custom which make temple culture so endlessly fascinating.

Temples are spaces of sacred beauty, yet if all one sees are relatively deserted temple buildings, with perhaps a few worshippers praying and casting divination blocks, then one is seeing this religion while it is sleeping. Only during ritual does the tremendous power of the religion fully awaken and reveal its spectacular creativity. And so, when travelling to Tainan, if one gets the chance to see some kind of ritual event – particularly a larger ritual procession, or a Presentation of Incense pilgrimage – this will likely be the most exciting and memorable thing you will see in the country. How to find such an event? Follow the fireworks, drums and chanting, down narrow alleys and into the temple. People will be welcoming and you'll have a tremendously memorable experience. Alternatively, go to the Yuhuang Temple on a weekend morning, or if it happens to be the second or eighth lunar month, go to the Xi Luo Temple 西羅殿 [202 A2]. Every year on or around 1 January there's usually a large ritual procession to conclude a Taoist offering ceremony, and throughout the year there are ritual processions and other fascinating events; listen for fireworks and drums, and you'll find where gods still reign in the world.

Stephen M Flanigan, a historian of religions, also contributed the What is Taiwan's Mainstream Religion? *box (page 30).*

and the interior is awkward because the Japanese colonial authorities – no fans of Taiwanese faiths – ordered the demolition of part of the shrine when they decided to widen Tainan's roads in the 1930s. On the right as you exit the shrine there's a workshop that turns out paper models of houses, cars and other items, which are burned during funerals to ensure the dead do not lack for shelter or furniture in the next world. This stretch of Minquan Road is where the pious do their shopping as several stores sell indispensables such as votive money, incense sticks and stainless-steel ghost-money burners. You may browse, but be respectful when taking photos or handling items.

Martial Rites Temple aka Official God of War Temple 祀典武廟 **(Sìdiǎn Wǔ Miào)** [202 B2] (229 Yongfu Rd Sec 2; ⊕ 07.00–21.00 daily) A gorgeous edifice that required major repairs after the 2016 earthquake (page 203), this temple used to be part of Prince Ning Jing's palace, but in 1674 the Ming pretender agreed to convert it into a shrine dedicated to Guan Gong. Walk through the main chamber to find a pavilion devoted to Guanyin on the left (note the delicate but weathered woodcarvings of dragons), behind which there's a delightful little rock garden. The small temple opposite at 200 Yongfu Road Section 2 honours an equine spirit – Guan Gong's steed.

Qing Taiwanfoo
As Taiwan's capital and economic centre for most of the Qing era, Tainan developed a large yet very traditional middle class that continues to influence the city.

Great Queen of Heaven Temple 大天后宮 **(Dàtiānhòu Gōng)** [202 B2] (⊕ 05.00–21.00 daily) When leaving the Martial Rites Temple, sightseers usually head next door to this timber-framed Mazu shrine. Established in 1684 by Shi Lang, the general who masterminded the defeat of the Kingdom of Dongning (page 12), it was also formerly part of Prince Ning Jing's mansion. Shi attributed his victory to the Mazu icons he carried with him during the campaign; he may have been sincere, but it's possible his conspicuous piety was contrived to win over Taiwan's Mazu-adoring population. Inside the temple a gold-skinned and sour-faced Mazu is flanked by the two demons she tamed. On the right as you face the goddess there's an antique set of 21 votive handbells. At the back of the complex, behind a red fence, stands Ning Jing's memorial tablet – he committed suicide here in 1683, aged 65 – but even if you read Chinese it's near-impossible to pick out amid the clutter of tablets and icons.

The alleyway that links the Martial Rites Temple and the Great Queen of Heaven Temple, Lane 227 of Yongfu Road Section 2, is known as 'fortune-tellers' alley' because at least three residents ply this trade in their front rooms. None of them speak English, so bring a bilingual friend if you want your fortune told.

Chikan Tower 赤崁樓 **(Chìkǎn Lóu)** [202 B2] (212 Minzu Rd Sec 2; ⊕ 08.30–21.00 daily; admission NTD50/25) Located across the road from the Martial Rites Temple and meaning 'red-roofed tower' in Chinese, this is where the Dutch built their second stronghold in 1653. Little remains of that bastion, which the VOC called Fort Provintia, although an exposed remnant will give you an idea of just how robust it was. In reality, Chikan Tower is a small complex of traditional Chinese buildings set in a Chinese classical garden; think moon gates, carp-filled ponds and manicured mini-trees. As such it works well, especially in the evening when the onsite coffee shop (EM; non-alcoholic drinks; $) draws a relaxed crowd. Two pagodas and a school were built on the Dutch ruins in the 19th century, and although only a small part of the school still exists, the pagodas have been kept up in good condition. The front tower was built in 1886 at the urging of local officials who credited the

Sea God with protecting Taiwan during the Mudan Incident of 1874 and the Sino-French War of 1884–85. The Sea God's services are no longer required but the other tower, known as the Wenchang Pavilion, still has a religious function: in addition to honouring education god Wenchang Dijun, visiting students climb the creaking wooden stairway to petition a statue of Kueixingxiang, the god of literature.

Shennong Street 神農街 [202 A1] Tainan's most traditional thoroughfare is lined on both sides by 19th-century two-storey merchant houses, some of which retain the original wood frames and steep staircases. A few have become shops and cafés but many are locked up and unoccupied. The street is especially atmospheric after dark. At number 94, **Taikoo** [202 A1] (✆ 221 1053; ⊕ 18.00–02.00 Mon–Thu, 16.00–02.00 Fri–Sun; $$) is a long-running retro-modern bar with a decent selection of beers.

Wind God Temple 風神廟 [202 A2] (8 Lane 143, Minquan Rd Sec 3; ⊕ 07.00–21.00 daily) This is the only temple devoted to the Wind God in Taiwan, which is surprising given the frequency of typhoons. Represented by effigies in the centre of the shrine, the Wind God is believed to have influence over the five elements of earth, fire, metal, water and wood. On the Wind God's right, the Thunder God holds a hammer in one hand and a nail in the other, while his wife, the Lightning Mother, carries a pair of circular mirrors on the left. At the time of the temple's founding in 1739, the ocean was a stone's throw away and the **Government Reception Archway** 接官亭 was where VIPs arriving from the mainland would disembark; take a close look and you'll find carvings of dragons, lions and sages. An equally ancient stone pavilion nearby collapsed after the 2016 earthquake.

Great South Gate 大南門 [202 B3] (Nanmen Rd & Shulin St; ⊕ gate 08.00–17.00 daily, surrounding park 24hrs daily) Served by bus #2, the South Gate is the best preserved of Tainan's four remaining city gates (there used to be 14). There's a segment of wall and even a pair of cannons, though presumably the latter were originally installed on top of the wall rather than pointing at it. The two-storey building in the centre of the surrounding South Gate Park dates from 1932 and features a slightly unusual combination: Art Deco windows and a tiled exterior. At the end of the park furthest from Nanmen Road there's a collection of stelae: inscribed stone tablets from the mid-18th to mid-19th century, each the size of a very large tombstone, that served various official functions. Some promulgated new laws, others recorded the visit of a high official or the suppression of a rebellion. Information panels beside each slab summarise the text in both English and modern Chinese. They're fascinating snapshots of Qing society: one decree, dating from 1767, stipulates that beggars shall not display corpses when soliciting alms; there's also a directive that people should not commit suicide as a way of repudiating their debts.

Five Concubines Temple 五妃廟 [202 C4] (Between Wufei St & Jiankang Rd; ⊕ 08.30–21.00 daily) This shrine, founded in 1748 and located in a small park full of gnarled trees, commemorates the ladies who, when the Kingdom of Dongning was destroyed in 1683, decided to accompany their lord Prince Ning Jing to the next world rather than take his advice to remarry or flee to a nunnery. Instead of the usual door gods, the entrance bears body-length portraits of two of the concubines; inside, all five are represented by doll-sized josses. Beside the tomb where the concubines are said to be buried there's a tiny shrine devoted to two eunuchs who also killed themselves rather than submit to the island's new rulers.

Taiwanese can drive when they're 18 and vote when they're 20, but according to one of Tainan's most popular customs, they become adults when they turn 16. In Qing-era Tainan, a child reaching that age was a cause for celebration because 16-year-olds working on the docks and in workshops were entitled to adult wages, not the half-salaries younger employees received. Since the 1740s, 16-year-olds and their parents have been going to the **Kailong Temple** 開隆宮 [202 C2] (56 Lane 79, Zhongshan Rd; ⊕ 05.30–21.00 daily) on the seventh day of the seventh lunar month to celebrate this coming of age, an event called *qìxī* in Mandarin because it coincides with a traditional lovers' day. In 2019, the principal rite will be on the morning of 7 August. In 2020, it'll be on 25 August.

Until quite recently those wishing to take part in the ceremony, which involves crawling under an altar three times, had to purchase special gowns, shoes and hats and prepare specific offerings to honour Qiniangma, the goddess believed to protect children under the age of 16. Nowadays the clothing can be rented and offerings need not adhere to custom so closely. The city government has been promoting the event as a way to bring visitors to Tainan. Even if watching teenagers wave joss sticks while their parents try to cram offerings on to tables already buckling under the weight of fruit, rice and seaweed doesn't appeal to you, some of the associated folk performances and concerts might.

Altar of Heaven aka Tian Tan 天壇 [202 B2] (16 Lane 84, Zhongyi Rd Sec 2; ⊕ 05.00–22.00 daily) Hidden in the backstreets but unmissable thanks to its egg-yolk yellow walls, this is said to be where Koxinga prayed to the Jade Emperor and where, in the 18th century, local people celebrated that god's birthday on the ninth day of the first lunar month. The temple, which was built in 1854, continues to be very popular today, and there's a good chance you'll run into some kind of religious event and see a Taoist priest crack a thick whip to scare off ghosts. These rites are invariably accompanied by deafening pipe-and-drum music; there are no hymns or requiems, just lengthy jams. Unusually, there's no effigy on the main altar, but rather an ornate tablet bearing the emperor's title: Yùhuáng Shàngdì. The shrine's most famous calligraphy tablet bears the character *yī* ('one'), which is written with a single left-to-right horizontal stroke.

Prefectural Cheng Huang Temple 都城隍廟 [202 C2] (133 Qingnian Rd; ⊕ 05.30–21.00 daily) While not as large as its counterparts in Chiayi or Hsinchu, Tainan's city-god shrine is to be seen as much for the serene back garden with its huge spirit-money furnace as for the interior art. Before going inside look at the corners of the frontage – the largest and highest of the figurines on both sides depict Europeans, although their attire looks more Chinese than Western. If you come here on or around the 11th day of the fifth lunar month, you'll see lively celebrations for the city god's birthday. The faithful confer offerings on the deity and get free sacks of rice in return.

Xi Hua Hall 西華堂 [202 C1] (92 Beizhong St, also accessible from 65 Xihua St; ⊕ 06.30–18.00 daily grounds only) A small 260-year-old Buddhist nunnery that's an oasis of peace despite its city-centre location, Xi Hua Hall is less than 50m from

Tainan Park 台南公園 (⏰ 24hrs daily). Inside the park there's an ornate memorial archway venerating literature and learning that was erected during the reign of Emperor Jiaqing (1796–1820).

Japanese Tainan
The city is rich in Japanese-era architecture and the highlights can be seen by taking a leisurely 2-hour walking tour. To begin, head southwest from the station.

Former Tainan Meeting Hall 原台南公會堂
[202 C2] (30 Minquan Rd Sec 2; ⏰ 10.00–22.00 daily; free admission) This 1911 French-influenced structure hosts occasional exhibitions while the adjacent wood building functions as a coffee/souvenir shop. The lawn, pond and rockery behind date from the 1820s and together are known as **Wu Garden** (⏰ 24hrs daily; free admission) after Wu Shang-xin (1795–1848), a salt tycoon who owned a major chunk of this neighbourhood. Wu's gravestone is now displayed in Great South Gate Park (page 213).

Old Weather Station 台南氣象站
[202 B2] (21 Gongyuan Rd; closed for renovation) Likely the oldest Japanese government building surviving in Taiwan, locals nicknamed this 1898 structure 'the pepper-pot' on account of its unusual shape. The museum inside, which has some old meteorological instruments, should reopen sometime in 2019. Behind the station there's a Japanese-style garden and a 1920s wooden building called **Ying Liaoli** 原鶯料理 (⏰ 13.00–21.00 Tue–Fri, 10.00–21.00 Sat–Sun; free admission) that housed a restaurant during the colonial period. It's been thoroughly renovated but nothing is sold here now.

National Museum of Taiwanese Literature 國立台灣文學館 (Guólì Táiwān Wénxuéguǎn)
[202 B3] (1 Zhongzheng Rd; 📞 221 7201; w www. nmtl.gov.tw; ⏰ 09.00–21.00 Tue–Sun; free admission) Externally and internally charming, Tainan's former city hall was built in 1916 and is distinguished by a European façade and a fine mansard roof. When the city government relocated in 1997, the structure was converted to a museum that has bilingual displays about the lives and works of both local and foreign writers. From here, a small detour south (turn right just before the Confucius Temple) brings you to the back of the **Old Tainan Martial Arts Academy (aka Butokuden)** 原台南武德 [202 B3] (Youai St; ⏰ usually closed to the public). This voluptuous piece of classical Japanese architecture was erected in 1936, though the current structure serves as an elementary-school auditorium.

Land Bank 土地銀行
[202 B3] (28 Zhongzheng Rd; ⏰ 09.00–15.30 Mon–Fri) This massive Art Deco edifice was built in 1937 as a branch of Japan's Kang Gyo Bank. The interior is worth a very quick look; you can change money upstairs.

Lin's Department Store 林百貨店
[202 B3] (Zhongzheng & Zhongyi rds; w www.hayashi.com.tw; ⏰ 11.00–22.00 daily) Known during the colonial era as Hayashi Hyakkaten, this department store won great public attention when it opened in 1932 because it boasted Taiwan's first passenger elevator (note the lift's mosaic floor). Do go up to the rooftop to see the restored Shinto shrine plus bomb damage and bullet holes from an American air raid in the last few months of World War II. Inside you'll find a restaurant, a couple of coffee shops and a good selection of upmarket souvenirs.

The outskirts Trekking out to any of the sights listed in this section takes a fair bit of time, but all are highly worthwhile for culture vultures.

National Museum of Taiwan History 國立台灣歷史博物館 *(Guólì Táiwān Lìshǐ Bówùguǎn)* [202 C1] (250 Zhanghe Rd Sec 1, Annan; ☎ 356 8899; w www. nmth.gov.tw; ⊕ 09.00–17.00 Tue–Sun; admission NTD100/50) The permanent exhibitions in this excellent museum go all the way back to prehistoric times. Of the many vivid models and images, most memorable is the full-size replica of a single-mast junk, the kind of vessel that transported goods between Taiwan and

A FORGOTTEN TRIBE CAMPAIGNS FOR RECOGNITION

For years, the leaders of the Xinhua-based Siraya Culture Association have been arguing that many Tainan folk are indigenous, even if they don't know it. When the Dutch arrived in the 1600s, Taiwan's southwest was the stomping ground of the Austronesian Siraya people – an ethnic group, the SCA argues, that didn't simply disappear as Han settlers poured into the region. Elements of its culture and language live on, and since the SCA's formation in 1999 the association has been striving to 'energise the Siraya tribe' and reconstruct the Siraya language, the last native speaker having died circa 1908.

Siraya had no written form until the 1630s, when Dutch missionaries devised a Romanisation system to aid their conversion efforts. One pastor wrote: 'Their language sounds pleasant, modest, measured, and extraordinarily graceful, so that judging them in this respect you would not think them to be savage but to be outstandingly wise men, filled to the brim with modesty and virtue.' Working from gospel fragments and contracts (for at least 150 years after the Europeans left, the Siraya used the Dutch-designed writing system when drawing up lease agreements and other transactions) the SCA has compiled and published a 3,500-word Siraya glossary. You won't hear Siraya spoken in Xinhua, but here are a few words to impress – or baffle – the locals: *tabe* is hello; *tatalag* means welcome; *alid* means god, while *alilid* means to thank.

According to a Han traveller who visited the region in 1603, Siraya society was matriarchal. There were no tribal chiefs or kings as such, and everyone was considered equal. Rather than cultivate rice in paddy fields, the Siraya subsisted on dry or 'upland' rice. Deer were hunted, but only in winter; skin and horns were bartered with Han settlers in exchange for cloth and other goods. Siraya homes were bamboo framed and the roofs were thatched with straw. Doors were left unlocked, he wrote, because society was so orderly. Unlike Han people, who have traditionally preferred to bury their dead at times and in locations they considered auspicious, when a Siraya died, his or her body was first preserved by smoking, then buried under the floor of the family home. Compulsory abortions were another unusual feature of traditional Siraya society; couples weren't allowed to live together or have children until the husband ceased being a warrior and became a community elder.

We have a good idea what the Siraya looked like before they became assimilated, thanks to the artists working for the VOC and Scotsman John Thomson (1837–1921). Later the British royal family's official photographer, Thomson toured Taiwan's southwest in 1871 and took some of the very first photos of the region. His images are preserved at the Wellcome Library in London and can be viewed online at w wellcomecollection.org/works.

the Chinese mainland during the Qing era. Several of the museum's 200 fibreglass human figures are in or around the boat; crew members negotiate with an imperial official who wears a mandarin's gown while stowaways hoping to start a new life in Taiwan cower in the hold. Elsewhere, dozens more waxwork-style figures form a religious parade or work on the land, and these mock-ups do a superb job of pushing one's imagination back to the Taiwan of yore. Other displays explore the 19th-century tea trade and the adoption of Alid, a deity revered by the indigenous Siraya people (see box, opposite), by Han Taiwanese who now worship him as Alizu.

The museum is 10km northeast of the city centre and can be reached by bus #18 from Tainan TRA station (12 departures per day Mon–Fri, 18 departures per day Sat–Sun; ⊕ 07.05–18.40; 30mins; NTD18).

Ten Drum Culture Village 十鼓文化村 [202 D4] (326 Wenhua Rd Sec 2, Rende; ☏ 266 2225 ext 101; w www.ten-hsieh.com.tw; ⊕ 09.00–17.00 daily; admission NTD399/380) Lauded in Taiwan for the way in which it has lifted zhentou culture (see box, page 32) to a new level, the Grammy-nominated Ten Drum Art Percussion Group has won a reputation overseas for electrifying performances that feature flutes, gongs and martial-arts moves as well as sensational drumming. The parent organisation is now based at this former sugar refinery where troupe full-timers give at least four performances every weekend (10.30 & 15.00 Sat–Sun). Drum groups from around Asia are invited to play here every summer. Also onsite is a workshop where an artisan makes buffalo-hide drums using the traditional method.

To get here by train, from Tainan there are around four departures each hour to Baoan TRA station (7mins; NTD15), from where you turn right and walk 1km towards the refinery's chimney stack – it's the tallest structure for some distance around and on it you'll see the English words 'Ten Drum'.

Chimei Museum 奇美博物館 [202 D4] (66 Wenhua Rd Sec 2, Rende; ☏266 0808; w www.chimeimuseum.org; ⊕ 09.30–17.30 Thu–Tue; admission NTD200/150) Reflecting the personal interests of a local acrylics/resins/consumer electronics tycoon, this museum houses a startling mix of stuffed animals and birds, weapons, armour, oil paintings and sculptures. The collection of violins, violas and cellos is one of the world's best, and includes the world's oldest still-playable cello, taken out of storage only on special occasions, which dates from 1566 and was once owned by King Charles IX of France. Some of the most valuable instruments aren't on display, however, having been loaned to musicians.

To get here, walk 15 minutes from Baoan TRA station (see above) or take the Red 4 bus from Tainan TRA station (10 departures daily; ⊕ 07.25–18.55 daily; 30mins; NTD59).

AROUND TAINAN *Telephone code 06*

The south's countryside and traditional lifestyles are highly accessible as day trips from Tainan or Chiayi. From central Tainan, Highway 20 goes east into the foothills to the first four sights listed below; km references are to distance markers on that road. If heading north, Highway 17 goes straight to Beimen and its pilgrim-magnet Nankunshen Daitian Temple. Meanwhile, Highway 19 is more direct if the quaint old town of Yanshui is your objective.

XINHUA OLD STREET 新化老街 (km12) This stretch of Zhongzheng Road continues to be the commercial heart of the little town of Xinhua, but to see it you'll need to leave Highway 20. Turn right when you see the bilingual sign to Guanmiao and after 250m you'll be on the old street. After the road was widened in 1920, the authorities encouraged local merchants to build new homes. Most of these two-floor abodes are in splendid condition and have Baroque and Art Deco features typical of the era, such as pebble-dash façades, shield motifs and plaster laurel wreaths. This kind of architecture isn't especially rare in Taiwan but Xinhua Old Street is almost unique in that the buildings' finer details aren't hidden behind advertising hoardings, and that the businesses along it are largely traditional. Redundant husking machines can be seen inside the rice shops at numbers 425 and 439 while other shops sell fabrics or herbal medicines. If you arrive before lunch, head down Lane 369 and explore the morning market that fills several alleyways.

To get here from Tainan, Green Line Yujing-bound services set out from Tainan TRA station every 15–30 minutes via Xinhua (⏰ 05.55–21.55 daily; 30mins; NTD43). Self-drivers should note parking on the old street isn't advised; continue south and you'll soon find a spot.

CAOSHAN MOONSCAPE WORLD 草山月世界 (near km22.5) The English name makes it sound like a theme park, but Caoshan Moonscape World is in fact an area of badlands, a striking exception to the tropical lushness found elsewhere in Taiwan. It gets more than enough rain but because the terrain consists of crumbly brown stone, vegetation tends to get washed away or drowned in slurry. Despite the desolation, the area is rich in birds and insects, and a few families grow bananas and bamboo between the gullies and ridges. Late afternoon is a good time to visit as the setting sun makes the eroded hillocks and steep ravines look truly lunar. Best explored by motorcycle or bicycle (the roads are narrow but those on four wheels will do fine if they drive slowly and cautiously), Moonscape World can be entered via several roads – look for bilingual signs on Highway 20 or continue past Yujing to **Beiliao** 北 寮, then take Highway 3 southwards until you see signs for **Hill 308** 308 高地 where you'll find restaurants (⏰ varies; no EMs; $$) with good views over the badlands.

KARMA KAGYU MONASTERY 噶瑪噶居寺 (km24.9; ☎573 2103; w www.lopon.org. tw; ⏰ 08.00–16.30 daily) Tantric Buddhism has a small but dedicated following in Taiwan and this monastery blends Tibetan and Chinese elements. It serves as the Taiwan seat of Ogyen Trinley Dorje, the young man accepted by most (but not all) Tibetan Buddhists as the 17th Karmapa Lama, the religion's third-most-senior figure. The white stupa can be seen from the highway but more interesting is the main hall with its *thangkas* (Tibetan devotional scroll paintings) and Buddha statues. The largest of the latter has a head of blue curls, such hair being one of the Buddha's 32 distinguishing physical characteristics. It's a short walk from the nearest bus stop (Ganlanshan 橄欖山) and there's free parking if you arrive by car.

HOLY GLORY TEMPLE 寶光寺 **(BǍOGUĀNG SÌ)** (km45; ☎577 2229; w holyglorytemple. org; ⏰ 05.00–19.00 daily) The hillside headquarters of one of Taiwan's main I-Kuan Tao sects is impressive in terms of size and setting. Ceiling paintings inside the principal shrine depict Christ and Muhammad alongside figures from Chinese mythology. Incense but not joss paper is burned here and visitors should take off their shoes before entering any of the shrines.

Green Line buses leave from Tainan TRA station for Yujing (every 15–30mins; ⏰ 05.55–21.55 daily; 1hr; NTD119) from where there are infrequent buses to Jiaxian (page 256) via Holy Glory Temple. A short distance east of the temple, Highway 20 crosses into Kaohsiung.

TAIJIANG NATIONAL PARK 台江國家公園 (TÁIJIĀNG GUÓJIĀ GŌNGYUÁN)

The wetlands and river mouths just north of Tainan offer some of Asia's best birding. Sicao, which is near Anping, and Qigu, the district immediately north of the Zengwen River, are Important Bird Areas; together they form the core of this oddly shaped national park, a reserve that stretches across the Taiwan Strait all the way to the southeastern corner of Penghu County. The name 'Taijiang' refers to a large lagoon that existed during and following the Dutch period but which was divided into smaller bodies of water after typhoons shifted huge amounts of silt.

Relatively close to Tainan and accessible by bus #10, the 515ha **Sicao Wildlife Refuge** 四草野生動物保護區 (**Sìcǎo Yěshēng Dòngwù Bǎohùqū**) is crowded with black-winged stilts (*Himantopus himantopus*) in late spring. Elsewhere, the **Black-faced Spoonbill Area** 黑面琵鷺保育區 (**Hēimiànpílù Bǎohùqū**), surrounded by mudflats, fish farms and abandoned salt pans, focuses on one particular migratory species (see box, below). The spoonbills gather here between late September and early spring and spend most of their time foraging on the mudflats. The management centre (⏰ 09.00–17.00 Tue–Sun) has useful bilingual presentations plus some specimens preserved by taxidermy. If you go further west you'll come across birdwatching platforms. Waterbirds are plentiful all year round and often-seen avians include Caspian terns (*Hydroprogne caspia*), brown shrikes (*Lanius cristatus*) and common greenshanks (*Tringa nebularia*).

Getting there and away If you're in Anping, drive towards the sea and follow the signs to Sicao. As you go over the bridge (the estuary here is designated a wetland of national importance) you'll see the white-walled national park headquarters (118 Sicao Bd; ✆ 284 2600; w www.tjnp.gov.tw; ⏰ 08.30–17.30 Mon–Fri). From central Tainan, take Highway 17 north and follow the bilingual signs to the various sections of the reserve. It's a fair way to the Black-faced Spoonbill Area – about 16km to the junction of Highway 17 and Road 173, then another 8km west on Road 173 to the management centre. The only public transport to this spot is the occasional #99 bus.

SOUTH TAIWAN'S STAR BIRD

The black-faced spoonbill (*Platalea minor*) has caught the public imagination like no other bird in Taiwan. Because of its handsome appearance and an avalanche of media coverage, it's now better known among local people than most of the island's endemic species. Black-faced spoonbills breed along the Korean coast in late spring, then winter in Taiwan, Fujian, Hong Kong or Vietnam. The birds start their lives with black feathers; some take six years to become fully white. Their bills change from brown to black and their irises become fully red. During the breeding season both males and females grow golden decorating feathers on their breasts, necks and heads. The adults are large, averaging 75cm in length.

On the face of it, efforts to protect the bird seem to be working. The number of black-faced spoonbills counted in east Asia climbed from 288 in 1988 to 3,941 in 2018, around half of which were in Taiwan, the vast majority in Tainan or neighbouring Chiayi. The species still faces threats, however, as construction projects cut into feeding areas. Also, the birds' stardom brings disturbance in the shape of large numbers of birders and photographers.

BEIMEN 北門 **(BĚIMÉN)** The heart of an area devoted to the growing of shallots and muskmelons, Beimen is so small a town that you'll have no problems finding your way around, although you'll probably only pass through en route to other sights. More information about the area can be found at Beimen Visitor Centre (200 Jiucheng, Beimen Li; ⊕ 09.00–17.30 daily).

Getting there and away From north or south, self drivers should take Expressway 61 or Highway 17 and follow the signs. It's almost always possible to park for free in central Beimen or in the grounds of Nankunshen Daitian Temple. It's a little trickier on public transport as there's no direct bus from central Tainan, but from Xinying TRA station (between central Tainan and Chiayi City) you can take the Brown 1 bus (8 departures daily; ⊕ 06.20–17.50) to Nankunshen (55mins; NTD92) and Shuangchun Coastal Recreation Area (1hr; NTD109).

What to see and do
Taiwan Black-foot Disease Socio-Medical Service Memorial Hall
台灣烏腳病醫療紀念館 (27 Yonglong Li; ✆ 786 2012; w www.blackfoot.org.tw; ⊕ 10.00–16.00 Thu–Sun; free admission) This museum occupies an elegant Japanese-style bungalow in the heart of Beimen, between the church and the telecoms office. You'll see a two-storey building with the words 'Pak-Mng Mercy's Door Free Clinic' on its façade; Pak-Mng is the Taiwanese pronunciation of Beimen. The memorial hall is on the same side of the road, a few houses further from the canal. The clinic operated 1960–86 and was run by King-ho Wang (1916–2014), a local doctor and lay preacher who received logistical and financial help from American missionary Lillian Dickson (1901–83). The museum celebrates their efforts to combat a peculiar local health problem: black-foot disease (BFD), which doctors describe as 'a chronic progressive arteriosclerotic vascular disease of the extremities'. The disease was caused by drinking well-water which contained a high concentration of arsenic, and BFD victims were more often men than women. The selective nature of the problem, coupled with Buddhist notions of rebirth and accumulated merit, caused many (including some of the sufferers) to assume it was punishment for bad deeds in a previous existence. Even when BFD was properly understood by doctors, some locals persisted in believing it was contagious (it was not), caused by evil spirits, or the result of being cursed. Some items are labelled in Chinese only but the amputated hand and feet preserved in formaldehyde need no explanation.

Wang's work went beyond treating sufferers' physical symptoms. With his late wife he ran a straw-mat workshop to provide employment. When an indigent patient died, he bought wood and made the coffin himself.

Shuangchun Coastal Recreation Area 雙春濱海遊憩區 (⊕ 24hrs daily; free admission) Variously called a recreation area and an ecology park, this is one of very few places in Taiwan where all four local mangrove species can be seen. A boardwalk takes visitors through the mangroves and over mudflats rich in crabs and mudskippers. The latter are fish that, when out of water, use their pectoral fins to propel themselves across the land. A few grow as long as a man's finger but most are less than half that size. There are thousands more mangroves between the park and the southern bank of the Bazhang, the river that divides Tainan from Chiayi County.

Nankunshen Daitian Temple 南鯤鯓代天府 (Nánkūnshēn Dàitiānfǔ)
(w nkstemple.org.tw; ⊕ 06.00–21.00 daily) Located 3km north of Beimen Visitor Centre on the inland side of Highway 17, Daitian Temple is one of the island's oldest

and liveliest places of worship and a must-see for anyone curious about Taiwanese religion. According to a leaflet published by the temple, its history goes back to the first quarter of the 17th century:

> One night the moon was full and bright and silence reigned supreme. Suddenly, there were sounds of bells, drums, pipes and strings passing from the sea. The sounds were clear and sweet. The fishermen on the island were very surprised. They went out to investigate the source of the sounds. There was a resplendent and magnificent yacht with three masts sailing slowly towards the port. Those fishermen guessed [...] it was an official's boat [...] and perhaps it had lost its direction and sailed to this port by mistake. Early the next day they wanted to find out what had happened to the boat. However, they couldn't find any large vessel, only a broken little boat lying against the coast. On the boat there were five statuettes of gods and a banner [bearing the names of the gods and the temple in mainland China they had come from].

The fishermen were delighted with their find. Convinced of the idols' efficacy (how could an unmanned vessel make it across the Taiwan Strait without divine protection?), they pulled the boat ashore and placed the effigies in a straw hut. They weren't disappointed: they enjoyed record catches, and prayers to the five gods, also known as the Five Kings, cured the sick better than any medicine. The gods' fame spread and in the 1660s a proper temple was built. Ever since, it's been a centre of the Wang Ye cult (page 33). Since 1818, a sixth god has been worshipped in a poky little temple to the right of the main hall of worship. Wanshanye ('ten thousand goodness lord') is a home-grown addition to the pantheon, a local orphan who had attained enlightenment a century earlier.

Great amounts of spirit money are burned at this temple and each day thousands of joss sticks are lit and sacrificed to the resident deities. It's often very noisy; the constant announcements may remind you of a busy airport. You might see a gaudily decorated truck park in front of the main shrine so a bikini-clad singer at the back can belt out pop songs through a karaoke machine – an everyday expression of popular religion in rural Taiwan. Visit on a Sunday morning and you'll see a constant stream of processions as effigies from affiliated temples arrive to pay tribute. The 26th and 27th days of the fourth lunar month – the birthdays, respectively, of the Great King and the Fifth King – are especially festive. During these events, don't be embarrassed to gawk or take photos; you'll be rubbing shoulders with plenty of agnostic locals who've turned up for the spectacle alone.

Many processions feature *tang-ki*, men possessed by gods. These spirit mediums wear nothing from the waist up; to show how their patrons protect them from injury, they cut themselves on the face, chest and back with swords, small axes and other sharp instruments. Some pierce their cheeks with long needles. Others speak in tongues. In the past, tang-ki (the term is Taiwanese) were sometimes asked to drive away phantoms or intercede when a relative fell sick, and although they weren't paid for such work, many accepted gifts. No-one chooses to be a spirit medium; there are stories of anointed individuals refusing to serve and suffering great misfortune until they accept their extraordinary role.

The complex has grown in recent years with the opening of **Da-kun Garden Hall of Culture and History** (⊕ 08.00–17.00 daily; admission by donation), in which you'll find a classical Chinese garden and some Chinese-language displays about the temple, and the **Lingxiaobao Hall** (⊕ 07.30–17.20 daily). The latter, an annexe to the rear of the main hall, was built to house a very special depiction of the Jade Emperor, a solid-gold tablet weighing 405kg. This icon is impressive but shouldn't distract you from dozens of fabulous beam and panel paintings. Some are truly top-notch, a few merely well-intentioned. Rather than repeat the myths and legends shown in many houses of worship, these pictures celebrate Taiwanese scenery, culture and heroes, including Jeremy Lin (page 71), even though Lin himself is an evangelical Christian.

YANSHUI 鹽水 **(YÁNSHUǏ)** Simply put, Yanshui is a charming old town. It's also a good size for exploring on foot; one can stroll from the Martial Temple on the northern edge of the town to Qiaonan Old Street in less than half an hour. Yanshui's side streets and alleyways are full of quaint houses, small shrines and old-fashioned shops. You wouldn't think it from the town's current size (population: 25,000) and relaxing somnolence, but as recently as the mid-19th century it was one of Taiwan's four most important settlements, a ranking expressed in a local idiom: 'First, Tainan; second, Lukang; third, Mangka [the old name for Taipei's Wanhua District]; fourth, Yuejin [the name of Yanshui's port].' Yuejin Harbour suffered from silting and closed for good in 1900.

Getting there and away Yanshui is 3km from the Xinying Exit on Freeway 1, 263km south of Taipei, 79km north of Kaohsiung. If you're on two wheels, approach by Highway 19 or Highway 19A. Parking near the centre isn't difficult except during the Beehive Fireworks Festival when police bar non-residents from bringing vehicles into the town.

Non-drivers will likely use a combination of train and bus. Xinying TRA station is well served by expresses, and there is also a visitor information centre inside (⏰ 10.00–18.00 daily). Trains take less than 25 minutes to/from Chiayi (NTD33–52) and around 45 minutes to/from Tainan (NTD56–87). Xinying's bus station is just across the roundabout from the TRA station; from it Brown Line buses leave about every half hour for Yanshui (⏰ 05.50–20.05 daily; 20mins; NTD29).

✗ Where to eat and drink A good place to find straightforward local food, including Yanshui's trademark comestible, *yì miàn* 意麵 – an unpretentious but

THE BEEHIVE FIREWORKS FESTIVAL 鹽水蜂炮

Fireworks and firecrackers are part of the Taiwan soundtrack, but just after each Lunar New Year the citizens of Yanshui takes things to an extreme. If you have a taste for huge crowds, mild danger and sensory overload, the Beehive Fireworks Festival is a not-to-be-missed experience. It isn't a fireworks display in the conventional sense, although there are plenty of colourful explosions high in the sky. It's an audience participation event, and it's every bit as dangerous as running with the bulls at Pamplona. Those who aren't prepared risk serious injury, and each year dozens of people suffer burns, eye injuries or temporary deafness. Don't go anywhere near the front line without a full-face motorcycle helmet, gloves, multiple layers of clothing and a towel or scarf to prevent stray rockets from getting under your visor. Don't worry if you're travelling light; you can buy everything you need in Yanshui on the night.

The festival has its origins in a cholera outbreak. Around 1885, a seemingly unstoppable epidemic had the townsfolk panic-stricken. They besought Guan Gong, the deified general regarded as the god of brotherhood and righteousness, to expel the evil spirits they blamed for the pestilence. They carried an effigy of the god through the town, burning piles of spirit money and igniting firecrackers satisfying and tasty noodle dish – is on the corner of Kangle and Zhongshan roads. Several eateries operate under awnings (🕐 approx 08.00–18.30 daily; no EMs; $) and options include seafood and vegetarian fare.

What to see and do The shortest route from the centre of Yanshui to Qiaonan Street is via Zhongzheng Road, a thoroughfare lined with 1920s shop-house combinations.

Martial Temple 武廟 (87 Wumiao Rd; 🕐 05.00–20.30 daily) This 325-year-old shrine is dedicated to Guan Gong – there's a huge statue of him on the right as you approach the front of the temple – but it isn't nearly as interesting as the Beehive Fireworks Festival (see box, below) that Guan Gong's devotees organise each year.

The Octagon 八角樓 (1 Lane 4, Zhongshan Rd; 🕐 08.00–17.00 daily; free admission) The town's most distinctive structure is all that remains of a sprawling mansion built in 1847 for Ye Kai-hong, Yanshui's leading merchant. Ye made his fortune exporting sugar to the Chinese mainland, and many of the materials used in the construction of this two-floor wood-and-stone residence – including the fir columns, roof tiles and limestone slabs – came to Taiwan from the mainland as ballast on his ships. The ground floor is open to the public; inside you'll see the original partitions and a portrait of Ye's son. The lanes behind the Octagon are among Yanshui's most photogenic.

Holy Trinity Catholic Church 鹽水天主堂 (19 Ximen Rd; 🕐 10.00–11.30 & 13.00–15.30 Wed–Sun) Of Taiwan's Christian places of worship, this church (founded 1955) is perhaps the one that most resembles a Chinese temple. The depiction of the *Last Supper* features men with Asian faces and hairstyles wearing traditional Chinese clothes, eating steamed buns with chopsticks. The crucifixion scenes are also thoroughly 'localised'.

at every turn. This exorcism by fire and noise worked and the epidemic soon receded and now each year, coinciding with the Lantern Festival, there's a re-enactment of this plague-expulsion parade. The event is sponsored by businesses and temples; participation is free. Residents cash in by selling snacks, soft drinks and protective attire.

The event now includes folk arts performances and other activities spread over two or more days. The fireworks parade begins around dusk on the 15th day of the first lunar month, and continues until dawn the following day. It features a series of 'beehives' – freight container-sized arsenals that fire tens of thousands of rockets over and into the crowd. Like angry bees, the fireworks scream in every direction, ricocheting off the tarmac and houses. When they hit, they hurt – even through two or three layers of clothing. The experience isn't quite the same as being in combat, perhaps, but those caught on the front line may feel they've been pelted with stones by an angry mob.

For some participants, the parade continues to be a demonstration of religious devotion and gratitude. Most of those who attend, however, are thrill-seekers 'pursuing experience and sensation', to use the words of a former culture minister.

Qiaonan Old Street 橋南街 The name of Yanshui's oldest thoroughfare means 'south of the bridge', and the bridge in question spans a small body of water that once formed part of Yuejin Harbour. A dozen of the street's single-storey wooden-framed houses date from the 1880s or earlier.

CHIAYI CITY 嘉義市 (JIĀYÌ SHÌ) *Telephone code 05*

Chiayi (population: 269,000) will never rival Tainan in terms of visible history, nor will it ever have the sophistication of Taichung. But spending a slow 24 hours here just after an energetic excursion into the mountains isn't a bad idea, especially if you want to see a way of life that's somewhere between Taipei's frenetic metropolitan existence and the languor of rural Taiwan.

HISTORY The written history of Chiayi begins in the 1640s, when Dutch East India Company officials passed through an aboriginal village here, collecting taxes and searching for potential exports. The Dutch spelled the village's name Tilaossen, and Han settlers, who were already arriving in some numbers, called it Tirosen and rendered it in characters which Mandarin speakers pronounce Zhuluoshan. In 1734 the settlement got its first city wall, a palisade of sharpened bamboo stakes. It earned its current name – which means 'right, fitting and proper' – from the emperor himself in 1787 when it defied Lin Shuang-wen's army (page 12).

After an earthquake flattened the city in 1906, Chiayi gained the straight but somewhat narrow roads it has today. The following year saw work begin on the famous logging railroad to Alishan. The timber trade had a big impact on Chiayi; buildings made of wood taken from the mountains can still be seen throughout the city. It also became a centre of art and scholarship; in 1926, Chiayi-born Chen Cheng-po (1895–1947) became the first Taiwanese painter to have a work included in Japan's most prestigious art exhibition. One of the city's most famous sons, he's now remembered as much for his grisly end (during the 2-28 Incident he was executed at the railway station by KMT soldiers) as for his pictures, which embodied both Chinese landscape-painting conventions and Modernism. Chen's works are still very popular – one fetched US$6.5 million when auctioned in 2007 – and reproductions have been set on steel easels at various points around the city.

GETTING THERE AND AROUND For details of trains on the mountain railway, see page 231.

By car, motorcycle or bicycle
By Freeway 1 Chiayi is 239km south of Taipei and 103km north of Kaohsiung. From the Chiayi exit at km264 it takes 20 minutes to reach the city centre. Parking isn't as difficult in Chiayi as in larger cities like Tainan. For two-wheelers, roads 163, 165 and 166 are decent alternatives to the often-busy Highway 1. If you need to hire a vehicle, check out the following:

🚗 **Car Plus Auto Leasing** 556 Linsen W Rd; ☎227 8855; w car-plus.com.tw; ⊕ 08.30–20.30 daily. General-use car hire & long-term leasing. There's also has a counter inside Chiayi HSR station.

🏍 **168 Vehicle Rental** 719 Zhongzheng Rd; ☎216 6689; ☎07.00–10.30 daily. One of several motorcycle-hire places across the road from the TRA station.

By HSR
Some 15km west of the city centre, Chiayi HSR station has three trains per hour to Taipei (1½hrs; NTD1,080); to/from Kaohsiung Zuoying is equally frequent

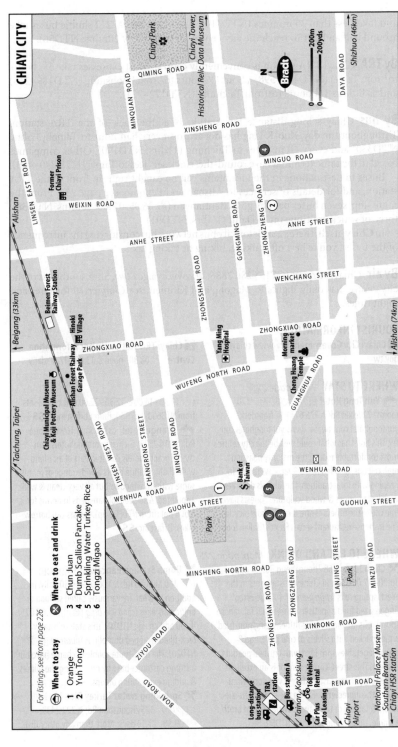

CHIAYI CITY

For listings, see from page 226

Where to stay
① Orange
② Yuh Tong

Where to eat and drink
3 Chun Juan
4 Dumb Scallion Pancake
5 Sprinkling Water Turkey Rice
6 Tongzi Migao

Chiayi Park

Chiayi Tower,
Historical Relic Data Museum

QIMING ROAD

MINQUAN ROAD

XINSHENG ROAD

MINGUO ROAD

Former
Chiayi Prison

WEIXIN ROAD

ANHE STREET

ANHE STREET

GONGMING ROAD

ZHONGZHENG ROAD

LINSEN EAST ROAD

WENCHANG STREET

ZHONGSHAN ROAD

Beimen Forest
Railway Station

Hinoki
Village

ZHONGXIAO ROAD

Yang Ming
Hospital

Morning market

Cheng Huang
Temple

GUANGHUA ROAD

ZHONGXIAO ROAD

Chiayi Municipal Museum
& Koji Pottery Museum

Alishan Forest Railway
Garage Park

ZHONGXIAO ROAD

WUFENG NORTH ROAD

LINSEN WEST ROAD

CHANGRONG STREET

MINQUAN ROAD

Bank of
Taiwan

WENHUA ROAD

①

WENHUA ROAD

GUOHUA STREET

Park

⑤
⑥ ③

GUOHUA STREET

MINSHENG NORTH ROAD

ZHONGZHENG ROAD

LANJING STREET

Park

MINZU ROAD

ZIYOU ROAD

BOAI ROAD

ZHONGSHAN ROAD

XINRONG ROAD

Long-distance
bus station

TRA
station

Bus station A

168 Vehicle
Rental

Car Plus
Auto Leasing

RENAI ROAD

National Palace Museum
Southern Branch,
Chiayi HSR station

Chiayi
Airport

Tainan, Kaohsiung

Alishan (74km)

Beigang (33km)

Alishan

Taichung, Taipei

DAYA ROAD

Shizhuo (46km)

N

0   200m
0   200yds

Southwest Taiwan   CHIAYI CITY

7

225

and takes less than 35 minutes (NTD410). The #7211 and #7212 shuttle buses take around half an hour to reach the city centre (departs every 20mins; NTD56).

By TRA Chiayi TRA station is conveniently central. Most expresses take 3½ hours to/from Taipei (NTD461–598), about 1½ hours to/from Kaohsiung (NTD189–245) and as little as 1¼ hours to/from Taichung (NTD172–224).

By bus Chiayi's long-distance bus station is at the back of the TRA station. Throughout the day, Kuo-Kuang has departures every half hour to Taipei (3½hrs; NTD330) and every 40 minutes to Taichung (1¾hrs; NTD190). Other companies based in the same terminal have round-the-clock services to Taipei (NTD240–450).

Buses to destinations in the mountains can be caught right in front of the TRA station, and for details of services to Alishan and Fenqihu, see page 231. From the same stop, seven buses per day go to Bantianyan (⌚ 06.05–17.05; 50mins; NTD58), three of which continue on to Dahu (1¼hrs; NTD91).

In Chiayi itself, there's a skeleton city bus network but considering the infrequency of the buses, you're best off walking, biking or taking taxis.

By air Chiayi Airport (CYI; ☎ 286 7886; w www.cya.gov.tw), 5km southwest of the city centre, has daily flights to Magong and Kinmen; see *Chapter 10* for fares and flight times.

TOURIST INFORMATION

⬛ **Chiayi City Government** w www.chiayi. gov.tw

⬛ **Chiayi TRA Station Visitor Information Centre** ⌚ 08.30–noon & 13.00–17.00 daily

---

 ## WHERE TO STAY *Map, page 225*

🏠 **Yuh Tong Hotel** 鈺通大飯店 (120 rooms) 7 Weixin Rd; ☎ 275 6111; e frontdesk. yuhtonghotel.com.tw; w www.yuhtonghotel.com. tw. This hotel has what could well be the city centre's most comfortable rooms, the majority boasting high ceilings, wooden floors & large windows. In keeping with local tradition, the lobby is decorated with koji figurines & wood sculptures. Guests have free use of the fitness centre & can borrow bicycles. The in-house restaurant serves French/Italian food

(⌚ 11.30–14.00 & 17.30–22.00 daily; meal sets from NTD600; $$$$). Buffet b/fast inc. **$$$**

🏠 **Orange Hotel** (83 rooms) 169 Wenhua Rd; ☎ 216 2323; e chiayi@orangehotels.com. tw; w orangehotels.com.tw. Part of an island-wide chain, Orange offers a wide range of rooms, some without windows but all very clean & well appointed. Also available are beds in dorms for 2, 4 or 6 ppl (from NTD600 pp). Guests can borrow bikes. B/fast inc. **$$**

✖ WHERE TO EAT AND DRINK *Map, page 225*

✖ **Chun Juan** 468 Zhongzheng Rd; ⌚ approx 10.00–17.00 daily. In Chinese restaurants in the West, spring rolls (*chūn juǎn* 春卷) are often finger-sized fried appetisers. Traditional Taiwanese spring rolls are bigger & healthier, being non-fried wraps packed with slivers of cold pork, egg & green vegetables sprinkled with crushed peanuts & sugar. This street-corner vendor is an excellent place to try them; just gesture if you don't want one of the ingredients. Eat on the spot (there are stools & tables) or take-away. With a cup of broth, a single, quite filling roll costs NTD50. **$**

✖ **Dumb Scallion Pancake** 啞煎蔥油餅 160 Minguo Rd; ⌚ 06.00–14.30 daily. In addition to what are variously called scallion or onion pancakes (*cōng yóu bǐng* 蔥油餅, NTD25; if you add an egg NTD30), this stall sells tasty leek-filled wrapped dumplings (*jiǔcài hé* 韭菜盒, NTD20). The deaf-mute couple in charge have built a strong customer base by minimising the oiliness & adding extra spring onions. **$**

✖ **Sprinkling Water Turkey Rice** 噴水雞肉飯 325 Zhongshan Rd; ☎ 222 2433; ⌚ 09.30–21.30 daily. More than any other dish,

Chiayi is associated with what locals call *huǒjī ròu fàn* 雞肉飯, shredded turkey & gravy served on white rice. Much of the turkey now eaten in Taiwan comes from the US but the meat served in this chain is sourced locally & reliably excellent. The Chinese-only menu lists 15-plus side dishes inc tofu, soups & vegetables. Soft drinks & beer available. $

✗ **Tongzi Migao** Cnr of Zhongzheng Rd & Guohua St; ⊕ 10.00–18.00 daily. If you've come for spring rolls (see opposite) but they've sold out, head to the adjacent vendor for a savoury snack popular in Chiayi. The name of this cup-sized delicacy is often but misleadingly translated as 'rice cake' but *tǒngzi mǐgāo* 桶仔米糕 (NTD20) is actually steamed rice topped with soft slivers of pork. To accompany it, order crispy pork ribs in soup (*páigǔ sū* 排骨酥, NTD35) or mushroom & pork thick soup with noodles (*ròu gēng miàn* 肉焿麵, NTD35). $

OTHER PRACTICALITIES
$ **Bank of Taiwan** 306 Zhongshan Rd
✚ **Yang Ming Hospital** 252 Wufeng N Rd; ✆228 4567; w www.ymhospital.com.tw; ⊕ 24hrs daily

✉ **General post office** 134 Wenhua Rd; ⊕ 08.30–19.00 Mon–Fri, 09.00–noon Sat

WHAT TO SEE AND DO Chiayi offers a good variety of sights including museums, places of worship, and remnants of the Japanese era.

Chiayi Municipal Museum 嘉義市立博物館 (275 Zhongxiao Rd; ✆278 0303; w www.cabcy.gov.tw/web/museumen; ⊕ 09.00–noon & 13.30–17.00 Wed–Sun; free admission) This museum has sections devoted to fossils, local geology and Chen Cheng-po, but more interesting is the collection in the basement of a building nearer Zhongxiao Road: the **Koji Pottery Museum** 趾陶館 (⊕ 09.00–17.00 Tue–Sun; free admission). Introducing the gorgeously colourful ceramic art that decorates many of Taiwan's finest temples as well as some of the form's leading artists, it's well worth an hour of your time. For detailed explanations of some of the most important works, go to w www.cabcy.gov.tw/web/English/ExhibitionEn.

Alishan Forest Railway Garage Park 阿里山森林鐵路車庫園區 (⊕ 24hrs daily; free admission) In this former marshalling-and-repair yard railway enthusiasts can get a close look at some of the forest railway's locomotives and carriages. This entire neighbourhood has been transformed in recent years: slum housing has been cleared and buildings associated with the logging industry have been renovated. Thirty Japanese-style bungalows built for forestry executives and their families on Linsen East Road have been refurbished and named **Hinoki Village** 檜意森活村

THE ALISHAN FOREST RAILWAY
Hopefully, the century-old railroad that links the lowlands with Alishan will be fully functioning when you're in Taiwan. The railway has been closed for years at a time following after natural disasters like 2009's Typhoon Morakot, when landslides cut the line in dozens of places, destroyed bridges and filled some of the 50 tunnels with mud. The 71.4km-long line took more than a decade to build, but by 1914 trains were taking workers and their supplies from Chiayi City (elevation: 30m) to Alishan (2,216m above sea level) and bringing timber and farm produce down to the plains. The most remarkable sections are those where the railway corkscrews its way around one mountain, then uses switchbacks and changes of direction to climb the next.

(aka Cypress Forestry Life Village; ⊕ varies but most closed Mon; free admission), home to shops and art spaces but you'll likely find the exteriors more appealing.

Former Chiayi Prison 嘉義舊監獄 (140 Weixin Rd; ☏ 278 9242; ⊕ 09.30–11.30 & 13.30–15.30 Tue–Sun; free admission) Built 1919–22, the only surviving Japanese-era prison in Taiwan housed up to 300 male convicts (and 30 women in segregated facilities) until 1994. The main doors, made of extremely valuable yellow cypress from Alishan, are original. Inmates were held in three wings arranged so the corridors could be observed by a single officer from his desk. The onsite workshops in which they laboured have been preserved, as has the bathhouse where they washed together. At the time of writing, visitors could only enter at certain times (⊕ 09.30, 10.30, 13.30 & 14.30) but this may well change. Get someone to call ahead if you'd like an English-language tour.

Cheng Huang Temple 城隍廟 (Chéng Huáng Miào) (168 Wufeng N Rd; ⊕ 05.30–21.00 daily) In the late 1930s, during the Kominka Movement (page 16), 63 of the 66 major shrines then existing in Chiayi were razed or converted to other uses. This city-god temple, central to spiritual life in the city since its founding in Emperor Kangxi's reign (1661–1722), was one of the three survivors. In the Qing era, government officials would reside here and take part in soul-purifying rites before assuming new posts. If you approach from Wufeng North Road, look to your left as you pass under the massive archway: you'll see two large panels inscribed with the names of those who donated money for the 1990 renovation. This list is proof of how broad a base popular religion still has in Taiwan; the nearly 3,000 names are arranged according to how much they gave, and the majority forked out what must have been at least a week's salary. To better accommodate its mini-pantheon the temple has expanded upwards.

Cheng Huang Ye, the city god, can be found right where you'd expect him to be – on the ground floor, in the very centre. High above the altar, almost lost in the gloom and soot, there's a four-character inscribed board presented to the temple on behalf of Emperor Guangxu. Dating from 1887, it reads *Táiyángxiànyòu* and means 'Protector of Taiwan and the Ocean'. It amounted to imperial recognition of the deity's power and benevolence; no other city god in Taiwan received such an accolade. Before heading upstairs, go into the rear chamber where there are icons of Mazu (in the centre) and Cheng Huang Ye's wife (on the petitioner's right). On what locals call the second floor, go behind the Guanyin shrine and you'll find, facing out the back of the temple, a large but amateurish painting that depicts smug-faced officials taking shelter in the temple while Lin Shuang-wen's rebels attack the city walls. One floor up, the rear altar on the right is devoted to the Old Man Under the Moon, heaven's matchmaker, whose birthday is celebrated on the second day of the sixth lunar month. The fifth floor is given over to a trio of bearded gentlemen, the Sanqing or 'Three Pure Ones' of Taoism, while the sixth and top level is unusual for a temple in that it's made largely of wood.

Every morning the neighbourhood east of the temple is a fascinating maelstrom of vendors and motorcycles, with several shops specialising in pickles or homemade noodles.

Chiayi Park 嘉義公園 (Jiāyì Gōngyuán) (Minquan & Qiming rds; ⊕ 24hrs daily; free admission) This pleasant suburban park wouldn't warrant a mention were it not for the adjacent arboretum and two eye-catching yet very different buildings. Covering 8.6ha, **Shanziding Botanical Garden** 山仔頂植物園 is home to mahogany and sandalwood groves criss-crossed by shaded pathways and there's

quite a bit of English-language information for the green-fingered. Rubber trees grown here from the 1920s onward supplied the Imperial Japanese Army during its Asian adventures.

The tallest structure on this side of the city, **Chiayi Tower** 射日塔 (⊕ 09.00–17.00 Wed–Fri, 09.00–21.00 Sat; admission to the observatory NTD50/25) is also known as Sun-Shooting Tower; an information panel inside explains the aboriginal legend behind this alternative name. If the weather's clear, do buy a ticket and ride the lift to the tenth floor for fine views. Near the tower stands the **Historical Relic Data Museum** 史蹟資料館 (⊕ 09.00–17.00 Wed–Sun; free admission), formerly part of a Shinto shrine complex. Don't bother with the displays inside about local education– there's scant English – but the exterior is sublime.

National Palace Museum Southern Branch 故宮南部院區 (Gùgōng Nánbù Yuànqū) (888 Gugong Bd, Taibao; ✆ 362 0777; w south.npm.gov.tw; ⊕ 09.00–17.00 Tue–Fri; admission NTD150/free) Rather than focus on the glories of China like its mother institution (page 103), NPM's Southern Branch aims to offer a pan-Asian perspective. If you've a strong interest in tea culture or Buddhist art, the permanent exhibitions alone justify coming here. The highlight of the latter section is a magnificent *kangyur* (a compilation of the Buddha's sayings) in Tibetan script that was created for a Chinese emperor in 1669.

Admission is free for all under-18s and anyone presenting a ticket stub from the Taipei NPM that's no more than three months old. If you plan to go to the Taipei NPM within three months of visiting the Southern Branch, buy a regular ticket for the Taipei NPM here and use it for both places.

Getting there and away The museum is connected to Chiayi HSR station by half-a-dozen bus routes (takes less than 10mins; NTD24). If instead you're coming from Chiayi City, take bus #7303 (departs 09.00 & 11.30 daily) or #7320 (7 departures daily; ⊕ 06.40–21.30), both of which take around 35 minutes (NTD60). The #106 Tourist Shuttle from Chiayi TRA station (4–8 departures daily; ⊕ 08.00–15.00; NTD148) takes an epic 1¼ hours. The museum is about 18km from the centre of Chiayi City; parking at the museum is never a problem. Whether you arrive by bus or car at the north or the south entrance you'll need to walk around 500m to the museum itself; if this is a problem, board the golf-cart shuttle (NTD50).

FROM CHIAYI CITY TO SHIZHUO BY ROAD 159A

For those driving or riding towards Alishan, Road 159A (159甲) is a highly attractive alternative to Highway 18 – the scenery is better and there are no tour coaches because the road is narrower. If you're starting from Chiayi City, get on to Minzu Road, which soon becomes Daya Road, and follow the signs to Fanlu. Don't panic if you find yourself on Road 159 by mistake – it joins Road 159A just before Bantianyan. Even if you're not stopping to hike, allow at least 2 hours to cover the 46km between Chiayi and Shizhuo.

Without your own vehicle you won't make it to the most scenic parts of this road; however, certain parts are accessible on public transport. From Chiayi TRA station seven buses per day go to Bantianyan (⊕ 06.05–17.05; 50mins; NTD58), three of which continue on to Dahu (1¼hrs; NTD91).

BANTIANYAN 半天岩 (**BÀNTIĀNYÁN**) Approaching this hillside spot, 428m above sea level, you'll see thousands of persimmon trees. However, for many Taiwanese visitors the main attraction isn't fruit but **Purple Cloud Temple** 紫雲寺 (km17 Rd 159A; ◷ 05.00–21.00 daily). Established in 1682, it's flanked by a 23m-high statue of Guanyin and at weekends there are never fewer than several hundred people in and around the temple, a good number of whom meditate for extended periods or join Buddhist or Taoist rituals. If you want a bit of a workout, follow the 2km-long **Qifu Trail** 祈福步道 up the hill behind the temple. It's clearly marked but sometimes slippery; at the far end you can either return via Road 159A (a distance of 3.4km) or continue 300m in the other direction to the trailhead for Three Treasures Mountain.

THREE TREASURES MOUNTAIN 三寶山 (SĀNBAˇOSHĀN) Past the temple, the
road becomes narrower and more twisting as betel-nut and persimmon groves give way to bamboo and mixed forest. At a large boulder bearing the English words 'Dahu Community' the road splits: turn right and you'll end up at Chukou on Highway 18; turn left to stay on Road 159A. The trail up Three Treasures Mountain begins with an obvious stairway on the left at km20.9. Allow at least 3 hours to get to the top of this 977m-high ridge and back to the road. Be prepared for many, many steps – but when it's clear the views are good.

DAHU SHARP MOUNTAIN 大湖尖山 (DÀHÚJIĀNSHĀN) Neither the tallest nor
the best-known peak in these parts, but offering good scenery for relatively little effort, this mountain is accessed just inland of the village of Dahu 大湖. Near km26, a small road veers steeply off to the right; there's no English signpost but on the relevant Chinese sign you can see '2KM'. Getting a motorcycle or a fairly robust car right to the trailhead (exactly 1,000m above sea level) isn't difficult. From there, it's an hour or so to the peak, where a sign gives the mountain's height as 1,357m. Much of the trail is shaded, making this an enjoyable hike even on hot days. From the ridge you can see several higher peaks and look down on tiny settlements to the south.

GANZIZHAI 柑仔宅 Past km32 tea is an important crop and landslides often
damage the road. Drive slowly around this tiny village and not just for safety's sake: the vistas around here are superb. Ginger, runner beans and cabbages also grow well here. Just after km40, the road turns sharply right to cross the headwaters of the Bazhang River.

SHIZHUO 石棹 (SHÍZHUŌ) (km63 Hwy 18) There's nothing really to see in Shizhuo
('stone table') but it's one of the better places to stop for supplies.

ALISHAN NATIONAL SCENIC AREA 阿里山國家風景區 (ĀLĪSHĀN GUÓJIĀ FĒNGJĪNGQŪ) *Telephone code 05*

Alishan's fresh, cool air and mountain scenery have been drawing tourists since the Japanese era, but this little town more than 2,000m above sea level has a history quite unlike the purpose-built hill stations of the British Raj. Both the settlement and the famous narrow-gauge railway that links it to the plains were built to facilitate relentless logging, and many of the area's ancient trees were felled to provide lumber for construction and furniture-making. During the colonial era, a number of Japan's most notable temples were rebuilt using red or yellow cypress from Alishan. The 415ha Alishan National Scenic Area encompasses tea-growing areas and indigenous villages as well as the eponymous forest recreation area.

GETTING THERE AND AROUND

By car or motorcycle Highway 18 is the area's main artery but Road 159A (page 229) and Local Road 129 (page 232) are recommended for views and lighter traffic. There are petrol stations at Shizhuo and just outside the forest recreation area. All of the region's roads are vulnerable to typhoon damage, so if you plan to explore by car or motorcycle, check conditions before setting out.

By bus You can catch buses to Alishan right outside Chiayi TRA station (⊕ 06.10–14.10; 2½hrs; NTD240); of the ten daily departures per day, four are Taiwan Tourist Shuttle services. From the same stop there are two services each day to Fenqihu (⊕ 07.10 & 15.10; 1¾hrs; NTD175). From Chiayi HSR station there are four Tourist Shuttle buses to Alishan per day (09.30, 10.10, 11.00 (via Fenqihu) & 13.10; 2½hrs; NTD278), all of which halt in Shizhuo (NTD197 from Chiayi HSR station).

The #6739 Sun Moon Lake–Tataka–Alishan bus leaves Shuishe at 08.00 and 09.00 (3½hrs; NTD350). You're advised to book your seat a few days or more in advance; an English-language form can be found online at w ntbus.com.tw/6739order-en. doc. From Alishan, the buses depart at 13.00 and 14.00.

By train The Alishan Forest Railway (see box, page 227) is slower and more expensive than buses but it's an experience that enraptures rail fans. At the time of writing, there was one daily departure from Chiayi (09.00, terminates Fenqihu 11.20; NTD292 one-way; begins return journey at 14.00), although on Saturdays, Sundays and national holidays, additional services set off at 08.30 (terminates Shizilu 11.25; NTD375 one-way; begins return journey at 11.40) and 09.30 (terminates Fenqihu 11.50; begins return journey at 15.00).

TOURIST INFORMATION Alishan National Scenic Area Headquarters and Chukou Visitor Centre (✆ 259 3900; w www.ali-nsa.net; ⊕ 08.30–17.00 daily) are just west of Chukou on Highway 18. There's another visitor centre in the busiest part of the forest recreation area (⊕ 08.00–17.00 daily).

WHERE TO STAY The Greater Alishan area has lots of homestays, although there's no compelling reason to stay inside the forest recreation area unless you want to see the sunrise from Zhushan.

Fenqihu and nearby

⌂ **Dadongshan Leisure Resort** 大凍山休閒渡假中心 (10 rooms) 214 Dinghu Vlg; ✆ 256 1151; w shop.okgo.tw/3046/. One of at least 3 homestays in Dinghu, a beautiful settlement inland of Shizhuo, this establishment makes a good base if you're staying to hike in the area. Rooms for 2, 4 or 5 ppl are perfectly adequate if unimaginative. B/fast inc; a set dinner of decent & filling Taiwanese fare can be ordered for NTD250 pp. **$$$**

⌂ **Arnold Janssen Activity Centre** (14 rooms, 2 dorms) ✆ 256 1035. This easy-to-find hostel is next to Fenqihu's Catholic church. Accommodation is clean & simple; the sgl & dbl rooms lack en-suite bathrooms, but the 4-person

rooms (NTD2,000) have them. Also rooms for 6, 10 & 12 ppl. Staying in the dorm costs NTD250 pp. No meals available but the hostel is 10mins' walk from the busiest part of Fenqihu. English spoken. **$**

Alishan National Forest Recreation Area

⌂ **Alishan House** 阿里山賓館 (150 rooms) ✆ 267 9811; w www.alishanhouse. com.tw. Centrally located, Alishan House is 3 bldgs stitched into 1. Rooms near the lobby are attractive & have a graceful simplicity, though perhaps not quite as much character as you'd expect given that the structure is a century-old Japanese colonial original. The sun deck on the 1960s annexe has good views & is popular with stargazers. Business centre, gym & coffee shop. 2 in-house restaurants (🕐 11.30–13.30 & 17.30–20.30 daily; EM; **$$$**) but you'll find better food elsewhere in the forest recreation area. B/fast inc. **$$$$$**

🍴 **WHERE TO EAT AND DRINK** Restaurants of varying quality are clustered around the main car park in the forest recreation area. In Fenqihu, vendors along the Historic Street serve up local snacks as well as the usual rice lunch boxes and noodle dishes.

🍴 **Shan Zhi Xiang Restaurant** 山芝鄉風味館 Opposite the post office inside Alishan National Forest Recreation Area; ↘267 9839; 🕐 10.00–21.00 daily. With many years' experience serving stir-fried mountain vegetables & dishes like 'crystal cold chicken' (*shuǐjīng yóu jī* 水晶油雞, NTD200) to tourists, this restaurant is a safe bet for a lunch or dinner to replace the calories you burned off hiking. If there's 2 or 3 of you, make your life easy by ordering the 3-dish, 1-soup set (*sān cài yī tāng* 三菜一湯, NTD600). EM. **$$**

🍴 **Yongfu Tea Oil Chicken** 永富餐飲苦茶油雞 km62.6 on Hwy 18; ↘256 1488; 🕐 11.00–19.00 Sat–Mon & Wed–Thu. This old favourite serves very good Taiwanese home cooking, the signature dish being chicken basted in tea-seed oil (*kǔcháyóu jī* 苦茶油雞); a standard portion is big enough for 3 diners (NTD350). The vegetables (from NTD50) & fried river shrimp (from NTD120) are excellent, as is the Shacha venison (*shāchá lùròu* 沙茶鹿肉, NTD250). No EM & no English spoken but the staff are used to foreign visitors who point to order. Solo travellers may want to order fried rice or noodles (NTD50) & a soup (NTD20–30). **$$**

🏕 **AjangHome** 阿將的家23咖啡館 129–6 Leye Vlg; ↘256 1930; w lalauyacou.wixsite.com/yangui; 🕐 09.00–16.00 Sun–Fri. This adorable coffee shop/campsite is a warren of stone walls & woodwork overlooking fields of tea. Even if you can't stay – as campsites go it's a bit pricey – dropping by for a cup of real Alishan coffee is a delightful experience (min spend NTD150 pp). **$$**

WHAT TO SEE AND DO The appeal of Alishan is undoubtedly its mountain environment, both the woodlands you can experience up close while hiking, and the valleys and peaks off in the distance.

Local Road 129 Near km50 on Highway 18 a side road drops southwards to three Tsou villages – **Shanmei** 山美, **Xinmei** 新美 and **Chashan** 茶山 – before hitting Highway 3 near Dapu, where there's a petrol station (🕐 07.00–18.00 daily). Xinmei is the prettiest of the three, but Chashan has more tourist infrastructure in the form of eateries and homestays (few have English signs, however). Despite Chashan's name ('tea mountain') not much tea is grown around here. The landscapes en route deserve not to be rushed.

Eryanping Trail 二延平山步道 (km53.3 Hwy 18) Just under 1km long but steep in places, this path leads to a ridge from where you'll get views over two drainages. It's best very early in the morning when you'll see much more of the lowlands. The viewing platform beside the highway, to the left of the trailhead, is a good alternative to hiking up. About 1km further along Highway 18 is Xiding 隙頂, a farming community where tea, jelly figs and peas are grown. A century ago charcoal was an important product hereabouts. To make it, groups of local men would head into the forests for days at a time, carrying little but tools, rice, cooking oil and moonshine. During these expeditions they also hunted and foraged.

Fenqihu 奮起湖 (**Fènqǐhú**) This little town, halfway between Chiayi City and Alishan, owes its existence to the logging railroad. Starting from the 1920s, outsiders came here to work in the railway depot or hawk food to ravenous train passengers (the uphill journey used to take 7 hours; replacing steam locomotives with diesel engines in the 1960s cut the journey time in half). Three engines are on display beside the railway station, including two antique units that began their working lives before World War I. Fenqihu's older buildings have walls of wood and roofs of tar paper or tin but relatively few have survived fires and redevelopment. The so-called Historic Street, just below the station (which is 1,405m above sea level), is a good place to search for something tasty if you've been working up an appetite on the boardwalk trails through the surrounding forests. For long-distance views, ascend 1,976m-high Mount Dadong. From Fenqihu it takes about an hour to walk to the trailhead where bilingual map boards show various routes, the longest of which is a 5-hour loop via the peak and other features of natural interest.

Dabang 達邦 **and Lijia** 里佳 The journey far outshines the destination. From Shizhuo it's a slow but very scenic 29km to the tiny settlement of Lijia via the more substantial village of Dabang. The road was in good shape at the time of writing but remains vulnerable to typhoons. There are a few B&Bs along the way but getting a meal isn't easy so bring something to eat. Cyclists contemplating this route should know the road plunges to around 700m above sea level before Dabang, climbs to an elevation of almost 1,500m, then drops steeply again to Lijia.

Dinghu 頂湖 A Hakka enclave about 1,650m above sea level, Dinghu is 4km off the main road and thus bypassed by tour groups heading for Alishan proper. There's nothing to do here except hike, gaze at the tea plantations and surrounding woodlands, and sink into a state of intoxicating relaxation. Allow 2 hours for a saunter along the **Dinghu Trail** 頂湖步道 encircling the settlement. If you want to go for a good walk but would rather not stray from Highway 18, park at km66.4 and head downhill along the 2.3km-long **Mihu Trail** 迷糊步道, which is popular with birdwatchers. Both are well signposted.

Alishan National Forest Recreation Area 阿里山森林遊樂區 (Ālǐshān Sēnlín Yóulèqū) (km88.2 Hwy 18; w recreation.forest.gov.tw; ⊕ 24hrs daily; admission NTD300/150/10)

When people talk about Alishan, they're usually referring to this 1,400ha reserve. It's an excellent place for people who don't consider themselves hikers but want to experience mountain woodlands. Clearly signposted trails wind through sublime forest, and before you know it, your gentle stroll has become a 3-hour circuit that, combined with the pristine air, will do you a power of good. Come prepared for cool, wet conditions as the resort gets rain 209 days per year and heavy cloud or fog 244 days. During winter, the average temperature is just 2–4°C, and while in summer the mercury seldom goes above 20°C, it can feel much warmer due to the strength of the sun. Unless you've a passion for white-pink cherry blossoms, avoid the sakura season in March and April when the Recreation Area gets packed out and room rates hit the roof. Sakura, a Japanese word adopted by the Taiwanese, means 'flowering cherry tree'.

To avoid the parking fee (NTD100 for cars, NTD20 for motorcycles), continue along Highway 18 as it veers right near the toll gate; you should find free parking after around 200m but at times you may need to go further. As soon as you enter the Recreation Area you'll see the railway station on your right and the main shopping/restaurant zone below you on the left; the information centre is in the latter. You'll need to go down some more stairs to reach the Hotel Area where Alishan's smaller inns are clustered.

Pre-dawn morning calls are standard as most tourists want to witness the sun rising from **Zhushan** 祝山, a 2,489m-high peak southeast of the resort. Some people walk – the trek takes 1½ hours and involves more than a few steps – but taking the forest railway is both a lot quicker and more fun (takes 25mins; NTD100/50 one-way, NTD150/100 return). The departure schedule is adjusted according to sunrise times and extra trains are organised during busy periods. Returning to Alishan on foot is highly recommended as the trail is very lovely mid-morning once the crowds disperse. The woodland it passes through isn't especially old as most of the peacock pines and cypresses were planted between 1920 and 1947, but among them you'll see stumps of giant cypresses logged during the colonial era. Most are slowly decaying and host ferns and mosses, but a few have sprung back to life.

Of the Recreation Area's several places of worship, the most interesting is **Tzu Yun Temple** 慈雲寺 (⊕ 06.00–19.00 daily). With its red tin roof and white plank walls, it bears a strong resemblance to shrines in the Japanese countryside, which is hardly surprising as it was built by Japanese Buddhists in 1919. Take your shoes off before entering the main hall and try not to disturb the resident nuns.

Zizhong 自忠 (altitude 2,280m; km96.1 Hwy 18) Hikers come here for the **Tefuye Historic Trail** 特富野古道, a 6.32km-long path that drops 600m en route to indigenous villages to the southwest. The first half of this glorious woodland trail is flattish because it follows a stretch of logging railroad that operated until the late 1970s; the second half is much steeper. There's no public transport anywhere near the western trail entrance, so most people park at Zizhong and content themselves with an hour-long stroll.

SEND US YOUR SNAPS!

We'd love to follow your adventures using our *Taiwan* guide – why not tag us in your photos and stories via Twitter (➤ @BradtGuides) and Instagram (◙ @bradtguides)? Alternatively, you can upload your photos directly to the gallery on the Taiwan destination page via our website (w bradtguides.com/taiwan).

8

Kaohsiung and Pingtung

Taiwan's tropical south contains much of what's great about the country: beaches, mountains, traditional villages and indigenous communities. You're more likely to see banana groves than factory chimneys and even the notoriously industrial city of Kaohsiung has become a pleasant place to stay and explore.

Kaohsiung City, which stretches all the way from the ocean to the south face of Mount Jade, has a population of 2.78 million and a land area of 2,946km². Pingtung County (population 828,000, of whom one in 12 is aboriginal; land area 2,776km²) is best known for Kenting, a national park that's an uneasy combination of beach-based hedonism and natural splendour, but many visitors find the mountain villages of the interior more alluring. If familiar food and other creature comforts are important, consider basing yourself in central Kaohsiung and venturing out for day trips; most of the destinations described in this chapter are no more than 2 hours from central Kaohsiung.

Kaohsiung and Pingtung's tourist sights aren't clustered like Taipei's attractions, so having a vehicle or the patience to use buses is essential if you're to make it to some of the more far-flung destinations such as the Buddhist complex at Foguangshan or the scenic but typhoon-vulnerable aboriginal districts of Maolin, Namasia and Wutai.

KAOHSIUNG 高雄 (GĀOXIÓNG) *Telephone code 07*

Kaohsiung used to feel like the place that got the polluting industries while Taipei got the investment and infrastructure. Three decades ago there was little point in visiting this oceanside conurbation unless you were doing business, but these days it's an entirely different story. Democracy has led to a fairer distribution of official resources; in terms of life quality the metropolis has almost caught up with Taipei, and if blue skies and sunshine are important to you, you may well feel Kaohsiung has leapfrogged the capital. In wintertime, Kaohsiung is far more pleasant than Hong Kong, which is at the same latitude.

HISTORY Like Birmingham, Los Angeles and other second cities around the world, Kaohsiung is an upstart. Two centuries ago it was nothing more than a fishing village, or rather a string of villages, one of which was located on what's now called Cijin. From 1603, Ming Dynasty admirals conducting anti-pirate sweeps referred to the region as Takau. This name, often spelled Takao and sometimes Dagou, stuck for more than three centuries, until the Japanese colonial authorities decided the written form – two Chinese characters with the literal meaning 'hit the dog' – was undignified. They replaced it with different characters meaning 'lofty hero', pronounced Takao in Japanese and Gāoxióng in Mandarin.

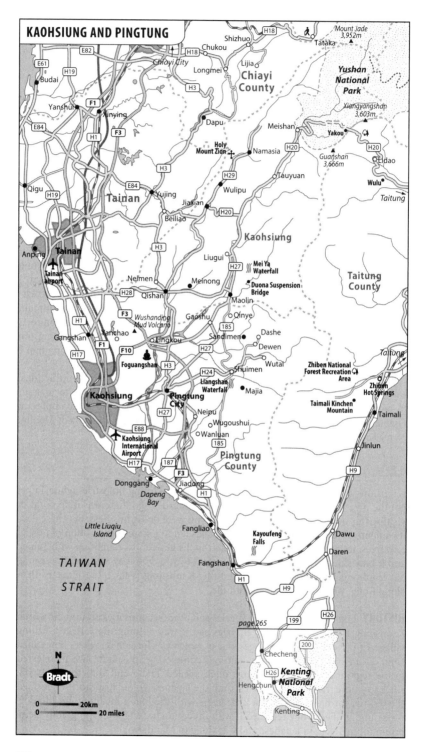

Mount Jade
3,952m
Tataka

Shizhuo   H18

Chukou

H18

E82

E61   H18
Chiayi City

H19   Longmei   Lijia   Yushan
Budai   Chiayi   National
Yanshui   H3   County   Park

F1   Xiangyangshan
Xinying   3,603m

H1   Dapu   Meishan   Yakou

F3   Holy   Namasia   H20   Guanshan   H20
E84   Mount Zion   3,666m   Lidao

Qigu   E84   H29   Tauyuan   Wulu
Yujing   Wulipu
H19   Tainan   Jiaxian   Taitung
Beiliao   H20

Kaohsiung

H3

Anping   Liugui   H27   Mei Ya   Taitung
Tainan   Waterfall   County
Tainan   Neimen   Meinong   Duona Suspension
airport   Qishan   Bridge
H28   Maolin
F3   Wushanding   Gaoshu   Qinye
H1   Mud Volcano   Dashe
Gangshan   Yanchao   Lingkou   185   Sandimen   Dewen
F1   F10   H27   Shuimen   Wutai   Taitung
Foguangshan   H3   H24   Zhiben National
Liangshan   Forest Recreation
Kaohsiung   Pingtung   Waterfall   Majia   Area
City   Zhiben
H27   Neipu   Taimali Kinchen   Hot Springs
E88   Wugoushui   Mountain
Kaohsiung   Wanluan   Taimali
International   185
Airport   H17   Pingtung
H17   Jiadong   County
Donggang   187   F3   Jinlun
Jiadong
Dapeng   H1
Bay
Little Liuqiu   H9
Island   Fangliao   Kayoufeng
Falls   Dawu

TAIWAN   Fangshan   Daren

STRAIT   H1

H9

page 265   199   H26

200

N   Checheng

Bradt   Kenting
H26   National
Hengchun   Park

0   20km
0   20 miles   Kenting

The colonial regime dredged the channel between Cijin and Kaohsiung proper, widened the harbour mouth and built the first breakwater. The city's industries developed and the population of the urban core multiplied sixfold to 1.5 million between 1950 and 2010. Whereas much of Taipei's growth can be attributed to the post-World War II influx of mainlanders, most of the migrants who relocated to Kaohsiung in the 20th century came from the interior of the country. Country folk who preferred factory work to farm labour were joined by Hakka from Meinong, Penghu islanders and thousands of indigenous people. In recent years a number of landmark buildings, among them a convention centre, have been added to the waterfront.

GETTING THERE AND AWAY

By air If you're coming from Europe via Hong Kong or Bangkok or from North America via Japan, arranging to fly into Kaohsiung International Airport 高雄國際航空站 (Gāoxióng Guójì Hángkōngzhàn) (IATA: KHH; ✆ 805 7631; w www.kia.gov.tw) rather than Taoyuan isn't difficult. Domestic routes include flights to/from Magong and Kinmen. The international and domestic terminals are linked by an elevated corridor. The international terminal has two money changers upstairs (⏰ 05.30–16.30 daily), a Bank of Taiwan branch downstairs (⏰ 08.30–midnight daily) and a post office on the third floor (⏰ 08.30–16.30 Mon–Fri). There are visitor information centres with free Wi-Fi in both terminals.

Airport transfers The most popular way of getting from the airport to central Kaohsiung is by metro. Kaohsiung International Airport Station is one stop from the southern end of the Red Line. Including waiting time and short walks at both ends, allow 35 minutes to get from the airport to Kaohsiung Zuoying HSR station (NTD50 one-way).

Buses to Kenting (depart every 30mins; ⏰ 06.25–22.15 daily; 2½hrs; NTD327) via Fangliao (1¼hrs; NTD144) stop at road level between the terminals, so there's no need to trek into central Kaohsiung if you're heading to the beach resort or the east coast. Buy your ticket when boarding; have exact change ready.

The tiny building between the two terminals houses two vehicle-hire companies: Car Plus Auto Leasing (✆ 801 0019; ⏰ 08.30–21.00 daily) and Hotai Leasing (✆ 0800 024 550; ⏰ 08.30–21.00 daily). Taxis are allowed to add NTD50 to what's shown on the meter, so expect to pay at least NTD400 if you're going beyond Love River.

By HSR To Taipei the bullet train usually takes less than 2 hours (4 departures per hr; ⏰ 06.40–22.10; NTD1,490), while to Taichung the journey time is around an

---

HIT THE DOG, HIT THE CAT

Kaohsiung isn't the only place in Taiwan to have had a strange name. Minxiong, a town just north of Chiayi City, was known as Damao ('hit the cat') until the Japanese colonial regime changed the written form to its current version, which means 'public hero'.

Odd toponyms can still be found in rural parts. One neighbourhood on the outskirts of Tainan is called Gourou ('dog meat') – perhaps its first resident was a butcher selling canine steaks – while in tea-growing country not far from Alishan there's a Niushihu ('cow dung lake'). Kaohsiung has a small valley marked on maps as Goushikeng ('dog faeces hole') plus a creek named Agongdian ('grandpa's shop').

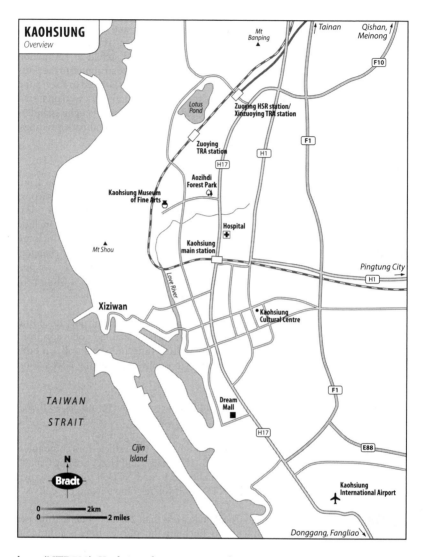

KAOHSIUNG
Overview

Mt Banping

↑ Tainan   Qishan, ↑
              Meinong

F10

Lotus Pond

Zuoying HSR station/
Xinzuoying TRA station

F1

Zuoying
TRA station

H1

H17

Aozihdi
Forest Park

Kaohsiung Museum
of Fine Arts

Hospital

Mt Shou

Kaohsiung
main station

Pingtung City

H1

Love River

Xiziwan

Kaohsiung
Cultural Centre

TAIWAN

STRAIT

F1

Dream
Mall

H17

E88

Cijin
Island

N

Kaohsiung
International Airport

0 ———— 2km
0 ———— 2 miles

Donggang, Fangliao

hour (NTD790). Kaohsiung has an integrated HSR/TRA/metro station at Zuoying, some distance north of the actual city centre. The rapid transit stop is called Zuoying but the TRA station there is called Xinzuoying.

By TRA By the time you read this, five new commuter stations should be operating but these aren't likely to make any difference to tourists. Most expresses will continue to stop at Kaohsiung Main Station (which is relocating underground) and Xinzuoying only; TRA passengers wanting to transfer to the HSR should get off at the latter. To/from Taipei, there's at least one express per hour between dawn and early evening (NTD650–843). Only Puyuma services complete the journey in less than 4 hours; around 5 hours is typical. A few additional expresses go no further than Taichung (2½–3hrs; NTD361–469), and there are 13 services daily to Taitung (⊕ 05.12–16.28 daily; 2¾hrs; NTD279–362). Trains to/from Tainan are frequent and usually take an hour (NTD68–106). Services to/from Pingtung are also frequent (NTD31–48) and take less than half an hour.

By bus The long-distance bus stations are on your left as you leave the TRA Main Station. From the Kuo-Kuang bus station there's a bus to Taipei at least every hour around the clock (5hrs; NTD530), to Taichung every 40 minutes (⏱ 05.40–22.20 daily; 3hrs; NTD330), and to Taitung four-times daily (⏱ 03.00, 07.00, 12.30 & 17.30; 3½hrs; NTD540).

Behind the Kuo-Kuang station, Kaohsiung Bus Co station serves Kenting and Kaohsiung's hinterland. More than 50 buses per day go to Kenting (NTD347–364) but not all stop at Donggang (NTD115).

For Qishan, Meinong and Foguangshan you're best off catching a bus outside Kaohsiung Zuoying HSR station/Zuoying metro station (page 252), from where services to Kenting include the #9188 (departs hrly; ⏱ 08.45–21.45 daily; 2½–3hrs; NTD343–382).

GETTING AROUND Note that eating, drinking, chewing gum and smoking are prohibited on metro trains, the light rail and city buses. Get an EasyCard (see box, page 54) if you plan to spend more than a couple of days in the Kaohsiung area. All fares mentioned in this chapter are one-way.

By metro Kaohsiung Rapid Transit Corp (w www.krtco.com.tw) operates two mainly underground lines, the Red and the Orange, and the incomplete circular Green Line. On the Red and Orange lines, which intersect at Formosa Boulevard Station, trains run every 5–8 minutes (⏱ 06.00–midnight daily; one-way fares are NTD 20–60). All signs and announcements are multi-lingual. Trips on the Green Line cost NTD30.

By bus The city bus hub is in front of Kaohsiung Main Station. Journeys are NTD12 per section; few trips are more than one section. Destinations are shown in English on the front of each bus, and inside the name of the next stop comes up in English on an LED board above the driver. A useful route is the #248 from Kaohsiung Main Station to Gushan Ferry Dock via the Love River (departs every 20–30mins; ⏱ 06.15–22.05 daily); #50 also goes to Gushan Ferry Dock via various Orange Line metro stations including Sizihwan (departs every 20mins; ⏱ 06.03–23.02 daily).

By boat In addition to the regular ferry from and to Cijin (page 244), there are harbour cruises (see w culturalcruise.khcc.gov.tw) that can be boarded at Pier-2 (page 243), which last up to 90 minutes and typically cost NTD549. Bicycles can be taken on ferries.

By hired car or motorcycle

🚗 **Car Plus Auto Leasing** [240 D2] Kaohsiung Main Station, 264 Jianguo 2nd Rd; ☎236 5510; w www.car-plus.com.tw; ⏱ 08.30–20.30 daily. There are also counters at the HSR station & airport.

🛵 **555 Scooters** [240 D2] 8 Lane 317, Linsen 1st Rd; m 0975 177 141; e service@555scooters. com; w 555scooters.com; ⏱ 11.00–21.00 daily. English-speaking outfit able to supply tourists with scooters of various types.

By hired bicycle
Bicycle-only lanes link Lotus Pond with Love River and run the length of Cijin. Shared bikes with baskets and lights (but without locks or helmets) can be hired through C-Bike (w www.c-bike.com.tw), which has rental points all over the city including metro and TRA stations, Lotus Pond and Kaohsiung

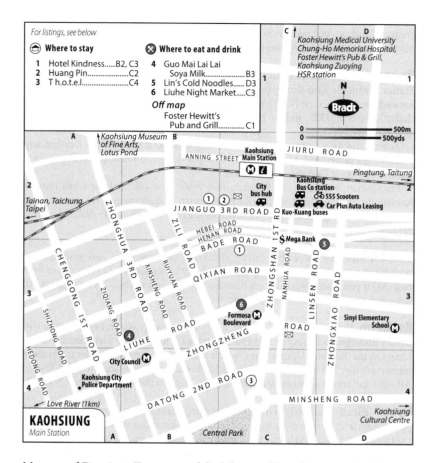

For listings, see below

Where to stay
1 Hotel Kindness......B2, C3
2 Huang Pin......................C2
3 T h.o.t.e.l..........................C4

Where to eat and drink
4 Guo Mai Lai Lai
   Soya Milk...................B3
5 Lin's Cold Noodles......D3
6 Liuhe Night Market.....C3

Off map
   Foster Hewitt's
   Pub and Grill..............C1

Kaohsiung Medical University
Chung-Ho Memorial Hospital,
Foster Hewitt's Pub & Grill,
Kaohsiung Zuoying
HSR station

Kaohsiung Museum
of Fine Arts,
Lotus Pond

Kaohsiung
Main Station

ANNING STREET

JIURU ROAD

Pingtung, Taitung

Tainan, Taichung,
Taipei

City
bus hub

Kaohsiung
Bus Co station

555 Scooters

Car Plus Auto Leasing

JIANGUO 3RD ROAD

Kuo-Kuang buses

ZHONGHUA 3RD ROAD

ZILI ROAD

HEBEI ROAD

HENAN ROAD

BADE ROAD

Mega Bank

CHENGGONG 1ST ROAD

ZIQIANG ROAD

XINSHENG ROAD

RUIYUAN ROAD

QIXIAN ROAD

ZHONGSHAN 1ST

NANHUA ROAD

LINSEN ROAD

ROAD

SHIZHONG ROAD

Formosa
Boulevard

ROAD

ZHONGXIAO ROAD

Sinyi Elementary
School

HEDONG ROAD

LIUHE

ZHONGZHENG

City Council

Kaohsiung City
Police Department

DATONG 2ND ROAD

MINSHENG ROAD

Love River (1km)

KAOHSIUNG
Main Station

Central Park

Kaohsiung
Cultural Centre

Museum of Fine Arts. To get one of the bikes, you'll need an iPass (Kaohsiung's version of the EasyCard) or a credit card. The first 30 minutes is free, after which you'll pay at an escalating rate; 2 hours costs NTD35.

Bicycles and electric mini-bikes can also be rented from the English-speaking folks at Happiness Bike [242 B2] (℡ 532 0969; ⊕ 08.30–21.00 daily) beside Sizihwan metro station Exit 1. For better and/or bigger bikes, try Giant Bicycles [242 D2] (16 Wufu 4th Rd; ℡ 521 8512; ⊕ 11.00–21.00 Fri–Wed).

By taxi Handy Andy (m 0931 827 808; e andys_cab902@yahoo.com.tw) speaks good English and is available for day tours in the region and shorter journeys.

TOURIST INFORMATION Kaohsiung City Government (w khh.travel/en) has a slew of visitor information centres, the most useful of which are in Kaohsiung Main Station [240 C2] (⊕ 10.00–19.00 daily) and by Exit 2 in Kaohsiung Zuoying HSR station (⊕ 08.30–20.30 daily).

 WHERE TO STAY
Near Kaohsiung Main Station
🏠 **Hotel Kindness** [240 C3] (195 rooms) 30 Tongai St; ℡ 288 5588; e kindness.hotel@msa.

hinet.net; w kindness-hotel.com.tw. Guest rooms in the biggest of this efficient chain's 3 branches near the main station (13 throughout the city) are kept spick & span. At 44 Jianguo 3rd Rd [240 B2] (103 rooms; ☎287 5566) some of the rooms are barely bigger than the beds but the location is better if you're walking from the bus or train stations. Room rates jump around; online booking can bring them under NTD2,500. Buffet b/fast inc & guests can borrow a bike for free. **$$$**

🏠 **Huang Pin Hotel** 皇賓旅社 [240 C2] (21 rooms) 40 Jianguo 3rd Rd; ☎288 3173. A little old-fashioned & with minimal English but clean. Solo travellers won't find a better deal as rooms with bath can be had for as little as NTD800 except on Sat night. Look for the white bldg sandwiched between 2 larger hotels. Inc a b/fast coupon for nearby McDonald's. **$$**

🏠 **T h.o.t.e.l.** [240 C4] (42 rooms) 177 Datong 1st Rd; ☎231 2141; e service@t-hotel.com.tw; w t-hotel.com.tw. Popular with businesspeople but the English-speaking staff are well able to handle visitors from afar. Room décor is mostly monochrome; all come with sofas, refrigerators & big-screen LCD TVs, while some also have jacuzzi, PC & CD player. Pool table in the basement; free self-service laundry with dryer & iron plus bike rental. Room rates are often below NTD1,800. Buffet b/fast inc. **$$**

✗ WHERE TO EAT AND DRINK
Near Kaohsiung Main Station
✗ **Guo Mai Lai Lai Soya Milk** 果貿來來豆漿 [240 B3] 186 Liuhe 2nd Rd; ☎281 8512; ⏰ 05.00–11.30 daily. In many ways a traditional b/fast shop – think crullers & egg pancakes – Guo Mai Lai Lai is especially known for its hot 'salty soya milk' (xián dòujiāng 鹹豆漿, NTD30). It comes adulterated with sesame oil, rice vinegar & chili oil then topped (if you wish) with shredded scallions, browned shallots & tiny dried shrimps. As you wait for it to cool the blend curdles into something resembling foamy cottage cheese. It tastes way better than it looks & is satisfying like a bowl of porridge. **$**

✗ **Lin's Cold Noodles** 林家涼麵 [240 D3] 278 Linsen 1st Rd; ☎235 5316; ⏰ 08.30–19.30 Mon–Sat. Order a bowl of cold noodles with shreds of chicken (jī sī liáng miàn 雞絲涼麵) or, if you're brave, cow's stomach cold noodles (niú dù liáng miàn 牛肚涼麵) & wash it down with a bowl of miso soup. There are plenty of conventional hot noodle options. **$**

✗ **Liuhe Night Market** 六合夜市 [240 C3] Liuhe 2nd Rd; ⏰ approx 17.00–01.00 daily.

Near the Love River
🏠 **Grand Hi-Lai Hotel** [242 F2] (540 rooms) 266 Chenggong 1st Rd; ☎216 1766; w www.grand-hilai.com.tw. Still Kaohsiung's swankiest hotel, Grand Hi-Lai's spacious rooms are just the right side of ostentatious. Big windows mean an abundance of natural light, & if you're on the southern or western sides of the building you'll pay extra for the engrossing harbour views. Book a health room if you fancy having access to your own exercise equipment. Rooms have separate shower cubicles & baths, but the latter are standard-size only. 13 restaurants, bars & bakeries, the most popular of which is **The Harbour Buffet** (☎2369 288; ⏰ 06.30–10.30, 11.30–14.00, 14.30–16.30 & 17.30–21.30; **$$$$**). Swimming pool, sauna & squash court. Buffet b/fast inc. **$$$$**

🏠 **Harmony Hotel** [242 E2] (31 rooms) 265 Chenggong 1st Rd; ☎216 6866; e harmony_hotel@xuite.net; w harmony-hotel.com.tw. Tastefully subdued colours, sinfully thick carpets, quasi-Art Deco styling & very substantial discounts that often take prices below NTD2,000 make this a hotel worth considering. Free parking. B/fast inc. **$$**

Kaohsiung's most famous night market is a great place for Taiwanese snack foods, of course, but that doesn't mean it isn't international. In recent years Turkish ice cream & Pakistani dishes have been available, as have sushi, sashimi & Japanese seaweed wraps filled with salad or roe. **$**

Love River
✗ **Chamonix Teppanyaki** [242 F2] 29 Wufu 3rd Rd; ☎221 8169; w chamonix.com.tw; ⏰ 11.30–14.00 & 17.30–21.00 daily. With a dozen branches throughout Taiwan, Chamonix's French–Japanese fusion meals have won a strong fanbase, despite the limited menu (diners must choose 1 of 3 meal sets) & high prices. Expect attentive service but call in advance if you require vegetarian options. EM, wine list. **$$$$$**

✗ **Ootoya** 大戶屋 [242 F2] Basement Level 3, 266–1 Chenggong 1st Rd; ☎215 4377; w ootoya.com.tw; ⏰ 11.00–22.00 daily. Located in the food court below Grand Hi-Lai Hotel, this is part of a Japanese restaurant chain that has spread throughout east Asia; you'll find branches in Taiwan's other major cities. Ootoya's Japanese

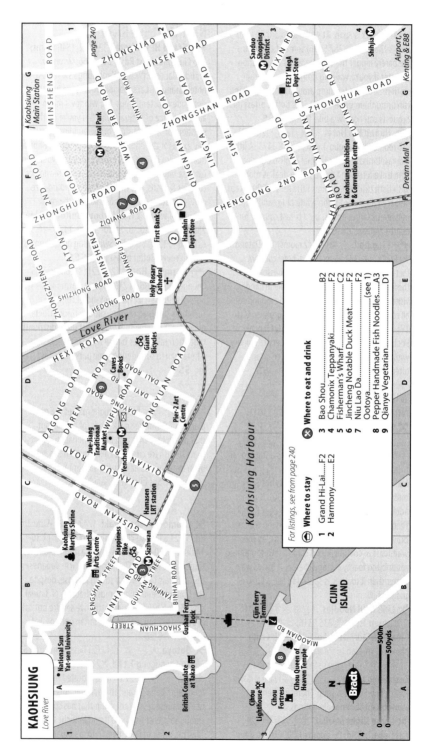

KAOHSIUNG

Love River

A National Sun Yat-sen University

Kaohsiung Martyrs Shrine

Wude Martial Arts Centre

Happiness Bike

Sizihwan

LINHAI STREET

DENGSHAN STREET

GUYUAN STREET

YANPING RD

BINHAI ROAD

SHAOCHUAN STREET

Gushan Ferry Dock

Cijin Ferry Terminal

MIAOQIAN RD

CIJIN ISLAND

British Consulate at Takao

Cihou Lighthouse

Cihou Fortress

Cihou Queen of Heaven Temple

N

Bradt

0   500m
0   500yds

GUSHAN ROAD

JIANGUO ROAD

QIXIAN RD

Hamasen LRT station

Yanchengpu

Jue-Jiang Traditional Market

DAGONG ROAD

DAREN ROAD

WUFU ROAD

DAYI ROAD

DALI ROAD

GONGYUAN ROAD

Caves Books

Giant Bicycles

Pier-2 Art Centre

HEXI ROAD

Love River

HEDONG ROAD

Holy Rosary Cathedral

SHIZHONG ROAD

GUANGFU ST

DATONG ROAD

MINSHENG ROAD

ZHONGHUA ROAD

ZHONGZHENG ROAD

ZIQIANG ROAD

First Bank $

Hanshin Dept Store

CHENGGONG 2ND ROAD

page 240

ZHONGXIAO RD

LINSEN ROAD

XINTIAN ROAD

WUFU 3RD ROAD

Central Park

QINGNIAN ROAD

ZHONGSHAN ROAD

LINGYA ROAD

SIWEI ROAD

Kaohsiung Main Station

MINSHENG ROAD

Sanduo Shopping District

YIXIN RD

FE21' MegA Dept Store

SANDUO RD

XINGUANG ROAD

ZHONGHUA ROAD

FUXINGYUAN ROAD

Shihjia

Airport, Kenting & E88

HAIBIAN ROAD

Kaohsiung Exhibition & Convention Centre

Kaohsiung Harbour

Dream Mall

Dream Mall & E88

For listings, see from page 240

Where to stay
1 Grand Hi-Lai......................F2
2 Harmony............................E2

Where to eat and drink
3 Bao Shou...B2
4 Chamonix Teppanyaki.......................F2
5 Fisherman's Wharf.............................C2
6 Jincheng Notable Duck Meat.............F2
7 Niu Lao Da..F2
8 Ootoya...(see 1)
9 Pepper Handmade Fish Noodles.......A3
  Qianye Vegetarian.............................D1

dishes (with a few Korean options) emphasise pork & chicken rather than fish, but one of the most consistently popular items is grilled eel on rice (*tàn kǎo mányú gài fàn* 炭烤鰻魚蓋飯, NTD520/410 depending on portion size). Other mains start at NTD240; if the meal sets look too large, go for a bowl of noodles in soup (from NTD150). Various child-friendly options are NTD200. Side dishes inc salads, soups & vegetables (from NTD40). **$$$$**

✗ **Niu Lao Da** 牛老大 [242 F2] 18 Ziqiang 2nd Rd; ☏ 281 9196; ⏰ 11.30–14.00 & 17.00–02.00 Tue–Sun. Renowned for its fried beef & beef hot pots, Niu Lao Da has in recent years gone a little upmarket; the décor & furnishings are far smarter than a decade ago. It still sources its meat from local cattle farms, promising no more than 8hrs from slaughter to table. The stewed rice & noodle options are good bets for solo travellers. Order with caution as the Chinese-only menu also lists cow's stomach, cow's heart & cow's lung. Local & Japanese beers available. **$$$**

✗ **Jincheng Notable Duck Meat** 金城鴨肉專門店 [242 F2] 62 Wufu 3rd Rd; ☏ 241 5419; ⏰ 10.00–20.30 daily. This wildly popular eatery has expanded along the pavement & on hot days opens an AC dining room upstairs. The staff recommend you get a whole/half cold salted duck (*yánshuǐ yāròu* 鹽水鴨肉, NTD480/240) so you & your friends can pull it apart with your fingers. There's every conceivable noodle option inc ban-tiao plus soups & side dishes of kimchi & tofu (NTD25–60). Spitting bones on to the table is OK yet everything is kept very clean. **$$**

✗ **Qianye Vegetarian** 千葉養生素食 [242 D1] 131 Dayi St; ☏ 521 3665; ⏰ 08.00–20.30 daily, closed 2nd & 4th Sun each month. Help yourself to salad, fried dumplings, tofu & meat-free Chinese dishes then show what you've got to the staff to find out how much you need pay (seldom more than NTD150). Come just before midday for the best pickings. Inc unlimited soup & black tea. Upstairs there's AC. No written menu. **$$**

✗ **Bao Shou** 包手 [242 B2] 15–1 Linhai 2nd Rd; 531 7912; ⏰ 24hrs daily. This chain specialises in the steamed breads many Taiwanese eat for b/fast but offers 25+ different fillings (NTD15–30). In addition to the traditional cabbage- & pork-filled buns there are cheese, curry & other flavours. Options for those with a sweet tooth inc chocolate & coconut. There's nowhere to sit but it's just a short walk to the benches at Takao Railway Museum. EM. **$**

✗ **Pepper Handmade Fish Noodles** 胡椒手工魚麵店 [242 A3] 44 Tongshan Rd, Cijin; ☏ 571 1711; ⏰ 10.30–18.00 daily. Consisting of little more than plastic stools & folding tables outside a single-storey building, this eatery is a good place to stop to/from Cijin's lighthouse. For more than 3 decades the owners have been serving delicious thick noodles made from fish dough in a broth flavoured with pork, chicken bones & seasonal greens. Crispy fried dumplings (fish or shrimp) also available & just as good. No EM so point to order. **$**

Bars

🍸 **Fisherman's Wharf** 漁人碼頭 [242 C2] Near Gushan 1st & Binhai 1st rds; ⏰ varies. Has a number of places where you can drink a beer & enjoy a bite to eat while watching the sun go down over the harbour. No EMs. **$$**

🍸 **Foster Hewitt's Pub and Grill** [240 C1] 30 Wenzhong Rd; ☏ 555 0888; ⏰ 18.00–02.00 daily. With bottled & tap beers from NTD100 plus a good range of scotches & wines this Canadian-run bar is a place for Western food in addition to a fine drinking establishment. Good burgers (from NTD160); starters, soups & salads (from NTD120). The EM also has steaks, Tex-Mex & Italian dishes. Most nights there's a min charge of NTD200 pp. Easily reached from exit 2 of the metro's Red Line Kaohsiung Arena Station. **$$**

ENTERTAINMENT AND NIGHTLIFE For high-brow entertainment, see what's playing at these venues:

Kaohsiung Cultural Centre [240 D4] 67 Wufu 1st Rd; ☏ 222 5136; w www.khcc.gov.tw. Municipal venue for exhibitions & shows of all kinds.

Pier-2 Art Centre [242 D2] 1 Dayong Rd, Yancheng; ☏ 521 4899; w pier-2.khcc.gov.tw;

⏰ 10.00–18.00 Mon–Thu, 10.00–20.00 Fri–Sun. An old harbour warehouse upcycled into an arts space, Pier-2 hosts exhibitions, rock concerts & the offices of cultural/creative businesses.

SHOPPING

Malls and department stores

Dream Mall [242 F4] 789 Zhonghua 5th Rd; ☎973 3888; w www.dream-mall.com.tw; ⏰ 11.00–22.00 Mon–Thu, 10.30–22.30 Sat–Sun & national holidays. The biggest shopping centre in Taiwan with 400,001m² of retail space, the Dream Mall is a very broad collection of international brands & mid-price eating options. Atop the roof there's a Ferris wheel that turns slowly enough to give riders – weather permitting – value-for-money views over all of Kaohsiung & a good part of the surrounding countryside. It's best reached by light rail to Dream Mall station.

FE21' MegA Department Store [242 G3] 21 Sanduo 4th Rd; ☎0800 000 563; ⏰ 11.00–22.00 daily. Incorporates a cinema & a good bookstore. Take the metro to Sanduo Shopping District station & leave by exit 1 to find yourself on the building's ground floor.

Hanshin Department Store [242 F2] 266–1 Chenggong Rd; ☎215 7266; ⏰ 11.00–22.00 daily. Directly beneath the swanky Grand Hi-Lai Hotel, Hanshin has the best food court of any department store in the city.

Bookshops

Caves Books [242 D2] 76 Wufu 4th Rd; ☎561 5716; ⏰ 10.00–21.00 daily. Postcards, magazines, quite a few books in English about Taiwan & a selection of novels.

Eslite [242 G3] 17th Flr, FE21' MegA Department Store; ☎331 3102; ⏰ 11.00–22.00 daily. Especially good for books on art & architecture in various languages & imported magazines, this branch is one of the most attractive bookshops in south Taiwan.

Markets

Jue-Jiang Traditional Market 堀江商場 [242 C1] Lane 239, Wufu 4th Rd; ⏰ varies, approx 11.00–22.00 daily. Nowhere near as busy as it was in its 1950s–70s heyday, this covered market is home to shops selling clothes & shoes that appeal to middle-aged locals, plus sweets & other packages treats imported from Japan, watches & Chinese medicines.

OTHER PRACTICALITIES

Banks and changing money

You can change money in the GPO & the post office beside Kaohsiung Main Station. Go to the airport if you need to change cash outside normal banking hours. Useful bank branches include:

$ **First Bank** [242 F2] 61 Wufu 3rd Rd
$ **Mega** [240 C2] 308 Zhongshan 1st Rd

Medical

✚ **Kaohsiung Medical University Chung-Ho Memorial Hospital** [240 C1] 100 Ziyou 1st Rd; ☎312 1101; w www.kmuh.org.tw; ⏰ 24hrs daily

Post

✉ **General post office** [240 C3] 177 Zhongzheng 3rd Rd; ⏰ 08.30–21.00 Mon–Fri, 09.00–noon Sat & Sun
✉ **Kaohsiung Main Station** [240 C2] On your right as you leave the station's front entrance; ⏰ 08.30–17.00 Mon–Fri, 09.00–noon Sat

Police

Kaohsiung City Police Department [240 A4] 260 Zhongzheng 4th Rd; ☎221 5796

WHAT TO SEE AND DO

Cijin 旗津 **(Qíjìn)** Fujianese fishermen began settling on this finger of land in the 17th century and it retains some of its old, salty character. Even if you turn around and immediately return to 'mainland' Kaohsiung, the ferry (departs every 10mins; ⏰ 06.00–midnight daily; 10mins; NTD15 one-way; motorcycles NTD20, bicycles free) from Gushan Ferry Dock 鼓山輪渡站 [242 B2] to **Cihou** 旗後, the main settlement, is worth taking for the views you'll get. The island is 9km from end to end but everything of interest is around the northern tip. Cihou can be explored on foot or by tourist pedicabs (drivers wait outside the ferry terminal and charge from NTD200 for a 20-minute tour but no English spoken) and bike rentals (from NTD50/hr). As you would expect in what was until recently a fishing village, seafood is a speciality, and Miaoqian Road, which leads from the ferry terminal to a sandy beach (swimming prohibited), is lined with restaurants. This thoroughfare's name means 'road in front of the temple', and the shrine alluded to is **Cihou Queen of Heaven Temple** 旗後天后宮 [242 A3] (93 Miaoqian Rd; ⊕ 05.30–22.00 daily), named after and dedicated to Mazu since its founding in 1673.

More interesting than the temple are **Cihou Lighthouse** 旗後燈塔 [242 A3] (⊕ 09.00–16.00 Tue–Sun; free admission) and **Cihou Fortress** 旗後砲台 [242 A3] (⊕ 24hrs daily; free admission). These two landmarks – the former was designed in the late 19th century by a British engineer and rebuilt in 1918, the latter was constructed in 1875 – stand near each other at the island's northwestern tip. The strategic importance of this craggy but lush hillock is obvious, and the views over the ocean and towards the former British Consulate (see below) justify the 10-minute slog up from the busiest part of Qihou.

Kaohsiung Martyrs Shrine 高雄市忠烈祠 [242 B1] (⊕ shrine: 08.00–17.00 daily, lookout: 24hrs daily; free admission) Like many other Nationalist memorials, this site was once a Shinto place of worship and the most recent renovation restored some of the Japanese-era features. Unless you've an obsession with KMT relics the only reason to come here is to enjoy fine views over the city and the harbour without the crowds that often gather at the former British Consulate. The only bus route up to the shrine is #56 from Kaohsiung Main Station (departs about hrly; ⊕ 09.03–18.03 daily). Alternatively, walking from Sizihwan metro/Hamasen LRT requires around 20 minutes. If you take Cianguang Road you'll go through a beguilingly higgledy-piggledy neighbourhood full of tiny homes. The alternative is to follow Linhai Road to Yanping Street, turn right through the morning market to Dengshan Street, then turn left until you see the elegant 1920s Kaohsiung Red Cross nursery at no 28. Between here and no 30, an unmarked lane with steps goes up to Cianguang Road. If you continue along Dengshan Street at no 36 you'll find **Wude Martial Arts Centre** 武德殿振武館 [242 B1] (⊕ 10.00–18.00 Tue–Sun; free admission). Built in 1924, it is perhaps the oldest and arguably the most beautiful of the dozen Japanese-era *butokuden* halls that survive in Taiwan (out of around 70 built prior to 1945).

British Consulate at Takao 前清英國領事館 (Qiánqīng Yīngguó Lǐngshìguǎn) [242 A2] (✆ 525 0100; w britishconsulate.khcc.gov.tw; ⊕ 09.00–19.00 Mon–Fri, 09.00–21.00 Sat–Sun; admission NTD99/39) A vestige of the Treaty Port era when Western powers forced China to open several towns and cities to foreign trade, these buildings at the southern tail of 354m-high Mount Shou are where British diplomats lived and worked between 1879 and 1897. The consular office on the waterfront at the bottom of this hill is a reconstruction; steps lead up to the consul's residence from where you'll get good views of the ocean and the city centre.

In 1911, the British government shifted all personnel and archives to Tamsui in the north. The residence and offices were sold to the Japanese government in 1925; a nearby cemetery for Westerners (marked on an old map inside the residence) remained in British hands but was overrun by squatters in the 1960s, and traces of only three of the 40-odd graves remain extant. Displays give a broad picture of trade relations between 19th-century Taiwan and the outside world; in addition to camphor, sugar and rice, the island's exports included lumber, salt, turmeric, sesame and peanuts.

To get here, bus #99 leaves Yanchengpu metro station (departs every 40mins; ⏱ 06.00–18.00 daily; 15mins) and stops by the consulate entrance before heading north along Caishan Avenue. Alternatives are taking a taxi or walking the 1.3km from Sizihwan metro station.

Caishan Avenue 柴山大路 From the car park below the old consulate it's possible to drive north through a university campus for 4.7km to where Caishan Avenue ends at a military base. Popular with cyclists, joggers and macaques – which sometimes dawdle on the edge of the tarmac – the road offers some agreeable ocean vistas. Consider heading up here for an afternoon coffee, but note that some businesses open only at the weekend.

Formosa Boulevard metro station [240 C3] (Zhongshan & Zhongzheng rds) This station's four tepee-shaped glass-and-steel entrances call to mind the little pyramids I M Pei controversially added to the courtyard of the Louvre in the 1980s. Japanese architect Shin Takamatsu titled these creations *Prayer*, and they do resemble church spires. Not everyone was impressed, however; nearby landowners complained about the impact on feng shui, saying the spires are like swords pointing into their homes. Inside the station there's a 667m² indoor ceiling installation called *The Dome of Light*. Said to be the world's largest piece of glass art, and representing 'birth, growth, honour, destruction and rebirth', it's a wash of colours and images that took Narcissus Quagliata, its Italian creator, more than 3½ years to finish. As with any other piece of art of this size, it's worth zooming in on details, then stepping back to appreciate the overall effect. It's not all joy and oneness with the cosmos, however – one section, partly obscured by a lift, features scenes of conflagration and a very messy car wreck. Perhaps the artist included the latter to impress upon people one of the reasons they should use public transport instead of driving. To learn more, take the 30-minute audio tour (NTD50). The station's Chinese name commemorates the Meilidao Incident of 1979 (page 19). In the Human Rights Learning Studio (near Exit 9; ⏱ 10.00–19.00 Tue–Sun) you'll find lots of English-language materials about Taiwan's recent history.

Kaohsiung Museum of Fine Arts 高雄市立美術館 [240 A2] (☎ 555 0331; w www.kmfa.gov.tw; ⏱ 09.00–17.00 Tue–Sun; free admission except for special exhibitions) Surrounded by parkland, this museum has a good mix of local, national and international artworks, including photography and installations. From Aozihdi metro station (5mins on the Red Line from Kaohsiung Main Station; NTD20) it's a long (35mins) but pleasant walk through Aozihdi Forest Park (⏱ 24hrs daily; free admission) to the museum. Red 32 and Red 35 shuttle buses link the museum and the metro station.

Lotus Pond 蓮池潭 (Liánchí Tán) [240 A2] Some visitors adore this 1.3km-long lake and the colourful shrines and pagodas that surround it; others find it all a bit kitschy. Most of the pond's landmarks are near its southern end, which is easily reached by train to Zuoying TRA station (not Xinzuoying where the HSR stops), connected by frequent services from Kaohsiung Main Station (8mins; NTD15). Get a leaflet from the visitor centre (⏱ 10.00–19.00 daily) on the southwestern shore, then make your way to the **Dragon and Tiger Pagodas** (⏱ 07.00–18.00 daily; free admission) and the **Spring and Autumn Pavilions** (⏱ 06.30–22.00 daily; free admission). At the former it's customary to go in via the dragon's mouth and leave by the tiger's jaws. The most attractive folk shrine in the city proper is nearby:

Qiming Temple 啟明堂 (🕐 06.00–21.30 daily) has a statue of Guan Gong in the main chamber, recognisable by his burgundy complexion. Upstairs, dead-centre, there's an especially fine representation of the Jade Emperor. Instead of going all the way around the lake, consider returning to the information centre and turning right. Almost immediately you'll see the **North Gate of Fengshan Old Town** 鳳山縣舊城 北門 (🕐 24hrs daily; free admission). Built in the 1820s, it boasts door-god images that are faded yet still august.

NORTH TO NEIMEN *Telephone code 07*

Beyond central Kaohsiung there's a tremendous variety of attractions, including religious sites, ethnic minorities and ecological wonders.

WUSHANDING MUD VOLCANO 烏山頂泥火山 (WŪSHĀNDĬNG NÍHUŎSHĀN)
(🕐 08.30–16.30 daily; free admission) Nothing between Kaohsiung and Tainan justifies getting off a train, but if you're in your own vehicle and curious about natural phenomena, do seek out this tiny nature reserve. You may be required to sign in at the entrance. Just a few metres high, the volcano is full of warm slurry (average temperature 28°C) that bubbles and occasionally spills over the edge of the crater; it's even possible to clamber up the sides and put your hand in. Rivulets of mud trickle across the clearing and into the surrounding forest, where you might see snakes hunting for frogs. Near the active cone there are two dormant volcanoes that have been baked rock-hard by the sun. Close by, the **Yangnyu Mud Pools** 養女湖 are gas-belching chocolate-brown pools that sound like wave-making machines. According to scientists, the slurry has a high chlorine content while the gas is mostly methane with traces of carbon dioxide and nitrogen. Taiwan has more than a dozen mud volcanoes, the precise number changing from time to time because typhoons and seismic activity occasionally reveal new volcanoes or shut down existing ones.

Getting there and away Cars on Freeway 1 should take the Gangshan exit and follow the signs to Yanchao. Take Local Road 38 for about 5km; when you see Jinshan Elementary School on your left, turn sharp right. Stay on the main road and follow the bilingual signs for 2.8km. This route is narrow and twisting, so drive carefully.

FOGUANGSHAN 佛光山 (FÓGUĀNGSHĀN) 📞 656 1921; 🌐 www.fgs.org.tw;
🕐 09.00–19.00 daily; free admission) A stop on many package tours of Taiwan and for good reason, Foguangshan is one of Taiwan's leading monasteries. Combined with the affiliated and adjacent Buddha Memorial Centre (page 248), it's an excellent place to learn about Buddhism. Its founder, Master Hsing Yun (b1927), was already well known in religious circles when he purchased this plot of land in 1967. Soon after arriving in Taiwan from the Chinese mainland in 1949, he became the first Buddhist monk in Taiwan to use radio programmes to spread his message. The propagation of Buddhism remains one of Foguangshan's main goals and the monastery now operates a television station, a worldwide network of Buddhist colleges and several publishing houses, while its charitable efforts include both a children's and a senior citizens' home. Unlike I-Kuan Tao, Buddhism wasn't suppressed by the government during the 1960s and its followers weren't harassed. However, Buddhists were looked down on by Chiang's pro-Western pro-Christian elite, and because of this many kept their beliefs to themselves. Hsing Yun chose the name Foguangshan, which means 'The Light of Buddha Mountain', because

he wanted Buddhists to be explicit about their religious affiliation. Foguangshan's overseas arm is known in English as the Buddha's Light International Association (w blia.org).

Monks and nuns who speak English and other foreign languages are available to guide individuals or small groups if given a few days' notice (↘ 656 1921 ext 6205; e fgs6205@fgs.org.tw; by donation), although if you roll up unannounced you'll still be welcomed and at the very least given an English-language map. The architecture isn't remarkable, but still it's easy to spend half a day here. Three parts of the monastery are essential viewing. The **Main Shrine** (⊕ 09.00–19.00 daily), externally grandiose, is stunning within. The three main Buddhas, each five times the height of a man, project a calming benevolence; 14,800 smaller Buddhas are ensconced in the walls. The other two must-sees appeal in very different ways. The **Cultural Exhibition Hall** (⊕ 09.00–17.00 Tue–Sun; free admission) is a large gallery that hosts new displays every two or three months. Some of the featured artists are world class, and while the works displayed are seldom overtly Buddhist, they are in keeping with Buddhist ideals. **Pure Land Cave** (⊕ 09.00–17.00 Tue–Sun; admission by donation) depicts the paradise described in Buddhist sutras, complete with flashing lights and animatronic figures.

At meal times, monks and nuns gather with lay people attending retreats. Before and after eating, sutras are chanted, and food is consumed in absolute silence. Casual visitors are permitted to watch and listen through the doorway. For a more conventional dining experience, head to the vegetarian tea house (⊕ 10.00–19.30 daily; **$$**) in the basement of the Dharma Transmission Centre. The menu lists tasty rice and noodle dishes, hot pots, teas, coffees and fresh juices.

Those staying in the monastery's **Pilgrims Lodge** (50 rooms; ↘ 656 1921 ext 6205; **$$** no meals inc) are welcome to watch the morning service in the main shrine at 05.50. The lodge accepts overnight guests willing to obey monastic rules – a vegetarian diet, no alcohol, no lying and no killing of living creatures. Coffee is permitted; the rooms have air conditioning and comfortable beds. Foguangshan occasionally organises English-language Buddhist retreats; for details call or email.

Getting there and around If you are travelling by car, take Freeway 3 then Freeway 10. Exit at Lingkou at km22 and go south on Highway 29. It's impossible to miss the memorial centre or the monastery. Motorcyclists can approach on Highway 29.

Buses to Foguangshan and the Buddha Memorial Centre include the #8501 (departs every 45mins; ⊕ 08.15–17.00 Mon–Fri, more frequent at w/ends; 1hr; NTD63) from Kaohsiung HSR station. If the driver stops you from boarding it's because that particular bus doesn't go all the way to the monastery. The Taiwan Tourist Shuttle's Dashu A route sets out from Fengshan TRA station (4 daily departures ⊕ 11.00–16.00 Mon–Fri, 10 daily departures ⊕ 09.30–17.30 Sat–Sun; 1hr; one-day pass NTD50). From Tainan, #8050 runs six times per day (⊕ 06.25–18.50; 1¼hrs; NTD190) and travels via Road 182 (page 250).

Many people walk the 1.6km from Foguangshan to the Buddha Memorial Centre. If you can't, ask and you'll be given a lift on one of the golf buggies that go back and forth.

BUDDHA MEMORIAL CENTRE 佛陀紀念館 **(FÓTUÓ JÌNIÀNGUĂN)** (↘ 656 3033; w www.fgsbmc.org.tw; ⊕ 09.00–19.00 Mon–Fri, 09.00–20.00 Sat–Sun & national holidays; free admission) This breathtaking complex, built to house a tooth believed to have belonged to the Buddha, has a lot to offer visitors interested in Buddhism,

Every spring, crowds pour into Neimen to watch dozens of teams take part in a multi-day martial arts display and competition. This is the Song Jiang Battle Array 宋江陣, one of the island's largest festivals. It's ostensibly a celebration of Guanyin's birthday, and so takes place around the 19th day of the second lunar month.

Rather than using karate chops to smash bricks or head-butts to break roof tiles, the event stresses teamwork and co-ordination. Performances feature ritualised duelling with swords, staves and pikes. Farm tools make occasional appearances, as in olden times battle-array members had to be able to fight using whatever was at hand, be it a hoe or even an umbrella. Fighters carry rattan shields and wear troupe uniforms, with long dark trousers and long-sleeved shirts as standard; participants also wear cummerbund-like sashes of brightly coloured fabric around their waists. Many battle-array members are senior citizens but capable of moving with the speed and grace of ballet dancers. Musical accompaniment is provided by drums, gongs and firecrackers.

There are three theories as to the origins of the battle array. Some think the tradition dates from the period Koxinga and his successors controlled southwest Taiwan (page 11). When that regime collapsed in 1683, some anti-Qing diehards decamped to the interior, beyond the reach of Taiwan's new rulers. Neimen was one of the places where they settled. Because it was on the front line between the Han-dominated lowlands and aboriginal hill districts, military knowledge was important and the frequent drilling needed to preserve such skills was held in temple forecourts. Other places in southwest Taiwan have battle array traditions yet nowhere have they remained as central to community life as in Neimen.

Some claim the battle array is a vestige of the time when towns and villages throughout Fujian maintained militias to fight off pirates. The third explanation, which is attractive if unconvincing, is that the battle array was inspired by one of the greats of classical Chinese literature, *The Water Margin*. This novel recounts the adventures of a band of outlaws during the Song Dynasty (AD960–1279) and the battle array seems to be named after the bandits' leader. Song Jiang was a genuine historical figure: his name appears in reports compiled by imperial officials but what happened to him after he surrendered in 1121 is a mystery.

religious architecture and art. The tooth itself is kept out of sight in a chalice-like container above the reclining Buddha image in the main building's Jade Buddha Shrine. Retrieved from the ashes after the Buddha's cremation, it was taken to Tibet in the 13th century when Muslim armies destroyed many of India's Buddhist monasteries. In 1959 the tooth returned to India in the pocket of a Tibetan lama fleeing the Chinese Communists; he gifted it to Master Hsing Yun in 1998.

Building this complex, which was inaugurated in late 2011, took a decade and cost an estimated US$300 million. The eight pagodas – four on each side of the plaza in front of the main building – represent a core part of the Buddha's teachings, the Noble Eightfold Path. Two sets of statues deserve some of your time. One depicts the founders of the Eight Schools of Chinese Buddhism; another shows 18 Arhats (individuals who have attained an exceptional level of enlightenment) but is unorthodox in that three members of the usual all-male line-up have been replaced with women to underscore modern Buddhism's support for gender equality. Overseeing all is a 108m-high bronze seated Buddha. The mini-mall at the front of the complex has tasteful souvenirs, plus places where you can get a coffee or a meal (all vegetarian). The four museums inside provide background about Foguangshan's history and founder, and feature some dazzling relics. No alcohol, tobacco or meat is allowed within the complex and visitors should dress respectfully. See page 248 for details on how to get here.

QISHAN 旗山 **AND AROUND** Whether you're driving or relying on public transport, there's a good chance you'll pass through Qishan – which boomed in the 1960s thanks to banana exports to Japan – on the way to or from Tainan, Meinong or Foguangshan.

Getting there and away
Self-drivers should take either north–south freeway to Freeway 10 and head northeast, then follow the signs to Qishan. Those on two wheels should note that if you're approaching from the coast via Highway 28, watch out for the scenic badlands around km18. From Tainan, consider Road 182 (see below).

From Kaohsiung HSR station, Freeway Bus #10 departs every 20 minutes for Qishan (⏰ 05.50–23.00 daily; 40mins; NTD70) with some services continuing on to Meinong (50mins; NTD88). Tainan–Foguangshan buses also stop at Qishan (page 248).

What to see and do
Shunsian Temple 順賢宮 (km403 Hwy 3; ⏰ 05.00–21.00 daily) If you go inside this large Mazu temple, which was inaugurated in 2008, it's likely that one of the shrine's volunteers will beckon you over to a television screen linked to a remote-controlled camera. The camera, high up in the roof, points at a square of unpainted concrete. If you look closely, you may be able to make out the eyes, nose and chin of a matronly looking woman. This, believers claim, is an apparition of Mazu that appeared during the building of the temple. Sceptics dismiss it as nothing more than random stains and discolourations, no more convincing than the Virgin Mary appearing on a grilled cheese sandwich in Florida. The temple, a major venue for the annual Song Jiang Battle Array (see box, page 249), can be reached by taking the #8050 Tainan–Foguangshan bus (page 248).

Jih Zhu Temple 紫竹寺 (⏰ 05.00–20.00 daily) The region's most famous and most central place of worship (Jih Zhu means 'purple bamboo') has served as the battle array's headquarters, parade ground and armoury for at least 300 years. Finding it isn't difficult: from Qishan, turn left at the 7-Eleven near km400.5 on Highway 3. and within 200m you'll see the ornate gateway. This house of worship is very much on the Buddhist side of the religious spectrum and you'll see pious individuals engaging in long, personal sessions of prayer and meditation. To get here, take the #8050 Tainan–Foguangshan bus (page 248).

ROAD 182 From Kaohisung's Neimen District the road to Tainan is clearly marked. The scenery along the eastern half of this winding but broad 34km-long road alternates between lush bamboo forests and denuded ridges like those in Caoshan Moonscape World. Between km26 and 27.5, bilingual signs (on the right if you're going to Tainan) point the way to **Wujian Hiking Path** 五間步道, a short, steep concrete track shaded by camphor and longan trees. If the weather's clear, the reward for your 30 minutes of hiking is near-360° views from the ridge. Take care not to step on the little freshwater crabs that scuttle across the path. The hiking path can be reached by the #8050 Tainan–Foguangshan bus (page 248).

MEINONG 美濃 *Telephone code 07*

Taiwanese tourists associate Meinong (population just under 40,000) with Hakka culture, tasty noodles and hand-painted parasols. For Western visitors, scenery and ecology are the main draws. Hemmed in to the north and east by forest-covered mountains and criss-crossed by creeks and irrigation ditches, Meinong is certainly one of the south's most appealing townships. The area is ideal for exploring by bicycle; pedalling slowly allows you to look down every side alley and stop at each tobacco barn. Along the way, you'll come across squarish ponds in which wetsuit-clad farmers cultivate a vegetable called the white-water snowflake, known to Mandarin speakers as *shui lián*. The spaghetti-thin stems are often sautéed with garlic, ginger, and/or sliced mushrooms.

HISTORY Accounts of Meinong's founding make no mention of indigenous people. Whether or not the land was truly *terra nullius*, two brothers surnamed Lim arrived here in 1735 and started growing rice, bananas, black beans, sugarcane and vegetables. They built 24 huts and a bamboo palisade to keep bandits out.

In the 1930s a new crop revolutionised the economy: tobacco. Soon one in four families was growing this cash crop, and tobacco earnings paid for temple renovations and college educations (it's said Meinong has produced more school headmasters and PhDs relative to its population than anywhere else in Taiwan). After Taiwan joined the World Trade Organisation in 2002, the island's cigarette-makers began sourcing from overseas, yet hundreds of redundant curing sheds still dot the landscape.

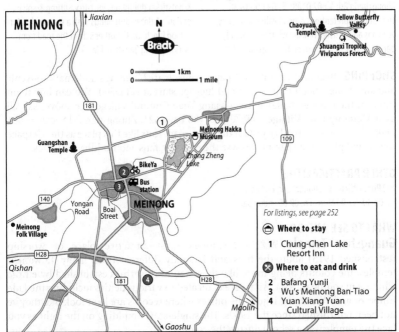

GETTING THERE AND AROUND
By car, motorcycle and bicycle Freeway 10 gets you within 6km of central Meinong. Two-wheelers can approach by Highway 28 or Road 185 from the south (page 257). Bikes can be rented from BikeYa (197 Taian Rd; m 0979 001 912; ⏰ 09.00–19.00 daily; from NTD100 per 3hrs), less than 200m east of the busiest part of the town.

By bus Some Freeway #10 services from Kaohsiung Zuoying HSR station/Zuoying metro station terminate in Meinong. The E28 links central Kaohsiung with Meinong via Qishan (departs hrly; ⏰ 07.00–21.40 daily; 1½hrs; NTD136).

 WHERE TO STAY AND EAT *Map, page 251*
Most visitors do Meinong as a day trip, but there are a handful of accommodation options should you wish to spend the night.

🏠 **Chung-Chen Lake Resort Inn** 中正湖民宿 (33 rooms) 30 Fumei Rd; ✆681 7783; w chungchen.mmweb.tw. Named after the small lake north of Meinong's old town centre, Chung-Chen Lake Resort Inn's bland rooms are more than made up for by the excellent views through the windows (or from the balconies that some rooms have). Showers only, no bathtubs. Rooms in the older building are significantly cheaper; a couple can stay on a w/day for NTD1,500. B/fast by arrangement. **$$$**

✗ **Wu's Meinong Ban-Tiao** 吳美濃粄條 20 Zhongzheng Rd; ✆682 0188; ⏰ 09.00–18.30 Tue–Sun. Unpretentious & good value for money, Wu's has all the usual Hakka favourites, not only ban-tiao. Very near the main bus stop. No EM. **$$**

✗ **Yuan Xiang Yuan Cultural Village** 原鄉緣文化村 km36.7 Hwy 28; ✆681 0888; ⏰ 09.00–17.30 daily. Consider the restaurant inside this souvenir-selling centre if there's 3 or more of you. Hakka staples at reasonable prices inc ban-tiao & pig's foot. For something different, order a portion of stuffed bitter melon (*kǔguāfēng* 苦瓜封). Coffees & teas inc *léi chá* (here called 'pestle cereal') start at NTD100. EM. **$$**

✗ **Bafang Yunji** 八方雲集 11 Zhongzheng Rd Sec 1; ✆681 8777; ⏰ 10.30–21.00 daily. This island-wide chain serves up a good range of boiled & potsticker dumplings inc curry, shrimp & spicy options. A dozen dumplings with a soup makes for a good lunch. On the other side of the road from Wu's Meinong Ban-Tiao. EM. **$**

SHOPPING Beautifully painted oil-paper parasols are Meinong's trademark souvenir and small ones that'll fit in your hand luggage start at NTD500. You can buy them (and see them being made) at Yuan Xiang Yuan Cultural Village (see above) as well as at **Meinong Folk Village** 美濃民俗村 (80 Lane 421, Zhongshan Rd Sec 2; ⏰ 681 7508; ⏰ 08.30–17.00 daily), just off the main road. Kids like this place as there's space to run and play, while parents browse the parasols, fans and Buddha statuettes.

OTHER PRACTICALITIES
✉ **Post office** 39 Zhongzheng Rd Sec 1; ⏰ 08.30–17.00 Mon–Fri, 09.00–noon Sat

WHAT TO SEE AND DO
Guangshan Temple 廣善堂 Meinong's most attractive place of worship (established 1915) abuts the hills and is subtly different from many Taiwanese temples, the colours being more like those found in shrines established by ethnic Chinese in southeast Asia. Altars are dedicated to various deities including the Jade Emperor and Wenchang Dijun; the offices where records are kept look like they've not been refurbished since the 1950s. The single-storey building on the right as you face the temple was a school during the colonial era.

Tobacco leaves have to be cured soon after harvesting, so from 1937 onward Meinong's farmers started building curing sheds. These slope-roof buildings typically cover about 40m², each of which has two floors and a ventilation shaft on top. Some sheds are brick, others are concrete while a few are made of wattle and daub. The wattle consists of slats of split bamboo; the daub is a mix of clay, soil, rice straw, chaff and pig dung.

The drying of the leaves was achieved by flue curing. A fire would be set under the floor of the shed's central chamber so hot air (but neither smoke nor sparks) would circulate around the leaves. Farmers or their wives would stay up throughout the night to monitor the temperature.

Yongan Road 永安路 **and Boai Street** 博愛街 Dozens of traditional single-storey houses, most of them still inhabited by the descendants of those who built them, can be seen on and near these two streets in central Meinong, just south of Wu's Meinong Ban-Tiao restaurant.

Meinong Hakka Museum 美濃客家文物館 (49-3 Minzu Rd; ✆ 681 8338; ⏰ 09.00–17.00 Tue–Sun; admission NTD40/20) The exterior of this museum was designed to resemble a curing shed and inside, the entire field-to-cigarette process is explained in detail. Other displays focus on traditional Hakka clothing. English-language tours are sometimes available; if you're hoping for one, get a Chinese speaker to phone a day or two before your visit.

Shuangxi Tropical Viviparous Forest 雙溪熱帶母樹林 (⏰ 24hrs daily; free admission) Just beyond the outskirts of Meinong, turn left at Chaoyuan Temple 朝元寺 and you'll very soon come to a small car park on your left. You can enter the forest here but if you're neither a botanist nor an arborist your stop will probably not exceed an hour. Nonetheless, it's worth noting the reserve's exceptional biodiversity and the reason for it. The Japanese colonial authorities brought in at least 270 tree species from as far away as South America and nurtured them here to learn which could thrive in Taiwan. Of the 97 exotic species that remain, 27 are found nowhere else in Taiwan. Unfortunately, few of the trees are labelled – to protect rare specimens from theft, perhaps. The trail leads to some benches; the able-bodied should follow the ropes and scramble up to a point 198m above sea level from which there are fine views to the west.

Yellow Butterfly Valley 黃蝶翠谷 Between May and July this lush valley near Shuangxi Tropical Viviparous Forest sees millions of lemon emigrants (*Catopsilia pomona*). Despite their name, these lepidopterans spend their entire lives within the watershed. During the summer you can be pretty sure of seeing small groups of butterflies lapping minerals from shallow pools; if you're lucky, you'll find yourself in a cluster of thousands. Farming and urbanisation have destroyed many of Taiwan's insect habitats, but the vast number of butterflies here is – like the diversity in Shuangxi Tropical Viviparous Forest – due to man's interfering with nature. Before World War I the colonial authorities planted hop-hornbeam trees in the area. The wood is exceptionally hard and was to be used for making railway sleepers and rifle stocks, but the leaves happen to be a favourite food of lemon emigrant larvae. More than a hundred other butterfly species can be spotted in the valley during the warmer months. Bring a picnic and spend a few hours here.

Maolin is best known for its remarkable Purple Butterfly Valley, one of the world's two major wintering spots for butterflies. Unlike Mexico's better-known Monarch Butterfly Valley, which attracts just one species, this valley draws swarms of dwarf crows, chocolate tigers, striped blue crows and other lepidopterans.

Even if you've no interest in butterflies, consider visiting Maolin for its rampant birdlife and meandering creeks. Throughout the valley you'll see snakes represented in carvings and images, for Maolin is a stronghold of the Rukai tribe. The Tapakadawane (Black Rice) Festival, the tribe's main annual public celebration, is held in November or December and features tribal songs and dances.

GETTING THERE AND AWAY
By car, motorcycle or bicycle From Meinong it's 19km to Maolin via Highway 28. If you're approaching from the south, Road 185 (page 257) is recommended. Once you reach **Dajin** 大津, follow Local Road 132 into the valley. Duona is 14.5km from the junction with Highway 28.

By bus On weekdays, H31 buses leave Qishan for Duona via Maolin at 08.50, 13.45 and 17.20 (25mins; NTD60). On weekends there are six buses (⊕ 07.50–15.45) but there's been talk of cancelling these services. Alternatively, take one of the seven daily #8218 buses from Pingtung to Dajin (⊕ 09.00–20.55; NTD106). Unless you've arranged to be picked up from Dajin, you'll have to walk or hitch a ride. It's 8km from Dajin to Duona Suspension Bridge.

 WHERE TO STAY AND EAT Almost all of the valley's inhabitants live in the villages of Maolin (Teldreka in Rukai), Wanshan (Oponoho) or Duona (Kungadavane). Noodles and other simple dishes are available at eateries in Maolin and Duona. The Maolin National Scenic Area website (w www.maolin-nsa.gov.tw) offers plenty of information about accommodation and eating options in the region.

De'en Gorge B&B 得恩谷的民宿 (14 rooms) Near Maolin Valley; m 0955 055 132; f @deengorge.guesthouse. With English-speaking environmentally conscious indigenous owners, De'en Gorge B&B has 2 kinds of room – basic but clean 4-person dorms with bath, & spacious rooms each with 2 dbl beds. No AC but none needed; no TV. Dinner available but must be ordered 3 days in advance so ingredients can be gathered. Camping allowed. To find this place, take the road down towards Maolin Valley but turn left instead of right after crossing the river; it's 700m up the road. **$$$**

SHOPPING
Ubake Creative Workshop 烏巴克創藝工作坊 116 Maolin Vlg; ☎680 1035; ⊕ 08.00–21.00 Sun–Fri. Acclaimed artists Ubake & his wife, who live below Maolin Village on a terrace overlooking the river, make & sell a wide range of indigenous glass-bead & leather arts.

WHAT TO SEE AND DO
Purple Butterfly Valley 紫蝶幽谷 **(Zĭdié Yōugŭ)** The 'valley' isn't a single location that people can point out on a map but rather a chain of hillsides where migrating butterflies feed and rest. At times, a single tree may host well over 1,000 lepidopterans. To find the best butterflying spots, enlist the help of those who know the area very well, such as the family that runs De'en Gorge B&B (see above).

The four purple-crow butterfly species that winter in Maolin spend the hot season 250km to the north where it's a little cooler. Eggs are laid at both ends of the route and left to fend for themselves; because few butterflies live more than eight months, the migration is a once-in-a-lifetime journey. A bilingual exhibition about the butterflies can be found in the lobby of the **Fengshan Farmers' Association Maolin Activity Centre** 鳳山區農會茂林辦事處 (✆ 680 1115; ⊕ 07.00–19.00 daily). There's no English sign outside but this tile-faced building, on the left as you approach from the lowlands, is the largest structure in the main village of Maolin. Rooms for two people are sometimes available here (**$$**) but often the place is fully booked by groups.

Maolin Valley 茂林谷
Opposite the fire/ambulance station just north of Maolin Village, a steep side road goes down to and across the river. Turn right and park. Hiking up the creek is a very pleasurable way to spend an hour or two.

Mei Ya Waterfall 美雅谷瀑布
Just past the village of Wanshan you'll see a bilingual signpost pointing 1.9km to this scenic spot. Follow the road to its very end. The little waterfall on the left isn't the main attraction; to get to Mei Ya Waterfall you'll need to hike for around 40 minutes. Typhoons often damage this path.

Duona Suspension Bridge 多納高吊橋
Tourists flock to this 232m-long bridge, roughly equidistant between the villages of Maolin and Duona, to enjoy dizzying views over the river far below. For locals it's merely another part of the road network, so watch out for motorcycles and even narrow-wheelbase trucks zipping across while you dally.

Hongchen Gorge 紅塵峽谷
At km14 on Local Road 132 turning right will take you to Duona; going left leads to a gorge where riverside hot springs were destroyed by Typhoon Morakot. Don't try to take a car all the way to the river but those on two wheels will do fine. At the turn-off on Local Road 132 an information board relates the discovery between 1978 and 2008 of 14 prehistoric rock carvings not far from here.

Duona 多納
This compact village, 450m above sea level, has considerable character thanks to its traditional slate homes. Admirable efforts have been made to get some of the modern buildings to fit in by covering their concrete walls with slate. If you go to the very end of the main street, which also happens to be the end of Local Road 132, you can look down over a large terrace where Duona's residents grow rice and other crops. The main reason to go beyond the village is to hike to **Ghost Axe Canyon** 鬼斧神宮, but this should not be attempted alone or without careful planning.

NORTHERN KAOHSIUNG *Telephone code 07*

SOUTH CROSS-ISLAND HIGHWAY 南橫公路 Formerly the most spectacular way of getting from southwest Taiwan to Taitung, the high-altitude sections of this road (Highway 20) were ravaged by Typhoon Morakot (page 21) and the highway has never properly reopened, although a few adventurous individuals on bicycles have made it all the way to the east. At the time of writing even that was impossible; how far you'll be allowed to proceed before being turned back at a police checkpoint depends on recent rainfall (which can trigger landslides) and whether reconstruction has progressed.

Do enquire if the road is open past Meishan as the alpine vistas beyond more than justify the amount of driving involved, even if you need to eventually turn

8

back. If you go further than Jiaxian you'll pass through a series of small settlements including Baolai, a hot-springs resort fallen on hard times, and mainly Bunun villages such as Tauyuan. Meishan (Mashowaru in Bunun) is 1,014m above sea level and just inside Yushan National Park, from where the road climbs relentlessly, the highest point being slightly over 2,700m above sea level.

HIGHWAY 29 If Highway 20 is closed, consider venturing north from Jiaxian on Highway 29. It needn't be a dead end – there's a back road to Chashan (page 232) – and soon you'll see some very fine scenery.

Jiaxian 甲仙 Coming from Tainan, this is the first town you'll encounter within Kaohsiung. Although there isn't much to see, it does have petrol stations, shops and a sideline in taro-flavoured ice cream. If you're approaching Jiaxian from the south, Local Road 128 is a scenic alternative that'll appeal to cyclists and others keen to avoid the heavy traffic where highways 20 and 29 meet.

Wulipu 五里埔 This plateau, some 5km north of Jiaxian, is now home to some of those who escaped when Typhoon Morakot obliterated the nearby village of Xiaolin. Before the calamity, Xiaolin had begun drawing the attention of scholars who realised its inhabitants had preserved a significant amount of indigenous Siraya culture (see box, page 216). Located on the right side of the road if you're approaching from Jiaxian, **Xiaolin Pingpu Culture Museum** 小林平埔族群文物館 (✆ 676 1168; ⊕ 09.00–noon & 13.00–17.00 Tue–Sun; free admission) isn't worth more than a very quick look unless you read Chinese and have a serious interest in Taiwan's aborigines. Just past the village on the right you'll notice **Jhen-hai Cemetery** 鎮海將軍墓 (⊕ 24hrs daily). The 70-odd tombs date from around 1886 when imperial soldiers were deployed here to take control of the mountains and reopen long-distance trails. Dozens died of malaria and the roughly hewn gravestones are touchingly simple. On each, crudely incised characters give the deceased's name and a few other details. The graveyard's location seems to prove the adage that in Taiwan, dead folk get the best places to live.

Around the next corner, **Xiaolin Memorial Park** 小林村紀念公園 is a sombre commemoration of the 462 Xiaolin residents who perished in the Morakot calamity. There are 181 Formosan cherry trees, one for each family, plus a simple shrine where relatives and survivors burn incense.

Holy Mount Zion 錫安山 **(Xīān Shān)** (⊕ 670 1218; w home.ziongjcc.org; ⊕ 06.00–17.30 daily) Bilingual signs point the way to this Christian commune, 2.8km from Highway 29 via a steep but safe side road. The sect based here is a non-mainstream denomination called the New Testament Church (NTC). Founded in the early 1960s by Hong Kong actress Kong Duen-Yee (1923–66), it has been led for four decades by Elijah Hong, a Taiwanese man whom some consider a fraud. According to the Church's multi-lingual website, Hong ('the Prophet of All Nations', as he's styled by his Church), was led by God to this mountain. Believers clashed repeatedly with the authorities but 'after more than a decade of labour and toil, this wild mountain was transformed into a beautiful Eden'. These days the 300-odd residents raise rabbits and ostriches and engage in organic farming. The entire site is extremely clean and orderly; if you're not curious about alternative lifestyles, however, it's of little interest. Non-Christian visitors, who can buy plums, aloe vera, reishi, mulberry juice and other products, are very welcome so long as they don't enter restricted areas, smoke, drink alcohol, gamble or picnic. Nor, the website warns, should they bring with them 'idols, charms, beads, incense sticks and other idol-related items'.

NAMASIA 那瑪夏 (**NÀMĂXIÀ**) The name of this district reflects the indigenous heritage of the valley's inhabitants, Namasia being the Tsou name of the river that drains this beautiful valley. The villages are also known by indigenous names: Nangisaru, Maya and Takanuwa. Nowadays Tsou account for one-sixth of the population; after the tribe was decimated by epidemics in the 19th century, Bunun clans moved in from the north and eventually became the majority. Further complicating the local ethnic map, in 2014 the Kanakanavu (who live in two of the three villages) and the Hla'alua (who reside in the adjacent district of **Tauyuan** 桃源) became the 15th and 16th tribes recognised by Taiwan's government. During the dry season, tourists come here to hike, buy plums and mountain greens directly from farmers, and pitch their tents at one of the several campgrounds.

NORTHERN PINGTUNG COUNTY *Telephone code 08*

PINGTUNG CITY 屏東市 (**PÍNGDŌNG SHÌ**) There's nothing wrong with Pingtung County's capital (population: 200,000) but to describe its sights would be to damn it with faint praise. Given its proximity to Maolin, Sandimen and other indigenous communities, spending more than an hour here would be a deplorable waste. Instead, it's better to use the city as a transport base and head inland. Everything you need is within 150m of the TRA station: for long-distance and local buses, turn left as you exit the station; to change money, walk directly away from the TRA station and keep an eye out for the bank on your right. For more information on the wider region, check out the Pingtung County Government website (w i-pingtung.com).

Getting there and away
By TRA Pingtung City is well served by trains from Kaohsiung (about 75 departures daily; ⊕ 05.12–00.19; 19–27mins; NTD31–48). Expresses to Taitung can be boarded here (16 departures daily; ⊕ 05.36–21.46; 2–3hrs; NTD242–314). There's also a visitor information centre inside the station (⊕ 07.00–21.00 daily).

By bus By the time you read this the city's bus stations should have been consolidated in a single building outside the railway station. Kuo-Kuang has services to Taipei (#1839; departs at least hrly; ⊕ 07.00–02.00; 5¼hrs; NTD610) and Taichung (#1873; departs hrly; ⊕ 06.30–21.30; 3¼hrs; NTD350).

Useful local services include buses to Donggang (various routes; at least 3 departures hrly; ⊕ 05.50–22.10; about 1hr; NTD82–106) and Wutai via Sandimen (#8233; departs at 07.45, 09.30 & 14.30 daily; 1¼hrs; NTD145). You can also get to Sandimen on some #8227 buses (50mins; NTD74). Of the four buses per day to Foguangshan, only the 07.40 and 11.00 departures would give you enough time to explore the monastery area (45mins; NTD78)

By car or motorcycle The Jiuru (km391) and Changzhi (km400) exits on Freeway 3 are both convenient. Motorcyclists are advised to take the more scenic Highway 3 rather than the faster but busier Highway 1.

ROAD 185 This north–south route connects Dajin near Maolin with Fangliao, hugging the base of the Central Mountain Range for most of its 69km and providing access to a number of intriguing indigenous districts. Traffic is usually very light. If you're short of time, skip the flatter southern half.

Getting there and around No buses run the length of Road 185. If you're using public transport, focus your energies on Sandimen. If you're driving from the north, consider approaching through Meinong as Highway 28 will bring you to Dajin where you can explore Maolin before heading south along Road 185. From the Changzhi exit on Freeway 3, Highway 24 will get you to Shuimen quickly, but be careful to follow the road as it veers left; many mistakenly continue straight on. Coming from Kenting National Park, the Road 185/Highway 1 junction is just inland of central Fangliao.

This region is perfect for exploring on two wheels. There are few gradients on Road 185 itself but cyclists aiming for Wutai need to be in top condition.

TOURIST INFORMATION

🔢 Maolin National Scenic Area w www. maolin-nsa.gov.tw

🔢 Rinari Visitor Centre Rinari Vlg, Shuimen; ⏰ 08.30–17.30 daily

🏠 **Where to stay and eat** While driving along Highway 24, it's likely you'll see various indigenous stone barbecues along the route. Rather than cook on a metal grill over charcoal, several vendors in Sandimen and other indigenous communities place choice cuts on a slab of slate right above the fire. Because the juices don't immediately drain off, the meat is basted as well as roasted. For keen carnivores the results are exquisite. Mountain boar and sausages are among items usually cooked this way.

🏠 **Dream House** 夢想之家 (5 rooms) 38 Wutai Vlg; ☎790 2312; m 0989 836 450. Neither the owner – who like many others in this village has the Han surname Du – nor his family speak English but they're used to accommodating Western guests. The interior is filled with indigenous artefacts; room rates inc both b/fast & aboriginal-style dinner. 2 ppl can expect to pay around NTD3,000 at w/ends. For about NTD500 the owner will pick guests up from Sandimen or drive them on to Maolin. **$$$**

✕ **Qingshun Mountain Cuisine** 清順山產 3–2 Tongxing Rd, Yuanquan Vlg, Gaoshu; ☎796 1419; ⏰ 10.00–21.00 daily. A bit of a drive from any attractions but serving ultra-fresh traditional fare, this restaurant is worth seeking out if you want to try mountain rat (*shān shǔ* 山鼠), muntjac (*shān qiāng* 山羌), mountain boar (*shān zhū* 山豬) or frog (*qīngwā* 青蛙). Fish & freshwater shrimp are also available, as are some vegetables you're unlikely to see in lowland cities. There's no EM but ingredients are laid out in a refrigerator so customers can see what looks

good. Beer & soft drinks available; the Chinese menu doesn't list prices but reckon on spending NTD200–300 pp. No English sign; if you're heading south out of Gaoshu on Hwy 27, the restaurant is just past km34 on the left. **$$$**

✕ **Windy Place: Autumn Moon** 風刮地秋月的店 km24.3 Hwy 24, Sandimen; ☎799 1524; ⏰ 10.00–midnight Fri–Wed. Owned by notable Paiwan artist Sakuliu Pavavalung & his Han wife Li Qiu-yue (her given name translates as 'autumn moon'), this long-established restaurant attracts people as much for the views that can be had as for the food, which is hearty rather than gourmet. It's said on some mornings you can see Little Liuqiu; even if it's hazy you'll be able to watch eagles swoop after prey. Hot dishes available 11.00–14.00 & 17.00–22.00; for individuals, the most authentically indigenous is the Paiwan flavour set meal (*páiwān fēngwèi fàncān* 排灣風味飯餐, NTD450). Coffees & teas from NTD100; occasional live music. Partial EM. Located on the right, 1km beyond Sandimen on the road to Wutai. **$$$**

What to see and do Sights are listed north to south.

Qingye 青葉 This Rukai community is well kept and little touched by tourism. At weekends and after 16.00 you can enter the elementary school to view a replica slate house. Look inland from here and you're sure to see crested serpent eagles circling above the forest. There are a few shops and eateries between the school and the slate- and pebble-faced Catholic chapel. The only way into the village is via a short road heading inland just north of km6 on Road 185.

Shuimen 水門 (km25.5 Rd 185) A gateway to points inland such as Sandimen and Majia, Shuimen is notable for its Hoklo-Hakka-indigenous ethnic mix. There are a few small hotels, eateries and shops. The **Taiwan Indigenous Peoples Culture Park** 原住民族委員會文化園區 (\ 799 1219; w www.tacp.gov.tw; ⏲ 08.30–17.00 Tue–Sun; admission NTD150/80), a highly regarded attraction managed by the Council of Indigenous Peoples (the central government agency responsible for the welfare of Taiwan's aboriginal population), is 20 minutes' walk from the bus stops. Inside there are replicas of traditional buildings and displays of handicrafts and costumes as well as the song-and-dance performances you'd expect at more commercial establishments.

Sandimen 三地門 About 94% of Sandimen's 7,500 residents are indigenous and among them are Paiwan artisans who've won a reputation for crafting beautiful keepsakes using leather, wild boar's teeth and delicately coloured glass beads (see below). The main village is a compact settlement laid out on a steep hillside in a way that gives almost every household an excellent view over the plains. It's a good place to see typical aboriginal families: middle-aged fathers who divide their time between building work on the plains and small farms in the hills; housewives who collect wild taros and dry them on the tarmac; and teenagers more conversant with Mandarin rap than the Austronesian language of their ancestors.

In the village, two shops of note are worth seeking. On the left of the main thoroughfare just below the heart of Sandimen, **Dragonfly Beads Art Studio** 蜻蜓雅築珠藝工作室 (9 Zhongzheng Rd Sec 2; \ 799 2856; ⏲ 08.30–18.00 daily) continues to make the glass-bead jewellery that represents a revival of an indigenous tradition. Until well into the 20th century coloured beads were treasured by both Paiwan and Rukai ladies, as wearing them signified high social status. Dragonfly now has more than 20 full-time employees who use Bunsen burners to soften and melt thin sticks of glass with which they decorate thimble-sized beads. Each pattern has a particular meaning such as honour or wisdom. The peacock (*kurakuraw* in Paiwan) symbolises eternal love while the earth pattern (*cadacadaqan*) represents the acquisition of wealth. The shop's bilingual leaflet explains these motifs. There's no English sign so look for the giant model dragonfly on the roof.

Hidden in the backstreets on the left as you enter Sandimen's main village but with bilingual signs pointing the way, **Sha Tao Zazurite Art Studio** 沙滔舞琉璃藝術空間 (45 Lane 29, Zhongzheng Rd Sec 2; \ 799 3332; ⏲ 09.00–18.00 Tue–Sun) is owned by Shatao Matilin, founder of a renowned indigenous dance troupe (if you're lucky you'll see them rehearsing here). Visitors are welcome to browse glass-bead art and wander into the workshop at the back where usually three or four women are busy creating necklaces, pendants and other items. Belts, shawls and CDs are also sold here; credit cards accepted.

From Sandimen, consider detouring further into the mountains via Highway 24 to visit indigenous communities set in superb scenery.

Dewen 德文 At km26.8 on Highway 24 a police checkpoint (⏲ 06.00–18.00 daily) controls access to the mountains beyond. If the road is safe you'll be allowed

8

to proceed after writing down some personal details; there's no need to show ID. Take the side road on the left to Dewen, a Paiwan village that during the colonial period was reputed to grow Taiwan's best coffee. The road continues on to another Paiwan settlement, **Dashe** 大社, 13km from the turn-off. There's little reason to stop in either village but the vistas along the way are superb.

Shenshan 神山 The Chinese name of this cluster of houses at km39 on Highway 24 means 'holy mountain', which is appropriate because it's the site of one of Taiwan's most appealing Christian places of worship, **Shenshan Roman Catholic Church** (⊕ for services only). The highway switchbacks through Shenshan, and the church is in the upper village. Like a lot of houses in the valley it's a squat slate-covered structure with small windows through which you'll see rows of hand-carved wooden chairs, each one made to resemble a tribesman in traditional garb.

Wutai 霧台 The border between Sandimen and Wutai townships is also an ethnic boundary – the former is Paiwan, the latter Rukai. Indigenous culture has survived better here than in many other parts of Taiwan because the road completed by the Japanese in 1942 was abandoned after World War II and not reconstructed until 1972. *Wutai* is a Mandarin rendering of the Rukai toponym Vudai, while in Chinese, *Wùtái* means 'fog plateau' and the valley often lives up to this name – expect sudden mists. Of the 3,100 people registered as residents of the township, fewer than 50 are Han. However, barely half of the township's population stays here year-round because jobs are scarce and the nearest high school is in Shuimen. The settlement from which the township takes its name is at km41 and it's perhaps Taiwan's most attractive village. Concrete-and-tile box houses are very much the exception; most residents live in slate-walled, slate-roofed cottages that blend in with the valley's greens and greys. On the homes that line Wutai Art Street you'll see certain motifs again and again: crucifixes, white lilies, boars and hundred-pacer snakes – but not Formosan clouded leopards (page 6), which once roamed the mountains hereabouts. The nearby terraces will give you an idea of the valley's agricultural limitations; the fields of millet, corn and taro are quite tiny. Wutai's main **Presbyterian Church** (⊕ 09.00–17.30 daily) is a slate-covered edifice with striking indigenous features; the external staircase is adorned with a sculpture of life-size tribesmen dragging a tree trunk up a hill. Inside, the crucifix, twice the height of a man, consists of two varnished logs, while the altar is a massive knot of tree roots and the bibles on the shelves are in Rukai. Underscoring the fact that this isn't a Han community, several of the grave markers in the adjacent cemetery bear not a single Chinese character, the name of the deceased being recorded solely in romanised Rukai.

Majia 瑪家 Between Shuimen's town centre and the petrol station on Road 185, Local Road 35 leads to a Paiwan-dominated district. If you turn right at km2.5 you'll enter **Rinari** 禮納里, a new village where indigenous people resettled after Typhoon Morakot (page 21) made up of attractive, mostly wood houses. In Paiwan, *rinari* means 'let's go and live together'. Continuing uphill on Local Road 35 there are waterfalls and, at km10, a two-storey pavilion where you should stop to take in the panorama. The road is fine for normal cars as far as Majia Village at km14; only those on motorcycle, bicycle, or foot can proceed further, and then not very far and only with great caution.

Liangshan Waterfall 涼山瀑布 This spot just off the highway attracts hikers during the wetter months and understandably so. There's plenty of parking near km29.5 on Road 185; follow the signs up the surfaced road. You'll get your first sighting of the cascade after 10 minutes' walking. It's then another 20 minutes on a mostly flat and entirely gorgeous trail; birdwing butterflies and blue dragonflies are numerous in autumn. The final stage is short but involves getting your feet wet and holding ropes as you clamber to the base of the fall.

Wanjin Basilica Minore 萬金聖母聖殿 (24 Wanxing Rd, Wanluan; ⏰ 06.00–21.30 daily; free admission) Bilingual signposts make finding Taiwan's oldest church very easy if you're coming from Road 185. When you see an army base on the left, prepare to turn right and drive about 1.5km. Located in what's probably the island's only Catholic-majority village – you'll see several Marian grottos – the current Spanish-style edifice, completed in 1870, is quite different from other churches in Taiwan. Spanish Dominican Father Fernando Sainz (1832–95) chose this village because he believed its mainly indigenous population would be more receptive to missionary work than nearby Hakka communities. He was right, making dozens of conversions in the first few years. He bought land here in 1863 but the adobe church he had built was destroyed by an earthquake two years later. In 1867 Sainz was kidnapped and held for ransom by Hakka bandits. The church suffered repeated arson attacks by anti-Christians (who alleged the Catholics made medicine out of human corpses) until 1874, when Emperor Tongzhi in Beijing ordered an inscription be added to show the mission enjoyed imperial protection. The stone on which the two-character message was engraved is little bigger than a notebook but can be seen high above the main entrance. A few ecclesiastical artefacts are displayed upstairs.

Wugoushui 五溝水 This splendidly preserved and extremely picturesque village, less than 2km from Wanjin, was founded in the early 18th century by Hakka settlers who dug a network of irrigation channels (Wugoushui means 'five ditches'). The most opulent structure is the Liu Ancestral Hall (near the elementary school; private but visitors usually allowed into the courtyard), built 1887–1921. The hall isn't easy to find but those who enjoy random exploring on foot or two wheels will enjoy the settlement and its surroundings. No 28 Xisheng Road (not open to the public) used to be a school.

SOUTHERN PINGTUNG COUNTY *Telephone code 08*

There's no need to hug the coast if you're heading towards Kenting but if you take Freeway 3 to its southern end you'll bypass the first two of the following destinations.

DONGGANG 東港 **(DŌNGGǍNG)** Unless you've a passion for seafood, the only reasons to visit this sizeable harbour town (population: 48,000) are to catch a ferry to Little Liuqiu or attend the King's Ship Festival, a triennial boat-burning extravaganza that will be held next in autumn 2021 (see box, page 262). If your stomach is rumbling look for the Huaqiao Seafood Market, which, like the ferry terminal, is in the township's northwestern extremity. Many of the market's smaller eateries (⏰ varies; $$$ specialise in sashimi, but for a broader range of options, including shark cooked with ginger, garlic and pickled cabbage (*suāncài chǎo shāyú* 酸菜炒鯊魚, NTD300) head to **Fuhaixian** 福海鮮 (m 0986 523 563; ⏰ 10.00–19.00 daily; EM; $$$), on the far left as you enter from the main road. If you need to park your car while you eat at the market or visit Little Liuqiu, the simplest option for travellers who don't speak Chinese is the multi-storey car park opposite the market. Signs point the way to **Donglong Temple** 東隆宮 (⏰ 05.30–

21.30 daily) where the main object of worship is Marshal Wen, a 7th-century scholar deified for saving the life of a Tang Dynasty emperor. This otherwise run-of-the-mill temple organises the King's Ship Festival and displays the vessel in the months before the burning.

Getting there and away Buses #9117 and #9127 from Kaohsiung stop in Donggang (around 4 departures per hr; ⊕ 04.15–22.30 daily; about 1hr; NTD111–125), and there are also frequent buses from Pingtung (various routes; takes about 1hr; NTD82–106). For those driving or riding, Highway 17 is the most direct route to Donggang from Kaohsiung but traffic can be heavy and the scenery isn't good. Consider exiting Kaohsiung via Expressway 88 (if in a car) or Highway 1 and then taking back roads southward. On the final night of the festival it's usually possible to park within walking distance of Donglong Temple if you get there before dusk.

DAPENG BAY 大鵬灣 Unlike some other parts of Taiwan's coast, which have been repeatedly reshaped by typhoons, Dapeng Bay has remained stable for centuries. One of Taiwan's largest lagoons (3.5km long and almost 2km wide), the bay is slowly developing into a centre for yachting and windsurfing. There's a 16.4km-long cycle path (free if you have your own bike), artificial wetlands that attract migrant waterbirds between November and January, and a camping ground.

Getting there and away Board a #9117 or #9127 bus from Kaohsiung and get off at km258 on Highway 17 (1¼hrs; NTD138), from where clear signs point the

BURNING THE KING'S SHIP

Ritual boat-burnings happen at several places in Taiwan's south, but no event is more spectacular than Donggang's King's Ship Festival. Preparations begin more than a year ahead of the burning with divination rites to ascertain the precise dimensions of the wooden junk that's to be constructed and sacrificed. Usually about 14m long and always fantastically decorated, recent boats have cost over £250,000 each. The eight days before the actual burning feature elaborate rituals throughout the town. On the final day, volunteers push the vessel through Donggang's streets as the ship is believed to act like a supernatural magnet, drawing disease and malevolence on board.

When it returns to Donglong Temple, offerings and supplies are loaded to placate the Wang Ye spirits (page 33) who've been hoodwinked into boarding. Among the items placed on board are dice for gambling, tobacco and pipes, inkstones and calligraphy brushes for writing, plus woks, food, oil and condiments for cooking. After midnight, the boat is dragged to a nearby beach; the masts are put in place, the sails unfurled and the anchors raised. Bales of joss paper (see box, page 98) are piled around the hull and, an hour before dawn, set alight with firecrackers. Flames consume the boat with surprising speed; seeing the hull blacken and collapse as the sky brightens is a truly unforgettable experience. The crowd soon thins because many locals wish to witness only the start of the conflagration. They leave as soon as they're confident the evils aboard have been consigned to another world. Stick around and by dawn you'll be able to get as close to the still-burning wreckage as the heat allows.

way to the Dapeng Bay National Scenic Area Headquarters (✆ 833 8100; w www.dbnsa.gov.tw; ⏰ 09.00–18.00 daily). Cars should take Freeway 3 to its southern end then turn right on to Highway 17 and follow the signs. Bicycles can be rented from Pen Bay Cycles (⏰ 09.00–18.00 daily; from NTD150/4hrs) about 200m south of the scenic area office.

JIADONG 佳冬 Hardly big enough to be called a town, Jiadong boasts south Taiwan's finest private mansion, the **Hsiao Family Residence** 蕭家古厝 (m 0932 200 024; ⏰ 09.00–17.00 daily; admission NTD50/30). Wealthy thanks to winemaking and cloth dyeing, the Hsiao family had this 51-room complex built in stages from the 1860s to the beginning of the 20th century. Several of the craftsmen who worked on it were brought in from Fujian and much of the wood in the five halls was imported from the Chinese mainland. Hexagonal and rectangular entrances link different parts of the mansion but are deliberately unaligned; it was believed that having one doorway facing another was like setting one person's mouth in opposition to the mouth of another, and would lead to relatives arguing. The vast ceramic pot that now stands in a hallway served as a one-person air-raid shelter during World War II. Get a Chinese speaker to call ahead if you plan to visit on a weekday as the clan members who staff the entrance and show visitors around sometimes take extra days off.

Once you're done at the Hsiao residence do go for a wander; there are other highly characterful old buildings within walking distance such as the tasteful century-old **Yang Clan Shrine** 楊氏宗祠 (⏰ most daylight hours; unbolt the gate if closed) on the northwestern edge of town.

Getting there and away Rail travellers will need to change at Chaozhou, from where 15 trains per day stop at Jiadong (⏰ 05.56–23.39; 45mins; NTD48). Kenting-bound buses (from Kaohsiung takes 1½hrs; NTD153) stop on Highway 17 about 400m from the mansion. Self-driving visitors should approach via Highway 17.

KAYOUFENG FALLS 卡悠峯瀑布 Visible from the South Link Railway (page 295), this pretty 40m-tall waterfall is perfect if you want to get out of heavy traffic on the coast road for an hour or more. There's no English sign at the turn off at km452.3 on Highway 1; look for the road heading inland just south of the petrol station and follow it through the mango orchards as it becomes a concrete track. It's fine for ordinary cars but watch out for pot-holes and trucks loaded with watermelons cultivated down by the river during the cooler months. After 3.95km a small Chinese-only sign directs visitors to the left. From there it's another 3.7km to the official car park which at the time of writing was closed due to typhoon damage. Two-wheelers could still approach the trailhead but larger vehicles had to stop a few hundred metres away; parking beside the road is possible but don't be surprised if a farmer asks for NTD200. The trail to the fall (where the pool is too shallow for swimming) is 510m long and includes many steps. Take care not to tread in monkey faeces; some farmers hereabouts have resorted to electric fences to keep macaques away from their fruit trees.

MUSEUM OF MARINE BIOLOGY AND AQUARIUM 海洋生物博物館 **(HǍIYÁNG SHĒNGWÙ BÓWÙGUǍN)** (Local Road 153, Checheng; ✆ 882 5001; w www.nmmba.gov.tw; ⏰ 09.00–17.30 daily; admission NTD450/250) This highly informative and child-friendly museum has interactive displays about coral reefs, the world's oceans and Taiwan's maritime environment. The English-language website has a schedule of shows and feeding times featuring whales, sharks and penguins.

Getting there and away The #101 bus from Eluanbi via Hengchun stops here (departs every 30mins; ⊕ 08.45–15.45 daily; takes 15mins from Hengchun; NTD26; from Eluanbi takes 45mins; NTD76). A taxi from Checheng, the nearest town served by Kaohsiung–Kenting buses, costs upwards of NTD200.

HENGCHUN 恆春 **(HÉNGCHŪN)** The compact town of Hengchun ('permanent springtime') has been given a facelift in recent years. At the same time, it's succeeded in making itself a destination in its own right rather than simply a place that feeds and waters through traffic and takes the overspill when Kenting is booked out. Coming from the north, just outside the town you'll see a model of a moon guitar, a two-stringed banjo-like instrument that features prominently in both Taiwanese opera and Hengchun folk. The latter is a traditional form of music that's been compared to Mississippi Delta Blues and which has enjoyed a minor revival in recent years. The town's main attraction is the city wall, especially the south and east gates. Bilingual signs guide those exploring on foot.

Getting there and away All Kaohsiung–Kenting buses stop along Highway 26 in central Hengchun; from Kaohsiung the journey time is at least 2 hours (NTD306). Self-drivers can approach by Highway 26 or Road 200 (page 268).

KENTING NATIONAL PARK 墾丁國家公園
(KĚNDĪNG GUÓJIĀ GŌNGYUÁN) *Telephone code 08*

Taiwan's first national park, established in 1984, has been more of a tourist-industry triumph than a conservation success, its record having been marred by squabbles over beach access. However, the park authorities have made some progress in recent years, closing down undesirable businesses (such as noisy go-kart circuits) and trying to balance environmentalist ideals with the rights of human residents, some of whom have lived in the area for generations and resent being told how they can or can't use their land.

Millions of visitors pass through the park each year, occasionally jamming the coast road, and much of the area suffers from congestion and overdevelopment. Nevertheless, there's plenty to do without dipping your toes in the ocean. If you can, escape to the hinterland to enjoy scenes of bucolic beauty, excellent birdwatching (the region has 31 of Taiwan's 33 diurnal raptor species) and some truly pleasurable motoring. Alternatively, head out to sea and under the waves with one of Kenting's English-speaking scuba instructors.

GETTING THERE AND AWAY
By car, motorcycle or bicycle Between Fangliao and Checheng, road users have no alternative to Highway 1 (which becomes Highway 26) along the coast, so be prepared for heavy traffic. Between early July and late October each year, Kenting National Park asks drivers to slow down, especially at night, because thousands of female land crabs from at least 25 species scamper across busy roads while making their way to the ocean where they lay their eggs. Around full moons, the coastal road is sometimes closed for a few hours to increase the crabs' survival chances.

By bus There are lots of buses from Kaohsiung, including the #9188 (every 30mins; ⊕ 06.00–22.00 daily; 2¾hrs; NTD340). Between 08.45 and 21.45, one of these services starts from Kaohsiung Zuoying HSR station (takes 3hrs to Kenting; NTD359). The #9127 and #9189 routes are slightly slower.

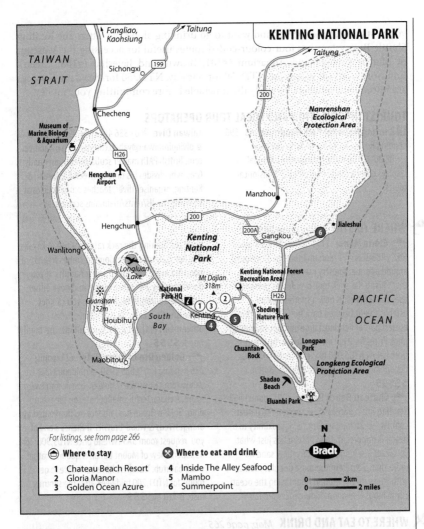

KENTING NATIONAL PARK

Fangliao, Kaohsiung

Taitung

Taitung

TAIWAN
STRAIT

Sichongxi · [199]

Checheng

Museum of
Marine Biology
& Aquarium

[H26]

Hengchun
Airport

Manzhou

Hengchun

[200]

[200A] Gangkou

Wanlitong

Longluan
Lake

Kenting
National
Park

Kenting National Forest
Recreation Area

[6] · Jialeshui

Guanshan
152m

National
Park HQ

Houbihu

Mt Dajian
318m

① ③

②

⑤

Sheding
Nature Park

[H26]

PACIFIC

OCEAN

*South
Bay*

Kenting

④

Nanrenshan
Ecological
Protection Area

Chuanfan
Rock

Longpan
Park

Longkeng Ecological
Protection Area

Maobitou

Shadao
Beach

Eluanbi Park

For listings, see from page 266

⊖ Where to stay
1 Chateau Beach Resort
2 Gloria Manor
3 Golden Ocean Azure

❌ Where to eat and drink
4 Inside The Alley Seafood
5 Mambo
6 Summerpoint

N

Bradt

0 ———— 2km
0 ———— 2 miles

By taxi Outside Kaohsiung's HSR and main stations you'll be approached by taxi drivers offering rides to Kenting for around NTD400 per person. Solo travellers may have to wait while the driver rustles up more passengers, but if you're a trio or a quartet you'll be able to leave right away. Compared with the bus, you'll save time and be delivered direct to your hotel.

GETTING AROUND

By hired motorcycle Many of the smaller hotels on Kending Road can help arrange scooter and/or e-scooter rentals (to guests and non-guests) and there are other rental businesses near the western end of the road. If the first place you try isn't satisfied with your papers, you can try another, but there's no guarantee any of them will be willing to rent to a tourist from overseas.

By bus The buses that ply the main road until late at night mean you can hop between South Bay and Kending Road (NTD23) at your leisure, a useful option if

Kaohsiung and Pingtung KENTING NATIONAL PARK

8

265

you're staying at the former and want to go drinking along the latter. The Kenting Shuttle Bus system has four colour-coded routes useful for accessing the Museum of Marine Biology and Aquarium (#101, Brown) and Jialeshui (#103, Green). Jump-on/jump-off passes are NTD150 for one day, NTD250 for two days. Services are infrequent, however, so study the timetable before committing your money.

TOURIST INFORMATION AND LOCAL TOUR OPERATORS

ℹ Kenting National Park Headquarters 596 Kending Rd; ✆886 1321; w ktnp.gov.tw; ⊕ 08.00–17.00 daily. Informative bilingual displays cover a range of ecological & historical topics.

Taiwan Dive ✆07 336 4571; m 0905 002 692; e divingintaiwan@yahoo.com.tw; w taiwandive. com. British PADI master scuba diver trainer Andy Gray, who divides his time between Kaohsiung & Kenting, organises dives, teaches scuba courses at all levels & sells/rents/maintains scuba gear.

🏠 WHERE TO STAY *Map, page 265*

🏠 Gloria Manor (171 rooms) 101 Gongyuan Rd; ✆886 3666; w gloriamanor.com. Developed around a former forestry management office that Chiang Kai-shek took over for his personal use, Gloria Manor is now a spotless luxury establishment situated back from & above the busiest part of Kenting. Large outdoor swimming pool. Prices for 2 ppl inc excellent b/fast range from below NTD6,000 to well over NTD12,000 depending on season, view & dinner option. **$$$$$**

🏠 Chateau Beach Resort (293 rooms) 451 Kending Rd; ✆886 2345; e service@ktchateau. com.tw; w ktchateau.com.tw. If proximity to a beach is important, the Chateau has just what you want – a long stretch of yellow sand no more than 50m from the most popular rooms, with those on the ground floor facing the ocean. Furnishings & in-room indulgences are fairly

basic considering the rack rates but use of kayaks & other watersports equipment comes free. 3 pools for kids plus a deep one for adults. If you decide to stay 2 or more nights midweek either side of the summer high season, you can get some great package deals. Neither b/fast nor other meals in the hotel's 3 restaurants are highly rated. **$$$$**

🏠 Golden Ocean Azure Hotel (21 rooms) 336 Kending Rd; ✆886 1050; e golden0933@ yahoo.com.tw; w www.golden-beach.com.tw/ azure. A characterful smaller hotel on the main drag, Golden Ocean has large rooms dominated by oranges, reds & wood-browns. If there's 3 or 4 of you, request room 3A5 (w/end price NTD3,900) for its superb view of Mount Dajian & quaint if rather small bathtub. Travellers have been able to get rooms for NTD1,200 midweek after the summer rush. B/fast inc. **$$$**

🍴 WHERE TO EAT AND DRINK *Map, page 265*

Kenting has a highly competitive dining scene so keep your eyes open for new bars and restaurants.

🍴 Inside The Alley Seafood 巷子內海鮮熱炒 9–3 Haibin Lane; ✆886 1536; ⊕ 11.00–14.30 & 17.00–21.30 daily. If you're not accompanied by a Chinese speaker, point to the pictures on the wall (or what others are eating) to order in this thoroughly local stir-fry joint, centrally located in a backstreet between Kending Rd & the sea. Prices are quite reasonable & they're willing to accommodate vegetarians. If you're not a fan of seafood, go for a pork dish or 3-cup chicken (*sān bēi jī* 三杯雞, NTD250/350). **$$$**

🍴 Mambo 曼波泰式料理 46 Kending Rd; ✆886 2878; ⊕ 11.00–14.30 & 17.00–22.00 daily. Having been around for the better part of 2 decades, this large Thai restaurant has got its act together. Service is polite & rapid, the food is consistently good. Few dishes – the range of Thai & Taiwanese options is broad – are priced more than NTD300 & there's no service charge. The music can be a bit loud, so grab one of the outside tables. Thai & local beers available. EM. **$$$**

✖ Summerpoint 252 Chashan Rd, Jialeshui; **m** 0936 160 006; **w** www.summerpoint.com. tw; ⊕ 09.00–approx 16.00 daily. The best eating option on this side of the peninsula & especially popular with surfers, Summerpoint is also a B&B (7 rooms, 1 dorm; **$$$**). Sandwiches, burgers, salads & all-day b/fasts start at NTD180. Indoor & outdoor seating; EM; located within walking distance of the Jialeshui ticket gate. **$$**

WHAT TO SEE AND DO Tourists interested in ecology would do well to start at the National Park Hedquarters (see opposite) where there are some in-depth displays.

Assuming you've arrived from Kaohsiung via Highway 26, you're likely to hit the sights in this order.

Longluan Lake 龍鑾潭 (⊕ 08.30–17.00 daily; free admission; parking NTD50/20) If you're more into waterfowl than birds of prey, this 175ha body of water is the place to go. The visitor centre, on the west side of the lake and 700m from the car park, has spotting scopes. In addition to ducks and egrets, birders have a good chance of seeing the Taiwan hwamei (*Garrulax taewanus*), a grey-brown thrush-like endemic. A variety of plants thrives near the visitor centre, including sisal.

Guanshan 關山 You'll need your own vehicle to get to the top of this modest ridge, a popular sunset-viewing spot. Before the sun sinks into the Taiwan Strait, make a point of also looking east over Longluan Lake and South Bay.

South Bay 南灣 (Nánwān) This 600m-long sandy beach is one of the park's nicest, though the view is marred somewhat by the nuclear power station and wind turbines. There are shower rooms and toilets. After dark the scene is less raucous here than along the Kending Road main strip.

Mount Dajian 大尖山 This 318m rock pyramid lives up to its name ('big sharp peak') and is one of the national park's most recognisable sights. Visitors are not allowed to climb the mountain, however, because of the risk they'll bring in livestock diseases that could harm the cattle that graze on its slopes.

Kenting National Forest Recreation Area 墾丁國家森林遊樂區 (Kěndīng Sēnlín Yóulèqū) (⊕ 08.00–17.00 daily; admission NTD150/75/10 at w/ends & national holidays, NTD100/75/10 Mon–Fri; parking NTD50/20) If you've visited some of Taiwan's mid-elevation forest recreation areas, you'll immediately notice the foliage in this monsoon rainforest is quite different. The land is uplifted coral reef and the soil is relatively thin, so many of the trees have exposed root systems. Make a point of climbing the stairs in the observation tower as, unless the weather's awful, from the top you'll see the Pacific Ocean and Bashi Channel as well as the Taiwan Strait.

Sheding Nature Park 社頂自然公園 (Shèdǐng Zìrán Gōngyuán) (⊕ 08.00–17.00 daily; free admission; parking NTD50/20) Properly exploring this hillside park takes over an hour but provides, at the very minimum, stirring views over the peninsula's east and south. The landscape is a mix of grasslands, uplifted coral reefs (including two narrow gorges you'll have lots of fun squeezing through) and mixed forest. Look closely at the trees and you'll see golf-ball-sized dark green fruit – they're wild guavas. The park is central to ongoing efforts to return Formosan sika deer (*Cervus nippon taiouanus*) to the wild, but there are usually too many people

8

around to spot either deer or macaques. Nevertheless, you're guaranteed to see a good range of butterflies and birds such as the Himalayan tree pie (*Dendrocitta formosae*). Wear proper shoes – the trails get slippery after rain.

Chuanfan Rock 船帆石 This squarish column is said to resemble the profile of the late US president Richard Nixon. It does, very slightly. The Chinese name, which means 'sail rock', is hardly more satisfactory, but the beach here is attractive.

Shadao Beach 砂島海灘 The foreshore here is fenced off to protect the only beach on Taiwan proper where the sand is overwhelmingly composed of crushed shells, coral and marine fossils. The **Shell Beach Exhibition Hall** (⊕ 08.30–17.00 daily; free admission) does a good job of explaining why shale turns west Taiwan's beaches dark grey, while those in the north are generally quartz sand and the south's shorelines are piled with shells and coral.

Eluanbi Park 鵝鑾鼻公園 (⊕ Apr–Sep 06.30–18.30 daily, Oct–Mar 07.00–17.30 daily; admission NTD60/30; parking NTD50/20) If you stay in a hotel near Kending Road, you'll probably notice Eluanbi's lighthouse blinking during the night. The surrounding park has geological and botanical attractions. A short distance east a side road on the right (if you're coming from Kending's main hotel area) leads to the 800m-long path to a monument marking Taiwan's southernmost point.

Longkeng Ecological Protection Area 龍坑生態保護區 (⊕ 08.00–15.30 Wed–Mon; free admission) Only 200 people each day are allowed to enter this 62ha reserve, which has ecosystems influenced by the area's collapsed limestone cliffs and coral reefs. If you're interested in entering either of the park's ecological protection areas (the other one is Nanrenshan), visit the national park website (w www.ktnp.gov.tw) and make an appointment between one day and six weeks in advance to view a multi-lingual briefing video. You won't be admitted to either area if you haven't seen the video. You also need to bring ID; children under the age of seven are not allowed in for safety reasons. Both Longkeng and Nanrenshan close for at least a month each year, usually in May or June.

Longpan Park 龍磐公園 (⊕ 24hrs daily; free admission) Not a park in the urban sense of the word but a wild realm of crumbling cliffs and wind-battered grasslands. The coastline hereabouts is so windswept trees don't grow. Bushes are snapped before they can grow taller than a man, and even if there were no trampling tourists, the near-constant gale would keep the grass flat. Hold on to your hat and if you're thinking of trying to clamber down to the ocean, think again – it's a very perilous scramble.

Roads 200 and 200A Taking Road 200 inland from Hengchun, you'll soon see the entrance for **Chuhuo Scenic Area** 出火風景區 (km2.8; free admission), one of at least four places in south Taiwan where natural gas seeps out of the ground and burns throughout the year. Staying on 200 will bring you to Manzhou 滿州 where there are several places to eat, even though the name of this pleasant little town has a distinctly unappetising derivation. It comes from the Paiwan word *manutsuru*, meaning 'stench', so given because local Paiwan used to gather here at the end of each hunt, skin their prey and discard unwanted body parts and bones. After a while, naturally, this debris stank. Manzhou is one of the best places to witness the raptor migration each October. Before you reach the centre of Manzhou, Road

200A veers southeast to **Gangkou** 港口, a seaside village very popular with surfers; you can rent a kayak and paddle around the estuary.

Jialeshui 佳樂水 (🕐 07.30–18.00 daily; admission NTD80/40 inc shuttle bus; parking NTD50/30) The forces of erosion have given this place an extraordinary selection of wind- and wave-sculpted rocks – look for the boulders and outcrops named after and resembling a dead pig, a human face, a snail and a frog. Some self-driving tourists park outside the ticket gate to avoid the parking fee. Before doing so bear in mind it's over 1km between the gate and where you can board an open-sided van that'll take you to the end of the paved road. The waterfall there isn't anything special but people who enjoy clambering over rocks will have lots of fun. If venturing more than 100m from the pagoda at the end of the road, take care.

Nanrenshan Ecological Protection Area 南仁山生態保護區 (🕐 08.00–15.00 Wed–Mon; free admission) This reserve, which accounts for more than one-quarter of the national park's 18,084ha of dry land, contains some of Taiwan's last remaining low-altitude primeval forest and para-tropical rainforest. For this reason, and because Nanrenshan continues to be an important ecological research site, visitors are limited to 400 per day. The procedure to enter is the same as that for Longkeng (see opposite). More than 1,200 indigenous plant species have been identified here, plus mammals like the endemic Coxing's white-bellied rat (*Niviventer coninga*). Allow 4 hours to walk from the entrance to the lake and back again.

UPDATES WEBSITE

You can post your comments and recommendations, and read feedback and updates from other readers online at **w** bradtupdates.com/taiwan.

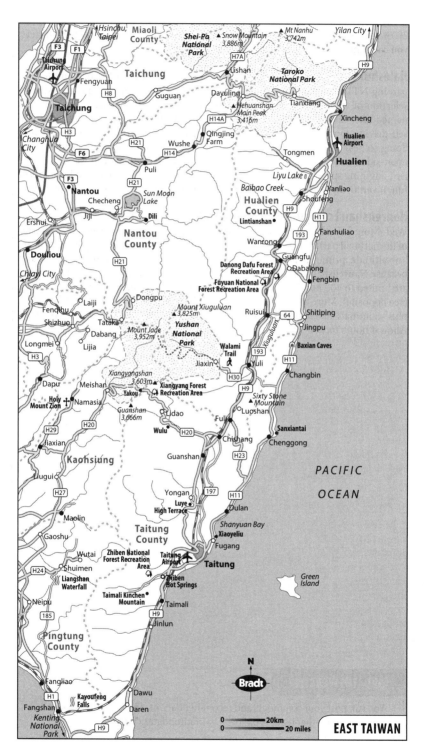

EAST TAIWAN

N

Bradt

0 — 20km
0 — 20 miles

9

East Taiwan

Thanks to the wonderful scenery and plenty of space in which to roam, the east is many visitors' favourite region of Taiwan. With fewer than 550,000 people spread over 8,144km², the two counties of Hualien and Taitung have less than 3% of the ROC's population but more than a fifth of the country's land, and in every sense nature is less tamed on this side of the island. Not only are the rivers and breezes cleaner, but the typhoons are stronger and the earth tremors more frequent. Relative to the Central Mountain Range, the Coastal Range is moving northeast at up to 13cm per year, while geothermal activity near the surface has created hot springs in places like Ruisui and Zhiben.

One in four residents here is Hakka and one in six is indigenous. Aboriginal cultures are strong draws but it's the scenery that impresses most. The top attraction is Taroko Gorge, a stunning natural composition of immovable rock and rushing water.

Until the 1950s, the easiest way for residents of Hualien to get to Taipei was to take a boat to Keelung, but nowadays there are fast trains and flights to both Hualien City and Taitung City. The authorities have done a lot to make the region more accessible to travellers who depend on public transport, and visitors in that category should look carefully at the various options set out on the Taiwan Tourist Shuttle website (w taiwantrip.com.tw). However, self-driving tourists should allow an entire day to get here from Taiwan's western plains, both because the motoring isn't always easy and there's a lot to see on the way.

HUALIEN CITY 花蓮市 (HUĀLIÁN SHÌ) *Telephone code 03*

Like every other population centre in the east, Hualien City (population: 110,000) doesn't have much history, so don't expect to stumble across time-worn temples or wander through quaint alleyways. However, what it does have is an appealing mix of people: the descendants of Fujianese who settled first in west Taiwan and then, a century or two later, migrated to the east coast; mainlanders who arrived in the late 1940s and the children they raised in Taiwan; Hakka families who appeared before and during the Japanese occupation; and members of the Amis, Truku and other indigenous tribes. There's some heavy industry around the harbour but the city centre is pleasant – just bustling enough to be interesting yet almost totally free of the air pollution and traffic jams that plague west Taiwan's cities.

GETTING THERE AND AWAY All fares mentioned in this chapter are one-way.

By air Hualien Airport (HUN; ☎ 821 0768; w www.hulairport.gov.tw) is served by two flights to/from Taipei Songshan Airport each day (40mins; NTD1,663), one service per day to/from Kaohsiung (takes 1hr; NTD2,170), and three per week to/

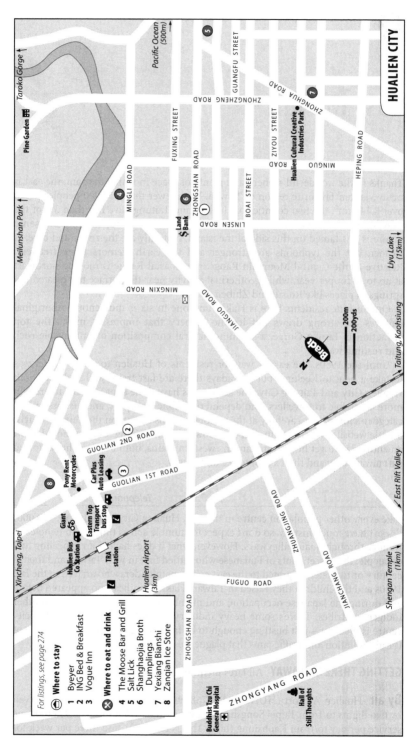

HUALIEN CITY

Taroko Gorge →

Pine Garden 🏯

Meilunshan Park ↑

Pacific Ocean (500m) ↑

GUANGFU STREET

ZHONGHUA ROAD

ZHONGZHENG ROAD

ZIYOU STREET

FUXING STREET

MINGLI ROAD

ZHONGSHAN ROAD

Hualien Cultural Creative Industries Park ●

BOAI STREET

MINGUO ROAD

HEPING ROAD

LINSEN ROAD

$ Land Bank

MINGXIN ROAD

JIANGUO ROAD

Liyu Lake (15km) →

Taitung, Kaohsiung →

N

Bradt

0   200m
0   200yds

East Rift Valley ⟋

Xincheng, Taipei →

GUOLIAN 2ND ROAD

Pony Rent Motorcycles ●

Car Plus Auto Leasing

GUOLIAN 1ST ROAD

Giant

Hualien Bus Co Station

Eastern Top Transport bus stop

TRA station

Hualien Airport (3km)

ZHUANJING ROAD

ZHONGSHAN ROAD

FUGUO ROAD

JIANCHANG ROAD

Shengan Temple (1km) →

ZHONGYANG ROAD

Buddhist Tzu Chi General Hospital ✚

Hall of Still Thoughts

from Taichung (1hr; NTD1,977). In addition to a few international charters, Hong Kong Express (w hkexpress.com) operates a scheduled flight from Hong Kong four times per week.

A taxi from the airport to a city-centre hotel shouldn't cost more than NTD250. Alternatively, there are 14 buses per day between the airport and Hualien TRA station (⊕ 08.40–18.10; 20mins; NTD39).

By TRA Of the 40-odd daily expresses to/from Taipei (⊕ 06.05–22.17; NTD340–440) the fastest are the Taroko and Puyuma services, some covering the distance in exactly 2 hours. Tickets should be bought as far in advance as possible; purchasing them in person at any TRA station is easier than doing so online. Five expresses from Kaohsiung via Taitung arrive in Hualien each day (4½–5¼hrs; NTD705), and more than 20 trains per day connect Hualien with Taitung (⊕ 06.09–22.28; 1½–3½hrs; NTD220–343). Those travelling light and staying in the city centre can probably walk from the station to their hotel.

By bus From the bus station next to the TRA station, there are hourly services to Guangfu (#1121; ⊕ 06.00–22.00; 1¼hrs; NTD140), three of which continue on to Ruisui (#1122; ⊕ 08.10, 11.20 & 19.20; 2hrs; NTD199). Buses head down the coast road about once an hour (⊕ 05.30–20.30 daily), of which the #1140 terminates in Jingpu (2hrs; NTD214) and #1145 in Chenggong (3hrs; NTD345). Just one Hualien Bus Co service a day goes all the way to Taitung City (#1127; ⊕ 09.30; 4¼hrs; NTD514), while Eastern Top Transport also operates one Hualien–Taitung service daily (#8119; ⊕ 14.10; 4hrs; NTD494). Ask at the visitor information centre where to buy your ticket and board the bus. Like the daily Hualien Bus Co service, it stops at Fugang, from where there are ferries to Green Island.

For details of buses from Hualien to Taroko Gorge National Park, see page 278.

By car or motorcycle Hualien can be approached from the north, south or west. The section of Highway 9 that links Suao to Xincheng (the Suhua Highway) is breathtaking but not much fun if you're on two wheels due to its narrowness and the number of lorries using it. That should improve in the next few years, however, as tunnelling and widening work continues.

GETTING AROUND If the place you're staying in offers you a bicycle, take it – the city is a bit too spread out for walking. Taxis are plentiful but will try to talk you into a half-day tour of Taroko Gorge.

By hired car, motorcycle or bicycle There's a branch of Car Plus Auto Leasing at 117 Guolian 1st Road (✆ 831 6688; w car-plus.com.tw; ⊕ 08.30–20.30 daily). The scooter-rental businesses around Hualien TRA station sometimes accept international licences. The bicycles that hotels and B&Bs offer to their guests aren't suitable for long-distance touring, so for better bikes go to Giant (35 Guoxing 1st St; ✆ 833 6761; ⊕ 09.00–18.00 Mon–Wed & Fri, 08.00–18.00 Sat–Sun) where weekday rentals begin at NTD150 per day; at weekends, you'll likely pay NTD200 for 2 hours.

TOURIST INFORMATION AND TOUR OPERATORS There's a visitor information centre in Hualien Airport (⊕ 09.00–17.30 daily) and another behind the TRA station (⊕ 08.30–17.30 daily), but by far the most useful in terms of English ability and location is the one on the left as you leave the front of the TRA station

(🕐 08.00–21.00 daily). Also try Hualien Tourist Service Network (**w** tour-hualien. hl.gov.tw).

Hualien Outdoors Matt Hopkins; 2–16 Guolian 5th Rd; ✆03 833 9037; **m** 0989 512 380; **e** hualienoutdoors@gmail.com; **w** hualienoutdoors.org.

This expat-run company offers river tracing, hiking & tea-focused trips in & around Hualien & Taroko Gorge National Park.

WHERE TO STAY *Map, page 272*

Hualien has experienced a hotel-and-hostel boom in recent years, so there's no shortage of accommodation.

Byeyer Hotel 百悅休閒飯店 (54 rooms) 361 Zhongshan Rd; ✆832 5185; **e** byeyer@ byeyer.com; **w** byeyer.com. Art Deco influences are evident in Byeyer's lobby & generally spacious rooms, only the most expensive of which have bathtubs. LCD TV sets are swivel-mounted so they can be watched from either the bed or the sofa that's in every room. B/fast & bike use inc. **$$$**

ING Bed & Breakfast 花蓮IN居民宿 (6 rooms) 27 Guomin 2nd St; ✆831 1185; **e** inghostel@gmail.com. This pristine homestay offers rooms with larger-than-average beds, fridges

& balconies. No need to lug your bags up the stairs – there's a lift. By booking ahead, couples can often get a room for less than NTD2,000. Inc b/fast at an eatery around the corner; guests can use the kitchen. **$$$**

Vogue Inn 嚮往時尚旅店民宿 (5 rooms) 93 Guoxing 2nd St ; ✆836 0668; **e** hualienvogue@gmail.com. One of at least 2-dozen accommodation options within walking distance of the railway station, Vogue offers excellent value for money. No b/fast, but there's never a danger of starvation in this neighbourhood. **$$**

WHERE TO EAT AND DRINK *Map, page 272*

Salt Lick 火車頭道地美式烤肉屋 147 Zhongshan Rd; ✆833 2592; **w** www.lickbbq. com; 🕐 11.30–15.00 & 17.00–23.00 daily. Carnivores will love this American-managed restaurant's selection of steaks, sandwiches & BBQ delights from NTD255. Meals come with fries & salad; side dishes of coleslaw, potato salad & US specialities like hush puppies from NTD85. Chicago-style pizzas from NTD300. Taiwanese craft beers as well as soft drinks available. Indoor & outdoor seating. EM. **$$$$**

The Moose Bar and Grill 麋鹿餐酒館 18–2 Mingli Rd; ✆833 2003; 🕐 11.30–14.30 & 17.30–21.30 Wed–Mon. Drinks in this Canadian-owned watering hole aren't cheap but there's an exceptional selection of whiskies, as well as imported beers & several intriguing Taiwanese microbrews. Food options include the highly rated fish & chips, a superb Reuben sandwich, pizzas & steaks. EM. **$$$**

Shanghaojia Broth Dumplings 上豪嘉小籠湯包 290 Zhongshan Rd; ✆835 0290; 🕐 11.00–01.00 Wed–Mon. Clean & reliable, this is one of the better options if it's late or you couldn't get your dumpling fix at Yexiang Bianshi. The friendly staff here will serve you broth dumplings

湯餃 (NTD70 for 8) or slightly more expensive sweet-&-sour broth dumplings (*suānlà tāng jiǎo* 酸辣湯餃) filled with cabbage or leek. There are also noodle dishes, wontons & seasonal greens. **$**

Yexiang Bianshi 液香扁食 42 Xinyi St; ✆832 6761; 🕐 10.00–13.30 & 16.00–21.30 daily. There's no menu here because the only option is soup containing 10 exquisite wonton dumplings (NTD70), the recipe for which has been perfected over the past 70-plus years. If you've never had them before, they're egg-sized packets of ground pork, garlic, chopped onion & spices. Expect to queue & come early at the weekend because this eatery often sells out before 19.30. **$**

Zanqian Ice Store 讚前冰坊 15 Guomin 9th St; ✆832 9986; 🕐 noon–21.00 daily. If you want to kill some time before boarding a train, do so here, over homemade ice cream (NTD30 per generous scoop) or a dish of snow-flake shaved ice (NTD50–80). If you go for the former, try the taro or pumpkin. Both flavours are mild & without artificial sweetening. Depending on the weather & the availability of produce, this family-run business closes down between sometime in Nov & Mar or Apr. EM. **$**

OTHER PRACTICALITIES

$ **Land Bank** 356 Zhongshan Rd
✚ **Buddhist Tzu Chi General Hospital** 707 Zhongyang Rd Sec 3; ✆ 856 1825; w www.tzuchi. com.tw; ⊕ 24hrs daily

✉ **Post office** 408 Zhongshan Rd; ⊕ 08.00– 21.00 Mon–Fri, 08.30–16.00 Sat–Sun. Money can be changed here.

WHAT TO SEE AND DO

Hall of Still Thoughts 靜思堂 **(Jìngsī Táng)** (703 Zhongyang Rd Sec 3; ⊕ 09.00– 17.00 daily; free admission) This externally simple yet striking grey temple is a must-visit for those interested in learning about contemporary Buddhism's interactions with mainstream society. Upon entering you'll likely be invited to watch an English-language DVD on the origins, activities and goals of the Buddhist Compassion Relief Tzu Chi Foundation (w tzuchi.org), Taiwan's biggest charity in terms of membership (four million supporters out of a population of 23 million in Taiwan; another six million overseas). Tzu Chi's founder, the Venerable Dharma Master Cheng Yen (b1937), has been based in Hualien since the early 1960s and the little cottage in which she lived at that time has been preserved nearby as part of **Tzu Chi Cultural Park** 慈濟文化園區 (⊕ 08.30–16.30 daily). Her shift away from a purely contemplative existence into relief work was prompted by some vivid encounters with extreme poverty. Sceptics and atheists will appreciate two aspects of Tzu Chi's approach: the absence throughout Tzu Chi properties of donation boxes and the emphasis on environmental protection. Take a look at the very detailed bilingual exhibition before stepping inside the multi-level Buddhist chapel at the heart of the building.

Meilunshan Park 美崙山公園 (⊕ 24hrs daily) The view inland and over the Pacific is one reason to come here, although another is to visit the colonial-era **Pine Garden** 松園別館 (⊕ 09.00–18.00 daily; admission NTD50/25). Established in World War II by the Japanese Navy as a communications post, this was where kamikaze pilots were wined and dined before setting off on their final missions. The café has hot and cold drinks (from NTD100; no EM) plus a few meal options.

Hualien Cultural Creative Industries Park 創意文化園區 (144 Zhonghua Rd; w www.a-zone.com.tw; park ⊕ 24hrs daily, display areas vary) This Japanese-era complex, a winery until 1988, now hosts exhibitions and performances, to which admission is often free. Finding out what's on isn't easy – the website's English pages are seldom updated – but the buildings are handsome so it's worth dropping by on the off chance you'll find something you like.

Shengan Temple 勝安宮 **(Shèngān Gōng)** (118 Cihui 3rd St; ⊕ 06.00–21.00 daily) By Tainan or Lukang standards, this exceptionally colourful complex of towers, pavilions and altars has almost no history. It traces its roots to precisely 06.30 on the 13th day of the sixth lunar month in 1949, when the Queen Mother of the West (a deity worshipped in China long before the emergence of Taoism) appeared in the form of a white light in a thatched hut. The cult that grew up here is now wealthy and engages in charity work in Taiwan and overseas. In an interesting reversal of Taiwanese or Chinese becoming 'rice Christians', Taiwan's media reported in 2009 that more than 50 Haitians have become disciples of the Queen Mother of the West. A comparative study of Haitian voodoo and Taiwanese folk beliefs would be interesting, as both religions have massive pantheons; followers venerate the dead and aim their prayers more often at lesser spirits than towards any supreme god.

Deservedly one of Taiwan's leading tourist destinations, Taroko Gorge is a true, not-to-be-missed geological spectacular. Of the many eye-popping sights, the most dramatic is the stretch where the gorge narrows from a classic V-shaped valley to a defile that turns the sky into little more than a sliver of blue, hundreds of metres above visitors' heads.

Tourists have been visiting the gorge since the 1930s, but only in meaningful numbers since the completion of the Central Cross-Island Highway in 1960. Most people spend their time gazing up at the clifftops or along the meandering Liwu River Valley. Yet the boulders that rest on the riverbed are also capable of making a strong impression, and not only because of their gargantuan dimensions. The Taroko area is synonymous with marble (quarrying used to be one of this region's most important industries) but because of mineral impurities and an abundance of schists and gneiss, you'll see rocks of pure white, dark grey, cream, silver, light brown and even soft shades of gold.

Visitor and tour-coach numbers peak in the middle of the afternoon so it's best to make as early a start as possible. The good news is that there's no bad time of year to come here. During summer the Liwu and its tributaries are full of vigour, but landslides sometimes close hiking trails or even the main road. The autumn can be very lovely indeed, and even in winter there are many dry, sunny days when a good number of the national park's 144 bird species and 251 kinds of butterfly are active and visible. Springtime sees an abundance of flowers, including purple azaleas.

Hard-core mountaineers should consider Taroko National Park's other attractions, such as Mount Nanhu (3,742m) or the notoriously dangerous Mount Qilai (3,605m). Permits must be obtained before you can climb either of these mountains; see the park's website for details.

HISTORY The geological processes that created Taroko Gorge began hundreds of millions of years ago with the accumulation of undersea sediment and volcanic lava, materials that eventually became the area's trademark layers of marble, schist and gneiss. About 6.5 million years ago, the Philippine tectonic plate collided with and began to slide under the Eurasian Plate, and as a result, the landmass we now call Taiwan emerged from the ocean. Rivers, among them the Liwu, formed and began chiselling down through the rock. That erosion continues today, but because of the tectonic uplift of the entire region the bottom of the gorge is rising by a few millimetres each year.

Austronesian people have lived on the few scraps of flat land around the gorge for at least 2,000 years. The existence of the Truku tribe, which takes its name from the gorge, can be dated from the arrival of Atayal and Sediq clans in the area three or four centuries ago. After their migration they were isolated from their brethren to the west and developed customs and a dialect of their own. Although they had some contact with the outside world – a Fujianese traveller who visited in 1697 wrote of Han Chinese mingling with the indigenous people, trading with them and panning for gold – the Truku remained the unchallenged masters of the Liwu catchment until 1914, when Japan sent a military expedition into the gorge. Once they'd taken control, they forcibly resettled many of the aborigines closer to the coast. The colonial regime built roads and began to exploit the gorge's hydroelectric potential. At the same time, they made plans for a national park that would have been triple the size of the one established by Taiwan's government in 1986.

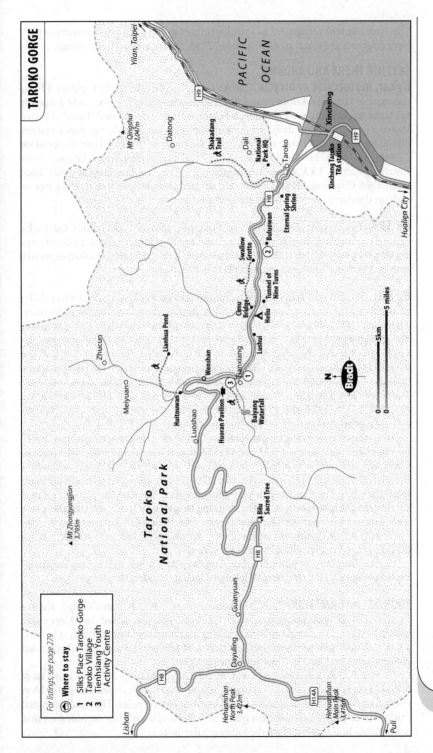

Yilan, Taipei

PACIFIC
OCEAN

Mt Qingshui
2,047m

Datong

Xincheng

Shakadang
Trail

Dali

National
Park HQ

Taroko

Xincheng Taroko
TRA station

H9

H9

H8

Hualien City

Eternal Spring
Shrine

(2) Buluowan

Swallow
Grotto

Gmu
Bridge

Tunnel of
Nine Turns

Heliu

Lushui

Lianhua Pond

Zhucun

Wenshan

Tianxiang

Meiyuano

(3)

(1)

Luoshao

Huran Pavilion

Huitouwan

Baiyang
Waterfall

N

Taroko
National Park

▲ Mt Zhongyangjian
3,705m

Bilu
Sacred Tree

H8

Guanyuan

Dayuling

Lishan

H8

Hehuanshan
North Peak
3,422m

Hehuanshan
Main Peak
3,416m

H14A

Puli

0   5km
0   5 miles

For listings, see page 279

ⓘ Where to stay
1 Silks Place Taroko Gorge
2 Taroko Village
3 Tienhsiang Youth
   Activity Centre

The Truku weren't recognised as a distinct ethnic group until 2004; previously they were categorised as 'Atayal'. As of autumn 2018, the tribe was 31,600 strong.

GETTING THERE AND AROUND
By car, motorcycle or bicycle Taroko Gorge can be reached by Highway 9 from the coast or Highway 8 from inland. Landslides sometimes close or cause delays on the latter so checking road conditions before setting out is advised. There's a petrol station (⊕ 07.00–19.00 daily) in the built-up area just outside the park's eastern boundary and another west of the gorge at Guanyuan (km116.8 Hwy 8; elevation: 2,374m; ⊕ 09.00–18.00 daily). There's at least one scooter-rental business near Xincheng Taroko TRA station but organising motorcycle hire is more easily done in Hualien City (page 273). Cyclists are advised to head up through the gorge as early in the day as possible when the traffic is light.

By TRA The nearest TRA station is Xincheng Taroko, 4.2km from the park's eastern boundary. From Hualien trains take 11–17 minutes (about 25 departures per day; ⊕ 05.09–22.50; NTD24–37), and about a dozen Taipei–Hualien expresses stop in Xincheng Taroko (2–3hrs; NTD311–403) daily.

By bus The Taiwan Tourist Shuttle Taroko service #1133A (7 departures daily; ⊕ 07.00–15.10) leaves from Hualien TRA station and takes 1¼ hours to reach Tianxiang (NTD149 one-way), a tiny village where you may wish to base yourself. The regular #1133 (departs 10.50 & 13.50; NTD172) follows an identical route. The #1126 goes beyond the gorge to Luoshao (departs 06.30; 2hrs; NTD189), and the daily #1141 is the only service all the way to Lishan just outside the park's western boundary (departs 08.40; 4½hrs; NTD453); both make several stops including Tunnel of Nine Turns and Tianxiang. One-/two-day passes (NTD250/400) for the #1126, #1133, #1133A and #1141 can be purchased at the bus station in Hualien and are a good deal as the one-way fare to Tianxiang is NTD149–172.

All of these services start from Hualien TRA station and reach Xincheng 30–40 minutes later, but only the #1133 and #1133A stop at Xincheng Taroko TRA station. Other services can be boarded at the stop on Highway 9 about 700m away; to find it, turn left when leaving Xincheng's train station and walk until you reach the main road, then turn right and walk a very short distance; the stop for Taroko Gorge is very near a 7-Eleven shop. If you're planning to arrive by train, you can also catch a #302 bus into the park at Xincheng Taroko TRA station (12 departures; ⊕ 07.10–17.10 daily; takes 45mins to Tianxiang; one-day pass NTD150). It's possible to leave luggage at the baggage office in the train station.

Taiwan Tour Bus (w taiwantourbus.com.tw) offers a one-day Taroko excursion from Hualien (NTD1,600 pp with foreign-language guide).

TOURIST INFORMATION Taroko National Park Headquarters/Visitor Centre (\ 862 1100; w www.taroko.gov.tw; ⊕ 08.30–17.00 daily, closed 2nd Mon every month), where you can get the latest hiking and transport information, is located a few minutes' walk northeast of the junction of Highways 8 and 9. Trail and road conditions are detailed in English on the park's website.

The national park service stations at Buluowan (⊕ 09.00–16.30 daily, closed 1st & 3rd Mon every month) and Tianxiang (⊕ 09.00–16.00 daily, closed 2nd & 4th Mon every month) can answer questions and assist in emergencies. The small bilingual exhibition at Tianxiang is worth a quick look. Both of these open on Mondays that are national holidays but close the following day instead.

WHERE TO STAY AND EAT A few places close to Tianxiang's bus stop sell hot meals and snacks (no EMs; $) but don't expect gourmet food. The restaurant in the national park headquarters (🕐 08.00–16.30 daily; EM; $$$) is a little pricey but reliable. Camping is allowed at **Heliu** 合流 (✆ 869 1359; NTD200 per tent; cold-water showers only) and **Lushui** 綠水 (free; no facilities) only. At you'll need to bring your own tent, food and cooking gear.

🏠 **Silks Place Taroko Gorge** 太魯閣晶英酒店 [map, page 277] (160 rooms) Tianxiang; ✆ 869 1155; e rsvn@silksplace-taroko.com.tw; w www.silksplace-taroko.com.tw. The only 5-star hotel inside the national park boasts a rooftop swimming pool & garden. One part is called The Resort, another The Retreat; rooms in the latter are more spacious & extra services are available. Room rates inc activities for kids, aerobics classes, demonstrations of indigenous crafts, b/fast & dinner. For non-guests the exceptionally good evening buffet is NTD800 plus 10% service charge. **$$$$$**

🏠 **Taroko Village Hotel** 太魯閣山月村 [map, page 277] (37 rooms) Buluowan; ✆ 861 0111; w www.tarokovillage.com. A collection of smart, tastefully decorated wood cabins spread out on a small plateau just above the Buluowan Recreation Area, Taroko Village Hotel is enjoyably remote. You can see the stars, hear the cicadas & sometimes glimpse wild animals. Pickup from Hualien TRA station or airport for a fee. Midweek room rates start at around NTD4,800 inc b/fast & dinner; meals are very tasty with lots

of meat cooked aboriginal-style (🕐 noon–14.00 & 18.00–19.40 daily; EM; for non-guests lunchtime set meals start at NTD280+10%). **$$$$**

🏠 **Tienhsiang Youth Activity Centre** 天祥青年活動中心 [map, page 277] (56 rooms) Tianxiang; ✆ 869 1111; e tsyac@cyc.tw; w tienhsiang.cyh.org.tw. Not a bad option in terms of price & cleanliness, but the bldg wins zero points for character. All rooms have TVs & fridges; most have tiny balconies. The smallest dbl rooms are NTD2,400. B/fast (NTD120 pp) & other meals (NTD180 pp) available. **$$$**

🏠 **Protestant Church Hostel** 天祥基督教堂 (2 rooms, 3 dorms) Tianxiang; ✆ 869 1203. Follow the signs to 'Tienhsiang Church' & you'll soon see a small stone chapel that wouldn't look out of place in northern Europe, & the hostel is on the left. The janitor doesn't speak English but is very helpful. The dbl with bath goes for NTD1,200 whether it's a w/day or hol, the tiny sgl (no bath) for NTD600. The dorms, which sleep 4–8, work out around NTD400 pp. Tianxiang's Catholic church operates an equally inexpensive but less characterful hostel. **$$**

WHAT TO SEE AND DO Ecotourists will find it easy to spend three days in the gorge hiking and trying to spot resident bird species such as the little forktail (*Enicurus scouleri*) and green-backed tit (*Parus monticolus*). Whenever there's a typhoon alert, park authorities tend to close all trails immediately even if the weather seems fine. If a typhoon strikes, trails stay closed until the authorities are sure there's no likelihood of rockfalls, which can take up to two weeks. Visitors should therefore track weather conditions and look at the park's website before setting out for the gorge.

Moving inland, you'll come across attractions in the following order:

Shakadang Trail 砂卡礑步道 The Shakadang drains from north to south and is one of the Liwu's major tributaries. This trail, constructed during the Japanese era to facilitate the building of a small dam, follows the river closely. The route begins with a long flight of steel stairs about 30 minutes' walk west from the national park headquarters. For the remainder of the trail's 4.5km length, the gradient is very gentle. Because so many people hike this trail you're unlikely to see much in the way of wildlife, but you will see Truku people tending small plots and selling bagfuls of an unusual local crop, a lettuce-type vegetable called bird's-nest fern (*Asplenium nidus*). Don't expect to reach 3D Cabin, the official end of the trail, and get back to the starting point in the 2½ hours mentioned in national park literature. If you've obtained permits in advance, it's possible to keep going to **Dali** 大禮 (elevation: 915m) and **Datong** 大同 (1,128m), two old Truku settlements. Nowadays there are no permanent inhabitants, just the occasional ex-resident returning to grow crops. Getting to either of these places involves serious uphill hiking. If you plan to stay overnight contact the national park headquarters as some of the rangers have family ties to the villages. Accommodation is rudimentary; do not expect English or electricity.

Eternal Spring Shrine 長春祠 (🕐 24hrs daily) Dramatically positioned near the base of what looks to be a highly unstable mountain slope, this small temple (marked on many maps as Changchun Shrine) is quite a sight. Water gushes through a tunnel between the two pavilions and into the Liwu River. It's possible to do an hour-long loop hike here. Walking from the Shakadang trailhead doesn't take long, but it does involve going through a tunnel that sees quite a bit of traffic.

Buluowan 布洛灣 A series of terraces 2km from and substantially higher than Highway 8, Buluowan Recreation Area has four very short but worthwhile trails, an exhibition of Austronesian weaving and basket-making, handicrafts for sale and a coffee shop. To get here, take the twisting side road that veers off to the south between km180 and km180.5 on Highway 8; Hualien–Tianxiang buses detour up this road.

Swallow Grotto 燕子口 (**Yànzǐkǒu**) This short (just under 0.5km) pathway takes you through one of the narrowest, deepest and most striking sections of the canyon. The cliff here is pock-marked as a result of abrasion by sand and grit carried downstream when the river is high; the place name refers to the birds who nest in the cavities.

Tunnel of Nine Turns 九曲洞 (**Jiǔ Qū Dòng**) If you're going to park and stretch your legs at just one point in the gorge, do it here. The 2km-long walking trail here is in fact a vestigial stretch of highway, superseded in 1996 when a long tunnel was built to straighten and broaden one of Highway 8's more dangerous sections. If you're not impressed by the dimensions of the gorge, you're nigh impossible to please. The 'nine' in this toponym isn't literal but rather a classical Chinese way of expressing 'many'.

Zhuilu Old Road 錐麓古道 What's billed as the gorge's most challenging and rewarding hike starts from **Cimu Bridge** 慈母橋, so named ('motherly devotion') because it's where Chiang Ching-kuo had a small pavilion built as a memorial to his mother. The trail ('road' is a misnomer – it's too narrow for hikers, let alone vehicles, to pass) ends at a footbridge across the gorge near Swallow Grotto. It was cut high above the current highway by conscripted Truku labourers soon after the Japanese took control of the gorge in 1914. The views from it are superb, but it's not for casual walkers. Because hikers have to ascend from 300m above sea level to around 780m, 6 hours are needed to complete the 10.3km-long trail. National park notices describe the route as 'rugged [and] highly difficult' and note that the cliff section 'is narrow and dangerous and visitors are frequently hit by falling rocks'. Permits are required and should be applied for at least three days in advance (see w npm.cpami.gov.tw/en). Often only part of the trail is open, forcing hikers to retrace their steps.

Tianxiang 天祥 **(Tiānxiáng)** Variously spelled Tiansiang and Tienhsiang, this little settlement at km170 (elevation: 480m) would amount to half-a-dozen households and a pair of churches if you took away the tourist industry. It's named after Wen Tianxiang, a 13th-century Chinese scholar renowned for his loyalty to the Song Dynasty as it was being crushed by Kublai Khan's invading Mongols. (This kind of patriot, unwavering in his support of a legitimate but defeated regime, had an especial appeal to Chiang Kai-shek's Nationalists.)

A number of short but challenging hikes begin in or near Tianxiang. From the Protestant church it's less than 200m (part of which is very steep) to a small plateau where you can see the ruins of a tiny Truku settlement called Tapido. This was a genuine indigenous community, not a resettlement village created by the Japanese or the Nationalists, and so it's almost certain there are graves here. The Truku, like many of Taiwan's indigenous tribes, practised indoor burial. When an aged person appeared close to death, he or she was moved into a sitting position. Once they'd expired, they were interred in that posture right under the house in which they had dwelled. The grave was then covered with stone slabs.

Behind the youth activity centre you'll find the start of a trail to **Huoran Pavilion** 豁然亭, which is on Highway 8 west of Huitouwan. There's good butterflying along both this path and the approach to Tapido. On the other side of the river, good views justify climbing the stairs to the somewhat commercialised **Xiangde Temple** 祥德寺 (⏱ 06.00–18.00 daily).

Baiyang Trail 白楊步道 **(Báiyáng Bùdào)** In the late 1970s, just as the Interior Ministry was finalising plans for Taroko to become a national park, the Economics Ministry was pushing ahead with plans to dam the Liwu's main tributaries to produce hydro-electricity. Taipower, the state-run utility, cut a short road from just inland of Tianxiang to the Baiyang Waterfalls and beyond. The road, which passes through seven short tunnels, is now a beautiful 2.1km-long hiking trail but often closed due to typhoon damage. No permits are required but carrying a torch is advisable as some of the tunnels aren't straight. Water and snacks are a good idea as you'll be walking for at least an hour each way if you want to see the waterfalls. The spherical, basketball-sized clumps you'll notice on some of the trees are ants' nests.

Wenshan Hot Springs 文山溫泉 **(Wénshān Wēnquán)** These riverside hot springs, 3km up the road from Tianxiang, have been known to the outside world since they were discovered by a Japanese army officer in 1914. Don't disregard the bilingual signs that warn visitors to stay away from certain spots: In 2005, a deadly rockfall brought the number of people killed by falling debris while bathing here to at least four (several others were injured) and caused the park authorities to close the entire site for six years.

Huitouwan 迴頭彎 (km163.4) This is the jumping-off point for the hike to Lianhua Pond 蓮花池 (elevation: 1,180m). Allow at least 3 hours to reach the pond, which is just under 1ha in size. Along the way there's a rope bridge and some uphill hiking through sublime groves of Makino bamboo. As recently as the turn of the century a few indigenous families and a handful of mainland China-born KMT veterans lived and farmed up here.

Bilu Sacred Tree 碧綠神木 (km126.3) After Huitouwan (elevation: 720m) the road climbs steadily to this lovely spot, some 2,150m above sea level. Bìlù means 'greenish-blue' and is the name of the river down below, not a description of the tree, a Lunta fir (*Cunnhamia lanceolata var. konishii*) that's 50m high and more than 3,000 years old. The restaurant/shop here (⊕ 08.30–17.00 daily; EM; **$$**) serves meal sets (about NTD250 inc coffee or tea), simpler items like soup or noodles (about NTD100) as well as the usual hot and cold drinks.

At **Dayuling** 大禹嶺 (2,565m), you have the choice of either going through the tunnel and on to Lishan and Shei-Pa National Park (page 191) or heading southward to Hehuanshan and Puli (page 188).

THE EAST RIFT VALLEY

The broad and largely unspoiled expanse of lush countryside between the Central Mountain Range and the Coastal Range is indeed lovely. More than 150km long, the valley is drained by three waterways: the Hualien River flows into the ocean near the city of the same name; the majestic Xiuguluan dominates the centre; and the southward-flowing Beinan cuts through some of Taiwan's best rice-growing country.

Guangfu 光復 (Guāngfù) is a good base for exploring the valley. Two-thirds of the township's 14,000 inhabitants are indigenous. The substantial Hakka minority came here to work in the sugar industry, which until a few years ago dominated the local economy. The sugar refinery still stands, but most of the cane plantations are now being afforested. The hot springs at Ruisui, developed during the Japanese era, still attract substantial numbers of Taiwanese tourists. However, for Western visitors the main draws are the valley's natural appearance and opportunities to go hiking and white-water rafting.

Because the valley is divided between Hualien County and Taitung County, telephone codes are included in all listings.

GETTING THERE, AWAY AND AROUND

By TRA Most of the 17 trains linking Hualien with Guangfu each day take under an hour (⊕ 05.32–22.28 daily; NTD63–97). There's a similar number of services from Taitung (most take 1¾hrs; NTD158–245), many of which also stop in Yuli (most take under 1hr; NTD99–154).

By bus From Hualien, there's a bus to Guangfu about hourly (#1121; ⊕ 06.00–22.00; 1¼hrs; NTD140), three of which continue southward on to Ruisui (#1122; departures at 08.10, 11.20 & 19.20; 2hrs; NTD199). Several buses per day set out from Guangfu for Yuli (#1142; 1hr; NTD142) and Fuli (#1137; 1¾hrs; NTD216). From either town you can catch a bus or train to Taitung City.

By car, motorcycle or bicycle Four- and two-wheelers are advised to take Highway 11 south from Hualien and then Road 193 when it veers off to the right. The first 20km of this famous cycling route has numerous twists and turns and is almost completely unpopulated (meaning there's nowhere to buy snacks or drinks) but intensely scenic. Approaching Dabalong, just east of Guangfu, the road becomes flatter and straighter.

TOURIST INFORMATION

⬛ East Rift Valley National Scenic Area w www.erv-nsa.gov.tw
⬛ Liyu Lake Service Station ⊕ 08.30–17.30 daily

⬛ Luoshan Visitor Centre km310.5 Hwy 9; ⊕ 08.30–17.30 daily
⬛ Xiuguluan River Visitor & Rafting Centre km89.8 Rd 193; ⊕ 08.30–17.00 daily. See page 286.

WHERE TO STAY

Butterfly Valley Resort (42 rooms) Fuyuan National Forest Recreation Area; ⊠ 03 881 2377; e reserva-tions@bvr.com.tw; w www. bvr.com.tw. At first glance this looks like a very expensive place to stay – midweek rates start at NTD6,300 & a 10% service charge is added to every bill. However, the rooms are very comfortable indeed & inc b/fast & dinner, pickup from Hualien's airport or TRA station, entrance tickets for the forest recreation area & use of hot-springs pools. **$$$$$**

Goose Nest Garden B&B 雁窩民宿 (7 rooms) 5 Lane 51, Luliao Rd, Yongan; ⊠ 089 550 281; m 0937 389 953; w www.goose51599. com.tw. This place is a little difficult to find; once you reach Yongan, locate the elementary school & the homestay is less than 50m to your right on the opposite side of the road. Alternatively, follow the Chinese-only signs (white characters on a red background with the owner's mobile phone number). Little English spoken but the owners are very hospitable & the rooms (for 2, 4 or 6 ppl) are spotless. Reservations essential in peak season. B/fast inc. **$$$**

Yuan Hsiang Hot Spring Resort 原鄉溫泉度假村 (18 rooms) 325 Wufu Rd, Ruisui; ⊠ 03 887 6307; e yuan.hhs@msa.hinet.net; w www.yuan-hhs.com.tw. Clean, spacious & used to Western faces, this very friendly (but far from bilingual) hotel also has a set of public pools open to non-guests (admission NTD150 pp; swimsuits required). All rooms come with hot-spring tubs. Midweek, 2 ppl can sometimes stay for less than NTD2,200. Inc a generous but very Taiwanese b/fast. **$$$**

WHERE TO EAT AND DRINK

Shu Wu Restaurant 樹屋餐廳 2 Huantan S Rd, Shoufeng; ⊠ 864 1888; ⏰ 11.00–14.00 & 17.00–20.00 daily. Located between Highway 9C & the southwestern corner of Liyu Lake, this Amis-run restaurant lacks English signs or menus but offers good inland cuisine. Meal sets inc a 1-person *jiǎn cān* 簡餐 (NTD280). Portions are fairly generous: the 4-dish, 1-soup option (NTD1,200) can satisfy 4 adults. The chicken soup crammed with sweet potato & goji berries is a particular highlight. **$$$**

Dah Chi Bean Curd Sheet 大池豆皮店 39–2 Dapu Rd, Chishang; ⊠ 986 2392; ⏰ 07.00–13.00 Thu–Tue. Come here to see the production process as well as for b/fast or brunch. Soya milk made from beans ground before dawn is boiled until a film forms on the surface; Dah Chi's artisans then collect the yellowish skins & hang them up to dry. Selling these 'tofu sheets' to nearby households & restaurants is their principal business but visitors can order fried soya sheets (NTD65 per serving) or bean-curd pudding flavoured with syrup (NTD25) to go with a big cup of sweetened or unsweetened soya milk (NTD15). Look for the English sign outside the premises, due west of Dapo Pond (page 288) between Hwy 9 & Rd 197. **$**

Fengchun Ice Cream Shop 豐春冰菓店 79 Shoufeng Rd Sec 1, Shoufeng; ⏰ Apr–Nov 10.30–17.00 daily. If you've been breaking a sweat on foot or on a bike, do stop here & treat yourself to ice cream handmade using equipment that looks as if it hasn't been updated since man walked on the moon. The flavours are just as traditional: adzuki bean, taro sweet-potato paste & sugarcane juice are among the most popular. From Shoufeng TRA station it's less than 100m; turn right as soon as you reach the main road. **$**

Guanshan Meat Circles 關山肉圓 60 Zhonghua Rd, Guanshan; ⊠ 089 811 396; ⏰ 06.00–14.30 Thu–Tue. In the busiest part of the town, just west of Highway 9 & opposite a temple car park, this clean eatery serves decent beef noodles, fried rice & wonton dishes (NTD50–100) that many prefer to their signature meat circles (NTD35). **$**

OTHER PRACTICALITIES The **post office** in Guangfu (124 Zhongzheng Rd Sec 1; ⏰ 08.30–17.00 Mon–Fri) can change major foreign currencies and travellers' cheques.

WHAT TO SEE AND DO Travelling north to south, you'll pass near the following sights in this order:

East Taiwan   THE EAST RIFT VALLEY

9

AMIS HARVEST FESTIVALS

Sometime in July or August – the precise date and exact name of the event varies from village to village – Amis clans in Hualien and Taitung counties celebrate the taking in of the harvest with singing, dancing and feasting. As with harvest festivals worldwide, these events, which tribespeople call Ilisin, are celebrations of abundance and expressions of gratitude for the blessings of gods and ancestors.

There's more to these festivals than revelry and gluttony, however. At Chishang in Taitung County, for instance, for three days the men engage in fishing while the women prepare glutinous rice, salted pork and millet liquor. On the fourth day the tribe gathers to erect bamboo watchtowers and pavilions. Traditional songs and dances can be enjoyed on the fifth and sixth days, when you'll see groups in traditional attire but bare feet dance with interlocked arms. On the seventh and final day the menfolk go fishing once again, hoping to close the festival with a big catch.

If you happen across one of these events, you'll likely receive a memorably warm welcome, and possibly some good-natured cajoling to get you to join in. For a detailed explanation of Amis culture and social organisation (and other major indigenous groups), see w dmtip.gov.tw.

Liyu Lake 鯉魚潭 (⊕ 24hrs daily; free admission) Close to central Hualien and thus often quite crowded, this picturesque body of water is popular with families and couples on dates. You can rent a pedalo and cross the lake (NTD300/hr for a 2-seater inc lifejackets), or hire a bicycle (from NTD100/day) or walk along the 3.5km path that goes around it. The Chinese name means 'carp lake', but nature lovers will find the tufted ducks (*Aythya fuligula*) and various herons more interesting than the piscine forms of life.

Baibao Creek 白鮑溪 If you've an interest in ecology and how mankind can better manage the environment, you'll happily spend an hour or two here. Assuming you're approaching from the north, near km21.5 on Highway 9C (the road from Liyu Lake) you'll see English-language signs; turn right and go 4km to the very end of the surfaced road. On the same side of the creek, it's recommended that you follow a gravel path that becomes a narrow trail upstream; expect lots of butterflies as well as rich flora. The low, fish-friendly wooden weirs you'll see along this creek are strikingly different from the concrete barriers that disfigure many of Taiwan's waterways and have contributed to the decline of freshwater species including the Formosan landlocked salmon (see box, page 194). Between the 1960s and 1980s the creek was a valuable source of nephrite jade.

Lintianshan 林田山 After World War II, when Taiwan's timber industry was in full swing, almost 400 families lived in this loggers' settlement just west of the highway. Decline began not with changing government policies in the late 1980s but earlier, after fires devastated nearby forests in 1972. Clusters of Japanese-style homes and offices remain in place and several have been renovated; displays about local history and exhibitions of woodcarvings make this a good place to break your journey. A short stretch of track is all that's left of a narrow-gauge railway that once penetrated deep into the mountains, to an altitude of 2,600m. Trains and buses from Hualien City stop in **Wanrong** 萬榮, 2.5km away.

FaTai'An Wetland 馬太鞍溼地 **(Mǎtàiān Shīdì)** (🕐 24hrs daily; free admission) Several English-language sources refer to this ecotourism destination as Mataian, which is the Mandarin pronunciation. FaTai'An (sometimes written Fataan), the original Amis name, is also a kind of plant, the beans of which sustained the local aboriginal population during a long period of warfare with the Amis of Dabalong. This wetland is almost unique in Taiwan in that it's not on or near the coast. Unfortunately, among the 100-plus aquatic plants here are invasive species that are influencing the local ecosystem. If you come here with a guide, ask them to explain the traditional and quite unique palakaw fishing method. To explore this area turn inland at km251.6 on Highway 9. Cross the railway tracks and look for the small bilingual signs pointing to various sites of interest as well as the area's indigenous restaurants.

Dabalong 太巴塱 Located east of central Guangfu near where Highway 11A crosses Road 193, the Amis of Dabalong (sometimes spelled Tafalong or Taibalang) are the traditional enemies of the Amis of FaTai'An, with whom they quarrelled and fought throughout the 19th century. You'll notice the clan's symbol, a white crab, in several places around this village. Dabalong's inhabitants are renowned for their woodcarving skills and, although almost all of the houses here are modern concrete structures, you'll certainly see a few signs of traditional Amis lifestyles, such as bouquets of millet drying in courtyards and animal skulls decorating doorways.

Danong Dafu Forest Recreation Area 大農大富平地森林園區 (🕐 08.00–17.00 daily; free admission) During the heydays of the sugar industry, cane was grown on large tracts of land south of Guangfu. Since 2001, more than 1,000ha of former plantation has been afforested. As well as over a million trees, the woodland features 20-plus plant species native to Taiwan. Wild animals including yellow-throated martens have been spotted here. The forest is much too large to explore on foot, but everything is accessible by bicycle; the official opening hours don't appear to stop people staying nearby from entering very early in the morning when they've a better chance of spotting the birds that thrive here. Most visitors enter from Highway 9, 5.4km south of Guangfu TRA station.

Fuyuan National Forest Recreation Area 富源國家森林遊樂區 **(Fùyuán Sēnlín Yóulèqū)** (📞 03 881 2377; **w** recreation.forest.gov.tw; 🕐 08.00–22.00 daily; admission NTD100/60) If you come to this 191ha reserve expecting an arboreal wilderness, you're in for a disappointment. The area near the visitor centre and Butterfly Eco-House is more like a manicured garden than a semi-tropical forest, but if you hike the four trails (total length: 6.1km) you'll see camphor groves, wild orchids and possibly rare birds like the maroon oriole (*Oriolus traillii*). Birding here is very good throughout the year. March to August is peak season for butterflies but as late as November you'll still see plenty. Fireflies are especially active from March to early May and again in October and early November. Food and accommodation can be had at the onsite Butterfly Valley Resort (page 283). The turn off to Fuyuan is on Highway 9, 10km south of Guangfu TRA station.

Ruisui 瑞穗 The busiest part of Ruisui, with several restaurants, shops and the TRA station, lies east of Highway 9. West of the highway near km273 there are two neighbourhoods each with several hotels where you can stay overnight or soak in naturally hot, yellow carbonate water for a couple of hours then move on: Ruisui Hot Springs and, a little further inland, Hongye Hot Springs. Few establishments have English signs; there are no free, public springs.

Taiwan is ideal for white-water rafting, as the wet season brings huge amounts of rain and the island's steep mountains mean fast rivers cut through fantastic scenery. Hualien County's Xiuguluan River is Taiwan's best-known rafting venue and every day during the summer hundreds of people board inflatables for a wild river experience.

The Xiuguluan, which drains into the Pacific Ocean at Jingpu (page 292) has enough rapids, eddies and sudden drops to keep things exciting. It's also very scenic, though at many points during the 24km-long float you'll be too focused on staying aboard to appreciate the canyons and cliffs. It's an exhilarating experience – but not ideal for those who prefer contemplative encounters with nature. During rafting season there are often hundreds of people on the river at the same time and their behaviour can be quite boisterous. Expect screaming, shouting, water fights and deliberate collisions.

Saoba Monoliths 掃叭石柱 You'll probably spend more time gazing over groves of betel nut and pomelo trees on the mountains than at the two somewhat bland 3,000-year-old monoliths, so close to the road you needn't get out of your car to see them. A bit further south there's one of Taiwan's three Tropic of Cancer monuments and, 800m beyond that, the turn off for Local Road 61. This route cuts through tiny indigenous villages before joining Road 193 between Ruisui TRA station and the Xiuguluan River Rafting Centre.

Xiuguluan River 秀姑巒溪 Organised floats down this river (see box, above) are possible year-round and especially popular between June and August. In peak season bookings should be made at least a day in advance; you may want to do this in person at the **Xiuguluan River Visitor and Rafting Centre** 秀姑巒溪遊客中心 (♦ 03 887 5400; ⊕ 08.30–17.00 daily). The centre – located where Road 193 crosses the river, 3km from Ruisui TRA station – is also where rafting expeditions begin. In spring and autumn, provided you arrive before 09.00, it's usually possible to sign up and be on the river the same morning. Operators charge NTD700–1,200 per person; this includes life-jackets, helmets and lunch but not transport back to the centre afterwards; if you take one of the shuttle buses that return to the centre from near the river's mouth you'll need to pay an additional NTD150 per person. It's possible to rent footwear for the float to keep your own shoes dry. The centre also lends out bicycles (free; deposit your ID).

Yuli Jinja 玉里神社 **(Yùlǐ Shénshè)** If you're walking or biking from Yuli TRA station (a distance of 1.1km) consider bringing a picnic because the view from this Shinto place of worship, west of the town centre, deserves to be appreciated at leisure. You're unlikely to gain any sense of religious awe when approaching, however, because dwellings built after the colonial period crowd the lower *torii* (gate symbolising the entrance to sacred territory). The first set of stairs from the road has 37 steps, while the second has 36, the third 16 and the fourth just nine. These numbers have a religious significance that's so esoteric few can grasp it. Like other jinja, this 1928 shrine suffered grievously in the wake of World War II; the stone lions were removed and Japanese words engraved on the stone lantern columns scratched off. All that remains of the *haiden* (oratory) and *honden* (main sanctuary) are chunks of stone and concrete; a few bear engravings that suggest that what once stood here wasn't merely utilitarian.

Yufu Bikeway 玉富自行車道 This 9.8km-long and nicely level bike path follows an abandoned section of the Hualien–Taitung rail line. Rather than cross the Xiuguluan River near central Yuli the railroad now takes a more direct route toward Taitung. The rerouting not only cuts total distance but also avoids a geological boundary concealed beneath the rock-strewn riverbed. The land east of the waterway is part of the Philippine Sea Plate, while everything to the west is on the Eurasian Plate. Each year, tectonic forces drive a bit more of the Eurasian Plate under the Philippine Sea Plate, lifting the Coastal Mountain Range ever higher and causing the authorities great inconvenience and expense. What used to be the railway bridge – and now serves as part of the bikeway – had to be realigned approximately every two years, and the parallel road bridge still needs to be fixed every three to five years. You may not notice the gradient as you cross from one tectonic plate to another but if you pause at the 3.2km marker and look carefully at the bridge the disparity is obvious.

If you don't already have bicycles, rent from one of the shops right outside Yuli TRA station or 400m to the east at the Giant branch (47 Heping Rd; ☎ 888 5669; ⏰ 08.00–21.30 daily). Finding the bikeway is a cinch: Ride to the front of the TRA station, turn left and follow the narrow road that runs right beside the tracks. After crossing the river you'll soon come to the disused Antong TRA station; around here, locals often lay out *méigān cài* (Hakka-style dried pickled mustard greens) on the railing to dry under the sun. The former Dongli Station, where a shop sells coffee, snacks and postcards, is the official terminus. Tacking northwest on minor roads to Highway 30 and Nanan Waterfall (see below) will add nearly 30km to your day's cycling.

Walami Trail 瓦拉米步道 This path begins at the eastern end of Highway 30 and provides access to the ecologically rich eastern half of Yushan National Park and forms the eastern end of the Batongguan Historic Trail (page 197). On it, you've an excellent chance of seeing troops of Formosan macaques and small flocks of black-browed barbets (*Megalaima oorti*). After dark, you may hear the canine yapping of a short-tailed deer species no bigger than a mid-sized dog, Reeves's muntjac (*Muntiacus reevesi*). Leeches are an occasional nuisance. If you plan on going no further than Jiaxin, the site of a police station during the colonial era and just 4.9km past the trail entrance, you don't need any kind of permit. If you wish to go beyond Jiaxin, drop into **Nanan Visitor Centre** 南安遊客中心 (☎ 03 888 7560; ⏰ 08.00–16.30 daily, closed 2nd Tue each month) and register before starting your hike. At Walami (13.6km from the trailhead; elevation: 1,060m) there's a shelter with running water and electric lights. Accommodation is free but you should bring a sleeping bag. Because space is limited you should apply to the park authorities for a permit at least a week in advance; this can be done online. You'll also need to be self-sufficient in terms of food and cooking equipment. If you want to hike to Walami and return the same day, you're required to register at the visitor centre before 09.00.

The nearest TRA station is Yuli, from where a taxi to Nanan Visitor Centre costs about NTD300, and around NTD500 all the way to the trail entrance.

Mount Liushidan aka Sixty Stone Mountain 六十石山 The uplands here
are famous for one crop: daylilies. These protein-rich orange flowers are used to make soups and other dishes, but it's the sight of masses of them covering entire

hillsides that draws tourists. The turn off (on the left if you're heading south) is clearly marked near km308.5. At the height of daylily season in August and part of September the mountain is closed to private vehicles; minibuses shuttle visitors up and down the mountain.

Luoshan 羅山 (km310.5) The main attraction here is a waterfall nearly 5km from Highway 9. There's also a disappointingly flat and lifeless mud volcano and some of the prettiest rice fields anywhere in Taiwan. You'll need your own vehicle as the road up to the waterfall is steep and unshaded. Following County Road 79 east towards the waterfall you'll find the visitor centre on your left. On the right about 750m from Highway 9 there's a charming little ma-and-pa grocery shop; opposite are a land-god shrine and a pre-war mud-brick house. Look closely at the walls of the latter and you'll notice scores of holes made by blue-banded bees that inhabit the walls each May and June.

Highway 23 For motorists, this winding and little-used road is an excellent way of cutting between the East Rift Valley and the coast. Top up your tank if coming from Highway 9 because the only petrol station is at km38 (⏱ 07.00–noon & 13.30–16.00 daily). The gorge-like Taiyuan Hidden Valley (km40.3) is a scenic highlight; don't give anything to the macaques who hang around here hoping to be fed.

Chishang 池上 Acclaimed since the Japanese occupation for the quality of its rice – local grain was supplied to the Japanese royal household in Tokyo – Chishang's farmlands have gained extra attention in recent years after featuring in TV commercials. The area's beauty is all the more exceptional because there are few power lines and utility poles getting between you and the landscape. Farmers believe the shadows cast by cables and pylons interfere with the rice's natural growing cycle, and have been successful in keeping them away from their paddy fields. The most famous rice-field scenery is southwest of the town centre and can be accessed by Local Road 6, which connects Highway 9 with Road 197 and is sometimes crowded with tourists on bicycles or on foot. If you're coming from the north on Highway 9, the turn off is on the left just over 3km past Chishang TRA station.

The body of water that gives Chishang (literally 'on the pond') its name is 1km southeast of the railway station. **Dapo Pond** 大坡池 (Da Po Chih on some signposts) now covers about 20ha, less than half its size in the 19th century. Designated a wetland of national importance, it's protected on account of its biodiversity.

A 7.5km-long bike trail links many local sights, but if there's any place that rewards random riding it's Chishang. Three businesses on Zhongzheng Road, the thoroughfare that leads directly to the front entrance of the TRA station, rent out bicycles and e-bikes.

South Cross-Island Highway (Highway 20) Even if driving all the way to the west coast still isn't possible (page 255), fans of Taiwan's highlands may still want to explore the eastern stretch of this spectacular road. The turn off from Highway 9 is just north of Guanshan (page 267). Do find somewhere to stop near **Wulu Canyon** 霧鹿峽谷 (km182), where the cliffs bear yellow sulphur stains. At one time the road followed every twist and turn of the Xinwulu River but over the years tunnels have been bored to straighten out the highway. Take great care if you decide to stroll along one of the now-redundant stretches of road – they aren't maintained.

Beyond Wulu your best hope for a hot meal is **Lidao** 利稻 (km177 Hwy 20), a Bunun village on a plateau 1,068m above sea level and a major venue of the tribe's annual Ear-shooting Festival (page 67). From the park by the elementary school you can see the mountains very well; the artillery pieces here were made in Russia and seized by the Japanese during the Russo-Japanese War of 1904–05. In the 1920s, the colonial regime used them against truculent aborigines.

The entrance to **Xiangyang National Forest Recreation Area** 向陽國家森林 遊樂區 (km154.5 Hwy 20; **w** recreation.forest.gov.tw; ⏰ 08.30–16.30 daily; free admission) is at 2,314m. Inside there are hiking trails (the longest is 1.77km) and stands of Formosan cypresses, cardinal maples and Taiwan red pines. This 362ha reserve doubles as the trailhead for several splendid high-altitude hikes, most notably to the peak of **Xiangyangshan** 向陽山 (3,346m) and **Jiaming Lake** 嘉明湖, a sublime body of water that fills a meteor-impact crater 3,310m above sea level. If you've a week or more, the right equipment and sufficient energy and provisions (as well as permission), you can hike northwards across Yushan National Park to Dongpu.

Guanshan 關山 This town's 12km-long bike path (⏰ 24hrs daily; admission NTD50) predates Taiwan's bicycle revolution and continues to be a major attraction, showing off the area's best scenery and deserving of 3–4 hours. Following a gradual climb, an exhilarating downhill stretch brings you to a place where water buffalo laze in a marsh. Most of the trail is shaded by mahogany trees or betel-nut groves. Among the crops you might see along the way are millet, rapeseed, jelly figs, pears, sugarcane and oranges. Bikes can be rented near the TRA station.

Luye High Terrace 鹿野高台 **(Lùyě Gāo Tái)** This small plateau has become one of Taiwan's top paragliding spots, and even if you're not interested in leaping off the hillside, you should come here for the excellent views up and down the East Rift Valley.

Two nearby villages are of interest. One is **Yongan** 永安, to the north. A mixed Han-indigenous village sprawling at the base of steep mountains, there isn't much to do here except stroll through neighbourhoods separated by cornfields and banana plantations. To hike up to the terrace from the village, first find number 442 Yongan Road, opposite which is a one-car-wide concrete track that goes down to a small creek. Cross the river, turn left and keep walking past the newly planted saplings until you see a stairway disappearing up into the forest. Take it and soon you'll be at a two-floor wooden pavilion on the northwestern edge of a terrace. Weather permitting, you'll enjoy excellent views northwards. To reach Yongan from the south, turn inland at km348 on Highway 9 and take the twisty road going uphill to Yongan. If you're coming from the north, leave Highway 9 at km344.5 and keep driving until you see Yongan Elementary School.

The other village worth looking at is due south of Luye High Terrace. Now called **Longtian** 龍田, it was established in 1917 to attract settlers from Japan, then as now a crowded country. Scores of hopeful immigrants arrived, but the majority, deciding life in Taiwan's cities would be easier, left within a decade. A few Japanese-style wooden bungalows still stand, and the Shinto Shrine in the centre of the village (2.6km from Luye TRA station) has been restored.

HIGHWAY 11: THE COAST ROAD

The coastline between the cities of Hualien and Taitung has more than enough rocky shores, steep green hills and indigenous villages to fill a couple of days. All km-marker numbers refer to locations on Highway 11.

Rice accounts for one-fifth of all calories consumed by mankind, and for many Taiwanese the proportion is even greater. Even though affluence has now brought a varied diet, millions of Taiwanese still eat it almost every day of the year. In Mandarin, the act of preparing a meal is *zhǔ fàn*, literally 'cook rice'. For breakfast, rice is served as a watery gruel with pickles, peanuts, fried eggs and dried shredded pork, while steamed rice is the basis of a typical Taiwanese lunch or dinner. Rice ground into flour can be made into dumplings or noodles (nowadays most noodles are made from wheat flour).

Rice grows well in Taiwan's warm climate and fields of green stalks can be seen throughout the lowlands. In recent years, average annual rice production has been about one million tonnes, meaning the island is more than 90% self-sufficient – an impressive achievement given the island's topography and population density, and the fact that other crops are also grown in large quantities.

Rice requires a great deal of water compared with other crops and paddy fields produce worrying amounts of methane, a greenhouse gas. However, in other respects this form of agriculture isn't too bad for the environment. Paddy networks appear to stabilise water supplies and reduce the incidence of flooding, and while paddies may look as though they support no other forms of life, they're often full of frogs, spiders and tiny moths. Unfortunately, many places are also infested by a species of snail. Known in English as golden apple snails (*Pomacea canaliculata*), these gastropods are not native to Taiwan. Introduced to the island from South America in 1979 because it was thought they'd be a popular foodstuff (they're high in protein but taste awful, even when processed), they've become a major pest because they feed on young rice shoots. Unlike their dry-land counterparts, they have tubular snorkels which enable them to stay safely submerged. They reproduce very fast: vivid pink egg masses are deposited just above the waterline to protect them from predation by fish.

As demand for organically grown food increases, more and more farmers are embracing traditional methods such as raising ducks in their rice fields. Not only do these fowl eat golden apple snails and other pests, but their feet stir the soil and their excrement is a good fertiliser. Several places in Taiwan are promoting their organic rice, of which Luoshan (page 288) has been one of the most successful.

GETTING THERE AND AROUND

By car, motorcycle and bicycle Running from Hualien to Taitung, Highway 11 is 167km long, and you should allow 4 hours' driving time from one to the other. Be aware that petrol stations along Highway 11 tend to close at 17.00. The road is well maintained and popular with cyclists.

By bus Whether you start from Hualien or Taitung, reaching the major sights by public transport is quite straightforward but tiring if you try to do everything in a single day. See pages 273 and 295 respectively for details of those cities' bus services. The Taiwan Tourist Shuttle #153 connects Taitung's bus and TRA stations with attractions including Fugang, Shanyuan Bay, Dulan and Sanxiantai. There are five departures per day (⏰ 07.20–14.20) and a one-day pass is NTD299.

TOURIST INFORMATION

ℹ East Coast National Scenic Area ☎089 841 520; w eastcoast-nsa.gov.tw

ℹ Hualien Visitor Centre km9 Hwy 11; ⏰ 08.30–17.00 daily

ℹ Sanxiantai Visitor Centre Sanxiantai; ⏰ 08.30–17.00 daily

🏠 **WHERE TO STAY AND EAT** Between Hualien City and Taitung City, the best places for eating are Chenggong and Dulan. The former has good seafood whereas the latter has a blend of expat-run startups and typical Taiwanese eateries. In terms of accommodation, the coast road is dotted with homestays, especially the stretch through Yanliao between km8 and km15.

🏠 **Qi Li Xiang** 七里香民宿 (6 rooms) 43–2 Wushibi, Changbin; ☎089 801 118; m 0955 258 514. A sizeable property between the coast road & the ocean midway between Baxian Caves & Sanxiantai, Qi Li Xiang offers plenty of space indoors & out plus a laidback approach that means the owners are sometimes hard to track down. 4 rooms can take 4 or more ppl. **$$$**

🏠 **Sea-Hi B&B** 近月旭海民宿 (5 rooms) 152 Yanliao Vlg; ☎038 671 158; e seahi.hualien@ gmail.com; w www.seahi.idv.tw/english.php. On the ocean side of the coast road, Sea-Hi B&B has certain advantages over many of its competitors: an easy-to-spot English sign, split-level 4-person rooms & a large garden where guests can relax & watch the waves. Room rates NTD2,400–3,900. A little English spoken; b/fast & pickup from Hualien Airport or TRA station inc. **$$$**

OTHER PRACTICALITIES The **post office** in Chenggong (77 Zhonghua Rd; ⏰ 08.30–17.00 Mon–Fri, 09.00–noon Sat) can change major foreign currencies and travellers' cheques.

WHAT TO SEE AND DO Heading south from Hualien City, the first few kilometres are somewhat bleak. However, by the time you reach Hualien Visitor Centre at km9 you'll be making frequent stops to enjoy the scenery.

Henan Temple 和南寺 (km11; ☎03 867 1001; ⏰ 06.00–19.00 daily) This hillside shrine was founded by a Chan master in 1967 who asked the 20 or so resident nuns to propagate the dharma through art, literature and music. It's often possible to stay overnight; calling a few days ahead is best but individuals who roll up unannounced are likely to be given a space to sleep, most likely sharing a simple room with another non-monastic (no AC; donations accepted but not solicited; b/fast available). Guests should, of course, behave appropriately – it's a strictly vegetarian institution and once the gate is closed it's not possible to go outside until the next day.

Fanshuliao 蕃薯寮 (km29.5) Fānshǔ ('savages' potato') is the old, politically incorrect name for sweet potatoes (they're now known as *dìguā*), and here the Fanshuliao River has cut a 70m-deep gorge. About 2km south you'll come to **Baqi Viewing Platform** 芭崎眺望台. Because the road is so winding it's easy to miss this spot but do stop if you can to savour the view over the bay.

Shitiping 石梯坪 If you read Chinese, the place name will give you a strong clue as to what to expect. Shitiping means 'stone ladder terrace' and the coast here is dominated by rock platforms that interest both geologists and marine biologists. The local environment, which has both coral reefs and the remnants of

During the summer, whale-watching boats set out from Hualien, Chenggong and some other places along the east coast. Tours usually last 2–3 hours and cost NTD800–1,000 per person. Bring your passport and if you're prone to seasickness, don't eat much in the hours before the tour. A broad hat and sunblock are highly recommended.

Nineteen cetacean species have been recorded off Taiwan's east coast, and if you join a whale-watching tour you're almost certain to see Risso's, Fraser's and common bottlenose dolphins as well. With a bit of luck, you'll spot killer whales, pygmy killers or maybe a sperm whale. Useful websites include Whale Watching in Taiwan (w www.whalewatching.org.tw) and Turomoan (℡ 03 833 3821; w turumoan.com.tw). Ask at any visitor information centre on the coast to ascertain sailing times and other details.

One irony of these tours is that many of those on board have travelled from western Taiwan, and most of them know nothing about the west coast's beleaguered population of Indo-Pacific humpback dolphins. In recent years, the number of these pale pink legally protected creatures has dwindled to fewer than 70 as they face five major threats: pollution, land reclamation, underwater noise, interactions with fishing boats and fishing gear, and reduced freshwater flow into the estuaries within their habitat. The last is crucial because it's the fresh water flowing into salt water that creates the variable conditions that give rise to the high fish productivity of estuaries.

ancient volcanic outpourings, nurtures a wide range of tropical fish, crustaceans and algae. It's possible to join whale-watching tours at the fishing harbour here (see box, above).

Just around the headland, the Xiuguluan River flows beneath a landmark bridge from which the spot gets the name **Changhongqiao** 長虹橋 ('long rainbow bridge'), then empties into the Pacific Ocean. If you've rafted down the river (see box, page 286), this is where you'll disembark, and travelling by public transport between Hualien in Taitung often involves changing buses here. You can kill time at **Xibulan Visitor Center** 奚卜蘭遊客中心 (⊕ 08.30–17.00 daily) or wander around the Amis community called **Jingpu** 靜浦. Drivers and motorcyclists (and exceptionally strong cyclists) may consider detouring along Local Road 64, a lovely backcountry route through the Coastal Mountain Range to Ruisui, sometimes crossed by crab-eating mongooses.

Baxian Caves 八仙洞 (km76.5; ⊕ 09.00–17.00 daily; free admission; parking NTD60/20)

A place of tremendous archaeological importance but limited tourist interest, Baxian's 16 caves are collectively named after the Eight Immortals prominent in Taoism and Chinese mythology. Several now contain shrines, but between 5,000 and possibly 25,000 years ago humans dwelled here. Since the late 1960s tools made from stone and animal bone have been excavated here, as have fish bones left over from meals and rubbing sticks used to make fire. It's Taiwan's only confirmed Palaeolithic site. When these caves were inhabited they were much closer to the ocean, but tectonic uplift has pushed the highest to 130m above sea level. Reaching them means climbing a wooden stairway, on which there's a chance you'll encounter macaques or aggressive dogs. A few archaeological finds are displayed in the visitor centre.

Sanxiantai aka Terraces of the Three Immortals 三仙台 (km112; free admission; parking NTD60/20) Named after three of Taoism's Eight Immortals, what was originally a little peninsula was worn down by wind and water until it became an island that's now linked to the mainland by a distinctive eight-arch pedestrian bridge. If you're here when it isn't crowded, your stop may stretch from the anticipated 20 minutes to over an hour.

Chenggong 成功 (km114) Each year, in late autumn and early winter, the fishermen who are the backbone of this small town's economy head out to sea and harpoon large numbers of black marlin. Many are exported to Japan or shipped to high-end restaurants in Taipei, but some end up in local eateries, of which there's a cluster between Highway 11 and the fishing harbour. English signs or menus are unknown, alas.

Dulan 都蘭 (km145) There's something about this laidback little town, which developed thanks to the sugar industry, that inspires a certain type of traveller to stay for weeks on end. The population is now a mix of local Amis, artists from all over, and couples who've fled big cities and now run homestays or restaurants. Galleries and shops can be found in the former sugar factory (⊕ varies) inland of Highway 11, and among the several restaurants on or very near the highway are places that serve French, Vietnamese and Taiwanese dishes.

Shanyuan Bay 杉原灣 (km155) One of the east's finest beaches, this 1.5km-long stretch of sand is safe for swimming and surfing but not always clean. One point of access is 700m north of the empty multi-story eyesore that was a controversial hotel development backed by the local government; the courts eventually shut the project down. A side road goes down to a temple where it's usually possible to park.

Xiaoyeliu 小野柳 (km156.5; free admission; parking NTD60/20) So named because it resembles Yehliu on the north coast (page 135), Xiaoyeliu's eroded sandstone formations are pretty but the place can get crowded and the sun is often ferocious. If you want to stay at the campground here ask at the visitors' centre (⊕ 08.30–17.00 daily).

Fugang 富岡 (km161) This tiny fishing town between Highway 11 and the Pacific Ocean is the jumping-off point for trips to Green Island and Orchid Island (page 331), and there are half-a-dozen eateries, a couple of small supermarkets and a handful of accommodation options. You'll have no problems finding any of these, or the harbour itself. It's OK to leave your vehicle in one of the free car parks near the port for a day or more. If you're coming from the East Rift Valley, approaching via Road 197 is not only scenic but also saves you the trouble of entering Taitung City. Getting here from Taitung City isn't difficult thanks to fairly frequent buses (NTD23–38).

TAITUNG CITY 台東市 (TÁIDŌNG SHÌ) *Telephone code 089*

The importance of this sprawling medium-sized city lies in its location at the southern end of Highway 11. Whether you're journeying down the coast or exploring the East Rift Valley, you'll likely pass through this friendly, but not conspicuously prosperous, administrative and transport centre.

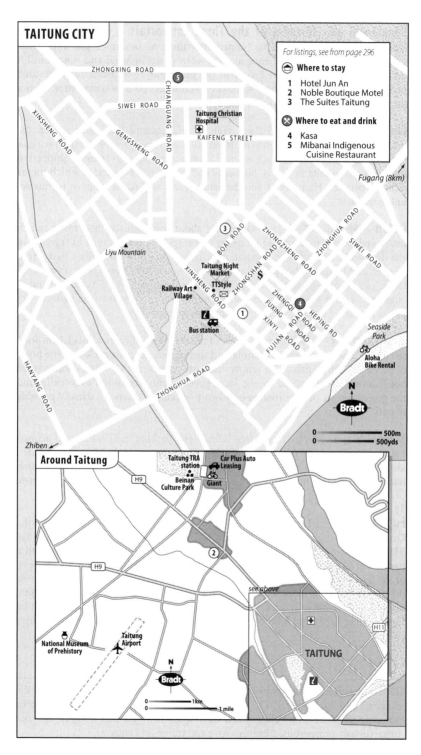

TAITUNG CITY

ZHONGXING ROAD

SIWEI ROAD

XINSHENG ROAD

GENGSHENG ROAD

CHUANGUANG ROAD

Taitung Christian Hospital

KAIFENG STREET

Fugang (8km)

BOAI ROAD

ZHONGZHENG ROAD

ZHONGHUA ROAD

SIWEI ROAD

Liyu Mountain

Taitung Night Market

XINSHENG ROAD

TTStyle

ZHONGSHAN ROAD

Railway Art Village

ZHENGQI ROAD

FUXING ROAD

HEPING RD

XINYI ROAD

Bus station

FUJIAN ROAD

Seaside Park

Aloha Bike Rental

HANYANG ROAD

ZHONGHUA ROAD

N

Bradt

0 — 500m
0 — 500yds

Zhiben

Around Taitung

Taitung TRA station

Car Plus Auto Leasing

Beinan Culture Park

Giant

H9

H9

2

see above

H11

National Museum of Prehistory

Taitung Airport

TAITUNG

N

Bradt

0 — 1km
0 — 1 mile

The population of 108,000 includes large aboriginal, Hakka and Hoklo communities, the last of which is behind the city's best-known cultural event, the annual Han Dan procession (see box, page 298). These parades are held after dark on the 15th and 16th days of the first lunar month and like Yanshui's Beehive Fireworks Festival, they coincide with but aren't a true part of the traditional Lantern Festival. The authorities, who initially discouraged the celebration, have in recent years latched on to Han Dan as a means of getting tourist dollars into the city. The event, which involves throwing firecrackers at a semi-naked man, certainly makes for good video clips.

Taitung is famous for its fresh fruit, the custard apple (aka sweetsop) being in season between December and February. If you head south from the city, you'll see fields covered with thick black netting under which betel pepper is grown. The betel pepper plant isn't related to the betel-nut palm, but its leaves are used for wrapping betel nuts before they're sold. Around the city you'll see local folk washing big baskets of these dark-green, fist-sized leaves.

GETTING THERE AND AROUND

By air Taitung Airport (TTT; ☎ 362 530; w www.tta.gov.tw) is 7km from the city centre and easy to reach by taxi or public bus. There are at least five flights each day to/from Taipei Songshan Airport (1hr; NTD2,280 one-way), but I'd suggest flying only if you're pressed for time because the rail journey is very pleasant. For details of flights to/from Green Island and Orchid Island, see *Chapter 10*.

By TRA The South Link rail journey from Kaohsiung (about 16 expresses; ⏱ 05.12–21.20 daily; most take 2¾hrs; NTD279–362) is one of Taiwan's most scenic. In the 98km between Fangliao and Zhiben, the track crosses 158 bridges and goes through 36 tunnels, the longest of which is 8.1km. You'll see uninhabited valleys and boulder-filled riverbeds, and after the 17th tunnel you'll catch glimpses of the Pacific. More than 20 trains per day connect Hualien with Taitung (⏱ 06.09–22.28; 1½–3½hrs; NTD220–343), many of which stop at Chishang (typically takes 45mins; NTD61–96) and Fuli (takes up to 1hr; NTD72–111).

There are at least 15 buses daily from Taitung TRA station (⏱ 08.10–18.25 daily; 20mins; NTD23) to the bus station in the city centre.

By bus Buses have an advantage over trains in that they bring you directly to the city centre. However, journey times are slightly longer and fares a bit higher. From Kaohsiung, there are four buses per day (⏱ 03.00, 07.00, 12.30 & 17.30; 3½hrs; NTD540). Eastern Top Transport has one bus per day to Hualien (#8119; 06.10; 4hrs; NTD494), as does Hualien Bus Co (#1127; 15.00; 4¼hrs; NTD514), both of which take Highway 11 along the coast.

Buses to East Rift Valley towns like Fuli are slower than trains, but if Luye is one of your objectives, look into the Taiwan Tourist Shuttle #8168 route (6 departures daily from Taitung bus station; ⏱ 08.30–15.30 daily; 1hr 20mins; NTD120).

By car, motorcycle or bicycle The absolute best way to enter Taitung is via the South Cross-Island Highway (page 255) but this route is unlikely to reopen soon so you'll likely take Highway 9 from the southeast. Be prepared to share the road with a significant number of lorries. If you're approaching from the north, both the coastal route (page 289) and the drive through the East Rift Valley (page 282) are extremely attractive.

There are car- and bicycle-hire outfits in the centre:

BIKING THE EAST WITH GIANT

Taiwan-based Giant Bicycles (w giant-bicycles.com), one of the world's leading bike manufacturers, offers bike-hire services at several of its shops around the island. With careful planning it's possible to pick up top-quality bikes, helmets, panniers and other equipment at certain branches in east Taiwan, use them for a few days, then return everything to a different branch. At the time of writing, Giant had yet to publish information about this facility in English, but if you send an email in English to one of the branches (Hualien City e giant. d21134@msa.hinet.net; Taitung City e giant.d21139@msa.hinet.net) well in advance of your arrival, it should be possible to arrange what you want.

Car Plus Auto Leasing Very near Taitung TRA station; \227 979; w car-plus.com.tw; ⊕ 08.00–20.30 daily

Aloha Bike Rental 22 Nanhai Rd; \323 273; m 0953 741 055; ⊕ 08.00–19.30 daily.

Located near the Seaside Park; decent, full-size bikes for NTD150/day.

Giant Beside Taitung TRA station; \235 879; ⊕ 09.00–18.00 Mon–Fri, 08.00–18.00 Sat–Sun; see box, above

TOURIST INFORMATION AND TOUR OPERATORS There are visitor information centres in the airport, the TRA station and Railway Art Village (all ⊕ 09.00–17.00 daily). Tour Taitung (w tour.taitung.gov.tw) is a useful official website.

Originally from California but now based in Taitung, Cheryl Robbins (m 0923 151 965; e specialtytourstaiwan@gmail.com) is an ROC-licensed tour guide and travel writer (see box, page 38) who specialises in multi-day cultural and ecological tours of Taiwan's indigenous areas.

WHERE TO STAY *Map, page 294*

There are a dozen homestays within walking distance of the train station but few have English signs.

Noble Boutique motel 貴築精品汽車旅館 (43 rooms) Km373.5, Hwy 9; \238 199; w noblemotel.com.tw. This plush motel is fairly convenient for Taitung's airport & TRA station. Rooms (not all of which have their own integral garage) are quite spacious & tastefully decorated in pale golds & browns. All have jacuzzis, big beds & big TVs. A few scratches here & there but very clean. W/day prices go as low as NTD1,780. Look for the big illuminated 'Motel' sign. B/fast inc. $$$

The Suites Taitung 地景泽行馆 (60 rooms) 18 Lane 362, Boai Rd; \356 589; e service@thesuites-taitung.com; w en.thesuites-taitung.com. Opened in 2017 & well maintained

so far, The Suites' claim to be a design hotel is more justified than most. This stylish bldg is within walking distance of Taitung's main night market (⊕ 17.00–23.00 Thu–Sat; $). Good for couples but adding a bed is a pricey NTD1,000. See their website for packages inc car or scooter rental. $$$

Hotel Jun An 君安旅店 (19 rooms) 96 Xinsheng Rd; \331 168. Basic, monolingual & not as quiet as you might like it but you're unlikely to find cheaper accommodation in the city centre. Even at w/ends you can often a get a room for 2 ppl for NTD700; a room that takes 4 at a squeeze is usually NTD1,200. AC, but no b/fast. One of the few budget inns with English on the sign outside. $

WHERE TO EAT AND DRINK *Map, page 294*

Kasa 102 Heping St; m 0980 085 878; ☐ @ KasaCafeTaitung; ⊕ 18.00–02.00 daily. Kasa has been around for some years & occupies an atmospheric old bldg that's ideal for a semi-outdoor

restaurant-bar. Very laidback & thus not ideal for anyone in a hurry. Not everything listed on the EM (which has curries & Western snacks) is available every day, but usually specials plug the gaps. $$

✕ Mibanai Indigenous Cuisine Restaurant 米巴奈山地美食坊 470 Chuanguang Rd; ✆231 084; ⏰ 11.30–14.00 & 17.30–21.00 daily. First the bad news: there's no EM, & while the workers speak a number of languages (including Amis & Puyuma) English isn't among them. Now the good news: this long-running indigenous restaurant is very clean & very popular with local tour groups. Enlist a Mandarin speaker or choose a set menu that fits your budget. **$$**

OTHER PRACTICALITIES
✚ Taitung Christian Hospital 350 Kaifeng St; ✆320 332; ⏰ 24hrs daily

✉ Post office 382 Zhongshan Rd; ⏰ 08.30–17.00 Mon–Fri. Can change major foreign currencies & travellers' cheques.

WHAT TO SEE AND DO
Round the City Bike Path Going anti-clockwise from the Seaside Park, the first point of interest along this 21km-long track is **Railway Art Village** 鐵道藝術村 aka Tiehua Village (⏰ 24hrs daily, gallery times vary). Housed in Taitung's original railway station (trains stopped coming here in 2001), the public art displayed isn't likely to bowl you over but the information centre here is convenient and there's often live music at the weekend (typical admission NTD250). Also worth checking out is **TTStyle** (105 Xinsheng Rd; ⏰ 10.00–22.00 daily) where 20-odd freight containers arrayed beneath a wood-and-steel membrane are occupied by craft shops and an all-day Western-style breakfast eatery serving coffees (from NTD80) and food (from NTD90). The bike path goes inland but not all the way to the National Museum of Prehistory before turning northeast and skirting the new TRA station. Pedalling onwards, you'll pass within sight of the topographical oddities of **Little Huangshan** and **Liji Badlands**, the latter somewhat like Tainan's Moonscape World. The final stretch through **Taitung Forest Park** is always pleasant.

National Museum of Prehistory 國立臺灣史前文化博物館 (**Guólì Shǐqián Wénhuà Bówùguǎn**) (✆ 381 166; **w** nmp.gov.tw; ⏰ 09.00–17.00 Tue–Sun; admission NTD80/50) About 7km from the city centre, this museum is worth visiting only if you're strongly interested in Taiwan's distant past. Skim the sections about Taiwan's geological history and prehistoric animal population (which included rhinos and horses) then head downstairs to read about the prehistoric cultures which flourished in Taiwan more than 2,000 years ago. Academics have yet to determine what relationship, if any, exists between the ancient Beinan people who inhabited this part of Taiwan and modern aboriginal groups such as the Puyuma (known in Mandarin as the Bēinán tribe). Traces of the Beinan culture were uncovered during the Japanese colonial era but there was no concerted effort to retrieve and catalogue the remnants until work began on Taitung's new railway station in 1980. Some 1,523 slate coffins were found, as were the jade knives and arrowheads now displayed in the museum. The main archaeological site, 4.5km northeast of the museum, has been turned into **Beinan Culture Park** 卑南遺址(⏰ 08.30–17.00 daily; free admission), where one of the original excavations has been preserved under a canopy. Don't go out of your way as there's very little to see, but if you've time to kill before boarding a train (the station's 400m away), the park's a lovely place to linger.

SOUTH FROM TAITUNG

If you've a spare day in the Taitung area but no plans to head across to Pingtung or Kaohsiung, consider heading to the southernmost part of the county, especially if you're a fan of rugged coastal scenery.

During the first few weeks of each lunar year in Taitung, volunteers take turns to have firecrackers hurled at their heads and bottle rockets fired at their bodies. Wearing nothing but red shorts, gloves, goggles to protect their eyes and wet cloths over their ears and throat, these men are carried through the crowd on a bamboo-and-rattan litter, which they share with the doll-sized effigy of a god. Han Dan's followers agree the deity they honour was once an ordinary mortal, but details of his earthly career are in dispute. Most think he was a general who died over 3,000 years ago and who subsequently became a god of war and wealth. It's said that, because he hates the cold, he bestows good fortune on whoever warms him by showering his icons with fireworks. However, a minority believe Han Dan lived much more recently, and that he was a thug guilty of extortion and violence. Eventually, showing remorse for his crimes, he urged the people he'd terrorised to scorch him with fireworks. They did so with a vengeance – the repentant ex-gangster was blasted to death.

The ritual bombardment sounds dangerous and it is: few of the human Han Dans can endure more than 10 minutes on the litter; all of them suffer wheals and minor burns. Unlike the shamans of Taiwanese folk religion, they are neither possessed by their patron deity nor in a state of trance – no wonder many swig liquor while waiting their turn. Each Han Dan wears several amulets and carries a bushy banyan branch. The latter has multiple functions: banyan leaves are said to ward off evil; the branch can be used to block incoming rockets; and when the Han Dan wants to throw in the towel, he waves the branch above his head.

According to Ho Chao-ti's superb 2006 documentary *The Gangster's God: A Film of the Taiwanese Underworld*, most of those who climb atop the litter are current or ex-mobsters. Some are new recruits; by taking part, they hope to show how tough and resolute they are, and so gain standing in criminal circles. However, her interviews with older participants revealed more complex reasons for wanting to have fireworks hurled at them: low self-esteem and a desire to suffer physical pain because they're overwhelmed with guilt about past misdeeds.

Nowadays the event is sponsored by local businesses who see it as a good way to get publicity. In addition to paying for the fireworks, they present each Han Dan with cash in a red envelope and sometimes a small gold medal. Over the decades, there's been a complete about-face in officialdom's attitude. The ritual, first held in 1954, was banned between 1983 and 1989 because of its gang links; however, in recent years the scorching of Han Dan has been heavily promoted by the authorities. Recent human Han Dans have included Taitung's mayor, an English teacher from South Africa, a German filmmaker and a local young woman.

GETTING THERE AND AROUND

By car, motorcycle or bicycle The distance from central Taitung to Taiwan's west coast is 96km. The going can be slow due to lorries and gradients. There are no petrol stations between Fenggang (⊕ 24hrs daily) and Daren (⊕ 06.30–22.00 daily). Driving time should be cut by 10% or more from the current 2¼ hours when a major tunnel is finished as vehicles will no longer have to climb to Shouka at

478m above sea level. The original stretch of road will be maintained and continue to provide access to Road 199 [see map, page 265]. Cyclists using Highway 9 need strong nerves because the road is narrow in places – widening and straightening projects are ongoing – yet traffic is sometimes both fast and heavy.

By TRA Several Kaohsiung-bound expresses stop in Zhiben, Jinlun and Dawu. Also, two local trains in each direction daily connect Taitung with Fangliao.

By bus Between Taitung and Dawu, travelling by bus has certain advantages over the train; for one, if you're staying in the city centre there's no need to trek out to the TRA station (Zhiben TRA station is also inconvenient), and on a bus you'll see more of the scenery because the rail line goes through several tunnels. Convenient southbound services from Taitung include 15 #8129 buses to Zhiben National Forest Recreation Area (🕐 06.00–21.15 daily; 50mins; NTD66) via the hot springs (NTD51). About a dozen buses per day stop in Taimali or Jinlun.

WHERE TO STAY AND EAT Accommodation options are limited south of Zhiben but you'll be able to find something to eat, usually within 500m of the TRA station, in each little town along the way.

WHAT TO SEE AND DO

Zhiben Hot Springs 知本溫泉 **(Zhīběn Wēnquán)** This perennially popular destination 17km southwest of Taitung City (sometimes spelled 'Jhihben') has a decent range of hotels, some of which have public pools where you can soak for a few hours provided you have a swimsuit; most charge around NTD300/150. That said, there are no standouts and before committing yourself to a particular establishment, you may want to ask whether it's possible to take a shower in ordinary tap water, as not every establishment offers an alternative to sulphur-tainted hot-springs water. If you feel like some exercise, follow the signs to Jade Waterfall aka Baiyu Falls 白玉瀑布, which is less than 900m from the main road along a steep but safe trail.

Zhiben National Forest Recreation Area 知本森林遊樂區 **(Zhīběn Sēnlín Yóulèqū)** (w recreation.forest.gov.tw; 🕐 Oct–Jun 07.00–17.00, Jul–Sep 07.00–18.00 daily; admission NTD100/50 Sat–Sun & nat hols, NTD80/50 Mon–Fri) Some 5km past the main cluster of hotels, this 111ha reserve encompasses patches of semi-rainforest and restored mixed forest. The highest point on the trail network is a pavilion exactly 500m above sea level. The less-than-180-degree views from this spot don't really justify the exertion required by the short, steep approach – but the macaques you'll encounter along the way, plus the giant banyan trees and numerous butterflies, certainly do. Leave enough time in your schedule for the delightful (and free) geothermal foot bath and the medicinal herbs garden.

Taimali Kinchen Mountain 太麻里金針山 This area gets busy in late summer when the daylily (*Hemerocallis disticha*) plantations are at their most spectacular. The orange buds are cultivated as a kind of vegetable, for cooking in soups with pork ribs, or for adding to fried rice vermicelli. In previous years the authorities have arranged shuttle buses up to the mountain from Taimali TRA station; ask at a VIC in Taitung for details if you're planning a visit.

Kiokai Ni Santo Josef 金崙聖若瑟教堂 (⏱ 07.00–19.00 daily) Established in the 1950s but thoroughly renovated in 2007, this Roman Catholic house of worship is known locally by its Paiwan name; English speakers would call it the 'Church of St Joseph'. In its current incarnation, it presents an unusual blend of indigenous and Catholic motifs: images of the Crucifixion, for instance, feature people wearing traditional Paiwan clothing, while snake emblems (the tribe's animal totem) appear in many places. The church is clearly marked, less than 500m inland of Jinlun TRA station; if you're arriving by train, follow the road that leads away from the station, past a couple of eateries, and you'll find it on your left. If you're approaching in your own vehicle, follow the signs for 'Central Jinlun'. Opposite the church, a road leads inland to five hot-springs establishments, all geared to local travellers, and a petrol station (⏱ 07.00–19.00 daily).

10

Minor Islands

Each of the ROC's minor islands has its own appeal, but a few generalisations can be made. All are thinly populated – less than 1% of the country's citizens live in the places described in this chapter – and apart from fishing, tourism and small-scale agriculture there's little economic activity. As a consequence, none of them suffer from industrial pollution or traffic jams.

Two kinds of Western visitor are drawn to these islands: those fanatical about watersports or birdwatching and those who want to see something quite different from 'mainland' Taiwan. Little Liuqiu and Green Island can be done as day trips, although staying overnight is recommended. The counties of Kinmen and Penghu deserve at least three days each, both quite different from Taiwan in terms of scenery as well as being exceptionally rich in history and architecture. The Matsu Islands and Orchid Island (the only ROC island to have an Austronesian culture being the homeland of the Tao people) are fascinating but difficult to get to, and because of these transport problems, if you're heading to either give yourself at least two spare days between your planned return to Taiwan and your flight out of the country.

The ROC has two other far-flung maritime outposts. Wuqiu (population: 685) lies midway between Kinmen and Matsu, 9km from the nearest PRC-held territory. Save for the ROC servicemen posted there, very few outsiders have been able to visit Wuqiu and obtaining permission to go there is practically impossible. Pratas, a single island and two submerged atolls 400km southwest of Kaohsiung in the hotly contested South China Sea, falls under Dongsha Atoll Marine National Park, and the only inhabitants are coastguard personnel and a few marine scientists. For years there has been talk of opening the park for small-group environmental-education tours but nothing concrete had been announced by the time of writing.

Between the KMT's retreat to Taiwan in 1949 and the 1980s, Kinmen, Matsu and Wuqiu were on the frontline of the Nationalist–Communist conflict. Now that Taipei–Beijing relations are more peaceful it's possible to travel by ferry between Kinmen and the Fujianese city of Xiamen, or from Matsu to Mawei near Fuzhou. In the short term, the easing of tensions hurt the islands' economies. As the ROC military presence on Kinmen, Matsu and Penghu shrank from more than 125,000 soldiers in the late 1950s to below 20,000, local businesses felt the pinch. However, all three archipelagos have in recent years benefited from tourist dollars.

Taiwan's domestic airlines offer some good flight/airport pickup/hotel packages to Penghu, Kinmen and Matsu, all of which can be booked online, although you'll need the help of a Taiwanese friend or local tour operator if you don't read Chinese. Changing money is easy in Magong and Jincheng, but if you're heading to any of the other islands do carry enough cash for the entire trip.

Located on the Tropic of Cancer some 45km west of Taiwan, all but one of Penghu County's 90 islands emerged from the sea as a result of volcanic activity. When the basaltic lava pouring from the ocean bed between eight and 17 million years ago cooled, it formed the hexagonal columns that give the archipelago's cliffs and tablelands a special appearance.

Han people began settling the islands nearly 1,000 years ago, but Penghu didn't become part of the Chinese Empire until a Yuan Dynasty official was sent to administer them in 1281. The population grew very slowly because life was harsh; farming was difficult and pirate raids were so frequent that in 1372 the imperial authorities commanded the inhabitants to return to the Chinese mainland. Not everyone left, it seems – in 1404 visiting officials ordered another evacuation, but again many stayed on. Dutch vessels visited in 1604 and in 1622 the VOC began building a fort. Two years later, however, the Chinese emperor ordered them to leave – and sent so many ships and soldiers the Dutch had no choice but to go. Because they couldn't set up a permanent base on Penghu, they landed at what's now Tainan (page 199). The Dutch weren't the first Westerners to set eyes on Penghu – during the 16th century, Portuguese sailors heading for Japan came here and named the islands Pescadores, meaning 'fishermen'. Seafood has always been a staple because the climate is too dry and the soil too sandy for many crops; you'll see no rice fields. Also, farmers have to surround their vegetable patches with high walls to keep out the strong, salt-bearing winds. Along with beaches and ancient, abandoned houses, these windbreaks – usually piled-up chunks of basalt – are one of Penghu's distinctive and recurring sights. During the Japanese colonial era, one of the archipelago's few non-fish exports was lime, produced by firing a mixture of sand, coral and sea shells. More recently, politicians and conglomerates argued that casinos would give the islands' economy a big boost, but in referenda in 2009 and 2016 county residents rejected the proposal to allow gambling.

Over time, Penghu's population (currently 104,000) has been shifting away from the remoter villages and islands and towards Magong, the county's administrative centre and a city rich in historical flavour. If you arrive by plane, you'll notice the county is pretty flat; the highest point on the main island (also called Penghu) is 48m above sea level. The islands used to be almost treeless, but in recent decades government-sponsored afforestation efforts have changed this. Among the archipelago's ecological attractions are turtles and avians; the endangered green turtles (*Chelonia mydas japonica*) that lay their eggs on Wangan Island between May and October are protected by ROC law. Cat Island, despite its name, is a haven for seabirds.

June is a good time to come, as is September, but the peak months of July and August are best avoided because of the crowds and the heat. Generally speaking, winter in the archipelago isn't much fun as chilly winds blast the landscape.

GETTING THERE AND AWAY

By air Even with the extra flights laid on during summer, to **Magong Airport** (MZG; ✆ 922 9123; w www.mkport.gov.tw) you can depend on at least 17 per day to/from Taipei Songshan (45mins; typical one-way fare NTD2,090), a similar number to/from Kaohsiung (40mins; NTD1,750), 12 to/from Taichung (35mins; NTD1,640), four to/from Tainan (30mins; NTD2,040), and at least one flight to/from Chiayi (30mins; NTD1,620). Most of the aircraft used are twin-propeller. Flights can be booked through the websites of carriers UNI Air (w www.uniair.com.tw) and Mandarin Airlines (w www.mandarin-airlines.com).

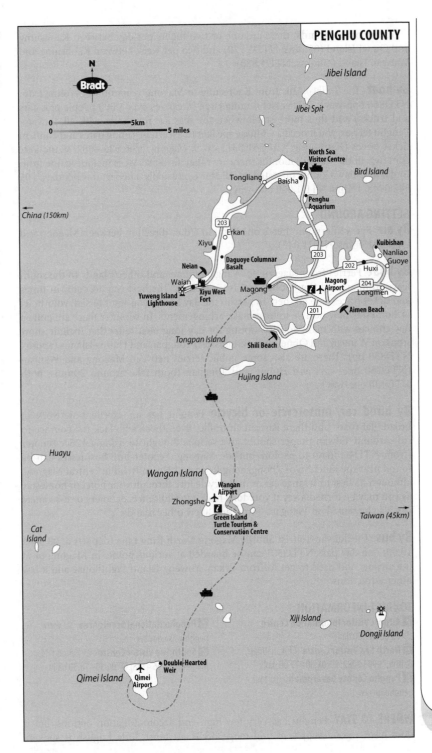

PENGHU COUNTY

Jibei Island

Jibei Spit

North Sea
Visitor Centre

Bird Island

Tongliang   Baisha

Penghu
Aquarium

← *China (150km)*

203

Xiyu   Erkan

Kuibishan

203

202   Huxi   Nanliao
Guoye

Neian   **Daguoye Columnar
Basalt**

204

Waian

Magong   Magong
Airport   Longmen

Yuweng Island
Lighthouse   Xiyu West
Fort

Aimen Beach

201

Tongpan Island   **Shili Beach**

Hujing Island

Huayu

Wangan Island

Wangan
Airport

Zhongshe

→ *Taiwan (45km)*

Green Island
Turtle Tourism &
Conservation Centre

*Cat
Island*

Xiji Island

Dongji Island

Qimei Island   **Double-Hearted
Weir**

Qimei
Airport

To the **other islands**, there are one or two flights per day between Kaohsiung and Qimei Island (35mins; NTD1,770) and two per week between Kaohsiung and Wangan Island (40mins; NTD1,880).

By boat The *Taihwa* sails from Kaohsiung to Magong year-round (4–6hrs; from NTD860 one-way). This vessel is quite large (it carries over 1,000 people plus cars and trucks) and thus more stable when the seas are rough. As with all Taiwan–Penghu ferries, you'll need a Chinese speaker to ascertain sailing dates and confirm ticket prices (Kaohsiung ✆ 07 561 5313 ext 9; Magong ✆ 06 926 4087; w tnc-kao. com.tw). In the warmer months there are other, faster services including one from Budai in Chiayi County operated by All Star Co (usually 3 departures per day; ✆ 05 347 0948; 1½hrs; NTD1,000 one-way).

GETTING AROUND
By air Every afternoon there's one flight in either direction between Magong and Qimei (15mins; NTD1,042).

By boat Ferries from Magong to Wangan, Qimei and other islands to the south leave from around the South Sea Visitor Centre. The best way to confirm times and ticket prices is to go there in person the day before you want to sail; your hotel or homestay may be able to help make arrangements. In summer there are quite a few choices with many tourists opting for day-long boat tours that include short stops on Wangan and Qimei, and perhaps also Tongpan and Hujing islands (approx NTD850 pp). There are also some public ferries between Magong and Wangan (NTD260 one-way) and Hujing and Tongpan (both take around 20mins; both NTD130 one-way).

By hired car, motorcycle or bicycle Penghu has an excellent network of broad, flat roads and there isn't much traffic. Even those who lack the courage to ride around Taiwan proper should give serious thought to using a 125cc scooter (from NTD400/day) to explore outside Magong. Scooter-hire businesses can be found near the junction of Zhongzheng Road and Huian Road in central Magong, although it's best to arrange car or motorcycle hire through your hotel or homestay as you may be turned away if you don't have a local licence. Scooters or e-scooters can also be rented on Wangan, Qimei and a few other islands.

By bus The Taiwan Tourist Shuttle Magong North Ring Line (departs at 08.30 & 10.00; one-day pass NTD350) can be boarded at various points in Magong or at the airport and used to get to/from Erkan, Yuweng Island Lighthouse and a few other attractions.

TOURIST INFORMATION
ℹ **Airport Visitor Information Centre**
⊕ 08.00–19.00 daily
ℹ **North Sea Visitor Centre** Chikan Wharf, Baisha; ✆ 993 3082; ⊕ 08.00–17.00 daily
ℹ **Penghu County Government** w tour. penghu.gov.tw

ℹ **Penghu National Scenic Area** w www. penghu-nsa.gov.tw
ℹ **South Sea Visitor Centre** 25 Xinrong Rd, Magong; ✆ 926 4738; ⊕ 06.30–18.30 daily

 WHERE TO STAY Penghu has very few high-end accommodation options, but it does have a good supply of mid-range B&Bs. At most, little English is spoken.

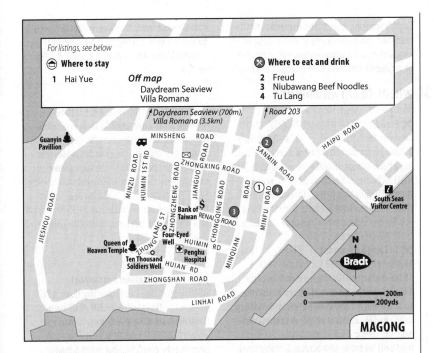

↑Daydream Seaview (700m),
Villa Romana (3.5km),   ↑Road 203

Guanyin
Pavillion

MINSHENG   ROAD

MINZU ROAD
HUIMIN 1ST RD
ZHONGZHENG ROAD
JIANGUO ROAD
ZHONGXING ROAD
CHONGQING ROAD
MINQUAN   ROAD
SANMIN ROAD
MINFU ROAD
HAIPU ROAD

JIESHOU ROAD

Bank of
Taiwan   RENAI RD

Four-Eyed
Well

Queen of
Heaven Temple
ZHONGYANG ST

Ten Thousand
Soldiers Well   HUIAN RD

Penghu
Hospital

HUIMIN

ZHONGSHAN ROAD

LINHAI   ROAD

South Seas
Visitor Centre

N

Bradt

0 _____ 200m
0 _____ 200yds

MAGONG

Camping hasn't caught on because of the strong winds that blow across the islands for much of the year.

Magong   *Map, above*

🏠 **Daydream Seaview Hotel** 白日夢海景民宿 (14 rooms) 237 Yangming Rd; ☎927 3371; m 0932 467 211; e daydream237@gmail.com; w daydream.tw. An imposing villa with Mediterranean-style décor & huge amounts of common space indoors, Daydream also has a small swimming pool, spacious garden & staff who speak a bit of English. The location is suburban enough to be very quiet yet near enough to the centre for nighttime sorties to Magong. B/fast inc. **$$$**

🏠 **Hai Yue Hotel** 海悅飯店 (79 rooms) 75 Minfu Rd; ☎926 9166; e hai.yue@msa.hinet.net; w haiyue.ool.com.tw. This town-centre hotel looks as if it was built in the expectation that hordes of gamblers would be beating a path to Penghu, & the fact they're not is good for travellers who want a degree of luxury. Good views, large LCD TVs & Wi-Fi in every room. Little English spoken but if you're arriving on an off-peak day it's worth asking for a room upgrade. B/fast inc. **$$$**

🏠 **Villa Romana** 西衛海岸民宿 (4 rooms) 581 Xiwei Li; ☎927 7429; m 0937 604 454; e penghu.villa@gmail.com; w www.villar.

com.tw. Some 15mins from central Magong, this homestay has an isolated location at the end of a peninsula. The 3rd-floor Ocean View suite with its 2-person bathtub is many guests' favourite but other suites also have excellent views thanks to extra-large windows. The entire building reflects the American co-owner's interest in the Greco-Roman period & eco-friendly architecture. Room rates NTD3,300–4,900. Can help arrange car & scooter hire & book activities. B/fast inc. **$$$**

Outside Magong

🏠 **Beach Corner 1–6** 峙裡沙灘轉角 **1–6** 民宿 (2 rooms) 1–6 Shili Vlg; ☎995 0026; e jung.1926@gmail.com. Being a stone's throw from Shili Beach makes up for the distance from central Magong (reachable by bus). Rooms are neither huge nor luxurious but thanks to the location you're unlikely to want to spend much time indoors. **$$**

🏠 **Sunrise B&B** 菓葉觀日樓民宿 (13 rooms) 129–3 Guoye Vlg, Huxi; m 0956 065 509; e sunrisebnb2005@gmail.com; w sunrisebb.idv.tw. Thanks to its oceanfront location &

English-speaking owners, this homestay attracts many Western guests, some of whom come for windsurfing or kayaking (equipment rentals can be arranged). No rooms have balconies but there's a big deck out front. 2nd-floor rooms are especially luxurious & so priced higher. Can arrange car/motorcycle hire; airport pickup, bike use & b/fast inc. **$$**

✖ WHERE TO EAT AND DRINK

Magong *Map, page 305*

✖ **Freud** 弗洛伊得音樂餐酒館 2–1 Xinsheng Rd; ☎926 4166; ⏰ 18.00–02.30 daily. In business for the better part of 3 decades, Freud has a decent range of local & imported beers (from NTD110/bottle) & a decent cocktail selection (from NTD150). Among the various beef, lamb & chicken dishes, you're bound to find something you like on the food menu (hot dishes available ⏰ 19.00–01.00 daily). **$$$**

✖ **Tu Lang Restaurant** 土銀小吃 6 Lane 38, Minfu Rd; ☎926 1832; ⏰ 11.00–14.00 & 18.00–midnight daily. The least obvious of the 5 or 6 seafood restaurants clustered around the southern end of Sanmin Rd but recommended by locals. No EM but lots of pictures of dishes on the wall. The shrimp & squid are obvious; the deep-fried balls are made with octopus & highly rated. Alternatively order by pointing at what you want in the tanks & confirm price beforehand. Local beer available. **$$$**

✖ **Niubawang Beef Noodles** 牛霸王牛肉麵 61 Minquan Rd; ☎926 9067;

⏰ 11.00–21.00 daily. Tired of fish & craving the flesh of land creatures? Squeeze in between the locals at this simple eatery for steamed dumplings, soups, thin rice noodles or standard noodles; the priciest item is the large portion of Imperial Feast Beef Noodles (*mǎnhàn niúròu miàn* 滿漢牛肉麵, NTD180). During peak season they often sell out of food before 19.30. No English sign (look for the bull horns among the Chinese characters) & no EM. **$**

Outside Magong

✖ **Longmen Seafood Restaurant** 龍門海鮮 58–2 Longmen Vlg, Huxi; ☎992 1277; ⏰ 11.00–14.00 & 17.30–20.00 daily. If you don't speak or read Chinese, ordering at a place like this can be hit or miss. There's no doubting the cook's skill but prices & quality of the raw ingredients fluctuate according to weather & season. The photos on the menu help & don't be shy about examining what others are eating. Very near the junction of roads 204 & 202. **$$**

OTHER PRACTICALITIES

$ Bank of Taiwan 24 Renai Rd, Magong
➕ **Penghu Hospital** 10 Zhongzheng Rd, Magong; ☎926 1151; ⏰ 24hrs daily

✉ **General post office** 70 Zhongzheng Rd, Magong; ⏰ 08.30–17.30 Mon–Fri, 09.00–noon Sat. You can change money at this branch.

WHAT TO SEE AND DO Penghu's main island is linked by bridges and causeways to Baisha and Xiyu. If you've two or three days only, you probably won't want to venture beyond this horseshoe-shaped landmass.

Magong 馬公 **(Mǎgōng)** If you spend a bit of time exploring the old centre of Magong, you'll find there's more to Penghu than the ocean, beaches and deserted villages.

Queen of Heaven Temple 天后宮 ***(Tiānhòu Gōng)*** (⏰ 06.00–20.00 daily) Until the 1920s, the city's name was written differently and meant 'Mazu temple harbour' – a reference to this shrine, Penghu's most famous place of worship. The temple has been around for at least 400 years and isn't especially large when compared with newer shrines in the county, but its charm lies in its obvious age and the delicacy of its finely carved wooden windows. A thorough restoration, the first since the 1920s, was completed in late 2013. Mazu, goddess of the sea and protector of fishermen, is the main object of veneration, but those interested in the history of interactions between China and the West will discover something more to their liking at the back of the temple on the right – a tall but narrow stele (a stone pillar used to make announcements) dating from 1604. The incised script on it is almost impossible to make out but the meaning is straightforward: it's a demand by a Ming Dynasty general that the Dutch expeditionary force, then anchored nearby, leave the islands. Those who read Chinese will notice that the stele describes the outsiders not as Dutchmen, Europeans or foreigners, but as 'red-haired barbarians'. The temple can be approached via Minzu Road of Lane 1, Zhongyang Street; the latter is where you'll also find the Ten Thousand Soldiers Well.

Ten Thousand Soldiers Well 萬軍井 The story is so much better than the reality. In 1683, Qing forces regrouped in Penghu before defeating the Ming loyalists then ruling Taiwan (page 12). They were short of water, but their commander, Shi Lang, ordered them to dig at this spot and amazingly a spring was found. These days the well is no more than a concrete ring covered with Perspex. The little temple across the street, **Lord Shi's Shrine** 施公祠 (⏱ 07.00–20.00 daily) is dedicated to the general.

Magong's other historic well, the **Four-Eyed Well** 四眼井, is likely older than the Queen of Heaven Temple, and gets its name from the four narrow openings through which water is drawn. There's said to be a population of goldfish proving the water is healthy. If that's true, they're good at hiding.

Guanyin Pavilion 觀音亭 (⏱ 06.00–19.00 daily) After the Queen of Heaven Temple, this is the Magong shrine most worth visiting. Founded in 1696, it's a timeworn place of worship with a sizeable cat population. The main focus, as you'd expect from the name, is the goddess of compassion, but among the deities worshipped in the side chambers are the lords of the North Pole Star and the South Pole Star, who sit next to each other. The North Pole Star Lord is a winter god in purple robes with a black face and a long black beard, while his southern counterpart is almost albino in appearance – pale eyes and skin plus white locks and facial hair, and orange-and-blue clothing.

Huxi 湖西
Kuibishan Geopark 奎壁山地質公園 Named after a steep hill next to the village of **Beiliao** 北寮, this is an especially dramatic location when the tide's high and the wind is up. At low tide it's possible to stroll along a basalt ledge to an islet almost 500m away. When driving to or returning from Kuibishan, do spend a bit of time looking at the dozens of abandoned coral houses in the largely abandoned village of **Nanliao** 南寮.

Guoye 果葉 This sleepy village's location makes it a favourite with those who like to see the sun rise over the ocean. The 7km-long bike trail that starts here goes southwards to the spot where the Japanese Army first landed in Penghu in 1895. The memorial erected by the colonial regime was converted after 1945 into a monument celebrating Taiwan's return to Chinese rule. It's then a short ride into **Longmen** 龍門 where there's a fishing harbour and a row of eateries around the junction of roads 202 and 204.

Baisha 白沙 **(Báishā) and Xiyu** 西嶼 **(Xīyǔ)** Sights in these thinly populated townships are listed in the order you'll encounter them if coming from Magong.

Penghu Aquarium 澎湖水族館 (58 Qitou Vlg; ☎ 993 3006; w penghu-aquarium. com.tw; ☺ 09.00–17.00 daily; admission NTD300/150/free for children under 6) The exhibitions in this aquarium focus on Penghu's marine life; some turtles and other largish sea creatures which were rescued after being found sick or injured are here, and there's a shark tunnel. For children, the pools where you can handle starfish and sea cucumbers provide the most fun.

Tongliang 通梁 Located at the northeastern end of the 2.5km-long bridge linking Baisha and Xiyu, this village is notable for the massive banyan tree that sprawls in front of the Baoan Temple, some attractive ruins and vendors who sell prickly-pear ice cream (*xiān rén zhǎng bīngqílín* 仙人掌冰淇淋), a purplish concoction that goes down a treat on hot days.

Erkan ancient residences 二崁古厝 *(Erkǎn Gcuò)* (near km30 Rd 203) This village's 50-odd enchanting traditional houses now outnumber its permanent inhabitants. The oldest ruin, which dates from 1690, is an interesting hodgepodge of coral, stone and mud bricks. Several of the families that used to live in Erkan established Chinese-medicine stores in Taiwan proper because local business and farming opportunities were limited. Among those who returned after making their fortunes were the two brothers who commissioned what's now called the **Chen Family Historical House** 二崁陳家古厝 (☺ 07.00–18.00 daily; admission NTD30/15) at number 6. Unlike most houses in the village, which face west, this 1910 Fujianese–Baroque courtyard abode looks southeast. The traditional bedsteads and washstands inside are still in excellent condition, as are the painted wall panels. The yellow-orange pomegranates depicted in one are symbols of fecundity, hundreds of seeds meaning hundreds of descendants; the pumpkin decoration is an emblem of wealth.

If you want something to eat or drink, get a bowl of bean-curd pudding (*dòu huā*豆花, NTD40) at the very quaint Erma Bean-Curd Pudding Shop 二馬豆花 at number 38 or some 'almond milk' (*xìngrén chá* 杏仁茶, NTD50) at the equally pretty Erkan Xingrencha 二崁杏仁茶. Both stay open throughout the day when tourists are around.

Daguoye Columnar Basalt 大果葉柱狀玄武岩 The far side of Erkan if you're coming from Magong, this is a miniature version of the basalt cliffs that distinguish Tongpan Island. The pond in front of the cliff is the result of quarrying; when it's full of water and the sun is shining, the cliffs reflect prettily.

Neian 內垵 Heading south on Road 203, as you enter this spread-out village about 3km south of Daguoye Columnar Basalt, you'll see a small brown bilingual sign pointing the way to the **Male and Female Pagodas** 塔公塔婆, a pair of stupa-like landmarks. It's said local residents built the first one to improve the area's feng shui, then added the second to ward off 'miasmas'. Some tourists attribute the camera malfunctions they've suffered when trying to take photos here to the pagodas' magical powers. A little further south there are boardwalks down to a decent sandy beach, wooden shelters where you can find some shade, and yet more basalt columns.

Xiyu West Fort 西嶼西台 (☺ 08.30–16.30 daily; admission NTD25/15) This bastion was built just after the Sino-French War of 1884–85 and equipped with four British-made Armstrong cannons. The current weapons are replicas and the massive stone-and-glutinous-rice walls have been patched up with concrete, but the views across the ocean make stopping here worthwhile. The turn-off is just beyond km34.5 on Road 203.

Yuweng Island Lighthouse 漁翁島燈塔 (grounds ⊕ 09.00–18.00 Tue–Sun; free admission) Yuweng is the former name of the island now officially named Xiyu and there's been a lighthouse on its westernmost promontory since 1778. Several of the lighthouse keepers who served here in the late 19th century were Westerners. The daughter of one died and was buried here in 1890, although it's hard to make out her name, Nelly O'Driscoll, on the grave marker. The current lighthouse is 11m high and dates from 1875; casual visitors aren't allowed inside. To see it, follow the signs and go behind the formidable-looking military installation found 2km down the turn-off from Road 203. Park on the bare earth and follow the track that goes to the right of the base. This area is battered by powerful winds all year round. One of the few plant species that can thrive around here is *Opuntia dillenii*, the cactus from which Penghu's signature prickly-pear ice cream is made. The flowers are yellow; the fruit have green skins and purple flesh.

Beaches Located on the southwest promontory, the 1.2km-long **Shili Beach** 時裡沙灘 is said to be the best on the main island for swimming. There are plenty of toilets, showers and other facilities but it's not overdeveloped nor does it get uncomfortably crowded. Just off Road 204, **Aimen Beach** 隘門沙灘 is another of the main island's longest strips of sand.

North of the main islands
Most visitors head straight for the 3.1km² island of **Jibei** 吉貝, where there are homestays, scooter rentals and watersports. It's best known for the 800m-long white **Jibei Spit** 吉貝沙嘴 (**Jíbèi Shāzuǐ**) that extends from its southern coast. Shaped like a human tongue, this sand bank is an entirely natural accumulation of tiny coral and shell fragments; it's a dazzling sight that attracts its share of coach parties. Don't ignore other parts of the island – which is small enough for some to explore on foot – as the beaches are less crowded and hand-built fish-trapping weirs dot the coast.

South of the main islands
It's possible to go directly to Qimei and Wangan from Taiwan; there's no need to transit through Magong. Tongpan and Hujing islands are served by regular ferries from Magong.

Tongpan Island 桶盤嶼 So named because it's shaped like the lid (*pán*) of a barrel (*tŏng*), this 0.4km² islet is famous for the imposing basalt columns that face the ocean in every direction. In 2017 the official population was 369, many of whom took the boat to Magong each weekday morning for work or school.

Hujing Island 虎井嶼 Most of this island's 400 residents live in the low-lying centre of the landmass, 1.9km south of Tongpan Island. There are yet more basalt cliffs at the eastern and western extremities along with a few remnants of the Japanese military presence before and during World War II.

Wangan Island 望安島 (**Wàngān Dǎo**) Wangan's grassy slopes are covered by wooden stairs and walkways that make for easy exploring. In the very centre of the island, **Zhongshe Village** 中社村 is a place for those who adore the picturesque past. The coral and stone cottages are hugely alluring but for some visitors it's all about the windows; in many cases they're neither square nor rectangular but the shape of a flag billowing in the wind, and adorned with elaborate stone lattices behind which are traditional sliding wooden shutters. Wangan's best-known ecological attraction is the Green Turtle Breeding Refuge, six beach locations where during summer and early autumn female turtles wade ashore after dark to lay and bury eggs. It's possible to witness this if you apply well in advance for a permit; access to the beaches is strictly controlled and there is a strict quota. Penghu National Scenic Area Headquarters can provide details, as can the **Green Turtle Tourism and Conservation Centre** 綠蠵龜觀光保育中心 (☎ 999 1368; ⊕ Mar–Oct 08.30–17.00 daily, Nov–Feb 10.30–15.30; admission NTD50/25). The centre, a short distance north of Wangan's ferry pier, educates visitors about the turtle population and provides information about other attractions on Wangan.

Qimei Island 七美嶼 **(Qīměi Yǔ)** The name of the fifth-largest island in the archipelago means 'seven beauties' and alludes to seven young women who, it's said, killed themselves by jumping down a well more than 450 years ago when Japanese pirates tried to ravish them. Don't bother with their tomb; spend your time enjoying the captivating coastal scenery. The most-photographed sight is the **Double-Hearted Weir** 雙心石滬, a fish trap on the island's northeastern side that represents a massive investment of human labour but requires little maintenance. Created by piling up chunks of coral and basalt, the principle is very simple: fish swim in when the tide is high but can't escape when the tide ebbs. This particular weir isn't unique but the vast majority of the 500-odd fish-catching weirs that still exist in the archipelago are far smaller and cruder.

KINMEN COUNTY 金門縣 (JĪNMÉN XIÀN) *Telephone code 082*

When it comes to enjoying these islands, some 277km from Taiwan but within easy shelling distance of mainland China's coast, an interest in Cold War history helps but isn't essential. Here, the Chinese Civil War continued long after Chiang Kai-shek's 1949 retreat to Taiwan (page 17). KMT forces dug into the island (quite literally – there are tunnels big enough to hide tanks and boats) and exchanged artillery fire with the Communists on the mainland until 1978. Beaches were turned into minefields and anti-paratrooper spikes were placed in farmers' fields.

Chinese civilisation here is relatively old; some local clans say they've been on the islands for almost 1,200 years. The archipelago's name translates as 'golden door' and alludes to a pair of towers built in the 15th century to keep watch for pirates. The toponym 'Quemoy', an anglicised rendering of how Kinmen is pronounced in the local dialect, is now seldom used except in the name of a local college.

Warfare has left scars but the irony is that, despite decades of conflict, Kinmen's traditional neighbourhoods are more intact than those in Taiwan, where much of the past has been bulldozed in the course of industrialisation. One does not have to go far from Jincheng, the main town, to find exquisite century-old houses. Between the 1950s and 1970s, Kinmenese weren't permitted to move away as the Nationalists feared the county would be depopulated. The official population has grown to 139,000 but it's hard to know precisely how many people really live here as many outsiders have registered as residents so they can enjoy cheaper air tickets and discounts on *kaoliang* (a strong, clear sorghum-based liquor made by an immensely profitable county-owned enterprise and enjoyed throughout the ROC). There's now a regular ferry between Kinmen and the People's Republic of China, so consider making the island your final 'Free China' stop before heading to the mainland.

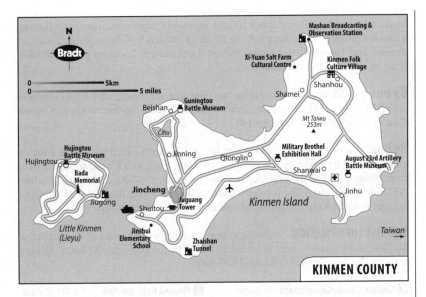

Both the ROC and the PRC regard Kinmen County as part of Fujian province. Three of the 15 islands are under Beijing's control; on the ROC side only the main island and Little Kinmen (also known as Lieyu) are accessible to visitors. The land area of the ROC-controlled portion of the county is a little over 151km². The islands are mostly granite and the highest point is 253m above sea level; the main island is 19km long but just 3km across in places.

GETTING THERE AND AWAY

By air Three airlines fly between Taiwan and Kinmen and travellers can depend on about 20 services per day from Taipei Songshan (from NTD2,136 one-way), eight from Kaohsiung (from NTD1,978), six from Taichung (from NTD1,990), and one or two from Tainan and Chiayi. Flight time in all cases is around an hour. Flights arrive at Kinmen Shangyi Airport (KNH; w www.kma.gov.tw) from where you can take a taxi (about NTD200 to Jincheng) or a bus (NTD12). If you're just transiting through Kinmen ask your airline about direct buses between the airport and Shuitou Pier.

By sea More than 20 services per day link Shuitou Pier with three destinations on the Chinese mainland (takes 45–60mins; US$36 one-way): Dongdu, near central Xiamen; Wutong, convenient for Xiamen Airport; and Quanzhou. Sailings are occasionally cancelled because of bad weather. Coming from China, travellers eligible for visa-free entry don't need ROC visas in advance and they can change their RMB into NTD at Shuitou. However, those leaving the ROC must obtain a PRC visa before boarding the ferry; at the time of writing, visa-free transit wasn't possible.

GETTING AROUND

By motorcycle or car Before you arrive, ask your hotel or homestay to arrange a scooter or e-scooter as many local businesses are reluctant to rent to anyone who doesn't hold a local licence. Few tourists use cars, but rentals can be arranged.

By bicycle The national park has been promoting cycling – riders can expect decent roads, light traffic and modest gradients – and bikes can be borrowed for free by anyone over 12 if they deposit ID and sign some paperwork from the following locations: Jinshui Elementary School; Shuangli Wetlands Nature Centre; Zhaishan Tunnel; and Lieyu District Rental Station. Locks and helmets are provided; bikes must be returned the same day.

By bus In addition to conventional bus lines that are inexpensive (most journeys cost NTD12) but infrequent, the Taiwan Tourist Shuttle has five routes in Kinmen County (w www.taiwantrip.com.tw).

By boat Work has started on a bridge linking the main island with Little Kinmen and it should be ready by the end of 2019. Until then, you'll need to take a ferry from Shuitou Pier to Jiugong (departs every 30mins; ⊕ 07.00–22.00 daily; 15mins; NTD60/30 one-way). The last ferry back to Shuitou leaves Jiugong at 21.30. Once you get to Little Kinmen it's easy to rent an e-scooter to get around.

TOURIST INFORMATION Visitor information centres are located at the airport, at Shuitou and Juguang Tower in Jincheng, and at Jiugong on Little Kinmen. All keep roughly the same hours (⊕ 08.30–17.00 daily).

Kinmen County Government w kinmen. gov.tw

Kinmen National Park 313 100; w www. kmnp.gov.tw

WHERE TO STAY Kinmen has several hotels, but none of them are comparable with the B&Bs that preserve and present several of the county's finest private homes.

Grace Kinmen B&B 新水調歌頭
(4 rooms) 35 Qianshuitou, Jincheng; 322 389; e sgrace_sun@hotmail.com. One of Kinmen's most attractive renovated antique residences is very clean & welcoming. Owner-manager Grace also manages other nearby homestays. Putting an extra bed in the room costs NTD600 for under-12s, NTD800 for anyone older. B/fast inc. **$$**

No. 45 Shanhou Guesthouse
山后邀月民宿 (5 rooms) 45 Shanhou Vlg, Jinsha; 353 745; m 0929 121 008, 0988

426 727; e joeyroland1117@yahoo.com.tw; w a353745.myweb.hinet.net. National park authorities spent over £300,000 renovating this gorgeous southern Fujianese-style compound in Kinmen's northeast before making it available as a B&B. It's old but guests don't rough it: a lot of the original woodwork remains in place, the furnishings are gorgeous & each room has an LCD TV & Wi-Fi. Rooms for 2, 3 or 4 ppl; b/fast available for a small charge. **$$**

WHERE TO EAT AND DRINK

Chiuan Min Fruit Restaurant
渼民水果創作料理 8 Lane 224, Boyu Rd Sec 2, Jinning; 324 489; ⊕ 11.45–14.00 & 17.45–20.00 daily. Set meals inc dessert & fresh juice are often priced at NTD600 pp. Common offerings are lamb cooked with papaya, chicken sautéed with rosemary & apple, pork ribs served with pear or seafood dishes flavoured with pineapple. Almost all the fruit comes from Taiwan's main island, not Kinmen. The unusual food, combined with a sleek, modern interior & fine presentation, make for a special experience. Reservations advised. **$$$$**

Jide Seafood Restaurant 記德海鮮餐廳
105 Cihu Rd Sec 2, Jinning; 324 461; ⊕ 11.00–14.00 & 17.00–21.00 daily. You'll need a Mandarin speaker to help you order as no English is spoken & the most interesting dishes are listed in Chinese only on a bulletin board. Among Jide's signature dishes are raw crab served in a slightly spicy *kaoliang*-based sauce (*gāoliáng qiàng xiè* 高粱熗蟹, NTD200–300) & sandworms (*shā chóng* 沙蟲, NTD250). Also worth trying are the small but flavoursome oysters & pork ribs with taro (*yùtóu pǎigǔ* 芋頭排骨). Local beer & liquor available. **$$$**

OTHER PRACTICALITIES

$ Land Bank 60 Minsheng Rd, Jincheng
✚ Kinmen General Hospital 2 Fuxing Rd,
Jinhu; 332 547; 24hrs daily

⊠ Post office 4 Minsheng Rd, Jincheng;
08.30–17.00 Mon–Fri, 09.00–noon Sat

WHAT TO SEE AND DO

Jincheng 金城 **(Jīnchéng)** Kinmen's main town is small enough to be convenient, large enough to have what you need, and sufficiently well preserved that you could spend most of a day here.

Memorial Arch to Qiu Liang-gong's Mother 邱良功母節孝坊 (Juguang Rd Sec 1) Commemorative stone archways of this type are called *páifāng* in Mandarin and can be found throughout the ROC. This, the largest and most ornate surviving arch anywhere in Taiwan or Fujian, is in the busiest part of Jincheng. It was built in 1812 to celebrate the loyalty and devotion Qiu Liang-gong's mother showed to the memory of his late father, who predeceased her by 28 years. Qiu, a Kinmen native who held important posts in the imperial civil service, died in 1817 and is buried in a tomb of near-imperial dimensions near Qionglin.

This neighbourhood is especially busy around breakfast time with both grocers and eateries doing a good trade. One of the best known of the latter, **Qiao Wei Xiang** 巧味香 (39 Juguang Rd Sec 1; 07.00–13.00 & 16.00–19.00 daily; no EM; $), has a reputation for oyster vermicelli. Also worth a quick look is **Kinmen Knife Creator** 金永利鋼刀 (30 Juguang Rd Sec 1; 08.30–21.00 daily). Inside the workshop you'll see shell casings which the proprietor turns into cleavers and other implements (see box, page 316).

Wu River Academy 浯江書院 (36 Zhupu N Rd; 09.00–21.00 daily; free admission) This walled compound is where male youths were schooled in classical literature, calligraphy, mathematics and other disciplines. Most sources say it was founded in 1780 but some believe it could date from as early as 1687; in any case it looks far newer thanks to a loving restoration a decade or so ago. People didn't come here just to study; they also sacrificed incense to patron deities for those sitting examinations and to Confucianist philosopher Zhu Zi (1130–1200). As the crow flies the academy, which now serves as a venue for neighbourhood cultural events, is 300m north of the memorial arch.

Juguang Tower 莒光樓 (08.00–22.00 daily; free admission) Located less than 1km south of central Jincheng, this quasi-classical pavilion was built in the early 1950s as a memorial to fallen soldiers. Inside there are displays about wind lions (see box, page 314) and other local traditions. Like the identically named Matsu township (page 317), the tower's name reflects Chiang Kai-shek's 'retake the mainland, restore China's legitimate government' ideology.

Around Jincheng

Shuitou 水頭 Exceptionally rich in mansions built by wealthy folk who returned home after making their fortunes overseas, this village (about 4km southwest of central Jincheng) is also where you catch ferries to Lieyu or the Chinese mainland. Number 37 Qianshuitou bursts with well-kept character; the geometric patterns on the Japanese ceramic tiles that decorate the front and the shape of some of the window lintels lend the sprawl a slightly Moorish look. Looking at it today, you'd never guess that soon after it was built in 1921 by merchant Huang Shun-tu, bandits

LIONS THAT TAME THE WIND

For centuries, Kinmen suffered the consequences of deforestation. A lack of trees meant strong winds lifted soil from fields and dumped it in ponds, hampering agriculture and exacerbating the shortage of fresh water. Islanders have traditionally blamed Koxinga for their predicament, saying he turned their woods into the fleet which carried him and his followers to Taiwan (page 11), but in fact the problem is much older. From the 14th century onward, local people were cutting down trees so they could boil seawater to obtain salt. The problem wasn't rectified until well after World War II when soldiers were put to work planting saplings.

Because of the sandstorms bedevilling Kinmen, the archipelago's inhabitants prayed to their gods for relief and began erecting lion-spirit statues to negate the winds sometime before 1400. Several were destroyed by communist shells in the 1950s but soon replaced. Almost all take the form of a lion upright on his hind legs, ranging in height from 22cm to 3.8m.

Particularly splendid wind lions can be found in Beishan and Shanhou while the one in Guanao near Mashan has become famous on account of his large penis. The majority of Kinmen's 69 wind lions are found in the north and east parts of the main island; most are on the northeastern edge of the villages they protect and face north or northeast. It's no coincidence that this is the direction from which winds blow, almost non-stop, between September and May.

Wind lions aren't found anywhere else in the ROC and they bear little resemblance to the playful-looking lions that guard the entrances of Taiwanese temples. Most are fierce-looking sentinels located in the gustiest parts of several villages. Many were hewn from granite but a few are cement or clay; several wear superhero-type red capes, donated by the faithful who worry the lions will shiver during gales.

Over time, Kinmen's wind lions have become generalist deities. In addition to countering the wind, villagers ask them for prosperity, baby boys, abundant harvests and protection from demons believed to cause mayhem. They're also believed to repel termites, useful given the amount of wood in Kinmen's traditional buildings. Like land gods, wind lions have birthdays that are celebrated with incense and prayers. Villagers also make offerings at the end of weddings and funerals. Not surprisingly, wind-lion models are a popular souvenir.

ransacked the place and kidnapped two of his relatives. After that they insisted on iron-plate doors and loopholes through which the residents could shoot at attackers. Number 34's white exterior contrasts with the Tuscan and terracotta reds that dominate this and other Kinmen settlements. The same clan now operates a B&B here, **Shuitou 37/53 Homestay** 水頭 37,53 民宿 (5 rooms; ☎ 328 131; m 0922 972 349; **$$**).

Zhaishan Tunnel 翟山坑道 (⏱ 08.30–16.30 daily; free admission) This 357m-long sea-level bomb shelter is a monument to what can be achieved if you've got a workforce that's healthy, strong and utterly obedient. Like the longer Jiugong Tunnel on Little Kinmen, it was chiselled out by soldiers in the 1960s so boats could bring in reinforcements and supplies even when the shelling was at its fiercest.

Cihu 慈湖 Birdwatchers head to this manmade brackish lake in the northwest to see great cormorants and other waterbirds. October to March is the best season for twitching as the majority of the 280 bird species regularly seen in Kinmen County are winter migrants. There's more for ecotourists a very short distance to the north at the **Shuangli Wetlands Nature Centre** 雙鯉濕地 (⏲ 08.00–17.00 daily; free admission), where displays expound on marine life as well as birds and aquatic plants; there's also a large semi-submerged window allowing you to see some of what's happening beneath the water surface.

Guningtou 古寧頭 This is where the Nationalist Army defeated communist units in a 56-hour battle on 25–27 October 1949, establishing a line of control that hasn't to this day changed, a story told inside the **Guningtou Battle Museum** 古寧頭戰史館 (✆ 08.30–17.00 daily; free admission). Also make a point of locating **Beishan Old Western-Style House** 北山古洋樓, which is far more interesting than its name suggests and not only because its designer blended Fujianese and 19th-century European architecture. It's riddled with bullet holes from the 1949 battle and much loved by shutterbugs.

East Kinmen For food and drink try Shamei 沙美 or Shanwai 山外.

Qionglin 瓊林 Kinmen is often described as being the shape of a dumb-bell and this ancient village is close to the narrowest part of the island. The Nationalists paid special attention to its defences, reckoning that if the Communists invaded, the attackers would try to cut the island in two here; in fact, the communist units involved in the Battle of Guningtou had intended to make their landings near Qionglin but were pushed west by the wind and current. **Qionglin Tunnel** 瓊林 坑道 (⏲ 08.30–17.00 daily; admission NTD10) was part of the fortification/bomb shelter system and it's fun to explore the underground corridors and chambers. The tunnel's total length is 1,355m and most of the network is around 6m underground. Near where you enter the tunnel there's an especially fine wind lion.

Military Brothel Exhibition Hall 特約茶室展示館 (126 Xiaojing Vlg, Jinhu; ⏲ 08.30–17.00 daily; free admission) Between the early 1950s and 1990, the ROC's armed forces ran a network of brothels on the front-line islands and this single-floor building housed one such establishment. The bilingual displays are interesting as far as they go. Charts comparing the price of 30 minutes' sexual services and soldiers' salaries show sex was considerably cheaper in the 1980s than in the early days. However, nowhere is it made clear whether soldiers had to buy the coupons with which they paid the girls (direct payment in cash wasn't allowed) or whether coupons were sometimes given out as rewards. The displays stress that no women were forced to work in the brothels yet fail to explain the recruitment process; some Taiwanese say many of the 'volunteers' were arrestees offered a choice – trial and probably jail, or two years' working in a military brothel. Inside the hall there's a coffee shop (⏲ 10.00–17.00 daily; EM; **$$**).

Xi-Yuan Salt Farm Cultural Centre 西園鹽場 (1 Xiyuan Vlg, Jinsha; ⏲ 09.00–17.00 Tue–Sun; free admission) Producing salt by evaporating seawater is an age-old but now defunct industry along the coast of southern China and Taiwan. These ponds in the northeast of the island were in almost constant use between the 13th century and 1995; they're now maintained as a tourist attraction and an educational site. If you don't read Chinese you may not learn much but the outdoors part is at least photogenic.

Mashan Broadcasting and Observation Station 馬山觀測站 (⏰ 08.30–17.00 daily; free admission)

From this vantage point – a bunker reached via a narrow tunnel on the northeast coast – you can look through telescopes at PRC fishing boats and people on the mainland going about their business. The distance to communist-controlled dry land varies between 1.8km and 2.1km, depending on the tide. From this same spot the Nationalists formerly used huge loudspeakers to make propaganda broadcasts that could be heard on the Chinese side. The observation post is part of an active army base, so take note of the rules posted at the entrance.

Kinmen Folk Culture Village 金門民俗文化村 *(Jīnmén Mínsú Wénhuà Cūn)*

(Shanhou Vlg; ⏰ 08.30–17.30 daily; free admission) Old villages in Taiwan and China tend to be higgledy-piggledy, so the symmetrical rows of perfectly maintained traditional homes that make up this very worthwhile outdoor museum come as a surprise. There are 16 residences, an ancestral shrine and a classroom where scions of the Wang clan – who built this complex after making a fortune by trading with Japan – were tutored in the Confucian classics. The exquisite swallow-tail roof ridges, which signified success in imperial civil-service examinations, were appropriate when the architects were commissioned at the very end of the 19th century. However, by the time the buildings were completed in the mid 1920s those examinations – like the empire itself – were a thing of a past. Inside you'll see some of the original furniture plus clothing from the same era.

Mount Taiwu 太武山

This isn't an imposing mountain by any standards but there's a fair bit to see around here, including a large cemetery dedicated to Nationalist soldiers who died in 1949's defensive battles, a memorial to Koxinga and Kinmen's largest freshwater lake. Beneath the mountain, protected from falling bombs by several metres of granite, there's a fully equipped hospital. You can ride a bike or motorcycle about halfway up the mountain and then continue on foot to the summit (253m above sea level). It's a pleasant hike that takes around half an hour one-way.

KINMEN CLEAVERS

If you visit Kinmen, the Taiwan-controlled archipelago that's just a few kilometres from the coast of mainland China, you'll be able to pick up a souvenir that is eminently practical and historically interesting but not something you should pack in your carry-on luggage: a meat cleaver.

Between 1949 and 1978, not a week went by without the communist forces on the mainland and the Nationalists on Kinmen exchanging artillery fire. Scavengers searched for shell casings and sold the fragments to blacksmiths, who turned the metal into cleavers and machetes. At first they were sold to locals, but when Kinmen was opened for tourism, the knives – which now come in fancy presentation boxes – proved a surprise hit. Indeed, so many have been sold that now some people wonder if the steel really is recycled war materiel.

Kinmen cleavers are available from several shops in Jincheng and also at the airport.

August 23rd Artillery Battle Museum 八二三戰史館 (1–10 Anmin Vlg, Jinhu; ⊕ 08.30–17.00 daily; free admission) Named for the massive artillery campaign that began on 23 August 1958, this thorough museum is filled with and surrounded by hardware used in the battle. The bombardment didn't take the Nationalists by surprise – mainland radio stations had predicted the imminent liberation of Quemoy and intelligence-gathering overflights of communist bases on the mainland confirmed something was afoot. Nonetheless, the garrison barely survived the onslaught and would probably have been overrun had it not been for Washington's moral and material support.

Little Kinmen/Lieyu 小金門/烈嶼 ***(Lièyǔ)*** Little Kinmen accounts for a fifth of the county's dry land and a tenth of its population.

Jiugong 九宮 You'll disembark beside a granite promontory that's not quite as solid as it looks. Five minutes' walk from the ferry dock, the entrance to **Jiugong Tunnel** 九宮坑道 (⊕ 08.30–17.00 daily; free admission) leads into Kinmen's largest underground military installation. Excavated after the 1958 artillery war, the main chamber here is 790m long, 11.5m high and 15m wide. Patrol boats, landing craft and small cargo vessels carrying supplies for the civilian population could moor here in safety during bombardments.

Bada Memorial 八達樓子 Located in the centre of the island, this memorial is an imitation of a tower on the Great Wall of China. The bronze statues on top celebrate seven Nationalist soldiers who died on the wall after holding back thousands of Japanese attackers for five days during a 1933 incursion.

Hujingtou 湖井頭 Unreconstructed Cold War hawks have two reasons to visit this village. Firstly, it's possible to gaze at the coast of communist China. Secondly, **Hujingtou Battle Museum** 湖井頭戰史館 (⊕ 08.30–17.00 daily; free admission), housed in a squat concrete building with crenellated walls, details some of the Nationalist Army's most heroic moments.

MATSU NATIONAL SCENIC AREA 馬祖國家風景區 (MǍZǓ GUÓJIĀ FĒNGJǏNGQŪ) *Telephone code 0836*

The northernmost outpost of the ROC is a cluster of 19 rocky islands 114 nautical miles (211km) from Taiwan. Life on the archipelago (total land area: 29.6km²) has never been easy as there's little flat land and the growing season is short. Pirates were a scourge in the Qing Dynasty, and during the 1950s and 1960s the islands were often shelled by communist forces. Gaodeng, just 9.25km from the mainland, is still off-limits to civilians because of the ROC military's presence. Nangan and Beigan have far more woodland now than before World War II; knowing trees can hide gun emplacements, the armed forces took the business of afforestation very seriously, and for a time, every conscript was assigned a sapling to care for and faced jail if his tree died.

The toponym Matsu derives from that of Mazu, the sea goddess revered throughout Taiwan and Fujian. Some believe Mazu's remains lie beneath a temple on Nangan, the largest island, and while a few Taiwanese come here for religious reasons, the majority of tourists are drawn by a combination of rugged scenery, distinctive and enduring granite cottages and military history. In June, July and August many birders come hoping to see the extremely rare Chinese crested tern,

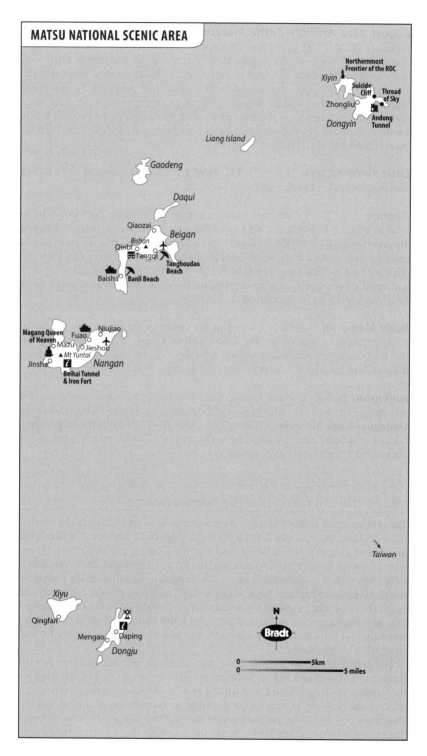

MATSU NATIONAL SCENIC AREA

Northernmost
Frontier of the ROC

Xiyin

Suicide
Cliff

Thread
of Sky

Zhongliu

Dongyin

Andong
Tunnel

Liang Island

Gaodeng

Daqui

Qiaozai

Bishan

Beigan

Qinbi

Tangqi

Tanghoudao
Beach

Baisha

Banli Beach

Magang Queen
of Heaven

Niujiao

Fuao

Mazu

Jieshou

Jinsha

Mt Yuntai

Nangan

Beihai Tunnel
& Iron Fort

Taiwan

Xiyu

Qingfan

Mengao

Daping

Dongju

N

Bradt

0 ━━━━━ 5km
0 ━━━━━ 5 miles

318

a species long believed extinct until it was rediscovered in these islands in 2000. To protect it and other avian species, eight uninhabited islands have been designated the Matsu Islands Tern Refuge.

Between 1974 and 2008, the archipelago's civilian population declined from 17,000 to below 10,000. Since then, as a result of closer transport and economic links with the Chinese mainland, it has bounced back to around 13,000, more than half of whom live on Nangan. Even when servicemen are excluded, there's a serious gender imbalance: males outnumber females 58:42. Most islanders are of Fujianese descent but rather than speak Taiwanese Hokkien, the day-to-day language is Fuzhou dialect.

In a July 2012 referendum, Matsu residents voted in favour of allowing gambling resorts to be built on the islands but so far no casino projects have broken ground.

GETTING THERE AND AWAY

By air Five or six flights per day (⏱ 06.30–15.55) leave Taipei Songshan Airport and land at Nangan Airport (LZN; ☎ 26522) while three (⏱ 06.50, 11.30 & 15.25) head for Beigan Airport (MFK; ☎ 56576). On both routes flight time is 50 minutes and a one-way fare is NTD2,007. There's also a daily flight from Taichung to Nangan (⏱ 12.10; 1hr 5mins; NTD2,455 one-way). All flights are operated by UNI Air (☎ 02 2518 5166; w www.uniair.com.tw).

Air travel between Matsu and Taiwan is often disrupted by weather conditions; allow at least one safety day if you've an international flight to catch.

By sea The *Taima Star* ferry (Keelung ☎ 02 2424 6868, Nangan ☎ 26655) is the cheapest way of getting to the islands. Passengers should arrive at Pier West 2 in Keelung before 20.00 as the boat sails at 21.50. On odd days of the month the ferry's first stop is Nangan around 08.00. After 2 hours the vessel leaves for Dongyin, arriving around midday. It then returns to Keelung, getting there about 8 hours later. On even days the ferry stops at Dongyin then Nangan before heading back to Keelung. Services are daily but on Tuesdays a smaller, less comfortable vessel takes the place of the *Taima Star*.

The cheapest one-way tickets entitle you to a seat in the lounge (NTD630) but these are only available if no bunk-bed spaces (NTD1,050 for a single, NTD840 pp if 2 share a large bunk) are available. The bunks have foam mattresses and curtains for privacy; there's a good chance you'll get some sleep. Fares are the same whether you disembark at Nangan or Dongyin; children and seniors pay half. Beer, instant noodles but not much else is available on board so bring some supplies.

There's a daily ferry between Matsu and Mawei near Fuzhou in Fujian (departure from Nangan 14.00, from Mawei 09.15; 1½hrs; NTD1,300 one-way). Currently the much quicker crossing from Beigan to Huangqi in Fujian (⏱ 10.00 & 15.00; 20mins; NTD675) is available only to ROC and PRC citizens. See page 45 for more about travelling between the ROC and the PRC by sea.

GETTING AROUND

By boat Ferries leave Nangan for Beigan every hour on the hour (⏱ 07.00–17.10 daily; 20mins; NTD160/80 one-way), and three ferries per day sail from Nangan to Xiju's Qingfan Port and Dongju's Mengao Harbour (⏱ 07.00, 11.00 & 14.30; 50mins; NTD200 one-way). These boats sometimes stop at Dongju before Xiju; confirm the first destination when buying your ticket. Sailing time between Xiju and Dongju is 15 minutes. Ferries return to Nangan right away. The main link between Nangan and Dongyin is the *Taima Star* ferry (page 319), for which one-way tickets cost NTD350/175. Between April and September there's usually an additional daily ferry between Dongyin and Nangan.

During summer peak season, private operators offer boat tours to Daqiu Island, around Dongyin and out to the Tern Refuge. Details can be had from Matsu National Scenic Area offices (see below).

By hired motorcycle Some homestays can help arrange scooter hire; ask before arriving in Matsu. Many rental businesses aren't willing to hire to visitors who have international but not ROC licences.

By bus There are infrequent public buses on both Nangan and Beigan (each journey NTD15). Schedules can be obtained from visitor information centres.

TOURIST INFORMATION There are several visitor information centres (most ⊕ 08.00–17.30 daily), including one on Nangan near the entrance to Beihai Tunnel where there are free shower facilities – nice if you've just come off the ferry – and one in Beigan opposite Banli Historic House. Matsu National Scenic Area (w www. matsu-nsa.gov.tw) has lots of tourist information.

 WHERE TO STAY

Nangan

🏠 **Matsu 1st Hostel** 馬祖1青年民宿 (10 rooms) 71 Jinsha Vlg; ☎23353; e admin@ matsuhostel.com; w matsuhostel.com. This picturesque option charges from NTD660 for a bed in a shared room to NTD1,320 for a 2-person room. Various packages inc b/fast, pickup from the airport or dock & 24hrs' use of a motorcycle. Shared bathrooms only. This hostel also accepts travellers interested in working holidays; they should be willing to commit for a month & do housekeeping, food preparation & other work in return for meals, a bed & airfare subsidy. **$$**

Beigan

🏠 **Chinbe No. 25 Guesthouse** 芹壁村25號 (11 rooms) 25 Qinbi Vlg; ☎55628; m 0975 421 178; e chinbe25@gmail.com; w chinbe25-eng. blogspot.com. Owner Sammi Chen, who speaks good English, returned to her birthplace from Taipei in 2009 to open this tastefully furnished homestay & later took over her father's old workshop to provide additional space. Wooden floors & stone walls give the rooms lots of character. Sea-view rooms usually cost around

NTD2,500; smaller traditional rooms without bathrooms are just NTD1,300. B/fast inc. **$$$**

🏠 **Banli Historic Homestay** 坂里大宅特色民宿 (14 rooms) 48, 50 & 52 Banli; ☎55663; m 0921 801 585; w banli.8898. tw. Wooden partitions & simple furnishings mean this restored mansion (page 322) may not be ideal for light sleepers or those who need en-suite bathrooms, but it's full of character & a good place to meet backpackers. Rooms for 2 ppl start at NTD1,200. Can help arrange motorcycle rental; b/ fast inc. **$$**

Dongyin

🏠 **Shangrila Inn** 香格里拉 (7 rooms) 128 Lehua Vlg; m 0919 280 767; e mouss0214@ yahoo.com.tw; w hotel.matsu.idv.tw/shangrila. Not to be confused with the high-end hotel chain, Dongyin's best accommodation choice has clean, comfortable rooms brightened by superb murals of local scenic spots. An extra bed can be added for NTD300. Attractive prices reflect the fact that not all rooms have en-suite bathrooms. Inc b/fast & pickup from the dock. **$$**

✖ **WHERE TO EAT AND DRINK** Matsu's climate and thus agriculture are quite different from Taiwan's, so there are some distinct local specialities, none of which are expensive. The dish called 'fish noodles' (*yú miàn* 魚麵) contains eel as well as saltwater fish. Westerners craving familiar carbohydrates enjoy 'Matsu bagels' (*jì guāng bǐng* 繼光餅), circular breads that have long been a favourite of soldiers posted to the islands because they keep well in kitbags and make a good snack for those on sentry duty. They're baked by being stuck to the inside of a metal barrel that is then heated by fire. Several places slice them open and stuff them with egg and meat to create what many call a 'Matsu hamburger'.

OTHER PRACTICALITIES
$ Bank of Taiwan 257 Jieshou, Nangan

✉ Post office 258 Jieshou, Nangan; ⊕ 08.30–17.00 Mon–Fri, 09.00–noon Sat

WHAT TO SEE AND DO
Nangan 南竿 **(Nángān)** Sights are described in the order you'd likely tackle them if arriving by boat.

'Sleeping With Spears, Awaiting Daybreak' 枕戈待旦 Approaching Fuao Harbour, you'll see four huge Chinese characters, red on a white background, up on the hillside. Read from right to left, they were installed at the behest of Chiang Kai-shek to remind everyone of his intention to retake the Chinese mainland.

Jieshou 介壽 At the southern end of the main street in Matsu's busiest settlement there's a morning market where ready-to-eat Matsu snacks and locally caught seafood are sold. The temple overlooking the nearby cove is dedicated to Baimazunwang ('the revered king of the white horse'), a minor deity worshipped in several shrines in Matsu but scarcely known on Taiwan proper.

Jieshou Park 介壽公園 The name of this park in the centre of the island means 'long live Chiang Kai-shek' and inside you'll find two major buildings. One commemorates Chiang Ching-kuo, the dictator's son; the other, the **Matsu Folklore Cultural Artifacts Exhibition Hall** 民俗文物館 (⊕ 09.00–17.00 Tue–Sun; free admission) has displays with some English about Matsu's traditional dwellings, customs and religious beliefs and multi-media introductions to the archipelago's dialect, poetry and songs.

Beihai Tunnel 北海坑道 (⊕ at low tide only; free admission) Soldiers using pickaxes and explosives hacked out this 10m-wide, 640m-long sea-level tunnel between 1968 and 1970 so boats could resupply Nangan's garrison during bombardments. The tunnel was never used, however – high tides washed in so much silt the openings to the ocean had to be sealed. The floodlit interior is somewhat like a water-filled cathedral and the special ambience is best enjoyed if you join one of the frequent gondola tours (NTD150 pp; takes around 20mins) or rent a kayak (NTD250 pp; May–Oct only). Tide times are posted on the Matsu National Scenic Area website ('tunnel info'). Two other ex-military sites within walking distance of the tunnel are also worth visiting: **Dahan Stronghold** and **Iron Fort** (both ⊕ 08.00–17.00 daily; free admission).

Mount Yuntai 雲台山 On a clear day you'll see the Chinese mainland from the top of this 248m-high mountain. The exhibition room near the peak is in a military building; at the time of writing only Taiwan citizens were allowed inside. By motorcycle, it's possible to get within a few minutes' walk of the summit.

Jinsha 津沙 One of the archipelago's most attractive villages, located in the southwest of the island, Jinsha has benefited from local government subsidies to preserve and restore traditional one- and two-storey granite houses. There's also a hostel here; see page 320.

Magang Queen of Heaven Temple 馬港天后宮 (⊕ 06.00–22.00 daily) This mid-sized temple north of Jinsha contains what's said to be the tomb of Lim Vo'g Niu, the Fujianese girl now revered as Mazu, the goddess of seafarers. According to one version of her life story, Lim swam out into the ocean in a bid to find her father but succumbed to exhaustion; her body washed ashore here. Some believe she was interred here while others say her remains were returned to Fujian and only her clothing was buried on Nangan. The putative grave, in front of the main altar inside the shrine, is marked by a flat granite slab covered by a sheet of glass; no excavation of the tomb was permitted when the temple was rebuilt in 2002. Effigies of Baimazunwang and his white horse are on the right. It's likely you saw the nearby Mazu statue (made of white granite and 28.8m tall) from the air or the ferry before setting foot on Nangan.

Beigan 北竿 (**Běigān**) Ferries from Nangan arrive at Baisha 白沙港 in the southwest; planes land at the other end of the island.

Banli 阪里 Situated in the southwest, this village's standout structure, the late 19th-century **Banli Historic House** 坂里大宅 (⊕ 09.00–21.00 daily; free admission), is on the main street opposite the school. Built by the Wang family, it was requisitioned by the army in 1949 and only returned to its owners in 1992. From the outside you'll see stone and tiles but inside it's all wood columns and partitions. Following a government-funded restoration, most of the complex now serves as a homestay (page 320). On the 13th day of the first lunar month, the village is the site of a unique religious ceremony that features locals burning straw to 'feed' the spirit of Baimazunwang's faithful steed. Banli's beach is a lovely strip of clean amber-colour sand behind the visitor information centre; do be careful if you go for a swim as the waves here can be big.

Qinbi 芹壁 The population of what could well be the ROC's most characterful village has shrunk dramatically but its distinctive stone cottages look like they'll last for eternity. The roofs, you'll notice, are covered with tiles held down by large stones, but because the tiles weren't sealed in place the houses are better ventilated than many dwellings of a similar age. Windows tend to be small and high up while walls are made of granite slabs that have been crudely squared off, or odd-shaped stones fitted together like jigsaw pieces.

Qiaozai 橋仔 The next community along if you're moving clockwise, Qiaozai has also suffered population outflow. It's said the village's gods now outnumber resident humans. Some of the colourful shrines where the former reside are noteworthy for having flame-shaped side walls that extend beyond roof level. These are said to reduce the risk of fire.

Tangqi 塘岐 Beigan's 'capital' has a post office, a few basic hotels and the island's best eating options. The road that goes under the runway leads to Tanghoudao Beach 塘后道沙灘, through a small village and then up a steep road to the **War and Peace Memorial Park Exhibition Hall** 戰爭和平紀念公園主題館 (⊕ 08.30–

17.30 daily; free admission). Even if you've little interest in the soldiers' uniforms and ordnance displayed inside, do walk up to this building for excellent views of the peninsula to the south.

Dongyin 東引 (Dōngyǐn)

About 1,300 people live in the eastern half of Dongyin and barely a dozen in the western half. The two parts are linked by a causeway, have few trees but an abundance of wild flowers. They're also still highly militarised, but don't take photos of soldiers, their equipment or army buildings and expect to be turned back at checkpoints.

Andong Tunnel 安東坑道 (⊕ 08.00–17.30 daily; free admission) On entering this former army base you'll take 400-odd steps down a tunnel that slopes at 30 degrees then emerges halfway up a cliff face where gulls nest each summer. In addition to sleeping quarters, ammunition depots and gun emplacements overlooking the ocean, the base had its own pigsty.

Dongyin Lighthouse 東引燈塔 (⊕ 09.00–17.00 Tue–Sun; free admission) If the weather's good you'll spend more time here than anywhere else on Dongyin. Reaching the lighthouse, designed by an Englishman and completed in 1904 (not 1877 as often stated), involves a little bit of walking on stone paths but the views are excellent. The cannon pointing out to sea weren't for firing at attackers but rather to warn shipping during fog.

Suicide Cliff 烈女義坑 A safe walkway from the car park leads to this dramatic viewing point where, legend has it, a fisherman's wife threw herself into the ocean rather than surrender to the pirates who'd killed her husband.

Thread of Sky 一線天 (⊕ 08.00–17.00 daily; free admission) The name of this dramatic spot gives visitors a good idea of what to expect and the narrow opening between two cliffs doesn't disappoint. Because this part of the island is under military control you should get a permit before entering. This can be obtained free of charge from Dongyin Visitor Centre (⊕ 08.00–17.30 daily) near the harbour.

Northernmost Frontier of the ROC 國之北疆 There's nothing here but expansive ocean views and a stone monument bearing four characters that mean 'the country's northern boundary'. The actual northernmost point is Beigu Reef, visible in good weather to the northeast.

Juguang 莒光 (Jǔguāng)

Matsu's most southerly township got its current name in the 1950s when Chiang Kai-shek made a speech comparing it to the ancient Chinese city of Ju, where more than 2,500 years ago a defeated king planned the counterattack that would restore him to the throne. The only islands of consequence are **Dongju** 東莒 and **Xiju** 西莒, similar in land area but quite different in shape; while the former is long and thin, the latter is much rounder and more suitable for exploring on foot. The ferry from Nangan stops at both. Dongju's ferry dock is at Mengao, just over 1km from Daping, where you'll come across restaurants, homestays and scooter rentals. Continue northeast to find the visitor information centre and, at the end of the road, a lighthouse built by the British in the 1870s to ensure the safety of ships approaching Fuzhou in Fujian. On Xiju you'll disembark at Qingfan where everything is conveniently close; veer east for accommodation options.

Whether you arrive at Baisha 白沙 or the smaller settlement of Dafu 大福, your first thought is likely to be that Little Liuqiu isn't very different from the rest of Taiwan. The town behind the ferry dock at Baisha is a dense collection of three-storey concrete boxes, and hundreds of tripod-shaped coastal fortifications have been piled up where the land meets the sea. Three temples are visible (Liuqiu has an amazing number of shrines considering its population, a mere 12,400), and the moment you step off the boat you'll find yourself in a whirligig crowd of people and motorcycles.

Don't let these initial impressions put you off. Fortunately, there's no more to Baisha than what you see from the boat – and it's the island's biggest settlement. Little Liuqiu is a jewel surrounded by clean seas. The 'little' is to distinguish it from Japan's Ryukyu Islands (now called Okinawa), the name of which was written using the same Chinese characters. The island is largely uplifted coral reef and thus unsuitable for farming, so you'll see not a single rice field and very few vegetable gardens. Nonetheless, food and other necessities are no more expensive on the island than in Donggang or Kaohsiung, so there's no need to haul lots of provisions with you.

The absence of industry and the tiny number of cars mean that the sounds of nature can be heard everywhere: waves, wind and birdsong. The vibe is unusually and genuinely relaxing. No wonder, then, that some expats head here rather than Kenting when they want a get-away-from-it-all weekend. Twenty kinds of coral and 300 fish species make Liuqiu a good place for snorkelling, and there's also superb scuba diving but little infrastructure for divers who don't speak Chinese.

English-language sources sometimes refer to the landmass as Lamay Island because its original inhabitants were the Lamayans, an Austronesian tribe. In 1621 and again in 1631, tribesmen massacred European shipwreck survivors. The VOC attacked the tribe in 1636. Most of those fighting on the Dutch side were recruits from other Taiwanese tribes that despised the Lamayans. The climax was a siege at what's now called Black Ghost Cave, where more than 300 Lamayans were massacred and the survivors were sold into slavery. After that, Little Liuqiu had no permanent human population until the ancestors of the current islanders arrived from Fujian in the late 18th century.

GETTING THERE AND AWAY

By ferry On a normal day there are eight services from Donggong to Baisha (⊕ 07.00–17.00; return fare NTD410/210) and five to Dafu (⊕ 08.00–18.45; return fare NTD380/190 inc admission to Black Ghost Cave, Meiren Cave & Mountain Pig Ditch); journey time on both routes is around 30 minutes. The return portion of your ticket doesn't entitle you to a seat on a particular boat, so you may have to queue for the next boat if lots of people are waiting. Don't worry that you'll be stranded on the island, though, as extra boats are laid on when needed. Each ferry takes around 90 people.

GETTING AROUND

By motorcycle or bicycle Scooters and e-scooters can be rented at Baisha. The standard weekday price of NTD300 per day for a 125cc model includes enough fuel to get you all over the island. You won't have to look for these rental businesses – they'll find you, possibly even before you've got off the boat. Helmets are provided but few people bother to wear them. There are very few cars on Little Liuqiu's roads.

Bicycles can be brought over on the ferry for free if they're bagged; unbagged bikes are charged NTD50 one-way.

TOURIST INFORMATION Maps of the island, which is part of Dapeng Bay National Scenic Area (w www.dbnsa.gov.tw), are available inside the ferry terminal at Baisha. For more detailed information, go to the information centre (📞 861 4615; ⏰ 08.30–17.30 daily); turn right as you leave the harbour and you'll see it on your right just as the road begins to climb. It's also worth checking out Little Liuqiu Township Office (w www.liuchiu.gov.tw).

🏠 **WHERE TO STAY AND EAT** The island can be done as a day trip but staying overnight is recommended.

🏠 **Loju Seaview Homestay** 小琉球樂嶼海景民宿 (6 rooms) 1–61 Sanmin Rd, Yufu; 📞861 2797; m 0905 979 161; w www.loju-seaview.idv.tw; 🟦 @lojuseaview. Best contacted through their Facebook page, Loju has spacious rooms (some with balconies & ocean views), a quiet location & a reputation for being super helpful when it comes to making arrangements for motorcycles, snorkelling & other activities. Within walking distance of restaurants & shops in the busiest part of Baisha. B/fast inc. **$$**

🏠 **Yucheng Hostel** 漁埕生態旅遊民宿 (5 rooms) 19 Sanmin Rd, Yufu; 📞861 4891; m 0982 096 908; e agogo77772008@yahoo.com. tw; w yhome.com.tw. This homestay offers simple but comfortable lodgings in rooms with wooden floors & roll-out beds. Packages that include a night's accommodation, b/fast, ferry tickets, motorbike rental & tours of the intertidal zone are priced around NTD1,900 pp for a couple. There's a lawn area where you can relax outdoors. **$$**

✕ **Baihai Restaurant** 百海餐廳 6 Minzu Rd; 📞861 2591; ⏰ 11.00–14.00 & 17.00–19.00 daily. If you're walking from Baisha's ferry dock towards The Vase (see below), this restaurant is the last building before you turn the corner to a temple. Surprisingly, not everything on the menu comes from the sea; island-made pork sausages are served chopped & mixed with lettuce. What's called a Little Liuqiu Pizza has neither tomatoes nor cheese, & is deep-fried rather than baked. However, it is circular & features seasoned prawns. There are also fish & crab dishes but you'll need language skills for the best results; no EM. **$$$**

🍷 **Wave Bar** 冰郎小酒館 308 Sanmin Rd; m 0921 124 435; ⏰ 10.30–16.30 & 18.00–02.00 daily. A stone's throw from Baisha's harbour, this watering hole focuses on smoothies & juices (from NTD80) during the day, then craft & bottled beers (from NTD150) after dark. Unusually several different ciders are also offered (from NTD180). **$$**

WHAT TO SEE AND DO You'll have no problems finding your way around Little Liuqiu. There are plenty of bilingual maps, signs and information boards. If you turn right out of Baisha you can make the scenic area branch office your first stop and then work your way around the island clockwise.

The Vase 花瓶岩 The island's best-known and most-photographed coastal feature is a rock outcrop that's shaped more like a giant mushroom than a flowerpot. Wade out towards it only if you're wearing good sandals or neoprene booties – the coral here is notoriously sharp and dangerous.

Meiren Cave 美人洞 (⏰ 08.30–18.00 daily; admission NTD120/80; ticket also valid for Mountain Pig Ditch & Black Ghost Cave) This section of coast on the northeast shore is pleasing but not stunning, yet kids love it because it's perfect for hide-and-seek. If you walk quietly you'll likely see crabs on the footpath. From the nearby plateau (where there's a campsite) you may glimpse green turtles bobbing a few metres offshore.

Mountain Pig Ditch 山豬溝 (🕐 08.30–18.00 daily; admission inc in Meiren Cave ticket) On the inland side of the road, this is another place where you can appreciate Little Liuqiu's coral-reef geology. There's plenty of shade and greenery. The place name is curious, as it's highly unlikely that wild pigs ever roamed the island.

Shangshan Fuan Temple 上杉福安宮 (🕐 05.00–20.00 daily) Inside this house of worship some 2km south of Meiren there's a huge amount of carved wood and, in addition to the land god in the centre, a statue on the left representing a very local deity. General Shuixing – he of the bushy crimson eyebrows, bulging eyeballs and dark-green face – has been worshipped since 1987, when a team of builders working across the road found the ground-breaking spike on their excavator kept snapping, even though the land was soft. Consulting Guanyin, the foreman learned an 'infernal soldier' dwelt here. That spirit has since been assigned a legion of divine soldiers with which he protects the area from misfortune.

The shrine backs on to a small fishing harbour where you'll find the photogenic remnants of Little Liuqiu's oldest house. Known as the **Tai Mansion** (not open to the public), it dates from the 1820s and was the abode of one of the island's most important families. It's said building the harbour's breakwater spoiled the mansion's feng shui and caused the family to scatter.

Geban Bay 蛤板灣 This cove on the southwest coast is extremely attractive but, as on most of the island's beaches, keeping your shoes on is advised because the sand contains fragments of broken coral. That said, do scoop up some grit and sift it carefully; you'll spot minute five-pointed yellow stars. These are foraminifera, the shells of organisms less than 1mm across. The scenic area administration urges visitors not to take shells, sand or foraminifera as souvenirs. During the warmer months fireflies can be seen around the bay and it's sometimes possible to witness green turtles coming ashore to lay eggs.

Black Ghost Cave 烏鬼洞 (🕐 08.30–18.00 daily; admission inc in Meiren Cave ticket) The best known of the three attractions that charge admission; local people still burn incense here because of the violent events of nearly 400 years ago (page 324). If you're squeezing into the cave itself, rent a torch (NTD20) from one of the vendors. There are good sea views from the platforms and stairways here. A few hundred metres off the coast you'll see fixed circular nets in the ocean used for breeding cobia (also known as black kingfish).

Guanyin Rock 觀音石 So named because of its resemblance to the Buddhist goddess, this outcrop is a short distance west of Dafu.

Dafu 大福 Situated on the east coast, the island's 'second city' doesn't have much of interest to tourists, but one of the nicest spots to paddle in the water is immediately east of here. If you take the wooden stairway down to the water's edge and hunt around, you'll come across fish and crabs, including some that wouldn't disgrace a table in a classy seafood restaurant.

Sanlong Temple 三隆宮 (🕐 05.30–21.00 daily) Once you've done a circuit of the island, explore the interior where the highest point is 87m above sea level. This multi-level temple is the largest and perhaps most colourful place of worship on Little Liuqiu yet certainly not the busiest. Among the deities worshipped here are the Jade Emperor (central position on what's labelled as the third floor) and Liuqiu's

Ecotours of the rocky platforms exposed when the tide goes out are so popular that the authorities now impose limits on the number of people allowed to enter these fascinating but sensitive places, which include Geban Bay and the environs of Yufu Fishing Harbour. All groups must be accompanied by qualified guides; B&Bs can make the necessary arrangements. Almost 700 marine species – among them crabs, starfish and sea cucumbers – have been recorded in the waters around Little Liuqiu and an experienced guide should be able to show you curiosities such as sea hares which squirt out purple ink when attacked. (The ink disorientates fish and in the past was used by locals as a fishing aid.) Don't touch anything unless your guide says it's OK – rock-boring urchins and other denizens can inflict nasty stings. Nighttime tours are also engrossing, especially if greenish bioluminescent plankton sparkles just beneath the surface.

town god (ground floor, on the left). Unlike the majority of shrines on the island, visitors need not take off their shoes when entering. Every three years this temple organises a boat-burning event similar to Donggang's (see box, page 262). The next event will be October 2021.

GREEN ISLAND 綠島 (LÙ DǍO) *Telephone code 089*

No-one can dispute the aptness of the name. Created by an undersea volcanic eruption, Green Island is dominated by rich verdure and dark mossy hues that go well with the black cliffs and grey pyroclastic boulders. And it's all alone, 33km from Taiwan's shores. There's no archipelago here, just a few rocks above water at high tide to keep the island company. It's been Green Island only since 1949 – previously it was known as 'Fire-Scorched Island' because the inhabitants used to light fires on the hillsides to guide fishing vessels home.

Since 1803 the islanders (current population 3,500) have been Han Chinese. Austronesian people certainly lived here a few centuries back and possibly as long as 4,000 years ago, but who exactly they were, and when and why they left, isn't known for sure. In 1951, Chiang Kai-shek's regime decided to use the island as a place of imprisonment and exile for communist agents, subversives and political opponents. Thousands of prisoners were shipped here for interrogation and re-education; torture was routine and executions commonplace. Prisoners broke rocks on the beaches and helped build the airport. The last political convict was released in May 1990 and visitors can tour the buildings where prisoners were held. Ordinary criminals, among them some leading mafiosi, continued to be housed in an off-limits high-security institution that's one of the island's major employers.

At high tide the island's land area is just 15km², while at low tide this expands to a little over 17km² as receding waters expose coral platforms rich in marine life. The fish, crabs and other creatures that inhabit the tidal zone make snorkelling a very popular pastime, second only to soaking in one of the world's three saltwater hot springs. Local tour operators have made the snorkelling so safe even non-swimmers can join in and get a glimpse of what's beneath the surface. Because the Kuroshio Current draws fish towards the island and then traps them just offshore, there's some excellent scuba diving. Many divers prefer the winter months when underwater visibility is often 20m. For general visitors, April and May are good months as temperatures and humidity levels are lower than during the summer peak season, and the strong winds that sometimes make winter ferry crossings extremely uncomfortable are seldom a problem. If the sky isn't hazy, from the boat you'll get capital views of the mountains that abut Taiwan's east coast; you may see flying fish skim the waves and perhaps a dolphin or two. Approaching the rugged coastline in gloomy weather provokes a stirring, ends-of-the-earth sensation. For convicts and dissidents this must have exacerbated their despair. For many visitors, however, it's central to Green Island's appeal.

GETTING THERE AND AWAY

By air Daily Air (℡ 07 801 4711, 089 362 489; w www.dailyair.com.tw) flies a 19-seat propeller aircraft three times each day between Taitung and Green Island (GNI; 12mins; NTD1,100 one-way). The schedule is on Taitung Airport's website (w www.tta.gov.tw).

By boat The shipping companies that operate ferries between Fugang and Green Island (50mins; NTD460/230 one-way) have offices in the passenger terminal at Fugang's small harbour. The waiting area has air conditioning. During summer there's a boat about every 2 hours (⊕ 07.30–15.30 daily) but in winter there's often just one boat each way per day. Local tour operator Green Island Adventures (see below) can help book tickets.

GETTING AROUND

By motorcycle Most visitors get the use of a 125cc scooter or an e-scooter as part of their package with Green Island Adventures or the homestay they've booked with. Rentals can be arranged just outside the harbour. The island's only petrol station (⊕ 08.00–18.00 daily) is very near Nanliao Harbour. Car hire isn't possible on the island.

By bicycle Bikes can be rented from some of the motorcycle-hire stores in Nanliao but Green Island is far from ideal for cycling as it can get very windy, there's not much shade and the round-island road has some steep gradients.

By bus Between April and September, a bus circumnavigates the island in a clockwise direction 11 times per day (departs from Nanliao Harbour; ⊕ 08.30–17.00; 2hrs), but during the low season there are only four buses per day. A one-day pass costs NTD100/50 and can be purchased on the bus.

TOURIST INFORMATION AND TOUR OPERATORS There are bilingual displays and leaflets inside **Green Island Visitor Centre** (outside the airport; ℡ 672 026; ⊕ 09.00–17.00 daily). If you want to stay at the campsite at the southern end of Green Island, you need to make the booking here. Try also East Coast National Scenic Area (w www.eastcoast-nsa.gov.tw).

Founded by Eddie Viljoen, **Green Island Adventures** (m 0972 065 479; e greenislandreservations@hotmail.com; w greenislandadventures.com) specialises in packages that include accommodation, scuba diving, ferry or flight tickets and pickup on both sides.

⌂ WHERE TO STAY AND EAT

⌂ **Sanasai Inn** 戀戀火燒島民宿
(9 rooms, 2 dorms) Nanliao; ℡672 189;

e sea672189@yahoo.com.tw; w loveinsanasai.
com. Winning plaudits from local & international

tourists, Sanasai has very comfortable rooms for 2, 4 & 6 ppl, as well as gender-segregated dorms with 8 beds (NTD600 pp). It's only disadvantage is that it's the better part of 1km from the core of Nanliao, so you'll need to walk a fair way if you plan to drink beer with your dinner. On the other hand, it's near a prime snorkelling location. B/fast inc. **$$$**

⚑ Zihping Campsite 綠島紫坪露營區 Near Jhaorih Hot Springs, this has shower facilities, power sockets & even a swimming pool, but you'll need your own tent. Staying overnight costs NTD400/200 per adult/child. **$**

✖ Green Island Bamboo House 綠島竹屋 Nanliao; ☏672 129; ⊕ 11.00–14.00 & 17.00–20.00 daily. Bamboo House has a reputation for good, quick service & generous portions. There's

no EM, so if you're at a loss as to what to eat, order a set for 2 ppl (NTD500), 4 ppl (NTD800) or 6 ppl (NTD1,200); all inc venison as well as seafood, rice & a soup. Located on the main road at the southern end of the runway; look for the bldg with lanterns strung vertically out front. **$$$**

✖ Mr Hot Dog 綠島哈狗店 Nanliao; ☏671 711; ⊕ 10.30–00.30 daily. Attracting a young crowd, this is perhaps the only restaurant in the world serving flying-fish pizza. Other pizza options inc venison, & there are also pasta dishes &, of course, hot dogs. Salads & side dishes round out the menu; all portions are quite small. Beers from NTD100, cocktails & shots from NTD120. EM. On the main road equidistant from the harbour & the airport. **$$**

OTHER PRACTICALITIES

✉ **Post office** 186 Nanliao Vlg; ⊕ 08.00–noon & 12.30–16.00 Mon–Fri. This branch can change major foreign currencies.

WHAT TO SEE AND DO If you arrive by ferry, turn left to reach **Nanliao Village** 南寮, the cluster of shops, eateries, hotels and private homes that has the island's only post office and police station. The village is also within walking distance of the airport; if you've flown in, before turning right to Nanliao, cross the road and drop into the visitor centre for maps and English-language pamphlets. It doesn't matter much which way you circumnavigate the island, but the following section goes clockwise. Near the lighthouse on the island's northwestern extremity there are some large tidal pools where you can cool off in the water, but elsewhere around the island there are very few spots where swimming is advisable, either because of currents or because you'll be stepping on coarse coral grit.

Green Island Human Rights Memorial Park 綠島人權紀念碑園區 **(Lǜ Dǎo Rénquán Jìniànbēi Yuánqū)** (⊕ 24hrs daily; free admission) Occupying a large slice of the island's north coast, the memorial park's most obvious sight is the curved semi-underground memorial wall with its immaculate lawns. Not all of the 1,000-odd names etched into the stone represent individuals incarcerated on Green Island (Annette Lu, a former vice president, is listed here even though she served her sentence in north Taiwan). Each one, however, was a political detainee during the martial-law era. Several spent two or three periods in jail and in one case the total comes to 26 years, just short of Nelson Mandela's term.

Green Island's first political jail, New Life Camp, functioned between 1952 and 1965. At times, more than 2,000 were incarcerated, including some women. Detainees left the camp to do farming and labouring work; they performed Taiwanese operas for island residents, and helped local children with their homework. Detailed information about prisoners along with photos of historical interest can be found at w 2011greenislanden.wordpress.com.

Oasis Villa 綠洲山庄 **(Lǜzhōu Shānzhuāng)** (⊕ 08.00–17.30 daily; free admission) Hurriedly built after a prison uprising in February 1970 convinced

the authorities all political detainees should be moved back to Green Island, this institution's Orwellian name won't fool anyone who looks around inside. There are four blocks, each with two floors and 52 cells; dissidents were held here, usually several to a cell, until the late 1980s.

Guanyin Cave 觀音洞 **(Guānyīn Dòng)** (⏰ 24hrs daily; free admission) This small Buddhist grotto attracts plenty of genuine pilgrims in addition to coach-loads of tourists. Inside there's a stalagmite that resembles, albeit very slightly, the goddess of mercy. The modest eatery (⏰ varies; **$$**) by the entrance has some very tasty fare, including venison with rice (*lù ròu fàn* 鹿肉飯), fried rice, venison soup (*lù ròu tāng* 鹿肉湯), and flying fish (*fēi yú* 飛魚), but there's no English-language menu or air conditioning.

East coast Very few people live on this side of the island, which is marked by a series of dramatic promontories. Several have been given names inspired by their shapes, among them Cow's Head Hill, Pekinese Dog and Little Great Wall. Between the road and the ocean you'll see impenetrable clusters of one of Green Island's most distinctive plants, the screwpine (also known as the fragrant pandam). Thousands have been planted as windbreaks. They bear fruit similar in size and shape to pineapples but are much harder and far less delicious.

Jhaorih Hot Springs 朝日溫泉 **(Zhāorì Wēnquán)** (📞 671 133; ⏰ Jun–Sep 05.00–02.00 daily, Oct–May 06.00–midnight daily; admission NTD200/100) Located in the island's southeast, these springs are a high point for many visitors who revel in watching the sun rise while soaking in sulphurous brine. Others leave disappointed because the water is often tepid or they feel the condition of the pools doesn't warrant the high admission charge (massage showers that don't work and less-than-pristine shower cubicles are common complaints). Come at dusk to avoid both the sun and the crowds; the place is often packed out after dinner. Apart from two small pools very close to the waves, most of the complex – which includes indoor and outdoor pools plus changing rooms – is above the beach.

Across-Mountain Ancient Trail 過山古道 At 281m above sea level, Green Island's highest point is closed to the public because it's occupied by a military radar station. This hiking trail comes close, though, and provides access to the unpopulated, unspoiled interior. Starting from near km11 on the ring road, the first quarter of the 1.85km-long path includes dozens of stone steps on which bask an incredible number and variety of lizards. A species easy to spot and recognise is Swinhoe's japalura (*Japalura swinhonis*), sometimes called the bamboo tiger. Often more than 20cm long, including tail, it has a thick yellow stripe on either side of its trunk.

ROAD-USERS AND CONSERVATION ISSUES

Visitors to Green Island are urged to ride slowly and give way to crabs and other creatures on the road. Among the species sometimes squashed beneath tourists' wheels are the black-spectacled toad (*Duttaphrynus melanostictus*) and the coconut crab (*Birgus latro*). The latter, a nocturnal animal weighing up to 1kg, is the world's largest terrestrial arthropod. Formerly hunted for food, it's now the only crustacean species protected by Taiwan's Wildlife Conservation Law.

Across-Mountain Trail 過山步道 This route is of a similar length but starts from near the campsite at the island's southern tip. Like the ancient trail, it hits the concrete track that serves the radar base. From there to the visitor centre it's more than an hour of downhill walking with very little shade. Bring water, snacks and a hat.

ORCHID ISLAND 蘭嶼 (LÁNYǓ) *Telephone code 089*

Linked to Taiwan by unreliable boat and air services, Orchid Island is a spectacular escape for the relatively few visitors who get here. Some 60km due south of Green Island and 63km east of the Hengchun Peninsula, it's unique among the ROC's islands in having an Austronesian culture. Most of the islanders are members of the Tao tribe, an ethnic group whose ancestors came here about eight centuries ago and who call their 46km^2 homeland Pongso no Tao.

In recent decades many Orchid Islanders have moved to Taiwan for work or higher education. The official population is a little over 5,000 but many adults are absent for months at a time because they earn their living elsewhere. Partly because of the geographical isolation, and partly because no tourists of any stripe were permitted to visit until 1967, the Tao have managed to preserve quite a bit of their culture. Among the most obvious manifestations of this are semi-underground typhoon-proof houses and ornate wooden fishing boats.

Tribal solidarity has been strengthened by anger over the island's use as a dumping ground for nuclear waste from Taiwan's atomic power stations. Between 1982 and 1996, almost 100,000 barrels of low- and mid-level waste were shipped to the island, and for years Taiwan's government lied to the islanders, telling them the storage facility was a fish cannery. Unusually high levels of radioactivity have been detected in the vicinity of the dump, which is at the southern end of the island, but this shouldn't deter you from visiting.

Young Tao dress no differently from other Taiwanese, yet some elderly men still go about their daily chores wearing little more than a traditional loincloth. During festivals tribal elders don rattan vests and conical helmets made of silver; the latter cover the entire head save for narrow slits that allow the wearer to see where he's going. Before taking a photo of a man in his loincloth – or of any other islander, in fact – do ask permission. Many Tao dislike being treated as tourist attractions rather than humans. However, visitors who show tact and sensitivity speak of being warmly welcomed.

Like Green Island, Orchid Island is a nub of solidified magma pushed up by an ocean-bottom volcanic eruption. There are eight significant mountains, the highest of which reaches 552m. Despite the rugged landscape there's quite a lot of forest, some real jungle and a few small but decent beaches.

In ecological terms, the island is as close to the Philippines as it is to Taiwan. The Bataan Islands, from where the Tao are thought to have migrated, are 110km to the south. Among Orchid Island's fauna is the Formosan flying fox (*Pteropus dasymallus formosus*), a large fruit-eating bat and Taiwan endemic. Birders will hope to catch sight of the elusive Lanyu scops owl (*Otus elegans botelensis*), an endemic subspecies of the Ryukyu scops owl. The wild orchids that gave the island its name aren't as numerous as they once were. The island is hot and humid year-round with summer highs of almost 40°C, nasty winter storms and an annual average rainfall of around 3,440mm. April is the driest month; October–November is likely the best time of year to go. When boarding the ferry or plane to Orchid Island, carry enough cash for your excursion and a bit spare; there's nowhere to change money and there's a significant risk the weather will delay your return to Taiwan itself.

GETTING THERE AND AWAY

By air Daily Air (✆ 07 801 4711, 089 362 489; w www.dailyair.com.tw) flies a 19-seat propeller aircraft six times each day between Taitung and Orchid Island (KYD; flight time: 25mins; NTD1,480). The schedule is on Taitung Airport's website (w www.tta.gov.tw), but note that flights are often booked solid, cancelled because of bad weather or delayed by military exercises.

By boat Boats leave from Fugang and there may be just one service per week (takes about 3hrs; NTD1,100 one-way). Boats are sometimes brought forward or delayed by a day or more to cater for large groups. A few services stop at Green Island on the outward or return leg, meaning it's theoretically possible, but very difficult in practical terms, to travel from one island to another without returning to Fugang. Be prepared for rough seas. Between April and September there are up to two ferries per day from Houbihu in Kenting National Park (takes about 2hrs; NTD1,000).

GETTING AROUND Hiring a scooter (NTD500/day) is by far the best option. If you don't make arrangements prior to arrival, rental businesses (which can also provide cars and minibuses) will find you as soon as you get off the boat or leave the airport. Drivers and riders should be wary of pigs and goats wandering across the road.

TOURIST INFORMATION Tour Taitung (w tour.taitung.gov.tw) has some useful information. If you see bilingual maps and leaflets about Orchid Island at visitor centres in Taitung City, take them – you might not find anything as good on Orchid Island itself.

WHERE TO STAY AND EAT A small number of visitors day trip to Orchid Island, but spending at least one and ideally two nights is highly recommended. If you're visiting in the peak summer season you should make reservations. At other times, you'll likely have hotel and homestay owners greeting you on arrival. There are simple eateries in the villages but no English menus, and as the food supply is uneven, don't expect everything listed on the Chinese menu to be available. All three of the establishments listed below are in Yuren, a subdivision of Imaorod in the southwestern part of the island.

Lamuran Homestay 魚飛浪民宿 (6 rooms) 76–2 Yuren, Hongtou Vlg; ✆ 732 610; m 0933 163 451; ■ @lamuran. Clean, simple accommodation but only 1 room has its own bathroom. 4 rooms have futon beds (max 4 ppl per room), 1 dbl has a king-size bed, bathroom & TV & 1 dbl is more basic. There's a deck with hammocks & sea views. Tao owner Syaman Lamuran speaks good English & can collect guests from the airport. B/fast available. **$$**

Lowgogai B&B 月台民宿 (8 rooms) 44 Yuren, Hongtou Vlg; m 0921 577 522;

■ @www.lowgogai.idv.tw. Basic but clean rooms cost around NTD1,500 for 2 ppl; the 4-person room starts at NTD2,400. Guests can use the washing machine. If booked in advance, the owner can help arrange car/motorcycle hire & provide b/fast. **$$**

✕ The Epicurean Café 無餓不坐 77 Yuren, Hongtou Vlg; ✆ 731 623; ⏲ 11.00–13.00 & 18.00–20.00 Thu–Tue. This long-established eating/drinking venue serves a mix of local, Taiwanese & semi-Western items. Individual dishes from NTD160. **$$**

WHAT TO SEE AND DO The ring road hugs the coast and links all six villages, each of which has a Tao name (given here with the Mandarin in parentheses). There's only one other route suitable for vehicles: a short cut from Imaorod on the southwest coast to Ivalion on the eastern side.

North coast Major features along the north and northeast coastlines have been given names like Crocodile Rock and Lovers' Archway. The lighthouse isn't officially open to tourists but even if the gate is locked the ride provides excellent views.

Yayo 椰油 **(Yēyóu)** This village includes the ferry dock, a petrol station (☺ 07.00–20.00 daily) and Orchid Island's only high school. There are a couple of small supermarkets, one to the north and one to the south of the harbour. The beach here is said to be good for body surfing.

Imaorod 紅頭 **(Hóngtóu)** The island's airport is just north of this village, which has a clinic, a post office and a few places where you can eat.

Weather Station 氣象站 **(Qìxiàng Zhàn)** Established in 1940 by the Japanese, who needed meteorological data for their war effort, this spick-and-span building is 322m above sea level and surrounded by manicured lawns. The views from here are an absolute treat. Take the short cut between Imaorod and Ivalion, then a steep side road on the north side.

Datianchi 大天池 **(Dà Tiānchí)** The hike to this little lake, the rainwater-filled crater of an extinct volcano, can be hot and tough-going, and the trail has been in

THE TAO AND FISH

Fishing is central to Tao existence. The building of fishing boats is surrounded by customs and taboos, as is the catching of fish and the sharing out of what's caught. Tao boats are shaped like large canoes but they're not dugouts. Each one is assembled from 27 pieces of wood, and pegs rather than nails hold the planks together because the islanders have no tradition of smelting and casting. (The tribe's distinctive conical helmets are made by beating Mexican silver dollars received when trading with outsiders in the 19th century.) The wood comes from longan or breadfruit trees and a kind of resin is used to caulk gaps.

Men do all the fishing. Women are absolutely prohibited from even touching a fishing boat as it's thought this brings bad luck. Traditionally, womenfolk were responsible for most land-based food production: cutting fish and readying them for drying, growing taro and raising the small black pigs you might see trotting around Tao settlements.

The annual flying fish season lasts about five months. During this period, other types of fish are not consumed; this gives stocks a chance to recover. In recent years motorised boats and trawlers from other parts of Taiwan have been banned from approaching Orchid Island between February and July. Flying fish are usually caught at night because they're attracted by light sources. Surface nets pulled behind the boats catch the fish as they fly.

Certain types of fish are reserved for certain members of the community, the elderly for instance. Black flying fish are considered the tastiest so they're usually cured and saved for guests or for consumption on the final day of the flying fish season, which traditionally is the first day of the fifth lunar month.

Minor Islands   ORCHID ISLAND

10

a poor state of repair in recent years. Those who complete it experience unspoiled evergreen broad-leaf forest and are often able to see a wide range of insects and plants. The entrance to the trail is on the main road, 1.2km south of the Yongxu Campus of Lanyu Elementary School, not far from Orchid Island's southern tip.

Little Orchid Island 小蘭嶼 (Xiǎo Lányǔ)
A little over 5km off the main island's southern tip, Little Orchid Island has long been uninhabited. Not that long ago, Taiwan's air force used to practise bombing runs on the island. Now it's sometimes possible to hire a guide and a boat and visit; asking at your homestay is often the best way to go about organising an excursion.

Ivalion 野銀 (Yěyín)
The villages on the eastern side of the island, Ivalion in particular, are the best places to see tribal culture and semi-underground stone dwellings. Just like modern sustainable homes that are built into hillsides, these small Tao houses are cooler in summer and warmer in winter than the concrete boxes that fill Taiwanese towns. Because of their low profile, they're far less likely to be damaged by typhoon gusts. The downside is that the interiors are usually cramped, dark and stuffy. That doesn't matter too much because cooking, eating and socialising are done above ground on roofed platforms.

Dongqing Bay 東清灣 (Dōngqīng Wān)
This broad bay on the east coast has an attractive 1km-long beach where many tourists go swimming and backpackers sometimes camp. During the flying fish-catching season it's a good place to see traditional boats come and go.

Birdwing Butterfly Conservation Area 珠光鳳蝶復育園區 (Zhūguāng Fèngdié Fùyù Yuánqū)
If you visit Orchid Island between April and September, you're much more likely to see Taiwan's largest butterfly than either the Lanyu scops owl or the Formosan flying fox. The wingspan of Magellan's iridescent birdwing (*Troides magellanus sonani*) often exceeds 20cm. The species, which is black and yellow with some red, is endangered because the plants it and its larvae feed on are harvested for use in Chinese traditional medicine. In this conservation area efforts are being made to provide it with a foothold where it can thrive.

Appendix 1

LANGUAGE

Many Taiwanese, possibly more than half of the population, speak Taiwanese or a blend of Taiwanese and Mandarin at home (page 25). Except for missionaries, few Westerners have learned Taiwanese. Mandarin, the official language of both Taiwan and the People's Republic of China, is the language of education and the one most often used in television and radio broadcasts. The only Taiwanese who don't understand Mandarin are those over 70 who received very little education.

If you attempt to speak Mandarin in Taiwan, you'll get various reactions, including shock and mirth, but also lots of genuine encouragement. If you're serious about practising the language, you'll find plenty of people willing to chat.

The Mandarin words and phrases in this section (and throughout this book) have been romanised according to the *hanyu pinyin* system of spelling. That system wasn't created with English speakers in mind. For instance, the letter 'x' is pronounced something like 'sh', while 'q' approximates 'ch' and 'zh' is a bit like 'j'. If the word ends in 'o', like *wǒ* (I, me), it sounds like 'or'. The word for have (*yǒu*) is pronounced like the casual greeting 'yo!' and not like the English personal pronoun.

When reading *hanyu pinyin*, one must also take note of the four tones. First tone, marked with a horizontal line (eg: *guā*) is flat and somewhat high. Second tone is rising and marked with an acute accent (eg: *bái*). Third tone is falling then rising, indicated in this book and many other resources by a breve (eg: *guǒ*). The fourth tone is falling and is shown by a grave accent (eg: *dòu*). The seldom-used fifth tone is neutral and so doesn't have any tone marking.

It goes without saying that the best way to master Mandarin pronunciation is to listen to native speakers, imitate and practise.

Much of this section is devoted to helping readers buy food and drink because this is an important part of any Taiwan experience as well as an endeavour in which many visitors struggle.

INTRODUCING YOURSELF As soon as people know you can speak some Mandarin, they'll be asking you questions like these:

What's your name?	你叫什麼名字?	*nǐ jiào shénme míngzi?*
My name is...	我叫...	*wǒ jiào...*
How are you?	你好嗎?	*nǐ hǎo ma?*
I'm very well	我很	*wǒ hěnhǎo*
Where are you from?	你是哪裡人?	*nǐ shì nǎlǐ de rén?*
No, not yet	還沒	*hái méi*
Bottoms up!	乾	*gān bēi*

In Mandarin, yes/no questions are answered affirmatively by simply repeating the verb or adjective in the question. Here are two examples: if someone asks you, 'Do you like…? (你喜歡… 嗎?/*nǐ xǐ huān… ma?*)', you can answer, 'like' (喜歡/*xǐ huān*); if they say, 'Are you happy?' (你高興嗎?/*nǐ gāo xìng ma?*), you can respond, 'happy!' (高興/*gāo xìng*).

ADDRESSING OTHERS

Unlike Japanese and some other languages, in Mandarin there are very few polite/familiar forms to worry about. Titles such as Mr or Miss (there's no Ms in Mandarin) are placed after the name.

Hello, Mr Lee	你好李先生	*Lǐ xiānsheng nǐ hǎo*
Hello, Miss Chen	你好陳小姐	*Chén xiǎojie nǐ hǎo*
Goodbye!	再見	*zài jiàn*

ASKING FOR HELP

Excuse me/I'm sorry	對不起	*duì bú qì*
Where's the toilet?	廁所在哪裡?	*cè suǒ zài nálǐ?*
Please give me…	請給我…	*qǐng gěi wǒ…*
I want to go online	我要上網	*wǒ yào shàng wǎng*
Can you speak English?	你會講英語嗎?	*nǐ huì jiǎng yīngyǔ ma?*
I don't understand	我聽不懂	*wǒ tīng bù dǒng*
Thank you	謝謝	*xiè xiè*
You're welcome	不用客氣	*bú yòng*
It doesn't matter	沒有關係	*méiyǒu guānxi*

SHOPPING

Do you have…?	你有沒有…?	*nǐ yǒu méi yǒu…?*
Can I see it, please?	我要看可以嗎	*wǒ yào kān kěyǐ ma?*
How much does it cost?	多少錢?	*duō shǎo qián?*
It's expensive!	太貴了	*tài guì le*
OK, I want to buy it	我要買	*wǒ yào mǎi*

NUMBERS

Numbers greater than ten are very easy. Eleven is *shí yī*, literally 'ten one', while twenty is *èr shí*, 'two ten'. Follow the same logic for larger numbers: 147 is *yī bǎi sì shí qī* – 'one hundred four ten seven'.

one	一	*yī*	eight	八	*bā*
two	二	*èr*	nine	九	*jiǔten*
three	三	*sān*	ten	十	*shí*
four	四	*sì*	20	二十	*èr shí*
five	五	*wǔ*	50	五十	*wǔ shí*
six	六	*liù*	100	一百	*yī bǎi*
seven	七	*qī*			

IN THE HOTEL

Do you have any vacancies?	請問有房間嗎?	*qǐng wèn yǒu fáng jiān ma?*
I have a reservation	我有定房	*wǒ yǒu dìng fáng*
Room for one/two people	單人房/兩人房	*dān rén fáng/liǎng rén fáng*
How much does it cost?	多少錢?	*duō shǎo qián?*
Does it include breakfast?	含早餐嗎?	*hán zǎo cān ma?*

DIRECTIONS

I want to go to…	我要去	*wǒ yào qù…*
… the bus station	公共汽車站	*gōng gòng qì chē zhàn*
… the TRA station	火車站	*hǔochē zhàn*
… the HSR station	高鐵站	*gāo tiě zhàn*
… the airport	機場	*jī chǎng*
… the hotel	旅館	*lǚ guǎn*
… the homestay	民宿	*mín sù*
Where is the…?	在哪裡…?	*zài nálǐ…?*

(The men's toilet will be labelled 男 (*nán*), the ladies' 女 (*nǚ*).)

… bathroom?	廁所?	*cè suǒ?*
… post office?	郵局?	*yóu jú?*
… bank?	銀行?	*yín háng?*
… restaurant?	餐廳?	*cān tīng?*
… visitor information centre?	遊客中心?	*yóu kè zhōng xīn?*

DRIVING

I want to hire…	我要租一輛…	*wǒ yào zū yī liàng…*
… a car	汽車	*qì chē*
… a motorcycle	摩托車	*mó tuō chē*
… a bicycle	腳踏車	*jiǎo tà chē*
Can I park here?	我可以停車嗎?	*wǒ kěyǐ tíng chē ma?*
92-octane petrol (two-star)	九二	*jiǔ èr*
95-octane petrol (four-star)	九五	*jiǔ wǔ*

EATING AND DRINKING
Meals

breakfast	早餐	*zǎo cān*
lunch	午餐	*wǔ cān*
dinner	晚餐	*wǎn cān*
small delicacies	小吃	*xiǎo chī*
snack	零食	*líng shí*
dim sum (Cantonese snacks)	店心	*diàn xīn*

Staples

steamed white rice	白飯	*bái fàn*
fried rice	炒飯	*chǎo fàn*
stewed rice; risotto	燴飯	*huì fàn*
braised pork on rice	肉燥飯	*lǔ ròu fàn* or *ròu zǎo fàn*
congee; rice porridge	粥	*zhōu*
breakfast rice gruel	稀飯	*xī fàn*
sticky rice triangles	粽子	*zòng zǐ* or *ròu zòng*
wheat noodles	麵	*miàn*
fried noodles	炒麵	*chǎo miàn*
rice vermicelli	米粉	*mǐ fěn*
ban-tiao (thick rice noodles)	粄條	*bǎn tiáo*
dry noodles with gravy	乾麵	*gān miàn*
sesame-paste noodles	麻醬麵	*má jiàng miàn*
ramen	拉麵	*lā miàn*
knife-cut noodles	刀削麵	*dāo xuē miàn*
steamed dumplings	餃子 or 水餃	*jiǎo zi* or *shuǐ jiǎo*

fried dumplings (gyoza)	煎餃	*jiān jiǎo*
soup-filled dumplings	小籠包	*xiǎo lóng bāo*
chicken's egg	雞蛋	*jī dàn*
hot pot	火鍋	*huǒ guō*

Flavours and condiments

spicy	辣	*là*
not spicy, please	我不要辣	*wǒ bù yào là*
salty	鹹	*xián*
black pepper	胡椒	*hú jiāo*
original flavour	原味	*yuán wèi*
tomato ketchup	番茄醬	*fān qié jiàng*
tofu	豆腐	*dòu fu*
dried tofu	豆干	*dòu gān*

Portion sizes and cooking styles

small	小	*xiǎo*
medium	中	*zhōng*
large	大	*dà*
vegetarian	素食	*sù shí*
offal, etc, braised in gravy	滷味	*lǔ wèi*

Meats

pork	豬肉	*zhū ròu*
pork ribs	排骨	*pái gǔ*
pig's foot	豬腳	*zhū jiǎo*
ham	火腿	*huǒ tuǐ*
bacon	培根	*péi gēn*
chicken	雞肉	*jī ròu*
beef	牛肉	*niú ròu*
steak	牛排	*niú pái*
duck	鴨肉	*yā ròu*
goose	鵝肉	*é ròu*
venison	鹿肉	*lù ròu*
snake	蛇肉	*shé ròu*
barbecue	烤肉	*kǎo ròu*

Seafood

	海鮮	*hǎi xiān*
fish	魚	*yú*
squid	魷魚	*yóu yú*
octopus	章魚	*zhāng yú*
oyster	蚵	*é*
clam	蛤	*gé*
seaweed	海	*hǎi zǎo* or *hǎi cǎo*

Vegetables

salad	沙拉	*shā lā*
cabbage	高麗菜	*gāo lì cài*
kimchi (pickled cabbage)	泡菜	*pào cài*
fried green vegetables	炒青菜	*chǎo qīng cài*
potato	馬鈴薯	*mǎ líng shǔ*

taro	芋頭	*yù tóu*
sweet potato	地瓜	*dìguā* or *fān shǔ*
carrot	紅蘿蔔	*hóng luó bo*
sweetcorn	玉米	*yù mǐ*
tomato	番茄	*fān qié*
mushroom	香菇	*xiāng gū*
bitter melon	苦瓜	*kǔ guā*

Soups

soup	湯	*tāng*
thick soup, potage	羹	*gēng*
egg-drop soup	蛋花湯	*dàn huā tāng*
miso soup	味噌湯	*wèi cēng tāng*
pork rib soup	排骨湯	*pái gǔ tāng*
wonton soup	餛飩湯	*hún tún tāng*

Hakka specialities 客家菜 *kè jiā cài*

| Hakka stir-fry (pork, squid and dried tofu) | 客家小炒 | *kè jiā xiǎo chǎo* |
| pig's intestine with ginger and vinegar | 薑絲炒大腸 | *jiāng sī chǎo dà cháng* |

Western foods

hamburger	漢堡	*hàn bǎo*
chips; French fries	薯條	*shǔ tiáo*
sandwich	三明治	*sān míng zhì*
cheese	起士	*qǐ shì*
spaghetti	意大利麵	*yì dà lì miàn*
pizza	比薩	*bǐ sà*

Breakfast food

	早餐	*zǎo cān*
fried egg	煎蛋	*jiān dàn*
egg pancake	蛋餅	*dàn bǐng*
steamed bread	饅頭	*mán tou*
steamed roll with meat	肉包	*ròu bāo*
steamed roll with vegetables	菜包	*cài bāo*
soya milk	豆漿	*dòu jiāng*
cruller	油條	*yóu tiáo*
cold (for food)	冷	*lěng*

Snacks and desserts

bread	麵包	*miàn bāo*
cake	蛋糕	*dàn gāo*
ice cream	冰淇淋	*bīng qí lín*
biscuits, cookies	餅乾	*bǐng gān*
chocolate	巧克力	*qiǎo kè lì*
sweets, candy	糖果	*táng guǒ*
chewing gum	口香糖	*kǒu xiāng táng*
pudding	布丁	*bù dīng*
bean-curd pudding	豆花	*dòu huā*

Drinks

	飲料	*yǐn liào*
boiled water	白開水	*bái kāi shuǐ*
fruit juice	果汁	*guǒ zhī*
cola	可樂	*kě lè*
coffee	咖啡	*kā fēi*
black tea	紅茶	*hóng chá*
tea with milk	奶茶	*nǎi chá*
tea with tapioca balls ('pearl milk tea')	珍珠奶茶	*zhēn zhū nǎi chá*
papaya milkshake	木瓜牛奶	*mù guā niú nǎi*
hot (for drinks and desserts)	熱	*rè*
cold; iced (for drinks)	冰	*bīng*
half sugar	半糖	*bàn táng*
no sugar	無糖	*wú táng*
less ice	少冰	*shǎo bīng*
no ice	無冰	*wú bīng*
cow's milk	牛奶	*niú nǎi*
beer	啤酒	*pí jiǔ*
kaoliang	高粱	*gāo liáng*
red wine	紅酒	*hóng jiǔ*
white wine	白葡萄酒	*bái pú tao jiǔ*

Fruits

	水果	*shuǐ guǒ*
apple	蘋果	*píng guǒ*
guava	芭樂	*bā lè*
longan	龍眼	*lóng yǎn*
lychee	荔枝	*lí zhī*
mango	芒果	*máng guǒ*
orange	橘子	*jú zǐ*
papaya	木瓜	*mù guā*
passion fruit	百香果	*bái xiāng guǒ*
pineapple	鳳梨	*fèng lí*
starfruit, carambola	楊桃	*yáng táo*
watermelon	西瓜	*xī guā*

Appendix 2

ROAD AND STREET NAMES

About a dozen road names appear again and again throughout Taiwan. Zhongshan Road honours Dr Sun Yat-sen, the founding father of the ROC, because Sun was also known as Sun Zhongshan. Zhongzheng Road does the same for Chiang Kai-shek. Minquan, Minsheng and Minzu roads are named after the three core principles of Sun's ideology, Sanminzhuyi (because of which we also have Sanmin Road). The 'Zhonghua' in Zhonghua Road means China; Aiguo equals 'patriotism'; Guangfu celebrates the return of Taiwan to Chinese rule in 1945. A few road names, including Chongqing and Nanjing, recall cities in mainland China. Heping means 'peace'; Wenhua means 'culture'; Zhongxiao is 'loyalty and filial piety'. Some road names are more prosaic: Beimen is 'north gate' while Miaoqian means 'in front of the temple'.

Academia Rd	究院路	Cisian	*see Qixian*
Aiguo E Rd	愛國東路		
Anbei Rd	安北路	Dagong Rd	大公路
Anhe Rd	安和路	Datong Rd	大同路
Anping Rd	安平路	Dihua St	迪化街
		Dongmen Rd	東門路
Bade Rd	八德路	Dunhua S Rd	敦化南路
Beian Rd	北安路		
Beimen Rd	北門路	Fuqian Rd	府前路
Binhai Rd	濱海路	Fuxing S Rd	復興南路
Boai Rd	博愛路		
		Gongyuan Rd	公園路
Changan E Rd	長安東路	Guangfu Rd	光復路
Changan W Rd	長安西路		
Chaozhou St	潮州街	Heping W Rd	和平西路
Chengde Rd	承德路	Hoping	*see Heping*
Chenggong Rd	成功路	Hsinsheng	*see Xinsheng*
Chengkung	*see Chenggong*	Huanhe N Rd	環河北路
Chienkuo	*see Jianguo*	Huanhe S Rd	環河南路
Chongqing N Rd	重慶北路	Huaxi St	華西街
Chongqing S Rd	重慶南路		
Chungcheng	*see Zhongzheng*	Jhonghua	*see Zhonghua*
Chunghsiao	*see Zhongxiao*	Jhongjheng	*see Zhongzheng*
Chunghua	*see Zhonghua*	Jhongshan	*see Zhongshan*
Chungshan	*see Zhongshan*	Jhongyi	*see Zhongyi*
Chungyi	*see Zhongyi*	Jianguo S Rd	建國南路
Cingnian	*see Qingnian*	Jianxing Rd	建行路

Jinshan S Rd	金山南路	Sihwei	*see Siwei*
		Simen	*see Ximen*
Kaishan Rd	開山路	Sinsheng	*see Xinsheng*
Keelung Rd	基隆路	Siwei Rd	四維路
Kending Rd	墾丁路	Siwei 3rd Rd	四維三路
Kuangfu	*see Guangfu*	Songjiang Rd	松江路
Linsen Rd	林森路	Taiwan Bd	台灣大道
Liuhe Rd	六合路	Tatung	*see Datong*
		Tungmen	*see Dongmen*
Meishuguan Rd	美術館路		
Miaoqian Rd	廟前路	Weixin Rd	維新路
Minchuan	*see Minquan*	Wenhua Rd	文化路
Minquan Rd	民權路	Wufei St	五妃街
Minsheng Rd	民生路	Wufu Rd	五福路
Mintsu	*see Minzu*	Wuquan Rd	五權路
Minzu Rd	民族路		
		Ximen Rd	西門路
Nanjing E Rd	南京東路	Xinle St	新樂街
Nanjing W Rd	南京西路	Xinsheng N Rd	新生北路
Nanking	*see Nanjing*	Xinsheng S Rd	新生南路
Nanmen Rd	南門路	Xinyi Rd	信義路
		Xitun Rd	西屯路
Pate	*see Bade*		
Poai	*see Boai*	Yanping S Rd	延平南路
Putou St	埔頭街	Yenping	*see Yanping*
		Yongkang St	永康街
Qingnian Rd	青年路		
Qixian Rd	七賢路	Zhonghua Rd	中華路
		Zhongshan Rd	中山路
Renai Rd	仁愛路	Zhongxiao E Rd	忠孝東路
		Zhongxiao W Rd	忠孝西路
Sanmin Rd	三民路	Zhongyang Rd	中央路
Shaochuan St	哨船街	Zhongyi Rd	忠義路
Shennong St	神農街	Zhongzheng Rd	中正路
Shuimei St	水美街		

Appendix 3

FURTHER INFORMATION

BOOKS Some of these books are impossible to find outside Taiwan or very expensive. Camphor Press (**w** camphorpress.com) publishes new titles and reissues classic Taiwan-related books in print and downloadable formats.

Literature

Chang, Ta-chun *Wild Kids: Two Novels About Growing Up* Columbia University Press, 2002. Critically acclaimed novellas by one of Taiwan's most popular and versatile writers.

Chu, Tien-wen *Notes of a Desolate Man* Columbia University Press, 2000. Prize-winning but somewhat difficult novel narrated by a gay man.

Pai, Hsien-yung *Crystal Boys* Gay Sunshine Press, 1993. A translation of the taboo-busting novel that bolstered mainstream awareness and understanding of Taiwan's gay community. The author, who is also known as Kenneth Pai, also wrote the sublime 1971 collection of short stories *Taipei People* (sometimes titled *Taipei Characters*).

Wang Wen-hsing *Family Catastrophe* University of Hawaii, 1995. First published in Chinese in 1972, this novel examines the expectations, resentments and tensions within a typical family.

Wood, Christopher *Taiwan* Fontana, 1981. Far-fetched yet entertaining thriller about a plot to steal priceless works from the National Palace Museum, by the man who wrote the screenplays for *Moonraker* and *The Spy Who Loved Me*.

Wu Ming-yi *The Man with the Compound Eyes* Vintage, 2015. Engaging environmentalist fantasy featuring Taiwan and its indigenous people.

Society

Blundell, David (editor) *Taiwan Since Martial Law: Society, Culture, Politics, Economy* National Taiwan University Press, 2012. An important collection of articles about how Taiwan has evolved over the quarter century since martial law was ended.

Caltonhill, Mark *Private Prayers and Public Parades* Taipei City Government Department of Information, 2002. An excellent book covering almost every religion – mainstream or otherwise – practised in Taiwan.

Crook, Steven *Dos and Don'ts in Taiwan* iGroup Press, 2010. A guide to modern Taiwanese customs, lifestyles and habits by the author of the Bradt Travel Guide to Taiwan.

Donnelly, Neal *Gods of Taiwan: A Collector's Account* Artist Publishing Co, 2006. Profiles of major and minor Taiwanese deities by a former US diplomat who collected god effigies during his 11 years in Taiwan, peppered with some excellent anecdotes.

Jordan, David K *Gods, Ghosts & Ancestors: Folk Religion in a Taiwanese Village* Caves Books, 2nd edition 1985. A brief and engrossing explanation of religion in Taiwan, written by an American anthropologist who did fieldwork in south Taiwan in the late 1960s. A 3rd edition e-book can be downloaded from **w** http://weber.ucsd.edu/~dkjordan/scriptorium/gga/ggamain.html.

Nature

Hsian, Mu-chi and Li, Cheng-lin *A Field Guide to the Birds of Taiwan* Forestry Bureau, 2017. This comprehensive guide is the first in English, and comes with English, Chinese and scientific nomenclature.

Food

Crook, Steven and Hung, Katy Hui-wen *A Culinary History of Taipei: Beyond Pork and Ponlai* Rowman & Littlefield, 2018. A 'food biography' explaining why Taiwanese eat what they do and how their diet has changed through the ages.

Erway, Cathy *The Food of Taiwan: Recipes from the Beautiful Island* Houghton Mifflin Harcourt, 2015. A cookbook with close to 100 recipes for both home-style dishes and street snacks.

Travel

Crook, Steven *Keeping Up With the War God* Yushan Publications, 2001. The author of the Bradt guide visits temples, attends traditional festivals and climbs high mountains.

Robbins, Cheryl *A Foreigner's Travel Guide to Taiwan Indigenous Areas* Taiwan Interminds Publishing, 2012–14. This three-volume series, by a full-time tour guide specialising in aboriginal communities, has very useful homestay and restaurant listings plus excellent photos.

Saunders, Richard *Taipei Escapes 1* and *Taipei Escapes 2* Community Services Centre (Taipei), 2011. Everything you need to know about reaching beautiful places in north Taiwan with an emphasis on day trips and short but spectacular hikes. The first volume covers the northeast, while the second deals with Taipei City and the northwest.

Saunders, Richard *Taiwan 101* Community Services Centre (Taipei), 2016. A two-volume guide to the country's 101 finest attractions. Very strong on the outdoors; the coverage of cultural and urban attractions isn't so comprehensive.

Saunders, Richard *The Islands of Taiwan* Community Services Centre (Taipei), 2013. A comprehensive guide to all of the ROC's minor islands.

Language

Books and audio materials about Mandarin Chinese available outside Taiwan tend to focus on Mandarin as it's spoken in the PRC, but this isn't a major problem (page 25). In Taiwan, the bookshops near Taipei's National Taiwan Normal University are a good place to find language-learning materials.

Easy-peasy Chinese: Mandarin Chinese Dorling Kindersley, 2007. Small and thus portable but probably contains more than enough for most travellers.

McNaughton, William *Reading & Writing Chinese: A Comprehensive Guide to the Chinese Writing System* Tuttle Publishing, 2nd edition 1998. Make sure to get the original version which covers traditional characters, not the alternative simplified-character edition. The Taiwan edition by Caves Books Ltd is considerably cheaper than the one available in the UK.

Meek, Catherine, Yan, Mao, Henlan, E and Hill, Brian *Breakthrough Mandarin Chinese* Palgrave Macmillan, 1999. Pricey yet effective introduction to the language.

Qian, Kan *Colloquial Chinese* Routledge, 2nd edition 2009. Highly rated book suitable for self-study; audio materials available on CD or as MP3 files.

History and politics

Brown, Melissa J *Is Taiwan Chinese?* University of California Press, 2004. An academic analysis of migration and the political manipulation of culture and how they influence Taiwanese identity.

Cole, J Michael *Black Island: Two Years of Activism in Taiwan* Amazon Digital Services, 2015. One of Taiwan's most active English-language commentators analyses the 'Sunflowers' and related movements.

Keating, Jerome F and Lin, April C J *Island in the Stream: A Quick Case Study of Taiwan's Complex History* SMC Publishing, 4th edition 2008. Covers Taiwan's history from the 1500s to the present, explaining how Taiwan overcame the odds to become a free democracy, but continues to be threatened by the People's Republic of China.

MUSIC Pop videos by scores of Taiwanese artists have been uploaded to YouTube and can be found by searching for their English names. Particularly worth listening to are **Bobby Chen** (Chen Sheng), a versatile singer-songwriter now in his 50s, and **Biung** (Wang Hong-en), a member of the Bunun tribe whose music ranges from gentle aboriginal tunes to raucous rock. Among the most successful Taiwan-born pop stars of the past 20 years are **Jay Chou** (Chou Chieh-lun) and **A-Mei** (Chang Hui-mei), both of whom have sold lots of albums throughout the ethnic Chinese world; the latter has also performed under the name **A-Mit** derived from her aboriginal name, Kulilay Amit. Not all Taiwanese pop consists of sugary ballads; there are punk bands, death-metal acts (notably **Chthonic**, who've toured overseas but have become less active since their leader was elected to Taiwan's parliament) and rappers like the controversial Nine One One. Multi-national Taiwan-based outfit **A Moving Sound** (W www.amovingsound.com), who describe themselves as a performance company rather than a band, have won considerable acclaim in recent years for their compositions and use of traditional Chinese instruments. Recordings of traditional indigenous polyphonic singing aren't hard to find in large CD shops. One that's especially good is *Who's Singing On Mountain* by Hualien Taiping Elementary School Chorus (Wind Records, 2004). The songs are entirely traditional and performed without any instrumental backing; liner notes in Chinese, English and Bunun explain the meaning of the lyrics.

WEBSITES
Official resources
W **immigration.gov.tw** Information for foreign tourists, students and dependants
W **np.cpami.gov.tw/english** National parks central website
W **www.cwb.gov.tw** Weather Bureau's bilingual site; forecasts, tide times and earthquake reports
W **www.ey.gov.tw** Taiwan's Cabinet
W **www.mofa.gov.tw** Ministry of Foreign Affairs
W **www.president.gov.tw** Taiwan's Presidential Office

Travel information
W **issuu.com/travelintaiwan** Download copies of *Travel in Taiwan* magazine
W **www.boca.gov.tw** Visa information from Taiwan's government
W **www.freeway.gov.tw** If you expect to spend a lot of time on the motorways, visit this site and read about traffic laws on the fast roads
W **www.railway.gov.tw** TRA's informative but clunky website
W **www.thsrc.com.tw** High-speed rail schedules and online ticket purchasing

Culture
W **dmtip.gov.tw** Digital Museum of Taiwan's Indigenous People
W **www.moc.gov.tw** Taiwan's culture ministry
W **www.tribe-asia.com** Handicrafts and arts made by members of Taiwan's indigenous tribes

Taiwan blogs Several of these blogs are no longer actively updated but all contain information that's useful for travellers.

w **bradttaiwan.blogspot.com** Compiled by the author of this guidebook; features some sights not in this guide

w **danshuihistory.blogspot.com** In-depth posts about little-known episodes in Taiwan's history

w **goteamjosh.com/blog** Photo-heavy coverage of many locations

w **hikingtaiwan.wordpress.com** Mouthwatering photos of Taiwan's scenery

w **hungryintaipei.blogspot.com** A female foodie reviews hundreds of Taipei restaurants

w **lifeoftaiwan.com/blog** Tourism-related articles and interviews

w **michaelturton.blogspot.com** Commentary on all aspects of life in Taiwan including political, historical, educational and environmental issues

w **synapticism.com** In-depth articles and excellent photos of little-known architectural and historical gems

w **taiwanbiking.blogspot.com** Cycling-only blog by Michael Turton

w **taiwanincycles.blogspot.com** Informative bike-oriented blog

w **taiwan-scene.com** Online travel magazine with a good amount of original content

w **taiwanoffthebeatentrack.com** Hikes and other expeditions written up by Richard Saunders, author of several Taiwan travel books

w **trickytaipei.com** Lots of opinions and some useful eating tips

News

w **taiwannews.com.tw** Covers politics and crime

w **www.taipeitimes.com** DPP-leaning newspaper

w **www.taiwantoday.tw** Government website updated daily; news and some interesting features

Get involved

w **spca.org.tw** Taiwan Society for the Prevention of Cruelty to Animals

w **tahr.org.tw** The website of the Taiwan Association for Human Rights, a long-established group campaigning, among other things, against the death penalty

w **www.volunteermatch.org.tw** Organises international work camps in various parts of Taiwan

For long-term residents There are dozens of English-language Facebook groups through which expatriates and visitors buy, sell, trade or give away items, as well as asking and answering questions and sharing tips.

w **forumosa.com** Taiwan-centric forums with lots of travel information

w **taiwaneasy.tw** Has a comprehensive directory of Taipei eateries and other businesses

MOBILE PHONE APPS

Eat Drink Taiwan Created by an American developer to help gourmets find delicious food in Taipei, Tainan and other cities

Index